This is a volume in

THE UNIVERSITY OF MICHIGAN HISTORY OF THE MODERN WORLD

Upon completion, the series will consist of the following volumes:

The United States to 1865 *by Michael Kraus*

The United States since 1865 *by Foster Rhea Dulles*

Canada: A Modern History *by John Bartlet Brebner*

Latin America: A Modern History *by J. Fred Rippy*

Great Britain to 1688: A Modern History *by Maurice Ashley*

Great Britain since 1688: A Modern History *by K. B. Smellie*

France: A Modern History *by Albert Guérard*

Germany: A Modern History *by Marshall Dill, Jr.*

Italy: A Modern History *by Denis Mack Smith*

Russia and the Soviet Union: A Modern History *by Warren B. Walsh*

The Near East: A Modern History *by William Yale*

The Far East: A Modern History *by Nathaniel Peffer*

India: A Modern History *by Percival Spear*

The Southwest Pacific: A History *by C. Hartley Grattan*

Africa: A Modern History *by Ronald Robinson*

GREAT BRITAIN TO 1688

A Modern History

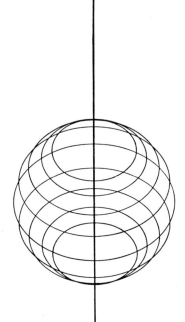

The University of Michigan History of the Modern World
Edited by Allan Nevins and Howard M. Ehrmann

GREAT BRITAIN TO 1688

A Modern History

BY MAURICE ASHLEY

Ann Arbor: The University of Michigan Press

Preface

Although I have written a number of history books and history has always been the occupation of my leisure and is my delight, I am not by profession a teacher: indeed I belong to what I fear may be a dying class, that of the intellectual journalist. So in preparing this book I have felt as if my youth has been renewed and I have been allowed to return in spirit to my old university of Oxford and study, as in happy bygone days thirty years ago, for the papers set in British history in the Honours School.

Alas! ghosts walk there. I have in mind in particular the Rt. Hon. H. A. L. Fisher, who was then Warden of my old college (New College as it is called) and encouraged me in the art and science of historical writing not only by precept but by example; for he lectured and wrote more clearly and more attractively than any other Oxford historian of that time. But I also cannot help paying tribute to my old friend and tutor, Sir Llewellyn Woodward, still active at Princeton, who inspired in me the joys of exploring the problems of modern history. I think he was disappointed that I never became a don or acquired donnish ways. But that was not his fault.

I have tried to recapitulate the early history of my country without assuming knowledge of the subject in my readers and without, I hope, treading upon the corns of those many experts whose books I have used and tried to understand. I am obliged to Mr. Edward Miller, Fellow of St. John's College, Cambridge, and Mr. Roger Schofield, B.A., of Clare College, Cambridge, for attempting to keep me on the rails, and to Professor Gerald Abraham of Liverpool University for helping me over my chapter on music.

I have been struck, as I have been writing this book, how quickly ideas about British history have changed over thirty years. It is not merely that vast quantities of books and articles have been published throughout the English-speaking world. Nor is it only that new generations ask new questions. For it seems to me that the form of presentation has changed, that university historians are less sure of themselves than they once were, that old patterns are no longer being followed, and that old shibboleths have been abandoned.

The focus also is important: we are now looking at matters in the light of the Nuclear Age in which we live and are reading history books written not in the buoyant, confident world before the first German war, but books written in what many of us in England regarded as the Age of Guilt. Thirty years ago we were brought up in the afterglow of Victorian optimism, supplemented by Germanic systems. It is those systems, I think, which have been most misleading to students of British history, especially in the period with which I deal here. Scholars of my generation were brought up to talk about the "feudal system," the "manorial system," the "mercantile system," and many other systems. It took me a long time to realize that these scarcely existed outside the minds of professional historians. Feudalism was invented by antiquarians in the seventeenth century, when the wickedness of the Norman Conquest was a commonplace of advanced political argument. We now know that the "manorial system," which for a generation took pride of place in the textbooks of economic history, had no universal application. The "mercantile system" derived from a rather patronizing attitude adopted toward government policies in the era of Free Trade, which died in England in 1931. Thus I have become suspicious whenever I see the word "system" in a history book and I have tried here to leave out words and phrases that imply such a thing. If they have crept into this book at all, it must be blamed on the historical education I received at school.

I have also tried, as far as possible, to limit my use of the phrase "medieval" in this book. For few scholars agree when they look at the broad continuity of British history what is meant by a medieval idea. It is true that I have given the title "Middle Ages" to the second book of this volume, but only because it is admirably vague and I could think of no more satisfactory way of describing the period between Anglo-Saxon times and the Tudor age. My personal view is that the outlook of men changed perceptibly in the period when this volume ends, when the great mathematician and physicist Isaac Newton published his *Principia*. The sudden spurt in science and mathematics in the latter half of the seventeenth century, the publication of more sophisticated political ideas, the birth of nonconformity, and the dawn of religious toleration all suggest to me the beginnings of modern times. Yet one recalls that Newton himself was often absorbed in theology, while the

Popish Plot showed how men could still be agitated by religious causes impinging upon politics.

Again, the structure of British history thirty years ago was profoundly "constitutional." Economic history was still thought of as a new and rather doubtful subject; there was no Professor of Economic History when I first went to Oxford. But constitutional history was *de rigueur*. Both at school and at the university we were invited to learn volumes of constitutional documents almost by heart. My father did, and so did I. Sir Arthur Haselrig, M.P., said once in the second Protectorate Parliament: "Princes are mortal, but the Commonwealth lives forever." In the same way we were taught that constitutions had more historical significance than mortal men. The history of England, it seemed, swung between the two poles of the Magna Carta and the Bill of Rights. I was not persuaded of that when I was young, although the present head of an Oxford college at that time assured me—I remember his saying this to me in St. Aldate's as if it were yesterday—that constitutional history was more interesting than any other kind because it was the embodiment of political ideas, and the history of political ideas was the very best kind.

But it is, after all, men and women who make history. I therefore offer no apology for pausing in this book from time to time to give brief character sketches of the rulers of England from Alfred the Great to King James II. I do not believe with Thomas Carlyle that history is a chain of biographies of great men, but certainly the personal character of rulers has always affected ideas and events. I have witnessed in my lifetime the age of Coolidge and the age of Franklin D. Roosevelt; I have lived through the ages of Ramsay MacDonald, Stanley Baldwin, and Neville Chamberlain, on the one hand, and those of Sir Winston Churchill and Lord Attlee, on the other; and I refuse to consider that it made no difference who our leaders were.

Yet what one would like to know is how the government of kings or other rulers has influenced the lives of ordinary people in the past. Modern historical research, which properly concerns itself with social and economic affairs and local history, as well as big political events and constitutional ideas or revolutions in thought, does its utmost to answer this question. But information, especially for the early period before the invention of printing, is sparse and will always be incomplete. Only occasionally even in the seventeenth century, which was a prolific time for memoir and letter writers, can we obtain a straightforward insight into the lives of "the common people." What made them cheer John Lilburne at his trials or follow the Duke of Monmouth into battle? Or why in earlier times did they rally behind Wat Tyler or Robert Kett? How did the Norman Conquest affect their simple lives? Were they better off under Queen Elizabeth I or under King Charles II? I have very tentatively tried to answer a few of these questions, but I am sure I shall be told they are unanswerable. As G. K. Chesterton wrote, "We are the people of England that never have spoken yet." Yet in our own Age of the Common Man we should dearly like to hear his ancestors speak.

My book, then, is an introduction into that modern world where the historian of Britain can draw upon newspapers and accurate parliamentary reports, as well as on so many White Papers and Blue Books and volumes of "lives and letters" as he cannot possibly hope to read in his whole life. Before then there are few authentic statistics and much is guesswork. Nevertheless, looking back on our early history, as I must do, from the vantage point of what we in Britain today call the Welfare State, I take an incurably optimistic view. I have reread what the experts have to say about early days and, having done so, I find it hard to believe wholeheartedly either in "golden ages" or in a "Merrie England." To my mind people as a whole are today better off in nearly every way, better fed, better clothed, better educated, more fully employed and yet with far ampler leisure and more freedom, than they have ever been before in British history. I know what has been said about the "myth of progress," about the benefits that have been conferred by the aristocracy or plutocracy of the past in patronizing the arts, in the pursuit of disinterested knowledge, and in the distribution of charity. I am aware that material improvements are not everything, that spiritual values have changed, and that the professional classes, to which I belong, are in some respects worse off than they were in my father's and grandfather's days. Progress has not of course been evenly spaced or uncheckered. One of the first things my history master at St. Paul's School in London told me when I was a boy was not to be superior about the "Middle Ages." Yet I think that ordinary Englishmen were in fact happier under the Normans than they were under Alfred the Great and happier in the reign of King Charles II than they were, say, under Henry VI.

But even as recently as 300 years ago the world was for the few, and the very few. Slowly order replaced disorder. Gradually the standard of living was raised. Imperceptibly knowledge increased and became more widely spread. Men and women became less inhibited and more intelligent. History itself ceased to be monkish chronicle or political controversy rehashed. It is to be hoped that our children will learn from the study of history that men can improve themselves, can overcome war and superstition, as they seem to be overcoming want and ignorance. Their problem is to ensure that physical science is their servant and not their master. Today at least we have left—most of us—the "kingdom of the fairies" described by Thomas Hobbes in *The Leviathan*. That is my approach to history, as I see it today. Now I shall begin to tell the story of Britain.

Contents

BOOK I: EARLY TIMES

Chapter

I   Prehistoric Britain to the Coming of Caesar   3

II   Britain under the Romans   8

III   The Coming of the Anglo-Saxons   22

IV   The Conversion of England to Christianity   26

V   The Rise of Wessex and Alfred the Great   32

VI   Origins of Wales, Scotland, and Ireland   41

VII   From Edward the Elder to Edward the Confessor   47

VIII   English Society Before the Norman Conquest   55

IX   The Foundation of Normandy and the Reign of Edward the Confessor   61

BOOK II: MIDDLE AGES

X   The Norman Conquest   69

XI   The Reigns of William II, Henry I, and Stephen   77

XII   The Reigns of Henry II and Richard I   88

XIII   The Reign of John and Magna Carta   96

XIV   The Reign of Henry III   103

XV   Wales, Scotland, Ireland in the Eleventh, Twelfth, and Thirteenth Centuries   110

XVI   English Life and Art in the Twelfth and Thirteenth Centuries   114

XVII   The Reigns of Edward I and Edward II   118

XVIII   The Reign of Edward III   128

XIX   England in the Fourteenth Century   135

XX   Richard II and the Great Revolt   145

XXI   The Reigns of Henry IV and Henry V   151

XXII   The Loss of France and the Wars of the Roses   159

XXIII   Wales, Scotland, and Ireland in the Fourteenth and Fifteenth
         Centuries   175

XXIV   Fifteenth-century England   180

BOOK III: THE TUDOR AGE: THE REFORMATION

XXV   English Society in the Early Tudor Age   187
XXVI   The Reign of Henry VII   194
XXVII   Henry VIII and Cardinal Wolsey   203
XXVIII   The English Church on the Eve of the Reformation   208
XXIX   The Beginning of the English Reformation   214
XXX   The Last Years of Henry VIII   225
XXXI   The Reign of Edward VI   232
XXXII   The Reign of Mary I   240
XXXIII   John Knox and Mary, Queen of Scots   247
XXXIV   The Early Years of Elizabeth I   253
XXXV   The Foreign Policy of Elizabeth I   259
XXXVI   Elizabeth I and the War Against Spain   268
XXXVII   The Economic and Social Life of the Elizabethan Age   276
XXXVIII The Expansion of England   285
XXXIX   Learning, Literature, and Art in the Tudor Age   293
XL   The Character of Elizabethan England   300

BOOK IV: STUART TIMES: THE ENGLISH REVOLUTION

XLI   The Accession of James I   309
XLII   The Last Years of James I   316
XLIII   The Reign of Charles I   321
XLIV   The Coming of the Civil War   330
XLV   The First Civil War   341
XLVI   The Execution of Charles I   349
XLVII   The Interregnum and the Protectorate   357
XLVIII   The Restoration of Charles II   368
XLIX   Charles II and the Rise of Political Parties   376
L   Economic and Social Life in Seventeenth Century
         England   382
LI   Education and Culture in the Seventeenth Century   389
LII   Music Through the Seventeenth Century   397

LIII Scientific and Political Ideas Through the Seventeenth
Century 400
LIV James II and the Revolution of 1688 412
LV Toward a British Empire 420
LVI Britain in 1688: Conclusion 427
Suggested Readings 433
List of Sovereigns 443
Index i

MAPS

Celtic and Roman Britain 15
Anglo-Saxon England 30
Early Wales 42
Scotland 44
Ireland 46
France: The Angevin Empire 90
France: The Hundred Years' War 163
England and Wales in Wars of the Roses 172
The World in the Reign of Queen Elizabeth 263
Tudor England 282
First British Settlements in America 290
England, Wales, and Southern Scotland in the Seventeenth
Century 346

BOOK I
EARLY TIMES

I

Prehistoric Britain to
the Coming of Caesar

"Well," said an American visitor once, when he first saw the cliffs of southern England, "it is a little island and it has often been conquered." The history of Britain up to fewer than 1,000 years ago is that of repeated invasions, in which different tribes, peoples, or nations moved in from the east, north, and south of Europe to conquer, settle, and impose their own ways upon a small but inviting land.

The invaders usually crossed what were to be known as the English Channel and the North Sea and spread across the lowland zone of the island. Those who came from modern France or Belgium were again in familiar country—indeed, upon the other side of a chalk ridge divided by the ocean. Their advance was simplified by the slow-moving rivers that led into the very heart of the country; alternatively they could beach their boats at the many excellent harbors and inlets which dotted the south coast and stretched as far east as the mouth of the river Thames. In early times Britain was exceptionally vulnerable to assault by peoples hungry for land and was therefore in the end inhabited by an extremely mixed population. "Saxon and Norman and Dane are we": Iberian and Celtic, Roman and Jutish, Frisian and Norwegian too— truly a melting pot of early Europe.

No one is certain about the origin of Britain's name. By the ancients the island was called "Albion," the White Land, and was supposed to be part of the lost continent of Atlantis. A Greek merchant, Pytheas of Marseilles, a forerunner of Columbus in the age of Alexander the Great and the first explorer known by name to have traveled to the island, described its inhabitants as the "Pretanic" or painted people. Julius Caesar, following perhaps wrongly and obscurely the geographers of the Classical World, called the country which he invaded "Britannia"; and Britain it has remained.

The country was first famous for its tin in which an export trade flourished from the earliest recorded times. Its forests afforded timber of many kinds; the damp, mixed, but never extreme, climate made the land green, wherever the forest was not king; it was lavishly watered and much of it was easy to cultivate with a primitive spade or plough. Throughout the lowlands it was a gentle and welcoming country, and it possessed rich coal and iron ore deposits, to be enjoyed by future generations.

The lowland zone of Britain extended across the south, middle, and east, bounded, apart from the sea, by a line running north-east from where the city of Exeter now stands to the site of Durham. The highland zone was far less attractive to invaders. Broken by the Midland Gap and the Cheshire plain, it was rugged and windswept, largely covered by hills, mountains, and moorlands, by Dartmoor and Exmoor, by the Cambrian mountains in Wales, by the Pennine chain and the Lake District, by the Cheviots, the Grampians, and the Scottish Highlands, with a heavier rainfall and a poorer soil; it demanded and obtained a tough and conservative people.

In prehistoric times only the coastal belts and glens of the highlands were settled. The first invaders preferred the chalk uplands or limestone plateaus of the lowland south where the light and porous soil could be quickly cleared to support man and beast. Thus the history of the early incursions into Britain is that of adventurers fanning out across the lowlands from the east or south and imposing their habits on those whom they vanquished. But upon the edge of the highlands they halted; and when they penetrated into these less hospitable regions their newer cultures were repelled or absorbed by the old.

⊗ THE STONE AGES

About 250,000 years ago *homo sapiens,* veritable man, first appeared in Britain. It was by no means one of his earliest homes; the British Isles, the last horizon of peoples coming across the world from the east, were infinitely younger than man, who has walked the earth for at least half a million years. Nor can we be sure precisely when he appeared in Britain. Apart from a few skeletal remains of dubious date, dug from the prehistoric slime, his presence has to be inferred from stone and bone tools, the making of which alone distinguished him from the apes. It was when much of the world was covered by a huge ice sheet, which spread southward until it froze northern Europe, four times to recede and return, that man is first assuredly detected dwelling in southern Britain amid tundra and steppe-like conditions of arctic cold. This was before Britain had become an island, when it was still joined to the mainland of Europe. In this oldest Stone Age primitive hunters mingled with the mammoth, the woolly rhinoceros, the bison and the reindeer, the wild ox and the horse; lived in caves that were warm in winter and cool in summer; and fashioned tools with the flints that were to be found embedded in the chalk hills of southern England. A population of perhaps 250 human beings lived by hunting game and by grubbing up roots and berries. They wrought spears, knives, hammers, harpoons, and needles. With these rude implements they slaughtered the wild animals and produced food and clothing; but they had neither corn nor cattle nor pottery. Few of them survived beyond the age of twenty or thirty. They believed in unseen powers controlling a dreadful existence and practiced magical rites to propitiate and ward off the devils. Such were the first men who dwelt in the land of Britain.

When the Ice Ages finally ended after many centuries and a warmer climate came, the barren landscape gave way to forests of birch, aspen, willow, pine, oak, and beech; the mammoths, rhinoceroses and reindeer disappeared; and other primitive men crossed the land bridge from what was later continental Europe or ferried over the fens that then covered the area now occupied by the North Sea. These men of the Middle Stone Age were sea fishermen as well as hunters, could fashion tools to cut down trees and light fires, knew how to build canoes and to shoot arrows, and dwelt at the edges and in the clearings of forests.

About six or seven thousand years before Christ, Britain was finally severed from the mainland of Europe. The glaciations of the Ice Ages had transformed the face of the land, causing the sea level to rise and reshaping rivers, valleys, and mountains. It is estimated that England sank 70 to 100 feet lower than it had been in the Old Stone Age. As the weather became sunnier, the country grew more attractive, the vegetation richer and more varied. Three streams of colonists poured over from the east. Whether they ousted the earlier cave dwellers we cannot say. Some of them had small stone tools known as microliths; they had dogs and other domesticated animals; they hunted the forest beasts, such as the red deer and the wild pig; they inhabited covered pits or rock shelters as well as caves. For three or four thousand years they lived much as the fowls of the air, neither sowing nor reaping, "poor little groups of hunters and food gatherers scattered round the fringes and in the clearings of the dripping forests." Then in the third millennium before Christ occurred the revolution of the New Stone Age when the first agriculturalists established themselves in Britain.

These earliest, nomadic exponents of the art of mixed farming crossed the sea as peaceful immigrants searching for new lands. They may have been delighted at the mild climate and rejoiced in the greensward. They avoided forest, marsh, and heavy clay, and rapidly scattered over the area in which it was easiest to settle in southern England, particularly upon Salisbury plain, always the center of civilization in earliest times. Later they ventured farther north to modern Yorkshire and perhaps Scotland and Ireland. These colonists lived primarily by breeding cattle upon the chalk uplands, but they also kept goats and pigs and they grew barley and wheat on the hillsides, milling them to make flour. They developed an elaborate flint-mining industry and boasted many tools, from polished axes to picks constructed from the antlers of stags. They were advanced in carpentry and could make elementary clay pots by hand. The colonists dwelt in villages of round huts or in summer camps. When they died, they were buried in long barrows which served as collective tombs. They practiced fertility rites and may have worshipped their ancestors and sacrificed human beings to their gods.

The colonists of the New Stone Age were thus enterprising farmers, industrious, skillful, and fiercely religious. They stayed in Britain side by side with the older hunting communities who benefited from the new arts but still practiced their old ways. A small, slender, long-headed people, the men of the New Stone Age were not great fighters. Less than a thousand years after their immigration they were attacked from the mainland of Europe by domineering round-headed warriors, taller men armed with bows and arrows and battle-axes who overran the whole of habitable Britain in the second millennium before Christ.

✂ THE BEAKER FOLK AND THE CELTS

These latest invaders came immediately from the Rhineland and modern Holland, although the cradle of their race was Spain. A ruthless and adventurous people, called by the archaeologists the Beaker Folk after the drinking vessels which they used, they dispossessed or enslaved the older inhabitants and scattered widely throughout modern Britain. Once they had conquered and were recognized as rulers, their restless energies were directed into many pursuits, including ranching, commerce, and building. They stimulated the manufacture of bronze, first made, it seems, by Irish smiths from a mixture of native copper and tin; they wore linen and woolen clothes fastened with jet buttons; and they rejoiced in jewelry and fine weapons. But their pottery was clumsy and the land was little cultivated. The vast and famous temples of Avebury and Stonehenge in modern Wiltshire, the latter built with large blue stones brought by sea from a sacred mountain in modern Pembrokeshire, are their most noble contribution to the inheritance of Britain. Whether in these prehistoric temples priests conducted the worship of the Sun only or of a whole pantheon of primitive gods is uncertain, but these impressive monuments were the dedicated work of men who felt the majesty of death.

The so-called Beaker people were followed into Britain by other pastoral warriors. The earlier part of the second millennium before Christ must have been a time of troubles, but by about 1500 B.C. a pattern of culture can be seen: a national religion with a reconstructed

Stonehenge as its temple, a common language, an age of bronze, perhaps even a single king. Whether the language spoken by these Beaker people was Celtic or not is uncertain. But by the first millennium before Christ the "Celtization" of Britain had begun. Expanding from their homelands in France and western Germany, under pressure from the Germans and Illyrians, the Celtic-speaking tribes of Europe saw the British Isles as a sanctuary from the upheavals on the mainland. The Celtic invaders were armed with double-edged swords and sturdy battle-axes, but did not necessarily have to fight their way in; they may have mixed peacefully with the existing inhabitants to whom they were culturally akin.

Thus during these last centuries before Christ wave after wave of Celtic immigrants disembarked along the east and south coasts of Britain and settled far and wide. For the first time the planting of crops became really important. The Celts introduced the two-ox plough and the silo; their small square fields can still be seen today through the magic of air photography. In their stone farmhouses a higher degree of civilization prevailed than ever before: cooking was done in bronze caldrons, woolen yarn was spun and then woven into clothes, ornate vessels with pleasing geometric patterns were fired, men wore tunics and began to shave, according to Caesar, all over their bodies. Iron, a cheaper and more plentiful metal than bronze, was discovered about 500 B.C. By the time the civilization of classical Greece reached its perfection in the age of Pericles, Britain had become inhabited by a largely Celtic community of simple farmers living either in walled homesteads or hut villages.

But as the pressure from the mainland of Europe increased, these Celts grew more warlike. Farmlands and hamlets had to be defended by hill forts against fresh armed incursions from overseas and in case of intertribal wars. Some quite large fortresses were built at Cissbury in modern Sussex and Maiden Castle in modern Dorset. The later Celtic warriors employed two-wheeled battle chariots, copied from the Etruscans, and many a struggle was waged for the best lands. To the victors went the spoils. The conquering tribal chieftains and their retinues, with bladed daggers and javelins, swords, shields, and horsed chariots, enjoyed a roistering life: they were served food on fine crockery and flagons of imported wine; they bought luxurious goods from abroad, and their women were sophisticated enough to use mirrors. The Druids were their priests and counselors; they preached immortality and the transmigration of souls, performed cruel sacrifices, worshipped their gods in sacred groves or temples, and made and administered laws to inspire unity among the warring tribes.

Such were the rulers of Britain in the last centuries before the Romans came—not, as was once thought, the veriest savages dyed blue with woad, though primitive enough. The population was mixed, the heirs of hundreds of groups of invaders, organized under tribal kings or chiefs, bellicose and quarrelsome. In 75 B.C., just before Julius Caesar's time, the Celts were joined by mightier warriors still, the Belgic tribes (Celtic with an admixture of Teuton) that introduced into Britain the heavy eight-oxen plough, the potter's wheel, a coinage of gold, and carved for themselves a kingdom in modern Kent, Middlesex, and Hertfordshire. Partly under the impact of these virile people the Celts scattered even more widely. When Caesar came to Britain he noted that the most civilized inhabitants (these new Belgic tribes with whom he had first to fight) lived in Kent and in the southeast corner of the island nearest to the mainland, whereas he thought that the tribes of the interior were more backward. The Belgae did not mind having to hew down the forests or to cultivate clay lands; the earlier, less enterprising inhabitants still preferred the simplicity of life on the chalk uplands.

II

Britain under the Romans

In 55 B.C. Gaius Julius Caesar, proconsul of the Roman Republic and governor of two of its provinces known as Cisalpine and Transalpine Gaul, a man who embodied all the power and majesty of the Classical World, decided to conquer Britain. The Roman Republic, originally a mere city state on the banks of the Tiber, had already become an empire covering two million square miles, comprising most of Europe and Asia, and stretching from the Rock of Gibraltar to the river Euphrates. Caesar, now in the prime of his life, was one of the three statesmen who virtually ruled this huge territory, a genius alike as a political orator and administrator, a general and a leader of men. In the first three years of his command in Gaul he had subdued much of France, Belgium, Holland, and Switzerland and ruled over an area from the Rhine to the Pyrenees and from the English Channel to the Alps. Now he was absorbed in consolidating his victories and contemplating new conquests.

The motives which induced Caesar to attack Britain were two: first, the Romans, though in fact knowing very little of this mysterious barbaric land on the outer edge of civilization, believed that it contained riches and that to occupy it would add prestige to their armies; secondly, it was an island that offered a refuge to rebels against the imperial might of the Romans and even a springboard for conspiracies and counterattacks in Gaul.

In the late summer of 55 B.C. Caesar therefore planned a reconnaissance in force. He had been able to extract hardly any geographical or political intelligence from the traders whom he interviewed: "he could not ascertain anything about the size of the island," he wrote, and indeed he believed in common with other authors of his time (and the later historian Tacitus) that it was triangular in shape with one of its sides facing Spain. After sending a warship to collect information about the coast of southeast Britain, at the end of August he ordered transports to concentrate at Boulogne upon the other side of the Channel in readiness for the assault.

Two legions (each with a nominal establishment of about 6,000 men) —the cream of the Roman armies; 500 cavalry, to be separately embarked; and a number of auxiliary troops, including artillerymen and archers who were assigned to galleys with special turrets—were allocated to this expedition with Caesar himself in command. The Britons were forewarned of the coming of the Romans not only because they had spotted the single ship spying out their coast, but because Caesar had sent over a Belgic king to require the submission of the more powerful tribes. Thus Caesar had abandoned any hope of surprise, and when he attempted to disembark his legionaries from eighty transports in the neighborhood of Walmer in modern Kent, they were confronted by painted warriors in chariots and understandably hesitated to plunge fully armed from their low boats into the deep water; Caesar then ordered up his galleys to outflank the Britons by enfilading them with artillery. Covered by catapults, the legionaries pushed on to the shore, but were still in danger of being overwhelmed by superior numbers. However, Caesar kept a mobile reserve in hand and eventually the Britons withdrew and sought an armistice.

But the formidable impression made by the valor of the legionaries and by the novelty of the galleys was soon dissipated. Caesar's cavalry had been delayed in starting and then was driven back by adverse winds to France. Most of his transports, anchored upon the water line, were shattered by high tides beneath the full moon and the Romans found themselves in peril of being stranded in a strange land, cut off from their base without equipment or provisions for a long war. Confined to an armed camp, the legionaries had to seize what corn they could find and many of them were ambushed as they did so. Caesar managed to have his transports repaired and covered a rather ignominious withdrawal in mid-September by once more exacting hostages and promises of submission from the local tribes. In Rome a thanksgiving service was ordered in honor of his exploit; the mission had been successfully accomplished, even if only a handful of Britons in a corner of the island had been met, and next year Caesar determined, having digested his lessons, to occupy Britain with a larger force.

Julius Caesar's aim in 54 B.C. was to subdue the island, but he was unable to hold it. He took immense risks. Of the eight legions under his command in Gaul he left only three behind and he brought half his cavalry with him. Throughout the winter soldiers and slaves had sweated to construct both wider and shallower transports, designed by Caesar himself to carry more men and enable them to land more easily. Together with the Roman warships nearly 800 vessels bore down upon the Kentish coast in July. Intimidated by this armada, the Britons did not this time attempt to resist the invasion. Profiting from his initial success, Caesar beached his boats on the highwater mark and thrust inland, making a twelve-mile night march to surprise the hill fortress of Bigbury, two miles west of Canterbury. The Gaulish cavalry disposed of the British defenders who lined the woods and the legionaries occupied the fort, but meanwhile a storm had severely damaged the beached ships and Caesar was obliged to return to the coast to arrange their repair and ensure against any fresh disaster.

The fall of Bigbury persuaded the tribes of southeast Britain, who habitually warred among themselves, to unite against the Romans. Cassivellaunus, king of the Belgic tribe of the Catuvellauni, was appointed commander-in-chief, although the neighboring tribe of the Trinovantes hastened to come to terms with Caesar. Battle was joined after a Roman foraging party had been attacked and so many Britons were killed that they never dared again to meet the Romans in the open field. Caesar now determined to crush his chief enemy by thrusting across the river Thames and occupying his tribal capital. The Thames was forced and the capital fell. But King Cassivellaunus had not yet shot his bolt; gathering a force of 4,000 charioteers, he carried on guerrilla warfare and sent orders to four petty kings to surprise the Romans' naval base. Only when this last brave maneuver failed did Cassivellaunus seek terms from Caesar. The Roman commander, who had learned of trouble approaching in Gaul, was glad enough to accept tribute and hostages. As soon as the hostages were delivered and his ships repaired, he packed his men as tightly as he could on board and hastened back to unruly

Gaul. This time no celebrations were ordered in Rome. The first real attempt to conquer Britain with an armada had been abandoned.

The Romans were disappointed with what they had found in Britain. Cicero, the orator and friend of Caesar, wrote at the time: "I hear there is no gold or silver in Britain" and later: "the result of the British expedition is a source of anxiety. For it is notorious that the approaches to the island are ramparted by astonishing masses of cliff; and besides, it is now known that there is not a pennyworth of gold in the island, nor any hope of loot except from slaves; and I do not suppose you expect any of them to be a scholar or a musician." Caesar himself, while he was impressed by the size of the population, noted that many of them were savages who practiced polyandry and did not even grow corn. He had learned that he did not have sufficient men at his disposal both to occupy Britain and to hold down Gaul, and he knew that the Celtic tribes on both sides of the Channel conspired together to harass his movements. And though the Roman army could always win a pitched battle, the Celts were adepts at guerrilla warfare and skirmishing. What remained was the knowledge that the Romans could conquer Britain whenever they wished, if they were prepared to devote time, men, and money to the purpose.

After Caesar left, ultimately to return to Rome, to be named imperator, and to be assassinated on the steps of the Senate, Roman influences spread throughout Britain. The tribal chieftains imported Roman goods—necklaces and bracelets, glassware and wine—and heard more about Roman ways from merchants and traders. They imbibed Roman culture and even in some cases accepted Roman overlordship. The terror inspired by the legions was remembered, but the lesson was not grasped that political independence needed the kind of unity they had momentarily accepted under Cassivellaunus. As Tacitus wrote later of the Britons under the Roman Empire, "nothing helped us more in the war with their strongest nations than their inability to cooperate. It is seldom that two of their states unite to repel a common danger; fighting in detail, they are conquered wholesale."

So the Britons resumed their wars with one another and awaited with indifference the time when one of the new Roman emperors should decide to gratify a thirst for glory by carrying through the conquest denied to mighty Caesar. Julius Caesar's successor, the Emperor Augustus, contemplated it; the mad tyrant Caligula resolved upon it only to cancel it suddenly; at last in 43 A.D. the emperor Claudius came.

✥ THE COMING OF CLAUDIUS

As a result of Caesar's invasions some of the mists begin to lift from early Britain, which now entered the mainstream of European history. Roman authors like Caesar and Tacitus sketched the characteristics of the country, and the portrait of its people was no longer dependent upon the spade of the archaeologist. To the south lay the virile kingdom of the Catuvellauni which, after the departure of the Romans, absorbed the territories of the neighboring Romanophil Trinovantes and covered much of southern England, which was ruled from a new capital at modern Colchester in Essex. The grandson of the heroic Cassivellaunus, Cunobelin—Shakespeare's "Cymbelin"—wielded so wide a supremacy that he was actually described as "king of the Britons." Another Belgic tribe, the Atrebates, whose leader Commius had first been an ally and later an enemy of Caesar, founded a new kingdom about 50 B.C. in modern Hampshire and Wiltshire which rivaled that of the Catuvellauni. Beneath or beside these bigger kingdoms modern Sussex was inhabited by a tribe called the Regni, and in the southwest Dorset contained the Durotiges, Devon and Cornwall the Dumnonii, and Somerset and Gloucestershire the Dobuni. The middle kingdoms included the Coritani of modern Leicestershire and Lincolnshire, and the Iceni of East Anglia. In Wales were to be found the Silures, the Ordovices, and the Degeangli. The Cornovii (of modern Shropshire) and the vigorous Brigantes occupied much of the north except for the area east of Yorkshire inhabited by the Parisi, an advanced people, as their name suggests, who came from the banks of the Seine. Of these tribes the most cultured were the latest invaders—the Belgic tribes, the Catuvellauni, the Atrebates, and the Parisi. Both Caesar and Tacitus remarked on the size of population produced by these numerous tribes as well as the pleasantness of the island's climate, which allowed corn to be grown, cattle to be pastured, and hunting dogs to be raised. Tin and other metals, wheat, cattle, dogs, and slaves were exported from Britain in return for the luxuries of the Roman Empire. Thus Britain seemed a more attractive prospect and an easy prize when Claudius made up his mind to annex it.

For nearly a hundred years the project had been on the Roman agenda. Now that Britain had many Roman traders and some client princes, knowledge about it was broader than in Julius Caesar's day. Its continued independence appeared to be a source of danger to the security of the Roman Empire, especially in Gaul. And Claudius, who was not one of the brighter of the Roman Emperors, was eager for personal glory.

The expedition was carefully planned. Fifty thousand men were put under the command of an experienced officer, Aulus Plautius, and a landing was made at Richborough in Kent, simultaneously with other landings or feints at other ports. Richborough was a safe landlocked harbor and an excellent naval base for the Romans. Cunobelin, king of the Catuvellauni whose rule extended to Kent, had recently died and his sons, Caratacus and Togodumus, had inherited his kingdom. Though they were determined to resist the Romans, they were disunited and defeated separately. A decisive battle was fought on the line of the Medway, a tributary of the Thames. Then Plautius halted to await the coming of his emperor.

Claudius came, saw, and conquered. The Roman army forced the crossing of the Thames and marched on Colchester, the capital of the Catuvellauni, where, accompanied by a corps of elephants, the emperor received the submission of many tribes. The kingdom of the Catuvellauni was declared to be a Roman province, Colchester was converted into a military settlement (Camulodonum), and Plautius was appointed first governor of Britain. But the Roman system of colonial administration was eclectic. Some tribal chieftains were recognized as client kings and some Roman military settlements were established and linked with each other by military roads. The aim was to divide and rule.

After sixteen days the emperor departed and left Plautius to complete the conquest. Having occupied the southeast, he pushed out two columns northward. Many battles were fought, and most tribes submitted before the advancing legions. The Romans' progress was slowed as they reached the highland zone. Caratacus, the Belgic prince who had escaped after the battle of the Medway, constituted himself the leader of a resistance movement centered in Wales, where he carried on a guerrilla war. Ostorius Scapula, who succeeded Plautius as the Roman governor in 47 A.D., planted one of his legions at Gloucester and cornered Caratacus in northwest Wales. Here the Britons were outnumbered, surrounded, and crushed, and the wife and daughter of Caratacus captured. Caratacus got away only to be surrendered in chains to the Romans by the Queen of the Brigantes—a typical act of betrayal in this divided land: he died in honorable captivity at Rome.

Caratacus had been "worshipped by his followers as a national hero, the champion of their liberty, and their heaven-sent leader against the invaders." British resistance to the Romans did not end with his death. In 61, provoked by the conduct of a brutal Roman financial official, or procurator, the Iceni of East Anglia revolted. Their queen, Boudicca, had been flogged, her daughter raped, and her palace sacked. While the new Roman governor Suetonius Paulinus was away suppressing Druid worship in Anglesey, an island off north Wales, the Iceni rose and, joined by the Trinovantes, Catuvellauni, and other tribes, swept down to kill the Roman military settlers in Colchester and set the town on fire, to burn the rising commercial center of London, and to wipe out the newly built Roman town of Verulamium (near modern St. Albans in Hertfordshire). In these three towns 70,000 people are said to have perished. But the Roman governor kept his head. He returned from Anglesey, collected 10,000 men, and forced the Britons to fight on ground of his own choosing. The blood-sated host was massacred and Queen Boudicca committed suicide. Vengeance was executed upon the tribes who had dared to rebel against their Roman masters.

Though a more clement policy was followed after the recall of the procurator who had provoked the uprising, about ten years later the Brigantes rose in the north and, just as a legion had previously been stationed at Gloucester to control Wales, another legion had now to be moved to York to hold down the north of Britain. This move took place about the year 71 and the conquest of south Wales was completed in 75. In 78 a powerful governor named Julius Agricola, who had served his apprenticeship in Britain in the war against Queen Boudicca, took up his appointment. More is known about this fine and incorruptible Roman soldier than about any other governor of Britain because his son-in-law happened to be a historian of genius named Tacitus.

Under the direction of the soldier-emperor Vespasian, who had himself served for a time in Britain, Agricola adopted a forward policy. The south was now at peace. He completed the conquest of Wales and moved into modern Scotland, reaching the Forth-Clyde line in 81. Next year he contemplated the subjugation of Ireland, which he thought might be held by one legion and a modest number of auxiliary troops. But he found that he had not the men to spare. Instead he pushed into the north of Scotland, breaking the resistance of the highlanders at a great battle on some unknown site called Mount Craupius, perhaps in the Moray Firth. Tacitus claimed that after this battle the whole of Britain was subjected to the Romans. In the following year Agricola was recalled.

Such was the virtual end of the original Roman military advance through Britain. Agricola had at his disposal four legions and an army of some 70,000 men. The garrison was reduced. One of the legions was withdrawn to Germany and the policy was adopted of making a permanent frontier to the new province and renouncing conquest beyond it. This policy was symbolized and promoted by the building of the magnificent wall named after the Emperor Hadrian.

The three Roman legions that remained in Britain were stationed at Caerleon-on-Usk (whence it had been moved from Gloucester) in the extreme south of Wales, at Chester lying to the north of Wales, and at

R. Forth

ANTONINES
WALL · · · · · · [Edinburgh]

HADRIAN'S
WALL · · · · · ·

Solway Firth

Durham •

BRIGANTES

•[York]

Isle of Angelsey

DEGEANGLI

CORNOVII

•Chester

CORITANI

the Wash

ORDOVICES

• Wroxeter

ICENI

CATUVELLAUNI

SILURES   DOBUNI

TRINOVANTES

•Colchester
(Camulodunum)

Caerleon •

• Gloucester

Verulamium •

[Cardiff]

R. Thames

London
(Londinium)

Silchester

Richborough

Medway R.

[Canterbury]

ATREBATES

[Walmer]

REGNI

DUROTRIGES

Exeter •

DUMNONII

Isle of Wight

CELTIC AND ROMAN BRITAIN

York: all these fortresses were strengthened and supplemented during the reign of the Emperor Trajan with the aim of holding in check the warlike tribes in modern Wales and modern Scotland. Agricola's gains in Scotland were abandoned and, encouraged by the withdrawal, the tribes in the modern Lowlands of Scotland launched an attack upon the Roman army. The legion at York was cashiered for its failure to suppress this fresh revolt and was replaced. The Emperor Hadrian, who succeeded Trajan in 117, and was known as the great consolidator, himself visited Britain and ordered the creation of a northern frontier with a wall stretching some 73 miles from Newcastle upon Tyne in the east to Bowness on the Solway in the west. This remarkable engineering feat took five years to complete and involved the shifting of millions of square feet of soil and rock. The line of defense consisted of a solid high stone wall, protected by a deep ditch and with another ditch or "vallum" to its hinterland. Garrisons were stationed in forts set out at intervals and there were sally ports, turrets, signal towers, and a traverse fortified road. The exact size of the garrison assigned to the wall itself is not known, but it was of considerable strength. The general strategic aim was to restrain the unsettled northern tribes and to protect the Roman province of Britain, now blossoming into prosperity, from attack by barbarians. This famous wall, much of which still remains visible today, set amid desolate moors, was the extreme limit of the Roman world, and it was "to guard the fabric of civilization through the long menace of darkness and dissolution."

The building of Hadrian's Wall was a defensive move inspired by a military disaster. Soon after it had been completed the Romans again moved forward, seeking to make a desert and call it peace by subduing the Scottish Lowlands, as earlier they had reduced the tribes in Wales. The Roman army advanced as far as the Forth-Clyde line where an earthen rampart, known as the Antonine Wall, was constructed in 143. But the Romans had overstretched their resources: fortified lines need garrisons and mere walls do not frighten a determined enemy. The tribes both in the Scottish Lowlands and in Yorkshire again rebelled; the Antonine Wall was penetrated and overrun; reinforcements had to be sent to Britain; and about 184 the Emperor Commodus had to dispatch one of his best generals to stem an invasion of the province from the north. After the death of Commodus in 193 a struggle between two claimants for the imperial succession involved the withdrawal of troops from Britain. The emperor Severus, who won the civil war, then himself came over to direct operations against the Scots, rebuilt Hadrian's Wall, and repaired the fortresses of York and Chester, both of which had suffered severely during a prolonged series of revolts and disturbances on the frontiers. Severus died at York in 211 after many crippling and exhausting battles, but he had achieved more than most of his predecessors and for nearly a century afterwards peace prevailed in Roman Britain.

✿ THE CHARACTER OF ROMANIZATION

Before the Roman conquest life in Britain had been extremely primitive. Cunobelin, who most nearly approached being a paramount king, lived in a shack and his subjects for the most part dwelt in slums. Tacitus remarked tartly, "One must remember that we are dealing with barbarians." But once the legions had established order, the Romanization of Britain, if far less intense than in the Mediterranean lands, made fairly rapid headway. The army of occupation, consisting of about 50,000 men, was concentrated mainly on the western and northern frontiers, and the tribes were allowed to govern themselves subject to the military and fiscal requirements of the Roman governors, who were directly responsible to the emperor.

The principal instrument of Romanization was the town. Towns were virtually unknown in Britain before the coming of the Romans, but now under imperial stimulus they were built in the valleys and on the plains and occasionally on the sites of former hutted settlements. For the Roman soldiers themselves settlements or *coloniae* were built, for example at Colchester, Gloucester, and Lincoln. Colchester was originally the Roman capital of Britain. But London, a natural center of commerce, soon became the largest town and the effective seat of civil government. There were also one or two full-fledged *municipiae,* Roman towns with a recognized legal status. Most of the towns, however, were tribal centers known as *oppida* which enjoyed local self-government. Spas or holiday resorts were created at Buxton and Bath for the delectation of the Romanized Britons.

The towns were beautified by impressive buildings and furnished with mass-produced goods. "Agricola," wrote Tacitus, "gave private encouragement and official assistance to the building of temples, public squares and private mansions. . . . He trained the sons of the tribal chiefs in the liberal arts. . . . The result was that in place of distaste for the Latin language came a passion to command it. . . . Our national dress came into favour and the toga was everywhere to be seen. And so the Britons were gradually led on to the amenities that make vice agreeable—arcades, baths and sumptuous banquets. They spoke of such novelties as 'civilization,' when they really were only a form of enslavement."

A typical town was Silchester, the capital of the tribe of Atrebates, lying at the crossroads of western England. Here was an *oppidum* of some ninety acres surrounded by a wall a mile and a half long, containing not only a number of large houses, shops, and places of amusement, but cottages set among gardens and paddocks. The most important building was the forum or market which was combined with a basilica or town hall. The forum was a big open court surrounded by porticoes with shops and offices on three sides and on the fourth side the town hall, built of bath stone with red tessellated floors. The town contained four pagan temples and by the time of the fourth century also a small Christian church. There were centrally heated public baths and an amphitheater outside the walls, where sporting events and pantomimes took place, and an inn. The basilica was large enough to hold the entire population of the town at one time—perhaps 4,000 people.

These towns, built under the direction of Roman surveyors upon a chessboard pattern with guttered streets, were the ambitious and privileged vehicles of a superimposed civilization. They were linked by roads first constructed for military purposes but developing into a network admirably conducive to trade. Since the towns were erected on natural sites and connected with each other by the most direct means, many modern British roads still lie upon the same foundations and follow the same general lines as the Roman roads.

These splendid roads encouraged industry to develop, as for example the production of lead (from which silver was refined), copper (in Wales), tin (in Cornwall), iron (in Sussex), shale (in Dorset), and jet (in Yorkshire). Metals and corn were exported; wine and olive oil and manufactured goods such as glass, pottery, and silverware were obtained in return. Roman Britain was nonetheless fundamentally an agricultural community still principally concentrated in the chalk uplands. A traditional field system was practiced in farms or villas of all shapes and sizes ranging from large and relatively luxurious estates to squalid small holdings, but it was improved by better communications, construction of canals, and the draining of fens. It is estimated that in spite of the exposure of unwanted children a million people may have dwelt in Britain and flourished under the protection of the Roman peace.

The Romans do not appear to have imposed their own religion upon Britain, although they suppressed the Druids and expected a proper respect to be paid to the emperor. The Roman gods mingled agreeably with the crowd of Celtic gods. As Gibbon wrote, "The various modes of worship which prevailed in the Roman world were all considered by the peoples as equally true, by the philosopher as equally false, and by the magistrates as equally useful." In 313 the emperor Constantine published an edict granting toleration to the religion of Christianity that had come into Europe from the east, and the Christian church at Silchester is supposed to date from that time. Three British bishops attended the Christian Council of Arles in 314. Exactly when Christianity first came to Roman Britain is uncertain, but Tertullian, one of the early fathers of the Church, claimed that it penetrated to parts of the island inaccessible to the Romans. It prospered among the poorer rather than the wealthier classes in the towns and villas; the rich remained pagans.

The Romans clung to Britain as part of their empire for nearly 400 years, maintaining a garrison there even after they had been obliged to withdraw troops elsewhere upon the continent of Europe under the pressure of barbaric attacks on their frontiers. It is doubtful if they stayed for economic reasons. Appian, a Roman lawyer, wrote about the year 150 that "even the half of the island which the Romans now hold is not profitable to them." They acquired slaves and a substantial number of recruits for their armies from Britain and heavy taxes from citizens (in 212 the emperor Caracalla had conferred Roman citizenship on nearly all the freemen of the Empire) and the island was in fact treated as a kind of strategic reserve from which reinforcements and supplies could be sent to threatened points on the continental mainland.

The Britons were brought for the first time into the orbit of classical civilization. They learned Latin and Christianity, they were taught how to build on a large scale, and they took part in mass entertainments. The Britons of the second century after Christ were at least as Romanized as the Britons of the twentieth century became Americanized. The art of gardening in Britain owes much to the Romans, who introduced among other things the cherry and the rose. Yet a great deal of the Roman civilization was too artificial to survive and some of it was cheap and distasteful. The tendency of the Celtic tribes to quarrel among themselves was not eradicated; the bread and circuses offered in the ephemeral life of the towns was enervating; the well-paid and equipped garrisons who guarded the frontiers and coasts for them left the Britons incapable of relying upon themselves. Thus when the Romans finally withdrew the Britons lacked any pattern of unity and possessed little effective leadership; they were therefore quite unable to stem the new tides of invasion which lapped all around them and came in to scatter or destroy them. Demoralization set in and town life decayed more than a century before the Anglo-Saxons began to occupy Britain in the middle of the fifth century.

⌘ THE WITHDRAWAL OF THE ROMANS

After the devastation of Scotland and the rebuilding of Hadrian's Wall by the Emperor Severus, Roman Britain had enjoyed a fitful peace. Severus had divided the country into two parts—Lower Britain with its capital at York and Upper Britain which included the west, the south, and London. Each was under a separate command, and possibly the aim was to prevent power from being concentrated in the hands of one ambitious general; during the third century when the Roman Empire as a whole fell into a decline there were not only economic depression and monetary inflation, a failure of town life, and an increasing threat from the barbarians on every side, but also constant civil wars between emperors and would-be emperors who recruited rival armies composed of discontented soldiers.

Although the dangers had not yet become insistent, the province of Britain was beginning to feel the menaces of barbaric invaders—Scots in Ireland, Picts in Scotland, and the Anglo-Saxon or Frankish pirates from Germany. In the last years of the century the towns were decaying. The ambitious projects of the age of Agricola were forgotten. By 300 the forum at Wroxeter (in modern Shropshire) had been burned down, the theater at Verulamium had been destroyed, and deterioration had set in at Caerwent, Silchester, and London. By the time of the next century squatters occupied ruined towns and the richer Romanized Britons had abandoned their town houses and retired to their estates in the country.

To cope with disturbances upon his eastern frontiers the emperor Diocletian, the sturdy son of a farmer who ruled until 305, appointed a colleague named Maximinian to take command. Not only had he assigned to him the armies of Britain, Gaul, and Spain, but also a fleet that was known as the *classis Britannica* based upon Boulogne, which had been in existence since the time of Claudius. The admiral of this fleet, Carausius, took advantage of the opportunity to acclaim himself an emperor by winning over the legions stationed in Britain to his side. He succeeded in maintaining order and defending his short-lived empire in Britain until he was murdered by his own finance minister, who in due course was overthrown in turn by the emperor Constantius. Carausius, Constantius, and his son Constantine the Great reorganized the defenses of Britain once again. A ring of forts between twenty and thirty feet high was built along the coast from the Wash to the Isle of Wight. Hadrian's Wall was regarrisoned; the fortress of York was rebuilt; a new fortress was constructed at Cardiff. The legion so long stationed at Caerleon was removed to Richborough, still the finest port in the southeast, where Aulus Plautius had landed 250 years earlier.

Britain was now divided into four provinces. There was a garrison army and also a mobile field army largely consisting of cavalry. Three commanders were appointed, the Duke of the Britons with headquarters at York, the Count of the Saxon Shore in charge of the coastal defenses in the east, and the Count of the Britons in charge of the field army. In addition there must have been a fleet of some kind—scout ships are known to have existed—while later a system of signal stations was set up along the Yorkshire coast. Yet all these defenses, which sound so impressive, were barely adequate to fend off the menace of the barbarians. In the first place, the Romans no longer had sufficient trained forces to garrison them. To guard the Saxon shore Wales and the west had to be denuded of soldiers. Secondly, the long line of forts and signal stations was useless to withstand the daring and skill of pirates unless it was strongly manned or afforded bases for a first-class fleet. Indeed these coastal defences have been compared to the sand castles built by children at the seaside to keep out the tide. In addition to taking such military measures as they could the later rulers of Britain confessed their insufficiency by trying to buy off the barbarians, allowing them to settle under treaty (as *federati*) in various parts of the island, notably in Wales and East Anglia.

In any case these arrangements held good for only 50 years. In 360 the emperor Constans (who succeeded Constantine) had to send a force to Britain to attack the Picts and Scots. Seven years later the Anglo-Saxons from the west combined with the Picts and Scots from the north and launched an assault on Britain from three sides; they killed the Count of the Saxon Shore and defeated the Duke of the Britons. When the emperor ordered an able Spanish soldier named Theodosius to retrieve this disaster he discovered London in a state of siege and the barbaric bands swarming all over the south of Britain. Theodosius found that the army was corrupted and demoralized, but managed to restore some order. The next Roman general in supreme command betrayed his trust in the cause of personal ambition and took away the garrison. Once more a Roman soldier, by name Stilicho, came, conquered and reorganized.

At the beginning of the fifth century the end of Roman Britain was at hand. Neighboring Gaul was aflame and the barbarians were marching on Rome itself. The last troops were withdrawn from the island and the Britons left to fend for themselves. In vain they appealed to Rome for help. Some shadowy Roman government may have persisted in the southeastern part of the country until ten years after the sack of Rome in 410, but the curtain of the "Dark Ages" was rapidly coming down. In the middle of the fifth century the event took place known in history as the Adventus Saxonum—the permanent occupation of southern Britain by the Anglo-Saxons, from whom England took her name.

III

The Coming of the Anglo-Saxons

The pressure of the barbarians upon Britain had become intense as early as the middle of the fourth century, but it was only when the Roman Empire declined and fell that their attacks grew irresistible and the Anglo-Saxons streamed into the island to change the character of its people for all time.

Who were the Anglo-Saxons and from where did they come? In the Venerable Bede's *History of the English Church and People,* written in the early eighth century, a circumstantial story is told, but Bede also speaks in broad terms of "the Saxon nation" or the "Anglo-Saxons" who came from "Germany." We can call them if we wish either a Teutonic or a Nordic people; we know for certain only that the invaders were men of aggressive, stirring, energetic natures who had dwelt in parts of modern Scandinavia, Germany, and Holland and that they were representative of the numerous barbarians who swept westward to overwhelm the Roman Empire in the fourth and fifth centuries after Christ.

"Angel" itself was a part of modern Schleswig; the Saxons derived originally from modern Holstein but had drifted west and multiplied. They mingled with the Frisians and the Frankish pirates. But inundations along the coast of the North Sea discomforted them as they sought new homes; they therefore searched for more attractive lands than the sandy dunes and "terp mounds" where they proliferated: they heard tales of an emerald isle not far across the sea.

These Anglo-Saxons were pagans and farmers, claiming descent from the great god Woden. As pirates their name had long spelt terror to more civilized or less warlike peoples. They were sailors of immense courage and skill who crossed the seas in shallow boats without decks or masts, some eighty feet long, in which they could not only move swiftly across the high seas but could also row up the deep rivers that led into inhabited Britain. "To these men," it has been said, "a shipwreck was a capital practice rather than an object of terror" and "the dangers of the deep ... were their intimate friends." Wearing woolen cloaks and skirts and armed with spears, longbows, and curious wooden shields, chanting their songs of war, they were loyal followers of their chiefs or petty kings, who were men of honor according to their own code. Fever to emigrate, hunger for land, and overpopulation brought them to Britain in their long narrow boats while Rome fell and unrest perplexed the souls of men.

In the last days of the Roman occupation the rulers of Britain had, as we have seen, invited some pagan tribes as allies or *federati* to settle among them in the hope that they in turn would ward off other pirates. It was in this manner that the Anglo-Saxons had heard of this little-known part of the western world. A story has survived that after the Romans left, a proud Romano-British tyrant, Vortigern, invited two chiefs named Hengist and Horsa, said to be Jutes from northern Denmark, to help repel the incursions of the Picts and Scots. The tale is that Horsa was killed, and that Hengist married Vortigern's daughter whom he loved, but later treacherously betrayed his host and occupied Kent, which thus became the earliest of the new settlements. This story has been exhaustively examined by modern historians. Hengist and Horsa, it is thought, may well have been historical figures, but whether they were Jutes, and who the Jutes really were, nobody agrees. But probably it was in this sort of manner that the Anglo-Saxons first established themselves in Britain.

In general these invaders never broke through in one vast flood under a united military command, or as an organized host eager to settle. They came over in relatively small groups, fought their way into different parts of the island, often ferociously crushing everything before them, but sometimes coming to temporary terms with the old inhabitants.

Why then was it that the Britons, who learned many of the arts of war and defense from the Romans and indeed served as recruits in their experienced armies, failed to repel the invaders and drive them back into the sea, as their ancestors 500 years earlier had checked and humiliated mighty Caesar? The answer in brief is that they were disunited and demoralized. They had grown accustomed to the protection afforded by the Roman eagles, to the security given by the Roman walls, to the coastal defenses and the Britannic fleet. The civilization that the Romans had built had long since decayed; the garrisons had vanished; the country folk were leaderless and the townspeople were no more; and the Britons fought against each other under leaders like Vortigern. Moreover they were not confronted merely by the Anglo-Saxons, who landed at points from the extreme northeast to the far southwest, but also by Scots ranging the western coasts and Picts coming from beyond the Tweed. Much of the land was depopulated and the Britons who were left had neither a central government nor a unifying religion. The Welsh monk Gildas, writing about the first half of the sixth century, blamed his countrymen for forgetting Christianity and living by the rule, "Eat, drink, and be merry, for tomorrow we die."

If the acquisition of east Kent was the earliest triumph of the Anglo-Saxons, the occupation of modern Sussex (the land of the South Saxons) and of Wessex (the land of the West Saxons, comprising modern Hampshire and Dorset) followed not many years afterwards. At the same time other marauders penetrated the rivers of East Anglia and settled along the banks of the Wash and the Ouse. These warrior bands were assisted not merely by the demoralization of the British people but also by the relatively easy travel provided both by the rivers and the Roman roads. According to the Anglo-Saxon Chronicle, a king or powerful chieftain named Aelle landed at Pevensey in Sussex in 477 and founded modern Chichester. Another king named Cerdic, the son, possibly, of a Welsh mother, came to Hampshire in 495 and was the progenitor of the later rulers of Wessex.

Whether these ancient traditions are to be exactly credited or not, there is little question that Kent and Sussex and the areas near the rivers Wash and Ouse were the earliest sites of Anglo-Saxon settlements, to be followed soon by the occupation of most of southern Britain, including the Isle of Wight, lying off the south coast, and Northumbria. In the latter part of the fifth century the Anglo-Saxon invaders were fought for a time upon equal terms. The Britons had first appealed vainly for help to the soldiers of the Roman empire who were still in France. Then under the command of Ambrosius Aurelanus, described by Gildas as "the last of the Romans," they held up the Saxon advance somewhere in the eastern Midlands. About 500 a chieftain named Arthur, converted by later chroniclers into the legendary King Arthur of the Round Table, won a resounding victory at Mount Badon, of which the location is unknown. Arthur may have been a cavalry leader and the battle may have been fought upon the Upper Thames. If this was so, it was the last contest fought in the afterglow of Roman Britain. Though resistance continued in western England and in Wales for many years, the battle of Mount Badon was the last considerable defeat inflicted upon the all-pervasive Anglo-Saxons who, again according to Gildas, for decades swept the land from sea to sea, massacring its people, laying waste its homes, and setting fire to its fortifications.

The second phase of the Anglo-Saxon conquest opened in the middle of the sixth century. The West Saxons expanded northward, defeating the Britons first near Salisbury and then near Swindon. From there they moved into the plain of central England, but as late as 571 the Britons were still fighting fifty miles north of London. A wedge was soon driven between the Britons in Devon and Cornwall and those north of the Bristol Channel in south Wales after a decisive battle near Bath in 577. Three British kings were killed and the sites of the formerly Roman towns of Gloucester, Cirencester, and Bath fell to the Anglo-Saxons. Parallel with the Anglo-Saxon advance from the south of England was the consolidation of another group of invaders north of the Humber. Here two kingdoms, Bernicia and Deira, were established, but in the following century these peoples came to be known as Northumbrians. A king of Bernicia moved forward into the Scottish Lowlands early in the seventh century; after that the only pocket of resistance in north Britain was in the area around the Clyde river known as Strathclyde. Other kingdoms were set up in the Midlands, later to be known as Mercia. As soon as they pressed forward throughout the island, the invaders also began to fight among themselves.

Thus the picture of England, as we shall now call the southern part of the island, 150 years after the first coming of the Anglo-Saxons, is of two large stretches of territory gradually occupied and consolidated against the Britons. In the south the new kingdoms were congested, and virile leaders thrust the Britons back into modern Cornwall or Wales. In the north other Anglo-Saxon conquerors repelled the Scots and the Irish. Occasionally a strong king, known as a Bretwalda or overlord, might impose some temporary form of unity over the warring tribes. The first two Bretwaldas, Aelle of Sussex and Ceawlin of Wessex, commanded at most a shadowy form of allegiance and their influence did not extend north of the Humber.

To what extent did the Britons survive among these aggressive new-comers? Was any of the Roman culture left? If we are to believe the lamentations of the monk Gildas, they were wiped out by the sword, fire, and pestilence, thus paying the penalty for their sins. But the Britons were still resisting two centuries after Gildas wrote, and it is likely enough that during these years some intermarriage took place between the Anglo-Saxon conquerors and the Celtic women. Yet the evidence of far-reaching devastation is unquestionable and many mas-sacres took place. The small groups of bold adventurers who headed the invasions can scarcely have been able to take many prisoners or make many slaves. There is no evidence of treaties or agreements, only of interminable war.

The Roman towns were already long in decay before the Anglo-Saxons came, and not one of them survived except as a ruin to be un-covered by modern archaeologists. If London had a continuing history, it was not as a thriving market town or a center of government but as a derelict port inhabited by squatters. The Anglo-Saxons did not occupy the former Roman villas or even the sites of Romano-British villages. As a rule they settled in the valleys, along the banks of rivers or at the foot of hills, while the Celts had always preferred the higher ground. The

Britons made no attempt to convert their conquerors to Christianity. Only in the west do Celtic names survive in any large numbers. The Anglo-Saxon methods of agriculture differed from those of the Celts, as air photography shows. Some Britons are known to have fled over the sea away from the wrath of the Anglo-Saxons and to have settled in modern Brittany.

It has been said that the Anglo-Saxon migration to Britain was "more a colonization than a conquest." Possibly it was both. If that were true, then one might assume that these colonists would have mixed with the original inhabitants and acquired some of their characteristics. But they came only as farmers in a relentless search for good land; they brought with them their own laws, institutions, and religion; they knew nothing of town life; and they soon brought their own women. No doubt some Britons were absorbed, but many were certainly killed or withdrew westward over the Channel. Neither philology nor anthropology offers convincing proof of any marked degree of Celtic survival in central England. When Gildas cried to his God, "Thou has given us as a sheep to be slaughtered and among the Gentiles has Thou dispersed us," he spoke truly enough. Outside modern Wales, Scotland, and Cornwall, the Celts remained as shattered remnants of a once civilized people.

IV

The Conversion of England to Christianity

At the beginning of the seventh century while England was still occupied by many warring Anglo-Saxon kingdoms, with Welshmen and bellicose Irishmen on their western flanks, some form of order was slowly emerging out of the chaos and the light of civilization began to reappear. North of the river Humber, King Ethelfrith, who reigned from 593 to 617, was a powerful ruler who subdued the Scottish Lowlands, while his successor and conqueror, King Edwin, became the founder of the modern city of Edinburgh. South of the Humber King Ethelbert of Kent is a recognized historical figure—the third of the Bretwaldas or overlords who commanded the allegiance of other kings and petty kings of his time.

All these rulers were pagans, though Ethelbert married Bertha, a Frankish princess who was a Christian and brought her own bishop with her from Paris to Canterbury. This pagan religion, the names of whose gods (Trig and Woden, Thor and Frig) survive in the names of our days of the week, extolled the virtues of courage, loyalty, and honor, but not of gentleness, charity, or mercy. It despised the coward and the liar and exalted the hero as a comrade of the gods. Its priests were not deferred to as the Celtic Druids had been, nor did they, like the Druids, perpetrate human sacrifices. It was neither a violent nor a cruel religion, it did not attempt to proselytize, and its very tolerance was a source of weakness. Because it concentrated on the heroic virtues and had nothing to say of an afterlife, it offered little defense against the magic of the Christian gospel.

The Anglo-Saxons were surrounded by Christians of varying sorts. St. Columba was an energetic and attractive descendant of an Irish king: he followed in the footsteps of St. Patrick, patron saint of Ireland (who first came to Ireland from Wales) and set up a monastery of beehive huts in Iona off the northwest coast of modern Scotland in 563 as a center of missionary zeal. Another similar monastery was built on the island of Skye, and these became sanctuaries for criminals and schools for priests as well as bases for evangelization. In the tradition of Gildas and his contemporary St. David, the patron saint of Wales, the Welsh Christians were not evangelists. Rather they were austere idealists chiefly concerned with saving their own souls. They gloried in their aloofness. "It was a consolation to them to think that the Anglo-Saxon invaders who had stolen their lands and slain their clergy were heading straight for hell fire and an eternity of punishment." On the continental mainland where an eastern Byzantine empire had replaced the old Roman one, a great man had been born in the ruins of imperial Rome, a nobleman and monk who became the bishop of that city in 590 and was thus a younger contemporary of St. Columba. Pope Gregory I, as he was called, decided to revive the glories of Rome in the ecclesiastical sphere and to assert the supremacy of his see over all the other bishoprics in the world. His predecessors had been obscure; Gregory was the founder of the modern Papacy, making the see of St. Peter stand out in the western Europe of the "Dark Ages" "like a lighthouse in a storm." In order to extend Latin Christianity to a pagan people he dispatched a mission to England in 597 under the leadership of a learned prior, once his cellmate in a monastery, by the name of Augustine.

The road to the conquest of Britain from Europe had always run through Kent; and by the end of the sixth century Kent was certainly the most civilized, perhaps the only half-civilized part of England.

Whether it was originally settled by the Jutes, as the first chroniclers recorded, is less certain, but the archaeological evidence shows that from the earliest times it had enjoyed a distinctive culture, possibly the result of close commercial relations enjoyed with the mainland of Europe, with which it was a bridgehead.

Thus when Augustine, the missionary sent from Rome, landed on the Island of Thanet in 597 and came into Kent, he encountered the most influential of the Anglo-Saxon kings and the most advanced of the English peoples. No doubt Gregory the Great had realized this, for his was the brain behind the mission. Augustine and his retinue of forty monks had hesitated and lingered upon a Christian island on the French Riviera before venturing forward into the little-known island territories of the pagan Saxons. Indeed Augustine himself had returned thence to Rome in an effort to obtain release from his unwelcome duties, but Gregory had thrust him on. In the end all went well for Augustine. The missionaries found a friend at the Kentish Court in the Christian queen Bertha. The king was already imbued with the notion that the Romans had magic to purvey. He gave them the abandoned British church of St. Martin in his capital at Canterbury in which to worship, and was soon converted himself.

Nothing reveals the statesmanship of Gregory the Great more plainly than the interchange of letters between himself and Augustine. Realizing fully that the Roman Catholic faith could not be imposed brutally upon the ignorant, he instructed Augustine to go slowly and even to embody some pagan habits or rituals into his services. Thus both Yuletide and part of the Easter festival have pagan origins. Some clergy were permitted to marry. The robbery of churches was not to be heavily punished. Women were not to be forbidden to go to church "whilst they have their monthly courses" or to receive the Communion. In general a realistic approach to evangelization was to modify the rigid idealism of the Italian monks.

The initial triumphs of Christianity in England were undoubtedly derived from this cautious approach, from the fact that the Anglo-Saxons were not intolerant savages, and from the promises held out to them of a future life of eternal glory. In a world where life was short and brutal the Christian faith brought the hope of relief from suffering, and its gentleness appealed especially to women, who were not then despised. In the same way that King Ethelbert's Christian wife smoothed the way for Augustine, so later the wife of King Edwin of Northumbria, also a Christian princess (and Ethelbert's daughter), assisted in the conversion of her husband and her country.

But the conversion of the English was gradual and at first superficial.

When King Ethelbert of Kent died in 616 it looked as if heathenism, its heroic virtues rooted strongly in the soil of central England, would regain the day. Ethelbert's son married his dead father's second wife and reverted to pagan habits. Laurentius, who succeeded Augustine as second Archbishop of Canterbury, was not apparently approved in Rome. Other members of Augustine's original retinue fled back to France. Only one other English king had by then been converted.

Christianity owed more to the second Archbishop of Canterbury than is generally realized. Laurentius stuck it out, and eventually King Ethelbert's son was converted. The frightened monks returned, one of them to succeed at Canterbury, another to become the first Bishop of Rochester. Gregory the Great had planned that England should have two coequal archbishops, one in London, the other in York, with a dozen bishops under each. Although the first St. Paul's church was now built in London, the seat of the archbishop remained at Canterbury, and it was not until a generation later that York, the Northumbrian capital, became a Christian city and had its own archbishopric.

In 627 King Edwin of Northumbria was converted by Paulinus, a monk who had come to England under Gregory's orders to reinforce Augustine. The king was baptized in the wooden church of St. Peter in York which he had built for the occasion. In 634 Pope Honorius I (Gregory I died in 605) confirmed Paulinus as Archbishop of York. As in Kent, there was a reaction against Christianity in the north of England, which occurred after Edwin was killed in battle at the age of forty-seven. His conqueror was the pagan King Penda of Mercia in the Midlands, a skillful warrior. Archbishop Paulinus fled to Kent. Like all these pagans, King Penda was tolerant. His son Peada became a Christian in 653. Edwin's successor Oswald—again through the influence of a woman —was converted to Christianity, this time not by the missionaries from Rome but by the monks who had come over from Ireland. Meanwhile East Anglia was also converted and soon afterwards Wessex, where the king was baptized by a Roman missionary in 635.

Thus by the middle of the seventh century virtually the whole of England had by one means or another been converted to Christianity. No doubt the baptisms of individual kings did not ensure the destruction of deeply rooted pagan customs and superstitions, some of which are still the background to rural life in England. Much missionary work remained to be done. The Roman Catholic bishops, directed from Canterbury, labored to build the diocesan system envisaged by Gregory the Great, while Irish or Scottish missionaries independently set up monastic schools in the north and east of the country. As the princesses had played their parts in the courts, so also the abbesses—one of the most famous

ANGLO-SAXON ENGLAND

was Hilda of Northumbria who ruled a "double monastery" of men and women at Whitby—helped to spread and confirm the faith. Early England owed its Christianity largely to women, who instinctively rejected the warrior religion of Woden and Thor.

After the middle of the seventh century "the conflict between heathenism and Christianity gave place to a conflict between one type of Christianity and another" (Hodgkin). Northern England, under the patronage and encouragement of King Oswald of Northumbria (d. 641), who became the first English saint, and then of his brother Oswy, had been converted by the monks from Scotland who settled on a bleak headland at Lindisfarne. Here the saintly Aidan created a training school for preachers and used it as a headquarters from which he wandered on foot, expounding the mysteries of his faith. But his patron King Oswy discovered the awkward fact that the Celtic missionaries had a different date for Easter from that adopted by the Roman Christians, so that while his wife, brought up by the Romans, was fasting at Lent, he himself was feasting. Another difference was that whereas the Celtic Christians shaved their heads in the middle with a wisp of hair at the front and thick curls at the back, the Romans shaved their heads all over. In addition to these grave discrepancies King Oswy was conscious of the magnitude of the papal power and had an uneasy feeling that, in spite of their pious lives and humble manners, the Celtic missionaries might not after all command the road to heaven. For these reasons King Oswy summoned a conference at Whitby in 664 at which the Celtic and Roman Christians confronted each other in theological debate. The effective leader of the Romans was a handsome, if quarrelsome, young nobleman named Wilfrid, who was the Abbot of Ripon. He insisted that the Pope of Rome sat in the seat of St. Peter, to whom Christ had assigned the keys to the door of heaven. He also pointed out that the whole world celebrated Easter at the same time except the Scots and ancient Britons (who remained aloof from the debate in their Welsh fastnesses). These arguments convinced the king, who decided that thenceforward Easter must be celebrated after the Roman manner.

King Oswy's decision at Whitby settled the matter immediately only in his own kingdom of Northumbria, although, being a Bretwalda, his example was a telling one. Five years afterwards the pope appointed as Archbishop of Canterbury the first outstanding administrator in the history of the English Church, a Greek scholar named Theodore of Tarsus. At the age of sixty-six this learned and honorable man came to England and set about reorganizing its bishoprics, making appointments to vacant sees, reforming abuses, promulgating canons, and, in general, showing a statesmanship in which moderation and common sense were the principal ingredients. Schools were set up, new churches built, and clergymen encouraged to stay where they were instead of wandering, as the Celts had done, all over the land. Thus the basis was laid for the modern parish system, which did not, however, come into being for many years.

Through the work of Theodore of Tarsus and other devoted Christians, including the petulant but energetic Wilfrid, a pattern of cultural unity was achieved in central England. Synods were held to discuss Church questions and, as Bede wrote later, "This was the first archbishop whom all the English Church obeyed." While the secular rulers still fought each other to attain political supremacy, the primacy of Canterbury was recognized everywhere and Canterbury in turn accepted the ultimate authority of the pope in Rome, thus making England an integral part of Christian Europe at the very time when it was threatened by the rise of the Moslems. The English Church began to flourish in vigor and in culture. It sent missionaries abroad and took up the task of education at home. It produced poets, artists, and men of letters. Civilization had again returned to Britain by way of Rome.

V

The Rise of Wessex and Alfred the Great

After the conversion in the seventh century, the English kingdoms, whose history since the arrival of the Anglo-Saxons about 450 had been so confused, were groping toward some form of political confederation. Strong kings or Bretwaldas had effectively asserted overlordship from time to time. Gradually out of the chaos there arose three dominant kingdoms—first Northumbria in the north, then Mercia in the Midlands, and finally Wessex in the south.

The defeat of the fifth of these Bretwaldas, King Edwin of Northumbria, by Welsh and Mercians at the battle of Hatfield Chase in 632 heralded an era of Mercian supremacy that lasted intermittently for nearly 200 years. The successful kings of Mercia were Penda (632–654), his son Wulfhere (657–674), Ethelbald (716–757), and Offa (757–796). Penda and Wulfhere consolidated the power of their dynasty in the midlands. Ethelbald was the grandson of a brother of Penda. He exacted obedience from the kings of Wessex in the southwest and Kent in the southeast, lived an immoral life tempered by Christian benefactions, and was murdered by his own bodyguard after a reign of over forty years. Offa re-established and indeed extended the supremacy attained by his predecessor.

Ethelbald had been known as "king of the southern English" or "king of Britain," but Offa came to be acknowledged as "king of the whole of the land of the English" or "king of the English" even by the pope himself. Offa was not merely a conquering soldier; he was also a statesman. He battled with the weak and negotiated with the strong. He defeated Kent, Sussex, Essex, and East Anglia one by one, while he arranged marriages of convenience with the royal families of Northumbria and Wessex. He drew a boundary line upon the western side of his dominions which marked the frontier of the Britons (who still vigorously survived and had fought fiercely against both Mercia and Wessex in the eighth century) which was known as "Offa's Dyke," an earthwork stretching from North Wales to the Bristol Channel of which remnants may still be seen. Offa was on friendly terms with both Pope Hadrian I and the creator of a new empire comprising much of western Europe, the King of the Franks, Charles the Great or Charlemagne, who was crowned emperor at Christmas, 800. From the pope King Offa exacted the creation of a new midland archbishopric at Lichfield (although it did not last for long) and with the emperor Charlemagne he eventually concluded the first commercial treaty in English history. In general King Offa promoted foreign trade and improved the coinage of the realm; coins with his name upon them are numerous, but the English penny derived from another Mercian king, Penda. When Offa died in 796 at the height of his success, he was described as the greatest English ruler of the "Dark Ages."

Unfortunately we know very little of either King Offa or King Egbert of Wessex, to whom in the first quarter of the ninth century the overlordship of the English peoples was to pass. Both of these men were unquestionably significant figures in the evolution of the united political England, patterned upon a united English Church, which was finally consummated by the triumphs of King Alfred the Great of Wessex.

The influence of the middle kingdom of Mercia shrank after the death of Offa. King Egbert, who came to the throne of Wessex in 802, claimed descent from the royal founders of Wessex as well as Kent and he had studied the art of statesmanship in exile at the court of Charlemagne. In two swift campaigns he defeated the Britons of Devon and Cornwall and in another two he shook off the supremacy of the Mercians. Though he laid the foundations for the rise of Wessex by expanding into Cornwall and annexing Kent, he did not wield as much power as Offa had done or his own great-grandson Alfred was to do later.

The ninth century saw the consolidation of Wessex under Egbert's son Athelstan and grandson Ethelwulf, but already the English people were menaced by a new threat of invasion from abroad; even before Egbert died, the piratic Danes or Vikings, who had become the terror of the European mainland, had made their first raids into England.

✂ THE COMING OF THE DANES

The Danish invaders of the ninth century may be compared to the Anglo-Saxons' own ancestors when they first assaulted and conquered ancient Britain in the fifth century. Like them they came originally from northern Europe, were a mixture of farmers and pirates, commanded the sea, were adventurous, hardy, and pagan. In some ways the Vikings were more cultured and sophisticated than their predecessors. Their ships were bigger, better built, and provided with sails as well as oars. A Viking ship could cross the Atlantic in four weeks, and Vikings are known to have reached America. Their leaders achieved a high standard of material comfort; nevertheless they were in essence barbarians imbued with primitive beliefs. After the strong hand of Charlemagne had been lifted, they scoured the whole of Europe and beyond in search of booty. Unlike the early Anglo-Saxon pirates, they do not appear to have been motivated by the pressure of population in their homelands; their piracy was simply a well-organized and conducted business enterprise. First they pillaged the wealthy monasteries conveniently situated near the English coast; then they circled Scotland to attack Ireland, which was a prey to incessant internal strife. The Vikings fed on their successes and grew bolder. They invaded Spain; they attacked Paris; twice they sacked London. But the English did not crumple before them, as the Britons had yielded to the Anglo-Saxons. Charlemagne had won a respite for Christian Europe, and the kings of Wessex, who were the most vulnerable to attacks from the sea, were forewarned. Before he died King Egbert had inflicted a check upon the Danes at the battle of Hinxton Down in 838. In 850 Ethelwulf defeated a Danish host at the battle of Aclea and his son Athelstan, who was then the king of Kent, also repulsed them. In the same year both London and Canterbury were sacked. The peril was severe; it has been estimated that over ten thousand Vikings in some 350 ships bore down upon England during these campaigns.

King Ethelwulf decided that he must appeal to the Christian God for help against an enemy so numerous, so agile, and so profane. He sent his four-year-old son Alfred to Rome in 853 and later followed himself, marrying a Frankish princess on the way back. In his absence his son Ethelbald, who must have thought it an inappropriate time for his father to leave home, rebelled against him, but the family quarrel was patched up and the House of Egbert crusaded against the ever-swelling Danish hordes, thereby winning their own immortality in the first heroic age of the English people.

KING ALFRED'S CHARACTER AND ACHIEVEMENT

Alfred the Great was born in 840 at Wantage in Berkshire near the ancient Icknield Way along which men had traveled before the Romans came and which was the very route by which the first Anglo-Saxons had entered this part of Britain. Alfred was the youngest son of King Ethelwulf, one of four brothers who became kings of Wessex. Alfred's only sister was married as a child to the neighboring king of Mercia. As a boy Alfred had twice been to Rome where Pope Leo IV "girded him as his spiritual son with the honour and outward array of nobility after the manner of the Consuls at Rome."

Alfred grew to manhood at a time when the pagans were everywhere beating at the gates of Europe, the Saracens from the south, the Magyars from the east, the Moors from the west, the Vikings from the north. When Alfred was twenty-two the Danes first wintered in England, in the Isle of Thanet. Then each year their "great armies," as mobile on land as they were on the sea, encamped more or less where they wished. In 867 they set up a puppet king in Northumbria; the next year they wintered at Nottingham in Mercia where Alfred's brother-in-law invoked the aid of Wessex; in 870 they subjugated East Anglia so that much of the north and east of England came under their control. If they could now overcome Wessex, the whole of England was theirs.

After the death of his father Alfred fought with his brothers against the Vikings, and after the succession of his brother Ethelred he was recognized as his "viceroy." Brought up in this age of strife and stress, Alfred was evidently a man of intensely neurotic disposition who endured mental and physical ill health through much of his life. He suffered from piles; later he was afflicted by neuritis or some other form of nagging pain. He was a prey to sexual doubts (unlike his eldest brother, who had no compunction about marrying his father's young widow), and collapsed during his own wedding festivities. Nor was he well educated in spite of his early visits to Rome. He did not learn to read until he was twelve and was largely self-taught. But Alfred was no morbid valetudinarian. He had the courage to overcome his daily pain; he was eager, quickminded, a lover of learning, but at the same time a skilled soldier and statesman.

His first test came at the beginning of 871. The Danes were wintering in Reading and threatened Wessex both by land and by sea. Alfred and his brother Ethelred collected an army and marched to confront them. At first they were repulsed, but later the Vikings sallied forth from their base and battle was joined that January at Ashdown. King Ethelred, following his father's habit, refused to fight until he had heard Mass in his tent, but Alfred led an uphill assault. The conflict centered around a single stunted thorn bush where the shield walls of the two sides clashed and finally the Danes fled the field, leaving many dead. This was a famous victory in early English history, for it was the first time that the all-conquering Danes had been convincingly defeated. But much fighting was still to come. Soon Alfred was left to fight alone, for at Easter his brother died. In the summer a fresh Danish army came upon the scene. Altogether nine battles were waged. Eventually a truce was concluded, probably by the payment of a tribute or "Danegeld" as it was later called. The Vikings spent the next winter in London, which then belonged to Mercia, and for four years Wessex enjoyed a respite.

When the Vikings returned to Wessex in 875 the menace to English survival had increased, for meanwhile the Vikings had overrun Mercia and appointed another puppet king, while King Alfred's brother-in-law had fled the country to die in Rome. Now the Vikings' plan was to assault Wessex by concerted movements over land and sea. They slipped past Alfred's army to occupy a fortified base at Wareham in Dorset and then moved on to Exeter in Devon, but their fleet was dashed to pieces in a storm off the coast of Dorset. It seemed to the Christians as if God had at last intervened on their behalf. At Exeter the Danish land army submitted, made peace, gave hostages, and left.

But within six months the Vikings were back again in Wessex. Under their new leader Guthrum they found a base at Chippenham in Wiltshire and from there overran the whole of Wessex. The Christians had been surprised during the festivities of Twelfth Night and the men of Wessex were wearied after many years of almost ceaseless war. King Alfred with a select band of warriors withdrew to the west of Somerset, where, covered by swamps and forests, he harried his enemy and prepared his revenge. Tired of plundering, the Vikings now aimed to complete their conquest of England by overcoming the last center of resistance in the southwest. Perhaps they hoped to invoke the help of the Welsh and the Cornishmen and to overwhelm King Alfred by attacks from land and sea, as they had failed to do five years earlier. At any rate they had met their match.

At Easter the tide of fortune turned. An attempt by the Vikings to land a force from South Wales by sea in Devon was frustrated and soon afterward Alfred called together his forces at a point near which the counties of Somerset, Wiltshire, and Hampshire met. Battle was joined at Ethandun or Edington on Salisbury Plain. Here in this primitive home of the islanders Alfred's men "closed their ranks, shield locked with shield, and fought fiercely against the entire heathen host in long and stubborn stand." Many Danes were killed and the rest fled to their camp at Chippenham, which was besieged by men of Wessex for fourteen days. In the end Guthrum and his Vikings surrendered and not only promised to leave Wessex, as they had often done before, but undertook to be baptized as Christians. King Alfred received his enemy Guthrum at the font of a village church as his "son in the Faith." After conqueror and conquered had feasted together, Guthrum led his army away into Mercia. Such was the so-called "treaty of Wedmore," the undoubted turning point in the prolonged struggle between the Christian English and the heathen Danes.

King Alfred's victory belongs not merely to the history of England, but to that of the world, for in these years the Saracens were threatening Rome and the Vikings besieging Paris; and had England succumbed, the light of Christianity and perhaps of civilization might have been blotted out of Europe.

The war against the Danes continued sporadically for the rest of King Alfred's reign. After the "treaty of Wedmore" Guthrum and his men went from Mercia into East Anglia where an Anglo-Danish community was built up. In 884, however, another Danish host came ashore in Kent and Alfred marched successfully to the relief of Rochester. Apparently Guthrum was tempted to join with the new invaders to seek his revenge; at any rate in 886 Alfred organized a counteroffensive by sea and by land. He advanced "with burning of towns and killing of men" upon London, which had now fallen into Danish hands. King Alfred placed an ealdorman or subruler named Ethelred in charge of western Mercia and married him to his eldest daughter. Thus "all the English people submitted to Alfred except those who were under the power of the Danes."

Afterwards King Alfred concluded a fresh treaty with Guthrum defining the boundaries of his kingdom and the Danish lands or "Danelaw." Broadly the Danes held East Anglia, Essex, the eastern midlands or Mercia, and the land north of the Humber, while King Alfred ruled the whole of southern England and the western Midlands. By the same treaty it was agreed that in the simple laws of those times the two peoples should be treated as equals.

Peace did not last for long. Fresh Viking armies from the European mainland, tired of their prodigious and fluctuating struggles in France, once more arrived at the mouth of the Thames aiming to take London and to force the south of England from Alfred's grasp. Meanwhile Guthrum had died and the Danes of East Anglia, who regarded London as a menace to their security, were induced to disregard their pledges and ally themselves with their comrades from France. The new threat to Wessex was grave; Alfred, his son Edward, Ethelred of Mercia, and Alfred's other ealdormen had to contend with three Viking armies as mobile as they were daring. At first King Alfred tried to divide his enemies and to buy them off with diplomacy, but in this he failed. Soon a confused and bloody contest was being waged over the entire face of England. At one time an amphibious force from East Anglia was attacking Alfred's stronghold of Devon on two sides; at another a combined Danish army dashed across the country, occupied the old Roman city of Chester in the northwest, and penetrated into Wales. Although Wessex was attacked on every side, the Danes never took London nor defeated Alfred's men in open battle. The English king carried on a defensive war and divided his own army as little as possible. By 896 both sides were exhausted and lands laid waste, and disease had decimated men and cattle. Guerrilla warfare continued until the death of King Alfred at the end of the century. It is hard to assess the character of his last campaigns, but King Alfred had proved himself one of the outstanding generals of early English history.

Generalship consists not merely in campaigning but in the organization of victory. King Alfred had been able to fight off the superior and diverse forces of his enemies by reforming his own army, building a navy, and planning elaborate systems of fortification. King Alfred's army or fyrd (its Anglo-Saxon name) was not a national army of militiamen. It consisted in actuality of the king's own bodyguard and the fighting men of his royal household, supplemented by the forces of his ealdormen or subrulers and by the retinues of his thanes or nobility. One of King Alfred's reforms was to divide his fyrd in two, so that a body of trained men was immediately available at any time of the year and would not disperse as soon as the immediate danger had passed. While there is little evidence whether or not Alfred improved the weapons of his army, he took trouble to construct a navy capable of meeting the Vikings on their own terms. Since their original invasions the Anglo-Saxons had surprisingly neglected sea power and, although King Alfred's navy was at first beaten, toward the end of his reign Alfred deliberately aimed to outbuild the Danes with a fleet of longer, bigger, and swifter fighting vessels. He himself went to sea in his own long ships and may fairly be described as a founder of the English navy.

At the same time King Alfred worked out a system of land defenses by building burhs or forts at strategic points all around his kingdom. One such burh was at Oxford (hence perhaps the legend that Alfred founded Oxford University), another at Worcester. Use was made of the remains of old Roman walls, but most of the fortifications were fairly crude earthworks with banks and ditches which needed effective garrisons to hold them. Still they were skillfully and coherently planned and sited to cover the whole of Wessex, and so were capable of holding up the enemy until the field army arrived.

Alfred by no means dedicated the whole of his life to military measures. In the interludes of comparative peace he gave his time and energies to codifying the laws and promoting religion, learning, and education. Earlier kings like Ethelbert of Kent, Ine of Wessex, and Offa of Mercia had published codes of law. King Alfred collated such codes and imbued them with his own brand of Christian patriotism. The basis of these laws, insofar as they dealt with personal injuries, was that, in place of an older recourse to feuding between the parties, they sought to secure compensation to an injured person and his family group. For this purpose not all men were of the same worth. If a man were killed, his slayer had to pay a "wergild" to the dead man's kin; and the sum was higher for a noble than for a commoner. The same held true with other injuries. The penalty for violating a nun was double that where the offense had been committed against an ordinary woman; and it was more expensive to knock out the front teeth of a nobleman than those of a mere peasant. The guilt of the accused man was determined by his success or failure in getting a body of men to swear to his character by a solemn oath or by an appeal to the divine judgment in the form of an "ordeal." The king was the supreme court of appeal, and the worst of all crimes was treason against him. The king did what he could to protect the Church and the poor, but in those days of war, devastation, and pestilence the maintenance of law and order was very difficult.

King Alfred was much concerned to uphold public morality, according to Christian principles, and to instill at least elementary education among his subjects. His contemporaries complained that the first half of the ninth century had been an age of religious and intellectual decay. Pope Formosus is believed to have written about 895 that "abominable pagan rites were rampant" in England and that the English bishops behaved like "dumb dogs that cannot bark." One must not exaggerate the picture, for accounts of demoralization are to be read at most times of stress in English history, but the terrible and widespread Danish raids had undermined law and order and, as in the days of Gildas, caused men to lose their faith. As for education, it had always been dependent upon the clergy, particularly the monks, who were alone capable of teaching.

Under the impact of perpetual invasion monastic life had been almost completely destroyed and learning and discipline undermined.

The king believed that a revival of Christianity was needed, and it was characteristic that he prefaced his codification of the laws with a recital of the Ten Commandments given to Moses. But he does not appear to have set much store by the foundation of monasteries; he founded one at Athelney, the historic spot in Somerset where he prepared his great counteroffensive in 878, but he had difficulty in staffing it, and, according to his biographer, Asser, two of the foreign monks whom he imported attempted to murder their abbot. Later the king aimed to stimulate education by direct and personal leadership. His first move was to induce educated men to come to his court. Asser was a Welsh monk from St. David's in Pembrokeshire who showed his master how to translate Latin. Other qualified clerics were found in Mercia, while a saintly figure named Grimbald came over from France and is said to have refused the archbishopric of Canterbury. With the aid of such savants Alfred founded a court school, probably upon the model of that of Charlemagne. The sons of the king and of noblemen, as well as boys of humbler birth, were taught reading and writing, and hunted as an outdoor exercise. The king expected his officials to follow his own example and educate themselves as well. According to Asser, "almost all the ealdormen, reeves, and thanes who had been illiterate from their childhood took to their books, preferring to study laboriously the unaccustomed learning rather than have to give up their posts." Thus by precept and example King Alfred secured a revival of learning and expected his bishops and clergy to carry it far beyond the confines of his court.

He also saw that it was important, as he wrote, "to translate the books which are most needful for all men to know into the language which we can all understand" and he confessed that "very few could understand their mass-books in English or translate even a letter from Latin." Under his guidance therefore a variety of books, such as the *Pastoral Care* of Pope Gregory I and the *Soliloquies* of St. Augustine, were translated from Latin into Anglo-Saxon. The *Church History* of the Venerable Bede, the unique authority for the early history of the English Church and people, completed in the monastery of Lindisfarne in 731, was translated at an early stage. At the same time an Anglo-Saxon Chronicle was drawn up, embodying part of Bede and bringing the narrative down in detail to Alfred's own reign. If we add to the translation of Bede and the compilation of the Chronicle the value of Asser's life of King Alfred and of the information supplied by the prefaces which the king wrote to some of the translations, we may surely hail this versatile man as the true founder of English history. Alfred's interests ranged beyond the limits of his own kingdom. He was always in touch with Rome, the fountainhead of the Christianity in which he so fervently believed, and the site of his childhood pilgrimages. He paid tribute to Rome, as had some earlier English kings, in the form of Peter's pence. He also sent gifts to the Patriarch of Jerusalem and is said to have planned a mission to India. Though he believed in an almost puritan form of Christianity, there was no limit to the intellectual tastes of this extraordinary man; they included philosophy, science, and poetry, and his mind darted from the seeds of the earth to the stars in the sky. Thus Alfred created more than a mere political kingdom of England; he fashioned a world of the mind and the spirit. He was the greatest Englishman in early history.

VI

Origins of Wales, Scotland, and Ireland

It was at the time of the Danish invasions that three nations which are bound up with the history of England started to emerge from their obscurity: Wales, Scotland, and Ireland.

Wales received a distinct identity when the Anglo-Saxons drove the Celts westward but did not follow them into their mountain fastnesses or into Cornwall. King Arthur, who fought the Anglo-Saxons as Caratacus had fought the Romans, is the hero of early Welsh history. The Welsh had continued to resist the Anglo-Saxons, particularly in Mercia, for more than 250 years, but little political unity ever prevailed in Wales (any more than it had done among the Britons when the Romans came). Its rulers were petty kings or chieftains and Celtic tribalism was strong. "They are above all things devoted to their clan," it was recorded in the twelfth century, "and will fiercely avenge any injury or dishonour suffered by those of their blood." The Welsh were, however, conscious of Roman culture and had their own notions of law. The position of women was remarkably advanced. A woman's marriage portion was protected by her clan; she could not be beaten by her husband except for specified offenses; and she received compensation if divorced. Broadly speaking, the Welsh chiefs managed to maintain order in their dominions and a rudimentary code of law was enforced. The Welsh Church, as we

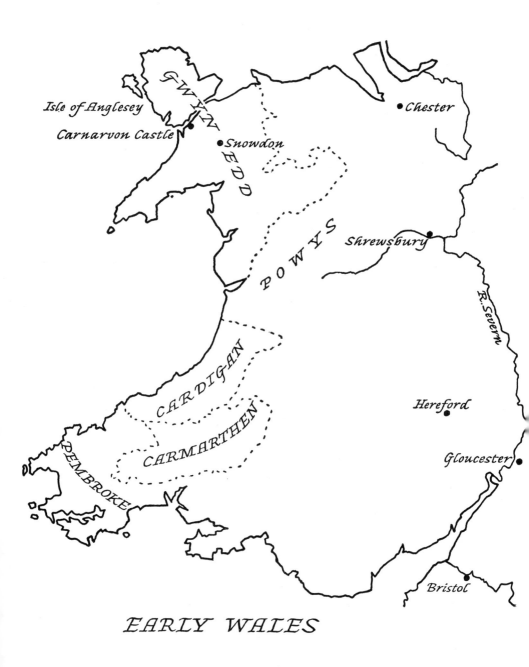

Isle of Anglesey

Carnarvon Castle

GWYNEDD

• Snowdon

• Chester

POWYS

Shrewsbury

R. Severn

CARDIGAN

CARMARTHEN

PEMBROKE

Hereford

Gloucester

Bristol

EARLY WALES

have seen, long held itself aloof and it was not until the end of the eighth century that it fully accepted the Roman discipline and the Roman Easter. It possessed some clerics of ability. Asser, the biographer of Alfred the Great, had come from Wales.

Gwynedd, the beautiful fertile land in north Wales where Mount Snowdon or "the haunt of the eagles" towers over the scene, was always important among the Welsh kingdoms, and for a time a king of Gwynedd, Rhodri the Great (844–878), succeeded in uniting much of Wales into one realm. After his death, however, his possessions were divided among his six sons and his kingdom broke up. Meanwhile the incursions of the Norsemen, who attacked Wales from Ireland, had become violent and the Welsh felt the need of a protector. They had long been in contest with Mercia, even after the days when King Offa had defined the boundary line between them with his dyke, but their enmity with Wessex had been only intermittent. Therefore the princes of Wales turned to Wessex and acknowledged the supremacy of King Alfred and later of his son, Edward the Elder. Thus, in the words of J. E. Lloyd, the historian of Wales, "the basis was laid of the homage which later was demanded from all Welsh princes by the English Crown."

Scotland or North Britain, as it was originally called, was given a separate character by its geography, since it was a part of the highland zone and most difficult to conquer. When the Roman general Agricola led his army there in the second century the country was covered with forests, bogs, and lakes, and the local tribes were able to frighten the experienced Roman legionaries. As the Roman power receded the indigenous Picts and the Scots from Ireland swarmed south and even overran Hadrian's Wall. By the seventh century, when the Anglo-Saxons had established themselves in southern Britain (outside Wales and Cornwall), northern Britain was divided into four kingdoms, that of the Picts in the north, the Scots in the northwest, the Britons of the southwest in the valley of Clyde, known as Strathclyde, and the Angles of Bernicia, a kingdom that stretched across the later Scottish border and covered modern Lothian.

These four kingdoms were at constant war with one another, but the introduction of Christianity by Irish saints like Columba, Mungo, and Aidan helped to formulate a common culture. After Bernicia became part of the English kingdom of Northumbria early in the seventh century it looked as if its virile ruling dynasty might conquer the whole of northern Britain; but in 685 King Ecgfrith was defeated by the Picts at a battle near Forfar; and in the end it was the Scots, not the Northumbrians, who achieved supremacy in northern Britain. Kenneth MacAlpin (843–860), a contemporary of King Alfred, became king of the Picts as

HIGHLANDS

Forfar •

Perth •

R. Forth   Stirling

Edinburgh • • Pinkie   Dunbar

Glasgow   R. Clyde   Berwick

R. Tweed   Flodden

ROXBURGH

LOWLANDS   Otterburn

Newcastle •
R. Tyne

Carlisle
NORTHERN ENGLAND

▮▮▮ Roads to Edinburgh

SCOTLAND

well as the Scots and contended with the Angles of Lothian. King Edgar the Peaceful, great-grandson of King Alfred, granted Lothian to King Kenneth I about 973 in order to ensure security on his northern frontier. It was not until the beginning of the eleventh century that another Scottish king, Malcolm II, finally consolidated the frontier of his kingdom as far south as the river Tweed. He also succeeded to the throne of Strathclyde, and thus virtually ruled the whole of modern Scotland, apart from the outlying islands.

Little is known about pagan Ireland. It was originally populated by the Celtic-speaking people known as Gaels, and was divided among local kings, provincial kings, and a high king whose seat was at Tara in modern Meath. The first high king was reputedly Cormac Mac Art who while king of Connaught conquered Tara in the fourth century. In the fifth century St. Patrick, a Romanized Briton, was taken a prisoner somewhere in Britain and carried off to Ireland where he was miraculously converted to Christianity while tending sheep. Trained as a missionary in France, he returned to Ireland and in due course founded the Archbishopric of Armagh. The Church that he established, like that founded by St. Columba in Scotland, was an agency of civilization. It was essentially a monastic Church where the monks were scholars and artists as well as missionaries. The Irish saints maintained literature and promoted art, as exemplified by the beautiful Book of Kells which has been preserved until this day. But this monastic Church did not, perhaps could not, afford a pattern of political unity, as did the later Scottish and English Churches.

The high kings of Ireland were never more than the first in order among equals and a Roman Catholic hierarchy was inappropriate to the tribal system. The disunity caused thereby proved fatal when the Norsemen launched their first assaults upon Ireland at the beginning of the ninth century. About 834 the Danes built Dublin at the mouth of the river Liffey. The names of the provinces of Ulster, Leinster, and Munster all have a Danish origin. In 853 Olaf the White from Norway became the ruler over all the Scandinavians in Ireland. Early in the next century these Irish Norsemen adventured into Wales and northern England, for a time holding a kingdom at York. The east coast of Ireland was their base, and early town life in that country owed much to these seafaring adventurers. After nearly two centuries of complicated conflict the Irish hero-king, Brian Boru, at the age of seventy-four defeated the Scandinavians at the battle of Clontarf (1014), but he himself was killed along with his son and heir, and once again internecine wars followed.

Londonderry

ULSTER

Armagh

CONNAUGHT

Drogheda

Dublin

LEINSTER

Kilkenny

MUNSTER   Clonmel

Waterford   Wexford

Cork

IRELAND

VII

From Edward the Elder to Edward the Confessor

While the Norsemen still flourished in Ireland, their hold upon the north-east of England was short-lived, for they were driven back and eventually subjugated by the son and grandson of King Alfred the Great. They were never united in the tenth and eleventh centuries and were defeated piecemeal. Edward the Elder, the oldest son of King Alfred, who reigned from 899 to 924, was a mighty warrior. He had first to suppress an internal revolt engineered by his cousin Ethelwald with Danish support. Then he attacked the Danes in the Midlands and defeated them at the battle of Tettenhall in Staffordshire. In the same year, 910, the Anglo-Saxon Chronicle records that "King Edward took possession of London and of Oxford, and of all the lands that owed obedience thereto. And a great [Viking] fleet came from Brittany and ravaged by the Severn; but they there afterwards almost all perished." Edward continued his father's policy of fortifying as he conquered and of maintaining a navy as well as an army. He was helped by his sister Ethelfeda, who was known as "the Lady of the Mercians" and must have inherited much of her father's genius and dedication to duty. She carried out the fortification of the Midlands and expelled the Danes from Derby.

Meanwhile the Norsemen from Ireland had occupied northeast England under the Viking chieftain Raegnald; but once King Edward's military control reached out as far as Derbyshire both Raegnald and the rulers of Strathclyde and Scotland thought it politic to acknowledge him as "their father and their lord." Thus before Edward the Elder died he reigned over the whole of Britain south of the Humber and was the respected ally of all other rulers in the land.

Edward's son, the flaxen-haired Athelstan, was crowned at Kingston on Thames in 925. There was a tradition that as a child he had been invested by his grandfather with a scarlet cloak, a belt set with gems, and a Saxon sword sheathed in gold. Again Alfred's genius was clearly transmitted to his descendant, for Athelstan was not merely the acknowledged ruler of both Wessex and Mercia (since his aunt Ethelfeda's death), but he also crushed the new Danish kingdom at York, received the homage of both the Scots and the Welsh, and suppressed a revolt by Cornishmen. When in 934 the Scots rebelled against him Athelstan summoned an impressive host to his court at Winchester, which included Danes as well as English and Welsh, and led a military expedition northward by land and sea which was so awe-inspiring that the Scots yielded without giving battle. By way of revenge three years later the Scots and the Britons of Strathclyde allied themselves with the Norsemen of Yorkshire in a vain effort to overthrow Athelstan and his army. A tremendous battle was fought at Brunanbuhr, celebrated by a still extant poem, though no one knows for certain the exact site of the ground. The English won after a hard struggle, and three kings, five earls, and a son of the king of the Scots were left dead on the field.

Thus Athelstan could claim to be "king of the English and ruler of all Britain." He became an outstanding figure in the world of his time. His sister was married to the emperor Otto the Great, a successor of Charlemagne in Germany, but nevertheless Athelstan sent military aid to the King of France against the Germans and for the first time a naval force from Britain was engaged against the European mainland. At home Athelstan's court moved majestically through southern England. He held large national assemblies with his magnates and bishops at which the affairs of the many different parts of his realm were discussed; he even had a staff of clerks who have been called the earliest English civil servants. He published many laws, punished crimes severely, promoted trade, and maintained discipline over his more powerful subjects. He was a friend of the Church and a collector of holy relics. Like his grandfather, he shines forth in the sparse charters and chronicles which tell of his reign as an undoubted leader of men.

With the death of King Athelstan in 939 there was some reduction in English power. His son Edmund I was only eighteen when he came to the throne and reigned for fewer than seven years before being murdered. Edmund's brother Eadred reigned for nine years and was succeeded after a long illness by his nephew Eadrig who is supposed to have been three years old at the time of succession. It was only when King Edgar ruled from 959 to 975 that comparative prosperity and peace returned to the land.

In the course of the short reigns of Athelstan's successors many confused campaigns were fought during which the north of England again struggled to throw off the supremacy of the south. For a time a Norwegian hero named Eric Bloodaxe managed to revive an independent kingdom in Northumbria and again link York with Dublin. He was finally defeated at the battle of Stainmore in 954 and his kingdom fell. Indeed Alfred and his immediate heirs had built up such a complete military machine and tradition that for nearly a century the ascendancy of Wessex survived alike the renewed violence of the Norsemen and the choice of minors as its kings.

The reign of Edgar (959–975) is also known as the Age of Dunstan, because this pious and influential prelate, who became Archbishop of Canterbury in 961, made a profound impact on the English history of the later half of the tenth century. Dunstan was born in Somerset in 909. His father was a thane and his uncle Athelm was the first Bishop of Wells and afterwards became Archbishop of Canterbury. As a young noble Dunstan was frequently at court where he became unpopular, it is said, because of his bookish habits. When he was twenty-six he was accused of practicing black magic and expelled from court. His enemies tied him up, threw him in a bog, and kicked him until they were tired. This incident was a turning point in his life. Dunstan decided to become a monk and retired into the quiet of a clerical house at Glastonbury.

The English Church had been founded by monks and its early bishops were monks. But the system established by Archbishop Theodore was based on large dioceses, that is areas ruled by bishops, and the intention was to divide them into smaller units or parishes as in Italy. While churches were built both on royal and private estates, the development of the parochial system in England was slow and little is known about it. The service of the Church was largely performed by groups of clergy or clerks living together in houses or minsters. Most of these clergy were married men, not well educated but a cut above the ordinary peasantry. Until the terrible scourge of the first Danish invasions fell upon England the monasteries had been centers of learning and missionary activity, but under the lash of the heathen they were wiped out and not even King Alfred was able to revive them. It was not until the Danes were beaten back into eastern England and a time of comparative peace prevailed in the tenth century that there was an opportunity for a resurgence of monasticism. It was with this monastic revival that the name of St. Dunstan is associated.

⌘ ST. DUNSTAN

Dunstan, in spite of his reputation for saintliness and religious devotion, cannot have been an easy man to get along with. When he returned to court under the young King Edmund I he was shortly again expelled by royal order. But a miracle, or at any rate a change of heart, induced the king to forgive and recall him; and he was appointed abbot of Glastonbury, which he transformed into a monastic house where he ruled for fifteen years. His duties as abbot did not prevent him from being often at court, where he became a valued royal adviser. But the next king banished him for interfering between him and his future wife, and Dunstan retired to Ghent where he learned more about the purified and improved monasticism practiced on the continental mainland. In western Europe as a whole the first half of the century was a period of peace and reform, and the monasteries of Cluny and Fleury in France provided examples of ascetic life and rule in accordance with the original ideals of St. Benedict of Aninae. Dunstan absorbed all this, and when he was re-called to power in England by King Edgar, who was king of Mercia before he succeeded to the throne of Wessex in 959, he persuaded the king to promote, encourage, and support monastic order so as to strengthen and sustain the Church of England. It was a measure of his success that at the end of the century thirty monasteries were flourishing in southern England.

Edgar himself was no saint; his sexual life was complicated and he is reputed to have fathered an abbess illegitimately. But he appointed Dunstan first Bishop of Worcester, then of London, and finally Archbishop of Canterbury, and accepted his advice on Church matters. Throughout the south of England abbeys were restored or set up according to the reformed Benedictine rule. Dunstan had two fine men as his assistants, St. Oswald of Worcester (later Archbishop of York) and St. Ethelwold of Winchester. Together these three compiled the Regularis Concordia, a new code for the use of the English monks and nuns, and inspired by their own example a high standard of clerical life and service. It was Dunstan too who planned and formulated the coronation service for the monarchy which was to endure in England for more than a thousand years. He presided over the coronation of King Edgar on Whitsunday in 973, late in the reign, at Bath in Somerset. He strengthened the ritual by presiding over the coronation of the next two English kings. Thenceforward it was recognized that by the act of anointment at his coronation the sovereign of England was peculiarly endowed with the divine right of kings.

Two years after his coronation King Edgar the Peaceful died. This was the tribute paid to him by the monk Aelfric at the end of the tenth century:

The time was happy and pleasant among the English when King Edgar furthered Christianity and raised up many monasteries. And his kingdom dwelt in peace; one did not hear of any fleet, save of one's own people holding this land. And all the kings which were on this island of Cambrians (Welsh) and of Scots, came to Edgar one day, eight kings were they, and they all bowed to Edgar's rule.

A story has survived that these eight kings rowed Edgar on a royal barge along the river Dee, while he held the tiller.

After King Edgar's death came a reaction. According to the Anglo-Saxon Chronicle, his son Edward, a bad-tempered boy of thirteen, "God's law broke, and rule monastic quashed, and monks drove out, and God's servants put down." King Edward was murdered at Corfe Castle in Dorset with the connivance of his stepmother and dishonorably buried at Wareham. Ethelred, a youth of "elegant manners, handsome features, and comely appearance," known in history as Ethelred the Unready or Redeless (uncounseled), succeeded, but the dark deed that heralded his boyish accession to the throne hung over an unhappy reign which lasted for nearly forty years.

It was not unnatural that the monastic system built up by St. Dunstan should have been unpopular with the lay nobility of England, for while the best of these monasteries were devoted not only to religion but to art, literature, and learning, the vast properties with which the king endowed them were necessarily at the expense of the rest of the community. Although abbots were not supposed to marry, they often were married before they were ordained priests and their properties were passed on to their children or other relatives. Nepotism was rife and monasteries were convenient refuges for nobility who had committed crimes. Privileges and immunities were showered upon them which could easily be abused. All this created much jealousy and even divided families against each other. Bishops and abbots were given large powers and they shared the perquisites of justice. Nor did they shut themselves from the secular sphere of influence; Dunstan himself has been compared with the group of great ecclesiastical statesmen of European history that culminated in the seventeenth century in Archbishop Laud and Cardinal Mazarin. In the tenth century bishops took to the field and saw battle. And it is possible that it was Dunstan's advice that lay behind what proved to be the ephemeral imperial policies of King Edgar.

After the death of Edgar, Dunstan withdrew into the background and busied himself more with purely church business. He is said to have been both stern and gentle, and full of kindness to the poor. Undoubtedly he gave an impulse to what has been called the reformation of the tenth century, from which flowed a cultural rebirth of the English people. But his statesmanship is harder to measure. Perhaps overconfidence was fostered by King Edgar's era of peace and reform. At any rate the fiber of national resistance had weakened when toward the end of the century the ravaging Norsemen once more swept in from oversea in search of prey.

🍀 THE ASSAULT OF THE VIKINGS

For more than thirty years England was subject to attack, terror, treachery, and famine. It is said that one reason why the Norsemen began a new wave of invasions was that Harold Bluetooth, then king of Denmark and Norway, was so severe a master—among other things, he compelled his people to become Christians against their will—that the Viking warriors were tempted to leave their homes and search for freedom and adventure abroad. Already they had set up the duchy of Normandy in France under a chief named Rollo. Their compatriots had established a more or less autonomous regime in northern and eastern England which was to be known as the Danelaw, although for the time being this region had been brought under the control of the Saxon kings of England. Now they sought to extend their hold on this rich and peaceful island. Among the invaders were the bloodthirsty Swein the Forkbeard, a son of Harold Bluetooth who overthrew and succeeded his father, and Olaf Fryggvason, descendant of a former king of Norway.

The raiding began sporadically in 980 and swelled into a systematic ravaging of the whole English coastline by the end of the tenth century. To offset this constant and unremitting pressure King Ethelred first signed a treaty with one duke of Normandy and then married Emma, the sister of another duke. He vainly attempted to buy off the invaders with tribute—first 22,000 pounds of gold and silver, then 26,000 pounds, then 36,000 pounds (this tribute was later called "Danegeld")—and he even hired Viking mercenaries. In 1007 King Ethelred appointed an ealdorman of Mercia to be responsible for the defense of the Midlands and the next year he organized a large fleet. His own servants were irresolute and some of them betrayed him; one thane took part of the new fleet over to the enemy. "When the general grows fainthearted," recorded the contemporary chronicle, "the whole army is checked." Moreover Ethelred's policy was an ill-judged mixture of cowardice and cruelty. In 1003, for example, he ordered a massacre of Danes in which Swein's sister perished. Under such leadership the morale of the English people collapsed. In spite of the wealth of the land, the traditions of Alfred the Great, and the period of consolidation under Edgar, the English lost faith in themselves and longed for the strong arm of a monarch capable of governing. In 1013 after King Ethelred himself had fled to Normandy, the English submitted to Swein as their king, but he lived only a few months longer. One of his sons, Harold, succeeded him as king of Denmark, and his second son, an ambitious young warrior named Canute, withdrew from England to reconstitute an army, while Ethelred returned to die in 1016 after a long and miserable reign.

King Ethelred the Unready had a son named Edmund Ironside in whom the spirit of Alfred and Athelstan fitfully glowed. Edmund fought valiantly against Canute when the Danish prince returned with his army, but he was defeated at the battle of Ashingdon in Essex. A treaty was then signed dividing the country between Edmund and Canute, but in that same year of 1016 King Edmund suddenly died on St. Andrew's Day, leaving no grown heir, and was buried in the tomb of Edgar the Peaceful at Glastonbury. Thus Canute, son of Swein, was chosen sole king of England, "the first Viking leader to be admitted into the civilized fraternity of Christian kings" (Sir Frank Stenton).

✂ KING CANUTE

Canute was a ruthless king with a good deal of the Slav in his make-up, but he was a soldier who knew how to govern. England was only part of the northern European empire which he carved out for himself before he died when he was forty. At first he treated England like a conquered country; he divided it into provinces, one of them under the Anglo-Saxon ealdorman of Wessex who had betrayed King Ethelred, another under his foster father, a Dane named Thorkell the Tall who later tried to betray him. Canute imposed on the English a heavy tribute to buy off or pay off the host of Vikings who had long harried the land. About 1019 his brother Harold, the king of Denmark, died and Canute left England to secure the succession there. In 1026 he finally defeated a coalition of Swedes and Norwegians, which was joined and perhaps inspired to fight and destroy him by the regent he left behind in Denmark, Thorkell the Tall. After an initial setback Canute overcame all his enemies, drove the king of Norway from his own country, and reached the peak of his power when he ruled over the three nations of England, Denmark, and Norway. Those who conspired against him were subdued, conciliated, or killed. The treacherous ealdorman of Wessex was put to death. The only surviving son of King Ethelred's first wife, a brother of Edmund Ironside, was assassinated at his order; and "the King commanded the widow of the late King Ethelred [Emma of Normandy] .... to be brought to him so that she might become his wife"; he ignored the fact that he was already married to the daughter of a former earl of Northumbria, and indeed he appointed her for a time as his regent in Norway.

In the intervals between battle, murder, and bigamy Canute did what he could to please his English subjects. He promulgated a code of law based upon the laws of Edgar the Peaceful; he allowed the bones of St. Alphege, who had been murdered by his fellow Vikings, to be re-buried with full canonical honors; and he inserted Dunstan's name in the calendar of the saints. He exacted the submission of the king of Scotland. He paid a pious, or at least diplomatic, visit to Rome. Above all, he gave the impression of being a devoted son of the English Church. As his modern biographer has pointed out, however, "the moving passion of Canute's life was not a fiery zeal for the exaltation of the Church but a yearning for personal power and imperial honours." What he offered the English was "security to the common man, new markets to traders, and the chance of an exciting career to young noblemen."

Canute's empire was already collapsing before he died. His first wife was unable to hold on to Norway. In England his favoritism of the Danes, the substantial taxation he demanded to pay for his armies, and the severity of his rule alienated the English nobility. Yet his standing army and small but capable fleet maintained the peace and safety of England as long as he lived. As soon as he died the future darkened. A son by his second marriage, Harthacanute, had to stay in Denmark to ensure the succession of his house, and a son by his first wife known as Harold I or Harold Harefoot, who was technically a bastard, was after an interval recognized as king of England. Canute's Norman widow fled abroad.

Harold Harefoot inherited his father's ruthlessness and policy without a fraction of his ability. A grim incident marked the beginning of his reign, when two of his Danish soldiers enforcing the collection of tribute were murdered by a mob in Worcester Cathedral, and he burned the town and harried the neighborhood as punishment. On his behalf a son of King Ethelred who came to England to visit his mother was blinded and put to death. Harold I died at Oxford after a reign of four years when he was still in his twenties. His half brother Harthacanute, king of Denmark, succeeded him in England, but as the Chronicle laconically recorded in 1042, "he died as he stood at his drink and he suddenly fell to the ground with a horrible convulsion." Exasperated by their experiences with these two worthless sons of King Canute, the whole English nation then welcomed with relief Edward, son of Ethelred the Unready and Emma of Normandy who had managed to escape the murderous intentions of Canute and his sons, as king "as was his right by birth." This last undisputed, if undistinguished, king of the English was crowned at Winchester in Easter, 1043. He was the son of a Norman mother and brought up in Normandy; his reign proved to be the prelude to the Norman conquest of England.

VIII

English Society Before the Norman Conquest

The population of Britain in the eleventh century is estimated at between a million and a million and a half; it would have been larger if the country had not been so often torn asunder by war and invasion. At the apex of English society, as it existed before the Norman Conquest, stood the king, who wielded full, but not despotic powers. His murder or the murder of any member of his family could not be compounded; treason against him was the worst form of crime; even an infringement of "the king's peace" was punishable by death. But no early king, in spite of proud boasts, was supreme in the British Isles. He might be acknowledged as an overlord or Bretwalda by other kings, but they merely required his assent to the alienation of their lands, attended his court if asked, and offered their services as allies in time of war. No king of Wales or Scotland, let alone Ireland, was at that time the subservient vassal of the king of England.

The king governed with the advice of a council of wise men or a witan, which usually met at the time of the principal Christian festivals or, when summoned, wherever the king happened to be "wearing his crown." To the witan the king might call whom he liked, but naturally they were usually his noblemen, bishops, and court officials. The kingship itself was elective, although the dead king's eldest son was usually chosen. But that might not be the case if the heir was a minor. Alfred had been preferred to his older brother's son; the Danes, Swein and Canute, were preferred to any Anglo-Saxon prince. Thus a splendid opportunity came to the witan when a king died.

It is evident that beginning at least with the reign of King Athelstan a rudimentary form of civil service existed, ranging from the officials of the court to the shire reeves. The king had a scriptorium (writing office) or secretariat served by his chaplains or clerks. They kept his seals and were responsible for drawing up charters and writs and for maintaining the royal archives. The king, although he may not have kept his money under his bed, for a time did carry his treasure around with him; but later a treasury was set up at Winchester, the capital of

Wessex, possibly under a royal chamberlain. In these institutions may be detected the germs of the later Chancery and Exchequer. The king also had his own bodyguards, called "housecarles" by the Scandinavian kings, who were paid for by a special tax and housed together. They were to be the cream of the army that fought with King Harold II against the Norman invaders.

The king obtained services from all his subjects, unless they were compounded for, either directly from his nobility and Churchmen or indirectly through the village communities. His most ancient right was a "feorm" or food rent which fed him and his court. He could also require services for his officials as they moved about the country on royal business. The men of Dover, for example, provided passage by ship for royal messengers when they visited the Continent. Then the king might need roads and bridges built or military services ranging from the furnishing of men and arms in time of war to the building of local defenses or fortifications. But no general taxation was imposed, other than the tithe for the Church—a tenth of the harvest—and the collection of tribute or Danegeld when the Vikings had to be bought off. In general the king was dependent for local government and justice on his nobility, lay and ecclesiastic, because so long as communications were primitive and a standing army or police force nonexistent, he could not exert his will over his subjects except through his more powerful servants, to whom he granted lands and other privileges in return for their rule on his behalf.

His leading servants were the ealdormen or earls, as they were called later, who governed large territories, comprising several shires or districts, in his name. When a strong king reigned they were obedient and serviceable; they detracted from a weak king's power. The Earl of Mercia served Alfred well; but Ethelred the Unready was betrayed by his Earl of Mercia. The king also had officials known as reeves, who ruled over his towns or "ports" and over his royal estates, and presided over the shire courts as his shire-reeves or sheriffs. These men were drawn from his nobility or thanes (thegns).

The thanes were a mixed class. The king had court thanes who followed him from place to place; other thanes were well-to-do landowners with clearly defined obligations; but some were small landholders. Roughly the status of the thane corresponded with his economic position. He lived in a great barn-like hall with his own servants, had a chapel and a kitchen, and a minimum landholding. Wergild, the amount of money payable according to ancient Anglo-Saxon law by a slayer or his kindred to the kindred of a man slain, was in the case of a thane six times the amount required for the death of an ordinary freeman or churl.

The churl (ceorl) was the English peasant landholder or artisan. If he prospered, he might attain the status of a thane; if he declined, he might become a slave. Most churls farmed, both keeping cattle and growing their own corn. They lived in wooden cottages, usually occupied about thirty acres of land, attended village meetings, shared a common plough, served in the fyrd or local shire defense when needed, and were not originally bound to the soil—though later the claims of custom and overlordship became the effective guides for their daily lives. Some had no lord but the king, but in later times most recognized a duty to a private lord. Not all freemen were full-time cultivators; some were craftsmen, ranging from the king's goldsmith to the village blacksmith. Beneath this free class were the slaves—captives in war, persons punished for crime, or the victims of economic necessity. Slaves might be freed upon the death or at the will of their masters or they might be given limited rights. Thus the records speak both of freedmen and half-freedmen. In general the freedom of the churls was compromised by their need for protection against the harshnesses of the times. "The general drift of English peasant life in these centuries," observes Sir Frank Stenton, "was undoubtedly from freedom towards servitude."

This was roughly the structure of Anglo-Saxon society after the consolidation of England. One further fact is worth noting. English women had greater rights then than they have ever had again until modern times. An Anglo-Saxon lady could hold land in her own right and defend her claim in the law courts. She could make donations for religious purposes and free her slaves. By one set of Anglo-Saxon laws a widow with a child was entitled to half her husband's property; and one of King Canute's laws laid down that "no woman or maiden shall ever be forced to marry a man whom she dislikes," nor might a widow be thrust hastily into a nunnery. By law and custom Anglo-Saxon men and women were on terms of rough equality.

The chief source of livelihood for all these people was the land. Agriculture generally followed a two-course rotation; one year the fields were sown, the next year they lay fallow. In the Midlands the peasants' strips were mixed together in the open fields and cultivated under a common scheme. Here there was a strong "nucleated" village community; elsewhere, in Kent for example, scattered hamlets where kinfolk owned compact fields were customary. In either case extensive farming was costly. The majority of men must have lived on a low level of subsistence. Life was broken by war and pestilence. Famine as well as sudden death at the hands of marauders or pirates was a menace to all. Trade developed slowly. Apart from iron and lead mining, the production of salt was the most important native industry, for salt was the only means for preserving meat and fish, as the beehive was the source of sugar. London was the only really sizable town, a center of international trade which managed to survive the wars that year after year beat against its walls. Other towns grew up because they were fortified strongholds or the quarters of garrisons where markets could be held in safety or, on the contrary, because they were market places that needed and obtained defenses. These burhs or "ports" received special protection and legal recognition from the king; they might also have their own courts and mint money, although the dies had to be cut in London.

The Anglo-Saxons were not by nature townsfolk or merchants; the Danes were. The Anglo-Saxons had conspicuously failed to reoccupy the old Roman towns. The Danes, who as pirates bestrode the world, showed themselves to be internationally minded when they settled in England. They exported surpluses of food from England in exchange for gems, spices, and other luxuries; they established a number of towns in the Danish part of the country; they made York into the second largest town in England with a population of eight or ten thousand; they created the five "boroughs" of Derby, Nottingham, Lincoln, Leicester, and Stamford; they helped too to enhance London's pre-eminence as a port. In the Danish parts of England—the northeast, East Anglia, and the eastern Midlands—different customs, laws, and social habits prevailed long after there ceased to be separate kingdoms. They seem to have had a high proportion of relatively free peasants with a distinctive system of agriculture; and they had their own methods of computing money. It has been argued that the superficial unity of England before the Norman Conquest concealed a racial cleavage between the Danish north and east and the English south and west. Certainly a sense of local patriotism or particularism showed itself in the north at the time of the Conquest and very frequently in later British history.

✂ THE LAW AND THE CHURCH

The administration of the law in early England is a difficult subject. Much of it was a matter of custom. The pagan Germanic code of law, based on the notion of an eye for an eye and a tooth for a tooth, was modified by Christian concepts and occasionally by new laws promulgated by the kings and their witans. Wessex, Mercia, and the Danelaw all had different codes, and a variety of courts existed. Shire courts met under the presidency of an earl or bishop or perhaps a sheriff twice a year; the shires, in turn, were divided into "hundreds"—relatively small territorial areas, where courts were held every four weeks. These hundred courts may have grown out of earlier popular assemblies. They not only administered customary law but also formed a focus of local government. A final appeal lay with the king, but he was not yet the "fountain of justice," for he was bound by the immemorial customs of his realm. In addition, kings granted the right of holding private courts to wealthy landowners, to ecclesiastics, and to towns. In the cause of justice, both plaintiff and defendant produced "oath-helpers" or "compurgators" to swear to the truth of their cause. If the oaths did not settle the matter one way or the other, the defendant might have to undergo an "ordeal" supervised by the Church which might consist of his being thrown into water to see if he floated or being tested for his capacity to carry a glowing iron without acquiring a festering wound. A failure in these cruel tests would lose him his case. Punishments ranged from hanging to enslavement, but were given generally only if the guilty party was unable to pay his wergild or fine. This was, it has been said, a "rough-and-ready" system of law.

To some extent the influence of Christianity and the Church modified the brutality of early English life. The common sense of Pope Gregory I and the wisdom of Archbishop Theodore helped to teach the need for moderation and mercy, for decent standards of family life, for consideration toward the poor. The ease with which the Anglo-Saxon kings submitted to conversion leaves a feeling that the conversion was superficial, and the Danes of the Danelaw were not converted until the tenth century. Just as monasteries were subject to abuse as valuable forms of property, so individual churches were treated as private properties: "some men let out churches for hire, just like common mills," complained the monk Aelfric. Consistent complaint was made about the corruption of the Church and the decline of morals, and although the Church boasted martyrs like St. Alphege, the Archbishop of Canterbury who was pelted to death with cattle bones by the Vikings in the early eleventh century, Christian leaders did little to mitigate the desolation and degeneracy that pervaded the land during the long years of the heathen invasions. Moreover the religion taught by the monks was narrow and superstitious. They doted on miracles and were more concerned with saving their own souls than tending the poor. A good deal of Bede's famous history of the early Church is sheer hagiography. The monks sought the safety of their souls by fasting and prayer; the well-to-do laymen sought salvation by building churches with their own personal and family priests to serve them, or went upon pilgrimages to Rome. Kings often lived lives of flagrant cruelty and sexual promiscuity while they founded monasteries and defended the rights of the Church. Canute was not an exceptional example of this ambivalent behavior. While monks were often accused of laziness, of fox hunting or playing dice, the ordinary village priests were for the most part half-literate clerks, married men glad enough to receive the meager perquisites of their profession. Bishops were few (only fourteen bishoprics existed in 1042 and some of these were held plurally) and they rarely visited their dioceses to impose discipline on their clergy.

The Church's principal contribution to civilization in the Anglo-Saxon period is to be found in what it gave to learning, literature, and the arts. The earliest schools were set up by the Church; instruction was, it is true, confined to subjects needed for a clerical career, such as Latin, Scripture, and sacred music. But the knowledge of men like the Venerable Bede and Aldheim, Abbot of Malmesbury, who taught in the latter half of the eighth century, included Virgil and Pliny, and probably some Greek. It was in the monasteries that literature was preserved, that books were copied and illuminated, and sculpture and architecture received a stimulus. King Alfred had personally supervised translations from Latin, and about a hundred years after his death Aelfric, Abbot of Eynsham, followed in the footsteps of Bede as a historian and commentator on his times. The reformation of the tenth century under King Edgar the Peaceful was another period when Latin literature was revived, copied, and taught.

In addition to the study of Latin, basic to the needs of the Roman Catholic Church, a small but significant English or Germanic literature was growing, equally under a Christian impulse. The famous epic poem *Beowulf* was written by a Christian, although it was imbued with pagan tradition. Caedmon is the first English poet known by name; he was a Northumbrian oxherder of the seventh century whose reputation rests on a few lines repeated by Bede. Other later English poetry has survived, including an account of the heroic battle of Maldon where an English earl died resisting the second wave of Viking invaders. If early English poetry stems from the obscure Caedmon, Alfred the Great was undoubtedly the father of English prose. Nearly all early English poetry and prose, like other early English arts, is in the debt of Christianity.

Not much can be said with confidence about Anglo-Saxon art, for after more than a thousand years all too little of it can be seen or judged. Some churches were built of wood, others showed the influence of wooden models. Anglo-Saxon churches often had small chancels, no transepts, and horseshoe arches. A number of lovely sculptured crosses and illuminated manuscripts, mostly from the north of England, have survived. But little of this art is considered to be as good as the naturalistic Celtic art of pre-Roman times. A naturalistic school of sculptors and illuminators flourished at Winchester in the tenth century, and the Anglo-Saxon use of "expressive outline" has recently been commended, but many of the artistic achievements of the Anglo-Saxon period derive from Byzantine or Frankish models, since after the Norman Conquest English art was indebted to the Romanesque style.

Such, in rough outline, was the portrait of Britain on the eve of the Norman Conquest. To the Celts Britain owed those independent racial fringes which were to form Scotland, Wales, and Cornwall. From the Romans it acquired a system of roads. The Anglo-Saxons gave it a language and agricultural habits. The Norsemen contributed towns and trade and a spirit of adventure. The Church offered learning, literature, and the arts and some modification of the ruthlessness of the pagan world. Only one figure of genius looms out of the early historical fog, that of Alfred the Great. The Normans destroyed a great deal and transformed everything. Possibly the men who thought and wrote about these matters later in British history—lawyers like Coke, political agitators like John Lilburne—were not so wrong when they looked back to the reign of King Alfred as an age of progress and liberty.

IX

The Foundation of Normandy and the Reign of Edward the Confessor

Just as the Viking chief Guthrum had won for himself and his followers a kingdom in the east of England in the days of Alfred the Great, so during the first quarter of the tenth century another Scandinavian adventurer, Rollo or Rolfe, known as "the old pirate," had carved for himself and his followers a duchy which was to be called Normandy— the land of the Northmen—on the northwestern shores of the kingdom of France. About 911 Rollo was acknowledged as a vassal by Charles the Simple, a descendant of Charlemagne, and, like Guthrum, was afterwards baptized in the Christian faith.

Normandy was one of the outgrowths of an extraordinary period of Scandinavian conquest which embraced finally England, much of France, Sicily, and Iceland. It gradually developed into a flourishing state. The ducal palace was at Rouen in western Normandy and the settlers, pagan when they arrived, were slowly transformed into a distinctive community by Latin culture and the Catholic religion. Under a succession of able dukes the Normans widened and consolidated their territories. Rollo was followed as duke by William Longsword, and Longsword by his illegitimate son, Duke Richard I, who encouraged monasticism in the duchy at the same time that a monastic revival was taking place in the England of St. Dunstan. Duke Richard II of Normandy, who came to the throne in 996, was the brother of Emma, the princess who married two kings of England, first the Anglo-Saxon, Ethelred the Unready, and afterwards the Dane, King Canute.

A nephew of Queen Emma, Robert the Devil, who came to the throne of Normandy in 1028, had previously fallen in love at the age of eighteen with Arlette, the daughter of a tanner of Falaise. She gave birth to a son, the future William the Conqueror. The fact that William was a bastard mattered little, for in the annals of Normandy most of the dukes were bastards, a fact which may have accounted for their vigor and aggressiveness. The line never weakened, and William was the most capable of them all.

William the Bastard became Duke of Normandy in 1035, and twelve years later, when he was only nineteen, he suppressed a revolt by his nobility with the help of his overlord, King Henry I of France, and earned a reputation as a soldier in a campaign against neighboring Anjou. In addition to asserting his claims against Anjou, William later became Count of Maine, and repulsed the attacks of French kings who were jealous of his successes. He also invaded Brittany and defied the Papacy by marrying Matilda of Flanders against its wishes. The dukes of Normandy relied for their position and prestige not upon a sanctified heredity but upon their own fighting skill and diplomacy. They did not expect loyalty from their subjects; they demanded and exacted it. In return for grants of land from the duke the Norman nobility undertook to furnish their overlord with armed cavalrymen or knights whenever he needed them. This form of land tenure by knight service was known as a fief and was the essence of feudalism, although the word feudalism itself was invented by the antiquarians of the seventeenth century.

Thus Normandy was governed by militant rulers, furnished with a hardy aristocracy, Christianized late and feudalized early, enjoyed a rudimentary Latin culture, and formed a society essentially organized for war and conquest.

⊗⊗ EDWARD, GODWINE, AND HAROLD

It was in the Norman court at Rouen that Edward, son of King Ethelred the Unready and Queen Emma of Normandy, later to be known because of his piety as "the Confessor," had been brought up. King Canute had married his mother, after she was widowed, more from passion than from policy, and she always preferred her Scandinavian to her English children. She is even said, though on doubtful authority, to have preferred the somewhat obscure claims of King Magnus of Norway (the Normans are now believed to have originally been Norwegians) to succeed to the English throne above those of her own son, Edward. Edward was already in middle age when he was called to the throne, and his character must by then have been fully formed. The two influences that dominated his life were his antagonistic relationship with his Norman mother—one of his first acts as king was to confiscate her English properties because "she had been too strict with him" and for a time to disgrace her—and his education in the court of Normandy. But recent evidence suggests that he may have been a more normal man than he was once supposed to have been. In any case he came to a dubious and contested heritage.

Edward the Confessor's election to the English throne in 1042 had been largely brought about by a group of earls who first held sway under King Canute, including Godwine, Earl of Wessex; Leofric, Earl of Mercia, son of the legendary Lady Godiva of Coventry; and Siward, Earl of Northumbria, a Danish warrior. Godwine was a remarkable man who had been the son of a thane of Sussex, had married a relative of King Canute, and by her had a number of strong and ambitious sons, the eldest a rogue named Swein and the second, the future King Harold II. Their sister Edith was married to Edward the Confessor, presumably as a part of the price of his succession.

The first years of King Edward the Confessor's reign were devoted to warding off threats from abroad exerted by rivals for his throne. Luckily for him the kings of Norway and Sweden quarreled among themselves; and wisely refusing help to either, Edward kept a fleet intact and repulsed the occasional incursions of Vikings. By 1049 the danger had passed and the king dispersed his fleet. Naturally enough the new king invited Normans to serve him at his court, though he may well have wished to offset the influence of Godwine and his sons and the rest of the more or less hereditary English nobility. He planted Norman colonies in Sussex and Herefordshire; he appointed a Norman, Robert of Jumièges, first as Bishop of London and then as Archbishop of Canterbury; he made an earl of his nephew Ralf, son of Drogo, Count of Vexin; and he employed many Norman chaplains as his clerks. While it may be an exaggeration to say that Edward the Confessor surrounded himself with French or Norman favorites, he did pave the way for the future Normanization of England.

On the whole the early years of his reign were creditable to the statesmanship of King Edward. After the reigns of three Danish kings it might have appeared that the royal Scandinavian lines had a prescriptive right to the throne of England, and no doubt that was what they thought.

But by careful diplomacy, military preparedness, and general restraint a long war was averted. The king's Norman advisers counterbalanced the influence of the English earls and in any case the menace from without united them all in his service.

In 1051, after the external dangers had receded, a crisis arose at home. The spark that lit the revolution of 1051–52 was an incident at Dover. The king had received a visit from one of his French friends, his brother-in-law Count Eustace of Boulogne; on his way home Count Eustace and his men-at-arms were involved in an affray with the townsmen of Dover in which some twenty were killed on each side. Count Eustace complained to the king, who angrily ordered Earl Godwine to punish the town. Godwine, whose earldom included Kent, and believing that the fault did not lie with the men of Dover, refused to obey. He demanded to put his case before the king and his witan and summoned his sons and his troops to his side. "But the foreigners were the first to gain the King's ear," recorded one of the Anglo-Saxon chroniclers, and Earl Godwine and his sons "made a strong show of force in opposition, though it was hateful to them to be forced to oppose their royal lord." Whether they planned to exploit the episode to carry out a *coup d'état* is uncertain. But the king acted astutely. He summoned the other great earls to his aid, declared a truce, and called another meeting of the witan in London later that September, in the meantime ordering out the militia. At the London meeting, after the two sides had glared at each other and rattled their swords, the king outlawed Earl Godwine and his sons (who were outnumbered) and afterwards deprived their sister, Queen Edith, of all her possessions and sent her to a nunnery. Thus he treated his wife much as he had treated his mother; but just as he forgave his mother, he later took back his wife.

The king's triumph did not last long. Earl Godwine and his eldest son, Earl Swein, went oversea to Flanders, and Earl Harold with his other brothers crossed into Ireland where they planned their revenge. Edward looked to the Normans for support. It is believed that at this time he offered the Duke of Normandy the throne (sending a message by the Norman Archbishop of Canterbury who was on his way to Rome). The duke had no children and had "put away" his wife. But the king's patronage of Normans, to whom he gave large estates and whom he employed as sheriffs, proved his undoing. He alienated those English earls who had stood behind him when he defied Earl Godwine. After one false start Godwine and his sons concerted a triumphant return. The seamen of Kent rallied to them and the sailors of the king's own fleet refused to fight their fellow countrymen. Through the mediation of Bishop Stigand of Winchester a settlement was arranged: Earl Godwine and his sons were restored, upon terms, to all their possessions; the Archbishop of Canterbury, who was the king's principal Norman adviser, fled abroad and Stigand was installed in his place. Thus the House of Godwine was re-established and the revolution "reduced the Normans in England to political insignificance, and thereby decided that if the Duke of Normandy were ever to become King of England it could only be through war" (Sir Frank Stenton).

The rest of the reign was more or less peaceful. Indeed England at this time has been described as one of the most civilized states in Europe, eminent in the arts and in the production of books. Earl Godwine died in April 1053 and his rascally eldest son Swein passed away in a spurious odor of sanctity as he returned from a pilgrimage to Jerusalem. Harold became Earl of Wessex in his father's place, and when Leofric, Earl of Mercia, died in 1057, he was followed by his son and then by his grandson Edwin. Harold was active in suppressing unrest on the Welsh border where a prince named Gruffyd or Griffith aimed at a united kingdom. Malcolm III, king of Scotland, paid a friendly visit to the English court. Eventually both the Welsh and the Scottish kings acknowledged King Edward as their overlord, and later another Norwegian invasion was frustrated.

Although Earl Harold of Wessex was the most powerful of the king's subjects and had won a reputation as a warrior in the Welsh campaigns, the king's favorite was now Earl Harold's younger brother Tostig, whom the king named Earl of Northumbria when Earl Siward died in 1055. Tostig eventually made himself unpopular in the north, and in 1065 the thanes of Yorkshire rose against him and proclaimed him an outlaw. Earl Harold, possibly jealous of his brother, lent him insufficient support, and the king reluctantly agreed to accept Morcar, the brother of Earl Edwin of Mercia, as Earl of Northumbria in place of Tostig. Tostig left for Flanders and spent the rest of his life conspiring against his brother and his native land.

The Northumbrian revolt of 1065 exemplified the historical tradition of northern independence, which dates at least from the days of the Northumbrian kingdom in the seventh century and had been accentuated by the Danish influences centered in York. The loss of the earldom weakened the House of Godwine, although the hostility between the two brothers makes it doubtful whether its retention by Tostig would have made any difference in the later course of events. (Indeed throughout English history the rivalry of brothers or brothers-in-law has been common.) The outlawing of Earl Tostig is said to have broken King Edward's heart. The whiteheaded king with his becoming pink face, an ambivalent attitude toward women, and a reputed gift for curing the blind and the scrofulous was now taking on the attributes of sainthood. He was too ill to attend the consecration of Westminster Abbey, the building of which had been one of the chief cares of his last years, and he died in January 1066. In the end, disregarding whatever promises he may once have given to Duke William of Normandy, the dying king named Earl Harold as his successor. On the very day after the funeral king Harold II was crowned; he was to be the last Anglo-Saxon king of England.

BOOK II

MIDDLE AGES

X

The Norman Conquest

Earl Harold succeeded to the throne in the face of many obstacles, and his claim was contested. In earlier times the witan had selected a king from among candidates of royal blood. The best qualified candidate in 1066 was Edgar, a grandson of Edmund Ironside, the last heroic Anglo-Saxon king, but he was a mere stripling. His father, Edward the Atheling, spent much of his life in Hungary and had returned to England in 1057 only to die. Had he lived, Edward the Atheling might well have been chosen king, but, as it was, there was no unchallengeable full-grown prince descended from the ancient royal line of Wessex. In 1064 Earl Harold had visited Duke William of Normandy and, according to Norman accounts which no one contradicted, taken an oath of allegiance to him and promised to help him secure the throne of England. It has even been argued that Earl Harold had been sent to Normandy by Edward the Confessor to confirm the promise of succession made by the king to Duke William in 1051. (If so, why did the saintly king change his mind on his death bed?) In any case the Normans naturally said that King Harold II was a perjured usurper.

If Harold turned within two years from promising the crown of England to Duke William to accepting the throne for himself, he succumbed to an understandable temptation. The witan may have argued that they did not want another "foreigner," like the last cruel Danish kings to rule over them, for such kings invariably dragged England into the orbit of their own imperial ambitions. It is clear from the Anglo-Saxon Chronicle that antiforeign feeling existed. Duke William had no hereditary rights; his great-aunt, it is true, had been the wife of Edward the Unready and of King Canute, but he himself was a bastard; Harold's mother, the wife of Earl Godwine, had at least been a Scandinavian princess. Whatever Edward the Confessor promised and Harold himself swore, the ruling caste in England had no obvious reason to bow to Duke William unless he compelled them to do so.

King Harold hastened to do what he could to enlist support. He sent away his mistress and married the widow of King Gruffyd of Wales, who was a sister of Earl Morcar of Northumbria and Earl Edwin of Mercia. He prepared to repel the invasion he knew was coming from Normandy. But first he had to contend with his own brother, the exiled Tostig, who had been deprived of the earldom of Northumbria. In the early summer

Tostig harried the coasts of Kent and eastern England, but then sailed away to concert an attack with King Harold Hardrada of Norway, who also fancied he had a claim to the English throne. King Harold called out the fyrd, gathered a fleet, and took up his headquarters in the Isle of Wight. Meanwhile Duke William was patiently preparing for invasion.

William had many allies. Not only did he neutralize the French king and the king of Denmark, but the imperial regency in Germany promised him assistance and the pope, to whom Gilbert, Archdeacon of Lisieux, presented the duke's case, sent him his blessing and a banner. In Normandy an armada of 3,000 warships and transports, capable of carrying horses as well as men, was assembled. William invited volunteers to join his army for pay and adventure, and men from Italy as well as France flocked to fight under him. Whether the aim of this expedition was to subdue the entire island or merely to seize some rich territory and booty, as the Vikings had done of old, is not certain. But William put forward his claim to the English throne and demanded of Harold to know why he had repudiated his oath. Slowly the forces of these crusaders—or plunderers—gathered at the harbor of St. Valery, in the estuary of the river Somme, to await a favorable wind.

The delay that occurred between the date of King Harold's accession to the throne and Duke William's invasion proved advantageous to the Norman, for after waiting two months in the Isle of Wight, King Harold was obliged to dismiss the fyrd, either because their terms of service had expired or because they had run out of provisions or because the king believed that the moment of danger had passed. The English fleet was sent to London to be laid up. In the middle of September news reached Harold that another Scandinavian chieftain, the king of Norway, guided by Harold's own brother Tostig, had landed in Yorkshire. The forces of Earl Morcar of Northumbria and his brother Earl Edwin were overwhelmed at the battle of Gate Fulford, two miles south of York, on September 20, 1066. Leaving York an open city, the Norwegian army withdrew to Stamford Bridge upon the river Derwent. Here they were surprised and wiped out by King Harold's English army; both their leaders were killed and a shattered remnant crept away over the North Sea.

The battle of Stamford Bridge was fought on September 25, 1066. Two days later, after the bones of St. Valery had been invoked, the wind shifted to the south and Duke William's fleet and transports ploughed unmolested across the English Channel, reaching Pevensey Bay near Hastings in Sussex on the following day. When King Harold heard these dire tidings in York he was at the other end of England. He immediately rode south at the rate of about twenty miles a day and reached

London in the second week of October. Meanwhile Duke William, who was fortifying a position in Hastings, was told of King Harold's victory and warned that a vast host was approaching.

But the host was not vast. The English forces had received a buffeting in the two northern battles. Moreover Harold could only bring back with him soldiers upon horseback; the foot soldiers and the two earls were to follow him later. Nor could he have had time during the day or two he spent in London to collect many of the loyal militiamen from the southern shires. It is variously estimated that between six and eight thousand men fought on each side in the Battle of Hastings.

Why did King Harold not wait longer to gather his forces before he marched? The probability is that he hoped to surprise his enemy as he had done at Stamford Bridge, feeling sure that Duke William would not be ready for him so soon in view of his swift ride south from York. But William had been forewarned and it was the English, not the French, who were surprised at the Battle of Hastings. The English came out of the Sussex forest and formed on a ridge with a narrow 600-yard front, where they were securely covered on both flanks. The Normans were grouped in three lines with archers to the fore, then heavily armed infantry, and finally mounted knights. On one side fluttered a red and golden dragon, on the other the papal banner. The English had only a few archers and the king's bodyguard of housecarls was disposed to stiffen the ranks of the militia or carry out a countercharge. "All," admitted William of Poitiers, "were inspired by the love of their country which they desired, however unjustly, to defend against foreigners."

Much nonsense has been written about the Battle of Hastings, in particular about the better trained, heavier armed, and more highly skilled Norman knights. It is likely that the two sides were about equally equipped. The Normans had more archers, but they had no cavalry in the later sense of the term; the French knights were "mounted javelineers." The English aim was to break up the Norman attack on their shield wall and then to counterattack, and in this they very nearly succeeded. A "dog fight" continued throughout that autumn day, October 14, 1066. Duke William, although he had several horses killed under him, fully controlled the battle and repulsed his enemy whenever it broke rank. In the end it was the discipline of the Normans under their duke and the wearing tactics of his archers that gained the victory. On both sides there was generalship of a high order, but when King Harold was slain, perhaps by a stray arrow, and his body trampled upon in the twilight, the English cause was lost. Two of his brothers had fallen earlier. Afterward his body was buried in unconsecrated ground near the Sussex seashore. An outstanding soldier, with fine victories in Wales and York-shire to his credit, he had been outmatched by another, equally experienced but wiser.

The English leaders would still not submit to the foreigner and chose the youthful Edgar the Atheling as their king. But Duke William exacted the submission of Dover and Canterbury, and of Edward the Confessor's widow in Winchester. Then he outflanked and encircled London. At Berkhampstead the English leaders came to him and surrendered. The Archbishop of York, the earls Morcar and Edwin and young Edgar himself took oaths and gave hostages. On Christmas Day Duke William was crowned king in Westminster Abbey. The congregation was asked in English to acknowledge him their king. When the mounted guard outside the Abbey heard the shouting they thought the king had been attacked and set fire to the surrounding buildings. No oaths or ceremonies could conceal the fact that England was a conquered country.

✂ REVOLTS BY THE ENGLISH

Once he had been crowned, King William I quickly began to strengthen his rule and to divide the spoils. He had at his disposal all the possessions of King Harold and the House of Godwine as well as other properties confiscated from those who had fought alongside Harold at the Battle of Hastings or who rebelled later. A general land tax or geld (on the lines of the old Danegeld) was imposed. The new king employed his old friend William Fitz Osbern, whom he made Earl of Hereford, and his half brother, the warlike Bishop Odo of Bayeux, as his chief advisers. At the same time he held out a friendly hand to some of the English. Waltheof, son of Siward, the former Earl of Northumbria, was allowed to marry the king's niece and Earl Edwin was offered one of his daughters. A few of the English clergy were given administrative duties and some of the English nobility that fought against him were allowed to compound for their lands. But in general Normans were appointed to all the important strategic posts. Castles were built by either the new king or his barons wherever it was thought necessary to overawe the native population or command lines of communication. These castles, with their wooden towers and stockades, surmounting earthen mounds and protected by ditches and ramparts, could be rapidly erected. The Tower of London dates from the early years of the reign.

King William had only been in England for six months when he found it necessary to visit Normandy. His lieutenants proved incapable of maintaining order, and uprisings broke out in the north, the west, the southwest, and even at the vital port of Dover. But the risings were not concerted. As soon as King William returned he laid siege to Exeter, the chief town in the southwest, and obtained its submission upon terms. Then he marched north, scarifying the Midlands on his way. In 1069, however, the Northumbrians rose again, invoking the help of their old friends, the Danes, whose king dispatched a naval expedition; all the malcontents joined in; and the whole of northern England was aflame. King William himself suppressed this rebellion and punished the people with widespread devastation of the land from the Midlands northwest as far as Chester. The scars of his awful punishment long remained. The last of these anti-Norman risings took place in eastern England in the neighborhood of Ely. Here an obscure English thane, Hereward the Wake, carried on guerrilla warfare for many months. Morcar, once the Earl of Northumbria, surrendered to the Normans at Ely, while his brother Edwin, former Earl of Mercia, was killed on his way to Scotland, where King Malcolm III had given aid and comfort to all of King William's enemies. But in 1072 King Malcolm himself was obliged to submit and swear allegiance to the Norman conqueror.

The vain revolts of 1067–71 completed the ruin of the English nobility. If William had hoped for and tried to found an Anglo-Norman state, as King Canute had earlier set up an Anglo-Danish state, he failed. Henceforward the old English nobility was destroyed or submerged by the French overlords, and England became an occupied country. Drastic methods of military repression were employed so that within five years of his landing King William was able to dismiss the mercenary portion of his army and leave the regency to his wife, Queen Matilda, or to Norman earls, while he himself spent much of his time in France. While he was away from England in 1075 three earls, two French and one English—Waltheof, Earl of Huntingdon, who had conspired against him before—plotted an elaborate rebellion in which they were promised help from Norway, Flanders, and Denmark. But the plot misfired or was betrayed; the Danes arrived too late. The aim of this rebellion was said to be the restoration of conditions that had existed in the "good old days" of King Edward the Confessor. Earl Waltheof was executed for his part in it, and he rather than Hereward the Wake may be considered the last English hero to defy the Norman conqueror.

The last years of King William's reign were anticlimactic. The Conqueror passed most of his time in France where he was harassed by the undutiful behavior of his eldest son Robert "Curthose" and the machinations of his overlord, the French king Philip I. William's wife Matilda, for whose love he had defied the pope and to whom he was faithful, died in 1083. In 1086, threatened with yet another Danish invasion of England, he was compelled to gather a large army and ordered "all the landholding men in England, no matter whose men they might be" to swear an oath of fidelity to him upon Salisbury Plain. Meanwhile an inquisition was carried out to discover the wealth of the kingdom and its liability to tax. Already heavy taxation had been imposed to sustain his interminable wars. Now the price of conquest was brought home to every man.

The king eventually died in a priory on a hill outside the Norman capital of Rouen within earshot of the cathedral bells, after having taken part in a frontier raid carried out as a reprisal. It was an appropriate ending to a fighting life of over sixty years. Normandy was left to his eldest son Robert, but the kingship of England was bequeathed to his second and favorite son, William Rufus or William the Red-Faced, who was immediately crowned in 1087 as King William II.

"William I," wrote Professor Frank Barlow, "was more than a Norman Duke and more than an Old-English King. He took the prerogatives of each and made himself more powerful than either." The powers of the Anglo-Saxon monarchy had been wide, especially its right to collect taxes and command military services from the whole population; the Conqueror made lavish use of the land tax or geld; and he acquired large royal estates which he increased by confiscations and by extending the area of the royal forests. Moreover in distributing lands among his friends and followers he made sure (whether or not by deliberate intent) that he created no such concentrations of political strength as had been possessed by the Anglo-Saxon earls; only on the frontiers of his kingdom, or marches, as they were called, did he permit compact baronial territories or "honors." He governed the country with the aid of a Great Council which replaced the old witan. His principal officials were the sheriffs—not the earls, as of old—and the keepers of his royal castles.

When King William bestowed lands on his followers, he allowed them to retain all the traditional rights—the private jurisdiction, for example —that commonly went with them. At the same time he attached to them specific and defined duties. He expected each holder of an honor—each baron—to provide him with a number of knights, that is to say, well equipped and trained mounted soldiers, a body of men instantly ready for war. Knights were either attached to the baron's household (they were to be known as knights bachelor) or were granted land by the baron in return for their military obligations. This system of tenure by knight's service was uniformly applied in England, as it had not been in Normandy. The total number of knights made available to the king was at least four thousand, and these had to be provided not only by the lay tenants-in-chief but also by the leading clergy—the bishops and many of the abbots.

Thus the king asserted the principle, never expressed by his Anglo-Saxon predecessors, that all land was held directly or indirectly by him and the tenants owed him service. This was made plain in his insistence on the provision of knights and also in the Oath of Salisbury, wherein not only the king's own vassals but all the landowners of any importance in the country, whoever's vassals they might be, did homage to him. Moreover, by a survey carried out in 1086, later known as "the Domesday Inquest," the king made certain that he knew of what the wealth of his kingdom consisted, where the ownership of land lay, and what rights attached to it. Commissioners were sent out to the different counties and exacted the required information from local juries. Later royal clerks rearranged the information in two volumes, known to history as the Domesday Book. This unique early statistical survey is a tribute both to King William I's constructive administrative wisdom and to the realities of his power. Here was the groundwork of a centralized government for England.

If the king thus made sure of his hold over his barons, he was equally determined to assert his rule over the Church. Whatever the feelings of different kings might have been, the Anglo-Saxon monarchy had governed the Church, except that the archbishops had needed to receive a pallium or badge of office from the pope at Rome. To secure papal support for his invasion of England King William had given certain vague promises, but had never intended to grant additional rights to the pope. Both Pope Alexander II and Pope Gregory VII, who gave a new depth to the authority of the papacy, sent demands to King William for his "fealty"—indeed they hoped that he would regard England as a "papal fief"—but William repudiated every political claim. On the other hand, he allowed a papal mission to come to England and depose the English Archbishop of Canterbury, Stigand, who had been put into office by Earl Godwine without ever receiving the pallium. In Stigand's place King William appointed, with papal approval, Lanfranc, an Italian monk learned in the civil law. One of the first things that Lanfranc did in his turn was to insist upon his primacy over the Archbishop of York. The latter was deprived of three sees, including that of Worcester, that had traditionally been his, but was given in return the dubious compensation of the right to rule over the Scottish Church. Other bishoprics were redistributed at this time, being moved from smaller places into "towns" or "cities." Thus the principle of centralization, insofar as it was compatible with the political realities and ideas of the time, was extended to the ecclesiastical sphere. Another Norman administrative reform was the publication of a royal writ whereby the jurisdiction of the bishops was clearly separated from that of the old English law courts in the counties and "hundreds." This was the origin of the English church courts; lay courts were forbidden to interfere in spiritual causes, a source of perpetual future trouble.

By the end of King William I's reign most of the large estates had been transferred from English to French hands; only one or two barons and bishops were still Englishmen. England had been conquered by a few thousand knights at arms and was ruled by a few thousand more, who held nearly all the offices or positions of profit and much of the land. A feudal superstructure consisting, in simple terms, of a foreign aristocracy organized for war, had been built into the old English state; but many of the English laws and customs were preserved and accepted by the Norman monarchy. The new Norman lords acquired the rights that had previously belonged to the English earls and large landowners, such as the rights to make men work upon their land, pay them tribute or fines with stocks and cattle, and attend their courts.

One should not exaggerate the centralization or simplification that had been brought about by the Norman Conquest. Possibly as many political problems were created for the future as were solved. The common people of England no doubt acquiesced in the new order, as their ancestors had been inured to invasion and devastation, battle and sudden death, pestilence and famine, from immemorial times. Their way of life was little altered; the methods of agriculture remained unchanged; the structure of shire and diocese, of hundred and village survived. It is possible that the poorest people were even slightly better off under their new masters. The 25,000 slaves noted in the Domesday Book soon disappeared from the records. The centralized Norman monarchy afforded more security than the common man had ever known before: "a man of any substance," wrote a Saxon chronicler, "could travel unmolested through the country with his bosom full of gold" and "no man dared slay another, no matter what evil he might have done him." England was never again to be ravaged by invaders as it had been so often during the previous thousand years. By the time the Norman kings had ceased to rule the two races had been virtually merged.

XI

The Reigns of William II, Henry I, and Stephen

William the Conqueror had left three sons: his eldest, Robert, nick-named Curthose, was his mother's favorite, a brave soldier with a weak character who inherited the Duchy of Normandy and soon allowed it to fall into anarchy; William Rufus, the second Norman king of England; and Henry, a clever and ambitious prince who received from his father a large sum of money which he began to count immediately and invested in a rich territory acquired from his eldest brother.

William Rufus had been educated by Lanfranc, the Archbishop of Canterbury who had been the Conqueror's principal adviser in England and his effective regent when he was not there. It was to Lanfranc that the dying king had written a letter telling of his choice of Rufus as his successor on the English throne. But the real love of these Norman princes was not England but Normandy, and all three of the Conqueror's sons aimed at winning dominion over Normandy and enlarging their continental territories. Consequently they conspired and fought against each other while their barons, faced now by a dual allegiance, sided first with one and then with the others in order to improve their own positions.

King William II was an able man, though less a soldier than his elder brother and less a diplomat than his younger one. He was not a Christian, and his veneer of chivalry wore thin; he was a homosexual and never married. During his reign, although much of it was spent in Normandy, he consolidated the hold of his dynasty upon England. In 1088 he suppressed a revolt led by his uncle, Bishop Odo of Bayeux, who had been exiled from England by the Conqueror but had returned at the beginning of the new reign; the rebellion failed because Duke Robert of Normandy lent inadequate support. At the same time, however, the English recognized the need for a strong king. They resented the disloyalty of some of the Norman bishops and barons and when William Rufus promised them good laws and kind treatment "the Englishmen came to the assistance of their lord the king." Thus he was able to impose discipline upon his unruly baronage.

William II was severe and greedy in his attitude toward the Church.

After the death of Lanfranc in May 1089, he left the archbishopric of Canterbury vacant for four years until, thinking he was dying, he summoned the pious and learned Anselm, Abbot of Bec, to the see. He employed a capable cleric, Ranulf Flambard, later Bishop of Durham, as his chief minister, who made himself unpopular by the way he exacted taxes. Other bishoprics and abbeys were left vacant so that the monarchy might enjoy their revenues, and taxation was imposed upon the Church as heavily as upon the laity. William II quarreled with his new archbishop because he wanted to go to Rome to visit the pope; Anselm's estates were confiscated when he insisted on doing so. It is not surprising that the king was not congenial to the monkish chroniclers of his time and that he was long reckoned in the annals of English history as a bad man and a bad king.

By the standards of his day he was certainly not a bad king. He compelled Malcolm III of Scotland to do him homage and when King Malcolm died in 1093 secured the friendship of his sons by supporting their claims to the Scottish succession. The frontier between the two countries was fixed on the Solway, further north than it had been before. In 1095 and 1097 King William II himself led expeditions into Wales, and although he could not subdue the northern fastnesses, he established peace in the south. Finally in 1096 he obtained full control over Normandy by giving his brother Robert 10,000 silver marks to enable him to go on the first Crusade, during which many French knights, flocking confusedly across the Mediterranean, took part in the conquest of the holy city of Jerusalem from the Mohammedan Saracens. Just as King William achieved order on the frontiers of England, he also consolidated his power in Normandy by fighting with a fair degree of success on its borders, notably in Maine (to the south of Normandy) where he restored the position attained by his father. Thus by suppressing rebellions in England in 1088 and 1096, by exerting a strong hand over the Welsh and Scottish borders, and by keeping the baronage in subjection, William Rufus confirmed his father's conquest while he paved the way for the reunification of England and Normandy by his brother Henry.

Of the three brothers it was Henry, starting last, who triumphed in the end. After many abortive intrigues he seems to have conspired with a noble family named Clare to have his brother William murdered while he was hunting in August 1100; the accusation, though made by later historians and not by contemporaries, is plausible. After Rufus had been slain by an arrow as he hunted in the New Forest, his body thrust into a farm cart by peasants and hastily buried, Prince Henry, conveniently upon the spot, rode quickly to seize the royal treasury at Winchester and three days later had himself crowned in Westminster. Here where a new palace had been constructed, looking down the river towards the Conqueror's Tower of London and the stone-built London Bridge, the youngest son of William the Conqueror, a man consumed by a restless and unscrupulous urge for power, began his remarkable reign.

✿ KING HENRY I

Walter Map, a scholar who served in the royal household later in the century, wrote of King Henry I that though his entry into his kingdom was "faulty," "he surpassed all his predecessors in the tranquillity of his rule, in his wealth, and in the great sums he laid out all over Christendom." He was easy of access and kept good order. "No one but an idiot was poor in those days." His contemporary Peterborough chronicler says much the same thing: "He was a good man, and was held in great awe. In his days no man dared to wrong another. He made peace for man and beast."

When he first came to the throne King Henry I had to offer concessions, for his claim could be challenged and he required friends. He promised in his coronation charter that he would abide by the laws of King Edward the Confessor; he repudiated the unjust oppressions of his brother; he announced that the Church would be "free." Hastily crowned by the Bishop of London—Anselm, the Archbishop of Canterbury, was in exile and the Archbishop of York too old and far away—the king at once recalled Anselm to England and imprisoned the unpopular Flambard, Bishop of Durham. Next the king married Edith, daughter of Malcolm III, king of Scotland, who was also the great-granddaughter of the English hero Edmund Ironside. Archbishop Anselm was delegated to take her out of a nunnery. After the marriage the king returned to his mistresses and the queen to her religion.

Women and money were the new king's weaknesses. He had twenty illegitimate children, and one of his liaisons, with the wife of a "marcher" earl, proved useful during his Welsh campaigns. Otherwise he was abstemious in his behavior and careful in his expenditure. He explored every means of acquiring wealth, including debasing the coinage. In spite of severity to his enemies and sexual expansiveness, he won the reputation of being a good Christian.

In February 1101 the agile Bishop of Durham escaped from the Tower of London and crossed over to Normandy where he joined Duke Robert. Robert Curthose, Henry I's eldest brother, had just returned triumphantly from the first Crusade, having married a Sicilian heiress on the way back. It was natural that he should attempt to assert by force his claim to his father's throne in England. He managed to land at Portsmouth, but when the two brothers and their armies confronted one another at Alton in Hampshire, war yielded to diplomacy. Henry was recognized as king of England, Robert as Duke of Normandy. Not only was Duke Robert freed of the debts he had owed to William Rufus, but Henry promised him a large pension. King Henry also offered an amnesty to those of his vassals who had sustained his brother's cause.

But the Treaty of Alton soon proved meaningless. The king found excuses for punishing the rebel barons; he forgave the Bishop of Durham on the understanding that his astute mind be devoted to intrigues on his behalf in Normandy. Duke Robert's incompetence in the duchy was again disclosed and in 1104 King Henry I carried out the first of three successive invasions of Normandy. After wintering in England, he launched an attack in June 1106 with the aid of troops from Brittany and Maine. One of the few pitched battles of this age was fought in September at Tinchebrai and victory won by Henry I's deployment of his reserves. Duke Robert was taken prisoner, to die at the age of eighty in Cardiff Castle. Exactly forty years after the Battle of Hastings a king of England had conquered Normandy; Henry I ruled it for the rest of his reign.

A French king of the Capetian dynasty, which had ruled, in name, over the western half of Charlemagne's Empire since 987, had acquiesced in King Henry I's accession to the throne of England; and now the fifth Capetian, Louis VI or the Fat, who became king in 1108, was obliged to accept Henry as a rich and vigorous neighbor and vassal in Normandy. Though they were the overlords of many provinces, the actual territorial possessions of the Capetian kings were small. King Louis therefore maneuvered to undermine Henry I and expand his own power. Year after year desultory wars or diplomatic intrigues followed. William Clito, son of the imprisoned Duke Robert, was a pawn in the game, but Henry held his own. He found time too to suppress trouble on the Welsh frontiers or marches. But in 1120 it appeared that the empire he had built would collapse.

King Henry I had only two legitimate children, Prince William and Princess Matilda. Matilda at the age of eleven had been married to the emperor Henry V with the idea that an Anglo-German alliance would counterbalance French enmity. In November 1120 Prince William, returning from Normandy to England in an up-to-date "white ship" manned by a drunken crew, was drowned and the king's rival and enemies hoped that the Norman kingdom would expire. But Henry was not dismayed; he married again, as his first wife was dead; when this new marriage proved barren, he persuaded the English baronage to recognize his daughter, now a widow, as heiress to the throne. The barons agreed because they hoped to profit under a woman's rule. But in 1128 the king negotiated a second marriage for Matilda, this time to Geoffrey, the son of the Count of Anjou, who was known as the Plantagenet because his father planted broomplants or genistas to improve his hunting covers. Geoffrey was fourteen when he married Matilda, aged twenty-five, and with boyish distaste repudiated the marriage and sent away his wife, despite the fact that King Henry had promised his son-in-law the thrones of both England and Normandy. Later Geoffrey thought better of it and recalled his wife, who bore him three children in quick succession, the eldest being the future King Henry II.

King Henry I spent most of the last three years of his life in France delighting in being a grandfather. His position in England was secure. In his household arrangements some constitutional historians have detected the pattern of a future civil service. The king had a "justiciar" who acted for him in his absence, a chancellor, constables, and a treasurer. Details about his household have survived in a document called *Constitutio domus regis* drawn up for the guidance of his successor. His was a modest economy. The chancellor, for example, received for his services five shillings a day, a loaf of bread, four gallons of dessert wine and four of ordinary wine, one large wax candle, and forty candle ends. But in the king's court, attended by ministers of state who moved with him from place to place, were concentrated the highest deliberative, administrative, and judicial functions. It was the nucleus of the Curia Regis, the supreme royal court of justice; and when the leading barons and bishops attended to offer advice it became the Magnum Concilium, the great council of the realm.

King Henry's relations with his Church were not easy. The popes ever since his father's time had been staking high claims. In particular they insisted that the clergy should not receive its offices at the hands of laymen, as it had always done in Anglo-Saxon days. Lay investiture, as this was called, implied, so it was argued, that the king was spiritually superior to the pope. Neither Archbishop Anselm nor King Henry I wanted to make an issue of the matter. In 1106 a compromise was concluded. Bishops were henceforward not to be invested with ring and staff, symbols of their spiritual powers, by the monarchy; but they had first to pay homage to the king for their worldly estates or "temporalities" as his vassals before they received their spiritual appointments with appropriate ecclesiastical ceremonies. It was also agreed that the cathedral chapters might elect bishops, subject to the king's right to influence nominations and to veto. This agreement, known as the Compromise of Bec, was accepted by the pope and ratified in London. Afterward a number of vacancies in the Church were filled and later King Henry consented to the creation of new sees at Ely and Carlisle. Several monasteries were also founded during the reign.

King Henry I is sometimes described as devout. If he was a Christian, he was certainly a cruel, greedy, and lascivious one. He was a specialist in extracting money from the Church. After Anselm died in 1109 he left the archbishopric vacant for five years. He also discovered that to fine clergymen for being married, as many of them were, yielded an excellent revenue. The compromise he negotiated with Anselm merely papered over the cracks in the awkward relationship between the English monarchy, long accustomed to supremacy over the Church, and an aggressive papacy. Trouble lay in wait for Henry's successors and the problem was not settled until the reformation of the English Church in the sixteenth century.

The king's relations with his barons also remained ill-defined. Though Henry still demanded knight's service from his lay nobility, he started to take payment in money ("scutage" or shield-money) from the ecclesiastical baronage. The baronage, in turn, was beginning to exact money instead of military service from its tenant knights. Thus already, fewer than 100 years after the Norman Conquest, the basis of what later historians called feudalism, indeed the very reason for its existence, was being undermined. The next king, Stephen, was to fight his battles with mercenary soldiers instead of a "feudal" array.

器 KING STEPHEN

Stephen was a favorite nephew of King Henry I, who had made him Count of Mortain in Normandy and Earl of Lancaster in England. His mother Adela, daughter of William the Conqueror, had married the Count of Blois and her children, besides Stephen, included Theobald, who succeeded his father, and Henry, who became Abbot of Glastonbury and Bishop of Winchester. Stephen himself was married to a capable Scottish princess named Matilda, the niece of King David I and descended from the Anglo-Saxon royal line. If the other Matilda (the two Matildas were also, confusingly, cousins), the daughter of King Henry I, who was known because of her first marriage as the empress, was unable to establish her claim to the English throne, then either Stephen or his elder brother Theobald was a plausible candidate. King Henry I died suddenly on December 1, 1135, of an excess of hunting and shell fish while staying in the Forest of Lyons. In exactly three weeks Count Stephen had enterprisingly crossed into England, had been welcomed by the citizens of London, and was crowned by the Archbishop of Canterbury in Westminster Abbey. Meanwhile his elder and less enterprising brother Theobald had been recognized as Duke of Normandy.

Stephen owed his throne, as had his two predecessors, to the English Church and the English people. Pope Innocent II confirmed their choice. Like his uncle before him, Stephen had acted boldly and promised many concessions, while possession was still nine-tenths of the law. The empress Matilda, his rival, had a reputation for being haughty, grasping, and disagreeable, as well as being a woman, and her second husband Geoffrey, Count of Anjou, was disliked by all the Norman barons because he was the leader of their traditional enemies in France. King Stephen, for his part, was affable, generous, and brave, a genuine example of a chivalrous knight. But his very virtues were a source of weakness; it was no advantage for a king to be a gentleman in rough times. To maintain his throne he had to bribe both his barons and his clergy; but, as the Peterborough chronicler remarked, "the more he gave them the worse they behaved towards him." Because of the dubious nature of his title, the other barons looked on him as just one of themselves, only rather luckier. He lacked the single-minded unscrupulousness that enabled his uncles to exercise political control over all their subjects.

Yet for a time all went smoothly for him. His brother resigned the dukedom of Normandy in his favor and retired to Blois, thus preserving the unity of the Anglo-Norman state under one ruler. Stephen negotiated a truce with Count Geoffrey of Anjou and he defeated his Queen's uncle, King David I of Scotland, at the Battle of the Standard in August 1138.

At first his rival, the empress Matilda, had few friends. But the barons grew discontented or hoped to profit from civil war. Robert, Earl of Gloucester, the eldest bastard of King Henry I, who but for his "bar sinister" might have had a fine claim to the English throne, decided to lend her his support. Brian Fitz Count, illegitimate son of the Count of Brittany and Lord of Abergavenny, who loved the haughty Matilda and was loved by her, rallied to her side; and even the loyalty of the mighty Roger, Bishop of Salisbury, who had been the chief justiciar of King Henry I, was in question. King Stephen—unwisely, as it proved—first moved against Bishop Roger, whom he arrested, and thereby offended a powerful section of the Church. Therefore when the empress Matilda landed in England in October 1139, a number of barons turned against the king and desultory warfare broke out in different parts of the country. Ranulf, Earl of Chester, who had a grievance against the king and whose daughter was married to Robert of Gloucester, attacked him at Lincoln. Here in February 1141 the king was defeated in battle and taken prisoner. At a council held in Winchester and presided over by the king's own younger brother, Bishop Henry, now a papal legate, the king was deposed and the empress Matilda was chosen queen of England. But the other Matilda, Stephen's wife, hastened to her husband's rescue, and war raged between the two rivals to the throne. By the end of the year Stephen had been released from prison and he and his wife were recrowned by the Archbishop of Canterbury.

Henceforward something akin to anarchy prevailed throughout the country. Great barons like Ranulf of Chester, Henry of Huntingdon, Robert of Gloucester, Geoffrey de Mandeville of Essex (the Constable of London), Robert Beaumont of Leicester, Gilbert de Clare, Earl of Pembroke, all fished hopefully in the troubled waters. But in 1147 Robert of Gloucester died and the empress Matilda, rebuffed by fate, left England the next year never to return. Her son Henry of Anjou, however, now took her place; he came from France to stake his claims after winning a supporter in King David I of Scotland, who was eager to revenge his defeat by King Stephen. The pressure upon the harassed king was fierce. He was obliged to abandon Normandy to the young Henry, his father Geoffrey of Anjou having resigned his rights there in favor of his son. A succession of pointless sieges (the Norman castles were now fortified with stone and hard to capture), town burnings, baronial squabbles, and diplomatic marriages sustained or perverted the internecine war. Finally in November 1153 an agreement was reached between Henry, Duke of Normandy, on the one side, and King Stephen on the other. It was blessed by the English Church. Stephen was to be allowed to reign in peace for the remainder of his days, but Henry was to succeed him. King Stephen died in October 1154; thus the "nineteen long winters" of his unhappy reign reached an end. The grandson of William the Conqueror, he was the last and the least of the Norman kings of England.

✿ THE CHARACTER OF NORMAN ENGLAND

Under the Norman kings, until the unsettled reign of Stephen, the ordinary Englishman had benefited from a high degree of personal security and comparative freedom from wars and invasions. The price he paid for it was the performance of services closely defined and rigorously imposed. Most peasants were tenants of an estate or manor and paid their landlords not in money rents but with their own labor. Sometimes manors and villages would coincide, while at others a village would be under a divided lordship. In the first case village matters would be settled in the lord of the manor's own court, in the second at a general meeting of the villagers. The insistence of the Norman kings that obligation for payment of taxes and the provision of military services must be clearly defined and located tended to strengthen the chain of social responsibility and to that extent depressed the status of the peasants or villagers; but this depression had begun in Anglo-Saxon time when the habit of peasants "commending" themselves to the protection of a particular lord in return for specified services had first begun.

As in Anglo-Saxon times, an average peasant might hold some fifteen to thirty acres of arable land which were in some parts of England scattered in strips in the open village fields. These strips were shaped by the method of ploughing. Most peasants owned an ox or two which they contributed to an eight-ox plough worked in common, and a day's work by the communal plough might complete an individual strip; no doubt the good and bad lands were fairly divided among the village community, though some peasants might wangle something more than they were entitled to at the expense of a careless neighbor. The manorial lords also held arable land, known as their "demesne," in the open fields, and their holdings were cultivated by the villagers under the direction of a foreman or the village reeve. Some of the poorer peasants, cottagers or crofters with little land of their own, devoted most of their lives to laboring for others. To them the villager or villein owning thirty acres would be a figure to envy, despite his customary obligations.

Beyond his labor services to his lord each week and at harvest time, the peasant farmer was generally required to pay rent in kind; to give his lord a present when his daughter married or pay a fine when a son inherited; to use his lord's mill and his oven; and pay "tallage" or tribute on demand. The average villager could, no more than the leaseholder of a later era, "go with his land where he wished." In that sense he was "tied to the soil" and not "a free man." Some freemen existed, notably in East Anglia and in other parts of the former Danelaw, as well as in the towns. Modern research suggests that the pattern of these agricultural arrangements was by no means uniform throughout England, but the "tied" villager or villein was probably the characteristic peasant of Norman times.

Besides his arable holdings in the open fields, the peasant shared in the village commons on which the cattle grazed; in meadows, where they existed, which provided forage for the winter; and in woodlands where pigs enjoyed the acorns; and he might also have access to wasteland beyond the village. The problem of raising food for man and beast in the winter was a very considerable one, as was the maintenance of fertility in the open fields; hence the value of horse, cow, and sheep manure was high, as was the price of salt for the preservation of meat.

The question of the status of villagers in these early times is complicated. "There is very little contemporary evidence to show how the villeins of the twelfth century were faring and whether they were nearer freedom as the years passed" (D. M. Stenton). Nor can one measure precisely how onerous their customary labor services, their rent payments in kind, and other obligations were to them. Their obligations could be, and often were, limited by an appeal to the "customs" of the manor, which were sometimes remembered and sometimes invented. Men living on the margin of subsistence are rarely troubled by abstract ideas. The better-off peasant was certainly anxious to commute his services, that is to say, exchange his customary services for a money rent; the poor were most concerned to prevent themselves from starving each winter.

One grievance resulted directly from Norman rule—the forest laws. In primitive time arable land had been regularly extended by conquering the forests with axe and plough. The Norman kings, however, reserved vast districts for hunting deer and other beasts and prohibited the inhabitants of these areas from reducing the game preserves. Forest courts and officials saw that the law was obeyed. The royal forests were enlarged. The New Forest in Hampshire was created by William the Conqueror; almost the whole of Essex was covered by Epping Forest. At the end of the Norman period about one-third of England was covered by the forest law. The peasants who dwelt in the forest districts had some compensation for the severity of the law in that they were allowed access to the smaller game, invaluable for supplementing their diet in winter, but the law of the forest reinforced the common law and made the forester the most hated of men. Robin Hood of Sherwood Forest was to become a popular hero because he defied the forest laws.

The Normans contributed to the evolution of the English Church. The seats of the bishops were moved to more populous centers and new sees created, and the bishops, in order to administer the church courts, employed archdeacons who visited and supervised parishes. The manorial lords nearly all built churches to save their souls, so that where a village had more than one lord it sometimes had more than one church. The parish priest would be given land known as the "glebe," to support him, but he seldom enjoyed the whole tithe, which were payments in kind traditionally demanded out of the harvest for the upkeep of the Christian Church. These tithes were often granted by lords of manors to the monasteries, which provided such social services, medical care, and schooling as there were, or were engrossed by laymen. Therefore the village priest, though nominally a free man, was little better off than the average villager and had to cultivate his soil and even work for his patron in order to earn his keep. In spite of fulminations and prohibitions from above, the village clergymen were commonly married.

The Norman Conquest had stimulated the foundation of monasteries;

between 1066 and 1154 the number of religious houses rose from forty-eight to nearly three hundred. Some old Benedictine monasteries were taken over by French or Italian monks, and in the reign of King Henry I the Order of the Cistercians (the "white monks") established monasteries in England, the first built in Surrey in 1128. Archbishop Lanfranc has been described as "the father of the monks" and Norman influence is considered to have brought about progress and reforms. Complaints about the conduct of these houses and of breaches of their rules and vows were not uncommon, but on the whole this age of expansion was more virtuous than most; it has been called "a golden age." In general, the Norman kings strengthened and systematized the English Church without materially changing the life of the village community.

The Normans helped the slow development of town life. Pre-eminent was the city of London, joined to Westminster, with its abbey and royal palace, by a "populous suburb." King William I granted it a charter, as did King Henry I, and in the reign of King Stephen the citizens of London attempted to form themselves into a "commune" after a continental model. The city contained a great many churches including St. Paul's. Its citizens were known as barons and were exempted from taxes and granted privileges in return for an annual sum paid directly into the royal exchequer.

A common feature of other towns under the Normans was the merchant guild. These guilds regulated trade and commerce, but the members of the guild and borough tended to be the same, and thus the guild offered a road to self-government.

The introduction of buildings in stone by the Normans was an asset to the towns. Architecture was indeed the most distinguished of the arts during the Norman period. The Normans themselves, essentially fighting men and politicians, did not add greatly to the arts, and what used to be called Norman architecture is now more accurately described as Anglo-Norman Romanesque. The energies of the Norman administration were manifested in many a building, from their castles crowned by stone keeps to Battle Abbey, Tewkesbury Abbey, and Durham Cathedral. A good deal of the ecclesiastical architecture with its fat pillars, cushion capitals, and rounded arches is still to be seen; Kilpeck Church in Herefordshire and Studland Church in Dorset are notable examples. In Durham Cathedral is to be detected a precocious example of early Gothic. In general the Norman churches were bigger, twice as long and twice as wide, as corresponding Anglo-Saxon buildings. They were large and impressive, but their sculpture showed little delicacy.

The Normans made little impact on the graphic arts, and though their spoken language was French and their written or official language was

Latin, they did not offer much in the way of literature. Literary English suffered an eclipse. In fact the trilingualism of the Norman period—English, French and Latin—obstructed progress. On the other hand, the Normans did help to link England with western European culture. In essence, however, they were soldiers, administrators, and lawyers rather than artists or men of letters. It took time before the gifts and characteristics of the two peoples, conquerors and conquered, merged and gave birth to a new national pattern.

XII

The Reigns of Henry II and Richard I

When King Henry II, at the age of twenty-one, was crowned king of England, he became the ruler of an impressive empire and by his own efforts soon extended it. From his mother, the empress Matilda, he inherited Normandy; from his younger brother, Geoffrey, he extracted lordship over both Anjou and Maine, their father's inheritance; as his brother's heir he later acquired Brittany and consolidated that county by warring with its barons for three years; Touraine was also his by inheritance; by marriage he acquired the duchy of Aquitaine which stretched from the Loire to the Pyrenees; and finally in 1173 he also obtained the overlordship of Toulouse in the south of France. He expanded these territories by various means, including marriage treaties, and everywhere he kept his numerous vassals in check. He did not govern by remote control but moved his court from place to place, spending the larger part of his reign outside England; but he had a central chancery and reliable permanent officials and so was able to rule effectively over an area that reached from the south of Scotland to the north of Spain.

By contrast the king of France had still little more than his title; he owned a few thousand scattered acres and had a castle in Paris. Louis VII, Henry II's French contemporary, a pious monarch who nevertheless managed to quarrel both with the pope and the Church, did not improve his situation when, out of a sense of guilt, he embarked upon a Crusade to the Holy Land and in the process lost his rich and beautiful wife,

Eleanor of Aquitaine; their marriage was annulled after fifteen years and Henry II, on the eve of acquiring the English throne, had snapped up the heiress. Thus the so-called Angevin empire not merely dwarfed the dominions of the king of France—even though Louis VII was Henry's overlord for many of his possessions—but generated personal enmity and resentment between Paris and Westminster. When a stronger king succeeded Louis VII, King Henry II's reign was brought to an ignominious close.

But at first all went gloriously well for the young English king. In his own person he held his empire together and by his own skills he improved its administration. He was a squat man of medium height with red hair, freckled face, and grey eyes, and in his veins ran the blood both of the famous Norman and Anglo-Saxon kings. He was an indefatigable worker with a natural gift for government; an organizer rather than a warrior, he was master of all the diplomatic ingenuities of his age. He worked hard and played hard and was a man of passion, having besides his French wife, by whom he had several children who were valuable assets in the marriage markets of the world, a succession of mistresses including a lady known as Fair Rosamond and, it is said, the French princess Alice who was betrothed to his own son, the future Richard I.

In spite of the vast extent of his possessions across the Channel, England meant much to Henry II; the title of king carried many advantages so long as the barons were loyal. The first three Norman rulers had set a pattern of firm monarchical government, but it had been threatened with disintegration during the reign of King Stephen. The first thing that King Henry II needed to do in England was to restore order and create confidence. He expelled the Flemish mercenaries upon whom his predecessor had depended; he regained crown lands that had been alienated; he supervised the destruction of unlicensed castles; and he led expeditions to teach discipline to unruly barons. But he did not act vindictively, and the barons were encouraged to offer services and to expect benefits from their new master, just as ordinary people were led to hope for law and peace under the first of the Angevin or Plantagenet kings.

Two years after his coronation Henry did homage to Louis VII for his French fiefs; he then returned to England and himself received homage as overlord from both Wales and Scotland. Then in the 1160's he turned to making a series of reforms, financial, judicial, and military. There was now a central Exchequer at Westminster, as well as the king's personal treasury in the "chamber" of his itinerant court. King Henry sent out justices to report on the conduct of his officials—sheriffs, bailiffs, and foresters—and a number of them were removed for mis-

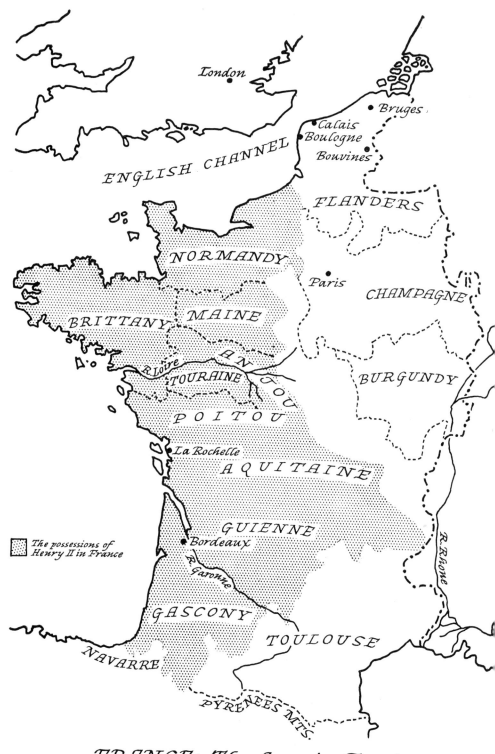

London

Bruges

Calais
Boulogne
Bouvines

ENGLISH CHANNEL

FLANDERS

NORMANDY

Paris

CHAMPAGNE

BRITTANY

MAINE

R. Loire

ANJOU

TOURAINE

BURGUNDY

POITOU

La Rochelle

AQUITAINE

GUIENNE

Bordeaux

R. Garonne

R. Rhone

The possessions of
Henry II in France

GASCONY

TOULOUSE

NAVARRE

PYRENEES MTS.

FRANCE: The Angevin Empire

conduct, while the Exchequer was reinforced by the selection of new sheriffs who gathered in much of the royal revenues. The king did not rely on the old Danegeld as his principal source of income, but concentrated on exploiting the widespread royal estates and drawing upon the profits of justice and other royal rights. He also obtained scutage or shield money, not only from the English ecclesiastical baronies as Henry I had done, but also from the lay barons, whose obligations for knights' fees were more carefully defined. The king reformed the coinage and suppressed unlicensed mints, while he exacted money from the townspeople, including the wealthy citizens of London, and from the Jews who, since the Conquest, had settled in England in considerable number.

Besides reforming the Exchequer system (its methods are described in a treatise entitled *Dialogus de Scaccario,* which was dedicated to the king), Henry made changes in administration of the law. Justices, who were sent out on eyre or circuit to enforce royal rights and sat with the sheriffs, began to hear criminal cases as well. By two assizes or royal edicts, given at Clarendon in 1166 and Northampton in 1176, trials for murder and other grave offenses were reserved to these justices on eyre. At first the king had to rely on his bishops and Exchequer officials as his justices, but gradually a body of trained lawyers was built up. To discover criminals, juries of twelve men representing each "hundred" and four men representing each village or township were invited to denounce wrongdoers to the justices for summary punishment. In the beginning this was no more than a rough method of maintaining justice and order, but at least the primitive Anglo-Saxon ideas of wergild were abandoned, the notion of the king as a fountain of justice was advanced, and a jury system was brought into general operation. Property rights were also safeguarded by a number of new procedures. Claims to freehold possession were investigated with the aid of juries, and writs were issued to restore to freeholders land wrongfully taken from them. "By making the smaller landowner's right to his property dependent on royal instead of the feudal courts" Henry "struck at the root of the great lord's power over his military tenants" (Bryant). Though the aim of most of these legal reforms was to secure royal rights and collect money for the Exchequer—since justice had, above all, to show a profit—the broadening scope of the royal jurisdiction and its centralization, together with the growth of case or common law, were to have momentous consequences for the future history of England.

Though these legal reforms did not interfere with the relations between a lord and his "unfree" tenants or villeins, they did act as a curb on the power of the greater barons. The king also prohibited military tournaments and trial by battle. He used shield money and ward money to hire soldiers instead of having a personal military service or castle guard, and thus freed himself from complete dependence upon his vassals in war. But at the same time he reaffirmed the principle that it was the duty of every English freeman to give military service to his king when it was needed, and the Assize of Arms of 1181 defined the equipment that he must have ready for that purpose.

In seeking to reform the law, restore order, and safeguard the rights of the Crown, King Henry II came into conflict with the Church, and in particular with his Archbishop of Canterbury, Thomas Becket. Becket was originally the king's chief clerk or chancellor and boon companion. He had been recommended by the previous archbishop Theobald whom he had served as an archdeacon, and when Theobald died the king appointed Becket to replace his old master. Becket was a versatile and capable administrator but a vain, obstinate, and ambitious man. The king wanted to arrest the pretensions of the Church to independence and to check abuses: he wanted to define more narrowly the jurisdiction of the church courts and to limit ecclesiastical appeals to the pope in Rome. The church courts, constituted by William the Conqueror, had by various means, especially during the reign of King Stephen, extended their jurisdiction to cover cases of contract, debts, and disposition of property and had also asserted the exclusive right to judge and punish all clergy for criminal offenses. Also during Stephen's reign a good deal of the royal control over the appointment of bishops had been lost, and King Henry II wished to reassert control. Since Pope Alexander III was engaged in a life-and-death struggle with the emperor Frederick Barbarossa and had been forced to flee from Rome to France, he certainly had no wish to alienate the English king. With a friendly archbishop and a complacent pope, Henry II had every reason to hope he could impose reforms on the Church.

However, he reckoned without Becket. As soon as he had been appointed Primate, Becket resigned his chancellorship and constituted himself the champion of the Church against the king. He saw his office as sacrosanct. The quarrel began when King Henry II demanded that clergymen who had been found guilty of criminal offenses in the Church courts should be handed over to royal officials for punishment. Becket argued that this was punishing the same man twice. When King Henry attempted to define the customs of the Church as they had existed before King Stephen's reign in the so-called Constitutions of Clarendon in 1164, Becket at first gave way, but then changed his mind, planning to appeal to the pope and to rally the other bishops against the king. Henry ruthlessly set out to ruin his recalcitrant Primate: Becket fled abroad while the revenues of his see of Canterbury were confiscated and his friends put in prison. The bishops were divided, since the king clearly had an arguable case, and the pope tried to arrange a reconciliation. After six years of contest a reconciliation did in fact take place and Becket returned to Canterbury, but he had already determined to sacrifice himself, as he believed, for the independence of the Church. He at once provoked the king. Henry, in a fit of Plantagenet anger, gave him the opportunity for the martyrdom he sought by encouraging four of his household knights to take the law into their own hands. The archbishop was murdered on the altar steps of his own cathedral.

This famous tragedy, delineated in recent times in T. S. Eliot's wonderful poetic drama *Murder in the Cathedral*—a tragedy which earned for Thomas Becket the title of saint and for the king, who admitted that his rash words had brought about, though unintentionally, the archbishop's assassination, a period of public humiliation—did not materially alter the course of later events. Most of the Constitutions of Clarendon were upheld. In effect the ability of clerks to escape the full rigors of the criminal law was restricted. On the other hand, the right of ecclesiastical appeal to the pope was reaffirmed, subject to a few minor qualifications. The king continued to control elections to bishoprics and the royal courts took much of the jurisdiction over contractual matters that the Church courts had been engrossing.

To offset the horror and indignation aroused by Becket's murder, King Henry II promptly embarked on a Crusade to conquer Ireland for the Church, a mission with which he had been earlier entrusted by the Papacy because the neighboring island was deemed anarchical and heretical. Afterward Henry returned to France, submitted to the pope, and was forgiven for his crime against Becket.

In 1173 Henry II had to deal with a widespread rebellion inspired by the king of France, who was encouraged by Henry II's quarrel with the Church, was aided by the king of the Scots, and was supported by Henry's own wife and children. For a time it looked as if Henry's splendid empire would fall to pieces, but while the king himself fought in France, his justiciar, Richard Lucy, and other officials and lesser nobility contended with the rebels in England; and the Church remained loyal. The king of the Scots was surprised and taken prisoner. The rebel barons, having surrendered, were mercifully treated, although the queen was placed under restraint.

For the rest of his reign the king had little trouble in England, but his French territories were riddled with disaffection stirred up by the new French king Philip Augustus, who succeeded Louis VII in 1180. In July 1188 Henry II left England to cope with revolts in the south of France. His eldest son Henry was dead and he preferred his younger son,

John, to his elder, Richard. Thus Richard was provoked into conspiring with the French king against his own father. Even John betrayed the father who loved him: "they cease not," Henry II exclaimed, "to persecute me even unto death." In July 1189 after a triumphant reign of over thirty-five years King Henry was humiliated by his French overlord and his own heir. Two days later he was dead. Though his empire was to disintegrate, his legal and administrative reforms long impressed themselves upon English society.

✇ KING RICHARD I

King Henry II's eldest surviving son, Richard, who had betrayed and abased his father, was invested as Duke of Normandy at Rouen in July 1189 and crowned king of England at Westminster on September 3. Richard I, known as the Lionheart, now a vigorous man of thirty-two, had inherited from his father his restless energy and hot temper but not his intelligence. He had spent much of his youth in his mother's home at Aquitaine and he saw life through the windows of tournament, chivalry, and war. A figure of immense arrogance, he was no more or less a Christian than his father had been, but the idea of a third Crusade to recapture Acre and Jerusalem, which had again been lost to the Saracen infidels, fired his sense of adventure. He sought personal glory and imperial majesty and England was to him nothing more than a mountain of gold to be dug to provide money. Thus England was dragged along by the leading strings of Angevin might. Its prosperity was attested in that it survived more or less unscathed the predatory habits of King Henry II and his two sons. The constitutional and legal reforms of King Henry II also surmounted the chaotic reigns of his two successors. But the barons grasped their opportunity to enhance their own positions and possessions when a strong king was not there to govern them.

Richard I's reign opened with a gigantic pogrom of the Jews, who had first settled in England at the time of the Norman Conquest and were courted and mulcted by Henry II; the reign ended ten years later with a disputed succession after the king had been killed in an obscure skirmish. Richard spent only six months of the intervening time in England.

His first action was to divide the responsibility for the administration during his absence. His brother John, whom he treated with lively contempt, was not only Count of Mortain in Normandy but was given exclusive control over six English counties (except for a few castles) and was Lord of Ireland as well. Two chief justiciars were appointed: in the north the Bishop of Durham, in the south William Longchamp, Bishop of Ely, a cripple of humble birth, administrative ruthlessness, and dynastic cupidity. Meanwhile an illegitimate brother of King Richard,

Geoffrey, became Archbishop of York, though he had to await the papal confirmation. As soon as all this had been arranged Richard embarked with King Philip Augustus of France upon the third Crusade. The emperor Frederick Barbarossa also joined in this European enterprise, but had the misfortune to be drowned on the way.

King Richard arrived first in Sicily where he rescued his sister Joan, widow of the late king, from imprisonment, and acquired some money. By a treaty concluded with the French king at Messina, Richard got out of his engagement to Philip Augustus's sister Alice (he married instead Berengaria, daughter of the king of Navarre) but promised full services to his French overlord for his numerous territorial possessions in France. In April Richard sailed to Cyprus, which he conquered and where he was married; but later he sold the island and went on to besiege Acre and Jaffa and to menace Jerusalem. By this time the French king had returned home from the Crusade, but Richard, who had made many enemies with his arrogance during the unsuccessful campaign, was taken a prisoner near Venice on his way back and for two years was at the mercy of the emperor Henry VI, son of Frederick Barbarossa, who demanded a huge ransom for his release.

Meanwhile turmoil prevailed in England. William Longchamp overthrew his fellow justiciar, made himself intensely unpopular with the barons, and then met with the opposition of Prince John. King Richard sent the Archbishop of Rouen back from the Crusade to patch up peace between his representatives in England, and an agreement was concluded at Winchester in July 1191. But further trouble arose when Geoffrey, Archbishop of York, returned from a visit to Rome and quarreled with Longchamp. Later that year Longchamp was overthrown, Prince John proclaimed regent, and the Archbishop of Rouen took over as chief justiciar. Excited by the thought of supreme power while his brother was a prisoner of the emperor, John now entered into negotiations with the French king, who invaded Normandy. The Archbishops of Rouen and York tackled John in England on behalf of their absent king, while a third archbishop, Hubert Walter of Canterbury, arrived in England in April 1194 with the news that King Richard had at last been released in return for a promise to pay the ransom.

Later in 1194 King Richard I came back to England for precisely three months; he restored order, arranged for the collection of money for his ransom, forgave his brother John, made Hubert Walter the chief justiciar, and had himself recrowned. By May he had gone. From 1194 to 1196 and again from 1196 to 1199 he fought against his old ally, the French king, for the preservation of his French territories.

During these years England was governed largely by Archbishop

Walter, who invented a number of expedients to collect money and men for the king's wars, and had to put down an insurrection in London which was partly provoked by the heavy taxation. Afterwards he resigned his office of justiciar in favor of Geoffrey Fitz Peter, Sheriff of Yorkshire and Staffordshire. Fitz Peter is said to have been less rapacious and less ingenious than Hubert Walter. But the country was wearied by taxes and neglect, just as the rest of the Angevin empire was tiring of perpetual war. When King Richard I died in April 1199, England was ripe for revolution and the French possessions of the Plantagenet kings ready to disintegrate. Richard had sown the seeds for the ruin of his brother, King John.

XIII

The Reign of John and Magna Carta

King John is one of the most controversial figures in English history. He was the victim both of circumstances and of his own character. To begin with, his succession had been challenged: some thought that his nephew, Arthur of Brittany, had a better claim to the throne; secondly, the kingdom had been bled white to pay for King Richard I's ransom and continental adventures; thirdly, it was an age of raising prices which fell hard on those with fixed incomes or rents, among whom was the king; lastly, it had only been by heroic efforts that his father and brother had held together their ramshackle "empire" and thwarted the scheming of Philip Augustus of France to destroy them. Thus King John inherited an empty treasury and a costly foreign policy, discontented subjects and unscrupulous enemies.

John, like his father and brother, had a fierce temper and restless energy. He was an assiduous ruler, a good soldier and diplomatist, and not without learning and culture of a sort. But he was a spoilt youth, the "Benjamin" of both his father and mother, and he had in added measure all the worst faults of the Plantagenets. Only five feet five inches tall, he had a shifty way about him; he was moody and sometimes cruel and sadistic. A contemporary chronicler wrote of him that "he was a very bad man, cruel toward all men and too covetous of pretty ladies." But he was a fair man, priding himself on his administration of justice, and not uncharitable to the poor. He had a high degree of intelligence, and relied on first-class officials. Archbishop Hubert Walter, Geoffrey Fitz Peter (the chief justiciar), and William Marshal, Earl of Pembroke, served him devotedly in his early years; and Peter des Roches, Bishop of Winchester, whom he chose to replace Fitz Peter as chief justiciar, was also an able administrator. The truth would appear to be that a defeated king was in as precarious a position as a discredited prime minister can be in modern times. In the end the barons took advantage of a favorable opportunity to air long-standing grievances against a weakened monarchy. Magna Carta, whatever its later and symbolic significance, was only one incident in a tragic reign.

During the first years of his reign King John lost most of the Angevin empire. King Philip Augustus of France made good use of his mistakes. John, for example, had married the betrothed of one of his own French vassals after repudiating his first English wife, thus giving offense to powerful families both in France and in England. He put to death his rival, Arthur of Brittany, possibly with his own hands, in a drunken rage. As his overlord, the king of France condemned him and declared all his possessions forfeit. After a long spasmodic struggle he lost all the provinces north of the Loire—Normandy, Maine, Anjou, Touraine, and Brittany—though he retained his mother's inheritance of Aquitaine (comprising Poitou, Guienne, and Gascony), while his mother, an indomitable old lady of eighty, fought in their defense.

The loss of Normandy and other French territories proved no great disadvantage to England in the long run, though for over 400 years English rulers fought to hold or regain a foothold on the European mainland; but the immediate consequences were profound. The Norman barons had generally owned property on both sides of the English Channel and were now faced with a divided allegiance. They blamed King John and came to terms, if they could, with the French king behind his back. To protect a now-exposed coastline a navy had to be created, almost for the first time since Alfred the Great. Royal prestige and personal honor demanded that King John should avenge his losses upon the French king and, to obtain the means to do so, he tightened the screw of taxation. Not only were the royal estates made to yield the utmost penny, but a new tax on movables as well as rents was exacted and many scutages, aids, and fines imposed upon the tenants-in-chief. Thus though England itself had enjoyed peace while King John was losing Normandy, after 1206, when a two-year truce was concluded with the French king, internal discontent mounted.

This discontent was exacerbated by a quarrel between the king and the Church. When Hubert Walter died, John wanted to name his own candidate as Archbishop of Canterbury. There was nothing revolutionary in that, but he nevertheless encountered opposition from the cathedral priory with its claim to select the archbishop, and from the most brilliant and demanding pope of early modern Europe, Innocent III. In effect the pope decided to pick the new archbishop himself, in view of the rival nominations from the cathedral priory and the king. Any English king would have resented such an extension of the papal authority. When an elderly theologian named Stephen Langton was consecrated by the pope, King John was provoked and refused to receive him. In March 1208 King John confiscated the revenues of the see of Canterbury, while the pope imposed an interdict on England which forbade the holding of ordinary church services and ceremonies. The papal interdict remained in force for six years and in 1209 the king himself was outlawed from the Church by excommunication. The king retorted by impounding the revenues of the churches on the ground that the clergy had been prohibited from carrying out its functions. Among other things he ordered that the clergymen's mistresses should be seized until their lovers ransomed them. These high-handed acts do not appear to have made material difference to the running of the kingdom. On the contrary, the confiscation of Church property eased the king's financial problems. The country remained at peace; a navy and an army were built up; dangers from Wales and Scotland were met expeditiously; a treasure chest (partly retained under the king's direct control in his "chamber") was filled in preparation for a renewal of the war with France.

Nevertheless the antagonism of the pope encouraged King John's enemies. While John was planning to fashion a coalition with his nephew, the German emperor Otto IV, and with the Count of Flanders to regain his lost territories, King Philip Augustus entered into an alliance with Frederick Hohenstaufen, king of Sicily, the rival of the emperor Otto, and contemplated the invasion of England. Might not King John be humiliated and beaten to the ground as the defiant foe of the Christian Church?

King John, who, after all, was by no means the only Christian king of his times to quarrel with the Papacy, now showed his resilience. He came to terms with the pope, welcomed Stephen Langton as archbishop, and received back his kingdom as a papal fief. Now the papal banner fluttered on his side as his new navy surprised and crushed a French invasion fleet at anchor near Bruges. This striking victory took place in May 1213. Both sides prepared for war. It looked as if the keys of victory were in King John's hands; but he reckoned without his barons.

Many of the barons had accumulated personal grievances or grudges against King John. During campaigns undertaken by the king against Scotland and Ireland in 1209 and 1210 a heavy hand had fallen upon the Marcher Lords. There is evidence that as early as 1209 conspiracies between English barons and the French king had begun. In 1212 Robert Fitz Walter, Lord of Dunmow in Essex, and Eustace de Vesci, Lord of Alnwick in Northumberland, had fled to France. When in July 1213, after the king's reconciliation with the pope, he was preparing to follow up his naval victory by invading France, some of his northern barons flatly refused to follow him. The king set out to punish them, but Archbishop Stephen Langton, newly arrived in England, persuaded the king to forgive them and the campaign was postponed until the next year.

It is necessary to distinguish between the relatively selfish outlook of these independent-minded magnates and the high ideals of Stephen Langton. Insofar as the phrase is applicable in early history, Langton believed in the rule of law. "He sought to have England governed by an orderly regime based on generally accepted legal principles." He thought that men should be reasonable and their rulers just. He hoped to reconcile the canon law of the Roman Church with the laws and customs of the English people. Though he had benefited from it, Langton was not pleased with King John's complete submission to the Papacy, for even after his long stay abroad he was at heart an English patriot. As soon as he arrived in England he addressed a meeting in St. Paul's Church drawing attention to the excellent precedent of King Henry I's coronation charter in which he had promised as a Christian king to uphold customary English liberties.

Such was the situation before King John embarked upon his campaign of 1214. His purpose was, in alliance with his nephew, the emperor Otto, to defeat the French king and regain all his lost ancestral possessions in France. While the emperor with English auxiliaries and other allies attacked from the north of France, King John landed at La Rochelle in the southwest and with his vassal barons of Poitou moved north across the Loire. In June the barons of Poitou refused to fight a pitched battle at La Roche-aux-Moines and on July 27 the emperor was decisively beaten at the battle of Bouvines, where the English commander, King John's half brother, was taken prisoner. This victory established the real power of the French monarchy and confirmed the loss of Normandy to England. A truce was patched up for two years, but King John returned home humiliated.

Several of the king's baronial critics had refused to accompany him to Poitou and protested when he demanded a large scutage from those who had denied him service. Now their opportunity for revolt had come: they did not so much wish to reform the government as to overthrow the king. In March 1215 they met under arms at Stamford and set out to capture the strategic royal castle at Northampton. After fifteen years of fighting and vain scheming the king was discredited and bankrupt. Undermined by the defeat at Bouvines, he offered to accept arbitration or submit to the judgment of the pope. The insurgents failed to take Northampton, but marched upon London where they were admitted by a section of the citizens. Yet it did not come to a headlong clash; for the king still had loyal and capable servants and supporters, while Archbishop Langton acted as intermediary between the two sides. On May 27 a truce was arranged and on June 15 the king and his advisers met the rebel leaders upon a meadow called Runnymede by the river Thames near Staines. Here he sealed a draft agreement known as the Articles of the Barons; four days later, after it had been skillfully worked upon by Langton and others, these articles were converted into the document known as Magna Carta—the Great Charter of Liberties.

Three generations ago an English historian wrote that the Great Charter was "the first great public act of the nation, after it had realized its own identity." It was a treaty between a king and his subjects, bringing a tyranny to an end. Modern writers no longer describe this essentially feudal document in quite such heroic terms. One scholar says that it was a "bargain" struck between the king and his barons seeking to redress private grievances, mainly selfish in motive. Another describes it as "an inadequate judgment on the past and an impracticable guide for the future." A third writes, "for John's reign the constitutional importance of Magna Carta is negligible. Its importance lay in the future."

The Charter was a document compounded of many strands. While in much of his conduct King John had merely followed the precedents of his ancestors, he had pressed his rights "up to the hilt" and beyond. Taxes and fines had borne so heavily upon his better-to-do subjects that they were driven to revolt. Just as it had been natural for the barons to expect King Henry I to repudiate the harsh methods of William Rufus, so with King John defeated in France and only recently absolved by the pope from the punishments imposed for disobeying the Church, the barons expected their king to modify his claims to high prerogative powers, the same powers that they had not criticized when they were exercised by King Richard I, the lion-hearted crusader. Like all reformers in early history, they appealed to ancient but vague customs that had been violated by the king; but there was a good case on his side.

In the sixty-two clauses of the Charter are to be found a reaffirmation of the king's duties to the Church, a definition of his rights towards his vassals, a list of reforms required in the royal administration, and promises of a more clearly articulated system of justice. It is not true that the

Charter was exclusively of benefit to the barons: the rights of cities and towns, including London, were affirmed; all "freemen" were guaranteed that they should not be proceeded against except by "due process of law" and that "to no one will we sell, deny or defer right of justice." Among the most important clauses were those that insisted that a council should be summoned to decide taxation. Though later generations exaggerated the meaning of the Charter, there is a good deal to be said for the view that it established, in the language of the day, the principle of consent to taxation through a representative body and a rule of law.

But the full meaning of these clauses lay in the future. The clause that caused most excitement at the time was that which set up a council of twenty-five barons to see that the promises given in the Charter were carried out by the king and to reduce the king to obedience if he broke these promises. Though this right to legalized rebellion against the crown was the only practical sanction available, it was a dangerous power to place in the hands of a group of magnates, most of whom were in fact the king's personal enemies. In any case neither side really intended to uphold the Charter, which was an incident in a struggle for power. The guarantees of peace offered at Runnymede in return for the signature of the treaty were not fulfilled. Some of the northern barons, who were not at Runnymede, immediately reopened hostilities against the king; the baronial headquarters in London were maintained; although Langton reproached the rebel leaders for their conduct, they at once prepared to renew the civil war. The king, for his part, also seems to have engaged in double-dealing. Copies of the Charter were circulated to the counties with orders that they were to be read in public. Yet no sooner had he set his seal to the Charter than he sent off an appeal to his master, the pope. Innocent III, who was planning a Crusade in which he expected the English king to take part, first threatened the barons with excommunication unless they submitted; then he quashed the Charter. The king enlisted mercenaries and accepted the challenge to battle.

King John now moved skillfully and boldly against the insurgents. By drastic military action he subdued much of the north and east. The leaders of the rebels replied by inviting over the French king's son, Prince Louis, offering to depose King John in his favor. Louis managed to land at Thanet and join the barons in London. The king prepared to resist from the Midlands but, after losing a convoy carrying much of his treasure and equipment across the river Nene, he died unexpectedly of fever at Newark in October 1216. He was buried at Worcester near the shrine of his patron saint, St. Wulfstan.

Was John a bad king? It is doubtful if he was either more vicious or more grasping than most of his predecessors. He pressed his powers, especially his financial powers, extremely hard, but then so had Richard I and Henry II, and his was an age of rising prices when a seller's market was not an advantage to the monarchy. The trouble with King John was that he was unsuccessful. It has been argued that it is a mistake to think of the king and the barons as naturally antagonistic in their interests; but what the militant aristocracy looked for was a warrior king to lead them to victory. The loss of Normandy and other French possessions had changed the whole map of English political life. It encouraged the Anglo-Norman magnates to betray their master in order to safeguard their own possessions. Whatever the Great Charter meant to the ideals of Stephen Langton and later reformers, to most of the rebel barons it was merely a milestone on their own road to a larger independence, such as some of them had enjoyed before during the reign of King Stephen.

The importance of the Great Charter to posterity was that it enshrined, in however crude a manner, the mighty principle of the rule of law: it suggested that monarchical government should not and need not be arbitrary, that it could be subjected to limitations more precise than the vague laws of Edward the Confessor or even the coronation oath of Henry I; it demanded the consent of those concerned to exceptional taxation; it required that the king should seek the advice of his natural counselors; it recognized that every section of the community that claimed to be free possessed its own prescribed liberties or privileges. In due course the Great Charter came to be revered as a symbol of English legal and political rights, as were the Twelve Tables in the history of the Roman Republic and the written constitution of the United States. Though the Charter may have been idolized and misinterpreted by future generations and though the twentieth century no longer thinks of King John and his barons in the black-and-white terms of the Victorian age, it justly occupies an honorable place in the history of western civilization.

XIV

The Reign of Henry III

The death of King John left England sundered by civil war, with Prince Louis of France in control of London and much of southern and eastern England. Nevertheless some of the ablest barons, headed by William Marshal, the octogenarian Earl of Pembroke, rallied to the cause of King Henry III, the nine-year-old son of King John. Moreover, by acknowledging himself to be a vassal of the pope the late king had brought the Church over to the side of the Plantagenets. Thus the papal legate Guala, a wise and intelligent man, William Marshal, and Ranulf, Earl of Chester, constituted themselves a triumvirate dedicated to winning back the throne for the royal line. The boy-king was crowned at Gloucester with a golden bracelet belonging to his mother. William Marshal became "rector" or Protector and Hubert de Burgh, appointed chief justiciar in the last reign, labored to support him. The Great Charter was reaffirmed with certain important omissions but with papal approval. A Flemish knight nicknamed Willikin of the Weald harassed the French in southeast England, while Hubert de Burgh, holding Dover castle for the king, stood astride the communications between London and France.

Thus Prince Louis's position was by no means comfortable, especially since his own father, Philip Augustus, king of France, anxious to propitiate the Papacy, repudiated him. Louis now made the fatal mistake of dividing his forces, sending part of them to besiege Dover and part into the Midlands. The royalists, headed by the aged William Marshal, won a telling victory at Lincoln and Prince Louis was obliged to abandon the siege of Dover. Hubert de Burgh intercepted reinforcements from France, winning a naval victory over a renegade monk named Eustace, who had twice changed sides. Peace was concluded in September 1213 at Kingston; Prince Louis agreed to leave the country in return for a payment of £7,000. The statesmanlike moderation of the peace terms, the self-restraint of the influential Earl of Chester, the sagacity of Archbishop Langton, who now returned from abroad, and the pardon extended to the rebels against King John all combined to produce a settlement of the kingdom and prevent a return to the anarchy of Stephen's reign. Indeed the loyal barons made a specific promise not to alienate the king's possessions, while treaties were concluded with the rulers of Wales and Scotland. When William Marshal died in May 1219, commending his royal charge to the care of the Church, he could depart in peace: England was recovering surprisingly, from the woes of King John's last years. On Whitsunday 1220 the king was again crowned at Westminster.

The minority of King Henry III was a formative period in the development of English institutions. Langton, who played an active part—at one time he was actually said to be redistributing the royal castles "by word of mouth" and placing some of them in the hands of his bishops— stamped the mark of his own integrity of principle, which had been enshrined in the text of the Great Charter, upon the government of the realm. Langton died in 1228, but eight years of internal peace prevailed while Hubert de Burgh remained chief justiciar. The king's high officials —justiciar, chancellor, and treasurer—administered the country on his behalf, but summoned a Great Council to meet when large questions had to be decided or financial aid was needed, and accepted the fact that they were responsible to it. At such Great Councils the king was later to indulge in "deep speech" or "parley" with many of his leading subjects, so that these wider meetings of the King's Council came to be known as parliaments.

In 1227 King Henry III declared himself to be of age. He soon showed himself to possess the restless ambitions of his family. Like his ancestors, he aimed to recover their lost provinces in France and to be more than an English king. "A magnificent potterer," he proved himself to be extravagant, his chief delight being in lavish building. Brought up under the protection of the Church, he was a good servant of the Papacy, always eager to go crusading. He was a devoted father and husband; he married the beautiful Eleanor of Provence, sister of the French king Louis IX or St. Louis in 1236. But he was seldom wise and never consistent or self-reliant. He turned first to one adviser, then another. He was petulant, unscrupulous, suspicious, cowardly, and unimpressive. Above all, he was never the master of the closely knit society of barons who fought both for and against his father. They did not respect him and were determined that he should not govern the country without their aid and counsel, as for a time he attempted to do. A distinguished historian has written that Henry III "got through all his troubles and left England prosperous and united," but it was more by luck than judgment. In the end it was his eldest son, Prince Edward, who by wise leadership preserved intact the throne that his father had owed to William Marshal and Stephen Langton.

Henry III's first actions after he declared himself of age were to quarrel with his abler younger brother, Richard of Cornwall, and with his justiciar. The masterful Hubert de Burgh, who was certainly not above feathering his own nest, was arrested, imprisoned, and disgraced, after having been dragged out of a chapel where he fled for sanctuary. Peter des Roches, Bishop of Winchester, an old favorite of King John and the former tutor of the new king, was brought in as principal counselor and his illegitimate son or nephew, Peter des Rivaux, was made treasurer of the royal household with the duty of overhauling the king's finances. Considerable changes were carried out in the years 1236–40. Crown lands were no longer administered by the sheriffs and other royal rights were allotted to fresh hands. Then new sheriffs were appointed. For a time important powers and resources were concentrated directly in the royal household, the king's "wardrobe" becoming an efficient financial department, more flexible but less responsible than the Exchequer. At the same time the Exchequer itself and the Chancery underwent reform.

Inevitably the industriousness of Peter des Rivaux and the new sheriffs provoked the resentment of the chief magnates, who regarded themselves as the natural rulers of the country with a prescriptive right to be called to the King's Council. The king was accused of betraying the Great Charter; demands were put forward that he must dismiss his new advisers and appoint officials approved by his barons. The Church intervened in the person of Edmund Rich, the saintly Archbishop of Canterbury. The king, ever fearful of having his father's fate, gave way. But his marriage in 1236 and the marriage of the Frenchman, Simon de Montfort, to Henry's sister Eleanor in 1238 opened the way to an influx of new foreign advisers whom the barons with little logic, since many of them were French or of French descent themselves, condemned as grasping foreigners. Still, once most of the French possessions of the Angevins had been taken from them, notions of English national independence and island patriotism began to sound more plausible.

The king had no consistent or well-thought-out foreign policy; in fact he managed only to confirm the loss of most of his house's ancestral properties abroad. In 1223 Prince Louis, who had nearly obtained the English throne, succeeded his father, Philip Augustus, as King Louis VIII of France, attacked Poitou and Gascony, and captured the port of La Rochelle. In 1226 Louis VIII died while his son Louis IX was still a minor. Henry III took this favorable opportunity to reassert his claims to Normandy and Brittany, but nothing came of an astonishingly lethargic military campaign. In 1234 Brittany finally submitted to Louis IX and in 1235 a truce was concluded between France and England. In 1242 Henry III's second and last military expedition in France took place. He was defeated in an attempt to regain Poitou, and another truce left him with only Gascony in Aquitaine, where the local baronage were proud and independent. Gascony in fact was an isolated duchy and though it was valuable for its wine trade—Bordeaux was the chief port—it was more a debit than an asset to the English Crown. In 1248 Henry III appointed his brother-in-law, the strong-minded and arrogant Simon de Montfort, Earl of Leicester, as its seneschal or governor. De Montfort proved himself to be courageous but ruthless, overriding private rights in causes that he deemed righteous, thus provoking and angering the Gascons, who complained to King Henry III about his administration. In 1252 King Henry intervened in affairs in Gascony; Simon de Montfort, although he had been given a seven-year tenure of office, voluntarily withdrew from it. Henry III spent a year himself in Gascony and then handed over its administration to his son Prince Edward, a promising youth of sixteen who had just been married to a Spanish princess, Eleanor of Castile. By this time King Henry's foreign ambitions had turned in another direction under the impulse of the Papacy.

The thirteenth century (like the twelfth) was a crusading age; one after another the kings, princes, and magnates of western Europe had taken their turn at trying to preserve the Holy Land from the infidels. But the popes were concerned not merely to reconquer the Middle East for Christendom but also to uphold their own domination in Europe. A prolonged struggle had taken place between Pope Innocent IV and Emperor Frederick II who, paradoxically, had been one of the most successful fighters for the Holy Land; yet he was deemed to be a heretic and enemy of Christ. When Frederick II died in 1250 the popes continued this contest with his sons. In particular they were eager to establish Sicily as a papal fief, taking it away from Manfred, one of Frederick's illegitimate children. With papal backing Henry III's brother, Richard of Cornwall, was elected king of Germany, while the throne of Sicily was offered to Henry's second son, Prince Edmund. In return for Henry III's military and financial support in Sicily the pope offered to put at his disposal the proceeds of a levy exacted from the English Church. Always a loyal servant of the popes and already committed to raise aloft the sword of a crusader, King Henry supinely agreed to all these proposals, but, before he launched upon his fantastic venture, he needed first to end hostilities with France by concluding a definitive treaty.

The new French king Louis IX was also a faithful servant of the Papacy—he is known in history as St. Louis—and was willing to make peace with England. The treaty of Paris, signed in 1259, left Henry III only in possession of Gascony, which he held as a vassal of the French king, but he finally surrendered all his claims upon Normandy, Brittany, Maine, Anjou, and Poitou. The treaty of Paris has been said to show the wisdom and generosity of St. Louis, yet it was in fact a humiliation for the once-imperial Plantagenets.

The failure of King Henry III's foreign policy was only one of several factors that weakened the position of the English monarchy in the thirteenth century. There had been troubles on the Welsh border where Llewellyn ap Gruffyd, Prince of Gwynedd, had defied the Lords of the Marches and was creating a Welsh nation. Henry III was in financial difficulties. He was expected to live on the rents of his own domains and his customary financial rights, but however severely these collections were enforced by his officials since the day of Peter des Rivaux's reforms, they were insufficient to cover the cost of adventures abroad. It is true that the king, in spite of some extravagant tastes, was not really a profligate and his expenditure was normally not more than a year in arrears, but he was in perpetual need of money and compelled to borrow from foreign merchants or Jews. Had his position been desperate, he would have been obliged to look to his Great Council for aid at an earlier stage than he did. As things were, he was able for a long time to rule without the full co-operation of his magnates, though the principle of close co-operation had been enshrined in the Great Charter and practiced during the king's minority.

During the long reign of King Henry III in fact the idea of established law and political co-operation between the king and his leading subjects slowly evolved. The conception of a common law or genuine English law, based upon judicial precedents in the king's courts, was expounded in a book written by Henry de Bracton, one of the king's judges, in the middle of the century. About the same time a plan of political reform was put forward by a group of barons (it is recorded in the chronicle of Matthew Paris under the year 1244) demanding that four conservators of liberties, officials elected by the baronage as a whole and only removable by the baronage, be added to the King's Council to ensure that the king governed in accordance with the Charters to which he had sworn; that his ministers, including the justiciar and chancellor, should also be elected; and that a number of the judges should be appointed by the Council. There is good evidence that such constitutional demands were put forward intermittently as a logical extension of the principles of the Great Charter ever after the king's weaknesses as a ruler became manifest.

The revolutionary proposal to restrict the powers of the king to choose his own officials and advisers was revived at Easter 1258 when King Henry III, now virtually bankrupt and in trouble with the pope because he was unable to fulfill his promises to him, turned desperately to his magnates for aid. Contemptuous of the king's follies, the barons, headed by Roger Bigod, Earl of Norfolk, met together and imposed harsh terms, known as the Provisions of Oxford. A council of fifteen members was to be appointed to advise the king on all matters relating to the government of the country and to propose reforms. In particular, the royal household, which had become the administrative center of prerogative power, was to be reformed, the king's so-called foreign advisers were to be replaced and expelled from the kingdom, and the Chancellor, now replacing the justiciar as the king's principal minister, was to be subject to the authority of the Great Council. Above all, the reinforced Great Council—or Parliament—was to meet three times each year, while another council of twelve was to be appointed to ensure that whatever should be decided in Parliament was carried out. Finally, all the principal ministers and judges were to be chosen with the approval of the baronial committees and both they and the sheriffs were to hold their offices for one year only. In putting forward these astonishingly far-reaching demands or provisions the barons were supported both by the knights of the shires and by other knights who were now taking the lead in local government and had come to Westminster earlier in the reign to expound local grievances.

The king reluctantly accepted the Provisions of Oxford. The new Council of Fifteen hastened to eject the king's foreign advisers, to repudiate the Sicilian expedition, and to make settlements with France, Wales, and Scotland. Hugh Bigod (younger brother of Roger) was appointed justiciar. But when the new government turned to internal affairs—to legal and administrative reforms and the consideration of the grievances of ordinary freeholders—the king's wealthier subjects began to quarrel among themselves, for it was one matter to overhaul the king's administration, quite another to tamper with baronial courts or baronial rights. In 1259 a "community of bachelors," said by Sir Maurice Powicke probably to have been "knights or other local gentry who were in Westminster at the time of Parliament," complained to Prince Edward on the eve of a meeting of Parliament at Westminster that whereas the king had accepted the provisions laid down at Oxford, the barons themselves had done "nothing of what they had promised for the good of the realm." By the Provisions of Westminster further reforms were introduced for the benefit of freeholders, who were permitted to invoke the assistance and protection of the royal courts and royal officers to stop exactions by great lords upon their tenants. In general the aim of the Provisions of Westminster was "to make everyday life easier for all kinds of freemen by protecting them in their free tenements and defining the limits of interference with their freedom" (Powicke).

All this sounded excellent on paper, but in practice such entirely revolutionary changes could not be achieved in a few months. The king had not expected that his freedom to govern the country would be permanently reduced. The magnates, for their part, were far less enthusiastic about restrictions being placed upon their own rights than they had been about limiting the rights of the king. When Henry III returned from a visit to France to conclude the treaty of Paris he profited from increasing signs of disunion he saw among his barons to undo much of the work of constitutional reform. On the other hand his brother-in-law, Simon de Montfort, after he returned to England in 1263, constituted himself the champion of the Provisions of Oxford: he wanted England to be ruled not by the king and his permanent officials but by a dedicated aristocracy. He rallied many of the younger barons, the knights, the citizens of London and of the southern ports, and even friars and scholars of Oxford—the new phenomenon of the age—to his side. After three years of political maneuverings during which the pope gave the king a dispensation for his oaths and the French king an arbitration (the Mise of Amiens) in his favor, civil war broke out. In May 1264 Simon de Montfort defeated a royal army at the battle of Lewes, where the king and his son were taken prisoners.

Simon de Montfort's triumph was short-lived. In January 1265 he summoned to London a parliament, including not only the chief barons and ecclesiastics, but two knights elected in the shire courts and two burgesses or citizens from each of the larger towns. The aim was to make final terms with the monarchy for the future government of the realm. But England was not yet ready for oligarchical leadership, however admirably intended. The arrogance of De Montfort affronted the other barons and he quarreled with his principal supporter, the young Gilbert de Clare, Earl of Gloucester. Prince Edward escaped from his imprisonment and was joined by Gloucester and the other lords of the Welsh Marches. In August 1265 Simon de Montfort was defeated and killed at the battle of Evesham.

This can be described as an unnecessary civil war. Prince Edward, its victor, recognized that the monarchy must come to terms with its greater subjects. By the Dictum of Kenilworth next year, those who had fought with Simon de Montfort, whose estates had been confiscated for treason, were conciliated, being allowed to buy back their properties; by the Statute of Marlborough in 1266 most of the Provisions of Westminster were re-enacted and the Great Charter was once again confirmed.

Thus it may be said that during the reign of King Henry III the country rejected alike an irresponsible and incompetent monarchy, the wildcat schemes for papal aggrandizement, and Simon de Montfort's plan for an enlightened oligarchy. The conception of regular parliamentary consultations and the supremacy of a common law were being very gradually evolved and accepted. Yet it was still a time when the Church Universal was the mightiest power in the Western world. It was under the benevolent guidance of a papal legate named Cardinal Ottobuono Fieschi that a settlement was completed in England and Wales after the civil war. As soon as that settlement was reached, Prince Edward, like his predecessor, King Richard I, left England to go on a Crusade, returning home only after the death of his father in November 1272.

XV

Wales, Scotland, Ireland in the Eleventh, Twelfth, and Thirteenth Centuries

Until its conquest by King Edward I of England the history of Wales swung between periods of relative unity and independence under vigorous chieftains and anarchy and internal war while its rulers fought each other. In the middle of the eleventh century Gruffyd ap Llewellyn became the master of all Wales and after doing homage to King Edward the Confessor was bold enough to defy his stronger neighbor. But in 1063 he was overwhelmed and defeated in a campaign by land and sea conducted by the future King Harold II of England and his head sent to Earl Harold by his enemies as the price of peace between the two nations. In the history of Wales Gruffyd became its first national hero. Although Harold did not conquer Wales he "reduced the Welsh question from one of national importance to its old status of a mere border difficulty."

That was the Norman inheritance. The chief effect of the Conquest was the creation of the Welsh Marcher Lords who were given by the Norman king considerable powers and compact territories in return for their maintaining order on the frontier. Among these lordships were those of Chester, Shrewsbury, Hereford, Gloucester, and later Pembroke. At times the Marcher Earls grew "too big for their boots" and had to be disciplined. The braver and abler rulers of Wales were, however, capable of holding their own against the Marcher Lords. Wales was essentially a pastoral society and could not easily be laid waste, overrun, or subdued by the troops and weapons of those times. Again and again the English kings themselves led expeditions into Wales. They seemed to conquer and exact the homage of the Welsh chieftains only for it to be found that the task had to be done over again by their successors. Thus after William the Conqueror subdued south Wales in 1081, in 1094 there was a revolt against his son William II in north Wales. Though this revolt was suppressed, King Henry I had again to fight against and conquer south Wales.

A "great revolt" and struggle for independence followed the death of King Henry I. Owain ap Gruffyd ap Cynan, Prince of Gwynedd, known as Owen the Great, was a wise ruler who did homage to King Henry II but obliged him to recognize the impossibility of conquering the whole of Wales. After Owain's death another Welsh hero, Rhys ap Gruffyd of Powys, took over the leadership of the Welsh princes, but when he died at the age of sixty-five in 1197 there was internal warfare between two princes each named Llewellyn. However, another Llewellyn (ap Gruffyd), who was the foremost ruler of Wales in the middle of the thirteenth century, managed during the confused reign of King Henry III to defy the Marcher Lords and even frustrate the English king himself. He entered into an alliance with Simon de Montfort, but after the defeat of Montfort at Evesham still retained his authority and influence. By the treaty of Montgomery in 1267 while he once more did homage to King Henry III, Llewellyn was accorded the title of Prince of Wales, which meant that he exercised overlordship over all the other Welsh chieftains.

Thus the Welsh emerged as a distinctive people with a language and literature of their own. Fine guerrilla soldiers, devoted Christians (the Bishop of St. David's had reluctantly acknowledged the supremacy of the Archbishop of Canterbury) who supported many monasteries, temperate, hardy, restless, and energetic men, they were ever defiant of their English neighbors along the old lines of Offa's Dyke. "The defence of their native land and liberty," wrote Gerald of Wales, the twelfth-century chronicler, "is their sole concern: they fight for fatherland and labour for liberty. . . . They deem it ignoble to die in their beds and an honour to fall on the field of battle." Throughout the centuries they have remained proud and by nature independent.

As with Wales, so in Scotland the Norman Conquest was to be followed by a series of frontier wars with the new English dynasty. Malcolm II, who had consolidated Scotland as a kingdom, was succeeded by Duncan and Macbeth, who still live today in William Shakespeare's tragedy *Macbeth*. But the Duncan and Macbeth of Shakespeare are not historical realities. Macbeth was a competent and vigorous ruler. He was nevertheless a usurper and in 1057 was overthrown by Malcolm III, known as Canmore or Bighead, the son of Duncan. Malcolm's long reign (1057–95) overlapped those of Edward the Confessor, William the Conqueror, and his son. He was twice married; his second wife was Saint Margaret, a sister of Edgar Atheling (grandson of Edmund Ironside) and therefore of the ancient Saxon royal family. Inspired by his wife and brother-in-law, Malcolm twice contended vainly with William the Conqueror, but was obliged to do him homage. During the reign of William II he and his son were treacherously killed.

A period of upheaval followed, but two of Saint Margaret's sons, Alexander the Fierce and David the Paragon, restored order, remodeled the Church, and lived on amicable terms with the Normans in England. Through his wife David became Earl of Huntingdon and Northampton and had a claim to the earldom of Northumberland. Thus he was an English magnate as well as a Scottish king and looked south for political guidance. But he made the mistake of allying himself with the empress Matilda against King Stephen. In 1138 he was defeated at the Battle of the Standard. Still his territories bestrode the river Tweed and he was able to give effect to his father's belief that the safety of Scotland required the possession of the English towns of Newcastle (in Northumberland) and Carlisle (in Cumberland). Because of his encouragement of Norman and Saxon settlers, the southern part of Scotland—Lothian—acquired a character distinct from that of the north.

King David I was succeeded by his grandson Malcolm IV (1153–65) and then by William the Lion (1165–1214). King John refused to concede control of Northumberland and Cumberland to the Scottish Kings, but the absentee Richard I involuntarily did much for the independence of Scotland. Alexander II (1214–49) married a sister of King Henry III, while his own sister Margaret married the justiciar Hubert de Burgh. For once treaties were honored and a period of peace prevailed so that the early half of the thirteenth century is reckoned a golden age in Scottish history. The reign of Alexander II's son, Alexander III (1249–86), was also remarkable for its quiet prosperity, and when he died the frontier with England appeared to be more or less settled along the line of the Tweed.

While the Norman and Plantagenet kings fought with the Welsh and came to terms with the Scots, they also conquered Ireland. The death of Brian Boru at Clontarf in 1014 was followed in Ireland by an age of profound political disunity. The most notable of the Irish kings was Turloch More O'Connor who was first king of Connaught and then high king, and attempted to exert political control by dividing the petty kings one against another. In this policy he gave particular offense to

Dermot, king of Leinster. It was Dermot who in 1166 invited the English to help him against his enemies.

Dermot's appeal was made at an appropriate time. Pope Adrian IV, concerned over the condition of the Irish Church, had given his approval to a plan for the king of England to crusade against Ireland. King Henry II interviewed Dermot in France and sent him back to England with letters patent permitting English barons to assist him in recovering his lost patrimony. The first to take advantage of this opportunity was Richard, Earl of Pembroke, known as Strongbow. The armed and mounted Norman knights supported by Welsh archers proved themselves to be infinitely superior in the art of war to the native Irish, so that by 1171 Strongbow had installed himself in Dublin as king of Leinster in succession to the now dead Dermot. It was then that King Henry II, eager to be out of England after the martyrdom of Thomas Becket, visited Ireland to ensure that the gains of Strongbow and other adventurers should be made to depend upon the English Crown and to obtain the submission of the Irish princes and the Irish Church. This he achieved with little difficulty and papal approval. He appointed Hugh de Lacy as his viceroy or justiciar and annexed the area around Dublin and Waterford as Crown domain. His son, King John, became Lord of Ireland.

But there was no proper central government. In the thirteenth century Ireland in fact consisted of a number of powerful Norman estates covering about two-thirds of the country and held down by castles and garrisons, surrounded on the north and east by Irish kings and chiefs who were unable to resist and were compelled to assent to the English advance. In the middle of the century the English conquered much of Connaught and Ulster, but the Irish managed to win a few local guerrilla victories. Thus the complete subjugation of the Irish natives to the English invaders was postponed until the reign of Queen Elizabeth I.

XVI

English Life and Art in the Twelfth and Thirteenth Centuries

The twelfth and thirteenth centuries were an age in which the Church of Rome attained the height of its authority in western Europe, when the pope succeeded in making himself the arbiter among its secular rulers. The Church was governed by a succession of able popes including Innocent III, Gregory IX, and Innocent IV. They launched four Crusades; they held countries from England to Sicily in vassalage; they abased kings and emperors; they exacted heavy taxation from clerics everywhere; at the same time the Church produced saints as well as statesmen and inspired art as well as conquest.

All this was reflected in the history of England. King Henry II paid humbly for the martyrdom of Thomas Becket but then compelled Ireland to submit with a papal blessing; King Richard I had been a lifelong Crusader; King Henry III had owed his throne largely to the Papacy and the peace of the country had been secured by papal legates like Guala and Ottobuono. Henry III's brother, Richard of Cornwall, and his son, Prince Edmund, were each offered thrones by the popes. While princes and barons left England to fight in the Holy Land, poorer people went on pilgrimages, notably to the shrine of St. Thomas at Canterbury. The Church could bind and could loose, could absolve kings from their oaths and save sinners. Whatever men thought in their hearts, whatever strange heresies might be wafting back from the east, the officers of the Church stood everywhere—at the king's side, in the courts of justice, as well as by the altars.

Art, learning, and agriculture were indebted to the leadership of the Church. The twelfth century saw English monasteries at their prime of life. In addition to the old Benedictine houses many new orders were established, of which the most influential were the Cistercians or white monks, whose real founder was an Englishman, Stephen Harding. Cistercian houses spread rapidly over England and Wales, their priors austerely seeking out wasteland in remote places, where they might make the deserts blossom. The Cistercians concentrated upon horticulture and sheep farming rather than upon learning, employing small freeholders as lay brothers. Other orders included the Gilbertine nuns, and the Knights Templars and Knights Hospitallers, brought into being by the Crusades. The Papacy sought to gain closer control over the orders in the monasteries, and in response to complaints about the conduct of religious houses the Fourth Lateran Council in 1215 arranged for their systematic visitation. On the whole the English monasteries emerged honorably from the visitations of the twelfth century, although there were numerous reports of mismanagement and loose living. Some canons were condemned for hunting and keeping hounds, while others were penalized for succumbing to the lures of the flesh and the devil. The prior of Newburgh "admitted immoral relations with several women, married and single. Nevertheless the bishop considered that the interests of the house and the prior's own deserts warranted further tenure of office" (Knowles). The prior of Abergavenny was an adulterer who absconded with monastic valuables. Altogether records of a fair number of lax and corrupt houses and immoral or absconding priors have survived, for the wealth, isolation, and relative freedom of the monasteries were a perpetual source of temptation.

It was because of these weaknesses in a valuable social institution and the relatively low grade of the village clergy that the wandering monks or friars received such a warm welcome in England. St. Francis of Assisi, the spotless founder of the gray friars, had preached repentance and urged purity of life and the practice of poverty. St. Dominic, a Spanish ascetic, ten years older than St. Francis, at about the same time founded an order of Black Friars to preach Christian truths and root out ignorance and error. Fra Agnellus of Pisa, who was the first Franciscan missionary to England, set up friaries at Canterbury, London, Oxford, and elsewhere. The Dominican preachers were also gladly accepted and received in particular the backing of Robert Grosseteste, the distinguished and learned Bishop of Lincoln. From the beginning the Dominicans wanted to spread knowledge; later the Franciscans followed suit. The early universities were indebted to the friars.

Though the coming of the friars gave a shot in the arm to English education, it had been promoted by the English Church long before they arrived. Early in the twelfth century the first master who is known to have lectured at Oxford claimed that there were "as many practised schoolmasters as tax collectors and other royal officials in the English towns." The cathedrals had "song schools" or grammar schools, and it is likely that few towns of any size were without schools of some kind where the rudiments of Latin grammar were taught.

In the realm of higher education the most notable event was the foundation of the ancient universities, of Oxford and Cambridge. Oxford was already a prosperous market town in the reign of King Henry I, and when during his quarrel with Becket King Henry II prohibited English scholars from going to Paris to study, many of them settled in Oxford and formed a *studium generale*. King John was much concerned over town-and-gown riots in Oxford: it is believed that the first university chancellor was appointed during his reign. Robert Grossteste, who died in 1253, is known to have been one of the earliest chancellors of Oxford University as well as a discerning patron of education generally. Cambridge was created by a migration of scholars from Oxford, just as the first Oxford scholars came from Paris. Both universities were recognized institutions by the time of King Henry III. The first Oxford college, Merton, was founded in 1264 and the first Cambridge college, Peterhouse, in 1284. But most of the students lived in halls or rooms. Neither university was a royal foundation, but in the course of time both of them were granted privileges by the Crown.

All the learned books and legal documents of those times were written in Latin, while French was the language of the court and upper classes— of romance and of chivalry. French influence was also dominant in architecture and sculpture. Both Canterbury Cathedral and Westminster Abbey were rebuilt after the French manner. William of Sens (in northern France) was the first mason employed on extending Canterbury Cathedral: flying buttresses were introduced and use made of Purbeck stone. At Westminster Abbey the decoration and traceried windows were said to have been intended to rival the elaborate Sainte Chapelle in Paris. (It is believed that King Henry III wanted to honor St. Edward the Confessor at least as lavishly as St. Thomas Becket was honored at Canterbury.) Lincoln Cathedral was modeled upon Westminster and at Wells and Peterborough the so-called Early English style of architecture, leading away from the Anglo-Norman Romanesque, was finely exemplified. Salisbury Cathedral stands out for its flawless unity. Though the English cathedrals may not have the perfection of Chartres or Rheims, they are more beautiful and more essentially English than their Norman forerunners.

On the west façade of Wells Cathedral a host of painted full-length sculptured figures from the Bible bore witness to a thriving if eclectic school of carving. The Annunciation group at Westminster is also striking. A number of skilled craftsmen are known to have worked at St. Albans where fresco paintings from the thirteenth century still survive. In drawings by Matthew Paris and other monks and in richly illuminated manuscripts the graphic arts of the period exemplify the Christian impulse. But it is the cathedrals and early Gothic churches that are the glories of thirteenth-century England.

England could, however, boast a few writers and thinkers. John of Salisbury (1120–80), a scholarly friend of Becket, wrote a book called *Policraticus* a "statesman's book," in which he dealt with principles of government, philosophy, and learning and reflected the culture and ethics of his age. To chroniclers like William of Malmesbury, Roger of Wendover, Matthew Paris, and Gerald of Wales we owe vivid if inaccurate histories that give life to those distant times. Walter Map was an early satirist. Henry de Bracton's exposition of the laws of England was a masterpiece of patient investigation that was consulted for many years to come.

On the whole, the reign of King Henry III was a time of progress. Stone was now in common use for building, and though glass was rarely found in domestic building, chimneys were coming in. Entertainments were provided by wandering minstrels as well as by court jesters and for indoor amusement there were dice, chess, and backgammon. English wool and corn were exported to pay for imported luxuries: the Crown's connection with Gascony made French wines popular.

It seems that, on the whole, prices were rising between 1150 and 1300. This suggests that the English farmer flourished. Rising prices may have hit English kings like Richard I, John, and Henry III who were dependent on fixed revenues and constantly needed to make purchases to support their armies and their officials, and may explain why they needed so often to appeal to their subjects for special aid.

Indeed the growing importance of the king's Great—as distinct from his private—Council and the regular meeting of parliaments were indirectly due to the pressure of royal necessity. The barons recognized their duty to assist their king in times of need, but asserted that they were the king's natural counselors and must be consulted by him. The king might be their anointed ruler, the vassal of the pope, and the largest land holder in the country, but they too were pillars of society. What they resented was the idea that the king should not consult them and should even attempt to govern without them. The rules must be preserved, the charters maintained, the common laws respected, the customs from time out of mind recalled. The king must never try to ignore his archbishops, his earls, or his tenants-in-chief or set up a purely personal administration directed by favorites, upstarts, or mere clerks. This claim was central to the political and constitutional history of the twelfth and thirteenth centuries, the essential fact that lay behind the Great Charter and the Provisions of Oxford. The remedy for all the ills of the land, it has been said, was always in those days thought to be a reconstruction of the King's Council. This struggle for power continued throughout the reigns of the Edwards and did not die away until the aristocracy committed suicide in the Wars of the Roses in the fifteenth century and the Tudors in the sixteenth for a time established a strong government.

XVII

The Reigns of Edward I and Edward II

A modern English constitutional historian has declared that the reign of Henry III saw "the collapse of feudalism as the basis of the practice and theory of political life." This naturally depends on what one means by the word "feudalism." But certainly the reigns of Henry III and his sons were of the highest constitutional significance; for during them were evolved, in however shadowy and primitive forms, three concepts which were fundamental to modern Britain: the idea of nationality, the institution of parliament, and the rule of law.

So long as the Norman kings had ruled and the early Plantagenets had governed or owned a large part of modern France, and while the aristocracy of England was mainly French in origin, the sense of English patriotism which had begun to be felt under King Alfred and King Harold had been submerged. But with the loss of most of the French territories that belonged to or were acquired by the Crown can be detected the growth of a native patriotism, exemplified by the genuine dislike of Henry III's "foreign advisers," and later King Edward II's; English chroniclers reveal these values; and leading barons boast that they are "Englishmen." Feelings of national instead of personal or local loyalties were sharpened by the long wars against Wales and Scotland that were to be waged by King Edward I and his son.

English parliaments first met regularly in the reign of King Edward I, but had begun to be used in his father's reign. Parliament, like centralized justice and administration, evolved out of the king's court. Originally a parliament was simply a special meeting of the king's official or sworn council and was concerned with dispensing justice that could not be done in the ordinary courts. The essence of parliament was the presence in it of the king and of no one else. Usually the royal officials were supported by a judicial element and a meeting of parliament was dignified by "a special peace." Sometimes the king in his council was reinforced by the presence of all the leading barons and prelates, often of only some, and not all the king's tenants-in-chief. Knights from the shires and burgesses from the towns ("the commons") first attended "parliaments" or "parleys" in performance of suit of court; that is, they arrived to report to the king on the administration of local justice or the results of local inquiries. Later they were invited, at least at times, to facilitate the levying of taxes by the Crown upon the entire property-owning classes of the kingdom when customary revenues proved insufficient for the royal needs. To begin with, parliaments which contained a wider representation than the normal reinforcement of the King's Council were known as "general" or "most general" parliaments. Such parliaments would contain a liberal representation of nobles and prelates, and ultimately of knights and burgesses too. But "parliament" long remained a loose term. In time full meetings of parliament were reserved not only for the resolution of judicial difficulties and the consideration of financial matters but also for the satisfaction of petitioners bearing their "plaints." Attendance by the commons at parliament was paid for and therefore not necessarily regarded as an unwelcome duty, especially as the meetings were short. Simon de Montfort had summoned knights and burgesses to parliament in 1265; they were called again in April 1275 and knights only in October 1275. Other parliaments containing knights and burgesses met later in King Edward I's reign. But the most recent view is that in the parliaments of King Edward I "the commons had . . . . only a shadowy, occasional and intermittent existence." Lower, as well as higher, clergy attended too. But to call these parliaments "legislative assemblies" is to anticipate history. King Edward I believed in holding general assemblies of his subjects not so much to consult them as to inform them of his wishes; and it was not until the reign of King Edward III that knights and burgesses constituting the commons began to meet for consultation separately from the lords, lay and spiritual, while the clergy then preferred to meet in their own convocations.

In the king's court too began the centralization of justice. While the King in Council was the fountain of justice, increasing judicial business meant specialized consideration under the king's chosen judges. The Court of King's Bench began to meet in Westminster early in the reign of King Henry III. The royal judges, now professionals, went out on assize, as they had done from the time of King Henry II, and although their visits were not frequent, they were imposing uniformity in the administration of a common law. During the reign of King Edward I the earliest year books reporting legal proceedings were written. Westminster Hall became the central place where justice was done, and in the course of the reigns of the first three Edwards the lawyers set up their own Inns of Court in London where they handed down the principles of the common law from generation to generation. In the reign of King Edward I too may be seen, if mistily, the beginnings of statute law—new laws promulgated by the king in parliament replacing or revising the customs of the past.

✸ THE POLICY OF EDWARD I

After King Edward I returned to England in August 1274 from a Crusade and a stay in France, he was responsible for the promulgation of a number of statutes (made in parliament) and ordinances (made in council) aimed at supplementing or clarifying the common or customary law of the realm. Fundamentally, however, the object of most of these statutes appears to have been to safeguard royal rights and prevent too large an accumulation of property, and therefore of power and wealth, from coming into other hands than the king's. For example, inquiries were instituted into baronial immunities and recorded in documents known as the Hundred Rolls. The Statute of Mortmain (1279) prohibited the grants of land to ecclesiastical corporations. But such statutes were difficult to put into effect. What the king really aimed to do was to publish a warning to his more ambitious or overweening subjects, to prevent the creation of fresh rights by his nobility or large alienations of property rather than to interfere with existing arrangements. The Statute of Mortmain, which would have been immensely damaging to the Church if rigorously enforced, was in fact modified by allowing churches to acquire lands paid for in cash.

Other statutes defined the administration of the public law. One statute dealt with the duties of the assize court judges; another statute limited the actions triable in the shire or county courts; a third imposed duties in crime prevention on the smaller administrative units—the hundreds and the villages. Other instruments were concerned with private property: *De Donis Conditionalibus* regulated "entailed" property; *Quia Emptores* affected the terms on which property might be alienated during the lifetime of the owner; writs of *Quo Warranto* were used to discover the precise extent of the rights of tenants-in-chief. Inquiries like those detailed in the Hundred Rolls or by the *Quo Warranto* writs had been made by earlier monarchs, at least from the time of the Domesday survey, and were aimed at restricting the power of the king's mightier subjects. Another writ, *Circumspecte agatis,* was intended to draw a clearer line between the secular and the ecclesiastical courts in order to prevent conflicts of jurisdiction.

On the other hand, the king was anxious to satisfy the new classes of the community who were now being regularly called to his parliaments. Thus the Statute of Acton Burnell dealt with the subject of merchants' debts; and the king's decision to expel the Jews from England in 1290 was popular with Londoners and other commercial communities and was commended in parliament.

Taken together, all this legislative activity, concentrated mainly in the first thirteen years of King Edward I's reign, constituted an impressive achievement, unique for some five hundred years of British history. A good deal of it was merely a logical extension of reforms introduced by King Henry II; part of it was aimed principally at safeguarding the rights of the Crown; much of it was honored in the letter rather than the spirit; many of the laws were unenforced or unenforceable. But the king earned the right to be called "the English Justinian."

He was indeed a remarkable man and vies with King Henry II for the claim to be the greatest ruler since the Norman Conquest. He had the quick temper and the unscrupulousness of others of his family— seen at their worst in King John. But he had a swift and tidy mind; he was hard working and receptive to new ideas. He was practical and sober in his outlook. "Of elegant build and lofty stature," a lover of hunting and an intelligent soldier, he deserved the description given by a contemporary of being "a valiant lion."

In foreign affairs he was, on the whole, a man of peace. He acquired a knowledge of Europe and of diplomacy during his early visits abroad. Being related directly or through marriage to other potentates of his time, he was in a position to act as a conciliator or mediator. His uncle, Prince Charles of Anjou, ruled Sicily; his cousin, Philip III, was king of France. By 1279 he had settled the outstanding differences between England and France and had established order in Gascony. In 1282 Peter, king of Aragon, ousted Charles of Anjou as king of Sicily and Edward tried to act as peacemaker between these two kings. In 1287 and 1288 it seemed that Edward had settled the Sicilian imbroglio by treaties concluded with the new king of Aragon, Alfonso III, but his younger brother James refused to abandon his hold on Sicily and the pope, who was a French partisan, quashed both the treaties. Meanwhile King Edward was involved in trouble with France. After Philip III died in 1285 his successor, Philip IV or "the Fair," had accepted Edward's homage for Gascony. But difficulties arose between the two nations both over Gascony itself and over disputes at sea, and in 1294 Edward prepared to wage war against France, being forced into it by the confiscation of Gascony by King Philip. In 1295 Edward's younger brother Edmund, Earl of Lancaster, led an unsuccessful expedition from Plymouth, and a truce left almost the whole of Gascony in the hands of the French king, who continued to hold it for nearly ten years. For a long time Edward was distracted by Welsh and Scottish affairs from attacking France. Eventually in May 1303 Philip the Fair, who had other problems to face, agreed, under the pressure of diplomacy rather than war, to restore Gascony to the English Crown, provided that his rights in Poitou were fully recognized. Edward I had married Margaret, sister of the French king, as his second wife and engaged his son to the French king's daughter; so for the remainder of Edward I's reign Anglo-French friendship was firm.

Edward I's foreign policy was confused and perverted by the problems presented by Wales and Scotland. In the earlier part of the thirteenth century each had acquired leaders and a nascent sense of nationality, but their relations with England were ill-defined and in Wales border warfare persisted. After the treaty of Shrewsbury in 1267 it had appeared that unity and freedom lay ahead for Wales under Prince Llewellyn ap Gruffydd, her accepted overlord. But the treaty had left questions unsettled upon the Marches; Llewellyn was reluctant to pay the full indemnity that had been promised or to do homage to the new king of England. His ambitions were unassuaged and he aspired to be independent both of Westminster and of Canterbury. In 1277 King Edward I organized a military expedition by land and sea, shut up Llewellyn in the Snowdon area, and dictated the treaty of Conway: Prince Llewellyn was compelled to yield territory, to do homage, pay an indemnity, and content himself with being a mere chieftain of north Wales. King Edward planned to impose English laws on the conquered territories known as "the four cantreds," since he regarded the Welsh customs as crude and outdated.

The Welsh resented their treatment and after five years of uneasy peace Llewellyn and his brother David, whom King Edward I had favored, rose against the English on Palm Sunday 1282. During a winter campaign Llewellyn was killed and in October 1283 David was betrayed, captured, and condemned to death. King Edward now established and fortified a "principality" in north Wales, centering upon the town of Carnarvon, where his son Edward was born in April 1284. A Statute of Wales defined the arrangements for the government of the principality. The English shire system was introduced and courts of Exchequer and Chancery set up in north Wales, although tribal customs were allowed to continue. The position of the Lords Marchers was also defined and limited, but their power remained substantial. John Peckham, Archbishop of Canterbury, concerned himself with the reform of the Welsh Church.

The Welsh did not take kindly to the loss of their independence, however tempered by benevolent reform. In 1287 when King Edward I was abroad, his brother Edmund, acting as regent, had to suppress a violent rising; in 1294 King Edward himself was obliged to postpone an expedition against France because of yet another rising, led by a bastard son of Llewellyn ap Gruffydd and provoked by the distaste both of the native Welsh and the Lords Marchers for being compelled to support the King in his projected French war. After a year of fighting the Welsh were again subdued. In 1301 King Edward created his son, Edward of Carnarvon, Prince of Wales and later ordered him to take part with a Welsh contingent in the Scottish wars. The discontented Marchers, whom King Edward I kept under strict control, nursed their grievances, troubled the peace of the land for years to come, and finally revenged themselves on Edward's son.

If King Edward I imposed peace of a sort upon Wales, he aroused a wasps' nest in Scotland. Here, after the death of King Alexander III in 1286, there was no obvious male heir to the throne. King Alexander's granddaughter, a child who was the offspring of King Eric of Norway, succeeded under guardianship and it was proposed that she should be married to Prince Edward of Carnarvon, the future King Edward II. Thus the two kingdoms might have been united in one island of Britain. The fond dream was not to be realized for more than 300 years; the Maid of Norway, as she was called, died on her way to Scotland. King Edward I was then invited to choose between thirteen candidates for the throne. In November 1292 he nominated John Balliol, undoubtedly the possessor of the best claim by lineal descent, who thereupon did homage to the English monarch as his overlord. One of the rejected claimants was Robert Bruce, the eighty-year-old Lord of Annandale.

The repeated and far-reaching demands for money and soldiers from their overlord to sustain his foreign policies, which had provoked the Welsh, also excited the wrath of the Scots. They retorted by ordering all Englishmen out of their country and by concluding a treaty with France, which was the foundation of a long-enduring Franco-Scottish alliance. As soon as he had suppressed the Welsh rising King Edward I marched north, slaughtered the garrison of the frontier town of Berwick, defeated the Scots at the battle of Dunbar, made their king a prisoner (he was later to die in France), and ordered the Stone of Destiny, upon which the Scottish kings were customarily crowned, to be sent down from Scone to Westminster, where it remains until the present day. The Earl of Surrey, the victor of Dunbar, was appointed governor or guardian of the kingdom, and the heads of all the chief families of Scotland were ordered to sign a roll—the "Ragman's Roll"—acknowledging Edward their king.

This was too much for Scottish pride; the Earl of Surrey was an incompetent, greedy, and absentee governor; it was only a question of time before the Scots revolted. Their first leader was Sir William Wallace, a modest and dedicated gentleman from Clydesdale. He started a guerrilla campaign, besieged Dundee, defeated the Earl of Surrey at the battle of Stirling Bridge in September 1297, and then invaded and ravaged the north of England. King Edward I was in Flanders at the time. He came home, led an Anglo-Welsh army into Scotland, and crushed Wallace at the battle of Falkirk in July 1298. Wallace himself was not captured until 1305 when he was hanged as a traitor and his head mounted upon a pole on London Bridge.

But the spirit of Scottish resistance was not quenched. It found a new and tireless hero in Robert Bruce, the grandson of the claimant against Balliol. He sacrilegiously killed one of his chief rivals among the Scottish nobility in a church, and had himself crowned at Scone. Undeterred by the ruthlessness of King Edward I, who deported his wife and hanged his brothers, he prepared to engage upon a prolonged struggle for his independence. At first defeated, he fled to Ireland, but soon returned to establish his supremacy in southwest Scotland. King Edward, who was now over seventy years old, set up military headquarters in Carlisle, where parliament met in January 1307. In July, hearing of Bruce's triumphs, he started for the Scottish border, but died on the way.

The last ten years of King Edward's life, from the time the Scottish revolt began in 1297, had been exceedingly stormy. To pay for his various wars the king had been obliged to make large demands upon his barons and people. The old methods of raising money and men had proved inadequate, and his parliaments were invited to contribute subsidies, usually in the form of fractions imposed on movable property—such as tenths and fifteenths; and there was also heavy taxation of the Church, imposed by grants in parliament or clerical assemblies. The more powerful subjects of the king reacted violently. John Peckham, Archbishop of Canterbury, and his successor, Robert Winchelsea, opposed the royal demands; the latter found backing after 1296 in the ban imposed by Pope Boniface VIII forbidding the lay authority to levy taxation without the consent of the Papacy. The Earl of Norfolk refused in 1297 to serve in Gascony unless the king came too, and he was supported by the Earl of Hereford and other Lords Marchers made restive by restrictions on their privileges. Norfolk and Hereford asked the king to confirm the Great Charter and the forest charters and forced Edward to accede to their request and make further concessions. But they distrusted the king's willingness to keep his word, and continued to press for guarantees, in particular for a reduction in the extent of the royal forests, where the special laws, brutally upheld, created a grievance throughout the land.

In 1301 the king yielded by giving his sanction to a number of articles, additional to the old charters, known as *Articuli super cartas,* by which he agreed to put a stop to arbitrary methods of government. He had already in 1297 given a promise not to exact taxes without parliamentary consent or to seize the properties of his subjects (he had taken wool from merchants and requisitioned cattle from clergy and laity to sustain his wars). But the king never seems genuinely to have intended to fulfill any of these promises extracted from him in time of dire need and he even invoked—as King John and King Henry III had done before him—the assistance of a compliant pope to quash the concessions he had made. He stuck by his ministers, repudiated his rebellious archbishop, and compelled his sullen barons to follow him into battle. But he died bankrupt and left a testament of troubles to his son.

Indeed in the reign of King Edward I, while the structure of the government of England remained intact, the functioning of a successful administration and the pursuit of a policy of territorial expansion had been shown to depend ultimately on the strength and personality of one man, the king himself. A weak king brought chaos.

✿ KING EDWARD II

Edward II, who came to the throne when he was twenty-three, had the character of a spoiled young man, son of a strong father who was too strict with him or else not strict enough. Vain and irritable, a gambler and a drinker, he loved to wear fine clothes, watch plays, breed horses and dogs, go driving, racing, and rowing. He was a coward with few brains, who depended on others for advice and comfort. His first favorite was a brave Gascon knight named Piers Gaveston, whom his father had banished from the court. Young Edward loved him dearly, made him Earl of Cornwall, and married him to his niece. Among Edward II's first actions were to dismiss Walter Langton, Bishop of Lichfield, who had been his father's treasurer, and to marry Isabella, daughter of Philip the Fair of France, as had been previously arranged.

The magnates of the realm, who had long chafed under the autocracy of King Edward I, were determined to discipline his weakling son. They were headed by Thomas, Earl of Lancaster, the king's first cousin, who held five earldoms, a dour and not particularly clever or competent man, terribly ambitious, jealous, passionate, and domineering, though a contemporary called him "discreet and pious." The barons obliged King Edward II to send away his favorite Gaveston to Ireland; and in 1309 they enlarged upon their grievances in parliament. Edward yielded on

some points and recalled Gaveston. Next year in 1310 an armed baronial parliament met at Westminster and demanded that the royal powers
should be put in the hands of a committee of twenty-one with the right
to enact ordinances. These Lords Ordainers, headed by Archbishop
Winchelsea, in effect moved a vote of censure upon many of the administrative methods employed by King Edward I and deliberately revived the policies of the barons of King Henry III's days. Their outlook
was broadly conservative. They wanted the traditional great departments
of state, such as the treasury and the chancery, to be supreme over the
royal household, where the wardrobe or chamber did the king's business
expeditiously, and they wanted to nominate the departmental heads as
well as other officials and judges. Above all, the Ordinances were aimed
against the King's foreign favorites. The King gave way to all these
demands; the Ordinances were published in every shire; the King reigned
and the Earl of Lancaster governed.

But this situation could hardly endure, especially as the principal
actors were not of the caliber of the earlier baronial leaders in English
history: Lancaster was no Simon de Montfort nor was the aged Winchelsea another Stephen Langton or Thomas Becket. In 1312 Edward II
again recalled Gaveston and defied the Lords Ordainers, but in vain.
Gaveston was caught, surrounded, and taken a prisoner at the rocky
castle of Scarborough, and in spite of solemn promises made to him by
his captors was put to death. This action brought about a split in the
baronial party, for two of the earls concerned with the capitulation at
Scarborough regarded Gaveston's murder as an affront to their honor.
So a "middle party" was created. And King Edward II was determined
to avenge the death of his favorite.

Meanwhile in Scotland a great king was fashioning a nation. Robert
Bruce, Earl of Carrick, was thirty-three when he was crowned. He had
successfully defied Edward I in all his glory, trained an excellent army,
chiefly of pikemen, and taken one by one every stronghold in English
hands. When Stirling Castle was threatened in the summer of 1314
Edward II at last felt compelled to come up and do battle, or disgrace
his father's name. The two armies met at Bannockburn, a brook to the
south of Stirling, on Midsummer Day. Fruitlessly the heavily armed
English cavalry thrust itself upon the Scottish pikes, while Robert Bruce
threw in his own cavalry to crush the English archers. The cream of
English knighthood was hemmed in without room to maneuver and
perished in marsh and stream. This famous Scottish victory gave the
land national independence for nearly 300 years. Robert Bruce won papal
recognition and a fresh alliance with France. Edward II had again to

bow before Thomas of Lancaster, who had refused to go with him upon the campaign.

But the Earl of Lancaster was no ruler. He quarreled with the other barons and refused to attend parliaments—indeed he held his own. Not only did Robert Bruce continue to make headway in Scotland, but one of his surviving brothers, Edward, "pricked the bubble of English power in Ireland." A truce had to be concluded with the Scottish king. For a time internal peace prevailed in England, but soon squabbles were renewed.

Edward II found himself a new favorite, an abler man than Gaveston, in Hugh Despenser, grandson of a chief justice of Edward I's reign. Greedy for land and titles and successfully accumulating large reserve funds which he entrusted to Italian bankers, Despenser alienated the powerful Lords Marchers; and Thomas of Lancaster patched up his differences with his fellow magnates and attacked the new favorite. In 1321 Despenser and his father were banished and their lands declared forfeit. Again the king tried to save his favorite. He managed to gather an army, rallied some of the middle party to his side, induced his new archbishop, Reynolds, to quash proceedings against the Despensers, and finally defeated Lancaster in Yorkshire, where this aloof, incapable aristocrat was put to death with three blows of an axe as a traitor and a rebel. Mocked at his death, he was later to be acclaimed a saint. For the moment Edward II had his revenge. A parliament meeting in 1322 at York revoked the Ordinances of 1310.

The triumph of Edward II and the Despensers was short lived. The French queen Isabella, not unnaturally incensed at her husband's love of his men favorites (who also seem to have engineered an attack upon her own properties), turned against him. Taking her son with her, she went to Paris ostensibly to treat with her brother, King Charles IV (the two countries were once more engaged upon the interminable war over Gascony), and then refused to return. She entered into a conspiracy with Roger Mortimer, the wealthiest of the Lords Marchers of Wales, moved into Holland, where Sir John de Hainault, brother of the Count of Hainault, raised soldiers on her behalf, and from there invaded England. Her swift triumph over her husband was astonishing, reflecting the complete and humiliating failure of Edward II as a king and as a man. She took Bristol and was welcomed in London. The Despensers were captured and put to death while Edward II was made a prisoner in Wales. A so-called parliament met at Westminster in January 1327 and deposed the king. Under pressure Edward II agreed to hand over his authority to his son Edward, Duke of Aquitaine, a lad of fifteen.

Edward II's reign of strife, confusion, and dishonor ended when, after two vain attempts to rescue him had been attempted, he was murdered in Berkeley Castle in Gloucestershire in September 1327. In the spring of the following year Robert Bruce was recognized as king of Scotland by the treaty of Northampton. Next year he died, immortalized as the architect of Scottish independence. Thus a notable era in British history had taken shape.

XVIII

The Reign of Edward III

Edward III was eighteen when he took over the government of his kingdom. He was already a husband and a father. He had married Philippa of Hainault, niece of the man with whose aid Edward's mother had seized his father's throne. In June 1330 Queen Philippa gave birth to a son, known to British history as "the Black Prince." For over three years Edward had in effect allowed his mother to rule. Now at last he had been provoked by the outrageous behavior of his mother's paramour, Roger Mortimer, who had created himself the first Earl of March—the name being taken from the Welsh March where his power lay. Mortimer's avarice betrayed him. By King Edward III's orders he was arrested in Nottingham Castle, tried before Parliament, condemned as a traitor, and hanged upon the common gallows. The Queen Mother pleaded in vain for his life. She herself was confined in honorable custody at a variety of castles and died nearly thirty years later, wearing the habit of a nun.

The young king was popular, charming, chivalrous, and magnanimous. He was not a strong man nor an intellectual. He loved fighting either in tournament or in war. Like Henry III he was fond of building in church and state: he was pious and devout. His praises were sung by the chronicler Sir John Froissart and by others. He managed his turbulent baronage because he never quarreled with them dangerously and led them skillfully to victory in foreign war; but he relied for advice and guidance chiefly upon his higher clergy, notably his first Archbishop of Canterbury, John Stratford. For a time he was able to restore the respect for the monarchy which his father had forfeited.

At first he was mainly concerned with Scotland. The conclusion of the treaty with Robert Bruce had been among the causes of Mortimer's loss of influence. Bruce's son David was only five years old when he succeeded to the throne under guardianship and he was soon thrust from it by Edward Balliol. First secretly, then openly, Balliol was supported by the English government against David Bruce's guardians. At the battle of Halidon Hill (1333) Balliol and Edward III won a decisive victory. This was followed in June 1334 by the treaty of Newcastle, whereby Edward Balliol handed over to English rule much of Lothian in the south and performed homage to Edward III for the rest of Scotland. Thus Edward had largely repaired the position lost by the Battle of Bannockburn. But the Scottish national spirit did not die, and resistance to English interference continued. Balliol was disliked as an English puppet and when David Bruce became a man he won back his throne. In 1341 the English were again swept out of Scotland. Thus Edward III's first military campaigns were unprofitable; but by the 1340's he was engaged upon a far more ambitious enterprise, the beginning of what came to be known as the Hundred Years' War against France.

The French kingdom had now reached a condition of strength and prosperity with a population four times as large as that of England, but the Capetian line, which had ruled the country long before William the Conqueror came to England and had gradually consolidated a half-despised monarchy, was now at an end. Charles IV, the last of three brothers to reign, had no son, and Edward III of England, being the son of Charles's sister, seemed to have a good claim to the throne. Indeed Queen Isabella had attempted to assert her son's rights. These were ignored and the late king's cousin, the first of the royal line of Valois, succeeded as Philip VI. Edward III's claim was not pressed; in fact he did homage of a sort to Philip VI for Aquitaine.

It was the possession of Aquitaine by the English Crown that was one of the principal reasons for the Hundred Years' War. It has been argued that Philip VI had no intention of overthrowing completely the English hold on Gascony, but so long as the kings of England owned land of any kind in France this was bound to be a source of trouble between the two monarchies. Aquitaine had long been an apple of discord. It was militarily vulnerable, the scene of frontier guerrilla activities, and had been confiscated more than once by the king of France as overlord in the past two reigns. Both prestige and trade—and the English trade with Gascony was particularly valuable—depended upon the English king's ability to uphold his rights. The French kings, on the other hand, were always anxious to shake off the influence of a rival monarch whose territory lay upon their flank and who was in a position to rally discontented vassals against them. In fact discontented French barons frequently took refuge in England, while the townsmen of Flanders in northern France, who relied upon the importation of English raw wool for the maintenance of their profitable cloth industry, also looked to England for help in quarrels with their count. Thus clashes of interest, both political and economic, produced hostility. France allied herself with the Scotland of the Bruces, and England with Flanders and the princes of the Netherlands.

Undeclared war began at sea: Norman sailors attacked the Channel Islands—which had been a possession of the English Crown since the time of William the Conqueror and lay near the French coast—and the southern parts of England. English sailors retorted by ravaging the coasts of France. The war is generally said to have begun in 1337 when the French king once again confiscated Gascony, but it was not until 1340 when Edward III formally assumed the title of king of France (chiefly to please his Flemish allies, who were thus absolved from the treason of fighting against their lawful overlord) and the English won a naval battle off Sluys in modern Holland that war flared up. To that conflict Edward III devoted much of the remainder of his life. To a large extent the war resolved his own political problems at home, for the barons admired a fighting king who could lead them on to conquest and plunder; while the king, for his part, was prepared to grant constitutional concessions, provided that his parliaments voted him the money he needed for his campaigns.

Was this the first "national" war? That depends on definitions. It was certainly "feudal" in origin, waged in "feudal" terms for "feudal" rights; and in it French barons and townsmen fought against their own king. But in the end it became a patriotic war as well as a struggle over dynastic prestige. France became the national enemy of England and a desire to humiliate her was a main factor in foreign policy.

In June 1345 the king's cousin, Henry, Earl of Lancaster, landed at Bayonne and for eighteen months carried on successful warfare on the borders of the duchy of Aquitaine. Next year Edward III, having raised a substantial army which was assembled at Portsmouth in the spring, planned—or so it was thought at the time—to join him there. Meanwhile one of the Norman barons, who had quarreled with the king of France, offered his assistance; King Edward therefore decided instead to land his expeditionary force in the Cotentin Peninsula in Normandy, where nearly 600 years later an Anglo-American army was to assault the western frontier of Hitler's Germany on D-Day. The English army occupied Barfleur, Saint-Lo, and Caen and, moving west, reached the Seine above Rouen to menace Paris. King Philip VI of France had prepared to meet his enemy with a larger army, although how much larger it was is difficult to say. Edward III crossed the Seine and the Somme and challenged his enemy to come at him upon the plain of Ponthieu in Flanders (Ponthieu was itself one of the English Crown's possessions in France, inherited from the wife of King Edward I).

It was near the village of Crécy that the battle took place. Because his forces were inferior the English king drew them up in a defensive position on the slopes of a valley with two "battles" or "battalions" forward and one, commanded by himself, in reserve. He dismounted his knights or men-at-arms and deployed his numerous archers on the flanks of each of his forward battalions. Sir John Froissart described how in the Black Prince's battalion (the king had knighted his son, a youth of sixteen, after they landed in Normandy) "the archers were formed in the manner of a portcullis." The French had made a long and tiring march; the once pro-English John de Hainault advised King Philip VI not to attack immediately on August 28, more especially as the English were fresh and had lain in wait for them all day. However, the chivalry of France was eager for battle. The Genoese crossbowmen engaged to fight for the French Crown were ordered to begin the offensive in the name of God and St. Denis and to prepare the way for the heavily armored cavalry. Under the evening sun they were outshot by the English archers. Thus when the French horsemen thrust forward they became enmeshed with their own archers and with one another. Struck down by the English archers and terrified by the noise of cannon—the first ever to be used, it is believed, by an English army—the French knights fought on gallantly. The English stood their ranks; the archers took to the sword; the men at arms supported the archers; and at the right moment the king threw in his reserve battalion. The victory was conclusive; few prisoners were taken; the chivalry of France lay scattered upon the field.

King Edward III turned to the siege of Calais, a better base for him than distant Bayonne or Barfleur. Here again a new page in early warfare was written, for the King kept the siege going throughout the winter, and a year after the battle of Crécy Calais surrendered honorably.

In 1348 the war was rudely interrupted by the coming of the Black Death, a bubonic and pneumonic plague which swept across Europe from the east and scourged England as well as France. It is estimated that between one-fifth and one-third of the inhabitants of the two countries were wiped out by it; its worst effects were upon the towns, where hygiene was unknown, but it also dislocated rural life. Scarcity of labor reduced the output of agriculture and industry; prices rose and rents fell; lords of manors abandoned the cultivation of marginal lands and tried to exact full services from their villeins and to prevent increases in the wages they paid to hired labor. The Ordinance and Statute of Labourers (1349–50) aimed at freezing both wages and prices and set up justices with the power to fix wage rates, but this was attempting to fly in the face of economic facts. The Black Death, though it did not have the revolutionary consequences once supposed, hastened existing social and economic tendencies, such as the commutation of labor services for relatively low money rents, the leasing of land by owners, and the turning from corn growing to sheep farming. The Black Death and later plagues which may have reduced the total population of the country by one-half helped to create a large class of small peasant farmers.

Damaging though the immediate results of the Black Death were, it did not after a year or two diminish the enthusiasm of the French or English monarchy for continuing the war. In the very year that the Black Death struck England King Edward III founded the Order of the Garter as a reward for valor, in the Chapel of St. George at Windsor. The king had been born at Windsor, which henceforward became one of the most decorative homes of the English monarchy. St. George, whom the historian Gibbon described as an infamous Middle Eastern merchant, became the patron saint of England. King John II, "the Good," of France, who succeeded his father in 1350, also dreamed gay heraldic dreams, and yearned for splendid feats of arms. But King Edward III found a new ally in King Charles the Bad of Navarre. The French king resigned himself to accepting a humiliating peace. However, negotiations broke down; war was resumed in 1355 with raids led by the Black Prince from Bordeaux and by Henry of Lancaster from Brittany. On September 19 a battle took place in the neighborhood of Poitiers where the French, though they fought dismounted, were again defeated after an all-day struggle, and their king taken a prisoner. In the same year as the battle of Crécy King David II of Scotland, who had attempted to create a diversion in favor of the French, had been beaten at Neville's Cross near Durham in northern England, and also made captive. Thus both the king of France and of Scotland found themselves fellow prisoners in the Tower of London. It was King Edward III's finest moment of military triumph.

Eventually both the captive kings accepted terms. By the treaty of Berwick (1357), David II, who was a poor son of his great father, agreed to pay a large sum as ransom and later even promised that if he had no male heir Edward or his son should succeed him on the throne of Scotland. After lengthy negotiations, during which Edward III asked for much more than he could hope to get, peace with France was concluded at Calais in October 1360. Edward III was confirmed in the possession of Aquitaine (much expanded by contiguous and long-debated territories), Ponthieu, and Calais. He was also promised a very large ransom for the release of John the Good and other royal French prisoners and hostages. In return King Edward renounced his claim to the French throne (never very seriously intended) and the French king gave up his overlordship of Aquitaine. But the exchange of these renunciations was supposed to take place subsequent to the treaty.

This peace, though reasonable enough upon paper, was difficult to fulfill. The French found it hard to raise the ransom money and their king ultimately returned a prisoner to London, where, fortunately for his country, he died in 1364. His son Charles V, an ingenious valetudinarian, no soldier, proved himself an altogether tougher character. Gradually he overcame the opposition of his more powerful subjects and of a discontented peasantry given to revolt. Meanwhile in Aquitaine the Black Prince, its duke and governor, had made himself unpopular by incessantly demanding money, while by involving himself in Spanish quarrels, he had created fresh enemies to the south of Aquitaine. In any case the Gascons, who had been willing enough in the past to play off the king of France against the king of England, did not care for the new position in which they found themselves under the unrestricted control of the English Crown. The French king, for his part, could argue that the English had been delaying the surrender of strongholds captured during the earlier campaigns, which they had promised by treaty to restore, and that they encouraged brigandage, since former mercenary soldiers were banding themselves together in "free companies" and pillaging the countryside. King Charles V took advantage of the fact that the renunciations envisaged by the treaty had never been exchanged to intervene in the affairs of Gascony. War broke out again in 1369 when Edward III's fourth son, John of Gaunt, advanced from Calais to Normandy and the Black Prince marshaled his troops in Aquitaine.

The situation now slowly changed in favor of France, which had a wise king, a notable military leader in his constable, Sir Bertrand du Guesclin, and a good admiral in Jean de Vienne. In England the king after a life of military ardor was approaching his dotage; the Black Prince, suffering from dropsy, had proved an incapable ruler of Aquitaine; and John of Gaunt conspired against his father's ministers. Adopting a sensible policy of avoiding pitched battles, the French refused to be provoked by acts of devastation, and attacked their enemy by the methods of guerrilla warfare. Ponthieu was lost and the English were defeated at sea.

So long as the French war had gone well the leaders of the English barons, who had humbled King Edward II, remained quiet. Edward III, whether deliberately or not, had strengthened the power of his family by intermarriage with the wealthier magnates and by distributing some of the richest estates in the realm among his sons. His eldest son was Duke of Cornwall and Earl of Chester as well as Prince of Wales and Duke of Aquitaine; his second son Edmund was Duke of York and Earl of Cambridge; John of Gaunt married the heiress to the Lancaster estates as his first wife and was created Duke of Lancaster. But this only transferred the jealousies of mighty subjects to his own sons: rivalry developed between the Black Prince and John of Gaunt. In 1371 the king's ministers were openly attacked and an anticlerical agitation was fomented. The king was always sensitive to baronial pressure and preferred to yield rather than imperil provision for his war. He abandoned his clerical ministers. William of Wykeham, the Chancellor since 1367 and Bishop of Winchester, famed among posterity for his foundation of Winchester College and New College, Oxford, was dismissed, as was also the Bishop of Exeter, who was treasurer, and lay barons were appointed to the chief posts. John of Gaunt lent his patronage to an Oxford don, John Wycliffe, who criticized the administration and the beliefs of the Church.

When the Commons, whose importance in the voting of taxes for the support of the war was becoming recognized, met in 1373 as a separate house of parliament, they expressed their wish to consult with the Lords on affairs of state. As soon as a fresh truce concluded in 1375 put a halt to the fighting, discontent with the government came to a head. John of Gaunt, who had now become the effective ruler of the kingdom, was unpopular and grasping, and resentment over the conduct of the war was expressed in the so-called "Good Parliament" which met in April 1376.

In the Lords the critics were led by Edmund Mortimer, Earl of March, in the Commons by his steward, Sir Peter de la Mare, who has been called the first Speaker of the House. The king's chamberlain and others were impeached, that is to say prosecuted by the Commons and condemned by the Lords, for corruption and peculation, while the king's mistress was sent away from the court. In June the Black Prince died and John of Gaunt managed to have the decisions of the Good Parliament reversed, his own steward becoming the Speaker of the House of Commons. The old king, whose reign twenty years earlier had witnessed the heights of military glory, thus died in the shadows, and the Black Prince's young son, Richard of Bordeaux, came to a shaky throne in June 1377.

XIX

England in the Fourteenth Century

The political facts of the fourteenth century had produced new institutions and constitutional principles. It had seen the evolution of parliament and its gradual division into two houses; the crystallization of great departments of state and courts of law; the acceptance of the principle of taxation by consent; and the recognition that new laws might be enacted by the king in his parliaments. But precisely when these institutions were completely established or these principles fully accepted no historians will be found to agree. Perhaps the contemporaries themselves did not know, because they scarcely realized that anything new or strange was happening.

Parliaments were special sessions of the king's court where, to begin with, he invited such subjects as he fancied to discuss matters with him. To put it another way, they were political bodies called together to treat with the king. Gradually parliament became more than a mere expansion of the court and represented the assembled power and majesty of the realm. The lords spiritual and temporal were summoned to parliaments by direct writs; the knights and burgesses, summoned through the sheriffs, were there to be informed what was going on, "to hear and do what might then be decided in the common council." During the reign of King Edward II the king's tenants-in-chief virtually insisted upon their right to be called to parliaments and Edward III, whose policy was to conciliate his influential subjects, summoned the same spiritual and lay lords time after time; but by the end of the century the lords had not yet fully established their hereditary claim to be summoned as peers of the realm, and so it might be said that the House of Lords as such still did not exist. It was the same with the Commons. During the reign of King Edward III the Commons usually retired and met separately, generally in the Chapter House of Westminster Abbey, while their superiors were meeting in Westminster Palace, but later they were called in through their speaker and informed what had been decided by king and lords. Equally during the reign of King Edward III the commons began to frame or sponsor petitions, but petitions could still be presented to the king in other ways. Sometimes the commons' petitions formed the basis for statutes, but not always. The powers and rights of the commons were in a formative stage.

It has been said that an administrative revolution took place in the fourteenth century. Naturally strong kings always tried to keep control over the organization of war, peace, and justice in their own hands or in the hands of officials whom they could trust. King Edward I's "wardrobe" proved to be a speedier and more efficient organ for transacting business than the elaborate and traditional procedures of the Exchequer and Chancery. When the barons complained about the powers of the wardrobe and the use of its insignia, the privy seal, in the reign of King Edward II, he turned to his chamber and used a secret seal to authenticate its decisions. Complaints about "private offices" or "inner cabinets" cover the whole of English history. But the Hundred Years' War proved to be a unifying factor in the national administration. So anxious was King Edward III for the wholehearted co-operation of his barons and for the collection of the maximum amount of revenue from his subjects that after 1338 the various administrative bodies were effectively coordinated: the chamber and the wardrobe ceased to be special instruments of royal administration and the keeper of the king's privy seal became a great minister of state.

In the Hundred Years' War the king no longer relied upon the ancient methods of raising an army. Edward III's grandfather had already discovered that these were becoming out of date and that good soldiers had to be paid. Troops were mostly raised by indenture, that is to say by contract, to fight in France, though every subject could still be called on to enlist by commissions of array under the Statute of Winchester of 1285.

The indenture system required large sums of money. The accepted early royal sources of scutage or aid were quite insufficient to meet the costs of prolonged campaigns oversea. Hence parliaments were called upon to vote subsidies to the king and these were collected either directly from the barons or the Church or from the counties through the sheriffs. In addition to fractions on movable property—the normal form of tax— the first export tax on wool (known as the Great and Ancient Custom) had been imposed in 1275, while in 1294 and again in 1336 a maltolte, as it was called, of forty shillings a sack was granted to the king by the wool merchants. In each case this heavier tax caused an uproar in parliament, for the merchants themselves were not directly affected by it since they were able to pass on the tax by lowering the price they paid for the wool to the growers; and after the middle of the fourteenth century parliaments preferred to grant the king additional subsidies rather than assent to an imposition agreed upon between the king and the merchants. This struggle over the wool taxes is one of the most significant episodes in the constitutional history of the time, for thereby it was decided that a single interest group, the wool merchants, should not be allowed to settle taxation by means of a separate negotiation when that tax was going to have repercussions upon the nation as a whole. By timely concessions to the king's government in the years 1339–41 the commons secured the right to control the levying of taxation and thus effectively asserted themselves. Taxation by consent, dimly foreshadowed in the Great Charter, was practically realized in the fourteenth century.

Legislation by king in parliament lay deeper in the future. Enactments might be made by king and lords on the petition of the commons; but the commons themselves did not draw up the precise terms of bills to be converted into statutes, while statutes might be suspended by the king or reinterpreted by the judges. The king or king's council remained the real lawmaking force in the fourteenth century.

If at the center of government parliament was gradually feeling its way to influence, in the counties and boroughs local government was also beginning to take on a more modern hue. By the regular summoning of knights of the shire or burgesses from the towns to meetings of parliament the court was brought into closer contact with local affairs. Hitherto chief reliance had been placed upon the sheriffs, but this proved unsatisfactory to the government since these men were often proved guilty of feathering their own nests or even of plotting against the Crown. Inquests into the conduct of sheriffs had been organized by both the Norman and the Plantagenet kings and the institution of justices "upon eyre" by King Henry II had lessened the sheriffs' powers. Other officials directly appointed by the Crown, such as commissioners of array to raise soldiers or exchequer officials to collect taxes, were used to link Westminster with the provinces, while in the late thirteenth century another office, that of keeper of the peace, was originated. In the reign of King Edward III these unpaid local officials became known as justices of the peace. They were given a wide range of duties, administrative as well as judicial: after 1361 or at any rate 1368 they met at quarterly sessions to discuss the business of the county. They stayed independent in spirit, and their expressions of opinion at quarter sessions were an excellent touchstone of the feeling of the English gentry, and remained so for hundreds of years. The boroughs too showed independence of outlook, while the guilds of merchants proved to be the instruments of constructive change in the towns.

Nevertheless the administration of law and the distribution of jurisdictions and franchises remained incredibly complicated and therefore largely ineffective: there were county courts and borough sessions and

assize courts, manor courts and church courts with much overlapping
and rivalry and a good deal of intimidation by the rich and powerful. Nor
were matters settled much more clearly in the central government. It
was not until the end of the fifteenth century that the king ceased actually to decide cases himself, wherever he happened to be, though even
before then most cases were delegated to judges, who had become a professional class. During the fourteenth century three common-law courts,
Common Pleas, King's Bench, and Exchequer, were sorting out their
different functions. Common Pleas dealt with actions between subjects,
the King's Bench with actions which concerned the king or great persons
privileged to be brought to justice before the king, and the Exchequer
with revenue cases. Because the King's Bench was intimately linked with
the King's Council, and for a long time was not differentiated from it, it
became the highest court in the land after Parliament; and the judges of
the Common Pleas, Barons of the Exchequer, and even the Chancellor
himself could be brought before it. It was not until the end of the fourteenth century that the King's Bench ceased to be directly controlled by
the king and his council. In the course of the fourteenth and fifteenth
centuries the Chancery Court became a tribunal which found remedies for
unforeseeable abuses in the working of the common law of the land. It
too stemmed from the king's court and its development was extremely
gradual. Only at the end of the fifteenth century did the Chancellor make
decrees upon his own authority.

If the thirteenth century was a Golden Age in the history of the English Church, the fourteenth century was a period of torpor and even
decline. The rot set in at the top. Boniface VIII, the last of the early
popes, died in 1303, and for seventy years the popes lived at Avignon
in France instead of at Rome and were under the obvious influence of
the French kings. When the "captivity" at Avignon ended in 1377 a
schism tore the Papacy asunder and Christian rulers were able to choose
between the claims to authority of rival popes. While it is no doubt true
to say that no one in Britain questioned the spiritual supremacy of the
pope—except for John Wycliffe and his followers, the Lollards—his
authority and influence were reduced. Though from the middle of the
century onward every bishop in England and Wales was appointed by
papal provision, the king invariably got the man he asked for. At this
time too kings and parliaments, convinced that the pro-French popes
were using their resources to the detriment of England, began to pass a
series of statutes of antipapal character. The Statute of Provisors (1351)
made the obtaining of a benefice in the Church by reservation or provision from the pope, in derogation of the rights of patrons, into a criminal

offense. Statutes of Praemunire (1353, 1365, 1391) imposed severe punishment on those who secured papal privileges contrary to the king's rights or who appealed to papal courts when the royal courts claimed jurisdiction. In 1366 parliament repudiated the annual payment of tribute to the pope agreed to by King John, though this had long fallen in arrears. These antipapal statutes were only enforced to a limited extent and were mainly used by the monarchy to exert diplomatic pressure upon the Papacy.

The bishops did not always agree with these antipapal measures, and they themselves, like the pope, were subject to attack by the laity on account of their secular interests. Bishops often served the king in high offices of state, and bishops and abbots actually formed the majority in the House of Lords. Their influence and wealth made them the envy of laymen—of barons, judges, lawyers, and merchants—and, as we have seen, toward the end of the reign of King Edward III they were temporarily forced out of office altogether. Meanwhile in the lower ranges of the Church pluralism and absenteeism persisted, although their evils have perhaps been exaggerated. The richer benefices frequently fell into the hands of lay proprietors or of royal servants. Before the fourteenth century the parish system had become more or less stabilized, but with the growth of population and of prosperity during the first half of the century new churches were built within the parishes. More churches did not necessarily mean the wider spreading of religion; many of these new churches were a source of convenient revenue to someone or other, and most of the parish clergy, especially the vicars and curates, remained poor and uneducated. The gulf between well-upholstered pluralists and absentees and the ordinary working clergy was marked. Nor were the monks and friars always a help from the point of view of personal spiritual comfort. The friars continued to preach, but their pristine enthusiasm was diluted. The different orders rivaled each other in the art of begging. They also managed to acquire property by one means or another in spite of their vows of poverty. The monks (except for the Carthusians who withdrew from the world into a life of contemplation) declined in austerity and often lived in luxurious leisure. Prohibition of meat-eating in the monasteries became a dead issue; monks enjoyed other creature comforts beside excellent meals and received pay and holidays. Instead of providing charitable hospitality they established inns, collected rents, and even lent money, and had wide business interests. At the same time broader opportunities attracted educated men away from the Church. After the Black Death the numbers of monks declined.

During the fourteenth century no English monk, friar, or bishop was canonized. Early English writers like Langland and Chaucer were caustic about the behavior of the clergy and the lewd conduct of people in church or on pilgrimage. Undoubtedly leaders of the Church had lost influence and some of them had been corrupted, but the basic beliefs of Christianity were not yet generally questioned. Religious zeal still glowed fiercely. When John Wycliffe, the first famous English heretic or Protestant, began to wield influence toward the end of the reign of King Edward III, he and his followers, the Lollards, while revealing a desire to reject the Papacy and some of the Church's mystical doctrines as well as to disendow the Church, also aimed at spreading a purified and exemplary Christianity and at reforming the abuses of the Church, but not at destroying it.

✿ ART AND LITERATURE

The fourteenth century saw steady development in art and literature. A new "Decorated style" was introduced into architecture, sculpture, and illuminated manuscripts. The fundamentals of the style were "a purely decorative use of architectural forms, a strongly three-dimensional sense, a love of graceful and flowing line, and of amusing and sometimes irrelevant detail." A large number of churches were built in this style in the reigns of Edward II and Edward III. Many-ribbed vaulting and curvilinear tracery are characteristic of the time. Among cathedrals, those of Wells and Exeter exemplify the new style; the chapter house of the former contains lovely palm vaulting, while in the nave at Exeter the vaulting sprang out from or was linked by ball-flowers. While in London churches the emphasis was chiefly upon the ornamental nature of the new architecture, in the churches of Norfolk elaborate tracery enriched the Gothic tradition. The creative gaiety of the Decorated style was shown particularly in the "babewyns" (from the Italian *babuino* meaning baboon), grotesque figures, usually monkeys, used to adorn tombs, psalters, or other manuscripts, which are said to have been peculiarly English. One of the mourners on the tomb of Philippa of Hainault, Edward II's queen, has a monkey attached to her by a chain; one of the windows in York Minster has a monkey blowing a horn; and several of the psalters in Norfolk are full of these comical figures.

In the reign of Edward III stained glass made rapid headway, and larger churches such as York Minster, Westminster Abbey, and Gloucester Cathedral were endowed with splendid windows. The tree of Jesse was the first design to be integrated in England to fill a large window. Later, battle scenes and tournaments were portrayed. Finally heraldic devices and banners were embodied not only in church windows, but also in the arches surrounding them.

About 1360 the Decorated style began to yield place to the more austere Perpendicular, which was cheaper to build: the flowing curves were exchanged for a rectilinear purity; the rib vault was followed by vaults of intersecting surfaces. The birthplace of this style is said to have been in western England, at Bristol, Gloucester, and Tewkesbury. When the nave at Canterbury Cathedral was rebuilt towards the end of the fourteenth century Perpendicular characteristics were introduced, as they were also at Westminster Abbey.

Progress in architecture was not confined to churches. Grand palaces were built for bishops and an aesthetic element was discernible in the castles of the nobility. Brick was used in building Caister Castle in Norfolk and Hurstmonceux in Sussex. The fourteenth-century manor houses also often took on a new form with gateways, a quadrangular pattern, and timbered framework. The great hall ceased to be the common living room for all its inhabitants: the lord of the manor had his own chamber and there were a separate kitchen, pantry, and buttery.

Sculpture flourished in this century. Its story begins in the last decade of the thirteenth century with monuments erected in memory of Edward I's queen, Eleanor of Castile, known as Eleanor Crosses; monuments line the route of her funeral from Lincolnshire to Westminster. These are notable for the curved rhythm of figures in the Decorated style. The Perpendicular style had its equivalent sculpture in the alabaster effigies (alabaster was quarried in the Midlands) of knights and their ladies lying in canopied tombs that filled churches and chantry chapels. This style also commemorated the passing of royalty, as in the effigy of King Edward II at Gloucester. Sculptured figures in bronze, stone, or wood, or engraved "brasses" were the principal forms of pictorial art. The early history of English painting is confused, but it appears that characteristic native English painting, both in panel and miniature, dates from the reign of King Richard II.

If in the England of the fourteenth century we can see a distinctive English style in art, if we may trace the growth of English patriotic feeling, engendered by the long war against France and demonstrated in the House of Commons, so too we may say that an English language and literature were born. In 1362 English superseded French as the spoken language of the courts of law; and in 1363 the Chancellor opened parliament with a speech in English. John Trevisa, writing in 1385, described how forty years earlier Oxford grammar-school masters had instructed their pupils to construe Latin into English instead of French; and he complained that boys at grammar schools then knew less French than their left heels. The heretical Lollards produced the first Bible translated into English; and Geoffrey Chaucer, born about 1343, was the first outstanding poet to write in English.

For many years monks continued to write their chronicles in Latin, people about the court spoke French, and the chancery transacted its business in Latin. But the spread of schools contributed to the use of English. Grammar schools were built not merely by the Church but also under the patronage of individual lay benefactors or of guilds. Winchester College—most ancient of British "public" (that is to say, private) schools—was founded in this century. Oxford and Cambridge remained the unique instruments of higher education; though often rent by internal feuds, they united to stop the setting up of any "upstart" universities.

It was at Oxford that John Wycliffe and a more notable thinker, William of Ockham, propounded ideas that were novel and even earth-shaking for their time. Ockham was an out-and-out "nominalist": he believed that universal concepts were mere names. He accepted religion as a mystery that could not be plumbed and thought that men could only philosophize on the basis of their own personal experiences. Wycliffe, who became a doctor of divinity in 1372, was, on the other hand, a realist for whom universals had an objective existence, and he thought religion a fit subject for the philosopher. In lectures delivered at Oxford in the 1370's he argued that human lordship, dominion, or ownership depended upon grace. Therefore, for example, popes and bishops had no right to hold vast properties unless they helped to propagate religion. This doctrine was a useful weapon against worldly bishops like John Stratford and William of Wykeham, who were employed by King Edward III as his ministers. Wycliffe was therefore patronized by John of Gaunt when he attacked his father's clerical government toward the end of the reign. But when Wycliffe began questioning some of the fundamental doctrines of the Roman Church, such as the doctrine of transubstantiation, he was repudiated or at least brushed off. Contemporary with Wycliffe were John Gower and William Langland, two poets in whose work may be seen implicit criticism of the society of their day. Gower, apparently upon the advice of King Richard II, wrote his later poems in English; Langland wrote his celebrated allegory *Piers Plowman* in a west Midland dialect and in the characteristic alliterative style of Anglo-Saxon poetry which had been preserved in the north of England.

Langland, it has been said, wrote in an archaic, even a dying language; Chaucer, for his part, speaks of human nature in an almost modern tongue. Geoffrey Chaucer, son of a merchant, had a varied career. He married a lady of the court and served with King Edward III in France. For several years he was a customs officer in the port of London, living over one of the city gates. At one time he was also a justice of the peace and member of parliament for Kent. He was a man of the world and no puritan. In his *Canterbury Tales,* an account of pilgrims who tell each other stories on their way to the shrine of St. Thomas Becket, we see the real men and women of the fourteenth century—knight and squire, priest and nun, sailor and miller, who may be contrasted with the chivalry of Froissart's chronicles. Sometimes Chaucer mocks the Church, sometimes he praises it. When one thinks of the behavior of the "lewd sots" in Canterbury Cathedral, described in Chaucer, at the one end of the scale of human conduct, and of the reverberations of Wycliffe's not-very-courageous preaching from Oxford at the other; of the anticlerical-ism of Edward III's parliaments and the humiliation of the Papacy after Avignon, one cannot help but feel a little skeptical about the pleas of those historians who warmly defend the virtues of the old English Church or fail to agree with Dr. Coulton that "the very fidelity with which Chaucer paints his own time shows the Reformation in embryo."

To turn from the spiritual to the material world: the beginning of the century was a time of higher prices, prosperous agriculture, growing wool-export trade, and rising population. Between the first half of the thirteenth and the first half of the fourteenth century the price of wheat rose by fifty per cent. More land than ever before was under the plough. Manorial demesnes were cultivated in a businesslike way both by bailiffs on behalf of large landowners and by ecclesiastical corporations with hired labor: food was needed to feed the retainers of the baronage, hired out to the king to help fight his wars, and to sustain the inmates of the monasteries and supply their inns; but surpluses were sent to the market for sale to townsmen or exported to Gascony and other places abroad. Soils were manured and dressed with lime and marl; there was thus in-tensive as well as extensive farming. Sheep were valued for meat and manure as well as for wool, and a primitive form of mixed farming ex-isted in some places. In these prosperous times landlords engaged in "high farming" often found it more economical to employ wage labor than to depend upon the customary manorial services; the villeins, for their part, were anxious to devote as much time as possible to the cultiva-tion of their own acres. Thus commutation of services for money rents had come about. Commutation began earlier in the north than in the south of England, but wage labor in one form or another henceforward played an increasing part in the life of rural England.

Even before the Black Death struck England in the middle of the century, an agricultural depression set in which affected the whole of western Europe. This depression was intensified by the heavy taxation imposed on account of the French war and then was worsened by the plague. The plague carried off half the population upon some manors; by the end of the century (owing to the reduction in the number of chil-dren born) the population of the entire country had fallen considerably.

The landlords' first reactions to the scarcity of labor were to reduce the acreage under cultivation and to try to exact the fullest services from their tenants in villeinage. When they found difficulty in obtaining agricultural workers they leased off their demesne lands. Before the Black Death there appears to have been a waiting list for good land, so that in spite of the plague sufficient tenants were forthcoming. Where labor was employed, higher wages had to be paid despite the new statutes. Villeins had often fled their homes to escape their customary obligations before the Black Death, and the flights continued afterward. By the end of the century "demesne farming" had practically disappeared and a property-owning peasantry had come into being.

Wool and corn continued to be the principal English exports, but the organization of the wool export trade was complicated by the king's wartime need of money and the manipulations of high finance in general. The middlemen wanted a monopoly and were prepared to pay for it, although the arrangement of the "staple" wool-market towns appears to have been of small benefit either to the English wool growers or to foreign buyers. A staple was a fixed place through which the export of wool was compulsorily directed. The first staple was established in the reign of King Edward I. Edward III changed the staple towns several times under pressure from various interests. Sometimes the staple towns were in England, sometimes abroad, finally at Calais, an English overseas possession. Broadly speaking, the king granted this commercial monopoly in return for loans, which eventually ruined most of the financiers who dealt with him. Earlier a group of Italian bankers had burned their fingers with Edward III's war loans. The institution of the various staples was once considered by historians to be proof of an enlightened royal economic policy, but a later view is that the king and the staplers "killed the goose that laid the golden eggs." The beginnings of a native cloth industry was probably the most important if unintended result of the staplers' monopoly, because English clothmakers were able to buy wool more cheaply than their foreign competitors. By the middle of the fifteenth century wool export had declined to one quarter what it had been in the early years of the fourteenth century. The woolen textile industry afforded the earliest investment opportunity to English capitalists, who bought wool and distributed it for spinning in cottage homes, afterwards disposing of the finished product.

All these economic changes, coupled with the ups and downs of the war with France, had profound effects on English society: the agricultural depression, the fall in population consequent upon the Black Death, the growing commutation of manorial labor services, the desire for freedom from serfdom widely seen in English villages, the decline of the wool export trade, the beginnings of a cloth industry, and the rise of early forms of banking and capitalism combined slowly to change the face of the land. These changes were reflected in the increasing significance of the House of Commons and historically are of more importance than constitutional arguments. The price paid for these profound social and economic changes was much discontent and widespread disturbance. In the Great Revolt or Peasants' Revolt which took place during the reign of King Richard II, ordinary English people, so long the playthings of the rich and politically powerful, made a first fleeting appearance in the pages of British history.

XX

Richard II and the Great Revolt

Richard II, like Edward II, succeeded to a doubtful heritage. The country was exhausted by the war against France and humiliated by recent defeats. The late king's sons had quarreled with each other during the closing years of their father's reign, pursuing their own ambitions with little regard for the general interests of the kingdom. Nevertheless the magnates rallied together when the child-king came to the throne. John of Gaunt was reconciled to William of Wykeham. Peter de la Mare, the able Speaker of the Commons in "the Good Parliament," was released from prison where he had been languishing. At first John of Gaunt— whether from modesty or caution—was not a member of the governing or "continual" council, but as steward presided over the coronation of the ten-year-old king. High hopes were expressed for the future of England under the boy Richard, who seemed "as fair as another Absalom" delighting in "a day of joy and gladness." But Richard, who belonged to the third generation, with a warrior father and grandfather, was to prove no soldier himself. Brought up in an atmosphere of flattery and grandeur by a beautiful but vapid mother, he was temperamental and spoiled and in the end balanced upon the edge of madness.

The bright hopes of the coronation were soon dimmed. The French war continued to go badly and the English might have been driven out of all their French possessions had it not been for the fact that in 1380 France was also burdened with a boy king, fought over by his quarrelsome uncles. In the first English parliament of the reign Sir Peter de la Mare demanded that the king's household officers as well as his ministers of state should be nominated by parliament, and that no measures agreed in parliament should be altered or repealed except by parliament. The second parliament of the reign complained about the scale of the royal expenditure, but the war—with defeat again suffered at sea and the southern coasts and Isle of Wight ravaged by foreign foes—made the levying of additional taxes unavoidable: in 1377 a poll tax of fourpence a head, regardless of individual income, was imposed; in 1379 there was a graduated poll tax; and in 1380 the rate was increased to a shilling. This tax, the equivalent of a laborer's weekly wage, touched off a political explosion.

The new tax caused general discontent and was evaded as far as possible. At the end of May 1381 the peasants and fishermen of three marshland villages in Essex rose against the tax collectors and drove them out with stones. The King's Council failed to send a strong force to restore order. Soon blood was shed and the rebellion against public authority spread from village to village throughout the shires around London. Wat Tyler, an ex-soldier with a gift for oratory, assumed the leadership of the Kentish rebels. Ten or fifteen thousand men marched on Canterbury, where they sacked the palace of the archbishop, Simon Sudbury, who was also the royal chancellor. The insurgents then moved upon London, releasing on their way a preacher named John Ball, known as "the mad priest of Kent," who propagated Christian-communist ideals derived from the teaching of the Franciscans. Momentarily the government was paralyzed. The king and his ministers took refuge in the Tower of London. Swollen as it went by artisans with grievances, by criminals, and by the riffraff of the city, the mob swept on; it forced its way across London Bridge, marched along Fleet Street, and burned to the ground the Savoy Palace of John of Gaunt (site of the later Savoy Hotel). Prisons were opened, lawyers' rolls—the bonds of servitude—were burned, and wine from bishops' cellars was drunk. At Mile End, an attractive village to the east of London, the rebel leaders at last foregathered at an invitation from their king.

On June 14 while another rebel leader, Jack Straw, was firing the northern suburb of Highbury, the fourteen-year-old king, accompanied by the mayor of London, a brave man named William Walworth, and a retinue which included the king's mother, met Tyler and yielded to all his requests. Richard II agreed to a petition for the complete abolition of villeinage or manorial servitude and granted the freed villeins the right to rent land at fourpence an acre. He also seems to have told the mob that it might "seize the traitors." At any rate Wat Tyler forced his way into the Tower, which must have been betrayed, laid hold of Archbishop Sudbury and Sir Robert Hales, the treasurer, and had them hacked to death. This was the high point of the rebellion. The mayor of London, the only man who had kept his head, was playing for time and rallying his forces. When Wat Tyler put fresh demands before the king on June 15, the mayor pulled him off his horse at Smithfield and he was killed: Tyler's head replaced that of Sudbury upon London Bridge; the rising in London was at an end. The young king had never intended to keep his promises, but was waiting for the passions of the mob to be sated. Later he told a deputation from Essex: "Villeins ye are and villeins ye shall remain."

The news of the rising had been heard throughout the land: there were sporadic outbreaks of violence in many places, ranging from Somerset to the Scottish border. At St. Albans the abbey was assaulted and the charters destroyed. Near Mildenhall in Suffolk the chief justice, Sir John Cavendish, was captured and executed, as was also the prior of the abbey at Bury St. Edmunds. At Ely a justice of the peace was murdered; in Cambridge, Corpus Christi College was sacked and set on fire; at Norwich the local rebel leader established himself in the castle while his followers plundered the town. But once the insurgents had been suppressed in London and an army had gathered at Blackheath in Kent, the rebellion soon blew itself out. Apart from Wat Tyler it produced no capable chiefs. One or two country gentlemen took the opportunity to work off local grievances, but they were not prepared to assume the leadership of peasants. Judges were sent out to discover and punish the guilty and to restore order. Possibly a couple of hundred were put to death; many others were imprisoned and fined before a general amnesty was granted. The governing powers had had a terrible shock, for they had suddenly witnessed a war of the masses, the desperate rising of common people revealing hatred of their masters.

The causes of the revolt undoubtedly lay in a long-smoldering resentment by the lower classes of their exploitation by landlords. They rebelled against bishops, abbots, and priors and murdered the Archbishop of Canterbury not because they were churchmen but because they were hard masters. A peasant rising in France two decades earlier, known as the Jacquerie, had been almost precisely the same kind, but the rising was sparked off not by desperate poverty, but by a realization of the great contrast that existed in wealth and status. As Sir Charles Oman wrote, "peasant revolts all over Europe were wont to spring up, not in the regions where the serf was in deepest oppression, but in those in which he was comparatively well off, where he was strong enough to aspire to greater liberty and to dream of getting it by force." Kent and

East Anglia, where the revolt was fiercest, were among the most prosperous parts of England. The aim of the rebels was to repudiate the
charters, whether of manors, ecclesiastical corporations, or boroughs, so
as to throw off the yoke of ages and achieve economic if not political
freedom. The incompetence and unpreparedness of the government, the
failure of the French war, and the inequitable taxes had all been factors
in the situation, but a sense of economic injustice lay at the root of it all.

Disturbances took place in many parts of England both before and
after the revolt. For a time afterward there was a reaction during which
some landlords actually tried to tighten the bonds of villeinage, but the
move towards emancipation had begun and later continued unabated.
Manorial serfdom had received a mortal blow from which it never recovered. The rule of law was shown to be shallow. Although the inspiration of the revolt came from the friars, with their doctrines of virtuous poverty, rather than from John Wycliffe, the antipapal propa-
gandist, the material riches of the Church had been nakedly revealed as
a subject of general jealousy. In spite of all that has recently been per-
suasively written about the continuing Christianity of England in the
later Catholic ages, in the Peasants' Revolt may be detected many signs
and portents of the Protestant Reformation that was to come in less than
two hundred years.

The tragedy of King Richard II, it has been said, began at Mile End,
or perhaps one should more correctly say at Smithfield, where he repudiated the promises made in panic to the rebel mob. The boy king,
having first been confronted with the shock of rebellion, then gave way
to fear, and finally learned the art of dissembling. This was ultimately to
become the pattern of his adult political life—dread and cunning, terror
and triumph. Throughout his reign he was under constant pressures, and
was never allowed to choose or at least to keep his own advisers. In
November 1381 parliament appointed Richard, Earl of Arundel, and
Michael de la Pole, later Earl of Suffolk, to be his governors and in the
following year he was married to the pious but nondescript Anne of
Bohemia. The king's favorite was Robert de Vere, Earl of Oxford, who
was even more foolish than Piers Gaveston. De Vere encouraged the
king to resent his tutelage and turned him against his uncles, John of
Gaunt, Duke of Lancaster, and Thomas of Woodstock, later Duke of
Gloucester.

During the following year foreign affairs got out of hand. John of
Gaunt, who had a claim of sorts to the throne of Castile through his
second wife, wanted to wage war against Castile on the side of Portugal
and to make peace with France. The leaders of the English Church were
anxious to launch a "crusade" on behalf of one of the two rival popes

against the other, and an expedition was sent into Flanders under the command of a pugnacious Bishop of Norwich. This was a fiasco and provoked the French. Soon England in turn was menaced with an invasion from France and with troubles upon the Scottish border. An English army entered Edinburgh, but King Richard II withdrew without achieving anything more. John of Gaunt was recognized as king of Castile and allowed to take a force to Portugal. This diversion did not stave off the threat from France. The king's youngest uncle, Thomas of Woodstock, Duke of Gloucester, supported by the Earl of Arundel and his brother Thomas, Bishop of Ely, and other magnates, now blamed the whole menacing situation, the failure of foreign policies, and the high expenditure of the court upon the king's ministers and demanded their dismissal. De la Pole, who was not incompetent, was made a scapegoat, removed from the office of Chancellor, and impeached in parliament. A commission of "moderates" was appointed to control the government, but the king resented his subordination and planned to shake himself free. He obtained a manifesto from the judges condemning the commission as illegal and roamed about the Midlands and north of England in search of military support. When he returned to London in November 1387, a trial of strength between the king and his critics in parliament followed.

These critics became known as the Lords Appellant because they "appealed" for the king's "evil counsellors" to be punished for treason—included were the Archbishop of York as well as De Vere and De la Pole—and accused them of "accroaching the royal power." De Vere tried to save the royalist party by bringing a force south, but it was defeated at Radcot Bridge in Oxfordshire and De Vere himself escaped the vengeance of his enemies only by swimming the Thames and fleeing to France. When parliament met in February 1388, all power was in the hands of the Appellant Lords. The Commons yielded to the wishes of these magnates, who included John of Gaunt's son—Henry of Bolingbroke, Earl of Derby—as well as the Duke of Gloucester and the Earl of Arundel, though they carefully refrained from attacking the king himself. This "Merciless Parliament" carried out murder by statute. The chief justice of the King's Bench, a former mayor of London, and others were put to death for no other crime than their loyalty to their royal master; the judges who had supported the king were sent into banishment.

For a time the Appellants themselves became the king's ministers and advisers: it was a change of government by violence. The King assented and accepted their counsel, but he did not forgive or forget what they had done. In May 1389, when he was twenty-two, he declared himself to be of age and exchanged some of his ministers in favor of "moderates" or "neutrals." In November 1389 when John of Gaunt returned home (having made a profitable private deal out of the war in Castile, marrying his daughters into both the Spanish and Portuguese royal families), he was used again as a buffer between the court and its critics. The next six years were ones of relative peace, although foreign affairs still went badly. The king interested himself in trying to obtain the canonization of King Edward II. In 1394 he visited Ireland where he acted as a conciliator of the native chiefs. After the death of his first wife he married the seven-year-old daughter of the king of France, Charles VI, and concluded a twenty-eight-year truce with that kingdom. Though this truce was not popular, the king's credit stood high in the year 1396. The parliament which met next year allowed him to recall the judges who had been banished by the Lords Appellant. He was on friendly terms with John of Gaunt and had created a new royalist party; he planned to ally himself with the French king, who had promised him support against any would-be rebels; and he even thought of making himself Holy Roman Emperor.

But the opposition of the Lords Appellant to his policies remained firm. Gloucester and Arundel withdrew from his council. Infatuated by his success in the recent quieter years, petulant at resistance to his personal plans, and motivated by a desire for revenge, the king now struck. Three of the Lords Appellant, Arundel, Gloucester, and Warwick, were arrested and the king organized their impeachment. Arundel was beheaded, Gloucester was murdered, Warwick, after abject groveling, was exiled; Thomas Arundel, who had been promoted to Archbishop of Canterbury, was also exiled. The king's friends, who now included Henry of Bolingbroke after he changed sides, were rewarded with dukedoms.

The victors proceeded to quarrel among themselves. Henry of Bolingbroke, Duke of Hereford, accused Thomas Mowbray, Duke of Norfolk, of treasonable conduct, misappropriation, and responsibility for the Duke of Gloucester's murder. The king found these charges not proved, but ordered Hereford to be banished for ten years and Norfolk for life; later he arbitrarily extended the exile of Henry of Bolingbroke to exile for life, and when Henry's father, John of Gaunt, died, he seized his entire inheritance. These were the acts of a lunatic or a tyrant. The king, who already showed signs of mental instability, had allowed his recent political triumphs to go to his head. He sent out agents to collect forced loans, exacted blank charters, forged parliamentary rolls, threatened outlawry upon all and sundry. Depending upon soothsayers for advice, he exhibited all the characteristics of a megalomaniac. While he knew that the exiled Henry of Bolingbroke and Archbishop Arundel were plotting against him in Paris, he elected to revisit Ireland, leaving his incompetent eldest uncle, the Duke of York, in charge of England. The expedition to Ireland, it has been suggested, was necessary because the native Irish had repudiated the promises made to the king in 1394 and were in open rebellion. Be that as it may, England was virtually denuded of all trained and loyal military forces when in July 1399 Henry of Bolingbroke landed at Ravenspur in the Humber and was at once joined by the northern lords. Indeed all the people of the north country were said to have flocked to welcome him in Yorkshire. Nominally he had come to claim his rightful Lancastrian inheritance; but the threat to the throne was clear.

Henry of Bolingbroke sent his forces westward to cut off Richard II, returning to England from Ireland, from his supporters in London and the south. The Duke of York supinely submitted to his nephew and some supporters of the king's party were captured in Bristol. The king eventually landed in Conway, where he was given to understand that he might keep his title and prerogatives if he restored to Henry of Bolingbroke the forfeited Lancastrian inheritance. However, as soon as he left Conway Castle he was ambushed and brought before Henry at Chester. Thence he was conducted to the Tower of London.

When parliament met—if it could be called a parliament without the presence of the king—it was announced that Richard II had abdicated. Henry of Bolingbroke claimed the throne both by virtue of his heredity, as descendant of a younger son of Henry III, and as a conqueror. His claim was agreed and Richard II was deposed; by February 1400 the late king was found dead in Pontefract Castle, whether by murder or suicide nobody knows. Thus in madness, murder, and tragedy ended the line of the Plantagenet kings, and the rule of the Lancastrians began.

XXI

The Reigns of Henry IV and Henry V

However cleverly the hereditary position may have been wrapped up and historically justified, Henry of Bolingbroke had won the throne of England by conquest. If heredity alone had counted, the young Earl of March, descended from an elder son of King Edward III, had a better claim to succeed. King Richard II had been forcibly compelled to abdicate. This "usurpation," as the enemies of King Henry IV called it, cast a blight over the whole of the new reign and poisoned English political history for a century. Henry himself, though he might have enjoyed unmolested the vast estates accumulated by his father, John of Gaunt, was by disposition a soldier of fortune. He had first sided with the Lords Appellant who humbled Richard II and then had turned against them. He was the most traveled of early English kings: he had fought with the Teutonic Knights at the siege of Vilna in Lithuania; he had served on embassies to France; he had visited Jerusalem by way of Vienna and Venice (and brought home a parrot and a leopard). Happily married at sixteen, he was now a harassed widower with six children, the eldest of whom was Henry of Monmouth, the future Henry V. Rich in political experience, he was suave and affable but at the same time practical and unscrupulous. He offered lavish promises to his first parliament, rewarded his friends (stimulating the chivalrous by founding the Order of the Bath), and made ready to contend with his many enemies.

Rebels immediately prepared to seize him at Windsor Castle, but the plot failed and King Richard II, on whose behalf the raising had been planned, was put to death. In due course the king appointed his fellow conspirator, Archbishop Arundel, to be his chancellor and at once gave offices to Henry Percy, Earl of Northumberland, and Ralph Neville, Earl of Westmorland, with whose aid he had won his throne. Parliament voted him taxes, but from the very beginning his income scarcely covered his normal expenses. These were soon increased by wars with Scotland and Wales and trouble with France.

The king of Scotland, Robert III, was a gentle old man whose country was torn by faction. Henry IV was tempted to use this opportunity for intervention and to reassert claims to overlordship abandoned by King Edward II. An expedition, which the king conducted in person, proved fruitless. The Scots retorted by invading Northumberland in 1402, but were defeated by the Percies at the battle of Homildon Hill. Later the heir to the Scottish throne, a boy named James, was captured by English pirates while on his way to France and sent to King Henry IV, who imprisoned him in the Tower of London. The son of the Scottish regent, the Duke of Albany, was also an English prisoner. These lucky captures spiked the Scottish guns and, although border warfare continued, Scotland was largely neutralized throughout the reign.

It was far otherwise in Wales. Here Owen Glendower, who claimed descent from two Welsh royal lines and had also been educated in England and served with the English king abroad, constituted himself a national leader. His rebellion rose out of a squabble with a neighbor, Lord

Grey of Ruthin, who had been favored by King Henry IV. Guerrilla warfare, which lasted for fifteen years, broke out. Glendower captured many of the royal castles in south Wales and defeated the Marcher Lords in battle. He allied himself with the Percies, who turned against their former patron and determined to place the young Earl of March upon the English throne. In July 1403 Henry IV marched north, defeated the Percies near Shrewsbury, and killed Henry Hotspur, the able son of the Earl of Northumberland; the Earl of Worcester was beheaded and Northumberland himself imprisoned. But Glendower fought on. In the spring of 1404 he captured Harlech Castle and the king was obliged to send his son, Henry of Monmouth, now Prince of Wales as well as Duke of Aquitaine, against him. The rebellion spread to the north of Wales, but gradually the young prince mastered the arts of mountain warfare. By the end of 1408 he had retaken Harlech and Aberystwith, though Glendower himself eluded capture.

France, like Scotland, was divided by factions. Her king, Charles VI, was insane most of the time and a struggle for power took place between the king's uncle—the Duke of Burgundy—and the king's brother, the Duke of Orleans. Although a truce with England prevailed, the Orleanists picked a quarrel with Henry IV. In 1403 a French fleet sacked Plymouth, French armies invaded Guienne and menaced Calais, and an attack on the Isle of Wight was repulsed with difficulty. The French gave help to the Welsh and the Scots. In 1407, however, the Duke of Orleans was murdered by the Duke of Burgundy, and both sides became eager for English help.

In 1408 the Percies and their friends once more rose against the king in Yorkshire and were defeated, Northumberland himself being killed. Thus after nearly ten years of trouble and strife the England of Henry IV subsided into a short period of comparative peace. But by this time the king himself, though still in his early forties, was a permanent invalid, wracked by a variety of diseases. His son, the Prince of Wales, who had already proved himself a soldier of genius, was beginning to assume the attributes of monarchy—for example, sending a force into France on his own authority. His allies and friends were his half brothers, the Beauforts, children of John of Gaunt's third wife, but technically bastards (until legitimized by an Act of Henry IV) because they had been born out of wedlock. One of them, Henry Beaufort, Bishop of Lincoln, demanded that the king abdicate. Another, Thomas Beaufort, Marquis of Dorset and admiral of England, for a time ousted the king's old friend, Archbishop Arundel, as Chancellor. The exact relations between the king and his eldest son at the time are obscure but were certainly antagonistic.

For a while the sick monarch aroused himself and dismissed both the prince and the Beauforts from his council, but he was reconciled to his son before he died.

These were not the only domestic woes that clouded King Henry IV's reign. The royal authority had been thoroughly weakened by Richard II's incompetence and arbitrary conduct. Though an act of parliament was passed against the maintenance by the magnates of the realm of liveried retainers—servants whom they employed to overawe the law courts and undermine justice—this act was pretty well a dead letter. A statute passed at the behest of Archbishop Arundel known as *de haeretico comburendo,* which allowed the Church to hand over heretics to be burned by the state, was, on the other hand, implemented. Wandering preachers known as the Lollards, who had been inspired by the unorthodox preaching of John Wycliffe, were the destined victims. William Sawtré, a London priest, was the first of a succession of martyrs to be burned alive at Smithfield in 1401. The parliaments of the reign were obstreperous.

The Commons were reluctant to vote the king money until he attended to their grievances, and parliament as a whole attempted to control appointments both to the King's Council and to his household. At one time the Commons nominated treasurers to administer taxes, while the parliament of 1406 tried to order the actions of the Prince of Wales. But Henry IV managed to borrow money from merchants and, on the whole, resisted the extremes of parliamentary pressure. That he was "a parliamentary king" is a historical misapprehension that has now been abandoned. When he died he had established his dynasty and had not betrayed the traditional prerogatives of the monarchy. Shakespeare made him say to his son—with broad historical justification—of his crown:

> To thee it shall descend with better quiet,
> Better opinion, better confirmation;
> For all the soil of the achievement goes
> With me into the earth.

✿ KING HENRY V

If Henry IV was a wise and fairly successful ruler, though not the premature constitutional monarch he was once supposed to be, his son was a soldier and diplomatist of outstanding qualities who gave his country a moment of excitement and patriotic triumph before early England moved into fifty years of confusion and disillusionment. Henry V's personal ambitions had colored the last years of his father's reign. When he succeeded at the age of twenty-five he had two high aims: to restore Christian order in the country and to conquer France as a preliminary to leading a Crusade to Jerusalem. He was a man of infinite determination and energy. He had learned the art of warfare in Wales and possessed genuine organizing ability. Wary-eyed and square-jawed, courteous and deliberate in his ways, he was much more like Oliver Cromwell than the chivalrous Tudor hero of Shakespeare's plays. He believed that he was predestined by God to conquer and to rule, though, as with Cromwell, doubts assailed him on his deathbed. He had a wide reputation for justice but, again like Cromwell, he could be ruthless upon the field of battle. One historian calls him "an honest fanatic," another "a bigot." Intolerance, however, was no uncommon thing in Christian Europe, and King Henry has rightly been called "steadfast in purpose and honourable in life."

Henry V appointed Bishop Henry Beaufort, his uncle, as his Chancellor but did not quarrel with his father's friend, Archbishop Arundel, whom Beaufort replaced. The new Chancellor made promises of good government to parliament, which voted the king generous taxes. King Henry appealed to parliament to support him against the heretical Lollards, whom he thought his father had treated too lightly. The Lollards, like the later Puritans, believed in the inspiration of the Bible and the right of every sincere Christian to interpret it for himself. They also questioned the Church's title to wealth, property, and power, following Wycliffe's doctrine that dominion (or ownership) was founded upon grace. These two doctrines undermined the whole structure of the Church, but the second of them appealed to laymen who thought that the confiscation of ecclesiastical property would reduce the need for taxation. The Lollards were not abashed by their early martyrdoms, and they had a leader in Sir John Oldcastle, who had fought alongside King Henry V when he was Prince of Wales, had married a rich widow, and was influential in Kent as well as in Wales. It was in Kent that the Great Revolt had been fiercest and it was from Kent that another rebellion was to come during the next reign.

Henry V conceived that the chief danger to his throne lay in the discontents of Oldcastle and his followers rather than in the unruliness in the north of England and the Scottish border country. After the king had vainly attempted to convert Oldcastle to more orthodox opinions, he ordered his arrest. Oldcastle escaped from the Tower of London and is said to have plotted to capture the king after a rising in the city. A number of Oldcastle's followers were hanged or burned to death. Subsequent inquiries indicated that this was to have been a "rising of the lower grades of society, the inarticulate people who came to life for a brief flash in 1381" (Jacob). After many adventures Oldcastle himself was captured in Wales in the autumn of 1417, hanged as a traitor, and then burned as a heretic in the fires of Smithfield. The Lollards were not the only danger to the peace of the realm. But in Wales Owen Glendower had been beaten and was in hiding; in Scotland the regent was kept quiet by the fact that the lawful king as well as his own son were still prisoners in London; Henry V was careful to give a public burial to King Richard II so that impostors should not be used to harass his dynasty. Though the north of England remained restless and lawless, after the first two years of the reign the king's authority was never really threatened.

Having dealt with the traitors and heretics, the new king turned to the realization of his foreign ambitions. The twenty-eight years of truce with France was now about to end. Expeditions carried out during his father's reign had shown that because of the civil war between the Burgundians and the Orleanists and because of the general weakness of the French monarchy the country was almost defenseless against a determined attack. It was a golden opportunity for aggression. On May 31, 1414, ambassadors were sent across the Channel to demand the restitution of the king's ancient rights in France: by these were meant not merely the full ownership of Aquitaine but the restoration of Normandy, Maine, Anjou, Touraine—the entire Angevin heritage. The king also demanded Ponthieu and part of Provence. But he offered to waive his hereditary claim to the French throne if he were allowed to marry Catherine, the daughter of the French king Charles VI. King Henry seems to have believed in the justice of these far-reaching claims and such was the powerlessness of the French Crown that it tried hard to buy him off. Nothing came of the negotiations, so after elaborate preparations had been completed a well-equipped English expeditionary force of 9,000 men landed near the mouth of the Seine in August 1415. King Henry V's plan was to subdue Normandy, the duchy of William the Conqueror, but his ultimate aim was the union of France and England. His first military objective was to secure a good base on French soil. His purpose was to convert Harfleur at the mouth of the Seine into a second Calais.

Harfleur surrendered on September 22, but its siege had cost King Henry one-third of his army. He now decided to advance to Calais by way of upper Normandy. It was a long and difficult march to undertake so late in the year. However, the English troops acquitted themselves well; they got safely past Dieppe and forced the passage of the Somme. The French army, which was at Rouen, decided to fight. Everything was arranged with the most delightful courtesy. Henry V had first proposed to the French dauphin or crown prince that the two of them should fight it out in single combat so as to prevent "the people of God" from destroying one another. The dauphin ignored the offer and French heralds came to the English lines with a formal challenge to battle. The battle took place on October 25, the feast day of Saints Crispin and Crispian, the martyr-cobblers of Soissons. The English king had at his disposal not more than 8,000 men whom he regarded, Cromwell-like, as soldiers of Christ. The contest ranged between two woods—one was named Agincourt—on the road to Calais. The English had the advantage of position, since King Henry was able to deploy three "battles" or "battalions," of which he himself commanded the center one (though he had no reserve), whereas the French had to dispose of their far more numerous army in echelon, since they could not deploy upon a broad front. As at Crécy, each English battle consisted of men at arms flanked by two wings of archers, while the archers were protected by stakes stuck in the ground. Theirs was in fact a defensive position. The battle opened when the French army advanced through the rain and mud in an attempt to ride down the English archers.

After a fierce struggle, during which the English first recoiled and then rallied, the archers were moved forward by King Henry, himself fighting on foot, to roll back the heavily armed French with axe and sword. Many were taken prisoner. When the English king detected a new move by the French cavalry at the rear of their echelon, he ordered that "in face of the new danger every man should kill his prisoners on the spot saving only the dukes, earls and others such high-placed leaders as fell to the King's own share." This was done: throats were cut, heads bashed, bodies "paunched," and once the massacre began even the highly born suffered. Such was the other face of chivalry. The total French loss is estimated at 7,000, the English at about five hundred. At the end of October the English army, depleted more by medical casualties than by battle losses, reached Calais; in the middle of November King Henry V returned to London to be greeted as the hero of Agincourt by cheering crowds of his subjects.

During 1416 Bernard, Count of Armagnac, the leader of the Orleanist party in France, laid siege to the new English base of Harfleur, but it was relieved by King Henry V's able brother, John, Duke of Bedford. Meanwhile diplomatic negotiations went ahead. A treaty was concluded with the German emperor Sigismund, who had vainly tried to act as a mediator between France and England, and a secret agreement was reached with John the Fearless, now the leader of the Burgundian party in France. King Henry V did not abate his high claims and was supported in parliament; he seems to have regarded the diplomatic maneuvers as a mere prelude to the renewal of the war. On August 1, 1417, he landed near Harfleur with an army of between 10,000 and 12,000 men, splendidly equipped and disciplined. Thence he invaded lower Normandy, took and sacked Caen, while John the Fearless, his ally, moved forward from the north to cut off Paris from upper Normandy. During a winter campaign King Henry V overcame the strong fortress of Falaise. By spring he was firmly established in Normandy.

In May 1418 the Burgundians took Paris, which was betrayed from within, imprisoned and killed Count Bernard of Armagnac, and occupied castles on the upper Seine. The question now was whether the victorious Burgundians would remain loyal to their English ally or turn against him in defense of the French monarchy. The English leaders did not doubt that Duke John the Fearless would engage in double-dealing if he could; he tried to save Rouen, the capital of Normandy, from an English siege and opened negotiations with the new French dauphin (who appears to have been a bastard). But King Henry V made steady military progress. In January 1419 he entered Rouen, which the Burgundians had failed to relieve, and then occupied Gisors and Pointoise, thereby threatening Paris. At the same time he stated his terms. According to one account, he said that if he were allowed to keep the whole of Normandy and Aquitaine, he would marry Princess Catherine (whom he had just met) and consent to permanent peace. By the autumn his position was immeasurably strengthened by a tragic event, for when on September 10, 1419, Duke John the Fearless went to meet the Dauphin he was treacherously murdered. His son and successor, Duke Philip, at once determined to avenge himself by coming to a full agreement with King Henry V.

The English king immediately made it clear to Duke Philip that he would not tolerate the double-dealing he had suffered at the hands of his murdered father. On Christmas Day a formal Anglo-Burgundian treaty was signed; this was followed in May 1420 by the Treaty of Troyes between France and England, whereby Henry V promised to marry Princess Catherine, daughter of the mad King Charles VI, and was acknowledged the heir to the French throne, in preference to the doubtful dauphin, as soon as his prospective father-in-law should die. The territorial clauses of the treaty were somewhat vague and became the subject of much future dispute. King Henry promised to reduce to obedience all parts of France which continued to accept the rule of the disinherited dauphin, while he seems to have assumed that the whole of Normandy was to be his in full sovereignty. But presumably nothing was more important than the grand prospect of the ultimate union of the Crowns of England and France. Henry V was but thirty and about to marry. No doubts existed that once the treaty had been ratified by the parliaments of the two nations, all would be finally settled and the long war would close in an English triumph.

Such are the vanities of human hopes. In the end the Treaty of Troyes proved an expensive burden to the English. Much blood was to flow and much money to be spent before the dreams of an Anglo-French union were dissipated. The dauphin continued to fight and in 1421 Henry V's eldest brother, the Duke of Clarence, was killed by his troops. Henry V had to collect funds and soldiers and return to France to push back his remaining enemy. The dauphin laid siege to Chartres and actually threatened to retake Paris. Henry V thrust him back behind the river Loire and set himself to subdue the remaining hostile fortresses in northern France. In May 1422 the English king forced one of them, Meaux, to the east of Paris, to surrender and hanged its governor on his own elm tree. During the drawn-out siege Henry contracted dysentery; by midsummer he knew he was dying. He commended the government of France to his brother John, Duke of Bedford, and that of England to another brother, Henry, Duke of Gloucester. They were instructed to care for the wonderful inheritance of the baby prince who had been born of his French mother in the previous year. Henry V died on August 31, 1422, in the country which he believed that he had conquered.

XXII

The Loss of France and the Wars of the Roses

With the early death of King Henry V, England was faced with a long royal minority during which the Council, ruling in a child's name, was responsible not merely for his kingdom but for the government of France as well. When King Henry VI, the only child of the hero of Agincourt, ultimately assumed authority many years later, he proved to be a simple-minded and petulant ruler, lacking in virility, unable to live in London, disliking hunting and war, dependent upon a narrow group of advisers, amiable but completely ineffective. Some called him a Maecenas, others a saint. He inherited little of his father's genius and a great deal of his mother's bad blood. In the end, like his grandfather, he went mad. But before all this occurred and finally made certain the overthrow of the Lancastrian monarchy, England was torn by dissensions and rivalries between the magnates of the realm and was weighed down with the heavy responsibilities that grew out of Henry V's conquest of France.

In his brother John, Duke of Bedford, King Henry V left a capable regent of France and a clever soldier. His outstanding abilities and the demoralization of the defeated French explain why the English managed to retain some hold upon France for more than thirty years. The mad King Charles VI soon followed Henry V to the grave; but the young dauphin, who assumed the title of Charles VII, retained control over much of central and southern France. The English held Paris and most of the area around the capital as well as Normandy and Gascony, while their ally Duke Philip ruled in Burgundy and lent them his support. Slowly Charles VII, a strange, degenerate, and unattractive prince, but not without a low sort of cunning, built up an administration at Bourges. Meanwhile the Duke of Bedford did his utmost to provide honest government and to give the French subjects of the English Crown reasonable treatment. He relied upon French advisers and officials and upheld French laws. But the resources at his disposal were not large; he had relatively few troops with which to maintain order and consolidate conquest. Since he received little money from England, he had to levy taxes which fell heavily upon the city of Paris and upon the Normans. All this created a sense of resentment and heightened the natural distaste for alien government.

Charles VII, the "king of Bourges," also had his problems. It is true that he had the support of the Orleanists and most of the appanaged princes of France, and that he had bigger resources at his disposal than Bedford. But he lacked an army. He was dependent upon brigand chiefs —survivors of the French civil wars—and on imported mercenaries supplied by the regent of Scotland. When he attempted to attack the territory of Burgundy he was defeated at the battle of Cravant in August 1423, and a year later the Duke of Bedford decisively defeated a force consisting mainly of Scottish mercenaries at Verneuil in southern Normandy.

Meanwhile Bedford's younger brother Humphrey, Duke of Gloucester, a man of broad ambitions and small capacities, except for his patronage of the arts (the Bodleian Library at Oxford owes much to him), added considerably to his difficulties. The duke elected to marry the divorced wife of a member of the younger branch of the House of Burgundy. This lady claimed to possess in her own right substantial territories in northern France and she encouraged her husband to lay hold of them. Gloucester landed at Calais, but on meeting resistance fled home, leaving his wife a prisoner of war and consoling himself with one of her ladies in waiting. This episode naturally provoked Bedford's ally, Duke Philip of Burgundy. Nevertheless the Anglo-Burgundian alliance endured for some years. Bedford himself married a sister of Philip of Burgundy. In 1425 the area of France under English control was extended by the capture of the city of Le Mans in Maine, to the south of Normandy: this was virtually the last conquest to be made in the name of King Henry VI.

Meanwhile Duke Humphrey of Gloucester, having done enough mischief in France, returned to England, where he had never been fully entrusted with the regency which had been assigned to him under the terms of King Henry V's will. He had to be content with the title of Lord Protector—except when his elder brother was in England—and not of regent, and his authority was strictly limited by that of the Council of State headed by his uncle Henry Beaufort, Bishop of Winchester, a scheming prelate of much ability, reputedly the richest man in the country. Gloucester himself, however, was not without resources: he was handsome and charming, popular with Londoners, artists, and women. At one time the rivalry between the two factions reached such a pitch that the retinues of Beaufort and Gloucester came to blows upon London Bridge. In 1426 Bedford had to visit England to patch up their differences.

On his return to France from his mission of conciliation, the Duke of Bedford concentrated upon consolidating his rule there. The outlook appeared to be good. The alliance with Burgundy was still reasonably firm; the release of King James I of Scotland from his long imprisonment in England, in return for a large ransom, created trouble in that northern kingdom, where the Albany family did not welcome his return, and this reduced the amount of Scottish assistance given to the French king. The conquest of Maine enabled English troops to threaten the whole of the middle Loire. There were many quarrels and much demoralization at the court of Bourges. Bedford now decided to lay siege to the city of Orléans.

The siege of Orléans began in October 1428. Suddenly and unexpectedly the initiative passed to the French. A young peasant girl named Joan of Arc, whom her admirers called a saint and her enemies a witch, appeared, dressed like a boy, to inspirit King Charles VII and his soldiers, offering them divine guidance in their war against the English and the Burgundians. She relieved Orleans and, after leading the king to be crowned in Rheims Cathedral, advanced with the army to the siege of Paris itself. The siege was repulsed; later at Compiègne the "Maid of Orléans," as she was called, was taken prisoner. In February 1431 she was tried and condemned as a witch by Norman judges. On May 30 she was burned at the stake in the market place of Rouen.

The temporary triumph and final martyrdom of Joan of Arc have been the subject of many splendid works of literature; but French historians have pointed out that they did not constitute the turning point in the war against the English in France. She had not succeeded in converting the guerrilla war into a war of liberation. For six months after her death little happened. Nevertheless the English army of occupation had been upset by her "miracles." The coronation of Henry VI as king of France scarcely offset the impact that she had made. However, the death of the selfless Duke of Bedford at Rouen six years later was certainly a turning point. Already Duke Philip of Burgundy had deserted the English alliance by making a truce with King Charles VII. The English had suffered defeats in Normandy and at last were forced to enter into negotiations with the French king at Arras. Here they were offered—and refused—the retention of Normandy if they would evacuate Paris; at the same time it was proposed that one of the daughters of King Charles VII should marry the English king. The offer was rejected even by the dying Bedford. Under the impulse of patriotic English fervor, exemplified in meetings of parliament, war continued and was declared against Burgundy as well as against France.

Richard, Duke of York, a descendant of King Edward III's second son, Lionel, Duke of Clarence, was chosen King Henry VI's lieutenant-general to renew the campaign in France, while Humphrey, Duke of Gloucester, was appointed captain of Calais. The French now turned to the offensive. There was a rising against the English in Normandy. After desertions by the garrison in Paris, which had been reduced to a state of starvation, King Charles VII at length entered his capital in 1437. The English, sustained with fresh supplies voted by parliament, counterattacked. When Philip of Burgundy, having changed sides, laid siege to Calais, he was repulsed by the exertion of English sea power; the Duke of York recovered some of the lost districts of Normandy; and a Scottish attack on the north of England, in support of the French, was defeated: after this King James I of Scotland was murdered and King James II sought peace.

After capturing Paris the French proceeded systematically to clear the English from the north, while the English clung on to Calais and Harfleur, to Normandy, and to Guienne in the south. Frequent changes of command were not conducive to English military success; the Duke of York resigned in favor of the Earl of Warwick, who was succeeded after his death by John Beaufort, Duke of Somerset; then the Duke of York again took command. In 1442 while York again had the title of lieutenant-general, Somerset was sent to Guienne. The King's Council had to decide whether the main effort should be directed to Normandy or to Guienne, both of which were now in peril, and to choose between

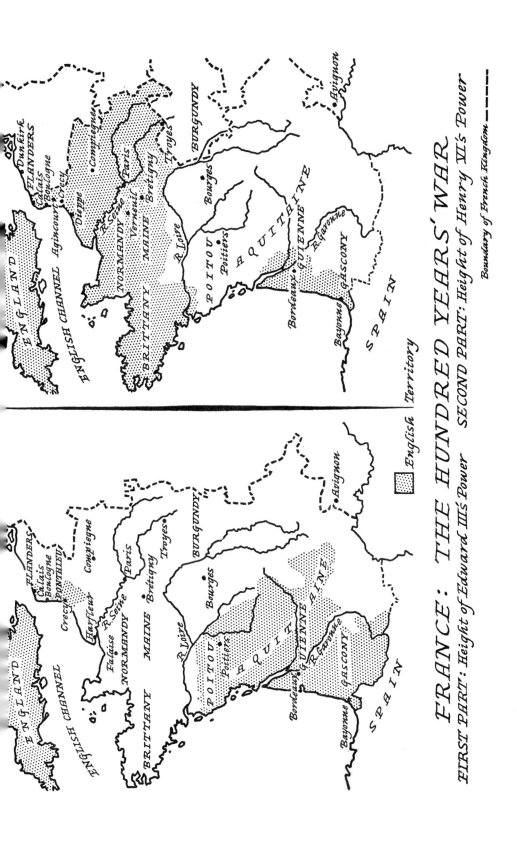

FRANCE: THE HUNDRED YEARS' WAR

FIRST PART: Height of Edward III's Power   SECOND PART: Height of Henry VI's Power

English Territory

Boundary of French Kingdom

the relative claims to precedence of the Duke of York and the Duke of Somerset. The decision went in favor of Somerset (his uncle Henry, now a cardinal, was the leading member of the Council at the time), but his expedition to Bordeaux proved to be a costly failure and soon afterward he died. Peace negotiations were then reopened with the French king. It was suggested that Henry VI should abandon the title of king of France; but retain Normandy, Maine, and Guienne in full sovereignty; and marry Margaret of Anjou, a niece by marriage of the French king. The principal English negotiator was William de la Pole, Earl of Suffolk. He found the French extremely stiff; but, anxious to achieve something to justify himself and his mission, he agreed at Tours to the marriage in return for a short two-year truce, secretly promising also to surrender English strongholds in Maine. This unhappy truce of Tours eventually cost Suffolk his life, though more immediately it earned him a dukedom.

King Henry VI was now twenty-three, an amiable, cultured, and even saintly nonentity who was dominated by his new French wife and by the Duke of Suffolk. The figures who had loomed so large at the beginning of his reign as a minor were passing away. In 1447 Humphrey of Gloucester, who had never recovered from his duchess's condemnation for witchcraft by the Church, was arrested and murdered; Cardinal Beaufort, his old enemy, died six weeks afterward. But the new regime did no better than the old. In 1448 Maine surrendered to the French; during the next two years the whole of Normandy was lost. A relieving force, dispatched by Suffolk, was overwhelmed at the battle of Formigny in April 1450. Three years later all the English possessions in southern France were lost as well. Of the wonderful conquest of King Henry V only Calais remained.

Why did the English lose the Hundred Years' War with France? It was a question of personalities, resources, and patriotism. Henry V had commanded wide loyalties—after all, nothing succeeds like success—and found an able successor in John, Duke of Bedford. But Bedford was not himself a king and had to leave behind in England a quarrelsome and divided Council which was unable or unwilling to raise the means for sustaining the English occupation. In the late 1430's England was riddled by famine and discontent, while her rulers were mostly selfish and incompetent. In France, on the other hand, the degenerate Charles VII was transformed from the despicable "king of Bourges" into a real master of his kingdom, not by some miraculous transformation of his own qualities, but because he found in the end such a capable group of soldiers and administrators that he earned the title of "the Well-Served." Saint Joan of Arc had helped to conjure up a sense of national patriotism. In the twenty years after her death France fashioned a standing army and a permanent system of taxation. Fighting upon inner lines in co-operation with Duke Philip of Burgundy, employing artillery in support of infantry, the French royal armies gradually shook off the pressure of English military power—now depending on a navy which, possessing bases in Bordeaux, Harfleur, and Calais, maintained the war against a more populous nation much longer than might otherwise have been expected; but ultimate defeat had become practically certain, and the price that had to be paid was anarchy and administrative chaos in England itself. The loss of the French war by the Lancastrian dynasty was one of the principal causes of the political demoralization which formed the background for the so-called Wars of the Roses.

THE WARS OF THE ROSES

The simple-minded King Henry VI and his French queen, Margaret of Anjou, were now left high and dry in the political world, flanked by two unsuccessful ministers, the Duke of Suffolk and Edmund Beaufort, second Duke of Somerset, who, though not a bad general, paid the penalty for having been governor of Normandy while it was being regained by the French monarchy. In 1450 Somerset was in Calais and Richard, Duke of York, was in Ireland, having been appointed Lord Lieutenant there three years earlier. Cardinal Beaufort and Duke Humphrey of Gloucester were dead. Parliament, meeting early in that year, sought a scapegoat for the national humiliation in the French war. The king vainly tried to protect Suffolk by sending him into banishment, but he was murdered by royal naval captains while trying to escape abroad. That the discontent with the king's government was not confined to the aristocracy was shown by the character of Suffolk's murder, by the behavior of the commons, and by the rising of "Jack Cade," which took place in the same year. "Cade" was a Kentishman, apparently of good birth, who persuaded the gentry and yeomen not only of Kent but of Sussex and Surrey as well to follow him.

The origins of the revolt are obscure, but the insurgents demanded that the king's debts should be paid and the Crown lands not alienated, that there be free election of knights of the shire to parliament and strengthening of justice throughout the land. The loss of the king's territories in France was blamed upon the treason of his ministers. All this reflected in a sharper and more threatening manner complaints and criticisms already voiced in parliament. Cade and his men marched into London almost without meeting resistance. They executed Lord Say, formerly the Lord Treasurer, in Cheapside and won a battle upon London Bridge. The king himself had withdrawn from London and was compelled to offer an amnesty to the rebels. But, like Wat Tyler before him, Cade was finally caught and killed. Nevertheless the local risings continued for some time. The Duke of York returned from Ireland and the Duke of Somerset from Calais; the profound dissatisfaction with the government meant that the lines were being drawn for civil war.

What were the origins or causes of the Wars of the Roses? The Wars of the Roses were so called because the emblem of the Lancastrians or followers of King Henry VI and Queen Margaret was a red rose, while the rose of the Yorkists or supporters of Richard, Duke of York, and his son Edward was white; although in fact the red rose was not adopted as a Lancastrian emblem until the wars were over. Fundamentally this was a dynastic struggle, for when it began King Henry VI was childless. The two claimants to succeed him were Richard, Duke of York, who, whether the royal descent were traced through the male or female lines, had an excellent claim stemming from his relationship to King Edward III. The other claimant was Edmund Beaufort, Duke of Somerset; the Beauforts were descendants of John of Gaunt. The difficulty was that they had been specifically excluded from the succession by an Act of 1407 passed with the approval of Henry IV, the founder of the House of Lancaster. But the position was even more complicated than that, for in 1453 Queen Margaret gave birth to a son. Unexpected this may have been, and the child's legitimacy was considered doubtful by many people; nevertheless, unless the baby prince could be proved a bastard, he was the unquestionable heir to the Lancastrian throne. But nobody wanted another minority. Henry VI's obvious incapacity for government cried out for a remedy. Moreover his incapacity was proved beyond a doubt when he went mad in the same year, 1453, after becoming a father; and the road was wide open for the most powerful of his subjects who had any plausible claim of royal descent to overthrow him. After all, though this was never stated in so many words, the kings of England had rarely paid scrupulous regard to the claims of legitimacy through primogeniture. Henry IV, for example, had possessed no unquestionable right to succession, any more than had King Alfred or Harold II, William II, or Stephen. The country had now become divided between two contending aristocratic factions. Law and order had largely ceased to prevail. The king was dependent for the enlistment of an army upon the retainers of the great lords of his realm: if they were not prepared to follow and obey him, then power reverted to the strongest on "the good old-fashioned plan." The weak character of the king, the disgrace of the lost French war, and the unpopularity of the French queen all helped to raise opposition to the governing set. The natural leader of this opposition was Richard, Duke of York, until 1453 the heir presumptive to the throne. On one side were marshaled behind the queen and the Lancastrians all the Beauforts, headed by the second Duke of Somerset; Henry Holland, Duke of Exeter; Jasper Tudor, Earl of Pembroke; James Butler, Earl of Wiltshire; John Talbot, Earl of Shrewsbury; Henry Percy, Earl of Northumberland; Richard Wyndeville, Earl of Rivers; Lord Clifford; Lord Beaumont; and Lord Egremont. On the other side, led by the Duke of York and his sons Edward, Earl of March, and Edmund, Earl of Rutland, were Richard Neville, Earl of Salisbury; Richard, his son, Earl of Warwick; Ralph Neville, Earl of Westmorland; John Mowbray, Duke of Norfolk; Lord Abergavenny; Lord Cobham; Lord Fauconberg; Lord Bourchier; Archbishop Bourchier; and the Bishop of Salisbury and of Exeter, who was the Earl of Warwick's brother. The Duke of Bedford, the Earl of Devon, and Lord Audley changed sides in the course of the wars. A certain pattern was given to these rivalries by a long-standing enmity between the Percy and Neville families, both of whom owned wide territories in the north of England.

Some historians have traced these aristocratic feuds back to the so-called "appanage" policy of King Edward III, who built up wealthy conglomerations of territory for the benefit of his sons. Others would place the emphasis, in considering the origin of the wars, on a general degeneration stemming from the English failure in the long struggle with France, which had undermined public and private morality and produced unemployed warriors ready to fight for whoever paid them best. Perhaps the central cause was the complete failure of the monarchy to provide political leadership, as had happened before under Edward II and to a lesser extent under Richard II. But the situation had deteriorated, it is argued, because old loyalties to the crown had ceased to exist. The retainer now fought for the magnate who employed him and the magnate fought for himself. It was a world of the few; on the whole, the lower classes from the gentry downward stood aside from these Wars of the Roses, which were fought out by the great men of the country and their immediate followers. When the dust of battle finally subsided, it was evident that ordinary life had gone on much as before and that less destruction had been done than the flow of "purple" blood might make a chronicler suppose.

In November 1451 the Duke of Somerset, King Henry VI's principal minister, was attacked at a meeting of parliament on account of the loss of the French war, and two months later a member of the House of Commons asked that the Duke of York be recognized as heir to the throne. The Duke of York, for his part, promised his loyalty to the king as long as he lived but sought the overthrow of his existing rival for the succession, the Duke of Somerset. This was the real beginning of the clash. York hoped that Somerset would be placed under arrest; instead he was arrested himself, though he was released after he had promised good conduct. In 1453, the year the Hundred Years' War reached its end with the loss of Bordeaux, King Henry VI had his first mental breakdown, York was appointed Lord Protector, and Somerset was imprisoned. Next year, however, the king recovered, Somerset was released, and the civil war began.

It was not a continuous civil war; nor did public administration collapse throughout the entire country. Although many eminent men were killed in battle or murdered, the battles were mostly upon a small scale: one side had only to show itself to be in a stronger position for the other to yield gracefully. The first battle was fought in January 1455 at St. Albans, where Somerset himself was killed. By the end of the year the king was again taken ill and York again became Lord Protector; but the following year the king recovered and York and his friends were relieved of their posts. Then an interlude followed during which the Percies and Nevilles engaged in their private war and there were many local outbreaks of violence. The civil war proper was resumed in 1459, but the Yorkists gave in after a skirmish at Ludlow in the Midlands and a meeting of parliament in Coventry passed bills of attainder against the duke and his chief supporters. This made certain a renewal of the fighting.

In 1460 the Yorkists invaded England from both France and Ireland. Richard Neville, Earl of Warwick who had earned himself a military reputation in the defense of Calais, landed at Sandwich in Kent, which had already been seized on behalf of the Yorkists, published a manifesto, and marched upon London. The royalists panicked and were beaten at the battle of Northampton (July 7, 1460), where King Henry VI was taken a prisoner. Richard, Duke of York, did not himself arrive from Ireland until September, although his eldest son Edward, Earl of March, had come over with the Earl of Warwick. The duke now showed himself both over-ambitious and irresolute. His claim to the throne was rebuffed by the House of Lords; a compromise was reached whereby the king recognized him as his heir and declared him Protector. But Queen Margaret, now the soul of the Lancastrian party, was made of sterner stuff. She retreated with her baby son into Wales and organized the resumption of the war. On December 30, 1460, York himself died heroically at the battle of Wakefield, the Earl of Salisbury was murdered, and the Earl of Warwick defeated in the second battle of St. Albans.

The Lancastrian triumph was short-lived; indeed the Royalists had already done their best. The Yorkist claim was taken up vigorously by Edward, Earl of March, who at the age of nineteen proved himself to be both a political and a military strategist of quality. Taking advantage of the Lancastrians' failure to advance on the capital after their victories in Yorkshire, he entered London in March 1461 and assumed the title of King Edward IV. He gathered an army and marched rapidly north to win decisively the battle of Towton in Yorkshire, the bloodiest battle of the Wars of the Roses, which was fought on Palm Sunday 1461. Many Lancastrian leaders perished there and the king and queen fled toward Scotland. Although King Henry VI lived on for another ten years, the battle of Towton signified the end of his abysmal reign.

✿ KING EDWARD IV

King Edward IV had many characteristics in common with a later English monarch belonging to another dynasty, the Stuart king Charles II. Like him, Edward was affable, easy of access, and had a sense of humor; like him he was lazy, though capable of outbursts of energy and decision. He was astute and enjoyed having his own way; he loved money and women. He owed his throne chiefly to the support of the mighty Neville family; since the death of his father the influence of his cousin, Richard Neville, Earl of Warwick, had been paramount. Warwick was an extremely ambitious man who had evident hopes of ruling in the new king's name.

The Lancastrians were still not beaten; indeed there were two kings in the land. The indefatigable Queen Margaret thought she might yet regain power for her husband either with the help of the Scots or the French. Twice the Scots invaded Northumberland and twice they were repulsed. These campaigns, directed by Warwick on Edward IV's behalf, were followed by further executions, a third Beaufort, Duke of Somerset, being beheaded on the field of battle. There were indeed "bloody assizes" in which more aristocrats perished. While these events were taking place the king had remained in the south of England and had unexpectedly found himself a wife in Elizabeth Wydeville (or Woodville), the daughter and the widow of Lancastrians.

It has sometimes been asserted that Queen Elizabeth was lowly born. In fact her mother was the widow of John, Duke of Bedford, and a French princess in her own right. Her father was Earl of Rivers. She was evidently a woman of strong personality and attraction. Edward IV, again like Charles II, was a man with many mistresses, but the widow, who was older than he was, knew her way about and had demanded and secured marriage. This marriage was the cause of a breach between Edward IV and the Earl of Warwick. Warwick had been anxious to negotiate an alliance between Louis XI (who succeeded Charles VII as king of France) and Edward IV and to seal it with a marriage of convenience. The king, however, was less eager for this, since at the back of his mind was a desire to reassert old English claims to French territories, perhaps in alliance with the future Charles the Bold of Burgundy, the successor to Duke Philip. Gradually the way was cleared for the king to follow his own bent. The capture of the lunatic King Henry VI in Lancashire appeared to bring the internal wars to an end. In 1467 Edward married his sister to the future Charles the Bold; in the same year he dismissed one of the Neville family, George, Archbishop of Canterbury, from the post of Chancellor and proceeded to promote his wife's relatives to important posts and to arrange the marriages of her sisters to some of the wealthiest men in the country.

The king's enemies were also making their plans. Louis XI, a clever intriguer known as "the Spider," aimed at embarrassing Edward IV by reviving the ebbing Lancastrian cause. Warwick, for his part, entered into a conspiracy with Edward's own brother, George, Duke of Clarence, offering him his daughter Isabel in marriage. In the summer of 1468 parliament met, the new Chancellor addressed it in patriotic terms, and war was declared against France. The tempo now quickened. Jasper Tudor, the Lancastrian Earl of Pembroke, landed in Wales and raised an insurrection; another independent rising took place in Yorkshire; and a conspiracy against the throne was discovered and crushed in London. Meanwhile an English fleet cruised the Channel under one of the Wydevilles, while Warwick and the other Nevilles openly declared against Edward IV. While the king's forces were moving north to deal with the rising in Yorkshire, Warwick entered London unopposed. The Yorkists were beaten at the battle of Edgcote and King Edward IV himself was taken a prisoner. But the Earl of Warwick's triumph was brief. He had taken fearful vengeance upon the Wydevilles—the queen's father was executed by his orders—but he unwisely permitted Edward IV to go free, evidently hoping to be allowed to govern the country in his name. Less than nine months after Edgcote, King Edward IV gathered an army together, declared Warwick and Clarence to be traitors, and forced them to flee the country.

King Louis XI of France, who had already been stirring up trouble for Edward IV, stepped in to do the obvious thing. He persuaded the Earl of Warwick to come to terms with Queen Margaret and the Lancastrians. The compact between them was signed at Angers in August 1470 and next month Warwick landed at Dartmouth in the southwest and marched on London, where he released King Henry VI from his prison in the Tower. In the spring of the following year Edward IV, sustained by his ally Charles, Duke of Burgundy, retorted by invading England from Flushing, disembarking in Yorkshire at the very same port where Henry IV had landed more than half a century earlier. The Duke of Clarence hastened to change sides once again. Warwick met his fate at the battle of Barnet, fought in April 1471, where after a prolonged struggle his army was beaten and he himself slain. A month later Queen Margaret, who had raised an army under the fourth Duke of Somerset, was defeated at the battle of Tewkesbury. Somerset was killed, as was also the queen's only son, Prince Edward. The queen herself was taken prisoner and within a month it was known that King Henry VI had died in the Tower, although the manner of death has never been discovered. Thus in a mighty holocaust most of the Lancastrians and much of the House of Neville had disappeared, and King Edward IV was left at last firmly seated upon his blood-stained throne.

For the next decade England emerged from her aristocratic blood bath into a period of comparative peace and prosperity. Between them the king's two brothers, Clarence and Richard, Duke of Gloucester, gobbled up most of the vast Neville estates under the respectable cover of marrying Neville women (though they quarreled over their shares of the booty). By confiscations from his defeated foes and by obtaining "gifts" or "benevolences" from those of the magnates who had survived—many of whom were compromised in one way or another—the king avoided any financial difficulties and was therefore in no hurry to call parliaments. (He was also said to have shown a neat hand at "touching" wealthy widows for money.) A council was set up to govern much of Wales, while Edward's able brother Richard was put in charge of the north. Business and commerce revived; merchants and ordinary country gentry were grateful. A treaty with the Hanseatic League in northern Europe opened the way to an expansion of overseas trade.

In 1475 Edward IV fulfilled his obligations to his brother-in-law Charles, Duke of Burgundy, and to himself by invading France, after extracting a large grant from parliament. Neither the astute king of France nor the king of England intended to carry his hostilities unreasonably far. In spite of Charles the Bold's indignant protests, they soon came to terms. Louis XI bought off the invader with substantial sums of money and allowed him to retain the empty title of king of France. Thus, like Charles II after him, Edward IV was able to live off French subsidies and enjoy his mistresses in comfort. The quiet of the last years of his reign was disturbed only by a quarrel with his brother Clarence, who, like so many others, met a mysterious end in the Tower of London. On March 30, 1483, this wealthy, successful, idle, and ruthless king died in his bed at the age of forty, worn out, it is said, by a life of self-indulgence.

Towns underlined
indicate where
battles occurred

Lancaster

York
Towton
R. Humber

Ravenspur

Wakefield

Stoke
Nottingham

Bosworth

Northampton

R. Severn

Tewkesbury

St. Albans

Milford
Haven

Edgecote

Barnet
London

R. Thames

Sandwich

ENGLAND AND WALES in Wars of the Roses

❀ KING RICHARD III

Prince Edward, the eldest son of King Edward IV, was a boy of twelve when his father died. The two strongest personalities left in the country were the Queen Mother, Elizabeth Wydeville, and the late king's brother, Richard, Duke of Gloucester. The queen and her numerous relatives had made themselves unpopular with many by reason of their greed, but Richard had been successful as a soldier and as the king's lieutenant in the north of England and had served his brother loyally even to the extent, according to some accounts, of carrying out the murder of King Henry VI on his behalf. He was a man of devouring personal ambitions, anxious to compensate himself for being smaller than most men and for having a slightly crooked shoulder and a withered left arm. Of a high-strung temperament and a melancholy, suspicious nature, he may well have imagined that the Queen Mother was planning to deprive him of the Protectorate which now seemed to be his by right.

At any rate his first action was to intercept Lord Rivers, the queen mother's brother, and her son by her first marriage, Sir Richard Grey, while they were bringing Prince Edward up to London from the west. With the aid of the Duke of Buckingham, Richard arrested both of them, dispersed the prince's retinue and himself carried the prince on to London. Here the Duke of Gloucester was recognized as Protector by the lords of the Council. Prince Edward was lodged in the Tower of London, pending his coronation, which was announced for June 22, 1483. Now Richard struck swiftly. On June 13 after another meeting of the Council, Lord Hastings, who had been a close confidant of King Edward IV, was arrested and put to death without trial for alleged treason. Other members of the Council including the Archbishop of York; John Morton, Bishop of Ely; and Lord Stanley were also arrested. Next the queen mother was forced to surrender her second son by the late king, Richard, Duke of York, who was put with his brother into the Tower. The preposterous argument was put forward that all the late king's children had been illegitimate, and were indeed the products of witchcraft, and that therefore Richard, Duke of Gloucester, was the rightful heir to his brother's throne. This doctrine was sold to the representatives of the city of London and a meeting of "parliament" or "estates of the realm" was held at St. Paul's Church. On the very same day Lord Rivers and other friends of the queen mother were beheaded in Yorkshire. On June 26 Richard III was enthroned. Troops were brought down from the north to overawe the capital; an amnesty was proclaimed. Tacit, but not enthusiastic, support was given to the new usurpation. On July 6 a splendid coronation was organized. The so-called reign of King Edward V was at an end. One of the bishops announced that God had sent King Richard III "to us for the weal of us all."

While the new king began a series of royal progresses in the Midlands and north to establish his authority, King Edward V and his younger brother were murdered in the Tower. At this point Richard III's fellow conspirator, the Duke of Buckingham, turned against him. His plan was to replace Richard III with Henry Tudor, Earl of Richmond, the representative of the line of Beauforts, and to marry the earl to Princess Elizabeth, the eldest surviving daughter of the late King Edward IV, thereby uniting the royal claims of both the Lancastrians and the Yorkists—blending the two roses. The plot failed. Buckingham was executed, and most of the remaining conspirators fled to France, where Henry of Richmond was already in exile. In January 1484 a parliament met, passed a bill of attainder against these rebels, and confirmed the title of the new king.

This parliament, the only one to meet during King Richard III's reign, was notable for a number of reforms. It passed acts to prevent the intimidation of juries and to abolish the "benevolences" exacted by King Edward IV. Promises were made that extortion would be stopped, that justice would be improved, and morality proclaimed. How far these statutes and promises were window dressing is hard to say. They form a basis for some writers to argue that Richard III was a humane and benevolent ruler.

Certainly the king attempted to induce the people at large to forget the violence with which he had seized the throne. He dangled concessions before the queen dowager, whose sons and brothers he had murdered. He is even said, after his own wife died, to have offered to marry his niece Elizabeth to prevent her espousal to his rival, Henry of Richmond, though he personally denied the story. He preached morality, announcing that it was his "fervent desire to see virtue and cleanness of living to be advanced, increased, and multiplied." But neither pious sentiments nor military preparations could avert the coming storm.

While King Richard III was collecting money—the means he used were called "malevolences" in contrast with his brother's "benevolences" —many clergy and gentry were escaping from the country to join Henry of Richmond in France. Richard III's only son died and he cast about desperately for a successor. He moved about the north of England, and in June 1485 published from Nottingham a proclamation against Henry of Richmond. But the sands were running out. In August, with the connivance of King Louis XI of France, the Earl of Richmond collected an invasion force at Rouen and sailed from Harfleur to Milford Haven in Pembrokeshire, where his own family was most influential. The two armies met near Bosworth in Leicestershire on August 21. Nearby hovered another army under Lord Stanley, member of a rising Lancashire family, who had entered into the conspiracy against Richard III but hesitated to declare against him because his son was in the king's power.

The king's army was demoralized, but not Richard himself. He found out where his rival was and charged him as he stood at the head of his personal bodyguard. With his own hands Richard III slew Richmond's standard bearer and engaged his enemy in mortal combat. At about this time Lord Stanley made up his mind to intervene; he carried out a flank attack which decided the battle. He had his reward, being created Earl of Derby on the field. The Stanleys have been among the rulers of England ever since. How Richard III perished is not known, but he fell pierced by many wounds. His crown was found hanging upon a hawthorn bush and placed upon the head of his conqueror, the future King Henry VII.

Richard III was a villain on the heroic scale. He had inherited the tradition, dating back at least to King Henry IV, that great magnates with a dash of the royal blood in their veins were entitled to fight with their retinues for the crown of England, if they thought that they were predestined to be its wearer. The Wars of the Roses, which almost ended on Bosworth Field, left the country disillusioned, exhausted, and deprived of many of its natural leaders. The hope remained that a king who was a real statesman would come forth and bring order and peace.

XXIII

Wales, Scotland, and Ireland in the Fourteenth and Fifteenth Centuries

Since the conquest by King Edward I of the principality, Wales, though inextricably mixed up in English political history, had only once found a national leader of its own. The Statute of Wales of 1284 had roughly divided the country into two parts—the principality, ruled directly by the English king and his officials, and the Marches, where rival English barons, at one time said to be over 140 in number, held virtually independent sway. The principality consisted of the ancient Welsh kingdom of Gwynedd in the northwest, including the island of Anglesey, and, separated from it in the southwest, the counties of Cardigan and Carmarthen. In these areas many military castles had been skillfully constructed under the direction of King Edward I to hold the inhabitants in check. At the southwestern tip of Wales, Pembrokeshire, colonized first by the English from the sea, was known as "little England beyond Wales." If the Welsh got out of hand it was always possible to attack them not merely from Pembroke and the Marches but also, through the exertion of sea power, from Bristol to the south or from Chester to the north. Indeed it was sea power that had sealed King Edward I's conquest of Wales.

The Statute of Wales divided the principality into six counties. According to Sir Maurice Powicke, "it imposed a system of order and justice which was wise and equitable." Welsh law and customs were maintained under the control of sheriffs and bailiffs. The creation of Edward of Carnarvon (Edward II) as Prince of Wales had been welcomed. On the other hand, much of Wales, under the rough care of the Marcher Lords, was still left isolated, in the words of Sir John Lloyd, "governed by countless lords and divorced from the English shire system and the courts at Westminster." Generally in these centuries it was from the Welsh Marches, where no royal writ was in effect, and not from the principality that threats to the authority of the king of England came.

The fourteenth century is considered to have been an era of peace in Wales. After 1343 there were sixty years of unbroken English ascendancy. Agriculture developed, boroughs were built, foreign trade increased. But the Welsh national spirit was not dimmed. Welsh fighting men served in the Hundred Years' War against France and thereby sharpened their skill. Welsh bards maintained the Celtic language and the flow of Welsh poetry and stimulated romantic memories of the glorious days when heroes like Arthur had flourished.

For the first sixteen years of the fifteenth century the Welsh found a national leader in Owen Glendower or Owain Glyn Dwr. Helped by English rebels against the new Lancastrian dynasty and with periodic assistance from the French, Owen Glendower maintained an uneven struggle against the future Henry V. But once he had been beaten, later English kings had little time for Wales. The memory of Owen's rule was long warm. A national literature persisted. Then an astonishing thing happened: a Welsh gentleman, Owain ap Maredudd ap Tudur, a handsome Anglesey squire, persuaded the French princess Catherine, who had been married to King Henry V and had been left a young widow, in whose household he was serving as clerk of the wardrobe, to take him as her second husband. He fought for the Lancastrians and was executed by the Yorkists. But King Henry VI created two sons of this marriage Earls of Richmond and of Pembroke. The Earl of Richmond married Margaret Beaufort, who was the direct descendant of John of Gaunt. After the death of her husband in 1456 Countess Margaret gave birth to a son, Henry of Richmond. This grandson of a modest Welsh gentleman was able to raise Wales against King Richard III and with the aid of a Welsh army to claim and win the throne of England.

The history of this period in Scotland was somewhat parallel to that of England. Here there was a long contest between the House of Steward or Stuart and its vassals for the realities of power. The intrigues, the battles, and the murders that took place during this struggle resembled those that punctuated the Wars of the Roses. The first Stuart, known as Robert II (grandson of Robert Bruce through his mother), was fifty-five when he became king. A virile man, he had six sons, eight daughters, and at least eight natural sons. His reign saw many changes in relation to England. A friendly truce was agreed upon with John of Gaunt. Then in 1385 came the alliance with France and an invasion of Scotland by the English King Richard II. In 1388 the Scots retorted with an incursion over the border and won a victory over the English at Otterburn or Chevy Chase in Northumberland, where the Percies were defeated. Both Robert II and his son, Robert III, are described by the leading historian of Scotland as "imbecile Kings." During the reign of Robert III (1390–1406) there was a contest for power between his brother, the Duke of Albany, and his son, the Duke of Rothesay. The accidental capture of James Stuart, the son of Robert III and heir to the throne, by the English, quieted the conflict between the two kingdoms for several years, but when James's father died, the Duke of Albany proved himself to be a ruler of ability, moderate, just, and generous. He died at the age of eighty-four, leaving a favorable heritage to King James I, who returned at last from England in 1424 at the age of thirty to begin his reign.

The Stuarts next turned upon the House of Albany and crushed it. James I proved to be an energetic king who kept his baronage under control, reformed the judicial system, and imposed fresh taxes. At the time of his murder in 1437 his successor, James II, was only seven. A new internal struggle began between the Stuarts and the Douglases, almost contemporaneously with the English Wars of the Roses. The Douglases won glory in the continuing border contests with the English. But in 1452 William, eighth Earl of Douglas, was murdered by King James II, who survived until 1480 when he himself was killed while laying siege to Roxburgh Castle by the unexpected explosion of a cannon. "At the close of the reign of James II," it has been said, "Scotland enjoyed a happiness and prosperity which she had not known since the last days of Robert the Bruce."

Relations with England continued to be checkered. King Edward IV lent his support to the ninth Earl of Douglas against the Stuarts, but in 1474 an Anglo-Scottish treaty was concluded, on the eve of Edward IV's expedition to France, and the future King James IV was engaged to a daughter of the English king, although marriage never followed. Meanwhile in 1472 the archbishopric of St. Andrew's was established, and the shadowy claim of the Archbishop of York to rule over the Scottish Church was thus finally shaken off. During the reign of King James III too the Scottish monarchy finally obtained sovereignty over the surrounding islands, including the Shetlands and Orkneys. King James III showed himself to be a discerning patron of the arts and Scottish poetry flourished. He was also ingenious in raising money for his own purposes. After the death of King Edward IV, James appeared to be the master of his kingdom; another truce was concluded with King Richard III. But the Scottish nobility thought their king was too strong and rose against him and his favorites. He was murdered in 1488 and his son King James IV was left to contend with the new English king, Henry Tudor.

After the conquest of Ireland under King Henry II and the active interest displayed in it by King John, who set up a permanent central government at Dublin, promising to extend the laws and customs of England to the country, this "emerald gem of the western world" tended to be overlooked and neglected by the English monarchs whose eyes turned toward the more inviting, richer soils of France. Ireland was described as a "lordship" attached to the English Crown and both Henry III and Edward I were named Lords of Ireland before they succeeded to the English throne. But the country was governed by either lieutenants or justiciars acting in the name of the Lord of Ireland, while outside the narrow arc surrounding Dublin mighty Anglo-Norman barons ruled almost independently of the English king: such men as the De Burgos (Lords of Connaught and Earls of Ulster) or the Fitzgeralds (Earls of Kildare) exercised almost untrammeled sway. The native Irish kings who had survived aimed to live on terms with the English Crown or the Anglo-Norman magnates, who themselves were becoming half-Irish.

Sir John Wogan, King Edward I's justiciar, who governed from 1295 to 1312, was the greatest of the early viceroys. It was he who, in order to help raise men to fight the English king's wars, summoned the first Irish parliament in 1297. But during the reign of King Edward II there was a setback when for three years Edward Bruce came from Scotland and conquered and ruled Ireland with the aid of the native princes.

After Bruce's defeat, Roger Mortimer, later Earl of March, became the king's lieutenant in Ireland and made concessions, promising the native Irish grants of English law and the Anglo-Irish all the rights guaranteed by the Great Charter. However, King Edward III, who put to death Roger Mortimer, his mother's paramour, was more concerned with the beginning of his war against France than with Ireland, and the native Irish rose and defied alike the justiciars and the Norman earls. In 1361 King Edward was compelled to send over his second son, Lionel, Duke of Clarence, "because our land of Ireland—by the attacks of Irish enemies and through the impotence of our lieges there, and because the magnates of our land of England, having lands there, take the profits thereof but do not defend them—is now subjected to such devastation and destruction that, unless God avert and succour the same, it will soon be plunged into total ruin. . . ." Clarence carried out campaigns against the native Irish and in 1368 summoned a council at Kilkenny which attempted to separate the English colonists from the Irish by forbidding English lieges to marry Irish, speak Irish, sell arms or horses to the Irish, or even entertain Irish minstrels. "The Statutes of Kilkenny," it has been said, "form the Great Divide in medieval Irish history. After a long attempt to conquer the whole island and after various attempts to bring the Irish within the law, the design was abandoned and the English Government decided to keep what it could of the country." But the Statutes were futile and ineffective. During the next 150 years there was a remarkable Irish revival.

The native Irish began to push back the English both in the "Pale" around Dublin and in the Anglo-Irish baronial colonies. In 1376 Art Oge McMurrough was declared "king of Leinster" and became the leader of Gaelic recovery. In vain King Richard II sent able lieutenants to Ireland; they met with defeat and disappointment, confessing that they could secure obedience only in the Pale. The king was forced to go over to Ireland himself in 1324 and temporarily restored order, exacting homage from McMurrough and the Irish chiefs. King Henry IV also tried to conciliate the native Irish, so that the colonies of the Anglo-Irish dwindled. The country came to be governed by an Anglo-Irish oligarchy.

One of the richest of the absentee landlords was Richard, Duke of York, who inherited the Mortimer estates: he was Earl of Ulster and Lord of Trim and Connaught. He came to Ireland in 1449 to act as the lieutenant of King Henry VI and remained there for ten years. He returned again in 1460 and during his years of power he won most of Ireland for the Yorkist cause. The accession of his son, King Edward IV, was enthusiastically welcomed in Ireland, where Edward's brother, George, Duke of Clarence, was lieutenant until his execution in 1478.

But the real rulers of Ireland were now the Earls of Kildare. Because of its Yorkist connections, Ireland was to become the scene of many serious attempts to overthrow King Henry VII and break the Tudor dynasty in England.

XXIV

Fifteenth-century England

The fifteenth century in England has often been described as an age of decline, decadence, and disillusionment. Of course such a generalization cannot be fully sustained. At the opening of the century the nation still rejoiced in the wonderful impulse given to English literature by the works of the poet Geoffrey Chaucer and his less distinguished successors and imitators, John Lydgate, the monk of Bury, and Thomas Hoccleve, the impecunious man-about-town. Toward its close the merchant William Caxton set up his printing shop "at the Red Pale" in Westminster and offered most of the treasures of the time in prose and verse to those who wished to read. The classical works, rediscovered by the Italian Renaissance, gradually penetrated into English society to stimulate new ideas. "So far as education is concerned," it has been observed, "the fifteenth century was not one of decadence, but of progress. A great development of educational foundations took place, alike in re-endowment and enlargement of old schools, and the erection of schools and colleges." About 200 grammar schools were then functioning. This was, in particular, a splendid period for the university of Cambridge. King Henry VI founded King's College, as well as Eton, today England's most aristocratic school: Queen's was founded by his wife, Queen Margaret of Anjou, and three other colleges were also established during the century. In spite of the interruptions of wars at home and abroad, foreign trade, notably the cloth export trade, was making progress. Much fine public and private architecture was completed. And as the old nobility died out, a vigorous gentry and yeomanry as well as a new nobility arose.

Nevertheless the decay of government at the center had a vitiating and widening effect on English public life. After King Henry IV had consolidated his rule and King Henry V had invoked a patriotism which reached its peak with the victory of Agincourt, civil strife became constant so that the forces of law and order were gradually undermined. It may be true that the mass of the people took no part whatever in the Wars of the Roses but watched their masters fighting them out, but a spirit of lawlessness was engendered and most aspects of life suffered. We can read in the illuminating letters of the Paston and Stonor families of the struggle for survival among the gentry. John Paston, for example, was left to execute the will of a friend who wanted him to found a college of priests at Caister Castle near Yarmouth. Other executors disputed his duty and it was only after endless litigation, during which he was thrice imprisoned, that he managed to retain possession of Caister: even then the college of priests was never established there.

The breakdown in government came even before the Wars of the Roses began in the middle of the century. The system whereby the magnates hired military retainers and used them not only to serve the king under indenture but also for their own private purposes dated back at least to the reign of King Edward III. What has been called by historians "bastard feudalism" arose; new loyalties or "affinities" cut across the old, undermining the monarchy by creating lordships which could overawe the courts of law, frighten the royal officials, and even terrorize parliament. Under King Richard II royal judges were losing their independence and sense of duty: justices of the assize were corrupted and justices of the peace bribed or intimidated. King Henry IV and King Henry V attacked but did not crush the system of "livery and maintenance," and the forces of disorder were revived during the minority of King Henry VI. "The justices of the Benches were retained in private interests, the justices of the peace were being made helpless by maintenances, the livery statutes were not kept, the election of shire knights [to parliament] were corruptly managed, assize jurors were bought, the sheriffs were the tools of the greater men, and, through their powers over juries, the law of the country was at their mercy" (Jolliffe). The Paston family three times found themselves besieged in their own houses by armed bands sent against them by peers of the realm. The Nevilles and the Percies carried on a private war in the north of England. The leaders of the Church, who were mostly statesmen with secular interests, involved with the ambitions of rival kings and lay magnates, did little to mitigate the general sense of confusion, although their comparative tolerance may have been commendable. It is no wonder that Lollardy, which questioned the virtues of the old order in the Church, and the spirit of the Peasants' Revolt and Jack Cade's rising persisted much longer than historians once thought.

In the Wars of the Roses a large part of the old nobility was wiped out and many great men were killed or assassinated. Apart from kings and princes, at least eight dukes, nine earls, and dozens of barons perished; a bishop of Salisbury, a sheriff of Kent, and two Speakers of the House of Commons were murdered. During King Henry VI's minority the Council itself became the stage for rival factions, and in the dark days of King Richard III the few magnates who survived did not dare to trust one another.

However ruthless and opinionated a king might be, no effective government could be carried on without the participation of a council of qualified advisers. But throughout the fifteenth century the King's Council varied immensely in character and quality. Sometimes it was a "continual council" of professional administrators; at other times it was a periodic meeting of influential magnates. Henry V relied upon a small, intimate council consisting chiefly of the great officers of state who were his personal and loyal confidants. But with his death the whole picture changed. Under King Henry VI the Council was an instrument of the nobility, chosen by the lords of parliament; members were sworn, salaried, and virtually unremovable. Contemporary political theorists—Sir John Fortescue, for instance—were wont to argue that no Council could be effective unless it was a reasonably compact body consisting of the most important lords temporal and spiritual in the realm; but rivalries and jealousies destroyed the Council in the late fifteenth century, and the failure of the Lancastrian royal council as an instrument of judicature was more or less complete.

Under King Edward IV the character of the Council changed again. It was a larger and looser body consisting of officeholders, some of the new nobility, and a considerable number of knights and esquires. Only the Chancellor and the Treasurer were paid for their attendances. The Earl of Warwick, who was the king's principal adviser in the first days of his reign, rarely attended the Council at Westminster. It was a complete contrast with the small, exclusive Council of magnates which had existed in the past. Naturally its powers and achievements were smaller. The emphasis in government was essentially upon the authority of the king himself. Even the judicial activities of the Council were reduced, and many cases relating to crime as well as to property were transferred to the relatively new court of chancery. But toward the end of the reign a number of important cases were dealt with by members of the King's Council sitting in the "Star Chamber" at Westminster.

Like the Council, parliament under the Lancastrians was largely, if not entirely, an instrument of the nobility. Many years ago a famous English historian wrote that "the house of Lancaster had risen by advocating constitutional principles, and on constitutional principles it governed." It was thought during the Victorian age that the fifteenth century witnessed the flowering of the House of Commons during an exciting period of constitutional experiment. Doubt has since been thrown upon that view; indeed it has been claimed that during the fifteenth century no recognizable "constitution" existed at all. However, it does seem fair to say that, in spite of the vicissitudes through which it went, the nature of the English parliament did become somewhat more clearly formulated during the century. The legal profession emphasized the theory that parliament was the king's highest court of law; and it also became not uncommon to regard parliament as composed of the "three estates of the realm"—spiritual lords, temporal lords, and commons—giving it an authority under the king that derived from the "natural order" of society. The three-estates idea, it has been argued, was grafted on to the idea of the king's high court. It can also be said that the House of Commons had been fully accepted as a distinct entity with a sense of corporate unity. Moreover there was a recognition that the knights of the shire and the burgesses came to parliament not merely as local representatives but as spokesmen of the country as a whole; the expression was used: "We that be comen for al the common of the land." The increasing importance of the Commons was signified by the fact that in 1429 an act was passed limiting the right to vote for members of parliament in the shires to freeholders possessing property worth at least forty shillings.

During the fifteenth century the House of Commons continued to exercise its right to present petitions to the Crown and many of these were directly translated into acts of parliament. On such matters as trade the influence of the Commons must have been considerable. But some of the petitions to the Crown were undoubtedly inspired by the nobility; therefore enactments based upon them do not necessarily measure the rising influence of the Commons. On the whole, the Commons seems to have done a useful job in overcoming legislative inertia on matters of social importance and in continuing to exert real control over taxation, but was anxious to keep out of political trouble. The Commons knew their place. They found that their liberty of speech and liberty of person were strictly circumscribed. For example, when their Speaker was arrested for attacking the interests of Richard, Duke of York, in 1453, they failed to protest and meekly elected a new Speaker in his place. At the beginning of the century the Commons "got Henry IV to put it on record that the judicial power of parliament resided only in the King and Lords" (Myers), and during the kaleidoscopic changes of the later half of the century the Commons were content to signify their approval of every change in the royal authority, no doubt hoping that sooner or later a strong king, capable of enforcing justice, would be discovered.

Thus while the importance of the House of Commons in the fifteenth century must not be exaggerated and certainly owed little to the deliberate policy of the Lancastrian kings, it had to some extent been strengthened, and that strengthening reflected the growing influence of the middle classes in the kingdom. It might indeed be argued that the rise of the gentry, which has been attributed by some historians to the Protestant Reformation of the sixteenth century, was at least clearly foreshadowed much earlier. The magnates had become a *rentier* class, who no longer farmed their demesne lands. This paved the way not only for the enterprise of the wealthier property owners among the knights and squires, but also for the emergence of a substantial "yeoman" class of small, more or less independent farmers, since the customary obligations of the peasantry to their landlords were increasingly commuted for money rents. It was among the "yeomen of England" that the famous archers were recruited who fought for King Henry V and John of Bedford. After the accession of King Edward IV not only were the gentry more active in public life, but merchants began to prosper and peasant proprietors to flourish; altogether a notable social advance was recorded after the political and economic depressions that prevailed in the middle of the fifteenth century.

In sum, the picture of the general demoralization of English society during the fifteenth century certainly needs qualification and modification. There was real promise for the future. When King Henry VII came to the throne, ordinary Englishmen were by no means badly off, in spite of the greed, selfishness, and incompetence of most of their rulers both in Church and state.

BOOK III

THE TUDOR AGE: THE REFORMATION

XXV

English Society in the Early Tudor Age

The early Tudor age may be described as a period of reconstruction in England. Its people as a whole were still not greatly advanced in their political outlook and its government did not yet differ in essentials, administratively or even constitutionally, from that which had prevailed under the Yorkist kings. But Englishmen were tiring of perpetual civil war. They had long looked for, and at last had found, a strong, competent, and energetic monarch.

Henry VII reigned over the kingdom of England, the principality of Wales, the lordship of Ireland, the town of Calais in France, and certain outlying islands, and after he had crushed the inevitable early rebellions with some ease, he ruled them in peace and well-being. His court was the center of his kingdom, the apex of society, the heart of culture and luxury. "The Tudor Court," writes Dr. Elton, "with its red-coated guard and its vast expenditure on silks, satins, and velvets was always a gorgeous affair, and ceremonial was one thing on which Henry invariably spent in a prodigal manner." "Not to have been at Court," said Shakespeare's Touchstone, "was to be damned." The English court, at least since the time of King Edward IV, had been profoundly influenced by the Italian courts of the Renaissance era, which delighted to promote scholarship and literature and to patronize the arts. The contrast between rude fighting men and learned clerics was disappearing. Here the old and the new nobility mingled. Although their political supremacy was past, the magnates of the realm remained socially important and impressively rich. At the Field of the Cloth of Gold, a famous scene in Henry VIII's reign, the English nobles were said to have "carried their manors on their backs."

While many leading peers had been killed or murdered in the Wars of the Roses and after, entire families had not been wiped out or indefinitely proscribed. King Henry VII was served by Lancastrians like the Earl of Oxford and Yorkists like the veteran soldier, the Earl of Surrey. He also created new peers from the higher ranks of the gentry. But he allowed no one to darken the sun of the Tudor monarchy itself. Avoiding the mistake committed by King Edward III and King Edward IV of entangling the royal family itself with the principal magnates, he did not hesitate to seek councilors among men of the "middle classes." The Tudors "tamed but did not destroy the aristocracy." The peerage was expected to consist of landed proprietors. "Decayed" peers were given grants of land to support their dignities. They remained the social and, to a large extent, the administrative leaders of the counties in which their great houses were situated or whence they had taken their titles. They were obliged to keep open house and hundreds of people were entertained in their halls and their park lands. Although they were kept in their places by the king, they were not excluded from public life. The Palace of Westminster never resembled the Versailles of King Louis XIV of France. And with most English peers a sense of social responsibility cut deep. For hundreds of years, until well after the political reform bills of the nineteenth century became law, they continued to be the mainstay of the British ruling classes.

Of course the peers and courtiers represented only a small fraction of the population of England, which is estimated at this time to have amounted to about three million. It would have been higher than that, had it not been for periodic plagues and epidemics. It took more than a century for the country to recover from the devastating effects of the Black Death in the middle of the fourteenth century. Other diseases swept the country too. There was particularly heavy mortality in London in the middle of the fifteenth century. A main source of infection was the black rat (said to have been introduced into England from the East—along with syphilis—at the time of the Crusades); these rats carried fleas which transferred infections to human beings, especially in closely populated areas. Consequently plagues fell severely upon towns and ports. Declining population had also caused whole villages and farmsteads to be abandoned in these centuries—lost villages only lately rediscovered by devoted scholars. It was probably not until the reign of King Charles II in the latter half of the seventeenth century that England began to recover from these terrible epidemics and underpopulation ceased to be considered a problem. Of these three million people nine-tenths were occupied in agriculture. Over 75,000 of them lived in London, Westminster, and their environs. London was by far the largest town: indeed it is said at this time to have been the largest city in Europe. Norwich, a great center of weaving, was the second largest English town, with a population of over 12,000; Bristol, the port for the west, had about 10,000 inhabitants, and York had fallen to a mere 8,000. These towns were little more than villages by modern standards. And in such towns as there were many of the inhabitants were not full-time industrial workers or shopkeepers, but were still intimately connected with the land.

This seems to have been a period of comparative affluence and expansion for the untitled landlord class, which is usually called the gentry.

As we have seen, there are indications that a rise of the gentry began in the reign of King Edward IV, long before it benefited from the dissolution of the monasteries or the sale of church lands. The English gentry was not a precise nor stratified legal class or caste. Some of them were "knights," but most of them preferred to pay a fine rather than undertake such obligations as pertained to knighthood. Others held the rank of "esquire," which carried with it the right to bear armorial insignia. But the gentry was a quite extensive class which ranged from the younger sons of the peers to landed merchants and yeoman farmers. The gentry looms large in history because it alone outside the aristocracy left family records for the edification of the social historian. Many of the gentry were both clever and careful. They might purchase land out of the profits of minor offices or obtain grants for services to the Crown. They had little landed snobbery, however, and it was a common practice, noted by foreigners, for them to turn their younger sons out of the family manor house to be apprenticed to merchants or skilled craftsmen or to learn the law in the London Inns. While the knights might come up to Westminster periodically to represent their counties in the House of Commons, the squires mostly stayed at home in the country looking after their own business or doing their duties as justices of the peace.

The breakup of the so-called manorial system of agriculture, with its villeins tied to the land, which had begun before the coming of the Black Death, had also created the yeoman class, long considered to be the backbone of England. The yeomen, like the untitled gentry, were a loose class and not a legal entity. They might be freeholders cultivating their own land, tenants-at-will or more commonly copyholders, that is to say peasants who held their lands on long leases with unalterable rents. The yeomen were frequently sheep farmers who profited by the continuing demand for wool cloth. Below the yeomen came the simple husbandmen or agricultural laborers who worked for others in return for a daily wage. Most of them had long ago achieved personal freedom in that they had ceased to be serfs, but inevitably they were often the victims of social injustice. On the whole, however, such evidence as we have of prices and wages suggest that wage laborers were fairly well off in the last decade of the fifteenth century. A day's pay, it has been estimated, would then buy three times as much wheat as it would have bought in 1300. Because in the records and literature of the time there was much talk about beggars who moved from town to town, alarming society and threatening lonely hamlets and farms, it must not be imagined that this was an age of exceptional poverty or unemployment. Many of the beggars were unemployables, discharged soldiers, or men who preferred to live lawlessly in the woods and forests or rogues and thieves who gained a livelihood by preying on the wealthy people in London. The general impression that may be obtained both from economic statistics and from the reports of foreign visitors (such as Polydore Vergil, an Italian who came to England in 1502) is one of rather widespread prosperity.

The most notable change in the character of English agriculture at this time was the progress of the enclosure movement. The fencing in of land by hedges or stone walls for the benefit of individual farmers might be carried out in a number of different ways. The oldest of these was by means of "assarts" or "intakes" from the wasteland or woodland that extended the size of the arable fields. Another method was for landowners to enclose common land belonging to a manor or village. This was generally considered legitimate provided that the lords of the manor did not encroach upon the customary grazing rights of the villagers' livestock. There was also consolidation of strips in open fields in order to improve cultivation and get rid of the "balks" or furrow marks that divided them. Finally, fields previously devoted to growing corn might be taken over for the pasturage of sheep, since the keeping of flocks was reckoned to pay better than tillage. Enclosure was a necessary stage in the progress of English agriculture. But it often meant injustice for the smaller man and was a source of much social unrest.

A good deal of enclosure had taken place before the Tudor period, although the consolidation of strips in the open fields does not appear to have gone very far. Enclosure was one of the grievances ventilated during the Peasants' Revolt of 1381. In the reign of King Henry VII protests were made against the enclosure of small peasant holdings for the purpose of more efficient arable farming or additional pasturage. It was said that such enclosures led to the destruction of villages and the reduction of rural communities, although in fact the fall in the agricultural population was mainly due to long-term causes. The shepherd, it was argued also, was a less skilled archer than a ploughman was and therefore less serviceable in times of war.

Two acts against enclosure were passed in 1489; one of them was in response to a fear that the Isle of Wight would be depopulated because of the concentration of holdings there in only a few hands. But these acts were ineffective and in spite of royal proclamations, commissions, and the protests of publicists like Sir Thomas More, who declared that sheep were devouring men, instead of men devouring sheep, the enclosure movement in one form or another went steadily forward until most of the open fields of the country, notably in the Midlands, were eventually covered with hedgerows.

Sheep farming was increasingly taken up. It has been estimated that there were now about eight million sheep in the country or about three sheep for each inhabitant. Woolen cloth was woven practically everywhere in the land: in Yorkshire, in the west country, and in East Anglia the industry was booming and even in the "home counties" around London many spinners and weavers were to be found: "all over Essex there lay villages famous for cloth making. . . . Hardly a week but the clatter of the pack-horse would be heard in the straggling streets, bringing in new stores of wool to be worked and taking away pieces of cloth to the clothiers of Colchester and the surrounding villages" (Power). Early capitalist middlemen bought the wool, gave it out to be spun, transferred the yarn to jobbing weavers who usually worked on domestic looms, and had it dressed and fulled. Finally the cloth would be dyed and sold on the home market or exported unfinished for sale in the markets of Europe. Just as the Merchants of the Staple had in earlier times done a flourishing trade in exporting English wool, sold chiefly at Calais (for the upkeep of whose garrison they were responsible), so the Merchant Adventurers, a fellowship created in the city of London in 1486, now promoted the sale of English cloth, chiefly at Antwerp, and thereby broke the monopoly of the German Hansa merchants. During the fifteenth century the total output of cloth in the country had remained more or less stationary, while exports of wool had declined. But in the sixteenth century cloth exports expanded again; this largely explains the movement to enclose arable land in order to keep more sheep. While cloth thus became the principal English export—and long remained so—supplemented by exports of corn in years of good harvests, imports were mainly confined to precious metals and luxury goods, such as wines and spices. These were highly profitable to traders and were easy to transport even over bad roads. And there was much smuggling.

Both commerce and industry were closely controlled and regulated. The belief that exports were of value only if they brought gold and silver into the country was widely held. Legislation had been introduced to prevent what was called "sumptuary" expenditure upon luxuries and was renewed. In the towns, notably in London, the corporations, consisting of large tradesmen and merchants, ruled with an iron rod, laying down restrictions upon apprenticeship and industrial employment. The livery companies maintained a jealous monopoly of trade and often opposed new methods. The craft guilds, which at first were intended to be open to all journeymen who had qualified to become masters and to be self-governing, increasingly tended to become narrow oligarchies of employers. Small guilds strengthened their positions by amalgamations. But broadly the state itself was, in the Tudor age, the principal regulator both of industry and trade.

Habits and pastimes varied from class to class—from the courtiers who drank French wines and read Italian poetry to the villagers who quaffed home-brewed ale and poached their landlords' rabbits. The Renaissance in Europe reintroduced classical Greek and some Latin authors and also had an impact upon architecture, which moved away from Gothic to classical styles. Caxton and his followers made books more common, and woodcuts and copper-plate engravings were bought and sold. Country houses were built upon a more lavish scale. The great halls lost their pride of place, and broad wooden staircases led up to bed-chambers or to long galleries where ladies exercised themselves and portraits of the owner were hung. Later, palaces after the Italian model sprang up and adorned the age of Cardinal Wolsey and King Henry VIII.

Furniture was broad, heavy, and hard, although the big beds were more comfortable than they looked. Farmhouses were constructed first of timber and plaster with thatched roofs and later of brick. An increasing interest was taken in gardening and many varieties of plants were grown. Hunting deer was the most popular outdoor sport, while hawking was the most aristocratic. Archery was still popular and tennis was played by kings. Football came in, but at first was considered "a bloody and murdering practice" rather than "a fellowly sport or pastime." Gambling for high stakes was not infrequent among the upper classes, but dicing and card playing were not thought suitable for the wage-earning class and forbidden to it except at Christmas. For indoor entertainment itinerant companies of actors moved about the country from inn to inn and paved the way for permanent playhouses like the Globe in the age of William Shakespeare.

In the towns the houses and shops were generally built entirely of wood so that fires were common and very destructive. But hygiene was improving somewhat. More conduits were built in London, while water was hawked from barrels in the city streets. Writers began to stress the value of clean air, although when the Dutch theologian Erasmus visited England he noted the stench of English houses. The policing system was still rudimentary; robbery and crimes of violence were common, though criminals were brutally punished when they were caught. Prisons were foul. Efforts were made to strengthen the town watches, but in general the parish constable was treated with contempt.

Men and women of Tudor times, at any rate in the upper classes, were enormous eaters. "In number of dishes and change of meat the nobility of England," noted William Harrison, "do most exceed, since there is no day in manner that passeth over their heads wherein they have not only beef, mutton, lamb, kid, pork, cony, capon, pig, or so many of those as the season yieldeth, but also some portion of the red or fallow deer, be-

side great variety of fish and wild fowl, and thereto sundry other deli-
cacies where in the sweet hand of the seafaring Portuguese is not want-
ing." Contemporary cookery books are prodigious and frightening; most
recipes required rich spices; fruit and flowers as well as meat and
vegetables were made up into pies and tarts; and meats were covered
with sweet sauces. Dinner was at eleven and supper at six o'clock, and
although a doctor gave warning that an hour was long enough to sit at
table, this was usually exceeded. Even craftsmen and yeomen had liberal
tables with big joints supplemented by bacon and eggs, fruit, and cheeses.
All this was washed down with vast quantities of ale, cider, or beer—
introduced by the Dutch in the fifteenth century—or among the wealthier
with French and Italian wines. Erasmus noted sourly that when he
traveled in England carriers were liable "to rob you of your wine" so that
you were forced to drink "health-destroying beer."

Erasmus and others who traveled in England in early Tudor times,
while noting the general prosperity, observed that the English were not
accustomed to overexert themselves. "Agriculture," remarked one of
them, "is not practised in this land beyond what is required for the consumption of the people." While landlords lived comfortably upon their
rents, derived from the old manorial demesne lands which they had ceased
to cultivate, the yeomen and wage-earning classes benefited from the glut
of land and scarcity of labor brought about by the reduction in population following the Black Death. Just as the old "feudalism" based on
military service had given way to a "bastard feudalism" based on hired
soldiers and servants, so too earlier methods of agricultural organization
involving labor services rather than rents yielded to a more straightforward and easy-going method of cultivation carried out by tenant farmers and agricultural laborers. The soil was good and the land ample in
relation to the number of people in the country. Thus there was a tendency to economic stagnation, to social self-satisfaction. No doubt
Englishmen were still better off in the lowland zone where the climate
was more propitious and the ground more fertile than in the more
rigorous and craggy north and in Wales and Scotland. The bulk of the
population was concentrated in the south, especially in the counties
around London, which offered a large market. The antiquary John
Leland noted during the reign of King Henry VIII the persistent economic and geographical contrasts between the south and the north. He
also noticed, however, that relatively little damage had been inflicted
upon the structure of the towns or the countryside by the Wars of the
Roses.

On the whole, the standard of welfare of the English people was high
for their time, but their spirit was low. In fact it may be said that the

reign of King Henry VII witnessed a false dawn; for a general rise in prices, chiefly owing to the influx of silver from the New World, which was then being explored, was to create many complications including lower returns in the real value of rents for landlords and a fall in the purchasing power of wages in the course of the sixteenth century. On the other hand, overseas adventures and expansion and the threat of the Counter Reformation were to present new and exciting challenges to the people of England. In the Tudor age they finally shook off their lethargy and revealed their genius.

XXVI

The Reign of Henry VII

"To the student of politics," wrote H. A. L. Fisher, "nothing is more interesting than the process by which a nation, demoralized by a long course of rancorous strife, is gradually recalled to peace and sanity. To do this was the function of Henry VII." To judge from a Flemish portrait, the victor of Bosworth had "a shrewd, hard face, wide-open eyes, a mouth tight at the corners, such a smile as Leonardo loved to paint" (Read). He was a "new monarch," a prince of the Renaissance, nearer to Machiavelli's ideal than to that of Froissart. Gracious, agreeable, and polite, he lacked personal charm. "His spirit was distinguished, wise, and prudent," wrote Polydore Vergil, the Italian chronicler whom he patronized, "his mind was brave and resolute and never, even at moments of the greatest danger, deserted him. He had a most pertinacious memory. Withal he was not devoid of scholarship. In government he was shrewd and prudent, so that no one dared to get the better of him through deceit and guile." His only "vice" was considered to be "avarice," which was not thought to be proper in a king.

Much paper and ink has been expended by specialist historians upon tracing and commenting on Henry VII's precise royal lineage. But so long as he had some shadowy claim to the Crown it did not much matter to him or to anyone else exactly what it was. He had gained his throne by conquest and he kept it by skillful government. By his very action in at once summoning a parliament he assumed that he was the king. The confirmation of his title by this parliament (this was one of those delightful constitutional paradoxes not infrequent in history) ignored the whole question of heredity. Indeed Henry VII was careful deliberately to delay his marriage to Princess Elizabeth, daughter of King Edward IV, who had, at any rate for Yorkists, an impressive title, until he himself had been crowned, lest there should be any doubt that he expected to reign in his own right. A coronation, said to have been more glorious than any held before, stifled all thoughts of illegality. The new king's duty was to show that he was capable of ruling and thereby restoring order to a distracted land.

Of course the technical defects in his title could not be concealed and were long exploited by his enemies. Although King Edward IV's sons had been murdered in the Tower by the orders of King Richard III, Edward had four surviving nephews, one his brother Clarence's son, known as Edward, Earl of Warwick, a boy of ten, who was lodged in the Tower, and three sons of his sister, who had been married to John de la Pole, Earl of Suffolk, the eldest of whom, known as the Earl of Lincoln, was actually nominated as his successor by King Richard III. Yet, to prove how little the possession of the authentic blood royal mattered to the ambitious or subversive, Henry VII's enemies preferred to deploy charlatans against him, who assumed various somewhat unconvincing disguises to hoodwink the ignorant. The chief sponsors of the "Yorkist" candidates were Edward IV's sister Margaret, widow of Charles the Bold, Duke of Burgundy, and Gerald Fitzgerald, eighth Earl of Kildare, Lord Deputy of Ireland, both of them champion mischief-makers.

The first charlatan to be employed against King Henry VII was Lambert Simnel, pupil of an Oxford priest, an amiable youth who pretended that he was the Earl of Warwick, although that gentleman was still alive in the Tower. The false Warwick was proclaimed king of England in Dublin, while the real Warwick was being paraded through the streets of London. The wild Irish rallied to Simnel and landed with him in Lancashire, while the dowager Duchess of Burgundy provided two thousand German mercenaries in support. The Earl of Lincoln, though he himself had an excellent and valid claim to the throne, constituted himself the military leader of this motley band of invaders. King Henry VII quietly enlisted an army, moved into the Midlands, and defeated the rebels at the battle of Stoke in June 1486. Lincoln was killed and Simnel was appointed a scullion in the king's kitchen.

The next charlatan, Perkin Warbeck, the mannequin of a Breton merchant, found in Cork, was more silky and more troublesome. He pretended that he was Richard, Duke of York, the dead younger son of Edward IV. Not only did he obtain the patronage of his alleged aunt in

Burgundy and of the restless Irish, but he was recognized by King Charles VIII of France (then at war with King Henry VII) and by the future Emperor Maximilian I. For a time the Yorkist malcontents, who used Warbeck as their mascot, had a base in the Netherlands and plotted to invade England. Henry VII discovered and crushed their fellow conspirators in England, but they still pressed on: first an attempt was made to land Warbeck at Deal in Kent and then at Waterford in Ireland; finally he was welcomed and received assistance in Scotland, where the king carried out border raids on his behalf. Henry VII now struck hard. In 1497 he called a parliament and demanded large grants so that he could levy war upon the Scots. This heavy taxation aroused resentment among the people of Cornwall in the southwest corner of England, since they thought that Scotland was not their business and in any case was a long way off. The Cornishmen killed a tax collector in Taunton and then marched across England to Kent, that ancient trouble spot for the English monarchy. Once again the king kept calm; London was solidly behind him; he raised an army and defeated the rebels in Deptford that June. Three months later Warbeck himself, who had turned up too late in the west country, surrendered, made a full confession of his imposture, and was placed in the Tower of London. Later he escaped from the Tower, but was recaptured.

Other conspiracies followed. In 1499 Edmund de la Pole, Earl of Suffolk, brother to the Earl of Lincoln who perished at the battle of Stoke, took it into his head to stake his claims to the throne and sought the patronage of Emperor Maximilian. But three years later Maximilian signed a treaty with King Henry VII and handed over the Earl of Suffolk to join the rest of the party of royal aspirants in the Tower. Later after yet another bogus Earl of Warwick had appeared and the real Warwick himself became involved in a conspiracy against the Crown, both Warbeck and Warwick were put to death. If one may judge by the conduct of former kings, Henry VII had been remarkably forbearing in permitting such spark plugs of revolt to survive so long. In general, this series of plots, impersonations, and risings revealed how tenuous the Tudor hold was. Yet Henry VII held on and won through.

Henry VII kept his position by sheer skill in statesmanship. He was neither as ruthless as Richard III nor, to begin with, as popular or wealthy as Edward IV. He instituted yeomen of the guard to police his court, but they were used more for ceremonial purposes than as a personal bodyguard. The king never possessed a standing army; he relied upon the loyalty of Londoners and others to produce soldiers when he needed them. He organized the beginnings of a fleet with half a dozen warships, but they did not provide for internal security. It is true that he gradually built up a sound financial position. His first parliament voted him "tonnage and poundage," or customs duties and a wool subsidy, while Acts of Resumption enabled the king to lay hold of Crown lands that had been alienated by his predecessor. After the alarums and excursions of the early years of his reign were over, he tended toward clemency: he sought to restrain the nobility and to invoke the loyalty of the country gentry and rising merchant class. He was empowered by parliament to enforce or reverse acts of attainder passed against conspirators guilty of treason. An act which was passed in 1495 declared that no subject faithfully serving a king of England "for the time being" in war should suffer for doing so either in his person or his property. The purpose of this curious act (optimistically trying to commit future parliaments in advance) was to assure such Yorkist partisans as still remained at large that the past was now forgiven and forgotten; in the words of Dr. Elton, it was "a notable step" in closing a chapter in the civil wars.

King Henry VII was able to overcome his domestic enemies partly because the other European powers of the time were too deeply absorbed in their own concerns to regard England except as a pawn in a complicated game of diplomacy. While England had been confused by the Wars of the Roses changes had been taking place in the political structure of Europe. The conflict between the Empire and Papacy which had dominated the Western world in earlier times had subsided. Important nation states were emerging and acquiring imperial ambitions. Louis XI, who ruled in France from 1461 to 1483, had consolidated the authority of the French monarchy; after the death of Charles the Bold of Burgundy the long dream of his House, which had been to create a "middle kingdom" in Europe, vanished, but his daughter Mary was married to Maximilian, son of the Habsburg emperor Frederick III, and thus Louis ruled over Flanders, Artois, Franche-Comté, and most of the Netherlands. When Maximilian succeeded to the Austrian territories in 1493, he had in his hands the nucleus of a vast, if scattered, empire. In 1469 King Ferdinand of Aragon had married Isabella, the queen of Castile, and thus formed the kingdom of modern Spain, whose dynasty also ruled over Naples. Italy was divided between the Spaniards, the popes, who ruled as secular monarchs in Rome, the Venetian Republic, the duchy of Milan, and the richly cultured Duchy of Florence. It was thus a prize for the greedy. Meanwhile in 1453 the Mohammedan Turks, sweeping in from the east, had conquered Constantinople and overrun Hungary, thus threatening the whole of eastern Europe. But two of the principal Christian powers, France and Spain, were far too much concerned with their own territorial ambitions to take part in a crusade against the Turks or to assist the emperor. So Maximilian's attention was distracted from the Netherlands. Henry VII was able to profit from all these difficulties and dissensions to unify his own kingdom and encourage the commercial enterprise of his subjects across the English Channel.

Enmity with France was the heritage of any English king of those times. This was not merely for sentimental reasons, arising from resentment at the loss of former French territories once conquered by Henry V, but also because so long as Calais remained in English hands its security was a main factor in English foreign policy. King Henry VII looked to the new Spanish kingdom as a potential ally against France. A marriage was therefore negotiated between Prince Arthur, the eldest son of Henry VII and Elizabeth of York, on the one side, and Princess Katherine of Aragon, the daughter of Ferdinand and Isabella, on the other.

The Spaniards were opposed to France because they were anxious to acquire provinces on the Pyrenean frontier between the two countries. When the French regent, the widow of King Louis XI, was embarrassed by a quarrel over the Duchy of Brittany, which she aimed to annex to the Crown of France, an Anglo-Spanish treaty was concluded at Medina del Campo in 1489, confirming the marriage treaty and appearing to commit England to a war against France upon somewhat disadvantageous terms. King Henry VII also made a treaty with Emperor Maximilian, and found himself for a time involved in desultory warfare in Brittany and the Netherlands. Both his allies promptly deserted him, so that for a time it seemed as if his foreign policy had collapsed. However, the king again kept his head. In October 1491 he personally appealed to a parliament for assistance against the French. Ships were hired; soldiers were raised; breweries were erected to supply the soldiers with adequate amounts of beer; and eventually in October 1492 he himself landed in Calais with what has been described as "an enormous army" and laid siege to Boulogne.

Within three weeks the whole war was over with scarcely any blood shed. Charles VIII, a half-mad hunchback who had now taken over the government of France from the regent, was at this time animated by thoughts of conquering Naples from the Spaniards and gaining an empire to the south: he therefore quickly came to terms with the English king. So long as the English left him alone he promised to pay large sums of money annually to King Henry VII and undertook to offer no further assistance to any rebels against him. The English troops returned home by way of Calais, a *"Te Deum"* was sung in St. Paul's Church, and Henry VII entered his capital in triumph. He had done much the same as King Edward IV in being realistic about the traditional Lancastrian claims to French territory and preferred a tribute in hard cash. But the English parliament was not too pleased with these very small gains in return for their own exertions in granting supplies; the treaty of Etaples, as it was called, was however ratified in 1495.

During the later part of his reign, when his domestic problems had been resolved, King Henry VII engaged in many elaborate schemes of foreign policy, hardly any of which bore fruit. He turned hot and cold with Spain. When his son Prince Arthur died, he arranged the marriage of his widow, Katherine of Aragon, to his other son, Henry, after having obtained papal sanction for the match. On the other hand, when Queen Isabella of Castile died in 1504 Henry VII himself thought of marrying her mad daughter, Joanna (his own wife having also died in 1503), and he also contemplated a marriage with the young queen of Naples and several other eligible heiresses. None of his varied marriage schemes was in fact realized; but his daughter Mary was betrothed to the grandson of Emperor Maximilian in return for the loan of a large sum of money. In 1506 he came to an agreement with Archduke Philip of Burgundy, son of the emperor, by which he exacted important trading concessions for English merchants in the Netherlands. Thus he acquired useful alliances both with Spain and the Habsburg emperor and had wisely kept clear of the Italian imbroglio in which all the other Western powers were involved. According to Professor Mackie, "in 1508 Henry stood before the world as the most successful diplomatist of his time." If that is true, it was more by luck than by judgment; most of his later plans proved futile—even the trade agreement was repudiated—and his grandiose dreams were never realized. His real achievement was nearer at home.

The help that Perkin Warbeck had received in Scotland and Ireland had brought to King Henry VII's notice the need to try to settle the relations between his kingdoms and those two countries on a more satisfactory basis. Scotland was fully independent and ruled by the cultured King James IV. Border troubles between the two nations were endemic, but there had been no clash until King James IV had embraced the cause of Warbeck and invaded England on his behalf. His disappointment with the result of his enterprise was considerable; for he seems to have believed that Warbeck really was Richard, Duke of York, and was astonished when the north of England did not rise enthusiastically in his favor and welcome the Scots as saviors. King Henry VII was justifiably annoyed at the intrusion into his affairs, but the Cornish rising saved the Scots from the punishment they might easily have received at the hands of an English army. Instead Henry VII brought pressure to bear upon James IV, not only threatening him with invasion, but also with supporting a pretender to the Scottish throne as a suitable retort to Perkin Warbeck. A truce was concluded, but border fighting continued. Spain offered her mediation, and at last in July 1499 an Anglo-Scottish treaty was arranged.

The treaty followed the lines customary in those days. It was one of "peace and alliance" in which both parties promised not to aid the enemies of the other or to receive rebels against the other; and, as usual, it was cemented by a marriage alliance. This dynastic marriage was more important than most, for King Henry VII's daughter, Margaret, was married to King James IV himself. This wedding of "the Thistle and the Rose" was celebrated with impressive magnificence in the chapel of Holyroodhouse in Edinburgh. The story is told that King Henry VII was warned that if his sons should die without issue, the kingdom might, through this marriage, one day fall to a king of Scotland. Henry VII is supposed to have replied: "If that should be, Scotland would be but an accession to England, and not England to Scotland, for the greater would draw the less"; and he added that it was a safer union for England than one with France. So indeed eventually it came about, for Margaret Tudor's great-grandson, James VI of Scotland, was to become King James I of England. Yet the treaty did not serve its immediate purpose of preserving peace between the two kingdoms. In the reign of King Henry VIII hostilities were renewed.

Ireland was an even harder nut to crack. Henry VII at first showed immense patience with Gerald Fitzgerald, eighth Earl of Kildare, his Lord Deputy. Kildare was an arrogant, restless, attractive, and able man, who had elected to support both the pretenders to the English throne. In 1492 the king at last decided to remove Kildare from his post, though he pardoned him for his grave offenses. In 1494, in an attempt to subdue the unruly Irish, he nominated his infant son Prince Henry as Lord Lieutenant of Ireland and sent over one of his most trusted and capable administrators, Sir Edward Poynings, to act as Lord Deputy. Poynings received instructions to conquer Ulster, punish the supporters of Warbeck, and impose order upon the island.

In Irish history the Lord Deputyship of Sir Edward Poynings looms large. He was unsuccessful in Ulster, but he summoned a parliament to meet at Drogheda in Leinster. This parliament attainted the Earl of Kildare, who was put under arrest and sent over to England. It also passed a number of acts which were intended to reform the English administration in Ireland. The general effect of these acts was to require that no Irish parliament should ever be summoned without the English king's permission; that no new laws should be discussed without the approval of the king in Council; and that all laws made in England should apply automatically to Ireland. All this sounded extremely tidy on paper, but, like most early statutes, had little immediate result and indeed never worked outside the Irish "Pale." King Henry VII was in fact more concerned over the immediate control of the country. After talking to Kildare in London and taking a liking to him, the king decided to send him back to Ireland to become Lord Deputy once again in place of the hard-working Poynings. This piece of realist opportunism worked out well enough, for the king had very little trouble with the Irish during the remainder of his reign.

What was the secret of King Henry VII's success in England itself? How was it that he was able to hand on to his son a stabilized government and a contented people after almost forty years of anarchy that had prevailed from the first battle of St. Albans to the battle of Stoke? In many ways his policy was not very different from that of King Edward IV, but he showed more patience, more application, and greater tolerance than his Yorkist predecessor. First, he carefully built up his finances. He recognized that he was expected to "live of his own," that is to say, manage with his hereditary revenues except in time of war. Apart from the customs duties and the normal "feudal incidents," he had resumed Crown lands, he had acquired the properties of attainted traitors, and once or twice he collected benevolences or gifts from his subjects. He also had the French tribute payable under the treaty of Etaples. Much of his revenue he now kept under his own personal control: many of his rents and normal sources of revenue were paid directly into his own chamber, which had an annual turnover of more than £ 100,000. The king employed experienced lawyers to ensure that he secured every penny he had a right to and he personally checked his own account books. It was no wonder that he died an extremely rich man.

The central government was directed by the King's Council and administered by various departments working under the king's supervision. He had a large and loose body of advisers and a smaller working council or inner ring of officials whom he trusted. While his dependence upon new men should not be exaggerated, he in fact drew several of his leading councilors from "men of lower rank and smaller fortune," such, for example, as Poynings. One of the accusations made in Warbeck's proclamation against Henry VII in 1497 concerned the "caitiffs"—the despicable persons—whom he admitted to his counsels. On the whole, he preferred consulting with his Council to summoning parliaments. Parliaments, though they were by no means incompetent, were not in fact called very often in his reign except when he needed money. But he only needed money in time of war because his so-called "avarice" paid off.

He used his councilors in many capacities. In the unruly parts of his kingdom, such as the Welsh and Scottish borders, conciliar government took a firm shape. And the Tudor Council, meeting in the Court of Star Chamber at Westminster, was employed to carry out the highest judicial work expeditiously without either fear or favor.

At the county level the king made much use of the justices of the peace, whose work he invigorated and whose duties he increased. They were even empowered to investigate and punish the misdeeds of sheriffs. These justices or commissioners of the peace were virtually unpaid and tended to be independent-minded. They were kept under fairly close supervision and were liable to dismissal, which meant a loss of prestige to them. The King's Council was assiduous in keeping all the local officials up to the mark. Throughout the sixteenth and the seventeenth centuries the justices of the peace were to remain essential instruments of government.

When King Henry VII's parliaments did meet, they passed a number of important statutes: the Statute of Fines for clearing up property disputes following the civil wars, statutes against "maintenance and retainers," statutes forbidding enclosures of land, statutes insisting upon the use of English ships to carry certain imports, statutes extending the powers and duties of the justices of the peace. Encouragement of one kind or another was given to trade. A treaty known as the Magnus Intercursus of 1496 temporarily improved relations with the Netherlands. Other acts were passed to stimulate the manufacture of cloth, to stop the export of bullion, and to prohibit what were considered to be undesirable imports. But too much attention should not be paid to the economic legislation, which was usually honored little either in the practice or the spirit. It has fascinated historians of economic ideas and perhaps should be remembered as an idea rather than a historical fact. Trade might have come to a standstill if some of the more unrealistic measures had been enforced; but they were nearly always circumvented either by licensing arrangements or by smuggling on a large scale.

The basis of King Henry VII's achievement really consisted in the fact that he created a sense of confidence in his leadership among his subjects. On the whole, he trusted them and expected them to trust him. With a few obvious exceptions he showed remarkable clemency in the later years of his reign—for example in his conduct towards the Earl of Kildare. He relied upon his subjects to furnish him with men, money, and arms when he needed them in times of danger, but he did not attempt to enforce a tyranny by calculated cruelty, by terrorism, or by a standing force of mercenaries. He believed that his ministers, his councilors, and his justices of the peace would serve him faithfully and, on the whole, they did. Above all, he was an opportunist who grasped all his opportunities. If his government should be called a despotism, it was certainly an enlightened one.

XXVII

Henry VIII and Cardinal Wolsey

King Henry VIII was not yet eighteen when he came to the throne. A handsome young man with an impressive presence, he had been excellently educated—John Skelton, the poet, had been his tutor—and commanded various languages, was knowledgeable about theology, and as a musician was even said to have played "on almost every instrument." He was an athlete too, a good shot, and a keen tennis player: "It is the prettiest thing in the world to see him play," wrote a contemporary, "his fair skin glowing through a shirt of finest texture." The first years of his reign were also said to have been devoted to "continual feasting." He was dominated by an insatiable lust for power, and his ambitions and appetites knew no limits. Ruthless and cruel, he had more of his maternal grandfather, Edward IV, in him than the temperate statesmanship of his father.

His inheritance was valuable. His father had left him a rich man. He also had a number of experienced administrators and councilors to guide him: Archbishop Warham of Canterbury, the Chancellor; Richard Fox, Bishop of Winchester, Keeper of the Privy Seal; and the veteran soldier, the Earl of Surrey, who was the Treasurer. The first royal decision of the reign was significant. To win good will, a proclamation was published inviting people to bring forward their grievances against the late king's servants. Richard Empson and Edmund Dudley, who had both been Speakers of the House of Commons and loyal officials of Henry VII whom they helped with his finances, were accused of extortion, although they had acted perfectly legally. A trumped-up charge of treason was preferred against them, an act of attainder was passed, and they were sent to their deaths on the block. So by murdering two innocent men the new king bought himself some cheap popularity. Next he sought martial fame.

Pope Julius II had formed the League of Cambrai and invited the

French into Italy in order to despoil the republic of Venice. Henry VII had stayed out of this so-called crusading enterprise. The pope, now embarrassed by the completeness of the French success, executed a change of front and formed another holy league with Spain and Venice to drive the French out of Italy. According to his father's wishes, Henry VIII had married Katherine of Aragon soon after his accession, and his father-in-law, King Ferdinand V, an extremely cunning politician, pressed upon the new English government the advantages of joining the new crusade. Though his Council was divided, Henry VIII agreed to do so, partly because France was England's traditional enemy, partly out of a desire for personal glory. In November 1511 the king bound himself to attack France before the following April. An English army was landed in Spain, but was kept occupied near Bayonne while the Spaniards assaulted Navarre in their own interests. The notion that the English could reconquer Guienne proved delusive. The expeditionary force was undermined by sickness, and after mutinies returned home with nothing achieved. The English navy was also defeated at sea and Scotland came in on the side of France.

An English parliament, which met in February 1512, had given support to the new king's crusade by voting a generous grant. Now in 1513 the king had to redeem himself. Although an attack on Brest from the sea was a failure, in May the king himself arrived at Calais with a large army and undertook the siege of the small town of Thérouanne. The bulk of the French army was still occupied in Italy and a force sent with supplies for the garrison (but not to fight the English) was beaten off with such rapidity that the action was known as the Battle of the Spurs. Thérouanne was captured and so was the more important town of Tournai. Meanwhile the Earl of Surrey won a larger victory by defeating a Scottish invasion of England at the battle of Flodden, south of the Tweed (September 1513), where King James IV of Scotland was killed. Thus King Henry VIII could make a triumphant return and was voted fresh supplies by parliament.

King Ferdinand of Aragon now arranged a truce with King Louis XII of France, thus leaving his son-in-law in the lurch, although he tried to persuade him to renew the attack on Guienne. But the English king was difficult to catch twice. Instead, in the summer of 1514, King Henry VIII made his peace with France. The French offered an alliance and a substantial sum of money, and the pact was sealed by the marriage of Louis XII, now a widower, to Henry VIII's sister, Mary. Being a young girl of beauty and spirit she made it clear to her imperious brother that when her husband, who was more than three times her age, died, she would marry whom she chose.

In 1515 King Louis XII duly died and was succeeded by a more romantic figure, King Francis I. King Francis, having confirmed the English alliance, promptly invaded Italy where he defeated the Swiss at the battle of Marignano. He also stirred up trouble for England in Scotland. The English government retorted by allying itself with Emperor Maximilian and by hiring more Swiss troops to resist the French. This complicated policy of trying to build up a coalition against France was a limited success. In August 1516 another young ruler, Archduke Charles of Burgundy, who had succeeded his grandfather Ferdinand V as king of Spain, came to terms with Francis I by the treaty of Noyon, to which Emperor Maximilian acceded, and it seemed as if England was left almost isolated in Europe. Eventually, however, in October 1518, a general treaty of peace was concluded in London; the possession of Tournai proved a valuable bargaining counter; it was sold back to France at a good profit. But after 1518 English influence gradually declined; the scene was set for a struggle between two young monarchs, both more powerful than Henry VIII—King Francis I of France and King Charles I of Spain, who in 1519 followed Maximilian as Emperor Charles V.

The victories of 1513 and the diplomacy of the subsequent years owed much to the hard work of the king's new councilor, Thomas Wolsey. Son of a butcher and cattle dealer of Ipswich, Wolsey was a self-made man. He became chaplain to the Archbishop of Canterbury and to the deputy governor of Calais, who recommended him to King Henry VII. He entered the King's Council in 1509 when he was Dean of Lincoln and threw himself with enormous energy into the king's business. He was rewarded by being appointed Archbishop of York in 1514 at the age of forty-one, a cardinal in 1515, and in 1518 legate *a latere,* which made him the principal papal representative in England. Besides the archbishopric, he held the sees of Bath and Wells, Durham and Winchester, and, for a time, Tournai. But he was not much concerned over his spiritual duties. He elbowed out the aging Archbishop of Canterbury, whom he had succeeded in 1515 as Lord Chancellor. Thus he accumulated a unique collection of offices. He was in fact if not in name the effective head, under the king, of both Church and state. According to the Venetian ambassador in England, writing in 1519, he was "the person who rules both the king and the entire kingdom." He was, the same observer noted, "very handsome, learned, extremely eloquent, and indefatigable." Above all, he retained his position by sheer hard work. The young king, after his military triumphs, reverted to pleasure—it was remarked that he cared for nothing but girls and hunting, the latter a sport which he was said to have converted into a martyrdom. In a sense

Wolsey was both prime minister and secretary of state for all departments, but his tenure of office was entirely dependent upon the king's favor; and the king judged his servant not merely by his ability to relieve him of tiresome routine, but also by the measure of his successes. Wolsey knew this, and though he was arrogant to all others—"the proudest prelate that ever breathed"—he was always deferential to his master.

What did Wolsey in fact accomplish? Was he a great foreign minister or war minister? After the general pacification of 1518 (which owed less to Wolsey's own skill than to the need felt for a quiet period during the forthcoming contest for the election of a new emperor) it was said that "nothing pleases him more than to be called the arbiter of Europe"; but in fact he was forced on to the side of the new emperor, Charles V, because of his fear of the growing power of the French in Italy and anti-French sentiments in England. Although King Henry VIII and King Francis I proclaimed their friendship for each other by a gorgeous display known as "the Field of the Cloth of Gold," held in Picardy in June 1520, in the following year a treaty of alliance was concluded by Wolsey with the new emperor, committing England to yet another war against France. As a bribe to Wolsey, the young emperor promised that he would support the English cardinal's candidature for the papacy, after which he yearned, but neither in 1522, when Pope Leo X died, nor in 1523 when Leo's successor, Adrian VI, died, did Wolsey come within any distance of being elected. Thus England was involved in a war with little real national purpose upon the side of the most aggressive monarch in Europe. Campaigns in France in 1522 and 1523 proved equally futile and the cardinal alienated the English parliament and the city of London with his insistent requests for money; an attempt to supplement the yield from parliamentary grants with a capital levy, known euphemistically as the Amicable Grant, angered the possessing classes and had to be countermanded by the king. In February 1525 the imperial armies decisively defeated the French in Italy at the battle of Pavia, where King Francis I himself was taken a prisoner. This complete upsetting of the balance of power in Europe compelled Wolsey reluctantly to accept a diplomatic revolution. First, peace was made with France, then in May 1526 England, France, and a number of Italian states agreed by the treaty of Cognac to contest the imperial domination of Italy. Wolsey was driven to this about-face partly by his propapal partisanship, for Milan, previously French, had now fallen into the hands of the emperor, and the independence of the pope himself was menaced.

The pro-French policy of Wolsey was by no means popular in London, for two reasons; one was the historical antipathy felt toward France, the other the disruption of the English cloth-export trade when war was declared on the ruler of the valuable markets of the Netherlands. Wolsey's policy was already seen to lie in ruins when in September 1527 Spanish troops occupied the Eternal City. Although in the next year a fresh treaty was made with France in the hope of rescuing the pope from the hands of the emperor, nothing was achieved and Rome itself was sacked. By now Wolsey was losing his influence with King Henry VIII. His policies were openly criticized in parliament. The ruling classes in the kingdom refused to fight with France against the emperor, and in the summer of 1529, France and Spain made peace without even consulting the English cardinal.

If Wolsey failed as a foreign minister, could it be said that he was more successful in domestic affairs? The immense ecclesiastical power that he had concentrated in his hands was never in fact used for any purposes of reform. It was clear that so greedy a pluralist was in no position to carry through the radical program that was necessary to sustain the authority of the existing Church if it were not to fall before the trumpets of Protestantism, already sounding in Germany. It is true that Wolsey suppressed a number of small monasteries, but his object was merely to raise funds to endow colleges at Oxford and at Ipswich which would reflect his own grandeur. In matters of finance too he was no genius. He had the advantage of being able to use what was called the "chamber system of finance," that is to say, the system whereby such resources as fines and revenues from Crown lands were paid directly into the king's own chamber and were under the control of able royal servants, instead of going through the older course of the Exchequer. It has been estimated that more than half of the royal revenues were dealt with in this way at that time, and indeed it was by such means that Wolsey was able to protect himself from parliamentary interference with his policies. Of course the money in the royal chamber was sufficient only for ordinary purposes of government; as soon as war spread, an appeal had to be made to parliaments. In 1514 a novel tax known as "the subsidy," distinct from the earlier "fractions," was imposed, a primitive form of income tax at the rate of a shilling in the pound. When in 1523 Wolsey demanded that this tax should be increased to four shillings in the pound, he met with stiff resistance in the House of Commons, and was given only half of what he asked. It was this pressure for higher taxation that created opposition to his war policy. His scheme to overhaul the royal household arrangements, known as the Ordinance of Eltham, also remained on paper. His only positive social act was to set up a commission to inquire into depopulation of villages brought about by the enclosure of land.

As Lord Chancellor, Wolsey extended the scope of the royal jurisdiction. He was not a lawyer himself, but he invigorated the juridical authority of the King's Council, reinforcing its capacity to deal with riots and to prevent oppression by the rich and noble: this was done in the Star Chamber. In the court of chancery or equity court, Wolsey also made his zeal and drive felt: "He trespassed and caused others to trespass wherever conscience found a loophole in the ruinous walls of mediaeval common law" (Pollard). Finally, he sustained the court of requests for poor men's causes—another offshoot of conciliar activity—and in general managed to encroach on the business of the ordinary law courts so as to mitigate the rigor of the common law. Here too, as in matters of public finance, he overreached himself by his arrogance; and though at first he might have done some good, he also created enemies who, in the end, helped to strike him down.

Wolsey was indeed an extraordinary historical character. Scarcely any minister had ever wielded such powers before, and certainly no churchman was ever to do so again. Because he was a cardinal, the "scarlet sin" to later generations, he was seen to be the embodiment of arbitrary government in Church and state, more so than any king except perhaps King John. At the very moment when the papacy was coming under attack from Martin Luther and others, Wolsey, as the servant and consistent supporter of the pope of Rome, seemed to stand for papal absolutism with "a plenitude of ecclesiastical power superimposed upon a corresponding secular authority." He made himself the target for envy. And once he lost the confidence of his king, the very memory of his flamboyant rule contributed to the destruction of the cause of papal independence to which he had devoted so much of his life. Later Roman Catholic monarchs, Queen Mary I and King James II, paid the penalty for Cardinal Wolsey's failures.

XXVIII

The English Church on the Eve of the Reformation

On the eve of the Reformation the relations between the English Church and the Papacy were by no means unfriendly. Their contests in the fourteenth century lay in the distant past; they had found a method of living and working together. The splendid days of the early popes—of men like Gregory VII and Innocent III—who once bestrode western Europe like colossuses had departed. After the healing of the great schism and the election to the Holy See of Martin V, the popes were always Italian prelates and the active rulers of their own secular states. One pope at the age of eighty put on armor and led his troops to battle; others attempted to win principalities for their illegitimate sons or nephews. Indeed the papal court was becoming a byword for extortion and corruption. None of this redounded to the credit of the English Church, but popes and kings were able to come to terms because the English Church paid heavy tribute to both. The successors of Martin V were at first careful not to infringe the fourteenth-century statutes of "provisors" and "praemunire" which forbade popes to interfere with the rights of English patrons to confer livings in the Church or with the jurisdiction of the king's law courts. The Lancastrian kings and King Henry VII, himself a pious monarch, needed papal assistance and did not press their claims too far; in fact these famous statutes had become largely dead letters. The culmination of this tacit understanding or working agreement came when King Henry VIII's chief minister, Thomas Wolsey, was appointed not only a cardinal but also a papal legate.

Most of the higher clergy of the English Church were, like Cardinal Wolsey, essentially statesmen and administrators, and wealthy landlords as well. First and foremost they were servants of the king. The struggles between the monarchy and archbishops like Anselm and Becket were long past. We have seen how Archbishop Arundel had helped to plot the usurpation of King Henry IV and how Cardinal Henry Beaufort had been the dominant figure in government during the early years of King Henry VI. Only once, and that was as long ago as the reign of King Edward III, had there been a successful attack upon the clerical advisers of the king. The reason was clear. The higher clergymen were the best educated and most capable administrators available in the realm: they had made themselves indispensable to the monarchy, and they invariably occupied the chief offices of state. Inevitably they neglected their dioceses. (England was now divided into twenty-one dioceses, eighteen under the Archbishop of Canterbury and three under the Archbishop of York.) They employed chancellors and archdeacons to carry out the administrative work in their sees and left to suffragan or assistant bishops the routine duties of the ordination of priests and the confirmation of young Christians. The higher clergymen were extremely well-to-do. It is estimated that the Church owned one-third of the land in England, that the rents due to bishops and abbots exceeded those of most temporal lords, and that the incomes of the two archbishops compared favorably with those of the richest lay magnates in the kingdom. It was no wonder that Wycliffe's doctrine of "dominion by grace" had struck a chord in many a jealous heart or that the House of Commons had at one time proposed the disendowment of the Church.

On the other hand, the ordinary parish clergymen were mostly poor. Between them and their masters a vast gulf was fixed. A number of rectors did adequately well out of the tithes paid by their parishioners, but the vicars, paid a salary by the owners of the great tithes, or the curates in charge received mere pittances. Most of the parish clergy were only a cut above the ordinary peasantry and spent much of their time farming their own "glebe" land. In any case there were far too many clergy: it is thought that there was an average of one clergyman for every fifty adults in the kingdom. Naturally they were not all parish priests. The Church was "the gateway to all professions" and clergy filled almost every professional post from that of Lord Chancellor to that of village schoolmaster. The parish priests were the worst paid. They had no special training, they hardly ever preached, they often performed their duties perfunctorily. No doubt many of them were good and popular men in their communities, but the services they provided can scarcely have seemed commensurate with the heavy cost of the Church to the nation.

The clergy as a whole was supposed to be celibate. Almost from the beginning of the English Church this rule had been ignored, although vain attempts had been made to enforce it. In fact the ordinary clergy took no vows of chastity, as the monks did. Most of them seemed to have lived with their wives and children in a normal way; but their wives were liable to be called "concubines" and their children "bastards." All this did not conduce to the setting of an example by the clergy of accepted Christian social morality in the eight thousand parishes of the country. To maintain their families the clergy were sometimes forced to such unsavory expedients as selling the sacraments or selling forgiveness for sins.

Thus the laity had many grievances about what they considered to be the burdens imposed on them by the Church. They did not find the bishops or abbots more generous or more considerate landlords than any others, and when the social surface cracked, as it did at the time of the Peasants' Revolt, the naked hatred of the Church's tenants stood revealed. Not only were the bishops and abbots strict landlords, but they and their officers were also magistrates wielding large powers that might be exploited profitably. Bishops frequently ruled in the court of chancery or served in the Exchequer Court. Nearer to the ordinary Englishman came the local Church courts, founded at the time of King William I, and the archdeacons' courts that had been developed since his time. There the laity was punished for spiritual and moral offenses. Probate of wills came within the purview of the Church courts, so that when a man died the Church was in a position to interfere with the deposition of his property as well as to take his best beast in payment of funeral dues. Men could be mulcted for matrimonial offenses or for alleged heresies. Payment of tithes had to be made to the clergy or to monastic landlords or to investors to whom the rights had been sold for a lump sum.

Apart from tithes, fees, and fines, other grievances against the Church persisted among the general population. One was "benefit of clergy," successfully defended by Becket when it was attacked by King Henry II, which allowed any clerk in holy orders to evade the full consequences of his first crime. The right of sanctuary in church or monastery also frequently helped malefactors to escape the arm of the law. In sum "the lesser clergy—parish priests and unbeneficed men—earned contempt and dislike by rapacity and pretensions with which their intellectual equipment, material means and private morality too rarely kept pace" (Elton).

Incumbents of livings represented only a modest proportion of the total number of clerks in orders. Roughly 800 religious houses of one kind or another existed, out of which 600 had only four or five inmates. Then there were the friars, the missionary clergy, who had won such golden reputations during the reign of King Henry III. The monasteries had in the earliest days of the English Church served many useful public purposes: they had offered education, hospitality, charity, and social services of many kinds. But to a large extent they had been superseded or corrupted. Usually the smaller monasteries had been founded so that the inmates could pray for the souls of their benefactors after they were dead. Such solemn obligations were not, and perhaps could not, always be fulfilled. For example, the abbess and convent of Barking once had to pass a resolution that the celebration of anniversaries of abbesses who had died more than 100 years before should be discontinued. The growth of inns had reduced the need for the provision of hospitality to travelers, while some monasteries actually established inns to save themselves the trouble of having to entertain. With the widespread establishment of grammar schools, the contribution of monks to education, which had in any case been small, was lessened. The amount of alms-giving by monks and nuns never seems to have been large and may well have been exploited by "sturdy beggars" rather than received by those genuinely in need.

It is difficult to measure the true character of the inmates of monastic institutions. Bishops were allowed only to visit some of them; Cluniac,

Carthusian, and Cistercian houses, for example, lay outside their sphere. Records that have survived of some of the visitations have been used to demonstrate a bad state of affairs, but this was partly because the visitors were more likely to notice the evil than to commend the good. Still it seems clear that some abbots and priors lived the lives of well-to-do country gentlemen, eating, drinking, hunting, and being merry with the best. Monasteries had been used, in effect, as hotels—far better hotels than most of the inns of the time—or as banks which both guarded money and lent it. Although the larger monasteries were often in debt, some monks at least proved themselves to be capable managers of sheep farms or horticultural estates. The prolonged researches of Professor Knowles lead one to conclude that the monasteries were neither as black as they have been painted by Protestant historians nor as misrepresented as has been alleged by Roman Catholic controversialists. They suffered in the fifteenth century from the general decline in population, for it was not so easy to recruit men of integrity and enthusiasm for a secluded and dedicated life when alternative and more profitable professions were becoming available. Again, monks and nuns frequently took their vows at an early age, and if they later succumbed to the "temptations of the flesh and the devil," it was at least natural and human for them to do so. Their characteristic faults were of minor significance, slackness and lack of charitableness being the most common. But undoubtedly the disillusionment and demoralization which were so general in the fifteenth century penetrated the monastic walls.

The friars had also declined in moral standards and intellectual quality since their great days. They still offered to preach, but many of them had become little more than ingenious beggars, exploiting their cloth and battening upon the weak-minded. The most capable among them had found niches in Oxford and Cambridge where they led a comfortable enough existence. All these understandable abuses of their profession among the clergy, secular or other, had made for recriminations. People could not fail to contrast the material side of clerical careers and behavior with the spiritual and moral opinions the religious were supposed to uphold. If Langland and Chaucer had poked fun at them in the fourteenth century, they presented far more obvious targets in the fifteenth. In fact, they probably conducted themselves better and committed far less flagrant sins or crimes than corresponding members of the laity. But their large numbers and vast possessions left them vulnerable to attack.

How far had the fundamental doctrines of the Catholic Church become the subject of criticism by this time in English history? In the fourteenth century William of Ockham, who had decided that the mysteries of God could not be defended on the basis of pure reason, "opened the door to free enquiry" and propounded a secularist theory of the state, denying the pope's supremacy over kings and even questioning the divine origin of the Holy See. John Wycliffe, as we have seen, was critical both of the pope and of the higher clergy and also supported the secular power against the Church. The Lollards had advocated the disendowment of the Church; in spite of the statute *de haeretico comburendo* their popular preachings survived right up until the eve of the Reformation in England. Dr. Rupp has drawn our attention to the latter-day Lollards or "known men," as he calls them, who were at once strongly anticlerical and simply pious. He also speaks of "Christian Brethren" who carried out propaganda in puritanical pamphlets. But it is questionable whether the theories of Ockham and Wycliffe or the views of the Lollards and their successors played much direct part in the reformation of the Church, which was organized by the king and his ministers chiefly for reasons of state. Theirs was not a constructive religious achievement, broad-based on new doctrines or the highest moral principles. But it certainly fed on the anticlericalism that had been endemic for 200 years, while Lollardism prepared the ground for the later triumphs of doctrinal Protestantism.

Nor did the higher criticism of the English Church owe much to ideas deriving from the Italian Renaissance and wafting over the sea. It was once claimed that the Renaissance crossed the Alps and became the Reformation. But in England the humanists, who benefited from the rediscovery of the classics, were mostly quite orthodox in their views. Dr. John Colet, the cultivated dean of St. Paul's Cathedral, was no Luther or Calvin. The Dutch theologian Erasmus, who carried great weight in English intellectual circles, lived and died an orthodox Roman Catholic. Sir Thomas More and Dr. John Fisher, both celebrated Christian humanists, were to be martyred for their Catholic beliefs. The true destroyers of the papal power in England were politicians and not humanist thinkers. "Kings of England," Henry VIII remarked in 1515 before the Reformation took place, "have never had any superior but God alone." "Times were merry in England before there were Cardinals," observed the Duke of Suffolk. It was indeed Cardinal Wolsey, Archbishop of York, who by monopolizing in his own hands the greatest powers of both Church and state and by squeezing the utmost penny out of all the clerical perquisites of his time was to open men's eyes (more than any political theories) to the corrupt condition of the English Church; but their eyes might not have been opened so easily had it not been for the suspicion and even detestation of English clerical privileges that had grown up from many causes during the fifteenth century.

XXIX

The Beginning of the English Reformation

"The Protestant Reformation," wrote H. A. L. Fisher, "was a revolt against papal theocracy, clerical privilege, and the hereditary paganism of the Mediterranean races." Intellectually and emotionally it was a revolt against the abuses of the old Church and an intense expression of the spirit of religious revivalism that has shown itself at many stages in world history. Politically, it coincided with the strengthening of nationalism in western Europe, while the conversion of the Papacy into an Italian secular state provoked the jealousies of other princes. Economically, the wealth of the Church aroused the avarice of rulers whose own revenues had been reduced by rising prices.

Such was the revolutionary atmosphere in Europe when in 1517 the Saxon monk, Martin Luther, fired the first shot by attacking the sale in Germany by papal agents of indulgences for the remission of sins—sales intended to pay for the rebuilding of St. Peter's Cathedral in Rome. In October 1517 Luther nailed ninety-five theses to the door of the castle church at Wittenberg. Opposing the purchase of salvation by Christians through their "works," he taught the doctrine of "justification by faith." By 1520 he was asserting that every Christian was a priest, that Rome was Babylon, and that the pope was Antichrist. On December 10, 1520, Luther was excommunicated. Next year his heresies had taken such a hold upon Germany that the young Habsburg emperor, Charles V, ranged himself on the side of the pope and by the Edict of Worms pronounced Luther an outlaw. But Luther was protected from punishment by the old Elector of Saxony and so escaped martyrdom. In Switzerland an abler theologian than Luther, Zwingli, began to deny some of the fundamental doctrines of the Roman Church; and in 1526 antipapal teachings had spread so far that a league of Protestant German states was set up at Torgau.

These events that shook Europe touched England very little at first. During the fifteenth century the English monarchs had lived on harmonious terms with the Papacy. With the approval of King Henry VIII Thomas Wolsey had become a Roman cardinal and legate and had concentrated his foreign policy and military resources on defending the popes from their enemies. Superficially England was among the most loyal Roman Catholic nations in Europe. In 1521 King Henry VIII himself had published a book entitled *Assertio Septem Sacramentorum* in which he answered Luther and for which he was rewarded by Pope Leo X with the title of Defender of the Faith.

It is true that in this same year meetings took place in the White Horse Tavern at Cambridge where university teachers discussed the doctrines of Luther, and that at about the same time William Tyndale, an Oxford man, planned to translate the New Testament into English and print and publish it for general use. But neither this group of intellectuals nor the humbler Lollards played much part in the repudiation of the papal authority by England which was now to come. It was occasioned by the king's need to obtain a divorce from his Spanish wife, and the process was aided by the strong feelings of anticlericalism in all ranks of society upon which the king's consequent contest with the Papacy fed.

In 1509 the king had been granted a dispensation by Pope Julius II so that he could marry his deceased brother Arthur's widow. Some doubt had been expressed at the time whether the pope had in fact the right to give such a dispensation. Did not the Book of Leviticus clearly state: "And if a man shall take his brother's wife, it is an unclean thing, he hath uncovered his brother's nakedness. They shall be childless"? Strictly, the verse appeared to refer to adultery; a contradictory verse in the Book of Deuteronomy actually ordered a man to marry his brother's widow, if she were childless: it was all very complicated. Moreover Prince Arthur had been only fourteen when he married Katherine of Aragon and he died less than six months later. So it seemed scarcely likely that the marriage had been consummated: certainly Katherine denied that it was. Thus neither the contradictory religious texts and their interpretation nor the facts of Katherine of Aragon's previous marriage entered very seriously into the question when in the middle 1520's Henry VIII made up his mind that he wanted a divorce.

The king's reasons were twofold. First, he was eager for a male heir; he was not content with one daughter, for the only queen of England had been Maltida, and she was a bad one. He was sharply aware of the disasters that had befallen previous royal dynasties when a grown prince was not available to succeed. Henry VIII had been married for more than fifteen years; time was getting on. His wife was over forty and had been given every chance. He had a bastard son, so he could not himself be blamed for the missing heir. Secondly, he had fallen in love with Anne Boleyn, a young maid of honor, descended through her mother from King Edward I. Historians are not in general agreement about what it was in her that appealed to the king. A Venetian observer wrote that she was "not one of the handsomest women in the world," although "her eyes were black and beautiful." An angular Englishwoman, she had acquired some seductive French ways. It was even more notable that she managed to keep the king on edge for five years and that she insisted upon marriage.

Gradually therefore the king's conscience gripped him—or at least so he said. He was convinced that he had never been properly married to his wife, even if this were a little difficult to prove, at any rate as a practical proposition, when they had lived together before the eyes of the whole world for so long and in such close intimacy. Henry VIII emphasized that he was profoundly concerned over the verse in Leviticus with its threat of childlessness—in spite of the survival of his daughter, Mary. It does not seem to have been until some time between 1525 and 1527, when hopes of the queen bearing a son had finally been abandoned and when he had fallen passionately in love with Anne Boleyn, that he pressed Cardinal Wolsey to secure a divorce for him, and he omitted to tell the cardinal that his desire was to marry the black-eyed Anne.

Wolsey was not in favor of the divorce, but he did not anticipate any trouble over it. The pope was in his debt. He thought that his simplest way was to summon the king before his own legatine court and, having found that the marriage was invalid, invite the pope's confirmation for its dissolution. Similar divorces had been granted without much difficulty and it was not the first time that a pope had repudiated the decisions of his predecessor. But Pope Clement VII was now the prisoner of Emperor Charles V, who happened to be Katherine of Aragon's nephew, and Katherine was by no means prepared to acquiesce in her humiliation. Wolsey's next idea therefore was to put through the divorce on his own responsibility with the backing of other cardinals; but that plan broke down, and in 1528 he again tried to extract a commission from the pope to dissolve the marriage. He had no wish for the question to be decided abroad, where all sorts of influences might be brought to bear on the papal court. Eventually Clement VII, who had escaped from the immediate control of the emperor, granted a commission for the case to be tried in England, and sent over Cardinal Campeggio, the Bishop of Salisbury, to act with Wolsey, but gave him secret instructions to procrastinate. In this Campeggio was remarkably successful. The case dragged on through the first half of 1529, and in July the court adjourned, never to meet again. By autumn the pope, who was anxious to offend neither the king of England nor Emperor Charles V, had succumbed to the influences nearer to him and revoked the matter to Rome. Henry VIII's patience was at last exhausted; he felt that his great servant had failed him. On October 9 Wolsey was indicted for "praemunire," that is to say, for having in the first place accepted the office of papal legate, to which King Henry himself had agreed; on October 18 he surrendered his seal as Lord Chancellor; and he soon lost all his other secular offices. That November he died. Meanwhile the king had summoned a meeting of parliament—the first for six years—with the intention of using it to bring pressure upon the Papacy by attacking the English Church. Whether ironically or not, it was at this point that Anne Boleyn at last yielded to the king's desires.

The question has often been discussed whether the House of Commons in what was afterward known as "the Reformation Parliament" was "packed." But this phrase is anachronistic and belongs to a later stage in English constitutional history. In general the knights of the shire were chosen with the approval of the great men of their counties to whom they might be related or be under obligations. Inevitably some of them held royal offices or were chosen upon the advice of important men at the king's court. Electoral contests, as they are known in Britain today, certainly never took place. To think in terms of differing political programs being presented to the electorate from which a choice might be made is completely wrong. But in most parts of the country anticlerical feeling was strong: it was natural enough that the knights and burgesses who came to Westminster should have many varying grievances against the Roman Church and be receptive to ideas of radical reform.

In any case the king had not yet determined to push matters to extremes. The advisers who immediately succeeded Cardinal Wolsey were mostly conservative in outlook—notably Sir Thomas More, a conscientious lawyer who replaced him as Lord Chancellor. In fact during the next three years the king had no precise policy. On the whole, he seems to have hoped that the pope might still show himself amenable on the question of the divorce: he persuaded himself that if pressure were brought to bear upon the Church, he could have his own way without, after all, having to associate himself with the archheretic, Martin Luther, whom earlier he had trounced.

During the first session of the parliament the commons were allowed or encouraged to set about remedying long-standing complaints against the clergy: the right of sanctuary for criminals was circumscribed; payments for mortuary dues and fees for probate of wills were reduced; the number of offices that might be filled by any one clergyman was limited to four. In the following year, however, the king himself turned the screw. That summer fifteen bishops, abbots, and leading clergy were accused in the Court of King's Bench of having broken the law by obeying Wolsey's authority as legate to the extent of paying him a part of their own revenues. Among those accused were the Bishop of Rochester, John Fisher, and others who were known to be in sympathy with Queen Katherine of Aragon. This move was followed by an indictment of the whole of the clergy for exercising its normal jurisdiction in the ecclesiastical courts. The two Convocations were compelled to buy pardons for this breach of the old statutes of praemunire with large sums of money. Thus the clergy were browbeaten by their imperious monarch; but they were not cowed. They paid their fines in installments; they asked that the statutes of praemunire under which these trumped-up charges were brought should be more clearly defined; they said that they would only acknowledge the king's right to be called Protector and Supreme Head of the English Church and Clergy so far as the law of Christ allowed.

Meanwhile the king had thought of a new device for securing his divorce: at least he had discovered an obscure Cambridge don named Thomas Cranmer, who suggested that he should consult all the universities of Europe about whether or not a man might marry his deceased brother's widow. Needless to say, the English universities thought that he could not, while the Spanish universities thought that he could. This knowledge did not get the king much farther, but it redounded to the credit of Cranmer, who was active in collecting favorable verdicts, and when in 1532 the aged Archbishop Warham at last died, Cranmer was appointed in his place at Canterbury. It was symptomatic of the continuing relations between the English monarchy and the Papacy that Pope Clement VII issued the bulls necessary for the confirmation of Cranmer's appointment.

By this time a stronger man than Cranmer had come forward as a minister of the king. This was Thomas Cromwell, who, although he had held office earlier, did not until then accumulate the posts that brought him to the forefront of public affairs. Son of a Putney brewer and blacksmith, Cromwell was a self-made man who began life as a soldier, accountant, and merchant and had traveled widely abroad. He entered the employment of Wolsey, for whom he acted as a business agent. Cromwell was also a member of parliament; his independence of mind was exemplified by the fact that he criticized the king's foreign policy and defended Wolsey when he was in disgrace. The king took him into his own service and he became his chief instrument in reforming the Church and breaking with the Papacy. Until recently his reputation among historians has been unsavory, but his latest biographer is of the opinion that he was "an administrator of tremendous energy, an institutional thinker, a patron of political philosophers, a bold and original statesman who thought of his own work as creative and who cast his shadow centuries forward upon the history of England." It is worth noting that his nephew was the great-grandfather of Oliver Cromwell, the future Lord Protector.

With Cromwell's advent to power it has been said that King Henry VIII "exchanged the lever for the hammer" in his dealings with the Papacy and the English Church, but another human factor also entered into the situation in 1533. In January the king was secretly married to Anne Boleyn. Soon she was known to be with child. It was now clear that no change of heart was likely to take place in Rome. The Commons, which had met again at the beginning of 1532, had produced what was called the "Supplication against Ordinaries," a document originally drafted by Thomas Cromwell, which enumerated grievances against the clergy in general and the two Houses of Convocation in particular. The king backed it up: indeed he sent for the Speaker and leading members of the Commons and informed them that though he had once thought that the clergy were wholly his subjects, he had now discovered they were only half his subjects, since they took an oath to the pope which was contrary to their oath to himself. The clergy then submitted to the demands made upon them, of which the most important was that Convocation should henceforward pass no laws without the king's agreement and assent. As soon as they had done this, Sir Thomas More resigned his office as Chancellor. Then followed an enactment which threatened to deprive the Papacy of the payments known as "annates" always made to it by newly appointed bishops. Next year came a most revolutionary act, that "in restraint of appeals," which forbade the English Church to refer questions to Rome and insisted that all matters affecting the king should be decided directly in Convocation. So at last the Rubicon was crossed and the "great matter" of the divorce was open for settlement. In May 1533 Archbishop Cranmer, with the approval of Convocation, annulled the king's first marriage; thus when the future Queen Elizabeth I, daughter of Anne Boleyn, was born in September she was deemed legitimate.

Now the antipapal statutes followed each other thick and fast. An act was passed abolishing annates, and later they were assigned to the Crown. A Dispensations Act cut off all other payments to Rome including "Peter's pence," which dated back as far as King Offa's time. No licenses of any sort from Rome were henceforward to be recognized in England. An Act for the Submission of the Clergy placed upon the statute book in precise form the promises given earlier defining the rights of Convocation. Finally, an Act of Supremacy affirmed that the king was the Supreme Head of the Church of England without any restrictions—a supremacy that was considered to lie beyond mere jurisdictional and financial rights and stretched into the spiritual realm. To sustain all this legislation against those who might not approve of it, a Treason Act was added, although its stringent terms, which extended the definition of treason to cover any statement in words or by writing that the king was a heretic, a schismatic, a tyrant, an infidel, or a usurper, even took the complacent Commons aback. The coping stone to the reforming legislation was an act of 1536 "to extinguish the authority of the Bishop of Rome." Henceforward the king in parliament was—as far as the law of the land could ensure it—as powerful in matters ecclesiastical as he was in matters temporal. The first stage of the English Reformation was completed.

Although there was no organized or united opposition to these revolutionary changes in the law in Church and state, they were resisted by a number of influential people. John Fisher, Bishop of Rochester, a scholar and lover of learning, had been the confessor of Queen Katherine of Aragon and never concealed his disapproval of the divorce; he thought that the reforms were destructive to the Church and he refused to take the oath of supremacy. Sir Thomas More was a cultivated lawyer, but also an ascetic who at one time thought of becoming a Franciscan friar. In 1516 he had published a book which became a classic entitled *Utopia,* in which ideals mingled with wit and fantasies. He too was opposed to the divorce and to the royal supremacy. A third critic was the king's own cousin, Reginald Pole, a younger man than Fisher and More, equally cultivated but less forthright. King Henry VIII wanted to have Pole on his side; he made him Dean of Exeter and later offered him the bishopric of Winchester and the archbishopric of York. Pole refused these tempting offers and in 1532 managed to obtain permission to go abroad. Here he published a book, *De Unitate Ecclesiae,* which firmly stated that no temporal prince could be supreme head of the Church in his own country. He kept out of the king's reach and was created a cardinal by the pope. From the safety of the Netherlands he brooded upon the loosening of the bonds between his native country and the Roman Curia.

King Henry VIII was not prepared to withstand opposition from any quarter. He chose first to attack Fisher and More through a madwoman named Elizabeth Barton. This young girl, who suffered from epileptic fits, seemed to regard herself as inspired. She entered a convent, had trances, and made revelations: she said that if the king were divorced, he would not live for another six months. In April 1534 she and her entourage were executed at Tyburn after she had "confessed" in the Star Chamber and a bill of attainder had been passed against her by parliament. On the most tenuous grounds the names of More and Fisher were included in the bill of attainder, although More's was withdrawn and Fisher was only fined £300 for misprision of treason. This was the first move against them. A year later a number of Carthusian monks who refused to take the oath of supremacy were imprisoned in the Tower of London, tied to hurdles, dragged to the gibbet at Tyburn, and tortured for treason before they were allowed to die; many friars perished in prison because of the ill treatment they received; then in the summer of 1535 both More and Fisher went bravely to their deaths. To balance the executions of these devoted Roman Catholics and convinced humanists and to preserve the king's reputation for doctrinal orthodoxy, thirteen Anabaptists (extreme heretics who did not believe in the existing methods of baptism) were also executed.

At this time too the dissolution of the monasteries began. Lord Herbert of Cherbury, who wrote a life of King Henry VIII, said that the members of the religious orders were "looked upon as a reserve army of the Pope's, always ready to appear in his quarrels." This was not, however, the main purpose of the dissolution, nor had it the conscious aim of binding the landed gentry and the middle classes to the Henrician Reformation by enabling them to purchase monastic lands cheaply. The object was simply to raise money for the Crown. The Reformation Parliament had been more generous in destroying the privileges of the Church than in voting the king subsidies. Although the clergy had been heavily mulcted with fines and the king had secured the annates and other papal sources of income, these proved insufficient for his many needs, more especially as he was now involved in trouble with Wales, Scotland, and Ireland, in guarding against possible attacks from Catholic enemies abroad, and in building a navy. Thomas Cromwell was created the king's vicar-general and special commissioner so that he might carry out a capital levy on the king's behalf. A general visitation of the monasteries with a view to their suppression began in the summer of 1535.

There were plenty of precedents. Both papal and episcopal visitors had reported unfavorably upon the monasteries in the past, so their shortcomings were notorious. Wolsey, himself a Roman cardinal, had suppressed some of the smaller religious houses. The visitors employed by Cromwell were lawyers of more than dubious character: a prurient Dean of York, a conceited Cambridge don with a "satrapic countenance"; and a former warden of New College, Oxford, who was to die in the Fleet prison, were among them. They carried out their task with incredible speed, tarring most of the religious houses with brushes dipped in venom; on this basis a bill was swiftly passed dissolving about 400 smaller houses and transferring their incomes and properties to the Crown. In November attention was turned to the larger houses. Here the abbots and priors read the writing on the wall. In 1537 the Abbot of Furness surrendered his house to the Crown: others rapidly followed suit. Some abbots, less adroit, were hanged. Ultimately most of the larger houses were either dissolved by commission or confiscated by statute. When King Henry VIII died, nothing of the great network of religious houses throughout England was left but a few chantries, and these too were abolished in the next reign.

What were the consequences of the dissolution? Many of the former functions of the monasteries, such as education and the social services, had already been largely taken out of their hands. But the monarchy did not use the resources that had been accumulated for the benefit of the English Church. Some promises were certainly given, but in the end all that happened was that six new bishoprics and a number of professorships at Oxford and Cambridge were founded. Yet the Crown had received about one-half of the entire wealth of the English Church and King Henry VIII had made himself probably the richest prince in the whole of Christendom. The extruded inmates of the monasteries must have suffered considerably. It is true that the leading abbots and priors received generous pensions or were moved to comfortable benefices, but the rank and file were poorly treated. Friars were not given pensions at all and nuns got miserable ones. Many monks were turned out into the cold world with a bare minimum on which to subsist. No doubt some of the monks received employment of a sort as secular clergy and a few of the nuns married. Still, if individual unhappiness is ignored as not coming within the scope of the historian, it can be argued that since the wealth of the monasteries was distributed directly or indirectly into other and often more businesslike channels, the general economy of the nation was not injured and only temporary unemployment was created.

It used to be said that the risings against the government which took place in 1536 were caused by the dissolution of the monasteries, but this view is no longer generally accepted. The risings were chiefly concentrated in the north of England. The north had long been unruly, little receptive to orders from Westminster. Economic and financial grievances had mounted there; resentment was expressed against the levying of taxation, against the spread of enclosures, against new legislation about the manufacture of cloth. Neither the Bishop of Durham, who had supported Queen Katherine, nor Henry Percy, Earl of Northumberland, had been able to maintain order in those parts. The smaller monasteries had been more popular with the laity in the north than they had been in the south of England, while wild rumors about stinging increases in taxation had begun to circulate there. In October 1536, riots broke out in Lincolnshire, and, although these were suppressed, a movement in Yorkshire proved much more serious because it found a capable organizer in Robert Aske, a lawyer who regarded his rebellion as a "pilgrimage of grace." He collected 30,000 men, but the monarchy repeated the tactics of duplicity employed of old against Wat Tyler and Jack Cade. Temporizing promises were given to the rebels, while an army was gathered against them. After a while the rebels dispersed and their leaders were dealt with piecemeal. Summary executions took place all over the north of England; a new prerogative council was set up at York to prevent further trouble. The danger had been real. Had Cardinal Pole—the only survivor of the leading opponents of the Reformation—acted quickly and furnished assistance from abroad, a civil war of considerable dimensions might have followed. As it was, the king's position was strengthened by the failure of the revolt.

Why did the first stage of the English Reformation pass, on the whole, so peacefully? In the first place, the Church itself was in a bad way and had long lacked real spiritual leaders. Cardinal Wolsey may have been, as the late Professor Pollard claimed, a diplomatist and administrator with few equals, but he was not an inspiring churchman: by engrossing both ecclesiastical and lay powers in his own hands, he had opened the way for the king to do the same thing. And Henry VIII was a man of astonishing magnetism, who put the fear of death into his servants: in a famous phrase used by Sir Thomas More, "if a lion knew his own strength, hard were it for any man to rule him." In Thomas Cromwell he found an ideal stage manager for all his projects. It was Cromwell who organized the Reformation Parliament to do his master's will. That the commons were not mere sycophants is amply proved by the way in which they resisted some of the demands made upon them by the king, notably for money. Moreover Cromwell was not content with mere management, with manipulation behind the scenes. By giving them arguments employed years before by the theologian, Marsiglio of Padua, Cromwell deployed a number of capable propagandists who put the case for the new church settlement with telling fluency: at least fifty books were published expounding the king's case, while the printing presses were denied to the other side. More important still, during the critical years the Roman Catholic rulers of Europe were distracted by their own affairs. The king of France and the emperor were still absorbed in conflict, and in any case the emperor had his own attention sufficiently occupied by the progress of the Protestant Reformation in Germany. King

Henry VIII was fully aware that his repudiation of the Papacy—not to mention the emperor's aunt—might inspire foreign intervention against him. He was thankful when the divorced Queen Katherine—the "old harridan," as he called her—died, since he believed she was the most likely magnet for imperial vengeance. Finally it has to be remembered that neither the king nor Cromwell nor the moderate Archbishop Cranmer had yet introduced any significant doctrinal changes. Men and women could still worship in their parish churches as they had always done or attend the Mass, crediting the transubstantiation of the Host, as they had from time out of mind. The extreme doctrines advocated by Luther and Zwingli had not merely taken no hold upon the English Church, but had indeed been rejected by it. "Ten Articles," which the king had published in 1536 to define his position, actually won the approval of the exiled Cardinal Pole. Thus the hope still faintly existed of reconciliation with Rome.

Only two noticeable changes took place in religious affairs in the late 1530's: one was that an attack was launched upon the use of images, the shrine of St. Thomas of Canterbury being ransacked; the other was that English Bibles were freely provided for reading—by those who could read—in the parish churches. Because the new leaders of the English Church were so conservative in their outlook, the assault on the authority of the Papacy and on ecclesiastical privileges had met with comparatively little resistance, once More and Fisher were in their graves. Indeed the spirit of nationality that had been bred in England during the Hundred Years' War against France was invoked, so that the repudiation of the pope as a foreign potentate was widely welcomed. This patriotic feeling was strengthened when Pope Paul III, who succeeded Clement VII, at last in 1538 published a bull of excommunication against the English king. Moreover the land settlement that followed the dissolution of the monasteries firmly anchored the interests of purchasers of church properties to the spiritual supremacy of the monarchy. Where men's treasures were, there were their hearts also.

No impartial historian can pretend that the Henrician Reformation makes an edifying story. It was motivated by lust and thrust forward by greed. The spoils of the monasteries went not to pay for education or social improvement, but for the rearmament necessary to protect the ecclesiastical settlement. If the "Gospel light" once shone "in Bullen's eyes," it soon faded away. Queen Anne gave the king another daughter and afterward produced a stillborn son, as Katherine of Aragon had done before her. The king then tired of his second queen. In May 1536 she was indicted before a grand jury allegedly for committing adultery with five men, including her own brother, and hurriedly executed. In the same month the king married Jane Seymour, a pale and modest young lady, who bore him a son, the future Edward VI. After Jane Seymour died the following year, from natural causes, Cromwell persuaded the king to marry Anne, sister of the Duke of Cleves, because he believed that it would strengthen England's position in Germany. Hans Holbein, the celebrated portrait painter, had been retained on salary to depict eligible ladies so that the king might inspect their portraits, but his picture of Anne of Cleves proved misleading. Not merely was this unfortunate German lady said to resemble a Flanders mare, but she dressed so badly that the king had to send to Paris to buy new clothes for her. That gave Thomas Cromwell's enemies, of whom he had many, the chance they had long awaited to turn upon him. Among them was Thomas Howard, Duke of Norfolk, who had distinguished himself in putting down the rebellion in the north and who had a niece, Katherine, believed to be capable of attracting the king.

Cromwell was arrested by the captain of the guard in the king's own council chamber. His colleagues, except for Archbishop Cranmer, deserted him as soon as he had been accused of heresy and treason. From his cell in the Tower of London he vainly begged the king for mercy. At the end of July 1540 this clever but repulsive statesman followed Empson and Dudley, More and Fisher, Anne Boleyn, and the rest of the long line of King Henry VIII's victims to death upon the scaffold. The architect of a new national state, the patron of the House of Commons, the Hammer of the Monks, the prophet of Erastianism in the English Church, the reformer of the Tudor administration is little remembered today; but, for good or ill, he was one of the founders of modern Britain.

XXX

The Last Years of Henry VIII

After Thomas Cromwell, who had been created Earl of Essex the previous spring, had been executed for treason in July 1540, King Henry VIII ceased to employ any one chief minister. His own authority over Church and state was supreme. He relied not upon a loose collection of advisers but upon a properly constituted Privy Council, which contained such men as the Duke of Norfolk, whose niece he married; Stephen Gardiner, Bishop of Winchester; Edward Seymour, Earl of Hertford, the brother of his third wife; and Thomas Cranmer, Archbishop of Canterbury. The Privy Council derived from King Henry VII's "inner ring" but had been converted into a formal body by Cromwell and acquired records dating from 1540.

Hitherto the king's leading minister had normally been the Lord Chancellor, but Wolsey was the last outstanding Chancellor. Cromwell had preferred to hold the position of Secretary, which ceased to be an office of the king's household and soon became a Secretaryship of State. Although after Cromwell's death this office was divided between two able members of his staff, later in Tudor and Stuart history the Secretary of State became one of the principal servants of the Crown and remained so for many years. In fact Cromwell had refashioned the king's administration in such a way that the household at last ceased to have the important functions it had performed in earlier times, while the Privy Council and the Star Chamber had become the main organs of government.

The king's counselors were divided between those who had what might be called conservative and those who held reformist opinions, at any rate upon matters of religion. The king himself tended toward conservatism, but Seymour and Cranmer were reformers. The king appears to have had a warm spot in his implacable heart for Cranmer. The sympathies of the archbishop, a twice married man, were against the celibacy of the clergy and directed broadly toward Lutheranism. He occupied part of his time in preparing a new liturgy for the English Church, but it was not until after the death of King Henry VIII that his prayer book was published. Encouragement was given to the reading of the Bible in churches, but the king did not approve of Tyndale's English version, which he thought savored too much of radicalism.

Even before the death of Cromwell the king had given publicity to his own theological views. An act "abolishing diversity of opinions"—generally known as "the Six Articles"—was passed in 1539 that upheld the belief in transubstantiation (to deny it brought the death penalty), Communion in one kind only for the laity, the celibacy of the clergy, the permanence of religious vows, and the use of private Masses and of the Confessional. The Six Articles were supported by Norfolk and opposed by Cranmer. After their publication Cranmer had to put away his wife, a number of Protestants were burned, and five hundred suspected heretics were placed under arrest. However an act of 1540 mitigated the severity of the Six Articles, the suspects were released, and a general pardon was granted. As he grew older, the king became a little more tolerant, though no less unpredictable: he was prepared to listen to arguments from both sides, and even swung at times a little to the left.

It is said that Katherine Howard, the king's fifth wife, was a conservative. It may be doubted whether any of these ladies who took the risk of marrying King Henry VIII held violent theological opinions. In any case by the middle of 1541 the king discovered that his latest wife had been guilty of unchastity before her marriage and adultery after it. Two of her alleged lovers were forthwith condemned for treason and hanged. The queen herself followed them to the scaffold after a decent interval: the statute under which she was condemned pronounced the novel doctrine that for the king's bride to be unchaste before her wedding was an act of high treason. The king's sixth and last marriage, which followed eighteen months later in 1543, was unusual because the lady concerned, Katherine Parr, though not technically unchaste before, had twice been a widow; her second husband had taken part in the Pilgrimage of Grace. Despite this, Katherine Parr reputedly leaned towards Protestantism, although that she did so any more than her predecessor leaned the other way is a speculative question. At any rate Katherine Parr succeeded in surviving her imperious and quarrelsome husband. If in the last years of his reign he moved away from extreme religious conservatism, the policy of the Six Articles was not officially altered and he died in effect a Catholic—but not a Roman Catholic—king.

Before the king died two acts of succession were passed. The first in 1534 had excluded Princess Mary, the daughter of Katherine of Aragon, from the throne on the ground that she was illegitimate, the marriage having been annulled. But in an act of 1543 King Henry VIII had second thoughts and provided for the succession of Prince Edward, Princess Mary, and Princess Elizabeth, his only legitimate children, in that order. He excluded the heirs of his sister Margaret (who had married King James IV of Scotland) and favored the heirs of his sister Mary, who had insisted upon wedding Charles Brandon, Duke of Suffolk, after her unlucky first marriage to the French king. He also expressed a wish that the Earl of Hertford should be the guardian of his young son and planned a carefully balanced council of regency to govern in his name. But kings have rarely provided satisfactorily for events after their deaths. Henry VIII's will was a source of much future trouble and was finally ignored when the Stuarts followed the Tudors upon the English throne.

During his last years too England was engaged in a singularly pointless war against France. At the beginning of 1539 the French king and the emperor Charles V, who was also the ruler of Spain, had signed a treaty at Toledo. Cromwell had been alarmed at this Catholic alliance and had advocated the king's marriage to Anne of Cleves, because her brother was related to the Elector of Saxony, the protector of Martin Luther, thinking it wise at that stage to enlist the German Protestants upon the side of England. This diplomatic insurance proved superfluous (hence the divorce of Anne of Cleves), since King Francis and Emperor Charles soon fell out. Nevertheless in 1544 a large English army was sent to France after an alliance had been made with the emperor; it managed to move from Calais to the conquest of Boulogne. A war with France both on sea and land developed. The French threatened the Isle of Wight. Finally in June 1546 a treaty was concluded at Ardes by which the English were allowed to retain Boulogne for six years, after which the French would be allowed to buy it back. Such was the fantastic ending to an extremely expensive campaign.

Before the war with France opened, the king had also turned his attention to Scotland. Here his nephew, King James V, had shown himself to be pro-French and anti-English: he had married two French wives and rejected the offer of the hand of Henry VIII's daughter, Mary; and his chief adviser, Cardinal David Beaton, Archbishop of St. Andrews, was strongly pro-French. In 1541 Henry VIII traveled north to meet his nephew, but King James failed to arrive. Thereupon an English army was sent into Scotland under the Duke of Norfolk to assert the ancient English claim to overlordship. However Norfolk did not reach Edinburgh and withdrew across the border after burning a number of villages. The Scottish king had difficulty in organizing a counteroffensive, as many Scots thought they had been dragged into the war with England on the tails of the French. Eventually he raised an army, but it suffered a disgraceful defeat at the battle of Solway Moss in November 1542. When King James V heard the news of the disaster, he retired to Falkland and took to his bed. At that time a daughter, the future Mary, Queen of Scots, was born to him by her French mother. When he was told of this he said, "It cam' wi' a lass, and it will gang wi' a lass"—meaning his own Stuart line. After that he expired. King Henry VIII now hoped to gain Scotland by negotiating the marriage of the baby Mary to his son, Prince Edward. But the pride of the Scots was affronted; they repudiated the marriage treaty; and with French assistance they defied the English under the leadership of Cardinal Beaton. Although Beaton himself was murdered, King Henry VIII made no headway in Scotland. Later Mary, Queen of Scots, was betrothed to the son of the French king, the future Francis II.

King Henry VIII was more successful in his policy toward Wales. A capable president of the Council of the Marches was found in Rowland Lee, Bishop of Lichfield and Coventry. An act of 1536 incorporated Wales into England. Four new counties (Denbigh, Montgomery, Brecknock, and Radnor) were added to the existing six, while the earldom of Pembroke and the lordship of Glamorgan were also converted into counties. Justices of the peace were set up, twenty-four members of parliament went to the House of Commons, and English laws and administrative methods were applied everywhere. Justices were sent to Wales on circuit and appeals were carried to Westminster. All these important changes were finally summarized in another act of 1543. Although there was some resistance to the new statutes, Wales was now completely united with England and its history became absorbed into the story of Britain.

It was not so with Ireland. Here the country was still ruled by the great Anglo-Irish lords, notably the Butlers, who were the earls of Ormonde, and the Fitzgeralds, earls of Kildare. For a time, from 1526 to 1528, Gerald Fitzgerald, ninth Earl of Kildare, was kept a hostage in London, but in 1532 after an English deputy had proved himself incapable of controlling the Irish, Kildare was reappointed Lord Lieutenant and thereupon resumed his customary feud with the Butlers. In 1533 Kildare was again recalled to London and imprisoned in the Tower, where he died. An Irish revolt followed, headed by the tenth Earl of Kildare. He declared for the pope and renounced his allegiance to King Henry VIII. The revolt was ruthlessly suppressed by methods dishonorable even for the sixteenth century. Seven of the Fitzgeralds were put to death. The new deputy enforced King Henry VIII's antipapal policy upon the unwilling Irish. For his pains he was ultimately put to death for treason. In 1541 King Henry VIII assumed the titles of king of Ireland and head of the Irish Church. But the Irish were far from pacified and revolts were only postponed by the continuing internal feuds. Henry VIII's settlement of the difficulties in Ireland was entirely superficial.

The king's campaigns in Scotland and Ireland and the war with France had been exceedingly costly. Personal extravagances, such as the building of palaces and colleges, including Christ Church, Oxford, and the upkeep of his six wives and various mistresses all increased the large bill that had to be met. Yet Henry was the richest king yet to have appeared in British history. Whereas under King Henry VII the yield from taxation averaged only £11,500 a year, in the last seven years of his son's reign it averaged nearly £100,000. This sum excluded forced loans and the taxation of the clergy. Beyond this were the king's own personal income and the revenues derived from fines imposed on the Church and sales of the possessions of expropriated monks. The king might perhaps have done better with regard to the monasteries. It has been calculated that the income obtainable from monastic properties could have amounted to at least £100,000 a year. Yet in 1540 to meet his current expenditure he started selling off the properties, for which in the end about £1,500,000 was obtained altogether. Some of the property was exchanged or given away as rewards for services, but much of it was sold to all sorts of purchasers. Although it might be supposed that a buyers' market was created, modern research does not confirm the view that the prices that monastic lands fetched for the king were much too low. Another source of capital was discovered in the debasement of the coinage —or, in modern terms, the depreciation of the currency. This had been carried out before in English history—sometimes, as under Cardinal Wolsey, because the currency was genuinely overvalued. The debasement that took place after 1542 was, however, arranged for no other reason than to help the royal finances; it showed a profit of well over £300,000.

The heavy sale of monastic lands had significant social consequences. The evidence suggests that a considerable amount of the land was bought either directly or indirectly by ordinary landed gentry or by merchants: how much it is hard to say because clearly a good deal was bought for speculative reasons and later changed hands. The result was that at least some of this land was developed in a more businesslike way than it had been before. The monks may not have been particularly easy-going or generous landlords, but neither were they necessarily competent business men inspired by enterprising ideas. It was common knowledge that in many parts of the country pasturage was becoming more profitable than arable cultivation. There was thus a pronounced tendency for the new landlords in some parts of the country to promote enclosures to make more grassland or establish "ley farming," which contributed to temporary unemployment and aroused local discontents. Enclosures had been one of the grievances aired during the revolts of 1536; although statistics indicate that the amount of enclosure in the reign of King Henry VIII was exaggerated at the time, undoubtedly it was a genuine cause of discontent.

If the dissolution of the monasteries, while doing no serious economic damage to the country, created unrest, even greater hardship resulted from the debasement of the coinage, although it also had some advantage from the point of view of the general economy. Prices had begun to rise owing to world causes at the beginning of the fifteenth century. By 1540 the price level may have risen by over 100 per cent, as compared with the thirteenth century. As a result of the debasement of coinage, the price level rose still higher in the decade 1541–50 and by the reign of Queen Elizabeth I it was about three times what it had been in the reign of King Henry VIII. It is difficult to translate the effects of such increases into modern terms. For Britain had not yet a fully monetary economy. The bulk of the population was still almost self-subsistent. Peasants grew most of what they ate and even produced their own clothes. Many rents were fixed by manorial custom and were not easy to increase, while any surplus produce grown by agriculturalists could be sold at the higher prices then prevailing. Therefore tenant farmers, for example, might not have been hit so severely as their modern counterparts would be. Nevertheless this general rise in prices did stimulate the new landlords to increase their rents when they could, while wages were controlled at least in theory and in law. Again increases in prices may have helped the cloth industry and thereby stimulated the movement to enclose land for sheep farming.

The reign of King Henry VIII therefore saw the beginnings of an agricultural, economic, and social revolution. It was a striking fact that Cardinal Wolsey's last war was frustrated because the House of Commons was reluctant to endanger the valuable cloth markets in the Netherlands. For the same reason there was a good deal of sham fighting between Henry VIII and Emperor Charles V, who ruled the Netherlands. Thomas Cromwell seems to have possessed some notion of the coming expansion of English commerce (after all, he had been a merchant himself) and he tried to bring the principal entrepôt markets back from Antwerp to England. The rise of modern capitalism has also been assigned by some historians to the sixteenth century: certainly some former monastic buildings were converted into rudimentary factories.

Thus the last years of the reign of King Henry VIII may have been, as Professor Bindoff has written, "as pregnant with change from the economic and social point of view as were the fifteen-thirties in the history of the King's government and creed." King Henry VII, after more than 100 years of internal conflict, had established the power of the English national monarchy and imposed law and order upon the land. His son, by defeating the Scots, by unifying Wales, and by asserting that he was king of Ireland, had moved toward the unification of Great Britain. By defying the pope and the Roman Catholic powers in Europe, he had also staked his claim to exercise a far more complete authority than had been enjoyed by any of his predecessors. Whether it is right to speak yet in terms of modern "nationalism" or "sovereignty" is questionable. These are terms that demand the very closest definitions. But assuredly by the monopolizing of many varied powers—for which Cardinal Wolsey had set the pattern—King Henry VIII enhanced the royal prerogative, while his ruthlessness had read lessons to the magnates of the realm which underlined those already taught them by his three predecessors. The English Church had become the Church of England, fully subject to the state, although the reform of its doctrines in a Protestant direction had scarcely begun. Finally, the position both of parliament as a whole and the House of Commons in particular had been strengthened.

It is scarcely true to say, as historians once did, that King Henry VIII took parliament into partnership; but he had made it the instrument of the Reformation and therefore raised its political importance. The character of the House of Lords had been changed because, with the disappearance from it of the abbots, it had ceased to contain a majority of spiritual peers. The House of Commons, increased in size by the members from Wales and also from Calais, had regularly been consulted, even if it had been used chiefly to strengthen the executive powers of the monarchy. On the whole, the Commons proved themselves to be tractable but not subservient. Many of the leading members were royal officials grouped around the privy councilors. Care was taken to see that men agreeable to the Crown were elected as far as possible. The Speaker was always, in effect, a royal nominee. But there was some foreshadowing of the members' rights of freedom of speech and freedom from arrest, rights not finally to be established until the seventeenth century. When Richard Strode was arrested by a court order for a speech made in parliament, the Commons secured his release and passed a bill in his favor; later the House secured the release of another member who had been imprisoned for a private suit. Thus, as Dr. Elton says, "began the long struggle of the Commons for control over their own privileges and for the powers of a court in ordering their own affairs."

When King Henry VIII died in January 1547 at the age of fifty-five it could safely be said that an exciting period in British history had opened in which new institutions and new liberties were to appear and the face of society was to be transformed.

XXXI

The Reign of Edward VI

"Woe to thee, o land, where a boy is King." It was ironical that after all King Henry VIII's exertions to secure a suitable heir to his throne— which brought about the rupture with the Papacy—when he died in

January 1547 he was succeeded by a boy of nine, who was to live only until he was sixteen. Edward VI received an excellent education that ranged from music to Greek; he was religious, bookish, and solitary, and not unnaturally became the tool of cunning advisers. Not only had King Henry VIII left the kingdom a prey to those internecine squabbles that always sprang up when there was a royal minority, but the government was faced with grave financial difficulties, an unsettled Church policy, social and religious unrest, and an unfinished war with Scotland.

When the Privy Council met, the late king's careful arrangement for a balanced group of moderates to act as an organ of regency was ignored, and Edward Seymour, Earl of Hertford, was chosen Lord Protector. The boy-king signed a commission giving his uncle full authority until he himself was eighteen years old; the rest of the Privy Council members then acted as his ministers or advisers. It was generally recognized that his only serious rival for power was John Dudley, Viscount Lisle, who had held the office of Lord High Admiral since 1543, even though his father had been one of the first victims of the late king's ruthlessness. Hertford assumed the title of Duke of Somerset and the office of Lord Treasurer; Lisle became Lord Chamberlain and Earl of Warwick.

Somerset was an ambitious man, but not very competent either as an administrator or a politician. In religion his sympathies lay in a Lutheran direction and evidently he was concerned to acquire popularity by reversing the severe policies of the late king. When the first parliament of the new reign met in November 1547, it proceeded, acting under the guidance of the Lord Protector, who became known as "the good Duke," to repeal the recent treason and heresy acts and to rescind an act passed during the last reign about royal proclamations. Somerset also sponsored public inquiries into enclosures of land for sheep farming, after he had published a proclamation condemning them. He revealed his religious colors by removing the principal Catholic sympathizers from the Council —such as the Lord Chancellor Wriothesley, a hater of heretics, who bided his revenge—and by encouraging Archbishop Cranmer to go ahead with his plans for an English prayer book. Somerset also showed indifference to family feelings by permitting his own brother to be executed for inept and unsuccessful conspiracy.

But his first big task was to resume the war with Scotland. Parliament voted him money and he led an army across the border to defeat the Scots by the deft use of artillery at the battle of Pinkie in September 1547. The English army reached a point within eighteen miles of Edinburgh, but then was bogged down at the fortified village of Haddington. Military pressure did not make the Scots any more amenable to English wishes, and in July the youthful Mary, Queen of Scots, was hurried out of the country so that she might be married, as arranged, in France. Soon after that Somerset's attention was distracted from Scotland by a renewal of war with France, compelling him to evacuate Haddington. War broke out in August 1548 and the French vainly tried to recapture Henry VIII's expensive trophy, the town of Boulogne. Once again the war got nowhere. In the end a treaty was concluded surrendering Boulogne four years earlier than had previously been promised in return for a sum of money. Internal difficulties were already confusing the protectorate; both in Scotland and France a diplomatic setback followed a military success.

These internal difficulties were the product of social unrest. There were risings in Cornwall and Devon, in Oxfordshire and in Norfolk. Although the peasants had other grievances, the western rebellion was chiefly a demonstration against the Protestant religious policy of the protectorate. In Norfolk, on the other hand, where the local leader Robert Kett gathered together a large force, the trouble was economic: language was even used reminiscent of the revolt of 1381, claiming that "all bondmen should be made free." Thus these risings arose from different motives, were not concerted, and were repressed without much struggle. The clement Duke of Somerset, who left the rounding up of the poorly-armed peasants and the execution of Kett to the ruthless Warwick, however, got the blame. Mercy and liberal-minded intentions did not command a high premium among the former servants of King Henry VIII; some of Somerset's attempted social reforms menaced the interests of the rich and powerful; an intrigue engineered by Wriothesley and others ended in October 1549 with the sudden fall from authority of Somerset and his appearance as a prisoner in the Tower of London.

Nevertheless Warwick did not yet oust his rival. The instruments of Somerset's fall were the Roman Catholics, and Warwick—who did not seem to have any profound religious convictions himself—hesitated to throw in his lot with the party of reaction. He actually released Somerset from the Tower, arranged for a marriage between their two families, and for eighteen months uneasily co-operated with him in the government of the kingdom. But Somerset still proved an effective obstacle to the realization of Warwick's own ambitions. "Somerset had courted popularity, while Warwick sought for power." The latter, an able soldier and intriguer, built up a party, posed as the champion of the possessing classes, and ingratiated himself with the boy-king. After having himself created Duke of Northumberland, he struck: the technique of the *coup d'état* against an inconvenient colleague had now been perfected; in October 1551 Somerset was arrested on a charge of treason and was beheaded in

February of the following year to the unconcealed sorrow of many ordinary people.

While Somerset and Northumberland engaged in their conflict for control of the government and vied with each other in pillaging the Church—Somerset, for example, blackmailed the dean and chapter of Westminster Abbey and appropriated the site of a parish church in the Strand, while Northumberland seized hold of episcopal revenues—the doctrines and practices of the Church were undergoing thorough reform. At one time King Henry VIII had entered into communication with German Protestant theologians, had invited Melancthon, Luther's friend, to England, and, according to Cranmer, had contemplated abolishing the Mass. But in fact he had done nothing positive, and Luther remarked tartly that the English king "does not seek the honour of God, but wishes to do just as he pleases." Still the Henrician Reformation was the beginning of dissent. It opened the floodgates. Even the monks in their religious houses before they were dissolved read Protestant pamphlets and discussed the news from Germany and Switzerland. Although ordinary people may have been more concerned over altering the machinery of the Church—with getting rid of papal taxation and ecclesiastical jurisdiction—than with doctrinal matters, informed opinion, ranging from that of the bishops to the university scholars, was being blown about by the warm Protestant wind.

The man in a position to influence theological decisions was Thomas Cranmer, Archbishop of Canterbury. When he was a don at Cambridge he does not seem to have taken any part in discussions of Lutheranism, and later when he worked for King Henry VIII he had been prominent simply as the instrument of his divorces and the agent of the break with Rome. But he was not devoid of thoughts of his own. He was, and has remained, a controversial figure. His enemies claim that he was an opportunist, the consumer and brilliant regurgitator of other men's ideas; a sycophant of the king and of Lord Protector Somerset; the supine coadjutor of Thomas Cromwell and of Northumberland. On the other hand, he interceded for the lives of Queen Anne Boleyn and of Thomas Cromwell; he never concealed his theological opinions as he formed them; and in the end he died like a man. "In theology," writes Professor Rupp, "his writings show him to have been slow-moving but tenacious. The charge of instability is a frivolous one, unless to move from one belief to another be instability, in which case every theologian of worth would be guilty, from the Apostle to the Gentiles to St. Thomas or Karl Barth." Certainly he was a weak man, but he earned the respect of King Henry VIII and others with less pliable consciences. It is difficult to believe that the archbishop who wrote much of the Book of Common Prayer and the Thirty-nine Articles, on which generations of Englishmen were brought up, was not a sincere Christian. As soon as his old master died, he turned his mind to a more complete reform of the English Church and to introducing some of the new ideas in vogue on the mainland of Europe.

The teachings of the Swiss theologians—in particular of Calvin (a Frenchman by birth) and Zwingli—made a considerable impact upon both Cranmer and Somerset. They were not so much concerned with the Calvinist view of the proper relations between church and state. That question had already been decided; their guide was neither Calvin nor Zwingli but an obscurer theologian named Erastus who argued for the supremacy of the state in religious matters. Henceforward parliament, not Convocation, was the accepted fountainhead of changing doctrines, while the bishops were virtually officers of a state department. As early as July 1547 a book of homilies, drawn up by Cranmer, was published, a general visitation was carried out, and injunctions to read the Gospels and the Epistles in English, to destroy images, and to abolish certain "popish" practices were imposed upon the Church. Other injunctions were less novel, but some of them were sufficiently disturbing to arouse protests by Stephen Gardiner, Bishop of Winchester, who had been pointedly excluded from the Privy Council, and by Edmund Bonner, Bishop of London. Gardiner was imprisoned in the Tower of London because of his views. Next followed a royal proclamation forbidding such symbolic ceremonies as the carrying of candles, the bearing of palms, or creeping to the Cross. Chantries, the last of the religious houses to be dissolved, were now confiscated; the use of Latin was reduced, and preaching was encouraged. Iconoclasm flourished and was officially approved. Much of the destruction of images, religious pictures, and sacred monuments in English churches, commonly ascribed to Oliver Cromwell, took place more than a century before he became Lord Protector.

The focus of theological controversy was the Mass. The Catholic doctrine of transubstantiation, which maintained that the bread and wine used in the service were changed in substance into the body and blood of Jesus Christ, had still been accepted in the reign of King Henry VIII. Some theologians believed in the Real Presence of Christ in the sacrament, though in an ineffable and spiritual manner rather than in substance. Zwingli, however, denied that there was any mystery in this traditional ceremony and regarded the service of the Holy Eucharist or Communion as a love feast commemorative of Christ's death. Calvin, on the other hand, thought that the only change that took place during the service was in the heart of the communicant when he received the bread and wine.

The first action of the English reformers, headed by Cranmer, was to add a Communion service—in which the congregation received the sacraments—on to a modified celebration of the customary Roman Mass. This was embodied in the first Book of Common Prayer. The blending of the old and new ceremonies was characteristic of this book as a whole, which was approved by parliament in 1549. It consisted of all the old liturgical books combined in one, simplified, revised, and translated into English. The daily offices were reduced to two, familiar in the later English Low Church—Matins and Evensong. An Act of Uniformity instructed the clergy to use this book and no other on penalty of fine, deprivation, or imprisonment. The imposition of the Book of Common Prayer on the English Church was a main cause of the uprising in the west of England in 1550. Yet so skillfully was it compiled that it seemed to be acceptable both to Catholics and reforming theologians; even Bishop Gardiner did not object to it.

After the suppression of the western rising the pace of reform became hotter. The Protestants gained control of the Privy Council; German and Swiss theologians arrived in England and were appointed professors at the universities; the rites of ordaining clergy were simplified and minor clerical orders were abolished; the destruction of images had been made official and clergy were allowed to marry. Gardiner was again imprisoned in the Tower and later he and Bonner were deprived of their sees. New and aggressive reforming bishops appeared, notably John Ponet, Bishop of Winchester; Robert Holgate, Archbishop of York; John Hooper, Bishop of Gloucester, a Zwinglian; and above all Nicholas Ridley, the new Bishop of London. Ridley busied himself by removing the altars from the east end of the churches and instead placing a communion table in the chancel, thus showing precisely how wrong he thought were the doctrines of transubstantiation and the Real Presence. In 1552 the reform movement reached its climax under the rule of the Duke of Northumberland. John Knox, the father of the Scottish Presbyterians, was offered an English bishopric. Only Princess Mary, the daughter of Katherine of Aragon, resolutely refused to be deprived of her Mass.

In 1552 the second Book of Common Prayer and a second Act of Uniformity were introduced. A revolution in ideas had taken place between 1549 and 1552. The first prayer book had been essentially a codification and translation of established practices. The Cornish had objected to it because they loved Latin or at any rate because they could not understand English. The first Act of Uniformity was one of the mildest measures in the history of the Tudors. Now the religious changes became more radical and far-reaching. The stimulus came from Northumberland himself and the inspiration from such foreign theologians as Martin Bucer and "Peter Martyr." When Northumberland offered John Knox the bishopric of Rochester, the object he said was for Knox to serve "as a whetstone to quicken and sharp the Bishop of Canterbury, whereof he hath need." But no doubt Thomas Cranmer's flexible and absorbent mind had reached its own conclusions. For instance, he had ceased to believe in the doctrine of the Real Presence, and the outstanding characteristic of the second prayer book was that it contained a new version of the Holy Communion service making it essentially an act of remembrance. The word Mass was left out: the Communion was henceforward to be celebrated, as Bishop Ridley wished, at a "table" and not an "altar"; ordinary bread was to be used for the purpose; and the clergyman who administered the bread and wine was not allowed to wear special vestments. Thus it became difficult if not impossible to interpret the rite any longer in a central Catholic sense. Yet even an instruction which was included in the book that communicants should kneel when receiving the bread and wine appeared offensive to extreme Protestants. To meet their criticism a Black Rubric was added explaining that to kneel implied "reverence and gratitude" but not the "adoration" of Christ's body and blood. In this book too a "general confession" replaced the "auricular confession" to the priest which had been permitted in the previous book, while vestments and the ceremony of baptism were made plainer. After the next reign this prayer book of 1552 was to provide the broad basis for worship in the Church of England until the present century.

The second Act of Uniformity was stiffer than the previous one. It permitted the ecclesiastical punishment of the laity for not attending church services as well as imposing punishments for the performance of unauthorized services. Once more this was a parliamentary act and it is by no means clear how far Convocation was consulted, any more than it had been clear earlier. Besides this, forty-two articles were published defining the faith of the Church of England. The articles were originally drafted by Cranmer but amended after they had been examined by six divines, of whom John Knox was one. In them such delicate matters as freedom of will, justification by faith, and good works were touched upon. Like the Prayer Book itself, many phrases, though beautifully written, were capable of varying interpretations: Cranmer was indeed a master of the art of verbal compromise, a pattern for latter-day diplomatists. The articles were eventually published in such a way that they appeared to command the authority of the English Church as a whole,

but that was disingenuous. They were pushed through by Northumberland and signed by the boy-king before he died. In such a rough-and-
ready manner the fundamental beliefs of the Church of England were
drawn up and defined; it is a tribute to the genius of Cranmer and his
colleagues that they have endured for 400 years. Ironically enough, the
layman responsible for dragooning them through the machinery of
church and state, the Duke of Northumberland, pronounced himself a
Roman Catholic on his deathbed.

However, not too much importance should be attached to Northumberland's own religion. He was moved by an insatiable lust for personal
power. In 1553 the crisis of his life approached. The boy-king, so long
his tool, was dying. King Edward VI had long been a consumptive and
his hacking cough was pitiful to hear. His health had been further undermined both by measles and smallpox. But in his clouded mind loomed
all the pride of the Tudors and the stubborn will of his father. He was
persuaded by Northumberland that he could determine the succession
as he wished. Northumberland's plan was to marry his own son, Guildford Dudley, to one of the granddaughters of King Henry VIII's sister
Mary, Duchess of Suffolk. The granddaughter therefore would also be a
great-granddaughter of King Henry VII. King Henry VIII's two daughters, Princess Mary and Princess Elizabeth, who had minds of their own,
were to be passed over as bastards. Thus Northumberland aimed to
acquire two more puppets through whom he might continue to rule the
nation. Lady Jane Grey was his chosen victim or instrument.

The king did as he was asked. The motives that induced him to agree
to the plan were to frustrate the papists and to prevent the return of
idolatry to England—for Princess Mary, the obvious heiress to the
throne, was a convinced Roman Catholic, like her mother. The judges
were terrorized and assented to the scheme. This "devise," as it was
called, was not only signed by the judges but by most of the Privy Council and other prominent personages, including Archbishop Cranmer, who
expressed some scruples but finally decided not "to stand against his
prince."

It was all entirely in vain. Lady Jane Grey reigned, if reign she did,
for only nine days. Northumberland had blundered by failing to lay
hold of the person of Princess Mary. Forewarned, she refused an invitation to be present at her brother's deathbed and instead fled into East
Anglia, where she quickly gathered round her a large and devoted
following. The Duke of Northumberland was reluctant himself to leave
London, which was restless, for he had never been popular there. His
own troops betrayed him. He got as far as Cambridge when he received
news that shocked him: members of the Privy Council, whom he had

locked up in the Tower, had managed to escape. Princess Mary was now proclaimed queen in the city of London. Everywhere the people were rallying to the legitimate Tudor heiress and revealing their pent-up hatred for the tyranny and terrorism of Northumberland and his minions. It was, writes a modern historian, "the greatest mass demonstration of loyalty ever accorded to a Tudor." In a hopeless attempt to save his own life, Northumberland threw up the sponge and declared that he too was for Queen Mary. She entered London on August 3, 1553. Evidently most English people were relieved that another bloodstained royal minority was at an end. But much more blue blood was to flow before England rose to a peak of glory in the reign of Queen Elizabeth I.

XXXII

The Reign of Mary I

Queen Mary was thirty-seven when she obtained the throne of England. She was small and very thin with reddish hair and a broad nose. She was shortsighted, and her voice could always be heard a long way off. On the whole, she had lived an unhappy life; she was embittered and prematurely aged. Marriages to various European princes had been planned for her and never realized: her theoretical bastardy, deriving from the annulment of the marriage of her mother, Katherine of Aragon, had stood in her way. A woman of immense courage, who had refused to become a Protestant during her brother's reign, the new queen was in fact largely governed in her policy by her religion and by the determination to undo her mother's disgrace. She wanted to restore the authority of the pope in England, and, being half Spanish herself, to ally herself with Spain.

Her first actions were to release from prison the Catholic bishops headed by Stephen Gardiner, whom she appointed Lord Chancellor, and to order the execution of the Duke of Northumberland and two of his henchmen. Archbishop Cranmer was soon charged with treason and placed in the same cell in the Tower of London from which the Duke of Northumberland had been led to the scaffold; Lady Jane Grey and her husband were also imprisoned. The principal judges, who had consented to Northumberland's plan to exclude Queen Mary from the succession, were deprived of their offices. But, on the whole, notes of caution, moderation, and even mercy were struck during the first months of the new reign.

The queen chose at first to preside over a large council, but so fierce were the squabbles within it that she found herself shouting to keep order. Later therefore she came to rely upon an inner circle of advisers, of whom Gardiner was the chief. Simon Renard, the capable ambassador of Emperor Charles V, who was Mary's cousin, also exercised substantial influence. He favored the policy of moderation, as did his master.

Emperor Charles V now dominated Europe. The two rivals of his younger days, King Henry VIII and King Francis I of France, were long since dead. He had built an empire comparable with that of Julius Caesar or Charlemagne: it stretched beyond the confines of Europe to Mexico and Peru. Charles V was a man without magnetism or charm and was not a soldier, but he was a consummate politician and a convinced Catholic. Hence he had troubles in Germany when the Lutheran movement took hold there; he was menaced by the Turks in his hereditary Habsburg dominions in eastern Europe; he had difficulties in the Netherlands; and he had been exhausted by a prolonged war against France in Italy. In 1552 he had been compelled to come to terms with the German Protestants by the treaty of Passau, while the French now attacked him on the Rhine instead of in Italy. In his troubles the idea of gaining the alliance of England appealed forcibly to him: indeed through marriage might not this country not only re-enter the Roman Catholic fold but become a part of his great empire? The French king, Henry II, did what he could to exert diplomatic pressure against Charles V in London, but all the cards were in Charles' hands. Yet he was slow to play them. He was an aging man, a prey to melancholy, and gradually losing interest in mundane affairs. "His single care and occupation," it was reported to his son, "day and night is to set his clocks and keep them going together; he has many, and they are his chief thought, with another new sort of clock he has invented and ordered to be set up in the frame of a window." So little was he concerned over politics that he did not at once press a marriage alliance upon his cousin Mary, but she had made up her mind to marry his son, Archduke Philip of the Netherlands, whose portrait by Titian excited her.

On October 1, 1553, Mary was crowned by Bishop Gardiner in Winchester Cathedral and at the end of the month she promised to marry Archduke Philip. Meanwhile she made it clear to her subjects where she stood on matters of religion. She proclaimed that she could not forsake the faith that she had practiced since her birth. Although she did not demand that her subjects should at once imitate her, she implied that they should; she ordered them to behave themselves circumspectly until fresh laws were made by parliament and in the meantime she prohibited the preaching of any sermons whatsoever. Thus the Protestants were handicapped and foreign theologians of this persuasion, seeing which way the wind was blowing, began to remove themselves abroad. But some of the leading English clergy, like Cranmer and Hugh Latimer, Bishop of Worcester, had disdained the chance to flee and preferred to face the wrath to come.

The Lord Chancellor, Gardiner, was by no means enthusiastic about the Spanish marriage, although it was he who was charged with negotiating the terms of the Anglo-Spanish treaty, which was the price of the marriage. Philip was given the title of king and was to assist in the government, but if Queen Mary died childless he was to have no further rights in England. The queen alone was given the authority to confer offices, which might be held only by Englishmen, and the country was not to be dragged into the emperor's war against France. In spite of all these precautions the marriage treaty was not popular with the first parliament of the reign. A deputation from the House of Commons had protested to the queen against a foreign marriage, and parliament insisted that the queen herself should not cease to rule after she had acquired her husband. A proposal put forward by Gardiner that the queen should be empowered to bequeath her crown as she wished was also defeated. There was little question that the marriage was greatly disliked, and the French ambassador optimistically reported home that rebellion was likely.

A widespread rising did in fact take place in February 1554, headed by Sir Thomas Wyatt, the son of a poet, and supported by the Duke of Suffolk, the father of Lady Jane Grey. The conspirators' plans were betrayed to the government and the revolt therefore was disorganized. However, Wyatt, who raised his standard in Kent, succeeded in thrusting into the very heart of London; Queen Mary had to appeal personally to the loyalty of the citizens before the rebels were overwhelmed and Wyatt sent to the Tower. It is not clear if the intention was to dethrone the queen and put either Lady Jane Grey or the queen's half sister, Princess Elizabeth, in her place. In any case the repression was severe. Not only were Wyatt, Suffolk, and other leaders of the rebellion put to death, but so also were Lady Jane Grey and her husband and many common people who supported the rising. Princess Elizabeth, a good-looking girl of twenty with golden hair and her mother's striking eyes, narrowly escaped with her life. She had been in correspondence with Wyatt, but nothing specific could be discovered against her, and Wyatt exculpated her upon the scaffold.

The way having been made clear for him at the expense of some common English blood, Archduke Philip arrived at Southampton in July 1554 in a galleon named "The Holy Ghost" and radiated Spanish courtesy and charm. He even sent for and drank some English beer without apparent distaste, then set off in the pouring rain for Winchester, where he was married to Queen Mary in the cathedral. The queen had persuaded herself that she had fallen in love with this daintily bearded Habsburg prince, experienced in the ways of love, and later believed that she was going to have a child by him. On both counts she was disillusioned. Philip dissembled as best he could, but could scarcely fail to be disappointed with his angular and unattractive wife, while it was far from satisfying for him to occupy an inferior position in England when the kingdom of Spain and much of Italy and the New World lay within his grasp. About two years later, as soon as he decently could, he took his departure, and when his father abdicated in January 1556 he became king of Spain. Though he conscientiously read his dispatches from London, he had little influence upon English policy.

Once married, Queen Mary turned to her other ambition of bringing the English Church back to obedience to Rome. Her first parliament had rescinded the ecclesiastical legislation passed in the reign of King Edward VI, but did not contemplate anything constructive. Her second parliament, meeting in March 1554, had proved obstreperous. Not only did it refuse to agree to proposed arrangements about the future succession, but it rejected the Lord Chancellor's request that it should revive the heresy laws, which had been dropped by the Duke of Somerset, and that it should reimpose the Six Articles of King Henry VIII. The first moves against the Protestants were therefore carried out by administrative action. The foreign theologians and their congregations were expelled or encouraged to leave the country and some English clergy followed them into exile. More Protestant bishops were deprived or arrested and Roman Catholics like Bonner were restored to their former positions. The ban on preaching was maintained and trusted bishops empowered to suppress heretical opinions. In particular, royal instructions were given that married clergy were to be deprived of their livings. It is estimated that one-fifth of the parish clergy of England were then deprived, although some of them may have been reappointed after they had given up their wives. Because of the glowing approval of the court, Catholic ceremonies were revived, the Mass was celebrated, and images were returned to the churches. It was ironic that all this should have been achieved not by statute law but by the exercising of the queen's authority as Supreme Head of the Church, which she found most distasteful.

Two primary difficulties stood in the way of a complete reversion to the situation that had prevailed in the Church at the beginning of the reign of King Henry VIII. The first was the reluctance of parliament to recognize the papal authority again. The other was the giving of church properties, including the possessions of the dissolved monasteries, into private hands. It has been stated that more of these properties had found their way into the possession of those with Catholic sympathies than those with Protestant opinions. Be that as it may, it was recognized not merely by the queen's advisers but by the Spaniards and the pope himself that this problem could not be solved. The first obstacle, however, was overcome. The third parliament of the reign, which met in November 1554, was much more complacent than its predecessors. The character of the House of Lords was changed by the restoration of the Catholic bishops. Governmental influence was brought successfully to bear upon the selection of members of the House of Commons. Therefore it was felt safe for Pope Julius III to send over Cardinal Pole as his legate to welcome an erring daughter home again.

The new parliament promptly reversed the act of attainder passed against Pole in the reign of King Henry VIII; it agreed to revive the heresy laws; and after it had been addressed by Cardinal Pole, it petitioned the pope that England should be received back into the Holy Church, after being absolved from the sin of schism. The only thing that it refused to do was to restore the former Church lands to their previous owners. The act of reconciliation took place in June, 1555. "And of, how many things, how great things," declared the papal legate, "may the Church, our mother, the bride of Christ, promise herself from these children! Oh piety! Oh ancient faith! Whoever looks on them will repeat the words of the prophet of the Church's early offspring, 'This is the seed which the Lord hath blessed.' " He then turned with a good will to promoting the punishment of heretics.

For the campaign that followed Queen Mary herself was primarily responsible. Heretics had first to be condemned in the church courts but were then handed over to the secular arm for punishment; and under the revived heresy laws the punishment was burning at the stake. Cardinal Pole approved and assisted, and so did the Bishop of London, Bonner, and others, but the policy commended itself neither to Stephen Gardiner nor to the Spanish ambassador nor even to King Philip of Spain. The burnings began with that of John Rogers, the editor of William Tyndale's translation of the Bible, in February 1555. John

Hooper, the former Bishop of Worcester, followed after refusing to recant his sins. Bishops Latimer and Ridley died in the autumn, Latimer on that occasion using the phrase that has inspired English Protestants ever since: "We shall this day light such a candle, by God's grace, in England as shall never be put out." Archbishop Cranmer did not perish until March 1556. He was torn between his acquired Protestant beliefs and his customary deference to the orders of the Crown. He fought a hopeless battle for his office and then for his life. The pope had excommunicated him, and even the abject recantations that he signed did not save him. In the end he admitted that what he had written was contrary to the truth as he saw it and had been forced out of him through fear of death. Then he faced the flames with quiet courage. Altogether three hundred victims were burned before the end of the reign.

Historians anxious to be impartial and not to pass judgments have done their best for the woman whom Protestants were to call "Bloody Mary." In human terms one can understand how this embittered woman, denied alike the affection of a husband and the promise of children, whose father had washed his hands of her and whose mother had been disgraced, could find her consolation in rigorously upholding the religion she had learned at her mother's knees. It is pointed out that in the Netherlands at the same time, Emperor Charles V had burnt not 300 but 6,000 victims, while his son, who testified to the unwisdom of heresy-hunting in England, had shown not the slightest mercy in Spain. Had not the heroic King Henry V set the example by burning the Lollards? Had not Henry VIII ruthlessly killed not for religious reasons but for mere reasons of state? It is argued also that we must not judge Queen Mary by the enlightened standards of the twentieth century when nothing worse has happened than the slaughter of millions of Jews in Hitler's gas chambers or the world's assent to the slow and steady miseries of the refugee camps of stateless citizens with no real homes and no possible future. But such crimes against humanity rarely redound to the benefit of the cause their perpetrators have at heart. The acts of the Protestant martyrs were long remembered. The heroic nature of their deaths rather than the horror of their punishments impressed the crowds that watched them, as it has also impressed posterity. Although nobody knew it at the time, the policy of persecution contributed materially to the permanent restoration of Protestantism in the Church of England.

The last years of Queen Mary I were far from happy for her or for her kingdom. Cardinal Pole, who had succeeded Cranmer as Archbishop of Canterbury, was unable to impose reforms upon the Church that were urgently necessary. Parliament not only showed its recalcitrance in this matter but was also extremely reluctant to vote the queen taxes, while she was trying to give back to the Church properties acquired by her father for the Crown. The queen's husband stayed abroad. What she had taken to be pregnancy turned out to be dropsy. In March 1556 another plot was discovered against her throne. Worst of all the ironies of her reign was that during 1556 a quarrel developed between Mary's husband, now the most Catholic king of Spain, and the Holy Father. The latest pope, Paul IV, was a fierce Neapolitan in his late seventies who decided to devote himself not to a crusade against the ever-menacing Turks but to expelling the Spaniards from southern Italy. He came to a secret agreement with King Henry II of France, which was later translated into a definitive treaty, promising him that if he would fight against King Philip of Spain, his sons would be rewarded with territories in Italy. King Henry was screwed up to the point of war and King Philip retorted with an attack on the papal states. In March 1557 Philip paid a fleeting visit to England, of which, after all, he was king, to induce his wife, Queen Mary, to join with him in his war against France. She greeted her husband with transports of delight and agreed to assist him—though when she reviewed her army she found it consisted of 400 men and she had the utmost difficulty in creating a war chest.

The pope responded by excommunicating King Philip and, after reducing the powers of Cardinal Pole, demanded his presence in Rome to answer charges of heresy. The queen herself, no longer able to claim that she was a papal crusader, devoted her attention to edifying Christian activities. She was, reported the Venetian representative in London, "a very great and rare example of virtue and magnanimity, a real portrait of patience and humility." At Easter she washed the feet of the poor; she also visited the wives and children of the poor of Croydon, giving them alms and advising them to live thriftily. War was declared upon France in June 1557. Forces were enlisted to assist the arms of Spain, but all that happened was that six months later, at the beginning of 1558, the last English possession in France, the port of Calais, was lost forever.

So this cruel, dismal, and barren reign came to its end. When the queen realized she was dying, she commended her country to the care of her absent husband and begged her half sister, Elizabeth, who she recognized would succeed her, to uphold the Church in the Roman Catholic faith. For some years Princess Elizabeth had been living in comparative isolation in her favorite residence at Hatfield, not very far from London. In the autumn of 1556 she suddenly found herself the magnet of gratifying attentions. "There is not a heretic or traitor in the country," reported a Spanish observer disagreeably, "who has not started as if from the grave to seek her with expressions of great pleasure." Queen Mary died in November 1558 and Archbishop Pole died within twelve hours of his mistress. When Princess Elizabeth learned the news, she exclaimed: "It is the Lord's doing and it is marvellous in our eyes." She had many problems, but a notable reign in English history, a precious memory to modern Britain, was about to begin.

XXXIII

John Knox and Mary, Queen of Scots

In 1558 John Knox, the Scottish preacher, published a book which caused much stir at the time entitled *The First Blast of the Trumpet against the Monstruous Regiment* [i.e., government] *of Women*. It was indeed a curious coincidence that in the latter half of the sixteenth century England should have been ruled first by Queen Mary I and then by her half sister, Queen Elizabeth I, while Scotland first had a regent in Queen Mary of Lorraine and then was to be governed by Mary, Queen of Scots. In fact these ladies did not rule so badly. Queen Elizabeth I was one of England's greatest monarchs. Queen Mary of Lorraine was no worse a regent than most; while if Mary, Queen of Scots, lost her throne through love, it was nobler than doing so out of incompetence.

When her father, King James V, died of a broken heart after the Scots' defeat by the English at the battle of Solway Moss, Mary had only just been born. A number of Scottish magnates, headed by Cardinal Beaton, were at first appointed to govern the realm, but then in January 1543 the next heir to the throne, James, third Lord of Hamilton and second Earl of Arran, took over as regent. By the treaty of Greenwich concluded in July 1543 it was arranged that when she reached a suitable age Mary, Queen of Scots, should be married to King Henry VIII's son, the future Edward VI. Thus it appeared that the long antagonism between the Scots and the English would be brought to an end and the two kingdoms on the island united, but instead Arran and Beaton linked arms in contesting this treaty and it was never ratified. King Henry VIII's retort was to send an army against the Scots under the command of the future Duke of Somerset; he captured Edinburgh and set fire both to the town and to Holyrood Palace. Next year, however, a French fleet appeared, and the English were repulsed at the battle of Ancrum; when King Henry VIII died the Anglo-Scottish war was still not ended.

The Duke of Somerset, after he became Lord Protector of England, returned to Scotland and won the battle of Pinkie, but once again the assistance of a French fleet put a halt to English progress. By the treaty of Haddington, concluded between the Scots and the French, it was decided that Mary, still a child-queen, should be married to the son of the French king, Henry II, instead of to King Edward VI of England. So Henry II was able to declare that "France and Scotland are now one country."

The political problems of Scotland had meanwhile been complicated by religious questions. Both the Reformation on the continental mainland and the Henrician reformation in England had made a profound impression on the Scots. The Scottish Church, like the English, was in many respects corrupt. Equally its huge possessions (it was said to have owned half the wealth of the kingdom) aroused the jealousy and cupidity of the laity. Lollardism had penetrated into Scotland and alarmed the ecclesiastical authorities there. The works of Martin Luther were widely read. A Scottish parliament, meeting in 1543, had permitted the translation of the Bible, and Beaton and Arran had thought it necessary to launch a campaign against heresy. The first popular Protestant clerical leader in Scotland was the graceful and dedicated George Wishart, who went abroad and then returned to preach the new doctrines to his fellow countrymen. He was martyred for his pains. But soon afterward Cardinal Beaton was murdered by his enemies in his own episcopal palace, the Castle of St. Andrews, and his dead body displayed on the wall. Arran determined to punish the murderers, who shut themselves up in the castle. It was in connection with the siege of St. Andrews that a friend and pupil of Wishart's, another popular preacher, John Knox, came to the fore.

Little is known of Knox's youth. He was born somewhere near Haddington and began life as a priest and a notary. He was nearly forty at the time of the siege, a keen reformer, a better preacher than a writer, and a sharp, fearless, and outspoken man. When the Castle of St. Andrews capitulated after a French cannonade from the sea, Knox was made a galley slave by the French for eighteen months. After that he dared not return to Scotland, but settled in England, first on the border at Berwick on Tweed, then in Newcastle upon Tyne, and finally in London. During these five years in England he won such a reputation as a licensed preacher that he was offered the bishopric of Rochester, which he refused. Before he finally returned to Scotland (he had paid a short visit in 1555) at the age of fifty-four, he spent a considerable time on the mainland of Europe imbibing the reformist doctrines and sitting at the feet of John Calvin, who ruled over Geneva as a theocracy. Knox returned home at one of the most critical moments of Scottish history.

Soon after her young daughter had been sent away to be brought up in France, Queen Mary of Lorraine was appointed regent of Scotland in place of the Earl of Arran. Supported by France, she governed the country with some ability and did her best to check the rising movement for Church reform. But her ultimate intention was to transform Scotland into an appanage of France. When in April 1558 the dauphin of France married the fifteen-year-old Mary, Queen of Scots, a secret treaty was signed by her whereby she promised that Scotland should become French if she died without children. The Scottish crown was sent to France. Moreover, on the death of Queen Mary I the French king declared that since Queen Elizabeth I, according to Roman Catholic opinion, was a bastard, he acknowledged Mary, Queen of Scots, as the rightful heiress to the English throne. He had the arms of England quartered on her shield. Before French eyes danced the tantalizing dream of France, Scotland, and England united forever under one sovereign.

It was safe enough for such grandiose notions to be bandied about at the royal court in Paris; they were far less comfortable for the French regent in Edinburgh. Mary of Lorraine did her best to soothe Scottish fears of complete absorption by the French monarchy and to steer a course between the old Scottish Catholic and the ever-growing Protestant movement. The first Protestant manifesto was published in Scotland in December 1557 and received the backing of Lord James Stewart, Queen Mary's half brother, and the powerful family of Argyll. Four nobles formed a group known as the Lords of the Congregation and placed their protestation before the Scottish Estates. The regent rejected the demands of the Congregation for far-reaching reforms in the Church and prohibited unauthorized persons to preach upon penalty of death.

It was at this point that John Knox, now a fully equipped and experienced evangelist, avid for reform, came back to his native land. He began with a sermon preached in the parish church at Perth, which was the center of the reform movement. When a priest tried to celebrate Mass there he was stoned, and an attack was directed against the friars and the monasteries. Both sides took to arms and civil war followed. The regent had a French army at her disposal; the Scottish reformers sought help from England. Reluctantly Queen Elizabeth I furnished assistance to the Scottish Protestants. Finally in July 1560 a treaty was signed at Leith, the port of Edinburgh, whereby the French promised to withdraw from Scotland. Queen Mary of Lorraine had just died and a council of twelve, consisting of both Catholics and Reformers, was set up to govern the country until Mary, Queen of Scots, should return from France. In the same year a Scottish parliament repudiated the rule of the pope, condemned all doctrines contrary to a Confession of Faith which was laid before the Estates, and banned the Mass. The first General Assembly of the Church of Scotland met in Edinburgh in December 1560. Scotland, like England, was not to become Protestant in a few years. The Highlands and part of the south remained Catholic. Thus when in the following year Mary, Queen of Scots, came back, she found many friends of the old religion.

Mary had blossomed in the French court. She was excellently educated in French, Latin, and music; she could write poetry and enjoyed embroidery; she was a keen horsewoman and most skillful in sport; a French poet wrote that "in her fifteenth year her beauty began to radiate from her like the sun in a noontide sky." In truth, as her portraits testify, she was no beauty, but she had the charm and spirit of many of the Stuarts, while passion burned within her. Soon after her first marriage her husband succeeded as King Francis II of France, but his health was wretched and he was destined to have only a brief reign. Mary nursed him through his last illness, but when he died in December 1560, her mother's relatives lost power: there was nothing for the eighteen-year-old dowager queen to do but sadly abandon the delights of Paris and go home to Scotland.

Her sea journey through a summer fog was perilous. Mary had deliberately failed to ratify the treaty of Edinburgh which required her to renounce her claim to the English throne and to recognize Queen Elizabeth I; Elizabeth naturally responded by refusing to give Mary a safe conduct should the rough weather compel her to land in England. Henceforward antipathy between the two queen-cousins mounted.

Though Mary had been away so long and the country had officially adopted the new religion, and though the Lords of the Congregation considered themselves the masters of the land, the people of Edinburgh, after giving their young queen a tepid reception, took her to their hearts after their own sober fashion. She was a resolute woman who knew no fear. She employed her half brother, James Stewart, later Earl of Moray, and William Maitland, Laird of Lethington, as her principal ministers; she interviewed the fanatical John Knox and told him that she intended to keep to her Catholic religion. She asked him: "Think ye that subjects having power may resist Princes?" "If the Princes exceed their bounds," was the stern reply.

The first three years of Queen Mary's personal rule over Scotland were astonishingly quiet. The main questions that arose were her relations with England and to whom she should be married again. Moray pressed his sister to come to terms with Queen Elizabeth. Elizabeth demanded that Mary should recognize her position according to the terms of the treaty of Edinburgh. Mary, equally proud, required Queen Elizabeth to accept her as her legitimate successor (since she was the great-granddaughter of King Henry VII) if the English queen had no children. Thus deadlock persisted; and Queen Elizabeth put off a meeting with her cousin. As to the question of marriage, there was no scarcity of suitors. Since royal husbands expected to be on a full equality with their wives, the rulers of France and Spain and other kingdoms were glad enough to offer princely bridegrooms, provided it was understood that Scotland might be absorbed into their kingdoms. For a time Moray wished for a Spanish match. Queen Elizabeth was also beset by suitors. They were the most marriageable women in Europe, but their subjects did not want them to have foreign husbands.

While Queen Elizabeth herself was warding off offers of marriage from abroad, she interested herself in her cousin's problem. In 1563 she made a surprising offer: she suggested that Queen Mary should marry her own favorite, Robert Dudley, Earl of Leicester, a widower with whom she herself had notoriously been in love. Dudley came of remarkable stock: his grandfather had been put to death by King Henry VIII for treason, and his father, the Duke of Northumberland, had perished upon the scaffold for conspiring against Queen Mary I of England. Robert Dudley's own wife had died in 1560, either from natural causes or possibly by her own hand, her mind having been distracted by her husband's relationship with the queen. Dudley was suspected of having murdered his wife and for that reason Queen Elizabeth thought herself barred from marrying him, though she might well have wished for the marriage. At any rate she caused Mary, Queen of Scots, to be informed, in effect, that if she married Dudley she would recognize her as her own successor to the throne. But Mary did not want Elizabeth's cast-off lover on those terms. Instead she decided to marry her cousin Henry Stuart, Lord Darnley, son of the Earl of Lennox, like Mary herself descended, though by a younger line, from King Henry VII of England. Queen Elizabeth, whether deliberately or not, had placed Darnley in her way, for she had allowed both Lennox and his son to leave England for Scotland. Whether Mary, Queen of Scots, actually fell in love with Darnley, who was tall, young, dark, vigorous, and a Roman Catholic, is disputed by her numerous biographers. At any rate such a marriage obviously would strengthen her claims to the English succession and even menace Queen Elizabeth's position, if the great Catholic powers of Europe elected to back her.

The sudden marriage of Mary to Darnley in July 1565 alarmed Queen Elizabeth, who tried to stop it, and infuriated the Protestant leaders of Scotland. The Earl of Moray and other Protestant lords then rebelled against their queen, but she herself led a force against them, beat them, and compelled Moray to withdraw into England to seek the help of Queen Elizabeth against his sister. But Elizabeth would not openly encourage a rebellion against a neighboring queen: the precedent was too dangerous. Therefore the Protestant lords planned to alienate Darnley—who soon proved himself an unstable, evil-tempered, and degenerate prince—from his wife by making him jealous of her Italian secretary, David Rizzio. Though Rizzio was murdered, the plot failed. Queen Mary, long with child, induced her husband to abandon his fellow conspirators and rallied some of the nobility to her side. In June 1566 she gave birth to the future King James VI of Scotland and King James I of England. She never forgave Darnley for what he had done. Next followed the tragedy that cost her the throne.

James Hepburn, fourth Earl of Bothwell, a recently married man, had been one of the nobles (though he himself was a Protestant) who had come to Queen Mary's rescue after Moray's rebellion. He was a bold and restless man who saw his chance to attain supreme power. Mary was grateful and fell desperately in love with him (though Scottish historians are for the most part unwilling to admit it). Bothwell, almost certainly with Mary's connivance, planned and carried through the murder of Lord Darnley. Bothwell was acquitted of the crime and three months later in May 1567, having obtained a divorce from his own wife, was married to Queen Mary. This was to provoke the Scottish Protestant leaders and to lose Mary most of her popularity with her people. The civil war that followed in Scotland was soon over. The two sides met at Carberry Hill, but Bothwell's men deserted him, and Bothwell fled to Denmark, never to return to his wife. The queen was imprisoned and forced to sign her abdication. Her baby son was crowned at Stirling, where John Knox preached a suitable coronation sermon. Queen Mary repudiated her abdication, escaped from prison and, after she had been defeated on the field of battle, rode into England to throw herself upon the mercy of Queen Elizabeth. The remainder of her life's story was thus bound up with the internal political history of England. Scotland was henceforward ruled largely by the Calvinist Church of John Knox, until King James VI grew to manhood and in 1603 united the Crowns of both Scotland and England.

XXXIV

The Early Years of Elizabeth I

Queen Elizabeth was twenty-five when she came to the throne of England in November 1558. Her character had clearly been shaped by her parentage and upbringing. Her father, King Henry VIII, had not treated her too unkindly; she evidently admired him even though he had beheaded her mother. She had his vitality, his driving force, and his courage. From her mother she inherited her share of feminine wiles: she became an actress of subtlety. She had been brought up partly by Henry VIII's last wife, Katherine Parr, who was married a second time to Thomas Seymour, brother of Lord Protector Somerset; but she missed a mother, and this may explain her masculine characteristics. When she was sixteen, her tutor remarked that "her mind had no womanly weakness, her perseverance is equal to that of a man." Her education was excellent. She mastered both the classics and modern languages. If she had not been required to become a statesman, she might have been a scholar.

When she was adolescent, Princess Elizabeth had an unfortunate love affair, or at least an elaborate flirtation, with Thomas Seymour. Not long afterward he lost his head. She grew resigned to hearing of people dying violently around her. At the time of Sir Thomas Wyatt's rising she nearly forfeited her own life, for Queen Mary had been convinced that her half sister was concerned in the plot. But nothing could be proved against her. She was placed in the Tower of London and later removed into the country under close surveillance. Born to danger, she had to take care over her every move lest she give cause for offense. Thus she learned to dissimulate: at one time she attended Mass to please the queen. She studied to become resourceful, self-reliant, and noncommittal. If her main weakness as a ruler was being dilatory in reaching decisions, there was certainly also an element of ingrained caution about everything she did.

As usual with a new monarch, the task before her was complicated. She had on her hands the unsuccessful French war that had already cost the country Calais. The treasury was more or less empty. Most important was the question of the future of religion. People asked themselves whether she would completely reverse her sister's policy and, if she did, whether she would wish to return to the position as it had existed in her father's time or in her brother's reign. A contemporary wrote at the outset of her reign of "the most dangerous divisions in religion among ourselves." Queen Elizabeth was under many pressures, though most of the advice that she received was to go cautiously about any reformation and not to tolerate startling innovations. She scarcely needed to be told, for it was obvious that foreign enemies would seize the least opportunity to intervene in English affairs, to proclaim that she was illegitimate, and to try to impose an avowedly Roman Catholic ruler, such as Mary, Queen of Scots, upon the country.

Queen Elizabeth did not select clerics to be her first councilors. All except one of her first Privy Council were laymen. Chief among them was Sir William Cecil, a supremely careful statesman who had somehow managed to survive the turmoils of the last two reigns, holding important offices during both of them and winning a reputation for administrative efficiency. Some historians have wondered whether the successes of the new queen's reign should be largely attributed to him. On the whole, however, Queen Elizabeth proved herself to be a good judge of her servants, and if she found that she had judged them wrongly she did not hesitate to get rid of them.

The Queen postponed an immediate decision on the religious problem until her first parliament met in January 1559. The House of Lords had a Catholic complexion, but the Commons soon showed themselves to be antipapal and eager for reform. Ultimately the decision was taken to introduce an Act of Supremacy whereby the queen became Supreme Governor instead of Supreme Head of the English Church—a difference without any deep significance, since in either case the Papacy was entirely repudiated—and to reintroduce with slight modifications the Common Prayer Book of 1552. The settlement confirmed the importance of parliament, and the queen herself had misgivings; Convocation was not consulted and the spiritual peers voted solidly against the new Act of Uniformity, which was passed by only three votes in the House of Lords. After that, nearly all the Marian bishops were deprived of their offices; several bishoprics were in any case vacant and a learned but moderate Protestant scholar, Matthew Parker, became Archbishop of Canterbury in the place of the dead Cardinal Pole. Inevitably most of the vacancies were filled by keen Protestants, some of whom had gone into exile during the previous reign and had mixed intimately with the reforming theologians of Switzerland and Germany. They returned with all the latest doctrines and the indignant emotions of émigrés. Exactly how many of the ordinary English clergy were deprived because of a refusal to take the new oath of supremacy is uncertain, but the number was small. Few of them were prepared to make personal sacrifices for the benefit of the pope, while the comparative moderation of the queen's ecclesiastical policy required little heart-searching. For example, the new prayer book in effect allowed either a Catholic or a Protestant gloss to be placed upon the precise meaning of the service of Holy Communion. When in 1563 Cranmer's forty-two Articles of Faith were revised and reduced to thirty-nine by a committee of the new bishops, it was found that they had been framed in such a manner as to allow varied interpretations of doctrine.

On the whole, the queen was thrust forward by events. She certainly held no vehement religious opinions herself, though she always gave pious thanks to Providence for her achievements and escapes. If indeed, as her best biographer seems to believe, Queen Elizabeth was a fervent Christian, her fervor was of a Cromwellian character: she was convinced that God was on her side. In matters of doctrine and ceremony she kept to the middle of the road and was opposed alike to Catholic stalwarts and later to Puritan evangelists primarily because she regarded them as enemies of the state rather than of the true religion. When in April 1559 the treaty of Cateau-Cambrésis put an end to the war between France on the one side and England and Spain on the other, it afforded her a breathing space. France was soon to be split by internal political machinations, while King Philip II of Spain, the widower husband of Queen Mary I, cast his cloak over the new queen and even offered her his hand in marriage. Sooner or later it was recognized that a Counter-Reformation movement, directed by a virile pope, might come, but meanwhile Elizabeth was firmly stationed by her advisers, her Commons, and perhaps by her people upon the Protestant side.

The choice, then, was made, at whatever the cost. Having made it, the queen would have liked to keep out of foreign entanglements while the nation licked over the sores of the last reign. By the treaty of Cateau-Cambrésis the loss of Calais was accepted. Nevertheless it was felt that help could not be refused to the Scottish Protestants when they pleaded for it. It was given somewhat reluctantly, but the treaty of Edinburgh of 1560, which forced the French troops to withdraw from Scotland, proved a good investment; not until the reign of King Charles I was there further serious trouble with the Scots. English intervention on the side of the French Protestants—the Huguenots—was less profitable. The temptation to intervene had been hard to resist. King Philip II of Spain was distracted in 1562 by an incipient rebellion in the Netherlands; after an agreement had been reached with the French Huguenot leader, Prince de Condé, an English force had been landed at Le Havre to assist him. Hopes arose of regaining Calais, but Condé came to terms with the French regent, and the decimated English garrison of Le Havre was obliged to surrender in July 1563. It was the one blot on Elizabethan foreign policy.

Apart from the religious settlement, the problem at the beginning of the reign was whether the queen should marry and, if so, whom. Her parliament favored her marriage not so much because its members wanted another king like Philip II, who might drag England into continental wars, as because they desired to see a royal heir to ensure the Protestant and Tudor succession. The heir presumptive to the English throne was Mary, Queen of Scots—even though Queen Elizabeth denied her recognition—but only the Catholics wanted this daughter of the Papacy. The obvious Protestant successor was also a woman, Lady Catherine Grey. But what was required was a Protestant prince. Should not the queen hasten to provide her people with one? The matter was not so simple. Queen Mary I's marriage constituted a bad precedent. Although there were Protestant candidates for the queen's hand, most of the foreign princes who offered themselves, from Philip II to the half-witted Scot, the Earl of Arran, were Catholics. To marry one of her own subjects, as parliament would have liked her to do, would have created jealousy. The only man Elizabeth desired to marry was Robert Dudley, but the tragedy of his wife's death stood in the way. Henceforward in spite of appeals to her from parliament, which sometimes she treated haughtily and sometimes evasively, it seems she decided never to marry. Her spirit was one of independence: men should serve her, but none should be her master. Thus she became the Virgin Queen.

The second parliament of the reign, which met in January 1563, was largely occupied with social legislation but continued to work over the question of the queen's marriage. It had been summoned because the war with Scotland and France meant that the government now needed money. The members of the Commons were willing to grant subsidies, but were genuinely anxious about the succession. In the autumn of the previous year the queen had been attacked by smallpox, yet no successor had been agreed upon. Thus both the Commons and the Lords separately pressed the queen to marry. She refused to give a definite answer, but assured them that she had not made up her mind against marriage. This House of Commons proved itself to be left-wing in its religious opinions. It contained at least forty members of an avowedly Puritan frame of mind, that is to say men who wished to "purify" the Elizabethan Church of all remaining popish "excrescences." When the government inserted into a bill aimed at increasing the size of the navy a clause establishing a compulsory "fish day" on Wednesday, ninety-seven votes were recorded against it on the ground that "fish days" were a Roman practice. Another bill "against those that extol the power of the Bishop of Rome and refuse the oath of allegiance" was made, in Cecil's words, "most sharp, penal, and terrible." The Commons also demonstrated their independence of the Crown by introducing a bill against the abuses of purveyors, officials who by prerogative right purchased food and other supplies for the royal household at well below the market prices. The queen vetoed the bill. In spite of such signs of restlessness Elizabeth did not dissolve this parliament at the end of the session; instead she prorogued it, so that it met again three years later. The retention of this body of men who "had learned to work together under radical leadership" was, Sir John Neale points out, a grave blunder on the queen's part.

When parliament was recalled in September 1566, no progress had been achieved in the matter of the queen's marriage. Public attention had been distracted to the events across the Scottish border where Mary, Queen of Scots, had married Lord Darnley and given birth to his son. Queen Elizabeth had been courted by Archduke Charles of Austria, son of the new emperor, Ferdinand I, had flirted with one of her courtiers, who was chosen King of the Bean for the Twelfth Night festivities, and had made Dudley the Earl of Leicester in the vain hope that this would make him palatable to her Scottish cousin. The object of recalling parliament was to ask it for more money. The Commons proved unco-operative. The election of a new Speaker, the queen's solicitor general, was carried by merely twelve votes. Then the House agreed to make the vote of fresh supplies dependent upon the queen's favorable answer on the question of the succession. The queen was angry. Her father, she asserted, would never have been treated in such a way. She told representatives of both houses that she would marry, but that this was no convenient time for talking about the succession. Still the Commons was discontented, and when she ordered the members to stop discussing the succession, Paul Wentworth, Member of Parliament for Buckingham, asked if such a command was not "a breach of the liberty of the free speech of the House." The queen yielded and revoked her command. The Commons then voted a subsidy, but when it tried to embody the queen's promises to marry in the actual text of the preamble to the subsidy bill she scotched the proposal. The Commons in the same session discussed six bills aimed at imposing yet more reforms on the Church. The queen would not allow them. She regarded religion, together with foreign policy and the succession, as matters that concerned the royal prerogative alone. In this exciting session therefore may be said to have begun that long struggle in England between Crown and parliament which resulted in the Civil War of 1642 and was not resolved until after the Revolution of 1688.

The battle in the Commons reflected a general movement outside in the direction of Puritanism. In 1567 Thomas Cartwright, the intellectual leader of Presbyterianism in England, returned to Cambridge to become the first theologian to advocate the removal of the archbishops as being inconsistent with the teaching of the New Testament. When in 1566 Archbishop Parker had published a *Book of Advertisements* instructing the clergy how they should conduct their services, it met with much criticism and even disobedience. The Puritans also attacked many practices which they considered "popish," such as the wearing of vestments, the playing of organs in churches, and the use of the ring in the marriage ceremony or the sign of the Cross in baptism. Gradually an influential if ill-defined Puritan movement arose, keenly backed in the Commons and even by some of the bishops and privy Councilors. On the other side, a hard core of secret Roman Catholics existed. To keep Roman Catholicism alive, a seminary was founded at Douai in the Netherlands by an exiled English priest with the purpose of training missionaries who could be sent by secret routes into England to proselytize or stimulate the ancient faith. Thus much disorder prevailed in the English Church. Queen Elizabeth was alarmed. It was she who had incited Parker to produce his *Advertisements*. Like her father, she was determined that her authority should be established in Church as well as state. In the end it was she, more than the ecclesiastical hierarchy, that sustained the existing settlement.

In the summer of 1568 Mary, Queen of Scots, had crossed the border into England. She demanded to see Queen Elizabeth in order to secure her help against her rebellious subjects and to clear her own name. She was an unwelcome visitor. Elizabeth neither wished to encourage the Scottish Catholics nor to give her approval to rebels against monarchy. She decided that an enquiry should be held at York under the presidency of the fourth Duke of Norfolk to hear both sides and, if possible, effect a compromise. Later the enquiry was transferred to Westminster, where the regent Moray produced letters, said to have been found in a silver casket after Mary's flight, proving her complicity in Darnley's murder. Queen Elizabeth refused to pronounce judgment or to intervene. Moray returned to Scotland and Queen Mary was placed in honorable captivity in Staffordshire. Here she became the magnet for plots against Queen Elizabeth.

The first of these plots resembled events of much earlier reigns. The northern magnates, headed by the Percies and the Nevilles, assented to a treasonable scheme that had wide ramifications. The queen's "evil and upstart counsellors" were to be overthrown; Mary was to be married to her former judge, the Duke of Norfolk, and to be declared successor to the present queen; England was to be Catholic again. The government got wind of the plot; Norfolk was arrested and sent to the Tower. The Earls of Northumberland and Westmorland rose in arms, as their fathers had done before them, occupied Durham, and planned to free Mary from imprisonment. A scratch force was raised against them by the Earl of Sussex, president of the Council of the North, and they soon fled across the Scottish border. By February 1570 the rebellion was over and six hundred wretched northern peasants were summarily executed. Many of them had been inspired by their devotion to the old religion. In Durham Cathedral they had torn up the new prayer books and celebrated Mass; but they had not yet received the blessing of the pope, which arrived afterward. In the same month that the humble peasants were hanged Pope Pius V published a bull excommunicating and deposing Queen Elizabeth I and absolving her subjects from obedience. Whether he had any right to do so in the terms in which he did it is arguable; at any rate he did so. Thus at last the peace of Elizabethan England was menaced. But the threat had come too late to be really dangerous. Over ten years had passed since the queen ascended the throne. In spite of Puritan criticisms and jealousies at court, her government was so firmly entrenched and so popular with her subjects that it could hardly be destroyed.

XXXV

The Foreign Policy of Elizabeth I

The bull *Regnans in Excelsis* published in Rome during February 1570, which deposed and excommunicated Queen Elizabeth I, had some singularly unfortunate consequences from the Roman Catholic point of view. Pope Pius V, who originated the bull, had been a Dominican friar and had served in the Inquisition. He was described by Ranke as "a strange medley of singleness of purpose, loftiness of soul, personal austerity, and entire devotion to religion with grim bigotry, rancorous hatred, and sanguinary zeal for persecution." He does not seem to have realized the kind of results that were likely to flow from his bull. Far from pleasing the leading Roman Catholic powers of Europe, it embarrassed them. They had no wish at this stage to lift a crusading sword against England, especially since the more aggressive English Roman Catholics had just been crushed when they rebelled.

It is true that relations between England and Spain had deteriorated since the earlier years of the reign. In 1568 a war "beyond the line" in the so-called Spanish empire had broken out because of the reckless behavior of English naval adventurers in search of booty; English discrimination against Flemish merchants had also been a source of dissatisfaction; and the queen was accused of giving secret help to discontented elements in the Spanish Netherlands. Moreover the queen had ordered the seizure or borrowing of bullion sent from Italy to pay the Spanish armies, while the Duke of Alva, the Spanish commander in the Netherlands, had replied by impounding English properties. Although it was ultimately the hope of the Spaniards that England might be won back to the cause of Roman Catholicism and even be absorbed into the Spanish empire, there was no wish at this stage to provoke the English queen. Thus neither King Philip II nor the Habsburg emperor Maximilian heartily approved of the papal bull.

The French government actually forbade the bull to be published in French territory, for the worsening relations between England and Spain offered a splendid opportunity for a diplomatic revolution—for carrying the English into an alliance with their nearest neighbors which would safeguard the kingdom against the ambitions of the Spanish monarchy and bury the hatchet used for hundreds of years.

That, however, was not the way in which the English government saw the situation. The queen and her advisers were very conscious of being diplomatically isolated. Not only were their French and Spanish neighbors more powerful with larger populations and armies, but England, it was felt, might at any time be under attack from Scotland or Catholic Ireland. So long as Mary, Queen of Scots, remained alive on English soil she was a possible rallying point for English, Scottish, and Irish Roman Catholics who could easily, as the northern rising had just shown, stir up trouble and open an opportunity for the invasion of England by their coreligionists abroad. Priests trained to convert England back to the old faith, coming in not only from Douai but also from centers in Rheims and Rome, naturally looked like the subversive agents of a foreign power. The intention of most of these dedicated missionaries was in fact purely spiritual; but once the bull of deposition had been published, it was difficult to distinguish them from spies and traitors.

The English government's deepest fears appeared to be realized in the course of 1570. The Duke of Norfolk, the only English duke and there-fore the highest ranking peer, had been released from his imprisonment in the Tower of London in August. Immediately he allowed himself to become involved in another plot against Queen Elizabeth concocted by an Italian merchant resident in England, by name Ridolfi. The plan was that Norfolk should declare himself to be a Roman Catholic, marry Mary, Queen of Scots, and then rule with her jointly over England and Scotland. To promote this far-reaching aim there was to be an internal rising in England and an invasion led by the Duke of Alva from the Spanish Netherlands. The pope, eager for an "enterprise" against Eng-land, approved the scheme, and the Spanish ambassador in London was concerned in it. Nevertheless Ridolfi's plot was largely a paper one and was cut off by Cecil before it had ripened. The Duke of Norfolk was again arrested and this time sentenced to death in January 1572. The Spanish ambassador was ordered out of the country. Only Mary, Queen of Scots, escaped. She was an inveterate plotter and in fact forfeited by her complicity any chance of regaining her lost power; for earlier in the year Queen Elizabeth had actually entered into negotiations with a view to restoring her to the Scottish throne, though on stringent con-ditions. The assassination of the regent Moray at the beginning of 1570 and divisions among the Scottish nobility had afforded this opportunity for a restoration. The Ridolfi plot put an end to all such negotiations, and Queen Mary was placed under closer surveillance.

The revelation of the Ridolfi plot, in which the Spaniards were im-plicated, compelled the queen and her council to reconsider English foreign policy. The queen now proved herself to be a diplomatist of genius. She had the advantage of an enthusiastically loyal following both in parliament, when it met, and in the country as a whole. She had highly capable ministers, including Cecil and her ambassador in Paris, Sir Francis Walsingham. She was able to play Spain and France against each other. By supporting the Protestant subjects of these two powers—the Calvinists in the Spanish Netherlands and the Huguenots in France—she could always weaken them in a military sense. She had the makings of the best fleet in Europe and could harass them both at sea. Finally, she had the advantage of being able to offer her own hand in marriage as a bribe to influential foreign suitors.

She used this last asset when England appeared to be isolated and in peril after the publication of the papal bull and the discovery of the Ridolfi plot. The Duke of Anjou, the brother of King Charles IX of France, though he was some eighteen years her junior, was then per-suaded to become her suitor. Walsingham conducted negotiations in

Paris. Though nothing came of the proposed match, the negotiations carried through by Walsingham resulted in the signature of a defensive treaty at Blois in April 1572, whereby England and France promised each other military and naval assistance if either was attacked by a third power. The way had been paved to more amicable relations when the French king had earlier established liberty of worship for the Huguenots and had indeed taken some of the leading French Protestants into his counsel. It was arranged that King Henry of Navarre, himself a Huguenot, should marry the French king's sister.

The treaty of Blois had hardly been signed when Europe was shaken by two awful events. That spring the discontented inhabitants of the Netherlands, leadership of whom was soon assumed by William the Silent, prince of Orange and a former protégé of King Philip II, flared into revolt. The motives for the revolt were not purely religious, for both Protestants and Catholics came to take part in it, but were largely political and economic: local patriotism had been affronted; local privileges had been ignored. Dutch Protestants and Flemish Catholics fought together against the Spanish Fury. In August of the same year when the Huguenots gathered in Paris to celebrate the marriage of Henry of Navarre, many of them were arrested and killed after the queen mother, Catherine of Medici, had persuaded her son that they were plotting against him. This was the signal for the massacre of hundreds of other French Protestants by a fanatical mob. But Queen Elizabeth was a "politique"; although the massacre aroused horror and indignant protests in England, it did not bring about a permanent breach in the new Anglo-French alliance. Indeed, after a suitable interval during which freedom of conscience was restored to the French Protestants, a new proposal was put forward for the English queen to marry another and even younger brother of the French king, this time twenty years her junior, by name Francis, Duke of Alençon.

Alençon was rather different from his brother, who had been a strict Catholic. The younger prince was ambitious, astute, and impetuous, and perfectly willing to change his religion if he could obtain some benefit from doing so. It was thought that he had Protestant sympathies, and the revolutionaries of the Netherlands hoped that he might lend them his active support against Spain. The queen, however, was anxious to prevent the Netherlands from falling completely into the hands of either France or Spain, since much English trade was transacted with the Netherlands, and it could easily be used as a springboard for a Catholic invasion of England. Thus she displayed an interest in Alençon's courtship partly in order to distract his attention from the Netherlands. When he first came to visit her she blew hot and cold and neither her

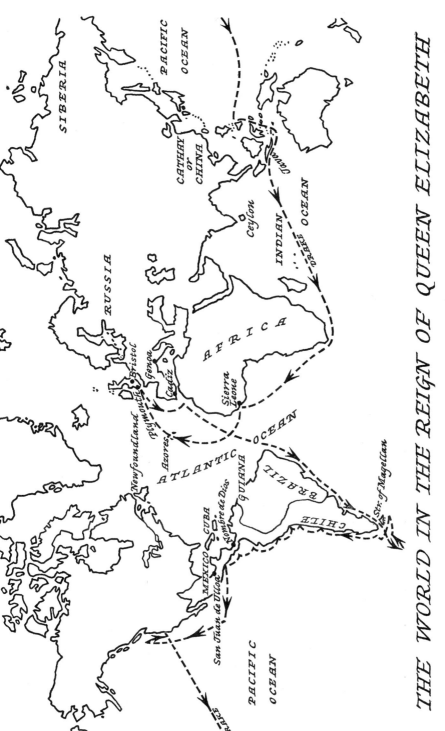

THE WORLD IN THE REIGN OF QUEEN ELIZABETH

council nor parliament could fathom her intentions. Such were the Machiavellian complications of Elizabethan foreign policy.

In 1580 the star of Spain was in the ascendant. Deaths in the royal family of Portugal caused this once-independent kingdom to come into the hands of King Philip II and with it the wide Portuguese overseas empire. In the Netherlands Philip had found a wiser governor and military leader than Alva in the Duke of Parma, who was a really great administrator. Now at last it seemed to Queen Elizabeth necessary, in order to redress the balance of power, to lend to the rebels in the Netherlands that positive support which for so long she had refused. Before Parma became governor, Don John of Austria, an illegitimate son of Emperor Charles V, had won a number of victories over the revolutionaries, after he had concluded a temporary but abortive pacification and an English mission of mediation in 1578 had failed. In May 1579 Parma had come to terms with the Catholic provinces of the Netherlands (which roughly constitute modern Belgium) and only the Protestants or Dutch were still fighting on. Queen Elizabeth therefore delicately broke off the Duke of Alençon's courtship, which had got so far as kissing in public, and induced him to borrow a sum of £60,000 and see first what he could do to help the Dutch. In fact he quarreled with his own allies and died of a fever in 1584. In that same year the real hero of the Dutch resistance, William the Silent, was killed by an assassin in the employ of Spain.

While these grave events were happening abroad, at home the English government's principal troubles related to religion. In purely material affairs the country was not unhappy. The first ten years of Queen Elizabeth's reign had been a period of comparative quiet. During the next fifteen years the queen's diplomatic ingenuity was successful in keeping her country out of open war. Thus a high level of economic prosperity prevailed. The debased coinage had been restored and English credit abroad had improved. Industry had expanded and trade was opening up all over the world. Capital had accumulated and was being invested in the thriving cloth industry and in the new coal trade. But the queen's "faithful Commons" were not content with material well-being. They demanded the fullest possible consolations from a purified Protestant religion.

Parliament met in April 1571 partly to deal with the leaders of rebellion and to counter the papal bull of deposition and partly to vote money to pay for the cost of repressing the rising in the north. The House of Commons now showed itself to be Puritan in sympathies with active "opposition" leaders in William Strickland, a Yorkshire M.P.; Thomas Norton, known as "the scold"; and Peter Wentworth, the most daring critic of the Crown until the days of John Pym. The queen, who had been far from anxious to summon a new parliament and still remembered her experiences with the previous one, made it clear at the outset that she expected members of the Commons not to interfere with "matters of state" or "prerogative" issues, but to confine their attention to questions propounded to them; that is to say they were not to initiate legislation. This did not at all suit the temper of the Commons. In fact Strickland at once demanded that the Book of Common Prayer should be further revised and that a committee should be appointed to confer with the bishops about the reform of the Church. The majority of his fellow members supported him. But the Privy Council sent for Strickland and warned him to stay away from the House. The Commons expressed their indignation at this order; the queen gave way and allowed Strickland to return to his seat; but she refused to waive her prerogative rights. She made it perfectly plain that she was the Supreme Governor of the Church and might do as she chose in collaboration with her clergy. Either she prevented bills on religion from being debated in parliament or she vetoed them. She would not be shaken from her view that religion—like foreign policy and the succession—was a matter of state and was the sole concern of the executive.

Thus the rising Puritan movement learned that there was little hope of reform through parliament. It therefore turned directly to converting the local congregations. A practice grew up in the south of England of holding weekly or fortnightly meetings at which the clergy of Puritan frame of mind interpreted passages of Scripture for the enlightenment of the laity and held private discussions afterward. These meetings were called "prophesyings" and were by no means agreeable to the queen, who regarded them as covers for subversion both of Church and state. When, however, she ordered Archbishop Grindal, the successor to Matthew Parker, to suppress them, he startlingly refused to do so; he was suspended from his office and virtually ceased to exercise his authority until his death in 1583. Meanwhile Thomas Cartwright, the Cambridge enthusiast of Presbyterianism, had come out into the open by publishing his *First Admonition to the Parliament,* which advocated the introduction into England of ecclesiastical government upon the model of Geneva. In the 1580's a more extreme movement grew out of the "prophesyings" and was known as the "classical" movement. The "class" was a kind of local presbyterian body out of which it was hoped to build a complete presbyterian organization within the Church extending up to a national synod or assembly. In the same period was seen the beginning of a separatist Puritan movement. Robert Browne, a clergyman in Norwich, and Henry Barrow, a London preacher, both believed that churches ought to be run by the local congregations without any elaborate hierarchy at all. They were thus poles apart from the Presbyterians who wanted, if anything, a tighter hold to be exercised over the English Church by a hierarchy devoid of bishops.

The queen herself would not stomach any of these novel ideas, though some of the bishops and several of the privy Councilors, notably the Earl of Leicester and Sir Francis Walsingham, were sympathetic to Puritan aims. She ordered that both the "prophesyings" and the "classical movement" should be put down. She let it be known that she preferred the clergy not to marry, that she liked them to wear vestments, and that she did not care for long sermons, which were the essence of Puritan services. Indeed on occasions she interrupted court preachers when they deviated into theological controversy. Cartwright, the Presbyterian, went into exile a second time; the Brownists were compelled to flee the country, though their leader conformed; Henry Barrow was later to be hanged for treason. Finally, in 1583, the queen appointed John Whitgift to succeed Grindal as Archbishop of Canterbury: Whitgift was a Cambridge don who had refuted Cartwright and was, if anything, more strictly anti-Puritan than the queen herself. It was he who built up a High Commission to enforce the discipline of uniformity upon the Church by supplementing the jurisdiction of the diocesan courts and by tendering to suspects and witnesses brought before it an oath obliging them to answer all questions truthfully: this was known as the ex-officio oath. If anyone refused to take the oath, he could be punished without right of appeal.

The queen did not encourage persecution on purely religious grounds: she would have liked to be tolerant and was always inclined to mercy. It was with the deepest reluctance that she had agreed to the Duke of Norfolk's being put to death. In June 1570, even after the papal bull had been published, she had actually ordered her Lord Keeper to declare in the Star Chamber that "Her Majesty's meaning 'was not to have any of her subjects molested by any inquisition or examination of their consciences in causes of religion.' " Although Catholics could be fined £20 a month for not attending church on Sunday or £66 for attending Mass, in practice these "recusancy laws" were not executed. The queen would severely punish either Catholic priests or Puritan clergy if she thought they were disturbing the public order or plotting treason, but she discouraged or prevented parliament from producing bills aimed at compelling Christians to violate their consciences. She sought "not to save their souls in the next world but to save her State in this" (Rowse).

That treason was in the air and that a movement was on foot to reconquer England and Scotland for the Roman Catholic faith were obvious in the 1580's. Jesuits visited Scotland to stimulate the Catholic nobles to conspire with the pope and the king of Spain. A large number of priests, including the selfless Edmund Campion, were tried and put to death for treason. Two Catholics, Esmé Stuart, Earl of Lennox, and James Stewart, Earl of Arran, managed to seize power in Scotland in 1580. Their plan was to overthrow the Protestant leaders and induce the king to become a Roman Catholic. In England a Roman Catholic named Francis Throckmorton acted as an intermediary among the French, the Queen of Scots, and the Spanish ambassador Mendoza to concoct a plot against the government. But in August 1582 Anglophils rescued the boy-king James I from the tutelage of the Catholics, arrested Arran, and forced Lennox to flee, while in November 1583 Throckmorton was put in prison and obliged by torture to confess his conspiracy. Walsingham was sent to negotiate with King James VI and the Spanish ambassador was ordered out of England.

So the more peaceable days of Queen Elizabeth I's reign neared a close. All her information, some of it garnered by spies, indicated that quite soon an "enterprise" against England, blessed by the pope and carried out by the Spaniards, was likely to be attempted. After the murder of William the Silent the cause of the Protestant United Provinces of the Netherlands was in peril. The Dutch looked in vain for help from France after Alençon's expedition had ended in confusion and failure. The queen's chief minister, Cecil, who had now become Lord Burghley and was not a warmonger, urged that England must plunge into the conflict upon the side of the Dutch so as to stave off the inevitable struggle with Spain. A treaty with the Dutch was signed in August 1585 and in September the Earl of Leicester was appointed lieutenant general to lead an expeditionary force against the Duke of Parma. In the same month Sir Francis Drake was commissioned to attack Spanish positions in America. Inexorably events moved toward the great war between Elizabethan England and Catholic Spain which was to overshadow the remaining years of the sixteenth century.

XXXVI

Elizabeth I and the War Against Spain

The parliament that met in November 1584 was more sober and sub-missive to the queen than the earlier parliaments of her reign. It con-tained a number of men destined to be famous in English history: Robert Cecil, Lord Burghley's son, Francis Bacon, Walter Ralegh, and Francis Drake. The Commons were still Puritan in outlook and tried to press through bills to reform religious practices in defiance of the queen's wishes. But they were at heart grateful to a sovereign who had made her-self thoroughly popular with her subjects and had given them peace "for full twenty-six years." Moreover they were deeply concerned for her safety. Pope Gregory had told the English Catholics in 1580 that the bull of deposition published by his predecessor might be suspended until a "public execution" was carried out, but this created alarm instead of lulling fears; moreover the papal secretary let it be known later that the assassination of Queen Elizabeth would not be regarded as a sin. The murder of William the Silent in the Netherlands—followed after-ward by that of King Henry III in France—offered a precedent, while the discovery of Francis Throckmorton's plot had already proved that the Roman Catholics in England were still hopeful of a revolution that would replace Queen Elizabeth with Mary, Queen of Scots.

Confronted with these threats, the Privy Council planned to protect the queen by drawing up a "bond of association," a document to be circulated for signature throughout the country: the signatories were to pledge themselves to obey the queen and to exterminate her enemies. Another clause in the bond was aimed directly at anyone pretending a title to the Crown who should make an attempt on Queen Elizabeth's life: the target was of course Mary, Queen of Scots. The Commons re-sponded enthusiastically to this proposal and finally a bill based upon it was agreed: significantly the bill was clearly intended to disable Queen Mary but not to exclude her Protestant son, King James VI, from the English throne.

Queen Mary had now been honorably confined in England for over fifteen years; she had lost her looks and her health, but never her spirit or her confidence in her own cause. She lived upon two hopes: one, that Queen Elizabeth might still some day restore her to her Scottish throne, the other, that her Roman Catholic friends at home and abroad would rescue her from captivity and win for her the Crown of England as well as that of Scotland. No intrigues were too laborious, no friends too dubious, no schemes too unscrupulous to serve her ends. But the ministers and parliaments of Queen Elizabeth were exasperated that Mary Stuart should be allowed to remain the focus for so much dangerous plotting. It was now felt that drastic action was necessary. Though she still enjoyed considerable privileges, she was placed under the care of a stricter governor than she had before in Sir Amyas Paulet, a loyal Puritan who ensured that his charge's every move was watched. In December 1585 she was moved to the manor of Chartley in south Derbyshire where Sir Francis Walsingham, who had become Queen Elizabeth's Secretary of State, devised a trap for her. He allowed secret correspondence to be smuggled in and out of the house in beer barrels and intercepted it on the way. By this means Queen Mary first received a batch of letters sent over in the French diplomatic bag. But Walsingham and his agents showed patience: eventually in July 1586 a letter arrived from a hair-brained Derbyshire adherent of Queen Mary named Anthony Babington offering to murder Queen Elizabeth and raise a rebellion, to which Mary sent an approving answer. To make doubly sure, Walsingham forged a postscript to Queen Mary's letter asking for the names of Babington's associates.

Thus the birds were caught and the trap was closed. Babington and his friends were arrested and barbarously executed; Queen Elizabeth was reluctantly obliged to agree that Queen Mary should be taken from Chartley to Fotheringay Castle in Northamptonshire and there put on trial under the terms of the new statute. Mary refused to recognize the jurisdiction of the court and pleaded her innocence; but the result of the trial was a foregone conclusion. The commissioners found her guilty and thus she became incapable of succeeding to the English Crown; but her punishment was left to Queen Elizabeth. A new parliament, summoned under the shadow of the Babington plot, demanded that "Jezebel might live no longer to persecute the prophets of God." The Privy Council was also unanimously in favor of the execution of Mary, Queen of Scots. Though appeals came in from Scotland and from France, King James VI's pleas for his mother's life were somewhat ambiguous and lacking in strength. Queen Elizabeth signed the death warrant on February 1, 1587.

The English queen now tried to cover herself as best she could. For whatever Mary Stuart might have done to her, was it not a dreadful thing to try to execute the dowager queen of France and the former queen of the Scots? What a terrible example it would be—and proved to be—for future revolutionaries. She tried to persuade Paulet that it was his duty under the bond of association to put Mary to death upon his own responsibility. He refused to be a party to murder. Lord Burghley, Walsingham, and their fellow councilors were made of sterner stuff; they got hold of the warrant and sent it off to Fotheringay. Early in the morning of February 8 Queen Mary was executed.

In London the news was received with rejoicing and the church bells were rung. Queen Elizabeth was angry—genuinely angry, it seems—with her councilors for acting without her permission and showed it, if only to impress foreign nations, but the repercussions abroad were, except in one respect, not serious. There was an uproar in Scotland, yet King James VI was determined to do nothing likely to jeopardize his own clear claim to the English succession. In France the king was not in the least anxious to become involved in a war with England when his own position at home was precarious. It was only in Spain that the death of Mary, Queen of Scots, had an important consequence, for King Philip II had long been meditating an out-and-out war upon England and had indeed discussed in detail plans to carry it through. Yet he had never been anxious to fight on behalf of Mary, Queen of Scots, whom he had regarded as a hopeless champion of the Catholic cause. Now the pope could be asked to declare that Philip II himself was the lawful Catholic heir to the English throne in virtue of his descent through his mother from the House of Lancaster. Thus the execution of Queen Mary was a prelude to the dispatch of a Spanish battle fleet, known as the Armada, designed for the conquest of Elizabethan England.

The motives that induced King Philip of Spain to set about the invasion of England were far from being purely religious. Certainly he needed the blessing and, even more, the financial help of the pope, Sixtus V, who, however, was cautious enough to say that Philip should not receive any part of the million crowns that were promised as a subvention until Spanish troops were actually fighting upon the soil of England. Still the pope himself was keen enough upon the enterprise and had indeed himself earlier sent an abortive expedition against Ireland. King Philip had been provoked by a long series of disputes with England and Englishmen, above all by Queen Elizabeth's open interference on behalf of his rebel subjects, the Dutch. Don John of Austria had assured him that the campaign against the Netherlands could be won only in England, since Queen Elizabeth was doing so much to keep the Dutch cause alive. Various plans were considered: a joint naval and military expedition to be sent direct from Spain, but that was thought to be too expensive; a sudden raid across the English Channel from the Netherlands, the troops to be carried in flat-bottomed boats under the cover of darkness, but that was deemed too dangerous; and a naval expedition sent from Spain to join hands with a military expedition prepared by the Duke of Parma, in the Netherlands: there the difficulty was that the Spanish Armada would have to pass through the Narrow Seas to make the rendezvous with Parma's force, which would require extremely delicate timing, more especially since no convenient port was open to the Spaniards.

After much thought the last plan was accepted by King Philip, though the military objections to it were fully realized. It was at least felt sure that once a landing in England was effected no soldiers would be available there capable of defeating the Spanish veterans from Parma's army. It was also believed that risings by English and Scottish Catholics would materially assist the Spanish operations. But three disappointments soon met the Spanish planners: their finest admiral, the Marquis of Santa Cruz, died on the eve of the expedition and had to be replaced by the less experienced Duke of Medina Sidonia (though the latter has usually been underestimated by historians); fewer than 150 vessels were collected instead of the five hundred for which Santa Cruz had asked; and the liaison between Medina Sidonia and Parma was to prove imperfect.

So large a military undertaking could not be kept a secret. Sir Francis Drake at once offered to interfere with the assembly of the Spanish Armada: in April 1587 he sailed to Cadiz where he created much havoc, sinking thousands of tons of shipping, destroying stores, and taking prizes. Then he demonstrated outside Lisbon, challenging the Spanish admiral to come out and fight. On his way home he captured a very valuable Portuguese galleon. Thus his partly private enterprise more than paid its way. It did not, however, distract King Philip II from his purpose. Whether it bought time for the English defensive preparations is not entirely clear. At any rate Queen Elizabeth's government hastily raised and trained volunteers, collected an army at Tilbury, where the queen herself carried out an inspection, and gathered a grand fleet at Plymouth under the command of Lord Howard of Effingham.

The English warships were faster, better built, and had guns of longer range than those of the Spaniards; many were designed for broadside fire at a distance. The Spanish galleons, though taller and stronger, were not numerous, and the Spanish fleet as a whole was weighted down by a great many soldiers who were a mere nuisance on board ship. The English had a fighting fleet with experience dating back to the reign of King Henry VIII, and its principal officers, who included men like Drake, Hawkins, and Frobisher—the Elizabethan "sea dogs"

—had not the slightest doubt in their minds that they could beat the Spaniards wherever and whenever they met them.

Although the bulk of the English navy was concentrated at Plymouth, a squadron was also stationed at Dover to keep watch on the Duke of Parma. In the summer of 1588 the Spanish Armada entered the Channel from the west and for ten days a running fight took place. Some of the queen's naval advisers would have preferred an attack launched earlier on the Spanish fleet in its own bases, as Drake had shown might have been done. But it was entirely understandable that the government felt nervous and preferred the fleet to remain existent and at home. The English admiral was not able to bring the Spaniards to a set battle in the Narrow Seas. Indeed Medina Sidonia handled his crescent formation with considerable skill, so that his losses were small, while the English naval commanders had some misunderstandings. The Spanish admiral's instructions were to get through the Channel and make contact with Parma. But Parma was effectively bottled up in the Netherlands, where English garrisons occupied the towns of Flushing and Brill, granted to them as pledges for Dutch debts. A French port was denied to the Armada and, with its ammunition and supplies diminished, it became a vulnerable target. On July 28—or on August 7 according to New Style dating—Howard's force did much damage to the Spanish galleons at anchor in Calais roadstead. Next day an even more decisive battle took place off Gravelines, where an English cannonade wrought havoc and threatened to drive the enemy on the shoals. Then the wind changed and the Spanish fleet was saved from annihilation.

Medina Sidonia's real difficulties were that he had no port in which to collect supplies and no means of replenishing his ammunition. Parma failed to co-operate with him and some of his captains betrayed him. He saw it was impossible to carry out his secondary instruction, which was to effect a landing in the Isle of Wight. Reluctantly he made the decision to sail for home, and in order to do so he carried out a long and dangerous voyage around Ireland. He managed to bring nearly half of his fleet safely back to his home port. It was to the credit of King Philip II that he did not condemn this devoted grandee, as many writers have done then and since. It was the measure of Medina Sidonia's selfless patriotism that he blamed no one for his failure but himself.

In England there was the greatest possible rejoicing over the retreat of the proud Spaniards—and justly so. The Armada had been one of the biggest expeditionary forces ever assembled; the heavy sailing ships had penetrated the English Channel and had never lost formation until the weather turned against them; if a rendezvous with Parma's veterans had been achieved, England might well have suffered invasion; no one could say how the scratch English militia might have fared against a trained Spanish army. But the defeat of the Armada was the beginning and not the end of the war against Spain. The resources of the Elizabethan government were severely stretched. The war in the Netherlands had to be sustained; the garrisons abroad needed support; further threats of invasion had to be warded off; and attacks needed to be launched upon the far-flung possessions of Philip II. It used to be imagined that Queen Elizabeth I's wars paid for themselves out of captured booty, but this was far from being the case. The queen's annual peacetime revenue was about £200,000 a year, out of which little could be saved for extraordinary purposes. Wartime parliaments patriotically voted taxes, but the utmost care had to be taken with all the resources available to sustain adequately the different campaigns. It is a proof of success of the queen's war-financing that her credit was always better than that of her enemies.

There was no immediate sequel to the defeat of the Armada. Measures against the English Roman Catholics were intensified, but the queen still refused to have anything to do with the Puritans and supported the rigorous repressive policy of Archbishop Whitgift, whom she called her "little black husband." In 1589, however, an impressive expedition was organized to attack the Spanish king in his home bases, as Hawkins, Drake, and other aggressive admirals had advocated. One hundred and fifty sailing ships and 18,000 men set out for Lisbon in the spring. It was a joint-stock enterprise, partly financed by the Crown and partly by London city merchants—for that was one of the means whereby the queen overcame her financial difficulties. The expedition was almost as much a fiasco as the Armada had been; the land army was wiped out by disease and Drake refused to risk his ships beneath the guns of Lisbon.

In that same year English commitments were extended still further when it was decided to lend assistance to the new French king, Henry IV, formerly Henry of Navarre. After the assassination of the ineffective Henry III, King Henry of Navarre, himself a Protestant, claimed the throne and struggled to enforce his rights against the league of Catholics. Queen Elizabeth promptly lent him money and dispatched an expeditionary force to his assistance. Next year King Henry IV won a victory over the Catholic league, but King Philip II of Spain was persuaded to move his forces into France and thereby possibly find himself a base for attempting another invasion of England. Parma swept down upon Paris, and, to protect herself against a Spanish assault, Queen

Elizabeth sent yet another force into France to be stationed in Brittany, ready to prevent the occupation of ports there or in Normandy by her enemy.

Meanwhile the war at sea continued mostly on a joint-stock or privateering basis. In 1590 and 1591 several squadrons visited the Azores to search for Spanish treasure ships. King Philip II replied by forbidding his treasure ships to sail except under escort. This convoy system had a success in 1591 when one of the marauding English squadrons was surprised. Sir Richard Grenville's ship, "The Revenge," was caught in isolation and fought a day-long losing battle against the entire Spanish fleet, an immortal feat of heroism. But while the English sailors harassed and disturbed the Spanish empire and captured some plunder, nothing of general importance was achieved; and in 1595 two of the most famous Elizabethan captains, Drake and Hawkins, died after a fatal expedition to the West Indies and Central America.

In the course of the war a new royal favorite arrived on the scene in the person of Robert Devereux, second Earl of Essex. He had replaced his stepfather Leicester in the queen's affections after Leicester had died in disgrace following his failure in the Netherlands in 1588. The queen was attracted by this handsome and virile young gallant who was handy both with his sword and his pen. He made his first martial appearance in defiance of orders when he served in the unsuccessful expedition against Portugal. Then in 1595, after the disaster in the West Indies and the sudden capture of Calais by the Spaniards, he took part in a fresh attack on Cadiz along with Sir Thomas Howard and Sir Francis Vere. The surprise was complete; a Spanish treasure fleet was destroyed, and the town was sacked. Essex earned much glory, but it was not enough.

Essex was a highly ambitious young man, delighted in the admiration of the queen; so too was Sir Robert Cecil, the hunchback son of the veteran Lord Burghley, the queen's most trusted minister, who had died in 1596 at the age of seventy-eight. Rivalry for political power developed between these two men: Essex received a rebuff when his candidate for the post of attorney general, Sir Francis Bacon, was rejected in favor of Cecil's candidate, Sir Edward Coke. But Essex obtained a signal honor when in 1598 he was appointed Lord Lieutenant of Ireland, where yet another front in the world war had opened.

On the European mainland things had gone fairly well for England in the late 1590's. Crozon in Brittany had been captured from the Spaniards and after King Henry IV changed his religion in 1593 he united most Frenchmen under him, but he still did not abandon the English alliance. Eventually in May 1598 a peace treaty was concluded between France and Spain at Vervins so that England and Holland were left to carry on the prolonged war against the Spanish empire on their own.

The center of the Irish nationalist movement was now in Ulster. Its leader was Hugh O'Neill, Earl of Tyrone. English by upbringing, this capable and ingenious man aimed to enlist the help of the pope and of Spain and to drive the English out of Ireland. At first the Spanish government provided only money and munitions, but after the peace of Vervins and the death of King Philip II, the new Spanish king, Philip III, sent an armada to Tyrone's assistance. The fleet failed to get through because of bad weather, and it was not until 1601 that a Spanish expeditionary force at last landed at Kinsale. Long before then the Irish had risen and an English punitive army had been wiped out on the borders of Ulster. In 1599 the Earl of Essex arrived with a splendidly equipped new army to begin a campaign not in Ulster in the north but in Munster in the south. Then he entered into a secret negotiation with Tyrone for a truce. The queen commanded him to stay and fight it out. Disobeying orders, he returned to court to plead his case. He was replaced by Lord Mountjoy, an able general, who defeated the Irish and the Spaniards alike and in the end compelled Tyrone to surrender. Thus it appeared that the English had finally conquered Ireland.

When Essex returned from Ireland to England he was put into prison for ten months and deprived of all his offices. He became the victim of Nemesis: all sorts of fantastic schemes germinated in his muddled mind. Apparently his intention was to gather together a group of adventurers and carry out a *coup d'état* against Cecil. In February 1601, on a Sunday, he dashed into the city of London with 200 men crying, "For the Queen! For the Queen! The crown of England is sold to a Spaniard! A plot is laid for my life!" It was evident that he was half mad, but the queen was remorseless; Essex and his fellow conspirators were punished with death.

That was the last exciting public event of the long reign. It was characteristic of the queen that she loved hopeless gilded adventurers like Leicester and Essex, but conducted herself toward them with caution and strictness, while she depended upon less showy and less attractive statesmen like Burghley and his son. After the so-called Essex rebellion, parliament was summoned once again. The queen was in a benign mood. She promised the members that she would abolish trading patents "commonly called monopolies," which had been abused by their holders and had thus become a widely felt grievance. In her last speech to parliament she ended with these words:

This testimony I would have you carry hence for the world to know: that your Sovereign is more careful of your conservation than of herself, and will daily crave of God that they that wish you best may never wish in vain.

Queen Elizabeth had indeed served her people well. She had staved off the Counter Reformation, preserved the independence of the English Church, defeated the machinations of the king of Spain, and afforded her country much peace and prosperity. She still refused to name her successor, just as earlier she recoiled from accepting a husband. She was married to her people, who loved her. In 1602 she was in her seventieth year, and on the anniversary of her accession, November 17, which was celebrated for many years to come as a notable date in British history, she was greeted "with as great an applause of multitudes as if they had never seen her before." But as winter came and the weather turned foul, she knew that she was dying. She refused both food and medicine. At last she did her duty by nominating King James VI of Scotland to succeed her. In March 1603 she passed peacefully away.

XXXVII

The Economic and Social Life of the Elizabethan Age

The reign of Queen Elizabeth I was a restless and exciting age in English history: to many it has since seemed to have been a golden age. On the whole, people were growing richer; the upper classes dressed themselves in fantastic clothes and spent their money with abandon; courtiers, merchants, and tradesmen—and the queen herself—speculated in daring foreign enterprises; large new houses were built that still survive for the amazement of posterity; theaters were opened for the first time; cock-fighting, bear-baiting, and the like flourished as never before; highway robbery and piracy were profitable and even admired pursuits; "large classes," Dr. Trevelyan has written lyrically, "freed as never before from poverty, felt the upspring of the spirit and expressed it in wit, music, and song."

Prices continued to rise, as they had been doing throughout the sixteenth century—a sixty per cent increase is estimated during the reign of Queen Elizabeth I—but this reflected the general economic expansion of the nation. Population was rising as well, particularly in the countryside: the death rate was heavier in the towns. The population of England and Wales at the death of Queen Elizabeth is variously estimated at between three and one-half and four and one-half millions. Between 200,000 and 300,000 people were concentrated in London and its environs alone, perhaps as much as one-twelfth of the population of the whole country. Some contemporaries thought that the country was overpopulated. Food was in demand and consumed in enormous quantities by those who could afford it. Subsistence farming ceased to be so common, and farmers supplied new markets in the towns, especially London, and exported abroad when the harvests were good. When harvests were poor, the export of corn was forbidden and gloomy observations were then uttered about there being far too many people in the country and about how desirable it was to establish colonies in Ireland or the New World. Although depressions occurred when harvests were bad or trade was interrupted, on the whole there seems little doubt that the general rise in prices—whether this was owing to the influx of silver from South America or to other causes—and the increasing population were highly stimulating to trade and industry.

Accumulation of capital out of profits brought investment in industry and commerce or in agricultural land which was acquired for the purpose of improvement. Interest rates became the subject of legislation. Theoretically at least, in Roman Catholic times to lend money was sinful, but now a maximum rate of ten per cent was imposed and accepted. The enclosure movement which had long been in progress became the subject of commendation by some writers and of adverse criticism by others. It was still quite widely asserted that enclosure for the purpose of converting arable land into pasture for sheep was a cause of hardship and depopulation in the countryside and was therefore socially disadvantageous; but experts on agriculture, such as Fitzherbert and Tusser, the author of *Five Hundred Points of Good Husbandry* (1573), advocated enclosure to make arable farming more compact and more economical. Fitzherbert urged the arable farmer to change fields with his neighbor so that he might "lay his lands together." Tusser wrote:

> The country enclosed I praise,
>   the other delighteth not me,
> For nothing the wealth it doth raise
>   to such as inferior be

Apart from enclosure, however, few advances in the science of agriculture seem to have taken place in the Elizabethan age. It is said that even the art of dressing fields with marl and other composts had fallen into neglect. Dung was often wasted by being used as fuel. No solution had been found, other than preserving loppings from trees and moss, for keeping cattle alive throughout the winter. After feasting themselves from Christmas until Twelfth Night, ordinary men and women could barely keep themselves nourished during the winter and eagerly awaited the promise of spring. Salted meat was a rare luxury. Beasts grew thin and died. Mixed farming was virtually nonexistent. Hops for making beer was the only noted new crop; potatoes were practically unknown.

The Elizabethan government itself insisted that enclosing land for sheep farming was antisocial. In 1563 a new statute was passed for the maintenance of tillage. But when corn became cheap and plentiful the main clause of this act, forbidding the conversion of land from tillage to pasture, was repealed. Two more acts were passed in the late 1590's, one of them condemning out-of-hand enclosures for pasture. Sir Francis Bacon, who advocated these measures, expressed himself as deeply concerned: "I would be sorry to see within this kingdom the piece of Ovid's verse prove true: 'crops grow where Troy once stood' " and "in England instead of a whole town full of people nothing but green fields, a shepherd and his dog." It seems likely, however, that the extent of these enclosures was exaggerated at the time. The Midlands, which were the scene of most "champaign" or "open-field" farming, were far from enclosed in the eighteenth century, when more than two thousand private acts were passed for that purpose.

The "improving" landlords benefited from the need for food and clothing which came from the growing population and the big demands from the capital city. Rentiers, who had long before disposed of their demesne lands, were, to begin with, less well off because they continued to draw their income from rents that could not easily be increased, while the price of things that they needed to buy steadily rose. There was, too, a certain amount of poverty owing to displacements of a population which was less mobile than in later times; such displacements led to a renewed outcry against enclosures for sheep farming; or again such rural poverty might have been brought about by periods of famine when the weather was as bad as it was in the years 1594 to 1596. The extent of such poverty is difficult to gauge, but it certainly existed and impinged upon legislation. Although the first statute of Queen Elizabeth I's reign dealing with the problem, dated 1563, only re-enacted earlier legislation permitting the punishment of "sturdy beggars," other acts passed at the behest of the Privy Council, notably that of 1572, required local authorities to raise rates to support the "impotent poor" and to establish workhouses as well as houses of correction for beggars capable of work. Another act of 1563 had laid down rules for apprenticeship and methods of fixing prices and wages. A comprehensive act of 1598 fixed the maximum poor rate at two-pence and instructed justices of the peace to appoint overseers of the poor to manage the workhouses. Thus after the destruction of the monasteries during the Reformation the care of the poor became recognized as a secular and not an ecclesiastical duty. By another act of 1601 the overseers of the poor were empowered to buy materials such as "flax, hemp, wool, thread, iron and other stuff" to set the poor to work. Attempts to control the prices of food were another contribution made by the Privy Council to the alleviation of poverty. But it was as difficult to stabilize prices as it was to import corn in time of dearth. Gradually the mitigation of poverty fell upon private charity.

Poverty was possibly more frequent in the towns than in the country-side. The cloth industry, for example, suffered several periods of de-pression during the later half of the sixteenth century when unemploy-ment became rife. Seasonal unemployment was also common in the ports, while mineworkers were poorly paid. On the whole, however, industry and commerce prospered in the Elizabethan age.

The cloth industry remained the busiest both in supplying the needs of the home market and in promoting exports. It was widely diffused and division of labor in it was far advanced. The industry was develop-ing at this time particularly in West Riding, Yorkshire, in Wiltshire in the west, and in East Anglia, where foreign immigrants—Huguenots or Flemings, driven from their native lands by the fury of the Counter Reformation—settled in considerable numbers. The principal English export was unfinished "white cloth"; but there was a setback in the trade in the later half of Queen Elizabeth's reign owing to the pro-longed disturbances in the Netherlands and the war against Spain. Nevertheless the value of cloth exports during the reign has been esti-mated at about £1,000,000 to £1,500,000 a year. The home market was stimulated by the introduction of lighter cloths that were then be-coming fashionable. The Flemings helped to develop these "new draperies" (says and bays), while in Lancashire wool and linen were mixed to make "cottons," and cotton itself was first mixed with wool to manufacture the rougher fustians.

The Merchant Adventurers Company, which had replaced the old Staplers as the chief export organization and consisted of a powerful group of London business men, received a royal charter in 1564, virtually giving it a monopoly on the export of white cloth to Europe, but it had to compete with the energetic German Hanse. When in 1576 Antwerp, their principal entrepôt, was destroyed by "the Spanish Fury," a decline set in. The Adventurers were also harassed by "interlopers" who refused to pay fees to the company and traded in its markets. Toward the end of the reign other companies came forward—the Eastland Company (1579) with depots first at Elbing and then at Danzig, the Levant Company (1581), trading in Venice and Turkey, and the East India Company (1599)—and began to tap new markets for the sale of cloth.

Other valuable industries included shipbuilding and coal mining. Expansion of foreign trade and the needs of war time stimulated shipbuilding at Newcastle upon Tyne and elsewhere. Though England was still thickly wooded, the demand for timber was insatiable: it was required not merely as domestic fuel, but for such industries as the manufacture of iron by smelting, the making of glass, and shipbuilding. Coal was being mined and shipped from Newcastle to London and was therefore known as "sea coal." Outcropped coal had long been used as domestic fuel in the neighborhood of the mines, but not elsewhere. Shipments of coal from Newcastle to London increased tenfold between 1545 and 1625; about a hundred collieries appear to have been in operation; a little coal was even exported; and companies like the Mines Royal and Mineral and Battery Works were established on a joint-stock basis to develop mining of various kinds or to make brass for cannon. The opinion has recently been expressed that "a minor industrial revolution" was taking place in the reign of Queen Elizabeth I.

Most classes of the community participated in the general economic and social prosperity of the times, but naturally some families did better than others and the fortunes of a few, the Roman Catholic Treshams, for instance, actually declined. The nobility, whether it was new or old, was expected to engage in conspicuous consumption. Peers had to uphold their positions in the community and entertain the queen and her courtiers. The Earl of Huntingdon died £20,000 in debt to the Crown and the queen's favorite, the Earl of Leicester, is said to have owed £70,000 when he died. Great men, like the Archbishop of Canterbury or the Earl of Derby, had to maintain retinues of hundreds of servants. Extravagant figures like Bess of Hardwicke, the Countess of Shrewsbury, showed their megalomania by building themselves palaces in which they rarely lived. Though some of the nobility suffered occasional inconveniences because of inflated prices and their own gross extravagances, most of them held on to their lands and successfully weathered the storms of the age. It was said of Lord Burghley that "by occasion of his office he hath preserved many great houses from over-throw by relieving sundry extremities."

After the Reformation the class usually called "the gentry" continued to expand, to play an increasingly large part in public affairs, and to accumulate more and more property at the expense of the Crown and the Church. The expansion of the gentry is the outstanding social fact in English history in the hundred years preceding the civil wars in the middle of the seventeenth century. Lord Burghley told his son that "gentility is nothing else but ancient riches," but it was much more often newly acquired riches. When after the dissolution of the monasteries large quantities of land were thrown on to the public market, they were bought up by all sorts of people who then became gentlefolk even if they were not so already. "As for gentlemen," wrote Sir Thomas Smith, "they be made good cheap in England." This was later underlined by Thomas Wilson, who asserted that lands were taken up and exploited as leases ran out, while merchants also aspired to be businesslike land-lords and higher gentry. Edmund Spenser's famous poem, *The Faerie Queene,* is said to have been intended as "a manual for the training of gentlemen." Later Peacham's *Complete Gentleman* (1622) summed up the Elizabethan teaching on the subject. The gentry invaded the universities and the Inns of Court. Heraldry flourished and the College of Arms was kept busy. Successful merchants bought themselves landed estates or offered generous dowries when they married their daughters into existing landed families. Whether the so-called "new gentry" was more businesslike than the old and whether it advanced in wealth at the expense of the nobility has been discussed and disputed. Some contemporaries believed that it did so advance, but on the whole, as Professor Habbakuk wrote, the old landowners "could stand a good deal of ruin." They often made up by judiciously negotiated marriages for the losses they had suffered through the sales of land. There is said to have been "a particularly rapid rise in landed incomes after 1590," which may have been brought about by rents catching up with prices. (On the Herbert estates in Wiltshire rents appear to have increased faster than prices throughout the sixteenth century, but these may not have been typical.) The Crown itself was the only landowner that was habitually obliged to sell capital to meet expenses.

The yeomen also prospered during the Elizabethan era. The yeoman farmer was not required "to keep up the port of a gentleman"; he could gradually acquire farms in small parcels, and was not ashamed to work upon the land himself. "The rich yeoman's wealth," writes Dr. Rowse, "lay in the fields, in his crops; the surplus he spent in adding to his holdings and buying more livestock. He lived like a husbandman in the

TUDOR ENGLAND

same kind of small house in the village street with a singular absence of comfort: a few pots and pans, a trestle table, a few stools, no chairs and boards to lie on." Some yeomen were actually better off than the gentry. In Leicestershire it has been said that the purchases of land by yeomen in the Elizabethan times was "the largest transference of land ownership since Domesday" (Hoskins).

While the nobility and court gentry did well enough out of the land, out of offices, out of patents granted by the Crown, and out of speculation, and new gentry and new yeomen were expanding their activities, there was certainly a depressed class at the bottom of the ladder. The literature that is available about depopulation and vagabondage was not written out of mere imagination. Nor were the various statutes introduced to cope with these problems without a real purpose. Men like Sir Robert Cecil and Sir Francis Bacon, who stood at the very center of public affairs, were much concerned over the condition of the poor at the end of Queen Elizabeth's reign. One speaker in the House of Commons of 1597 went so far as to assert that "the eyes of the poor are upon this Parliament and sad for the want they suffer." To preserve their own position in this age of steadily rising prices, all classes of landlords raised rents, imposed fines on their tenants when leases came up for renewal, and evicted those who were not prepared to pay. Enclosure created a measure of rural unemployment. If some small farmers were becoming bigger, others were compelled to leave their fields and seek employment as landless laborers or become beggars. If the rich grew richer, the poor often became much poorer. The north of England remained sparsely populated, backward, and lawless, while in the south there began "the destruction of the English peasantry." The sixteenth century, Dr. Elton has said, laid the foundation "for that characteristic structure of landlord, leasehold farmer, and landless labourer which has marked the English countryside from that day to this."

In the reign of Queen Elizabeth I the government and parliament engaged in industrial and commercial legislation. We have seen that one of the earliest roles of the House of Commons was to concern itself with economic affairs. Queen Elizabeth included these among what she called "Commonwealth matters," which she regarded as suitable for the attention of members of parliament, as distinct from questions of religion and foreign policy, which she thought belonged to the Crown. In her later parliaments initiative on enclosing, the poor laws, and similar subjects was taken in the Commons and was the precursor of a more definite legislative initiative seized by the House in the next reign. In any case national legislation on economic matters became more common at this time and was extended to industrial procedures formerly

dealt with by merchant or craft guilds. New industries like cloth manufacture and coal mining were in any case too complicated and too widely
dispersed to be controlled by local guilds. In the same way large commercial enterprises, beginning with the Merchant Adventurers and
culminating in the East India Company, required central control,
whether by the granting of royal charters or by acts of parliament.

The financial needs of the Crown also impinged upon the question
of economic control. Relations with customs farmers and holders of
profitable monopolies or purchasers of confiscated lands carried the
Crown into the world of business, while anxiety to maintain the nucleus
of a large navy explains such expedients as "fish days," navigation laws,
and ship money exacted from the ports. Thus the government was
brought directly into industry and trade. One historian has indeed
contrasted a period of "free trade" and local government of industry
that existed before the Elizabethan period with a national economic
control exerted in the interests of public finance and the protection of
native industries that prevailed afterward. It may be doubted whether
such a contrast can be sustained. Assuredly attempts by kings to
legislate on economic matters by statutes of laborers, sumptuary laws,
and the like can be traced far back into English history. On the other
hand, there is evidence of some tightening of state control during the
Tudor period.

In the Victorian age and indeed up to the time when Great Britain
abandoned free trade in the 1930's British economic historians were
wont to write at length on state control of industry in the sixteenth and
seventeenth centuries in terms of what they called "mercantilism," a
phrase invented in Germany and supposed to consist of a policy of un-
enlightened protection of the home market. Nowadays, however,
policies intended to promote a favorable balance of payments, the maintenance of the value of the national currency, the support of agriculture,
and the nurturing of "infant industries" are imposed by nearly every
government in the world. And these policies are usually practiced most
rigorously by the so-called "underdeveloped countries," such as England
was still in the sixteenth century; apart from unfinished cloth most
exports consisted of food and raw materials, while imports were mainly
finished goods and luxuries. Naturally therefore the Elizabethan government aimed at checking the importation of luxuries and at stimulating
the export of cloth, while helping fishermen, wheat farmers, ship-
builders and shippers by legislative means. How far this economic
policy was deliberately thought out and how far it was eclectic may be
a matter for argument; but, in general, it is safe to say that the House
of Commons tackled the different economic problems of the time as

they arose, often by panic measures. Nevertheless the nationalist feeling that arose in England during the Protestant Reformation and the wars against Spain and that was exemplified in the near worship bestowed on Queen Elizabeth I by her subjects was undoubtedly reflected in the economic sphere, as it was too in politics and in literature. England was self-conscious as never before in her history.

XXXVIII

The Expansion of England

Though the British Isles lay athwart the sea routes to the two Americas, her inhabitants were very late in entering the competition for the exploration, exploitation, and settlement of the new world outside Europe, the discovery of which transformed the history of mankind in the sixteenth and seventeenth centuries. The Portuguese, inspired by the republic of Genoa, had been among the first pioneers, and as early as the mid-fifteenth century, under the direction of Prince Henry, "the Navigator," had established settlements in the Atlantic islands of the Azores and Madeira and had opened up trade with Africa. Castile followed in the wake of Portugal and the Spanish court lent its patronage to Christopher Columbus, a Genoese adventurer who reached the West Indies and Central America in 1492. The Spaniards built a great overseas empire comprising Mexico, Peru, and Chile, Central America, Cuba, and the West Indies. Here they set up colonies and imported African slaves to supplement the native Indian labor and work in the silver and gold mines. Each year a treasure fleet sailed to Spain from San Juan de Ulloa in the Gulf of Mexico and from Nombre de Dios on the Isthmus of Panama bearing the wealth of Mexico and Peru to enlarge the treasury of King Philip II. In 1498 Vasco da Gama, a seaman in the service of Portugal, reached India by way of the Cape of Good Hope. The Portuguese began to trade rather than settle in Africa, India, and the Spice Islands of the East Indies. Already in 1493 Pope Alexander VI had published a bull dividing the newly discovered lands between Spain and Portugal, west of the meridian line passing through the Azores. Until the Reformation, at any rate, this bull was discouraging to the other European powers; in any case possession was nine-tenths of the law, and Spain, which absorbed Portugal in 1580, jealously guarded so immediately profitable a monopoly.

Only one minor discovery graced English history before the reign of Queen Elizabeth I. In 1496 King Henry VII granted a charter to a syndicate of Bristol merchants, headed by John Cabot, to seek new lands which did not infringe upon the Iberian monopoly. In 1497 Cabot set out in search of a northwest passage to the fabulous city of Cathay in China. In fact he landed upon the frozen and inhospitable north-eastern coast of modern Canada, which he called the "new-found land." Next year he set out again and is believed to have sailed as far south as Chesapeake Bay in modern Virginia. He never returned and certainly got nowhere near China. Henry VII continued to encourage these merchants of Bristol; in 1509 John Cabot's son, Sebastian, completed a voyage in which he is thought to have discovered Hudson Bay in Canada. Later he entered the service of Spain and did not return to England until 1548. The discovery of Newfoundland was not, however, wasted. Fishermen, chiefly from the west of England, sailed there yearly to catch and dry cod and in due course a settlement was built up which became the oldest British colony. Upon John Cabot's discovery too were based future English claims in North America.

After King Henry VII's reign there was a lull for about sixty years before further exploration was undertaken. In spite of England's geographical position and her naval traditions, no books of geographical importance were published: King Henry VIII was absorbed in Anne Boleyn and the Tudor succession while Cortez was conquering Mexico and Pizarro, Peru. Richard Hakluyt, a clerk in holy orders with a pronounced taste for geography who collected and wrote about the voyages of others, said in the first edition of his *Principal Navigations, Traffics and Discoveries of the English Nation* (1589) that he had "both heard in speech and read in books other nations miraculously extolled for their discoveries and notable enterprises by sea, but the English of all others for their sluggish security and continual neglect of the like attempts . . . either ignominiously reported or exceedingly condemned." On the other hand, it has been argued that the early half of the sixteenth century was a period of "apprenticeship" for English overseas merchants, seamen, and adventurers. In the reign of Queen Elizabeth I English shortcomings in these matters were put right; the sovereign herself and her ministers, Burghley, Leicester, Walsingham, and Sir Christopher Hatton (after whose crest Francis Drake's famous ship, the "Golden Hind," was named), lent active aid and encouragement to explorers.

One of the instances of this apprenticeship was in the voyages of William Hawkins of Plymouth, who managed to make friends with the Portuguese and to open up trade with Guinea and Brazil. In the early 1550's, in spite of Portuguese opposition, a steady trade was done with West Africa, and in 1564 William Hawkins' son John, with the blessing of the queen, boldly sailed into the Spanish Main on a trading mission and also reported on the prospects of profitable business on the Atlantic coast of North America. In 1567, however, when John Hawkins, accompanied by a young Devonian, Francis Drake, set out on a trip to buy slaves and was driven by bad weather to shelter at San Juan de Ulloa, he was treacherously attacked and lost most of his ships and his men, though he and Drake managed to reach home. Thenceforward English advances into the areas claimed by Spain were accompanied by piracy or open war or by a desire for vengeance.

The chief object of exploration at the beginning of Queen Elizabeth's reign was to find either a northwest or a northeast passage to the fabled riches of China. The way south, whether through the Mediterranean or around the south coast of Africa, was barred by the Spaniards and Portuguese. As early as 1520 the Magellan Straits to the extreme south of the Americas had also been discovered by a Portuguese in Spanish service: but the English hoped to reach and cross the Pacific from the north—though another much-talked-of project was to find a wonderful land called the Terra Australis which was believed to lie to the far south beyond the Americas.

After Sebastian Cabot returned to England in 1548, he became the head of a company which aimed to find a northeast passage. In 1553, as King Edward VI lay dying, ships belonging to this company left the Thames and one of them succeeded in getting as far as the White Sea and opening trade with Russia. This trade was developed by another merchant, Anthony Jenkinson, who became friendly with the czar in the 1560's: through his efforts English cloth was then sold both to Russia and to Persia. But now English enthusiasm and the urge for riches had been aroused. The search for a short sea passage to Asia, advocated by Robert Thorne and Roger Barlow in the reign of King Henry VIII, was taken up again by Dr. John Dee and Sir Humphrey Gilbert. As long as Queen Elizabeth I wished to be friendly with Spain, the routes south remained barred: instead, in 1576, Martin Frobisher received the backing both of the court and the city for a voyage of discovery purposing to reach Asia by way of the Arctic. He rediscovered Hudson Bay, near which he found a lump of black ore that was thought to be gold. The queen and many others hastened to invest in a promising speculation, but it proved a delusion and they burned their fingers. This put people off the northwest passage for some years.

Meanwhile Sir Francis Drake had set off on a voyage round the world. Drake, who was born in 1540, came of west country stock, but was brought up at Chatham in Kent where his father was a chaplain in the royal dockyard. He served his apprenticeship with Sir John Hawkins, during which he learned to hate the Spaniards; but he was in any case an enthusiastic Protestant who regarded his enterprises as those of a crusader rather than a pirate. In 1572 he decided to revenge himself for the disaster at San Juan de Ulloa and come to grips with his popish foe. Although he failed to seize the treasure in Nombre de Dios itself (where he was wounded), he later made a landing on the Isthmus of Panama where he stole Spanish silver valued at £40,000. His immediate imitators were less successful, and the court now interested itself in the project of discovering the supposed southern continent, Terra Australis, by sending an expedition into the Pacific by way of the Magellan Straits.

The queen herself selected Francis Drake to lead this voyage of exploration. She knew that it would mean challenging the might of Spain, but she is said to have told Drake that she "would be gladly revenged on the King of Spain for diverse injuries that she had received." Drake set sail from Plymouth in November 1577 with three ships, headed by the "Pelican," later rechristened the "Golden Hind"; he had the full backing of the court and secret instructions from the queen herself. When the ships at length reached the coast of Brazil and Drake revealed his instructions to his men, there was some muttering and then insubordination. Drake tried Thomas Doughty, an Irish adventurer who was second in command, for mutiny and ordered his execution. Having established discipline, he penetrated the Straits of Magellan, covering its 300 miles in the record time of sixteen days. But when he entered the Pacific Ocean he ran into heavy weather and lost two of his three ships. In November 1578 the "Golden Hind" turned north and carried out raids along the west coast of the Americas. He captured a carrack loaded with silver off Panama, which made the voyage pay. Then he turned north and laid claim to the possession of modern California. Deciding that he could not find a northeast passage back to the Atlantic, he next sailed west across the Pacific to the East Indies where he purchased a cargo of cloves and concluded a verbal agreement with one of the sultans. Once having found his way out of the dangerous waters around the East Indies, Drake traveled back south of Java, round the Cape of Good Hope to Sierra Leone on the west coast of Africa, and thence home to Plymouth Sound. He was the first

Englishman to sail round the world and the only European to do it since Magellan. It had been an astonishing adventure, made possible only by the sailing qualities and gunpower of the "Golden Hind" and the loyalty that Drake was able to inspire in his men. Nor did he live always in discomfort. He took with him artists to picture in their exact colors the coasts that he passed: indeed he painted himself. He ate his meals off silver plates with gold borders, kept his ship scrupulously clean, perfumed his cabin, and supped to the music of viols. He treated his Spanish prisoners with exquisite courtesy, explaining to them that if their king would not permit the English to trade in the Americas, they must expect to be robbed. When he got back to England, he was a national hero; the queen defended and knighted him; he had several imitators, but no equals. The only other Englishman to sail round the world was Thomas Cavendish, who returned in the year of the Armada's defeat, also bearing a rich cargo.

The reports received of the Americas from men like Drake and Hawkins, the beginnings of the settlement in Newfoundland, the example of the Spanish settlements, and a supposed threat of over-population at home all contributed to the idea advocated in the middle of Queen Elizabeth's reign of establishing English colonies overseas. Richard Hakluyt in his books advocated an English settlement in America, and a group of gentry, headed by Sir Humphrey Gilbert, his half brother Sir Walter Ralegh, and their cousin, Sir Richard Grenville, concerned itself with the proposal. In 1578 Gilbert was given a patent by the queen to discover and occupy land not possessed by any other Christian prince and permitting him to grant lands and make laws in any colony that he might establish. In 1582 Gilbert set out for Newfoundland, but his ships were wrecked off the uncharted coast and he himself lost in the tiny ship in which he was coming home through a storm off the Azores. Walter Ralegh, who at that time was a prime favorite of the queen, took over the plan from his half brother; he obtained a fresh charter and in 1585 Richard Grenville planted the first English colony in America on Roanoke Island in Chesapeake Bay. At first the native Indians were friendly and the colonists thought that they had found an earthly paradise, but in due course the natives became less friendly and the country did not prove so paradisial. Francis Drake, returning from his last raid in the Caribbean, took the disappointed colonists home, and when Grenville arrived there later in 1586 he found that it was deserted. He left behind a token force of fifteen, all of whom were killed by the Indians.

So the first settlement of Virginia—for so it was named in honor of the Virgin Queen—ended in disaster, and a second Virginian colony

HUDSON BAY COMPANY

Newfoundland

Mississippi R.

Missouri R.

Ohio R.

Maine

New
Hampshire
Massachusetts
New York
Connecticut
New Plymouth Colony
Rhode I.
Penusylvania
New Jersey
Maryland
Delaware
Virginia
Jamestown
North
Carolina
South
Carolina
Chesapeake Bay

Mississippi R.

Bermuda

New Providence

Santo
Domingo
(Sp.)

Jamaica

Barbad.

FIRST BRITISH SETTLEMENTS
IN AMERICA

also vanished. It was not until the reign of King James I that a permanent colony was established with difficulty in 1607. Ralegh consoled himself by dispatching an expedition to Guiana on the north coast of South America in 1595. It was believed that here by the Orinoco River was the land of El Dorado, as fabulous and as nonexistent as Cathay or the Terra Australis of Elizabethan dreams. Ralegh made friends with the Indians and fancied that he had discovered a gold mine. The queen and many of her subjects were impressed. Ralegh answered his critics by publishing *The Discovery of the Large, Rich and Beautiful Empire of Guiana* in 1596. He thought of the country as another Peru and a springboard from which the Spanish power in the Americas might be crushed. It was a mirage that eventually led him to his death in 1618. Though he failed himself, Ralegh may be called the founder of the first British empire. Of Virginia he wrote "I shall yet live to see it an English nation." And so he did.

In the reign of Queen Elizabeth I an area far nearer home than Virginia appealed forcibly to contemporaries, including Ralegh, as a suitable site for colonization: this was Ireland. King Henry VIII had assumed the title of king of Ireland and expected the system of tribal land tenure there to give way to that of England where the Crown ultimately owned all the land. This poor and backward but lush and convenient country seemed to be an ideal spot for new plantations. The natives could be bought out or dispossessed. Direct rule could be made a reality and English colonies could bring civilization to the benighted Irish. As Professor Quinn has written, "Ireland in the later sixteenth century was the severest testing ground for an England on the way to empire."

But in fact the English central government and local administration never had the resources to impose their will upon the Irish. The Protestant Reformation had made no impression upon either the natives or the Anglo-Irish, who were consequently basically hostile to the English way of life. Moreover the administration at Dublin always found itself dependent on the great Irish lords who invariably fought against each other. However able and tolerant the ministers of Queen Elizabeth were, they found themselves faced with an almost insoluble problem. Yet they had to try to establish order, since Ireland was a back door to England's enemies so long as it was not under proper control, offering a particularly attractive opening to the Spaniards and for intrigues by papal emissaries.

The same west-country group of rising gentry that concerned itself with American colonization took action on a far larger scale in Ireland. When one of the Irish lords, James FitzGerald, Earl of Desmond, was defeated in Munster in 1580, Ralegh, Grenville, and their friends all hurried to take up an offer of confiscated land to the south of the Pale. In 1587 Ralegh got a privy seal warrant giving him a provisional title to no less than 42,000 acres in modern Waterford and Cork. While, on the one hand, he was trying to settle Virginia, on the other, he was bringing men, women, and children into these Irish estates. Ralegh was not too particular in his methods of exploiting his properties and fell out with one of the queen's deputies, Sir William Fitzwilliam. When the Irish rebellion of 1588 broke out, Ralegh wisely rid himself of most of his Irish lands. The Munster venture had proved as unprofitable as the Virginian.

After Tyrone's defeat by Mountjoy at the end of Queen Elizabeth's reign, Ulster in Northern Ireland was also thrown open to English colonization. There settlements organized from London and from Scotland were to be established during the next reign. Further colonization was to be carried out during the middle of the seventeenth century. In Ireland, as in his war against Spain, the Lord Protector Oliver Cromwell was deliberately following in the footsteps of Queen Elizabeth, whom he admired. And indeed both Elizabethans and Cromwellians, when they thought in terms of large-scale colonization as a means to relieve an overpopulated England of its hungry mouths, looked first to Ireland. This, they believed, was preferable to trying to people the "howling wilderness" of the Americas or crossing the seas to despoil the Spaniards of the West Indies or the Portuguese of the East Indies. No one in those days imagined for one moment that it would prove easier for Englishmen to conquer and settle the American east coast or the Spanish-held West Indies than it was ever to be to subdue the unruly Irish in their Emerald Isle.

The voyages into different countries, the piratic raids of men like Drake and Frobisher, the attempts at colonial settlement in Ireland and much farther across the seas—all contributed to the development of English naval power and to the wide knowledge of seamanship and navigation upon which the first British empire was to be built. The continuous history of the British navy dates from the time of the Tudors. King Henry VIII was responsible for the construction of a considerable fleet and established two naval dockyards. He also created a Navy Board under the control of the Lord High Admiral. The Duke of Northumberland, who himself had been an admiral in King Henry VIII's reign, interested himself in the dockyard at Chatham; but by the time Queen Elizabeth I came to the throne the navy had declined in strength. As the menace of war with Spain loomed up, Lord Burghley found for the queen a capable professional adviser in the ingenious

Sir John Hawkins, who decided to build fast and navigable fighting ships —medium-sized galleons for the most part, which he preferred to the larger, more expensive, and less nimble ships that were favored by the Spaniards. Armed merchant ships were also used in substantial numbers to reinforce the queen's navy. English brass cannon too was of a high quality. Without the manpower and experience provided by the merchant adventurers and explorers, however, the place won in the world by Elizabethan England would never have been attained.

So began the influence exercised by sea power upon the modern history of Britain—a power that was to help create an English-speaking nation in the New World.

XXXIX

Learning, Literature, and Art in the Tudor Age

In the reign of Queen Elizabeth I literature flowered as never before in England: it was the age of Sir Philip Sidney and Edmund Spenser, of Francis Bacon and Richard Hooker, of Christopher Marlowe and William Shakespeare, and many others. Sometimes this magnificent outburst has been traced back to the European Renaissance and attributed to the influence of the humanists, the recipients of the "new learning" that flowed down from a pre-Christian civilization. Greek classics were introduced into England from the Mediterranean at the beginning of the sixteenth century; Ciceronian Latin replaced the dog Latin fashionable in the old Roman Catholic Church; "scholasticism" with its interminable discussions of nominalism, realism, and conceptualism fell into disrepute; and the Greek Testament was studied in the original. Erasmus of Rotterdam, who spent some years in England, Dean John Colet, the founder of St. Paul's school in the shadow of the London cathedral, Thomas Linacre, King Henry VIII's physician, and Sir Thomas More, Wolsey's successor as Lord Chancellor and the author of the Latin masterpiece *Utopia,* were all enthusiastic practitioners of the new learning. Under their impulse ideals of education began to change somewhat, while the Reformation reduced the hold of the Church upon national culture. Indeed it has been asserted that "the World, not the Church, called the tune to which the Age of Elizabeth danced and sang."

Dr. Rowse, who has studied the period deeply, has written how "all the myriad influences of Renaissance Europe . . . had come pouring in upon the English people, like so many waters finding their level: this island the last virgin soil to be fertilized"; he has also spoken of "a young people coming suddenly to maturity." Other scholars have stressed the uniqueness of the Elizabethan achievement and have questioned whether it ought to be connected other than loosely with the classical revival or with influences from Italy, France, and elsewhere. Professor C. S. Lewis has even claimed that "the more we look into the question, the harder we shall find it to believe that humanism had any power of encouraging or any wish to encourage, the literature that actually arose." Dr. Tillyard has shown how "medieval" many of the ideas and forms of sixteenth-century English authors remained and how religion still played a considerable part in formulating thought. The most that can safely be said is that the climate of the times produced men of genius, and that poetry and prose in the Elizabethan age was far superior to any that was being written when the Tudors first succeeded to the English throne.

To begin with, the dissolution of the monasteries and, in particular, the act of Edward VI's reign abolishing the chantries—small foundations that had often served educational purposes—were damaging to education in England. The intention of King Henry VIII and of his son's advisers had been to replace the monastic by other schools: officials of the Court of Augmentation were assigned to the project. But the financial difficulties of the Crown held up progress and in the end it was left largely to local influences and private individuals to repair the rent in the fabric of the nation's schools that had been torn by the Henrician Reformation. In 1563 the Speaker of the House of Commons said: "I dare say a hundred schools want in England, which before this time hath been." Thanks to the keen support of the expanding middle classes as well as to the patronage of a number of the wealthier clergy and nobility the position of the English grammar schools had been restored by the end of the century. There are estimated to have been 360 such schools in existence by then. Such famous schools as Harrow, Repton, Rugby, Uppingham, Merchant Taylors', and St. Paul's were founded during the sixteenth century. St. Paul's had its first high master in William Lily, godson of a celebrated Greek scholar, William Grocyn: Thomas Wriothesley, Earl of Southampton, Shakespeare's patron, was among Lily's pupils. Richard Mulcaster, first headmaster of Merchant Taylors', who was Edmund Spenser's schoolmaster, was a scholar and prosodist of distinction. Neither Mulcaster nor Udall, headmaster of Eton in Henry VIII's time, believed in sparing the rod.

At all these schools Latin was the regular fare. Lily and Colet wrote grammar books for the benefit of the scholars of St. Paul's. Aesop's *Fables* were studied in Latin; patriotic poems were composed in hexameters. Roger Ascham, whose book *The Scolemaster* was published in 1570 and who was the leading educationist of his time, recommended Cicero, Caesar, and Livy for sharpening wits in schools, and they have continued in most "public schools" until modern times. Mulcaster also strongly favored Latin, though he thought that a place might be found in the curriculum for English. Greek was taught only at such schools as Westminster, St. Paul's, and Eton. It was argued that Latin was essential for the professional classes, for men of letters, and even for budding merchants. Humanist influences long brooded over the grammar schools. Only Sir Humphrey Gilbert, the explorer, protested against the exclusively classical syllabus. Latin was reckoned indispensable for a gentleman.

It was the elementary or village schools that were most hit by the loss of chantry endowments. Children were expected to be able to read when they entered a grammar school (Shakespeare began at Stratford on Avon when he was seven). Some of the elementary schools vanished in the middle of the century, but others were founded to teach the three R's. Recent research suggests that more of these schools existed than was once thought; but they were only for boys. Girls were taught, in so far as they were taught at all, at home: marriage was their destiny; music and needlework their principal lessons. Only princesses and noble ladies, like Queen Elizabeth herself and Mary, Queen of Scots, received an advanced education.

Despite the Renaissance and the Reformation there were no startling changes at the universities. The curriculum of theology, Aristotelian philosophy, rhetoric, and the like was scarcely touched: corruption and indiscipline were common. Four new colleges, including Christ Church, conceived by Wolsey and completed by Henry VIII, were founded at Oxford. At Cambridge seven new colleges, of which Trinity was the largest, were established in the Tudor period: they included three, St. John's, Emmanuel, and Sidney Sussex (for which money was then left), which were definitely intended as breeding grounds for Protestantism, if not Puritanism. Both universities received the honor of royal visits: Leicester was chancellor of Oxford and Burghley of Cambridge. Oxford suffered more from the dissolution of the monasteries and the dispersal of the friars than did Cambridge. Indeed in Elizabeth's time Cambridge, which had long lagged behind Oxford in size and importance, almost caught up with her elder sister. Oxford boasted the better library; for while Duke Humphrey of Gloucester's collection of manuscripts was rifled from his library at the beginning of the Reformation, at the end of Queen Elizabeth's reign Sir Thomas Bodley, a retired diplomatist, started a work of restoration and set up the university library which bears his name to this day. In London what was in effect England's third university, the Inns of Court, was full of life and energy and virtually free from clerical inhibitions. It was in the Inner Temple that the first English tragedy in blank verse, *Gorboduc,* was performed in 1561. In 1596 Gresham College, intended to provide a more liberal education than the ancient universities, was founded out of a bequest left by a successful Elizabethan financier. Training in the common law and proximity to the fountain of culture at the queen's court gave students in London a better and more stimulating education than they received anywhere else.

English prose now covered a wide range of subjects—history and geography, allegory and fantasy, travel and religion, literary criticism, and even novels or what has been called "prose fiction." The pioneers in Queen Elizabeth's reign were John Lyly and Sir Philip Sidney, both of whom wrote in an ornate and elaborate style. Lyly, who was an M.P. and held a post at court, wrote two books, *Euphues* and *Euphues His England,* which gave the word "euphuism" to the English language. He was erudite and witty and obviously enjoyed his own inflated rhetoric. Sidney, nephew of the Earl of Leicester and a statesman and soldier as well as a poet and a patron of poets, wrote a pastoral story called *Arcadia* at about the same time as *Euphues* was written, and in a not-dissimilar style of scholarly fantasy. Robert Greene, a disciple of Lyly, later came down to earth with his "cony-catching" tracts dealing with the rogues of London's underworld. Thomas Dekker, author of the *Seven Deadly Sins of London,* also wrote in this vein, as did Thomas Nashe and Thomas Deloney, who offered realistic fiction to their age.

More interesting to posterity than the fictitious writers are the conscientious students like Leland and Camden, Hakluyt and Hooker. John Leland was an antiquarian, patronized by King Henry VIII, who traveled all over England and overseas for the purpose of recording all the facts he could collect about geography and history—taking notes, amassing manuscripts, and making maps. His *Itinerary* was a pioneering work of scholarship. Among his successors were William Lambarde, one of the earliest authors of an English county history, that of Kent, who received praise from Queen Elizabeth; William Camden, who began publishing his epic descriptive work *Britannia* in the 1580's; Lord Berners, who translated Froissart's *Chronicles;* Richard Hakluyt the

Younger, who dealt with the explorations of his time; John Stow, who wrote *Chronicles of England* and *Survey of London;* John Speed, who compiled a *Theatre of the Empire of Great Britain;* William Harrison, who wrote a *Description of England;* and finally Sir Walter Ralegh, poet and pirate, theologian and financier, who was to demonstrate his gift for prose in a *History of the World* written in prison during the reign of King James I. These chroniclers, geographers, and historians all wrote in a lively forward-looking manner. To examine the past of the country and stimulate further research a Society of Antiquaries was formed in the 1580's. These savants and others—the London group also included Edward Hall and Richard Grafton—met a demand for the writing of patriotic history in the age of the Armada and have earned the gratitude of later ages. "We are beholding to Mr. Speed and Stow," observed John Aubrey, the gossip writer of the next century, "for stitching up for us our English history."

To the Elizabethan age belong two books which have earned a permanent place in world history: the *Essays* of Sir Francis Bacon and the *Laws of Ecclesiastical Polity* by Richard Hooker. The *Essays,* like the epigrams of La Rochefoucauld, have been overrated, but even their critics admit that they are a triumph of prose style. Hooker, who was the nephew of the editor of Holinshed's chronicle, which Shakespeare used, furnished the classic apologia for the Elizabethan Church in a masterpiece of intellectual maturity which he left unfinished when he died in 1600. His arguments were reasonable, balanced, sympathetic, and judicious. It was a splendid piece of writing belonging to the golden period of the Elizabethan age. In the words of Professor Lewis, "the style is for its purpose perhaps the most perfect in English with a functional beauty and a structure that mirrors the real movement of his mind." On the Roman Catholic side the work of Cardinal William Allen deserves to be remembered; much of it is in Latin, but he also left some trenchant and vigorous English prose.

The most striking advances in English literature were in poetry and the writing of plays. Since Chaucer, most English poetry, and Scottish too, had become uninspired doggerel. Only John Skelton and Thomas Wyatt can claim distinction in the early Tudor period. Skelton's work, especially of the satirical or whimsical kind—for example his *Speke Parot*—has recently been revalued. The appeal he has made to such modern poets as Robert Graves and W. H. Auden suggests that he is, above all, a poet's poet. Wyatt, "the first of our Italianate poets" in England, had a genuinely lyrical gift, which has also received recognition in modern times. With Sidney and Spenser, both of whom took their writing with immense seriousness and used their imaginations for moral purposes, we enter into a higher realm. "Sidney," wrote Professor Lewis, "rises out of the contemporary Drab almost as a rocket rises: Spenser climbed out slowly and painfully, like Christian from the Slough." They wrote in a variety of styles, ballad and sonnet, hymn and epic. Sidney's best known work is *Astrophel and Stella,* but he also wrote an enduring *Defence of Poetry.* Spenser's poetry was rich, prolific, and difficult. His early work, *Shepherd's Calendar,* is ingenious if dull. His famous *Faerie Queene* is melodious, but obscure—a romantic allegory with a moral purpose suited to gentlemen. In Spenser was mingled a strain of pessimistic Puritanism and a sensuous love of beauty. It has been said that he was out of sympathy with the world in which he lived; certainly he lived in a dream. His eccentric genius contrasts with that of his more worldly contemporary, William Shakespeare.

Shakespeare, the greatest of English poets, was originally by profession an actor and apparently not a very good one. According to Nicholas Rowe, "the top of his performance was the Ghost in his own Hamlet." Born at Stratford on Avon in April 1562, son of a substantial yeoman who was also a glover, he married when he was eighteen and in due course joined a company of players in London, known first as the Lord Chamberlain's Men and later as the King's Men. Soon he proved himself to be an excellent natural writer (his education at Stratford had given him, according to his friend Ben Jonson, "little Latin but less Greek"). "Besides the advantages of his wit," says Rowe, "he was himself a good natured man, of great sweetness in his manners, and a most agreeable companion." The first play he wrote, *King Henry VI,* was performed in 1590. Altogether his plays have been divided into four groups, representing his period of dramatic apprenticeship and experiment, his later historical plays and "joyous comedies," his "grave and bitter comedies," and finally the tragedies and the romantic plays, culminating in *The Tempest,* plays that were both "grave and gay." The first of these two groups belongs to the reign of Queen Elizabeth I, the second to that of King James I. Shakespeare's extraordinary gifts received recognition both from the queen and from contemporaries:

Soul of the Age!
The applause! delight! wonder of our stage!

His poetry was interspersed with his profession as a playwright. *Venus and Adonis* (1593) and *Lucrece* (1594) were written in plague years when playgoing was interrupted. His sonnets cannot be precisely dated, but may also have been largely written then. Some of them are dedicated to a "lovely boy" who was also his patron, perhaps William Herbert, Earl of Pembroke, and others to a Dark Lady, "a married woman, who broke her bed-vow to take first Shakespeare and then his friend." "The boy, the stolen mistress, and the rival poet" of the sonnets are among the literary historical mysteries of the Elizabethan age. But of course they have no significant bearing on some of the finest poetry the world has ever known.

Shakespeare's plays were just a few among the many that enriched the Elizabethan stage. These ranged from Udall's comedy *Ralph Roister Doister* and Norton's tragedy *Gorboduc* to Thomas Kyd's *Spanish Tragedy* and Christopher Marlowe's *Jew of Malta*. Marlowe died when he was twenty-nine in 1592; some think had he lived he might have become as famous as Shakespeare. Among other playwrights of the age were Ben Jonson, Dekker, and Webster—the list of names extends, with that of Shakespeare, forward into Jacobean times. It was then that the first theaters were built in London after earlier performances had been given in the courtyards of inns. The Reformation had assisted a breakaway from the older passion and morality plays. The theater became a focus of wit and satire, of poetry and romance: it embodied all the liveliness and essential spirit of a national genius, which reached its peak of glory when Howard was defeating Medina Sidonia and Queen Elizabeth and her archbishop were repressing the Puritans inside and outside parliament. Its bright light was to be dimmed when the Puritans came to power half a century later.

The chief glories of Elizabethan England were her theater and her poets: they will endure when power politics and religious controversy are forgotten. But in other arts England was cosmopolitan; the wealth and expansiveness of the age opened the way for the introduction of many foreign artists as well as artisans who helped to beautify the country. Painters from continental Europe have preserved for posterity the features of leading men and women of the whole Tudor age. When Sir Thomas Gresham built the Royal Exchange, he brought in a Flemish architect and imported marble to pave its piazza. Nevertheless foreign influences did not prevent Tudor architecture from having a character of its own: it has been described as a compromise "between native tradition and vigour and classical form and integration." Church building was now reduced and the late English Perpendicular style in ecclesiastical architecture is held to have been uninspired (though some Cambridge colleges appear to refute this). The genius of Tudor architects shines out chiefly in purely secular buildings from palaces to humble farmhouses. Castles built chiefly for defense yielded place to noble homes dedicated to pageantry, hospitality, and entertainment: they range from St. James's Palace in London and Hampton Court Palace, which was built in the reign of King Henry VIII, to Wollaton Hall in

Nottinghamshire, Haddon Hall and Hardwick House in Derbyshire, and Montacute in Somerset. Manor houses varied in character according to the building materials that were locally available. In Cheshire, for example, one can see Moreton Old Hall with its elaborate black timbering or in East Anglia Elizabethan houses of cream plaster and peach-colored brick. The gables, the high chimneys, the mullioned windows, and the paneled halls all remind us of a proud and happy gentry, while some of the stately halls bear witness to the capabilities of native architects like Robert Smithson and John Thorpe.

Of the painters who came from abroad the most famous was Hans Holbein the Younger, who immortalized the features of King Henry VIII. Gheeraerts and Mytens came from the Netherlands in the reign of Queen Elizabeth I, but neither she nor Mary, Queen of Scots, live for us in paint in the same way as the second Tudor ruler. The best of the native English painters were miniaturists. It is indeed curious that more native painting has not survived, when it is considered how fond the Tudor gentry were of decorating their homes. They liked painting their walls, hanging them with tapestries and pictures, and placing heraldic devices over their doors and windows. Shops where books, pictures, and maps might be purchased did a flourishing trade in London. The Elizabethans loved jewelry, needlework, and fancy dresses. They worked hard, they fought hard, and they played hard. They loved music and song. When they died they built themselves elaborate tombs and monuments where the men still wear their armor and glory in their knighthood, the women modestly lying beside them in all their well-draped finery. Here in many a cathedral and parish church they speak to their descendants across the centuries, from the first Elizabethan age to the second.

XL

The Character of Elizabethan England

What is it that English and American historians have found so immensely attractive about Elizabethan times, which makes our habitually pedestrian pens scribble rhapsodically? Why do we speak admiringly of

"Gloriana" (Spenser's name for the queen), quote her "golden speech," and dilate upon her "golden age"? The late Sir Walter Raleigh, a Victorian scholar who thought better of his Elizabethan namesake than perhaps he deserved, wrote that "the Age of Elizabeth is the most glorious, and in some ways the most significant period in English history." Dr. Rowse speaks of "great themes" to which even he cannot do justice and of "a hundred images, a thousand memories" that "crowd in upon the mind" as he writes of the people in those distant days.

It was of course an age of immortal poetry and of material progress for the well-to-do. Yet the expansion of England can be exaggerated. It was not to Englishmen that the discovery of the New World is owed; nor did colonial settlement by English-speaking peoples have its origins in that time except as an idea and an unsuccessful experiment; if colonization was seriously planned anywhere, it was in Ireland. The growth of the royal navy, for which King Henry VIII was originally responsible, opened the way to exploration and to more development of British commerce, though piracy was as much admired as the more sober labors of merchant adventurers. One ought too to be cautious about the claim that an "industrial revolution" was already beginning, for industry was still on a modest scale and remained so for another century; most of the queen's subjects were still absorbed in agriculture. Although the historical evidence points to a considerable growth of national wealth and of population toward the middle of the reign, one must not forget the appalling plagues and famines, the unemployment and poverty in country as well as town, the administrative brutalities, and the lack of hygiene or medical knowledge.

If we turn from the material side of life to the evolution of thought, can it be said that the ideas of the time as expressed in poetry and prose, in philosophy, politics, and religion show a breaking away from what are customarily called the Middle Ages? The argument over continuity and discontinuity still rages. Dr. Tillyard has shown that it is wrong to think of the Elizabethan age as a secular period between two outbreaks of Protestant fervor and that much of the picture of the Elizabethan world order—though not all of it—was painted on "medieval" lines. "Raleigh's remarks on the glories of creation and on death [he says] . . . Shakespeare's on the state of man in the world . . . are the common property of every third-rate mind of the age . . . Spenser's philosophy is nearly as trite though rather more genteel." Such political writers as there were still talked for the most part of the divine right to rule and to obey and of an overriding natural law deriving from God. Most men still believed in sorcery and witchcraft. On the other side, the break with Gothic began; and anyone can measure the profound intel-

ligence of Cecil or Bacon, Hooker or Thomas Smith, Sidney or Shakespeare.

The advance that came—by advance one means movement toward
what we now think is good—was essentially in the material and political
aspects of life. The rise of the House of Commons has been made plain
to us by the lifetime researches of Sir John Neale and his master, A. F.
Pollard. Whatever the House of Commons did or did not do under the
Lancastrians and the Yorkists, it was not until the Tudor age that it
proved itself to be an important constitutional instrument in the state.
After King Henry VIII employed it to put through the reformation of
the Church, the House began to realize its influence. In the reign of
Queen Elizabeth I, though it did not meet frequently and was kept in
check by the government, it gradually perfected its procedure, laid
claims to freedom of speech and freedom from arrest for its members,
demanded the right to legislate on ecclesiastical affairs, and gave advice to the Crown on matters of state. Toward the end of the queen's
reign it started to seize the initiative in legislation, which had formerly
been exercised by privy councilors, and to impose its wishes, for instance on the question of limiting monopolies, upon the monarchy. It
used to be thought that it was not until the last parliaments of the reign
that the independence of the House of Commons was demonstrated, but
we now know that in fact there was an effective political group critical
of the government in the very first of Queen Elizabeth's parliaments.
Nonetheless it was admitted in the first parliament of King James I's
reign that members had restrained their criticisms when the queen was
old out of deference for a sovereign who had ruled so long and so successfully. The House of Lords continued to play its part in national affairs and to furnish many of the leading statesmen, as it has done until
modern times. But the rise of the House of Commons was the outstanding political fact in the reign of Queen Elizabeth I and pointed toward
the historical future.

The rise of the Commons reflected the expanding wealth and influence
of the English gentry. "Gentry" is perhaps a loose term that has recently
become overfashionable and perhaps oversimplified. In a typical Elizabethan House of Commons over half of the members are said to have
been "country gentlemen"; the next largest class were lawyers or at
least men who had been educated in the Inns of Court, while a smaller
number, chiefly those who represented the ports and the cities, were
merchants or tradesmen; the remainder were mainly royal officials. The
counties, where the electors were forty-shilling freeholders, were invariably represented by country gentlemen: to be a senior knight of
the shire was among the highest of social honors. But in the boroughs

too, where the electorate varied and usually had a narrower franchise than the counties, many members of parliament were also country gentlemen or lawyers, often the local recorders. Much of the work of local government was done too by country gentlemen acting as justices of the peace. The Tudors, however, created a new post, that of lord lieutenant of the county. The lord lieutenant was normally a peer and commanded the militia; the deputy lords lieutenant might be country gentlemen too.

If one groups together the gentry, the lawyers, and the merchants—the latter two classes usually bought themselves landed estates when they prospered—then one may say that the middle classes—the people whose incomes and social positions came in the middle between those of the nobility and the yeomen—expanded and flourished in the Elizabethan age. It is true that one or two historians have argued that there was no middle class at all, since all classes imperceptibly blended into one another, but that is an argument that seems to confuse class and caste. At any rate the country gentry, the merchants, and the rising professional men had managed to gorge themselves on sales of land by the Crown, much of it seized from the Church at the time of the Reformation, and since at one time there was a glut of property for sale they had the opportunity to buy fairly cheaply. Whether or not they then proceeded to exploit these lands in a more businesslike way than former owners had done—the abbots and priors in particular—is arguable; some contemporary writers thought that they did so. Insofar as they improved their incomes (and not all of them did), it does not seem to have been materially at the expense of the nobility. Still the general position of the peers did decline, both economically and politically, under the impact first of the Wars of the Roses and then of the repressive policy of King Henry VII. And though a new aristocracy was created, which ran from gilded gentry to the bastards of King Charles II, it never again exerted the same power that it once had. At the outset of Queen Elizabeth I's reign only one duke was left in England, and he was to perish upon the scaffold for treason. If the gentry rose at anyone's expense it was at that of their tenants. Some were "rack-rented" and some evicted to make room for sheep. In Leicestershire more than one in three of the 370 villages in the county underwent enclosure during the Tudor age. "The Midland peasant," it has been said, "saw rich farmers taking up more and more land but giving less employment than ever before to the agricultural labourer." Unquestionably the middle classes sometimes prospered in a rather ruthless way. The growing importance of the House of Commons and the relative decrease in the power of the House of Lords reflected this social revolution.

The increasing power of the middle classes did not yet mean that the authority of the monarchy had diminished. On the contrary, a suspicion existed that it had actually become stronger. One of the complaints voiced at the time of the Pilgrimage of Grace in King Henry VIII's reign was that there were too many "king's servants" in the House of Commons. If, as most parliamentary historians appear to believe, the House of Commons was not "packed" by the Tudor monarchy (although in fact Queen Mary I seems to have done so), it was because neither King Henry VIII nor Edward VI's two Lord Protectors nor Queen Elizabeth I had much need to do so. In their times the middle classes were more susceptible to leadership than the old ecclesiastical and lay nobility had ever been. They were flattered to be consulted; they limited their opposition to the floor of the House. But if the nobility proved obstreperous, the early English kings had been compelled to take up arms against them: sometimes it had been a choice between the leaders of the peerage ending on the traitor's block and a king's losing his throne to a usurper. Queen Mary I and Queen Elizabeth I were still faced with conspiracies led by the nobility; but it was precisely because they could count on the loyalty of the middle classes, concentrated in London, that they were both able to ward off these threats with comparative ease. Queen Elizabeth learned, after some harassing experiences in her first parliaments, to handle the Commons, and know when to be stubborn and when to yield gracefully. When, after she had given the country peace and order for twenty-five years, she appealed to their loyalty, they did not fail her. Indeed, since its very inception the English Commons always responded to capable and authoritative leadership, although they never much cared for voting taxes which fell on themselves. The queen's sex entered little into the matter. Sir Robert Cecil said of his mistress: "she was more than a man, and, in troth, sometimes less than a woman." She was, from her accession, wedded to her duties and possessed the same will to power as her father. "I have already joined myself in marriage to a husband," she said early in her reign, "namely the kingdom of England." She may have ruled intuitively and at times capriciously, but no one who considers her relations with her ministers and generals—with Leicester and Essex, on the one hand, with Burghley, Walsingham, and Drake, on the other—can doubt that it was she who ruled.

The "golden age" in Elizabeth's reign, if one may accept this phrase, was its last twenty years, the years which corresponded roughly with the war against Spain. That was the age of Spenser, Marlowe, Shakespeare, and Ralegh as well as of Howard, Drake, Frobisher, and the other "sea dogs." But the sixteenth century was also a great age in Europe as a whole—the age of Calvin and Erasmus, of Rabelais and

Cervantes, of Machiavelli, Bodin, and Montaigne. Some historians of civilization have argued that the century represented the apogee of Western culture and that civilization in the West has been declining ever since and is now passing away. Yet whatever gold may have glittered in the libraries, it was not a scientific age nor, by liberal standards, an enlightened age. In 1600 the scientist Giordano Bruno was burned at the stake. Men believed in sorcery but not in hygiene. In the reign of King Edward VI men were burned for being Roman Catholics, in the reign of Queen Mary I for being Protestants, and in the reign of Queen Elizabeth I for reasons of state.

What stand out in the British history of the sixteenth century are two political events. The first is the Protestant Reformation, begun by King Henry VIII, which after the vicissitudes of the reigns of Edward VI and Mary I produced the Elizabethan Church of England, as approved by the queen herself and by Richard Hooker. This Church was unacceptable to Roman Catholics either in England or in Ireland; at the same time there was born within it a Puritan movement which wanted to break more completely than ever with the episcopal organization and ritual practices of the old Church. The Puritan movement was not yet a doctrinal one, for by and large the Elizabethan Church, under the impact of the theologians who returned from exile in Switzerland and Germany, was Calvinist in tone and in faith. The "broad" Church of England, moving majestically between ritualism and evangelism, was to become part of the British way of life. So too was the Puritan rumbling, which goes on to the present day.

The second political event is the broadening of the middle classes and the rise of the House of Commons. The reign of Queen Elizabeth I began, in point of time, exactly half way between the ending of the Wars of the Roses, fought by the nobility, and the outbreak of the great civil wars, in which the bourgeoisie figured largely, in the middle of the seventeenth century. During the reign the Commons, more Puritan in their outlook than the queen, nationalistic, patriotic, jealous of their privileges, were beginning to savor their strength. This, in the long run, emerged as the factor that differentiated England from the countries of Catholic Europe where autocracies held sway. King James VI, who perceived only the high authority of the English monarchy and the growing wealth of the nation, was at first misled by the prospects before him. But finally, after he succeeded Queen Elizabeth on the English throne, he and the other Stuarts were to have their fill of parliaments. The middle classes continued their slow but significant rise to power. Only in our own times has their right to be the ruling class met with a challenge.

BOOK IV

STUART TIMES: THE ENGLISH REVOLUTION

XLI

The Accession of James I

James Stuart, the only child of Mary, Queen of Scots, had been crowned King James VI of Scotland when he was only eleven months old. The early part of his reign in Scotland, which lasted for nearly forty years before he succeeded to the throne of England as well, was a time of troubles: he had to contend, on the one hand, with the Roman Catholic lords and, on the other, with the leaders of the Presbyterian Kirk, who, in the tradition of John Knox, believed that the secular ruler should be subordinate to men of God. James could hardly repudiate his own mother, who was a prisoner in England and whom he had never seen since he was a baby, yet he dared not conspire against Queen Elizabeth I since on her goodwill depended his chances of succeeding to the English throne. Thus as soon as he became old enough to be aware of his problems, he was bound to try to play off the different Scottish parties and interests against one another and in doing so to suffer rebuffs as well as triumphs. He received a first-class education, chiefly from the tutorship of George Buchanan, a learned Presbyterian theologian, who ensured that he mastered the classics, modern languages, philosophy, and theology. In spite of the terrifying and rigorous discipline to which he was subjected, he proved himself precociously quick and intelligent. The main defect in his upbringing was lack of a mother's affection and care. Kept away from girls, he turned in search of love to young men older than himself. His recreations were hunting and riding, to which he was passionately attached, though in later life he frequently fell off his horses, and required deer and game rounded up and driven in front of him for the convenience of slaughtering.

James Douglas, fourth Earl of Morton, who succeeded James's grandfather, the fourth Earl of Lennox, as Scottish regent in 1572, was a fierce and tough old man firmly opposed to the extreme claims of the Kirk. He overcame several plots concocted against him, but in 1579 when Esmé Stuart, a cousin of the king, arrived from France, his authority was undermined and in 1580 he was executed on a trumped-up charge. Esmé Stuart, who was created first Duke of Lennox, was a fascinating intriguer and proved to be an evil influence upon the boy-king. He exploited the king's profound affection for him, drawing him "into a carnal lust" in sharp reaction against his Puritan upbringing by Buchanan. Lennox, though he declared himself to be converted to Protestantism, induced the king to enter into relations with France and other Catholic powers and to write affectionate letters to his mother, who then proposed that they should be associated together in the rule of Scotland.

Neither the Scottish Protestant nobility nor the Presbyterian clergy was prepared to acquiesce in the king's approaches to his mother and the Roman Catholics. In 1582 James VI was kidnapped when hunting near Perth; Lennox was ordered to leave the country; the Scottish ministers trumpeted their conquest from the pulpits. Their victory was short-lived. With the aid of James Stewart, Earl of Arran, and the Archbishop of St. Andrews, the Protestant lords were in turn defeated; a Scottish parliament in 1584 put an end for the time being to the Presbyterian system, declaring King James VI to be head of the Church. Again the situation rapidly changed. Arran was now defeated; the Protestant leaders and ministers returned; but the king remained free. In 1586 he concluded an alliance with England and accepted a pension from Queen Elizabeth. Thus when his mother was put to death for treason in February 1587 he had high hopes that if he were cautious and did not blot his copybook he would yet be Queen Elizabeth's successor in England. He weathered the storm of Scottish anger at the fate of Mary, Queen of Scots; he made it clear that in spite of public pleas and protests he had no intention of avenging his mother. And wisely he did not commit himself to the Spanish cause while King Philip II was preparing to invade England.

Complicated intrigues, plots, and conspiracies rent Scottish history in the 1590's; for a time the Catholics were in the ascendant and at another, the Presbyterians. King James VI married in 1589 a young blonde Danish princess named Anne who gave him several children, including Prince Charles, the future King Charles I of England, who was born in 1600. Gradually the king strengthened his own place in Scottish politics; first he overthrew the Catholic lords in 1595, then in 1597 he attacked the leaders of the Kirk and restored the bishops. He successfully frustrated fresh plans to kidnap, depose, or even kill him. When in 1598 and 1599 he published two books, *The Trew Law of Free Monarchies* and the *Basilikon Doron,* in which he set out lofty claims for the divine right of kings, he could fairly assert that he knew more than most men about the difficult art of monarchy. He had overcome a thousand intrigues and shown himself to be a master of his many unruly subjects. Moreover he had kept out of trouble in his tricky relations with Queen Elizabeth. Therefore in the spring of 1603 when he left Edinburgh for London to claim his throne at Westminster, he could fairly boast that at the age of thirty-nine he was an old, experienced, and successful king.

King James was delighted with his heritage and his new subjects appeared pleased with him. They greeted him enthusiastically, and swarmed along the roads to meet him: they thought of him as a good Protestant ruler with adequate progeny to ensure a Protestant succession, even if he was only a poor Scottish relative of the late queen of golden memory. The poet Dekker wrote:

> Blest God, when we for fear scarce
> looked to have seen Peace's moonshine
> Then send'st from the North, past all
> our hopes, King James his glorious sunshine.

There was a pronounced dualism in the character of the man who now became King James I of England. He was both uncouth and sophisticated, ribald and philosophical, clever and foolish: an "old young man" who craved love, but was unlovable. In his conduct of business he was nervous and excitable, willful and often lazy. Extravagant in his habits, he had a fine opinion of himself. Soon tiring of his wife, he reverted to his normal homosexuality. When he came to England he was dazzled by the opportunities that opened before him. Freed from the bullying of the Scottish nobles and ministers, no longer poor or despised, he expected his will to prevail in this wealthy kingdom just as Queen Elizabeth's had done. What he failed to understand was that in England the nobility did not count for as much as it did in Scotland, that the middle classes represented in parliament were already insisting upon their right to wider political authority than they had ever exercised before, and that it was only the skilled statecraft of his predecessor and her ministers that kept the government in command of events and the Puritan movement, which corresponded roughly to the Scottish Presbyterian, under control.

The House of Commons, for its part, when it met in 1604, contained a number of outstanding leaders in debate and committee who had also served in Queen Elizabeth I's last parliament, but very few privy councilors to represent the interests of the new monarch; it disclosed a nucleus of resistance to court policies and showed a determination to right grievances of which many members had long been conscious. Meanwhile the Puritans within the English Church hoped that their new ruler with his Presbyterian upbringing and background would be sympathetic to their demands for reform, especially for the abolition of Catholic ritual which the old queen had fought to preserve. In fact, the king himself naturally enough adhered to all Queen Elizabeth's policies: he had no intention of abating the prerogatives of the Crown; he had no wish to enhance the strength of the House of Commons; and remembering his own painful experiences in Scotland, he found the extreme views of the Puritans repugnant. Like Elizabeth also, he regarded the episcopacy as a bulwark of the monarchy. He coined the phrase "no bishop, no king." Thus the honeymoon, genuine enough in its way, between him and his new subjects did not last for long. The conflict between the Crown and parliament, which had been looming up in the early years of Queen Elizabeth but had been damped down by the exigencies of the war against Spain, reappeared. The character of King James I, whatever its weaknesses, was only one factor in a struggle which had begun before he arrived in London and was to continue throughout the whole of British history in the seventeenth century.

When the first parliament of the reign met in March 1604 the members crowded in to hear their new king. It proved to be an extremely active parliament. It held four sessions averaging about 100 days in length, as compared with the longest session of 76 days in the reign of Queen Elizabeth I; it set up many committees; and the first "committee of the whole House" met in 1607. King James I rubbed it the wrong way. When he published a proclamation for the elections of members he ordered that all returns should be made into chancery, which was to decide upon their validity. A case soon arose when an outlaw named Sir Francis Goodwin was returned; the House of Commons declared that he was properly elected and insisted that it was its right and not that of the court of chancery to decide upon the validity of the returns of members. In the end the king was obliged to give way, although a new writ was issued. Another constitutional case related to an M.P. who was confined in the Fleet prison for debt. The House of Commons summoned the warder of the Fleet and committed him to the Tower of London for a breach of its privileges. Again the king was compelled to intervene and to yield.

In its first session this House also raised an old grievance which had been expressed in earlier times, namely the prerogative right of the king to exact "purveyance," enabling royal servants to pre-empt for goods at low prices; the Commons also objected to the right of wardship whereby the king could draw profits from the properties of well-to-do minors who were orphans of tenants-in-chief. These wardships, like commercial and industrial patents, were usually conferred upon courtiers as rewards or perquisites. The king resented the complaints and scolded the Commons for ventilating them. They now retorted with an "apology" which was one of the most outspoken statements ever to be published by the House: it was, in effect, a reminder to a "foreign" king of what the powers and privileges of an English parliament consisted: their privileges, it was asserted, were "more universally and dangerously impugned than ever before." The conclusion was polite but firm: "let your Majesty be pleased to receive public information from your Commons as to the civil estate and government" for "the voice of the people, in the things of their knowledge, is said to be as the voice of God."

Before the parliament met for its next session an attempt was made by a group of Roman Catholic conspirators to blow up the king and both houses of parliament in what was known as the Gunpowder Treason or Plot. The plot was betrayed and detected at the last moment. Whatever the exact truth about its origins may have been, the episode shocked and thrilled the nation. The king explained that if he had been blown up, it would have been in the best of company and in the most honorable place in the country, far better than, say, an ale house or a brothel. Gratified by this lucid compliment, the House ended its second session peaceably: a financial grant was given to the king; and arrangements were completed for commissioners to discuss an act of union between the kingdoms of England and Scotland.

The third session of parliament was far less happy. The proposals for Anglo-Scottish union came to nothing because of the opposition of pressure groups, notably the merchants of the city of London, who were afraid of Scottish competition. Instead the king promoted a collusive action in which the courts found that Scottish subjects born since King James came to the English throne were entitled to the same privileges as his English subjects. But parliament was not pleased when it discovered that what it had refused to enact was declared in the courts to be the law already.

During this session too the Commons were perturbed by another legal case, this time in the Court of Exchequer, in which a merchant was condemned to a heavy fine for refusing to pay an "imposition" or an additional import duty on currants, a duty that had been levied by purely executive action. The judges found, however, that such a duty was clearly in accordance with the royal prerogatives: the ports were said to be "the gates" of the king "and he hath absolute power by them to include or exclude whom he shall please." In 1608 a new book of rates was published increasing such "impositions" so as to acquire more revenue for the Crown. Both the merchants and the Commons were upset by the terms of the judgment and by the new book of rates and insisted on debating them at length in their last session of 1610–11. The king, whose saving grace was that while he dilated upon principles, he was always prepared to indulge in compromises, now offered to limit his right to levy impositions and entirely to give up purveyance, wardship, and other ancient monarchical rights, provided that parliament would in compensation guarantee him an income of £200,000 a year and pay off his debts. In the end this bargaining for what was called the "great contract" broke down. Tired of being lectured and frustrated, the king lost his patience and dissolved his first parliament in January 1611 after it had sat intermittently for seven years.

Until this time the king had relied principally upon the advice of Sir Robert Cecil, the minister whom he had inherited from Queen Elizabeth I and had created Earl of Salisbury. The two at first were on intimate terms, but the king was alienated from this conscientious hunchback, who had become both Lord Treasurer and Secretary of State, by his Scottish favorites, the chief of whom was Robert Carr, Viscount Rochester, a man of physical attractions and low capabilities. Salisbury's death after much overwork left his master almost indifferent; but in fact he owed a great deal to him. It was Salisbury who negotiated in 1604 the ending of the long and expensive war with Spain; it was he who had tried to put the king's finances in some sort of order and had proposed the "great contract"; it was he too who had helped to suppress the usual early plots of the reign, in one of which an attempt had been made to place the king's cousin, Arabella Stuart, another descendant of Margaret Tudor, upon the throne: in that plot Sir Walter Ralegh had been involved and because of it had been condemned to death, though in fact he was confined to the Tower.

After the death of Salisbury the Treasury was put on commission. To begin with the king filled only one of Salisbury's other offices. As to the secretaryship, King James did not hasten to appoint anyone, but announced that "he was pretty skilled in the craft himself and till he be thoroughly weary will execute it in person." The Treasury commissioners proceeded to exploit "every artifice, however trivial or vicious for raising the wind which the ambiguities of the prerogative allowed." Nonetheless the royal expenditure was increasing and so were the king's debts. This was largely owing not so much to personal extravagance, although the queen and the favorites were greedy, but to the continuing increase in the cost of living. An additional expense was the marriage of the king's only daughter, Elizabeth, to the Protestant Elector Palatine in Germany, which was the consequence of King James's accession to the Protestant Union of states there. In 1614 therefore the king was obliged to summon his second parliament to ask it for money.

It is usually stated that the king tried to obtain a submissive parliament by influencing the elections to the new House of Commons. This is an exaggeration. What the king did was to try to obtain a larger official or semiofficial element in the House than had existed in the previous one. After it met, members themselves made the charge that "undertakers" had been employed to pack the House and that these "undertakers" were more dangerous to parliament even than the gunpowder plotters. A recent analysis suggests that about 160 members out of a total of 463 were connected in some way with the court. This does not prove that they would have automatically supported the government; indeed we know that they did not. The well-informed gossip-monger, John Chamberlain, said that undue exertion of pressure had actually worked to the disadvantage of the king in the elections. Many of the new members, of whom there were about 280, showed themselves stubborn and uncompromising. Supplies were refused to the king unless grievances were first remedied. The question of impositions was once more raised, while Puritan demands for reform were put forward. After a two-months' session the king dissolved this parliament; it passed no acts; it granted no money; and it is known in history as the "Addled Parliament."

In fact the king's financial difficulties were almost over. It is true that he tried to extract money from his subjects in the form of "benevolences" such as were obtained by King Henry VII, and had little success. But in 1618 a financier of genius, who had been a banker, merchant, and farmer of the customs—Sir Lionel Cranfield—joined the Treasury Commission and invented ways, largely by the manipulation of the customs revenues, to replenish the royal coffers. No longer was parliament urgently needed to vote subsidies. In that same year the Thirty Years' War between Catholics and Protestants began in Germany, darkening the face of Europe. England was dragged into the maelstrom of European politics for many reasons, above all through the king's German son-in-law. Religious problems, foreign affairs, and the king's peculiar attachment to his male favorites were to color the political history of the remainder of the reign. In 1616 the great poet and playwright, William Shakespeare, had died. Slowly the glory of the Elizabethan era was ebbing away. As the Puritan movement in the Church, sponsored by the new middle classes, surged forward, a more somber note was struck, heralding the civil war that lay twenty-five years ahead.

XLII

The Last Years of James I

"The brilliant flowering of European genius which we associate with the names of Shakespeare and Cervantes," wrote H. A. L. Fisher, "was immediately succeeded by a catastrophe which plunged a large area of central Europe into an abysm of barbarism and misery." That was the Thirty Years' War. A central figure in it was King James I's son-in-law, Frederick, the Elector Palatine.

Since Martin Luther had risen to fame in 1517, Germany had been uneasily divided into Catholic and Protestant principalities. Now, a hundred years later, a Protestant Union, to which King James I was a party, faced a Catholic League eager to put back the clock. The knowledge that a fanatical Habsburg prince, Ferdinand of Styria, who had been brought up by Jesuits, had become king of Bohemia and Hungary and was destined to be the next Holy Roman Emperor, provoked the deepest anxiety throughout the Protestant world. In Bohemia the Protestants, who had been granted toleration by an earlier emperor, were especially alarmed. A revolt was planned and two Catholic ministers and a private secretary were thrust out of a window of the palace in Prague. Trouble might yet have been averted, but the Protestant League failed to intervene to keep the peace. Instead the Bohemian Protestants, once in command, deposed King Ferdinand and invited the Elector Palatine, a Protestant, to accept the crown in his place. For one winter, therefore, King James I's daughter Elizabeth became queen of Bohemia.

King James himself might have prevented the war that was to follow if he had dissuaded the Elector Palatine from accepting this dangerous gift, so certainly calculated to incite the extreme wrath of the Habsburgs. Instead his first reaction appears to have been pride that his son-in-law had become a king. The vengeance of the Catholics was swift and terrible. An army commanded by Maximilian of Bavaria, the head of the Catholic League, was sent against the Bohemians. King Philip IV of Spain was asked by the emperor to create a diversion by attacking the Palatinate from the Spanish Netherlands. At the battle of the White Mountain outside Prague the Bohemians were decisively defeated. Afterward Emperor Ferdinand, as he now was, expelled Frederick from his Palatine territory and transferred it to the victorious

Maximilian. This was the most shattering blow received by the Protestant cause during the Counter Reformation: war flared up throughout
Germany.

All this was most disturbing to King James I both in his private comfort and in his public capacity. When he realized what had happened
he expressed his disapproval of his son-in-law's acceptance of the crown,
but how could he stand aside while he was being deprived of the Palatinate, the new home of his daughter? He found it all extremely inconvenient. He had reckoned himself to be a prince of peace. Moreover he
had no wish to offend either the emperor or the king of Spain, particularly since he was at that very moment contemplating the marriage of
his son Prince Charles to the Spanish infanta upon the supposition that
it would yield a handsome dowry.

In his pro-Spanish policy he had the support of his latest favorite
George Villiers, the son of a sheriff of Buckinghamshire. Villiers had
replaced Robert Carr, Earl of Somerset, in the king's affections. Carr
was rather a stupid young man, who, when he had been a page in Scotland, had been dismissed by the king for failing to say a Latin grace
correctly; but when he came to England he had impressed the king by
his conduct at a tournament, even though he broke his leg, and had
soon been loaded with gifts and honors. Before he was created earl,
Carr had set his heart on marrying Frances Howard, the young wife of
the second Earl of Essex; the king helped him by securing the annulment of her marriage with the aid of some singularly compliant bishops.
But when the lady, with or without her husband's connivance, arranged
for the poisoning of one of her husband's former friends in the Tower,
the king decided he had had enough. The fall of Somerset entailed the
fall of the Howard family, which since the death of Salisbury had been
engrossing many important offices of state. One Howard, Thomas, Earl
of Suffolk, had after an interval been appointed Lord Treasurer in Salisbury's place. About 1616 Villiers replaced Somerset as the favorite and
was created Earl of Buckingham. Originally the king did not trust him
as much as he had Somerset, but, unlike Somerset, Buckingham was
eager to shine as a minister, a diplomatist, and a soldier. It was upon
Buckingham's advice that Sir Lionel Cranfield was ultimately appointed
Lord Treasurer in October 1621 and created Earl of Middlesex. This
was Buckingham's only notable contribution to the king's service, though
he was to hold many offices, including that of Lord High Admiral.

The person who most directed the king's attention toward a Spanish
alliance was the Spanish ambassador in London, Count Gondomar.
Gondomar's attraction for the king was of a different order from that
of either Somerset or Buckingham. He was witty and clever and studied

to please the vain monarch: "The King," it was said, "took delight to talk with him."

While the negotiations for the Spanish marriage were first being discussed and before Buckingham had acquired full influence over the king, some of the anti-Spanish faction at court decided to back a project of Sir Walter Ralegh—who had been in the Tower ever since he was condemned for treason at the beginning of the reign—to go to the Orinoco valley in Guiana in search of a gold mine that he believed was there. It was obvious that such a venture could not be carried out without angering the Spaniards. The king was in need of money; Buckingham was bribed; and in 1617 Ralegh was released from prison. The king was persuaded that the Orinoco basin was not in fact in Spanish territory at all. But when the expedition proved a failure, and Gondomar protested, the king, who had never entirely trusted Ralegh, determined that he should be executed to placate the Spaniards. Buckingham did not object. Ralegh was put to death on the suspended sentence previously passed upon him and in October 1619 was beheaded as a sacrifice in favor of the pro-Spanish policy.

That policy received a setback from the Spanish attack on the Palatinate. Nevertheless the king was still in need of money and had not yet found anywhere to turn for it. Cranfield had not yet taken over at the Treasury and a severe economic depression had hit the country. A new House of Commons that met in January 1621 not only concerned itself with the general economic position and debated a considerable number of bills, but it also pressed the king about the proposed Spanish match before it would agree to vote him money. The king told the Commons in Elizabethan language that foreign policy was not their business at all and demanded subsidies to assist his son-in-law. The House became restless: it attacked the granting of industrial patents to courtiers; it impeached the Lord Chancellor, Francis Bacon, for accepting gifts; it published a protestation affirming its own liberties. Once again the king lost his temper and dissolved the House, subsequently tearing the offending protestation out of the official journal. Two leading members of the House, one of them the turbulent Sir Edward Coke, whom the king had earlier dismissed from the post of Lord Chief Justice for refusing to accept his commands, were imprisoned. Another member, John Pym, a wealthy west-country landowner who sat for a small Wiltshire borough, was confined to his own house.

While the Earl of Middlesex was engaged in improving the royal finances and the king was vainly attempting to mediate between his son-in-law and the Holy Roman Emperor, Prince Charles, the king's eldest surviving son, was sent to Spain, accompanied by the Duke of Buckingham, to complete the Spanish marriage negotiations. Charles had not at first cared for Buckingham, being jealous of his father's affection for him, but he had by now succumbed to the older man's charm. These two "sweet boys" were given permission by the aging and debauched king to ride incognito across France and, after creating an appropriate sensation in Madrid, to bring back the Spanish "angel" as the Prince's wife. Things did not work out as they hoped. Religious difficulties intervened. The Spanish princess shuddered at the idea of marrying an infidel and an effort was made to convert her suitor. Buckingham was arrogant and the Spanish king refused to give specific promises to obtain the return of the Palatinate to the Elector Frederick. Having suffered humiliation, Buckingham and Prince Charles, when they finally got back to England in October 1623, were violently anti-Spanish. Moreover Buckingham, indignant that his former crony, Middlesex, had failed to provide them with as much money as they wanted during their journey, surprisingly turned against him and demanded his impeachment. For the moment the royal favorite unexpectedly found himself a popular figure.

Thus the parliament that was summoned in February 1624, unlike the earlier parliaments of the reign, at first felt friendly towards the government. It was determined on a war against Spain in the Elizabethan manner; it was eager to assist the Protestant cause in Germany, where the long war was still raging; it was delighted to impeach the Lord Treasurer for peculation; it passed a fresh bill against monopolies, together with over ninety other bills; and it was allowed to debate foreign affairs to its heart's content, in spite of the king's earlier prohibition. One of the most promising new members of the House was a spruce young man, a client of the Duke of Buckingham, who praised the king, the prince, the duke and God, though he was inclined to be unduly verbose in the process. His name was Sir John Eliot; with John Pym, who was again returned, he was to figure importantly in the next reign.

This then was a "parliament of love," as King James had wanted the parliament of 1614 to be. In June 1624 a treaty was arranged with the Dutch whereby England undertook to dispatch six thousand men to assist in the recovery of the Palatinate. A subsidy was also promised to King Christian IV of Denmark for fighting against the German Catholics. Furthermore the Duke of Buckingham was sent to Paris to negotiate with the French government, then ruled by Cardinal Richelieu, for an alliance against the emperor and for the marriage of the king's sister, Henrietta Maria, to Prince Charles. During the spring of 1625 elaborate arrangements were being completed for an expedition against

Spain. But before a fleet could set sail King James I himself was dead.

Whatever his faults may have been, King James I did not betray the cause of the monarchy. Some modern American historians have emphasized that in the parliaments of his reign an "opposition" movement was being formed, and of course it is true that leaders like Coke and Pym, who were prominent in the next reign, had already made their mark on the political stage. But, like Queen Elizabeth I, the king had never allowed himself to be browbeaten by the House of Commons, although he had shown himself capable of compromise and did not press claims on the prerogative or make airy remarks about the "divine right of kings" further than was tolerable. Lately he had conceded the right of the Commons to debate foreign affairs. On the other hand, the Commons had not extended their privileges beyond the right to judge their own election returns; they had not yet won freedom of speech or immunity from arrest, although they now had the initiative in legislation. Toward the end of the reign criticism of the government had quieted down. The king had not yielded, any more than his predecessor had done, to the growing Puritan movement in the English Church. When the Puritan leaders had come to him at the beginning of his reign and asked that their grievances be considered, he had allowed them to be freely discussed at a conference in Hampton Court Palace and had agreed to some of their requests, including an authorized translation of the Bible. Furthermore he appointed in 1611 an Archbishop of Canterbury, George Abbot, who was known to have Puritan sympathies, while he did not show much enthusiasm for the High Church leader, William Laud, bishop of St. David's, who had been pushed forward by Buckingham. But the king would not tolerate anything that savored of Scottish Presbyterianism.

Until the economic depression of the 1620's and the outbreak of a new war against Spain, the reign had, on the whole, been peaceful and prosperous. Parliamentary grievances were not new. The influence of the king's favorites had been exaggerated, while in men like Francis Bacon, Lord St. Albans, and Lionel Cranfield, Earl of Middlesex, the king had capable ministers. They made the error, however, of quarreling with their friends and being found out in minor indiscretions, which most public servants of those days thought no more improper than adjusting one's income tax might be thought in modern times.

The king's weakness had been his own inordinate laziness. Toward the end of the reign the Venetian ambassador noted that "the King had always detested business and now hates it more than ever." His son's fault, on the contrary, was that he was unwilling to let well enough alone. King James I seems to have felt that a storm was coming and that in the future it would prove harder to restrain parliaments from reducing the royal prerogative or attacking ministers. It is doubtful, given the dissatisfied temper of the middle classes represented in the Commons and the restlessness of the Puritans, whether he could have done any more than he did to keep parliament under control or otherwise avert the storm. The Jacobean age was by no means one of the most discreditable in British history. When the first joint king of England and Scotland died, he might have said, as King Louis XV of France did later, but with less cause for self-deprecation, "After me, the deluge."

XLIII

The Reign of Charles I

On the surface, King Charles I was a more attractive and more dignified figure than his father, even if he were less colorful. As a boy he had not expected to succeed to the throne, for he had a promising elder brother, Prince Henry, who had died unexpectedly in 1612. Though fully conscious of the magnificence of his office, King Charles was a shy man who did not trust himself. He was hesitant in speech and small in stature. His prolonged silences and general indecisiveness derived from his lack of self-assurance; he was unable to come to terms with his people at large, as Queen Elizabeth I had done and King James I, with his vulgar excitability, had also been able to do. In private the new king was affable and condescending enough. It is notable that when Oliver Cromwell first met the king after he became a prisoner, the Puritan farmer succumbed to his monarch's charms.

Like his father, King Charles was a poor judge of men. At the beginning of his reign King Charles continued to depend upon his father's favorite, the Duke of Buckingham, the "Grand Vizier," as he was called, a man of more courage than diplomatic skill. After the death of Buckingham, he belatedly fell in love with his French wife and enjoyed a touchingly happy family life with her and their children. Both Buckingham and Queen Henrietta Maria proved poor counselors. If the king had used and trusted Thomas Wentworth, Earl of Strafford, or his nephew, Prince Rupert, more than he did, it is possible that he would never have become involved in, or ultimately have lost, the civil wars which were to cost him his throne. Later generations were to sentimentalize over him as a martyred hero, the sad figure portrayed in the intimate and sometimes tragic portraits of Van Dyck. Anti-Puritans were to commend him for the patronage which he bestowed upon art. They did not remember, if indeed they ever appreciated, that he was always a first-class actor playing a part to which he was little suited by nature. Basically a small-minded man, who lied and intrigued to keep the Crown that he thought had been given to him by God, he was to forfeit it because he never really tried to understand the people over whom he was called upon to rule.

His father had not undermined the position of the monarchy to any extent, but King Charles had inherited three problems which needed most careful handling. The first was a tradition established in the House of Commons since the first years of the reign of Queen Elizabeth I of opposition to court policies; the second was a restless Puritan movement within the Church of England that dated back to the Henrician Reformation, though held in check by both Queen Elizabeth I and King James I; the third was the most immediate difficulty—an ill-conceived and expensive foreign policy.

One aspect of that policy was the marriage alliance with France, which had been concluded upon a rebound from the rebuff administered to the new king's dignity by the court of Madrid. But at that stage Cardinal Richelieu, who ruled over France, had no intention of becoming involved in the war in Germany. Then there were sizable English commitments to the Dutch and the king of Denmark as well as those arising out of the war begun against Spain. King Charles married Princess Henrietta Maria, daughter of King Henry IV, two months after he came to the throne; instead of gaining any immediate political advantage from the marriage, he was saddled with promises made under treaty to allow the queen and her entourage to attend Mass at court and even to suspend the penal laws against English Roman Catholics. The hastily recruited army dispatched to the Netherlands was proving useless, while the naval war against Spain, now being organized by Buckingham as Lord High Admiral, moved with equal feebleness.

When the first parliament of the new reign met in June 1625 the king was already in desperate need of money to sustain the war, but since he thought that foreign policy, the waging of war, and the making of peace were royal prerogatives and since he believed that in any case the anti-Habsburg program had already been thoroughly approved by parliament, he did not attempt to justify it at Westminster. The House of Commons answered by voting him only one seventh of the money for which he asked (in the form of two "subsidies"), while it threatened to limit to one year the grant of "tonnage and poundage" or customs duties which his predecessors had received for life. The House of Commons deeply distrusted Buckingham because he had notoriously been the late king's favorite and also because it thought it sensed a rising pro-Catholic feeling at court. Members started to demand that the laws against "popery" should be more rigorously enforced, asked that Puritan measures, which King James I had refused, be introduced into the Church, and adversely criticized the High Church party led by William Laud, who was now Bishop of London. Even though Buckingham himself tried to soothe the Commons and pleaded hard for its assistance in the war against Spain, it remained unappeased. Thereupon King Charles I dissolved parliament, hoping that a swift success in the war would both please his subjects and put right his finances.

The first parliament of the reign had been asked for the sum of £40,000 to launch the royal navy against Spain. Since this had been refused, the king decided to use part of his queen's dowry for the purpose. The Duke of Buckingham was sent to The Hague to conclude fresh treaties with the Dutch and the Danes, to discuss the subsidies needed, and, if necessary, to pawn the Crown jewels. While the duke was in Holland, the first expedition against Spain met a disastrous fate. Following strategic lines that had proved acceptable in Elizabethan days, an armed force was landed from ships after some difficulty and set out to attack the town of Cadiz, but the soldiers were demoralized by the heat and the unfamiliar wine that they drank. On its way back the fleet was shattered by a storm; the soldiers on board were undermined by disease and starvation. Among those who, deeply moved, watched the return of the beaten fleet to Plymouth was Sir John Eliot, the vice-admiral of Devon, a friend and client of the Duke of Buckingham. Eliot was also M.P. for St. Germans in Cornwall; when in February 1626 a new parliament met, summoned because of the needs of war finance, Eliot launched a fierce attack on his former patron, blaming him as Lord High Admiral for the catastrophe at Cadiz. "Our honour is ruined," he declared, "our ships are sunk, our men perished, not by the sword, not by the enemy, not by chance but . . . by those we trust."

Not only was the country at war with Spain, but it was drifting into war with France. English warships had been searching French merchantmen on the ground that they were carrying Spanish goods; dissension had arisen over the fulfillment of the Anglo-French marriage treaty; and encouragement was being given to the French Protestants in revolt against their own king. In trying to meet their numerous difficulties and vast expenses—the king of Denmark alone had been promised £30,000 a month, a substantial amount for the time—King Charles I and the Duke of Buckingham optimistically hoped for help from the Commons. The precaution had been taken of preventing the election of one or two of the most violent critics of the government in the previous House by appointing them as sheriffs, since sheriffs were not allowed to stand as candidates. Still, Sir John Eliot's oratory rallied the new House to the condemnation of the government. In April a remonstrance was drawn up insisting on the right of the Commons to discuss and criticize all acts of policy, though the king had asserted earlier that "parliaments are altogether in my power for their calling, sitting, and dissolution; therefore as I find the fruits of them good or evil, they are to continue or not to be." Such haughtiness was a poor introduction to an appeal for money. The Commons ignored the question of subsidies and concentrated upon their grievances, which covered a wide range. They condemned the writings of a Dr. Richard Montague who had attacked Puritanism; they enlarged on the increase of "popery"; and they concerned themselves over the quarrels with France. Finally, Eliot and his friends planned to impeach the Duke of Buckingham for treason.

There was little question that as Lord High Admiral Buckingham had proved himself far from competent and the king might justifiably have replaced him. But was this treason? Thirteen charges were drawn up against him; one of them implied that he had poisoned King James I. Two members of the House of Lords, the Earl of Arundel and the Earl of Bristol, joined in the witch hunt. The king stuck by his friend. He accused Bristol of treason for his conduct when he was English ambassador in Madrid during the previous reign, and he ordered the arrest of Eliot and another member of the Commons for words they had used inside the House. Although Eliot was later released, parliament was dissolved and Buckingham was acquitted of the crimes alleged against him, not in a trial before the House of Lords but by collusive proceedings in the prerogative court of Star Chamber.

As the Commons had once again refused to vote the king supplies for the war, he now began to levy tonnage and poundage without parliamentary consent and tried to exact the subsidies denied to him by levying a "forced loan." This forced loan was widely resisted, whereupon a number of knights and rich men were arrested under royal warrant for their refusal to pay, while soldiers were quartered with the king's poorer subjects. Chief Justice Carew, who refused to admit the legality of these forced loans, was dismissed from his office; after this the Court of King's Bench denied bail to five knights imprisoned by the

Crown when they sued for their release on writ of habeas corpus on the grounds that the cause of their imprisonment had not been stated and that the king had the right to judge what was necessary in a time of emergency.

Meanwhile the war with France had finally broken out. This time Buckingham himself assumed command of a naval expedition that sailed uninvited to help the French Protestants; his attempt to relieve the town of La Rochelle on the west coast of France from a siege by the French royalists was repulsed by a smaller French defense force, and he returned home after having lost half his men. "Since England was England," it was said, "it received not so dishonourable a blow." Moreover the hope that English naval superiority would produce large prizes by laying hold of merchants' ships and treasure ships belonging to France or Spain proved delusive. Thus once again King Charles I was obliged to summon a parliament; and never had a parliament gathered in a worse mood.

Among the members of the new House of Commons were no fewer than twenty-seven of the men who had been imprisoned by orders of the Crown for refusing to pay the forced loan. In addition there were Eliot, who had been imprisoned during the previous meeting of parliament, Sir Edward Coke, the veteran paladin of the common law, who had once been attorney general and chief justice but was now an outspoken critic of the monarchy, John Pym, an astute and wealthy man of business who was to prove himself a master of parliamentary organization, and Sir Thomas Wentworth, a strong-minded and highly intelligent Yorkshireman who had resisted the imposition of the forced loan. None of these men were Puritans, at any rate in any extreme sense of the term, nor is there any reliable evidence that they had concerted a deliberate policy of opposition before parliament met, but all were conscious from their experiences in London and their constituencies of many general grievances—the failures in foreign policy, the forced loans, the billeting of soldiers, the imprisonments without cause by the Crown.

King Charles I, in his opening speech, naturally concentrated upon the grave dangers with which the country was faced when at war with both France and Spain; but he showed no tact when he addressed the two houses early in March 1628. He declared that it was their duty to find a speedy way of supplying the government's needs; if they failed to do so, he would have to "use those other means, which God hath put into my hands, to save that which the follies of particular men may hazard to lose." "Take this not as threatening," he added, "for I scorn to threaten any but my equals, but an admonition." Five subsidies were asked for: Pym was in favor of granting them; Eliot thought that they were too large; Wentworth proposed that they should not be finally agreed to until the king reaffirmed the liberties of parliament. At the same time an attack was made upon "projectors" who had contrived the plot against parliament and "extended the prerogative of the King beyond the just symmetry which maketh a sweet harmony of the whole."

The question that then arose was how the ancient fundamental rights of parliament could best be asserted. Wentworth wanted to introduce a statute, while others preferred a joint resolution by the two houses. Eventually an ingenious compromise was worked out: it was decided to draw up a "Petition of Right," which adapted to public use a private procedure. The petition invited the king to waive his prerogatives in favor of the operation of the normal course of the law. It dealt with arbitrary taxation, arbitrary imprisonment, billeting, and the employment of martial law. The king fought hard to save his prerogatives, especially his right to imprison his subjects without showing cause. In the end he yielded to heavy pressures, and after much wrangling and maneuvering the Petition of Right received the royal assent in the usual statutory form of a private bill. The subsidies were then voted and a bill for tonnage and poundage was prepared; but when a remonstrance was drafted demanding the dismissal of the Duke of Buckingham from all his offices, the king prorogued parliament to save his friend from ignominy.

Sir John Eliot had led the attack on his former patron and Lord High Admiral, under whom he had served as vice-admiral of Devon; he accused Buckingham of being the "great projector," the source of all the existing evils in the kingdom. He used extreme and violent language, which was widely repeated outside Westminster, but then left the House of Commons before the session closed, because of the death of his wife. During the adjournment the Duke of Buckingham, who was preparing a second naval expedition to relieve La Rochelle, was stabbed to death at Portsmouth by a fanatical naval lieutenant named Felton. How far the agitation sponsored by Eliot contributed to Buckingham's assassination is hard to say, although Felton was certainly influenced by general as well as particular grievances. Thus when parliament met again in January 1629 both the king and the Commons were in angry moods. To fiscal grievances were now added religious ones. The king had published a declaration enjoining peace and unity upon the Church, but Eliot and his friends insisted that so long as the king was advised by Laud, Montague, and other High-Church bishops, that policy would lay the road open to "popery."

Oliver Cromwell, a country gentleman of thirty, member of Parliament for Huntingdon, made what is believed to have been his maiden speech when he took part in a debate attacking these bishops. When the House attempted to question some of the king's officers about their seizure of merchants' goods for failure to pay customs duties, which members considered were being illegally exacted, the king ordered an adjournment. When the Commons met again early in March they knew that their days were numbered. The House was in a revolutionary frame of mind. When the Speaker again attempted to order an adjournment, two members thrust him back into his chair and held him down while three resolutions were passed: these declared that whoever should bring in "innovations" of religion or introduce popery or any other opinion disagreeing with Christian orthodoxy should be reputed a capital enemy of the kingdom, and so too should anyone who advised the levying of taxes not granted by parliament or, thirdly, anyone who had the temerity to pay such taxes. On March 10 this outspoken parliament was finally dissolved. Eliot and other parliamentary leaders were at once placed under arrest; and for eleven years King Charles I governed the country without calling a parliament, raising the money he needed by such prerogative means as he saw fit to employ.

How far did this intermission of parliaments constitute a royal tyranny? Both sides might appeal to history. The critics of the king made reference to an ancient constitution, which stretched back to before the Norman Conquest, to the sanctity of the natural and common law, to the Great Charter, and to the recent Petition of Right. The king, if he wanted to do so, could base his arguments on more concrete grounds; for the monarch had undoubtedly been the original legislator as well as the national executive and the fount from which all parliamentary powers and privileges flowed. Queen Elizabeth "of famous memory" had held parliaments only infrequently, had levied taxation by prerogative, and had imprisoned members without showing cause. The executive had always exercised the rights during all national emergencies to raise armies, to put dangerous men under arrest, and to collect money and arms for the defense of the kingdom. The only point that had been seriously argued in the courts was how the king could judge when there was an emergency. But times were changing. Both Queen Elizabeth I and King James I had been compelled to grant concessions to their parliaments if only because they found that they could not govern or raise sufficient funds for governing when the country was at war without their assistance. If mere precedent was to decide what was correct procedure, then by pinning down in his chair the Speaker of the House of Commons—who traditionally was the servant of the king—members of parliament had carried out a far more revolutionary act than any single deed committed by King Charles I.

A case for the king has been made out by some recent historians on other grounds than constitutional precedents. An American writer, for example, has said:

According to modern standards Charles was, in certain ways, an excellent King. After the death of Buckingham he attended to the routine business of the kingship as few English sovereigns have done before or since. And the fatherly care . . . he showed to one section of the people, the poor, was in such fashion that the results lasted long after him.

On the whole, it was the people of the middle classes, some moved by high principles, some, it is suggested, resenting their exclusion from the pickings of royal patronage, others indignant at different forms of taxation, who considered themselves the victims of an autocracy. Among their leaders was Eliot, whom the king refused to release from his imprisonment in the Tower of London, where his health broke down and he died. Unquestionably the king blamed Eliot for Buckingham's murder. On the other hand Sir Thomas Wentworth, once the Petition of Right had been granted, went over to the king's side and was promptly taken into his service. William Laud, Bishop of London, was promoted to Archbishop of Canterbury in 1633 and exercised considerable influence in the prerogative courts of both Star Chamber and the High Commission. But most of the king's ministers were corrupt nonentities, and he largely ruled his subjects himself as best he could.

In order to save money, peace was concluded both with France and Spain. The royal debt is calculated to have been about a million pounds, equivalent to less than two years' annual revenue. Money was obtained from the customs revenues, the payment of which merchants now more or less ceased to resist, and by exploiting to the full such ancient rights of the Crown as the profits of the Court of Wards, the imposition of fines on those who refused to accept knighthoods, and the proceeds of fines for offenses against the old forest laws. Servants of the Crown were rewarded with grants of land, sinecures, or shares in patents. The upkeep of the fleet was met by the levying of "ship money," imposed first on ports, then on inland towns. Protests against ship money were widespread. In 1637 John Hampden, a Buckinghamshire country gentleman of means, contested the levy as a matter of principle in the Court of Exchequer. The judges decided in the king's favor, although they were not unanimous. The amounts of ship money collected (it had at first proved a highly efficient form of taxation) decreased after the Hampden case.

During this period efforts were made by the king and his advisers to maintain peace and prosperity. The king set an example of family propriety at his court, which was elegant without being vulgar. After the death of Buckingham he turned to his wife for consolation and she rewarded him with a succession of children. The king showed himself to be a discerning patron of the arts and invited great painters like Rubens and Van Dyck to England. The versatile architect Inigo Jones was his surveyor general and worked out ideas for the embellishment of London. Peace with France and Spain contributed to the expansion of commerce; harvests were good; and trade flourished, even though there was competition from the merchants and seamen of the vigorous Dutch Republic. But the ship-money fleets protected the livelihood of English fishermen. The Court of Star Chamber took action against enclosers, who reduced the extent of arable land and thereby threatened to force up the price of corn. Proclamations to relieve the poor were published, although they do not seem to have been followed up. Sir Thomas Wentworth as president of the Council of the North imposed law and order upon that unruly part of the kingdom; and when he left for Ireland, where he took over as Lord Deputy in 1633, he proceeded to improve the revenues of that country and thus did not have to call upon the usual subsidies from England. The Elizabethan Church settlement was maintained, and Archbishop Laud and Archbishop Neile of York worked overtime to ensure uniformity of practices and to repress the irrepressible Puritans.

The chief criticism of the king's government during these years appears to have come from the left wing of the English Church and from those who had contributed to the ship money. But so long as peace prevailed the country was happy enough on the surface. Outside parliament there were, in any case, few means by which aggrieved subjects could express their complaints. The law courts, on the whole, were under royal control; the judges could be, and were, dismissed at the king's pleasure. Only in the pulpits might the king have occasionally heard the distant rumbling of thunder. It was when the peace was at last broken and religious agitation was provoked that the relatively quiet times ended and the meaning of the train of events which was to lead to the great rebellion against the Stuart monarchy became clear.

XLIV

The Coming of the Civil War

In spite of many obstacles and periods of repression when it was driven underground, the Puritan movement in England had made headway since it first came to light in the early years of Queen Elizabeth I's reign. Who exactly were the Puritans? And is it correct to speak of a movement? The ancestry of the Puritans may perhaps be traced back to the Lollards of the fourteenth century, but when they emerged under Queen Elizabeth I they consisted of extreme Protestants who believed in the need for the purification of the English Church by the elimination of all the remaining "popish" rites and rituals, which they regarded as idolatrous. Even the use of the ring in marriage or the sign of the Cross in baptism came under their ban. For ceremonial services they wished to substitute much more preaching, exhortation, and Bible reading than had ever been practiced before by ministers of the Church, and they also wished to stimulate individual Christians to pray directly to God without the intervention either of priests or elaborate worship. But "Puritan" was only a nickname and it did not at first describe a fully organized movement. The earliest Puritans had no new theological doctrines nor did they wish to alter the pattern of the Church. In the reign of Queen Elizabeth they had been prominent in the so-called "vestinarian controversy" when they tried and nearly managed to abolish all priestly vestments—even the ordinary surplice—and Puritan ministers took part in the "prophesyings" which the old queen disliked so much.

Between them the queen and Archbishop Whitgift had nearly halted the Puritan advance. When immediately after his accession a Puritan group put its case to King James I for the reduction of ritual and the encouragement of preaching, they presented to him a petition which was supposed to have been signed by a thousand ministers; yet when their claims were rejected and discipline imposed not more than 300 ministers were deprived of their livings out of a total of some nine thousand: it could therefore be argued that the recognizable Puritan movement in the reign of King James represented a relatively small minority in the Church. But by this time the Puritans were acquiring two new characteristics. In the first place, they were coming to favor the abolition of the bishops and much of the existing church hierarchy or, if not that, at least the taking away from the bishops of all their temporal powers, notably in the church courts. Some Puritans, loosely described as "independents" or sectarians, wanted the parishes to be autonomous; others favored the introduction of a system in which the Church was governed by a hierarchy of assemblies, presbyters or elders, and deacons. Secondly, because emphasis was laid upon the doctrine of predestination (though this doctrine had been accepted by almost the whole English Church in Elizabeth's time), Puritans reached the opinion that God's "chosen people" should show their faith by precise and exemplary conduct in their own lives: they sought to be witnesses to the reality of their conversions. They became the keenest of Sabbatarians and disapproved of games and sports upon the Lord's Day; they avoided excessive drinking in public or dancing around the Maypoles or swearing. They were ready to be reviled for the strictness of their Christian behavior. Since they regarded the leaders of the Church and many of the parish clergy as inadequate, they urged the employment of itinerant lecturers capable of bringing Christianity to the people at large by expounding the Holy Scriptures not merely on Sundays but on every other day of the week.

While this kind of strict Christianity was being built up in the first half of the seventeenth century, the Church of England was acquiring a distinctive faith or program with its own prophets. Richard Hooker had died before he completed his exposition of a temperate Anglicanism in the reign of Queen Elizabeth I, but men like Lancelot Andrewes, Bishop of Ely, the poets George Herbert and John Donne, the author Jeremy Taylor, and others were offering in prose and verse a reasonable defense of a religion that was less harsh than Genevan Calvinism and more English than Roman Catholicism. This was welcomed by the new monarch. King Charles I was the first English ruler to be brought up as a member of the Church of England and he took his title of Defender of the Faith seriously. He relied upon Archbishop William Laud to maintain order and put down subversive practices. Laud was an administrator rather than a theologian, who attached value to the beauty of holiness. At the same time this section of the Church, which may roughly be called the High Church, was influenced by the teaching of a Dutch theologian named Arminius, who believed in a Christian's freedom of will rather than his predestination. Since with very few exceptions the Puritans were keen predestinarians, there arose doctrinal as well as ritual differences within the Church. When Laud and his friends insisted that the Communion table should be treated as an altar and kept at the east end of the church, while the Puritans wanted to put it in the center of the church so that it should be accorded no sacramental meaning, the differences became accentuated. In the early years of King Charles I's reign various battles were waged between the king, Laud, and his friends, on the one side, and the Puritans, who were active in London and elsewhere, on the other. For example, the king decreed that only one sermon should be given each Sunday and that Christians should not wander away from their parishes looking for good preachers. When a group of Puritan sympathizers in London retorted by subscribing together to establish a fund for the payment of trained lecturers, this group was asked to explain its activities in the Court of Exchequer and was eventually dissolved.

Besides London and the ports, Puritanism had a considerable following in the clothing towns, for example, in the West Riding of Yorkshire and all over East Anglia, where refugee Protestant sects from France and the Spanish Netherlands had settled. It was at Huntingdon in East Anglia that Oliver Cromwell, most famous of the later Puritans, was born. Some Puritans left the country altogether and went to settle either in the Dutch republic, where there was more toleration, or sailed across the Atlantic to seek homes in what was to be known as New England. English Puritan exiles in Holland made use of printing presses there to produce pamphlets stating their opinions and attacking the bishops. These pamphlets were often vivid and scurrilous—they had models in the "Martin Marprelate" tracts that had been produced in Queen Elizabeth's time—and made a profound impression on those who read them. Thus, in spite of Archbishop Laud's efforts to clean up the Church by means of wide and regular episcopal visitations, the Puritan movement grew apace. The pamphlets were read, and between parliaments the pulpits where Puritan ministers or lecturers preached kept alive criticism of the prevailing order. "By 1632," writes Dr. William Haller, "the Puritans had succeeded in establishing within the church a veritable though unacknowledged and unauthorized order or brotherhood of preachers. . . . Its members were linked together by ties of youthful association, kindred, friendship, and marriage, as well as by conviction and interest. They looked mainly to Cambridge as their seminary and training-ground." They found sympathizers at many levels of society, while persecution (from which they had in fact been relatively free in King James I's time) only sharpened their ardor. Moreover they fancied that they saw in the practices of the "Arminians" and in the proceedings at the royal court, where the queen's Roman Catholic friends were the most privileged, a genuine revival of "popery." Fear of both Rome and Madrid ran deep.

In June 1637 the Court of Star Chamber elected to give a severe lesson to the Puritans. William Prynne, a keen Calvinist who had already lost his ears because of an attack which he had made on the theater in a book called *Histriomatrix,* John Bastwick, a popular London preacher, and Henry Burton, a physician over sixty, were all mutilated, put in a pillory, heavily fined, and finally exiled for writing against the bishops. Later a young apprentice named John Lilburne was brutally whipped and pilloried because he had been a distributor of Puritan pamphlets. The demonstration by Londoners in favor of the victims of these cruelties proved to be a warning of wrath to come.

It was in this same summer of 1637 that King Charles I and Archbishop Laud sought to impose a version of the English Book of Common Prayer upon the Church of Scotland. So far, King Charles I had tended to neglect his Scottish kingdom, although he had provoked the nobility by an act of revocation which meant the confiscation of some of their lands. Although King James, by enlisting the nobility on his side, had managed to impose a modified form of episcopacy in Scotland, the bishops cut little ice there and a presbyterian form of government functioned in the parishes. King Charles would have been better advised to leave well enough alone. An orgy of bishop-baiting began; and when an attempt was made to read services from the new book in St. Giles's church in Edinburgh, riots broke out. The Scots set up a resistance group known as "The Tables" and a covenant was drawn up inviting the Scottish Protestants to swear to resist to the death all religious innovations contrary to the word of God. King Charles retorted that he meant to be obeyed: although a long interval elapsed before he could gather an army together, eventually in March 1639 he traveled north to join his army at York with the intention of asserting his royal authority over his rebellious subjects. The English Puritans sympathized with the Scottish Presbyterians: the cloud over Scotland therefore presaged greater trouble for the king of England.

Although there was restlessness in England, King Charles was determined to punish his recalcitrant Scottish subjects and wonderful paper schemes were worked out for the purpose. The main difficulty was that he possessed neither an army nor a war chest. The Chancellor of the Exchequer informed him that the treasury was empty. The king therefore tried to borrow money from his wealthier subjects and called up a military levy. He hoped for a three-pronged assault on Scotland: troops sent from Ireland were to invade the west coast; Aberdeen on the east might be attacked from the sea; and in the meantime frontal advances could be begun across the border. The Earl of Strafford in Dublin did his best to serve the king, but by March 1639, seeing the way the wind was blowing, he advised that the expedition be postponed.

The Scottish Covenanters were far more efficient in their preparations. While King Charles I was appointing incompetents to overlapping military posts, Alexander Leslie, an experienced soldier, was chosen as commander-in-chief by the Scots. Although most of the Highlanders, being Catholics, did not rally to the Covenanters' side, one Highlander, Archibald Campbell, eighth Earl of Argyll, did so and his clan occupied a key position guarding the west coast against a possible Irish invasion. The Scots were aware that there was much discontent in England; indeed a friendly correspondence was opened between them and some influential English Puritans. The young James Graham, Earl of Montrose, who was to prove himself a brilliant general, stood ready to frustrate the attack on Aberdeen, Leslie took Edinburgh Castle, the Crown jewels of Scotland were seized at Dalkeith, and Aberdeen soon surrendered to the Covenanters. Thus by the time the king had advanced in the spring from York to Durham and from Durham to Newcastle his prospects were extremely gray and his officers totally demoralized. Early in June King Charles I reluctantly decided to abandon his campaign and a week later patched up a peace treaty. By the Pacification of Berwick (June 1639) both armies were to disband and a meeting of the Scottish parliament and an assembly of the Kirk to be called in the autumn. But everybody realized that the settlement was unreal, and the king was determined on revenge. Charles I summoned his ablest minister, Strafford, to come over from Ireland. Strafford offered as his advice that the king should call a parliament at Westminster and appeal to its members' native patriotism to lend him support against the Scots. He then hurried back to Ireland to organize a parliament in Dublin to set a good example.

Strafford was living in the past and the king was misled. Even in the reign of King James I the House of Commons had not responded to patriotic appeals by voting large sums of money. As parliament had not met for eleven years, a vast number of grievances had accumulated, especially over the payment of ship money. But the grievances of the gentry, merchants, and lawyers who gathered at Westminster in April 1640 were not confined to domestic affairs. They were suspicious too of the king's pro-Spanish policy. "All through the thirties Spanish bullion, for the payment of their troops in the Netherlands, had been shipped in English ships by way of London to Antwerp. English ships, being technically neutral, were immune from attacks by the Dutch. In this way King Charles's government had given valuable aid to Spanish arms against the Protestant cause" (Wedgwood). In the autumn of 1639 when a Spanish fleet had been chased into English waters by the Dutch, the king had allowed the Spaniards to replenish their stores of gunpowder and permitted their troops to be billeted in English coastal towns if they were forced to land. All this was known to the members of parliament; coming on top of their personal complaints over knighthood fines, "illegal" taxes, impositions, and the like, and resentment against the anti-Puritan policy of Archbishop Laud and his minions, an extremely unfavorable atmosphere had been created for the government. If an attempt was made to "pack" this parliament with royal supporters, it was unsuccessful. In any case the Crown had to rely on the ordinary country gentry who served as justices of the peace as its local agents, and they were in no mood to help.

The feelings of the House of Commons were expressed by John Pym, a veteran of the earlier parliaments, now the acknowledged leader of opposition to the Crown. After the king had made a short speech and Lord Keeper Finch had made a longer one appealing for assistance against the Scottish rebels and offering in evidence of their wickedness captured correspondence between the Covenanters and the king of France, Pym replied in a two-hour speech detailing all the many grievances of the king's subjects and arguing that no supplies of money should be voted until those grievances had been met. In vain the Earl of Strafford recommended the king to appeal to the House of Lords; for that was to affront the established right of the lower house to vote taxes. Then, more wisely, the king's ministers offered to give up ship money in return for a large vote of subsidies, but too much was asked too late and the negotiations broke down. In any case the majority of the House showed itself disinclined to renew the war against the Scots. After fewer than three weeks, the king dissolved the two houses. This therefore was known as the "Short Parliament."

Strafford had not been in favor of the abrupt dissolution of parliament. Nevertheless, having been the guiding force in a council of war, he now inspirited his master to a further military effort. He thought an Irish force could be landed in the western Highlands or elsewhere: he told the king, "you have an army in Ireland you may employ here to reduce this kingdom." Appeals were made both to the Spaniards and to the pope for a loan of money. Nearer home, the London city authorities were approached; but Puritanism was rampant in the capital, and refusals came from every quarter. The king pressed on. Bullion deposited by merchants in the mint was seized; courtiers were mulcted; the loyal gentlemen of the north of England, who were less friendly than the southerners to the Scots, were pressed for aid. Little came of all of this. The commander-in-chief fell ill and Strafford, who offered to take his place, was stricken with gout and hurried north in a litter. In August 1640 the Covenanters crossed the border and encountered no resistance. When the two armies eventually confronted each other at

Newburn, a few miles west of Newcastle, a cannonade proved sufficient to panic the useless English levies. Newcastle surrendered to the Scots and once more the king was obliged to come to terms with them.

Now for a second time the king was pressed to summon a parliament at Westminster. At first he compromised and called instead a great council of peers that met in the north of England and helped him to negotiate terms with the victorious Scots. By the treaty of Ripon the Scots were allowed to remain upon the English territory that they had conquered, while their army was to be paid by the king until a final settlement had been reached. This meant that—if only to supply the necessary funds—a new English parliament would have, after all, to be called together.

✿ THE LONG PARLIAMENT

The elections to what was to be known as the "Long Parliament" are said to have been eagerly contested, although our knowledge of them is by no means complete. In the end sixty per cent of the members of the previous "Short Parliament" were re-elected: it consisted, as usual, mainly of local gentry, but it also contained some seventy merchants and businessmen and many lawyers. The king's ministers tried to secure their usual quota of courtiers and officials, but some constituencies proved unexpectedly recalcitrant. Nonetheless the evidence of organized electioneering or canvassing by either the king's friends or critics is tenuous. Indeed the validity of speaking, as some historians have done, in terms of a court "party" and an organized "opposition" to the government is dubious. Even men who much later were to become acknowledged royalist leaders agreed with their fellow members on most issues in the early months of this parliament. After the first recess a young Oxford theologian, William Chillingworth, was actually sent to the Tower of London for asserting that there were "sides and parties" in the House of Commons.

The truth was that the whole of the new parliament was distrustful and critical of the king. His cavalier treatment of the Short Parliament, his humiliation in what was known as the "second Bishops' War" against the Scots, and a rumor that persisted of his negotiations with Roman Catholic powers and of an intention to bring over a "papist army" from Ireland to enforce his will on England all contributed to the mood of parliament. As soon as parliament met, John Pym determined that the king's ministers should be punished for what he regarded as the treasonable advice they had given their master to overthrow the "fundamental laws" of the realm. The chief culprit chosen was the Earl of

Strafford, himself a former member of the Commons and the principal architect of the "Petition of Right" of 1628.

Strafford actually welcomed the accusations that were brought against him; indeed he thought he might be able to bring forward counterac-cusations charging John Pym and his friends of intriguing with the Scots. If that produced no impression, then at least he could sacrifice himself for his king and thereby perhaps pave the way for a better understanding between the king and his leading subjects. But the atmosphere of the times was against him. Once again the grievances raised in the previous parliament were discussed and enlarged upon: ship money, monopolies, billeting of troops, the persecution of Puritans. Yet it was difficult to fasten any precise crimes upon Strafford, "the grand apostate." He defended himself effectively when he was im-peached by the Commons before the House of Lords. The attempt to prove (with the aid of one of the Secretaries of State, Henry Vane the elder) that Strafford had actually advised the king to use the Irish army in England was unconvincing. The Commons thereupon brought in an act of attainder against Strafford, which required no legal proof for its support, and persuaded the Lords to agree to it. It was passed on May 10, 1641 and on May 12 the earl, who, however much he might have filled his own pockets during his rule in Ireland, had served his king loyally and relentlessly, was executed. The act of attainder had required the king's assent. Charles I had promised on his word of honor that he would protect Strafford against his enemies, as once he had protected his friend Buckingham, but he allowed himself to submit to every kind of pressure, including Strafford's own willingness to sacrifice himself. With a Scottish army still in the north and a mob howling for blood in the streets of London, he feared for his queen and his throne and yielded. Though he was to invoke other loyalties from Englishmen, both in his own time and afterward, King Charles's character was never to be wiped clean after his betrayal of Strafford.

On the same day that he signed the act of attainder the king agreed to a bill whereby this parliament might not be dissolved without its own consent. Another act stated that parliament must be called every three years; virtually all the prerogative courts, the Star Chamber, the ec-clesiastical court of High Commission, the Councils of the North and of Wales were abolished; all taxes, from ship money to impositions, which had been levied without parliamentary consent were declared illegal; some royal ministers fled abroad, but others, like Archbishop Laud, were thrust into prison to await their trials; a humiliating treaty was concluded with the Scots. In effect a constitutional revolution was completed. The House of Commons, kept in check by Queen Elizabeth I and King James I, had risen to its highest peak of success.

During the summer of 1641 there was some reaction. While all his ancient prerogatives were being taken away from him, the king had remained calm and collected on the surface, sleeping and eating well, maintaining his habitual calm, but determined in his heart not to submit to a permanent reverse. It was, writes Dr. Wedgwood, "a time of play-acting and changes of mood. The King assumed the outward appearance of moderation, forbearance, and devotion to the Protestant Cause, while Pym tried to shake this poise without alienating those moderate men in the Commons who believed it." Divisions were in fact showing themselves in parliament, chiefly in relation to matters of religion. A group of Puritans in the House of Commons, among which Oliver Cromwell was one of the most prominent, was anxious to follow up the reconstruction of the constitution with a radical reform of the Church, including the abolition of the bishops. Other parliamentarians —such as lawyer Edward Hyde and Falkland, an attractive and cultivated peer—if by no means enthusiastic about the temporal powers of the bishops, were unwilling to accept revolutionary changes in the Church of England. Neither was the House of Lords, which rejected a bill proposing the exclusion of the bishops from its membership. The king played for time and hoped to obtain assistance either from abroad or perhaps, incredible as it may seem, from those very Scottish Covenanters whom he had twice fought earlier in order to regain his political position in England.

While during the later summer and early autumn the king paid a visit to Scotland, where he solemnly attended Presbyterian services and consented to the abolition of the Scottish bishops—but foolishly allowed some of his servants to get mixed up in a plot against the mighty Earl of Argyll—and while the English parliament was in recess, a rebellion broke out in Ireland which reached wide dimensions. The origins of this rebellion stretched far back into the past and were complicated. Broadly speaking, the outbreak arose from the resentment of the native Irish against English rule; against the impounding of Irish lands in the reigns of both Queen Elizabeth I and James I; on account of the lifting of the strong hand of Strafford, who had been an extremely efficient, if unpopular, Lord Deputy; and was based upon a hope that if the Scots were able to impose their own religious wishes upon King Charles I, the Catholic Irish could do the same. At any rate rebellion began in Ulster and spread like fire: a number of English were killed, English properties were seized, and many cruelties were committed. When news reached England of this Irish "massacre," as it was called, it had a profound impact upon the internal political situation. John Pym and his friends were convinced that although the rebellion must be put down it would be highly dangerous to place the control of an army for that purpose in the king's hands. The demand was therefore made that not only must the king's ministers be nominated by parliament (this, after all, was a demand that had been made and enforced in much earlier times) but parliament must control the militia and nominate the officers of the army as well.

While these extreme proposals were being formulated, divisions were beginning to appear in the House of Commons itself. There had already been disagreement over religious reforms being sought by the Puritans; now other differences arose about the distrust being shown of the king's intentions. To reaffirm their leadership, Pym, Cromwell, and their friends proposed to draw up a "grand remonstrance" setting out in detail every public grievance expressed against the Crown during the reign and embodying the demand that neither army officers nor ministers of state should be appointed by the king without parliamentary approval. After a hot debate the Grand Remonstrance was passed by the Commons on November 23, 1641 by a vote of only 159 to 148.

King Charles I had now reached the end of his patience. He regarded the Remonstrance as a personal insult and the final step calculated to deprive him of virtually every shred of executive power exercised by his predecessors. Moreover, he was made aware by the large number of members who had voted against the Remonstrance that now at last there had emerged a distinctive royalist party in the House of Commons; he also knew that the majority of the House of Lords was opposed to depriving him of his right to command the army and protect the established Church. He therefore returned a noncommittal answer to the Remonstrance and ordered the withdrawal of the guard that had been stationed at Westminster to protect the House of Commons. While the Commons were engaged in impeaching thirteen bishops and—so the king thought—planning to impeach the queen for treason, King Charles I summoned up his courage and at last struck. He entered the precincts of the Commons House and attempted to arrest five of its leading members, including Pym. But the members had been warned and escaped into hiding in the city of London. This abortive *coup d'état* advertised the coming of the civil war between the parliamentary leaders and the Royalists.

Early in 1642 the king left London and by March he was in England's northern capital of York, where he hoped to gather an army to assert his rights. He ordered the members of the courts of justice to follow him there. Gradually peers and friendly Commoners flocked northward to serve him. In June 1642 the remaining members of the two houses of parliament sent the king their proposals for a settlement, known as the Nineteen Propositions. These constituted an ultimatum requiring the king to surrender almost all his remaining prerogative powers: privy councilors, ministers, commanders of the military forces, and guardians of the royal children were all to be placed under the control of parliament, which was also to create peers and decide the future of the Church. When that ultimatum was rejected by the king as being a mockery, the two houses appointed a Committee of Safety and completed plans to enlist an army on their side. On August 22 the king moved south and raised his standard at Nottingham in the Midlands. Thus the great civil war began.

Many factors had contributed to the outbreak of the war. It can be, and has been, argued that it was essentially a struggle for power between the expanding and wealthy middle classes of the kingdom, on the one side, and the king and his advisers, clinging to their outworn prerogatives, on the other. An opposition to the Crown has been detected by historians of parliament at least from the first sessions in the reign of Queen Elizabeth I. Political discontent had been enhanced and sustained by the Puritan movement, but the king felt it his duty to maintain the structure of the Elizabethan Church, in which he heartily believed. The Puritan preachers had inspired an antiepiscopal mood that turned upon the king himself, who had inherited from his father the adage "no bishop, no king." Yet it must be admitted that not all the so-called middle classes, especially the country gentry, fought against the king when the war began. Had they done so, the king could scarcely have sustained the war as long as he did. Indeed families were divided among themselves; men were conscious of personal loyalties and of high principles. At the same time it was not a purely religious war. Not all the original Parliamentarian leaders—Eliot and Pym, for instance—were Puritans who wished to overthrow the Church, though when the war came the sword was ultimately transferred to Puritan hands.

Many political, financial, and constitutional grievances had accumulated during the first fifteen years of King Charles I's reign. The king's foreign policy, which showed favoritism toward Spain, was a factor in alienating his subjects. Ship money was a new and widespread grievance among almost all the classes of the community down to the peasant proprietors. The two "Bishops' Wars" against Scotland had aroused many resentments of a political as well as a religious nature. Above all, suspicions in regard to the court had reached gigantic proportions. The queen and the High Church bishops were genuinely believed to be conspiring to bring the kingdom back to the acceptance of papal supremacy. Hence the utter determination of Pym, Cromwell, and the rest not to permit control over the armed forces to remain with the king. What they feared was not so much an autocracy as a Popish Plot. It was over this crucial question—the control of the militia—which arose during the last hopeless negotiations between parliament and king during the spring and summer of 1642, that the final breach came.

XLV

The First Civil War

On the whole, the Parliamentarians controlled the larger resources for the waging of war. From the beginning they had the capital, London, and the financial power of that city and the biggest port at their disposal. Many of the other ports and towns in the kingdom were also Parliamentarian in sympathy. Hull in Yorkshire had refused to surrender to the king when he knocked at its gates; Portsmouth, the naval port, was soon lost by the Royalists; and it was not until the summer of 1643 that the king's army had an exceptional success in capturing Bristol, perhaps the second wealthiest town in the country. The navy, always of a radical frame of mind, went over to the Parliamentary side; the army did not in fact exist at the outset of the civil war. Until the Bishops' Wars the country had enjoyed a long period of peace and the only professional soldiers were those who had volunteered for service overseas on the Protestant side in the Thirty Years' War. The so-called "trained bands" or militia—relics from earlier times—were virtually untrained, except in the city of London. Even the weapons in the arsenals of the various county towns were few and largely antiquated. At the start soldiers were sometimes issued cudgels instead of muskets.

The king had less money at his disposal than the parliament had. He could only raise taxes in the counties where he was supreme. But he could call upon the loyalties of many of the leading country gentry and particularly of a number of peers who thought that their own fortunes were bound up with his and therefore provided him with money and service. For cavalry he could enlist the outdoor staffs of the big landowners—and cavalry was to prove the decisive arm in battle. He hoped to be able to borrow money and buy equipment abroad, notably in Holland, where his eldest daughter was married to the son of the prince of Orange. Somehow he managed to collect about twenty pieces of cannon, which made a noise, if they did nothing much else, at Edgehill and other battles. He had an army in Ireland. Above all, he could invoke the majesty of his name. Even men who doubted his cause were reluctant to betray him. The leaders of the Church knew that he was fighting for them. Roman Catholics in Ireland, in Scotland, in Lancashire, and abroad were aware that they had infinitely more to hope from him by way of liberty for their religion than from a parliament dominated by Puritans.

In assessing the resources of the two sides the personal element must not be left out of account. In his two young nephews from the Palatine —Prince Rupert and Prince Maurice—the king was to find officers of ability. Tribute has recently been paid by military experts to the versatility and ingenuity of Prince Rupert. A fine cavalry leader, he was also a master of the art of siege, and later was to show himself a notable admiral. This was an age of amateurs, when men learned the art of war chiefly in the hard school of experience. The Earl of Newcastle, a wealthy grandee who commanded for the king in Yorkshire, did not disgrace his new profession; Sir Ralph Hopton, who, like Oliver Cromwell, took up the art of war seriously in his early forties, won striking victories for the king. George Goring, whose reputation has been tarnished by Puritan aspersions upon his propensity for gambling and the bottle, did not—like the great General Ulysses Grant later—allow these habits to interfere with his soldierly prowess.

On the Parliamentarian side it was not the first commander-in-chief, Robert Devereux, third Earl of Essex, who proved the architect of victory although he had some right to call himself a professional soldier. Most of his military experiences had been or were to prove disastrous, and he was by nature pessimistic and uninspired. Edward Montague, Earl of Manchester, who was the second peer to be given a high command, like Essex, did not in his heart want to defeat the king, but only to teach him a lesson. By inclination, and perhaps by nature as well, he was lethargic. Sir William Waller, also a professional soldier of sorts, was not very competent. It was the young Sir Thomas Fairfax, who rose to fame in the northern campaigns, and Oliver Cromwell, who was among the first to enlist a cavalry regiment in the east of England, who in the end were to prove themselves the best Parliamentarian soldiers in the civil wars.

At first the Parliamentary armies were handicapped by committee rule; both a well-thought-out strategy and real generalship were lacking; whereas the Royalists could at least look to the king for united leadership; and insofar as any general strategic plan was ever followed by either side, it came from the king and not from parliament. The king's aim was to conquer his capital and compress his enemies into the southeast of the country, where their main strength lay.

At the beginning of the war the Parliamentarians controlled much of the east and south of the country, while the Royalists held sway over most of Wales and the west Midlands. The Earl of Essex led his army slowly northwestward in September 1642, uncertain whether he would need to confront the king's army in the Severn Valley or interpose between that army and London. A Royalist concentration was taking place in Worcester and it was outside that town, by Powick Bridge, that the first, as also one of the last, clashes of the civil wars was to occur. Here Prince Rupert took some prisoners, but later the Earl of Essex occupied Worcester in force. The king's army was growing fast, and late in the campaigning season Charles took heart and decided to advance on London, though pursued by Essex. On October 23 the king decided to try to shake off his pursuer: so the first important battle of the civil wars was fought at Edgehill near Warwick. The armies were evenly matched and in tactical terms the battle was drawn: Prince Rupert was victorious on the right wing of his army, the Parliamentarians on their right. But in strategic terms it was a Royalist victory, for Essex retired to Warwick, leaving some of his guns and his colors behind him. The king resumed his advance on London and occupied the city of Oxford, which was to remain his headquarters for the rest of the war.

If the king had now hastened upon London, he might have won a magnificent victory, but he was held up first at Windsor and then Brentford, to the west of London. Desperately throwing in all their resources to save the capital, the Parliamentarians managed to concentrate a large defense force, including London's trained bands, on the common at Turnham Green. But the battle of Turnham Green was never fought. The king recoiled before the host of grim Londoners guarding the river Thames and withdrew first to Reading and then to Oxford. During the winter the two sides glared at each other across the sixty miles lying between London and Oxford, and prepared for a renewal of the fighting next spring.

The year 1643 proved to be one of success for the Royalists. In the north the Earl of Newcastle defeated Sir Thomas Fairfax and his father at the battle of Adwalton Moor, and though later in the year he failed to take Hull, his hold upon eastern Yorkshire was firm. In the extreme west the Royalist Sir Ralph Hopton advanced from Cornwall into Devon, and in July the Parliamentarian Sir William Waller was defeated by the youthful Prince Maurice at the battle of Roundway Down near Devizes in Wiltshire. In that same month Prince Rupert captured Bristol and the Earl of Essex had to fight a drawn battle at Newbury to secure the relief of the city of Gloucester. Nevertheless, the Royalist hold over Wales and the west remained firm. Only in the east of England, where Oliver Cromwell, a dashing cavalry leader, was acquiring a knowledge of war, did the Parliamentarians have a number of small successes. Cromwell remarked upon the superior morale of the Royalists, the poor organization of his side in the provision of pay and arms, and the need to canalize the Puritan faith into pugnacity on the field. He always rated highly the factor of morale in war, but his genius as a general was to include all the details of supply. The contribution to be made by the men of the "Eastern Association," as the group of counties banded together in East Anglia was known, lay in the future. At the end of 1643 three-quarters of the kingdom was under the military control of Charles I, and in London much depression and uncertainty was felt by the Parliamentarian leaders; John Pym and his colleagues decided to seek help from Scotland.

Commissioners from Scotland and from the English parliament met at Westminster in September 1643 to sign a Solemn League and Covenant. The chief representative for parliament was Sir Henry Vane the Younger, son of the former Secretary of State of the same name, a man of high ideals and organizational ability who held unorthodox Christian views. The Scots entered the alliance partly because they feared that the victory of the king would mean the destruction of the Presbyterian religion which they loved so much and partly because they hoped to establish their own particular form of church discipline in England as well. Vane was aware that many English Puritans—notably the sectarians—did not care for this state religion, but to him the Solemn League and Covenant was essentially a military alliance. The clause binding the Church of England to conformity with the Church of Scotland was therefore phrased, "according to the Word of God and the example of the best reformed Churches," wording which left room for maneuver. The Scots understood the meaning of the interpolation, but hoped that once the war was over they might be able to induce the new rulers of England to come around to their way of thinking.

As soon as the Solemn League had been agreed upon, a Scottish army, led by Alexander Leslie, now Earl of Leven, was rapidly prepared and entered England in the depth of winter. The negotiators had been aware that at the same time Charles I's Lord Lieutenant in Ireland, the

Marquis of Ormonde, was concluding a truce with the Irish, which was known as the Cessation. This truce did not provide for Irish troops to be brought over to take part in the English civil war, but it released some of the king's royalist forces in Ireland for that purpose. Thus each side was freshened by new blood when the war was resumed in 1644.

The coming of the Scots affected the general strategy of the war, although it does not seem that the Committee of the Two Kingdoms, which now ran the war on behalf of the English parliament and the Scottish Covenanters, had an exact plan, even though it had several armies at its disposal. When the Scots came south the Marquis of Newcastle, as he had now become, marched north from York to meet them, but during his absence Sir Thomas Fairfax won a notable victory at Selby over the Royalist commander left behind in south Yorkshire; and the marquis was compelled to return to York. The northern capital was now besieged by three armies—that of the Scots, that of the Fairfaxes, and that of the Eastern Association, commanded by the Earl of Manchester, in which Oliver Cromwell was serving as lieutenant-general. Prince Rupert, who had been carrying out a campaign in Lancashire and making ready to welcome the king's reinforcements from Ireland, was ordered to go to the relief of York. The mere news of the prince's coming was sufficient to break up the siege: the three armies moved west in a vain attempt to intercept him. After Rupert had linked up with Newcastle he decided to confront his enemy, and entrenched himself upon the field of Marston Moor, not far from York.

At the battle there in July the Royalists were outnumbered and tactically surprised, for the fighting began in the early evening. Although the three Parliamentarian commanders at one stage fled the field on the assumption that all was lost after they suffered an initial repulse on each wing, Cromwell and Sir Thomas Fairfax fought on and changed the outcome of the struggle. Yet this did not prove to be a conclusive defeat for the king. The Earl of Essex, annoyed at being left out, had departed from Oxford, which he was supposed to be besieging, and marched to the southwest in the hope of winning glory there. He outran his lines of communication, was cut off, and abandoned his army before it surrendered in Cornwall. Meanwhile the Scots had returned to the north to clear their lines by besieging Newcastle, the Earl of Manchester had returned to the Eastern Association, and the Fairfaxes had taken themselves to the coastal town of Scarborough. In Manchester's army a quarrel broke out between Cromwell and a high-ranking Presbyterian officer, and finally when in October the armies of Manchester and William Waller tried to intercept the king as he returned from the vic-

Stirling

R. Forth

Dunbar

Edinburgh

Berwick-on-Tweed

Places underlined
indicate where
battles occurred

SCOTTISH
LOWLANDS

Newcastle

Carlisle

Scarborough

Marston Moor • York

Adwalton Moor • Selby Hull

Pontefract

Newark

Leicester

Naseby

Worcester

Cambridge

Edge Hill

Colchester

Gloucester

Oxford

London

Bristol

Newbury

Roundway Down

Taunton

Sedgemoor

Portsmouth

ENGLAND, WALES, AND SOUTHERN SCOTLAND IN THE SEVENTEENTH CENTURY

tory over the Earl of Essex, they lost another battle at Newbury in Berkshire, and even allowed the king to relieve a castle there under the very noses of its besiegers.

By this time King Charles I had found a champion in Scotland in a former Covenanter, James Graham, Marquis of Montrose. This skillful and handsome soldier, after seeing the king in Oxford, got across the border in disguise to carry out orders to raise the Scottish Highlanders for the royal cause with the sign of the fiery cross. The news of Montrose's successes with a minute army was soon to perturb the Covenanter Scots in England who refused to move far from the neighborhood of their frontier. Thus in 1645 the Parliamentarian outlook—in spite of the alliance with the Scots and the victories in the north of England—still appeared doubtful.

The Parliamentarians therefore decided to enlist a new army and to enforce some unity of command. After long discussions it was agreed not only to raise a "New Model Army" under the command of Sir Thomas Fairfax, but also to impose a "self-denying" ordinance whereby all existing officers who were members of the houses of parliament were required, after a specified period, to give up their commissions. This ordinance had the advantage that it not only made possible the countering of accusations put about by the Royalists that M.P.'s were profiting from the war to obtain well-paid posts for themselves, but it also enabled the Committee of the Two Kingdoms to get rid of the earls of both Essex and Manchester. The disadvantage was that General Cromwell was also required to give up his command.

The New Model Army was expeditiously created by Fairfax. Its nucleus was the army of the Eastern Association, but infantrymen also had to be pressed into service. Though Fairfax was a very popular commander (nobody knew what his religion was, so he appealed both to Presbyterians and to sectarians), and though its pay was at first regular and its supplies adequate, this army had only a short period of training and little experience as a fighting force. When it was led west to the relief of Taunton in Somerset during the spring of 1645 it failed to distinguish itself. Meanwhile the king, tiring of inaction in Oxford, was hesitating whether he should move east to overthrow the Eastern Association or north with a view to joining the victorious Montrose. When the Royalists suddenly sacked the town of Leicester, Fairfax, recalled from the west to Oxford, abandoned caution and decided to confront the Royalist army under Prince Rupert. The most critical battle of the whole civil war was therefore fought on a mid-June day north of the village of Naseby in Leicestershire.

At Naseby in the heart of England General Sir Thomas Fairfax, ably seconded by Oliver Cromwell, whom he had recalled at the last moment from his unwanted leisure in East Anglia, won a great victory: two out of three Royalists surrendered on the field of battle, so completely had they been outnumbered, outfought, and demoralized. This time the victory was followed up: Fairfax and Cromwell marched west to deal with the only large Royalist force still remaining. Lord Goring was beaten at the battle of Langport in July; soon afterward Prince Rupert surrendered the port of Bristol. Then all the Parliamentarian forces, other than those engaged in mopping-up operations, were concentrated upon the king's capital of Oxford. The king fled from the city in disguise to throw himself on the mercy of the Scottish Covenanters, who had now moved as far south as Newark. In June 1646 Oxford capitulated, and before the end of the year the Scots agreed to surrender King Charles I to the Parliamentarians and then went home. So the first English civil war came to an end.

The first civil war served the purpose for which it was fought: it compelled the king to accept the supremacy of Parliament. How did it affect the common people? In many ways it was a disaster. A great number of noble and beautiful buildings were destroyed; families were sundered; lives were ruined. How far the mass of the people were concerned by it is hard to gauge: no doubt in some quiet corners of the kingdom the agricultural laborer and the like scarcely realized what was going on. But in districts well fought over—Yorkshire, for example— small tradesmen and peasant farmers were conscious of interruptions in business and were made to feel the weight of wartime taxation. Each side imposed a "weekly assessment," a kind of land tax, or levied "excise," a sort of purchase tax. A popular ballad of the day reflected:

> Oh we shall have, if we go on
> In Plunder, Excise and Blood
> But few folks and poor, to domineer o'er
> And that will not be good.

The people's masters did not change greatly. Many of the same gentry who ruled before as commissioners of peace formed themselves into Parliamentarian county committees to collect the taxes, give the orders, and take the pickings. On the whole the efforts initiated at the beginning of the war to neutralize different countries were in vain, and even the so-called Clubmen who armed themselves against all comers in the west of England were unable to keep the war away from their borders. Men were apt to be pressed into the armies on either side and rarely received the pay they were promised. In Lancashire villages some men even drifted into the Parliamentary armies to escape the clutches of the local Royalist tyrant, the Earl of Derby. Once in the army there was little time for training, so that the pressed men easily got out of hand. The most humane commanders, like Fairfax and Cromwell, had to insist upon severe punishments for pillage and plunder. Otherwise they would have been disgraced by some outrage like the sack of Leicester.

The indiscipline and economic suffering caused by the civil war must not be exaggerated. Compared with the horrors of the Thirty Years' War in Germany or some of the later devastations on the mainland of Europe in the seventeenth and eighteenth centuries, it might all have seemed like a picnic. A London barrister noted: "We begin now to see that a kingdom according to human discourse is not so easily ruinated and will commonly hold by stronger roots than we imagined." The officers were, for the most part, gentlemen who knew each other and passed polite messages across the lines. There was little to choose between a Prince Rupert and a Thomas Fairfax, between a Ralph Hopton and a William Waller. Hard terms were rarely imposed after defeats. Toward the end of the war, for example, Fairfax granted generous quarter to Rupert after the siege of Bristol. Nothing like the same amount of fraternal blood was shed as in the American Civil War or the civil wars of the twentieth century. If the Royalists had been willing to accept the verdict of the first civil war, as they promised to do when they laid down their arms, England's struggle with herself could be regarded as one of the least cruel internal conflicts in history. Perhaps the Royalists did not accept the verdict because their losses were so few and their punishments so mild. When war broke out again heavier punishments were to be inflicted on the vanquished and the king himself was to pay for it all with his life.

XLVI

The Execution of Charles I

Although he had lost the war, King Charles I was not prepared to recognize that he was beaten. He still hoped to enlist help from the Scots or the Irish or to collect an army from abroad; above all, he expected to play off his enemies against one another. He was unwilling to betray the Church, at any rate in England; disconsolately remembering the fate of Strafford, he determined to be loyal to his friends and followers; but, above all, his aim was to regain power, and to do that he offered to sell the divinity that doth hedge a king on reasonable terms to the highest bidder.

Yet the tragedy of King Charles I was that, in the long run, no one was ever willing to trust him. He made it known to his intimates that his policy was to grant concessions that he did not intend to keep. To the Presbyterians in England he promised one thing; to the Independents in the New Model Army he promised diametrically the opposite. He held out grand hopes of equality for the Irish Catholics, while the Irish Protestants were informed, on his authority, that these need not be taken at their face value. The Papal Nuncio in Ireland had written significantly in October 1645 that he was "alarmed by the general opinion of His Majesty's inconstancy and bad faith, which creates a doubt that whatever concessions he may make, he will never ratify them unless it pleases him. . . ." Now, as a prisoner of the Scots, every fiber of his being was concentrated on diplomatic ingenuities aimed at spinning up some new material of hope for his side.

The victors in the civil war had as yet no intention of deposing the king: he still offered the best cement for a settlement. They had before them four immediate problems: one was how to come to some sort of an agreement with Charles I; the next was how to be rid of the Scottish army, encamped at Newcastle upon Tyne; the third was how to demobilize, or at least to reduce the size of, their own army; and the last was how to subdue the rebels in Ireland. With the approval of the Scots the English parliament presented the king with their terms, known as "the propositions of Newcastle": these required him to accept the Covenant, to abolish the existing Church of England, and to acquiesce in such an ecclesiastical settlement as might finally be agreed upon; to surrender all control over the armed forces for twenty years; and to consent to the punishment of his principal supporters. This was to invite him to betray both his Church and his friends, which he swore he would never do. Thus although he was eager to concoct some answer that would not be read as a refusal and might pave the way for negotiations in London, King Charles was obliged to reject the "propositions." It was then that the Scots were promised a financial arrangement satisfactory to them to meet the costs of their army; and they left Newcastle, handing over their royal prisoner to the English parliament.

The handling of the English army and the Irish question was more complicated. Since 1643 an assembly consisting of learned English and Scottish divines and representatives of the two houses of parliament had been sitting at Westminster to consider questions relating to the future of the English Church. It had already been decided that the bishops and deans should be abolished altogether and effect had been given to this decision by an act of 1643. But over whom or what was to be put in their place there were wide divisions of opinion. The Westminster Assembly was predominantly Presbyterian in sympathy and under Scottish influence, but the ultimate decision rested with parliament, where there was a strong sectarian minority led by Henry Vane and Oliver Cromwell, who obtained some support from lawyers and others known as "Erastians," who were against the subordination of the state to the Church upon the Covenanting model. The Presbyterian leaders in the Commons were fearful lest the New Model Army, which contained many sectarians, would be in a position to exert pressure in the shaping of the final plans for the new English Church, and thus had an added impulse to demobilize the army as quickly as they could. In March 1647, therefore, parliament voted that the bulk of the New Model Army was to go to Ireland, while a small garrison army was to be left in England on reduced pay. At the same time the majority voted that no M.P. and no one who refused to subscribe to the Covenant might continue to hold a commission. This was a direct insult to the great Independent leader, Cromwell, which he took lightly; but it provoked the New Model Army, which was already far in arrears in receiving its pay and was demanding other compensations before being demobilized.

At first Cromwell and other M.P.'s who had served in the army did their best to act as conciliators between parliament and the army. But the army's mood was ugly and realistic. Army men had won the war; why should they be fobbed off with the alternatives of being turned back to their homes unpaid and possibly to find no work or being shipped off to savage Ireland under Presbyterian officers? When the army leaders had made their position clear and a petition was presented asking for better terms, Denzil Holles, the Presbyterian leader in the Commons, proposed and carried a resolution that such petitioners might be "looked upon" and "proceeded against" as "enemies of the State." One can see in retrospect that this was a foolish act of statesmanship: it intensified discontent; it invited mutiny; immediately it deepened the character of the dispute. Parliament was then told bluntly that the soldiers would not serve in Ireland except under their old generals. Even when they were offered slightly better terms, it was made clear that they would not volunteer for service in Ireland and would only disband if all their arrears were paid. In May 1647, however, the parliamentary majority was still insisting on disbandment on unacceptable terms and even trying to raise a force in London as a counter to the New Model Army. Thus less than a year after the first civil war had ended the victors had fallen out among themselves.

It was at this stage that Oliver Cromwell had to make one of the most critical decisions in his life. He was already a man of forty-eight who had fully proved himself both as a soldier and as a statesman. He had been a loyal second-in-command to General Thomas Fairfax in the last stages of the war, but the Scots and others had recognized his great personal contribution to the victory. His statesmanship had been shown when he accepted the Self-Denying Ordinance temporarily depriving him of a command and when he made genuine efforts to act as intermediary between the House of Commons and the New Model Army. Now that the bishops had been abolished and he had come to recognize the importance of toleration for the many different kinds of Christianity brought about by the Puritan triumph, the fanaticism of his youth had been tempered. He was an earnest Christian and also a mature man; unlike his friend and superior, Fairfax, he was not a non-political soldier, and he embraced the responsibilities and ardors of leadership.

In the New Model Army there was a ferment of ideas. As the soldiers read their pocket Bibles and discussed matters of life and death by their camp fires, new questions arose. Every variety of religious faith was to be found in the New Model Army. Nor did questioning stop there. Pamphlets poured out from more or less unlicensed presses, written by well-educated men like William Walwyn, the Plato of his time, or by self-educated agitators like the former fiery apprentice, John Lilburne, who rose to be a lieutenant-colonel but had refused to sign the Covenant. Many of these pamphlets dealt with individual grievances or theological fancies. But after reading them and holding debates in camps and taverns, the soldiers developed a more fundamental sense of social dissatisfaction. Furthermore, they had seen the old ruling classes without their wigs and robes in undignified postures and awkward situations. The king was a prisoner, the queen an exile. "An atmosphere of challenging discontent inevitably grew from the experience and propaganda of the war, an atmosphere in which it was natural for other kinds of complaint—at economic loss or commercial depression—to be linked with an angry questioning of the social order" (Wedgwood).

Such was the atmosphere that existed when Oliver Cromwell decided in the summer of 1647 to break with the parliamentary majority and throw in his lot with an army verging upon mutiny. A general rendezvous of the army was held at Newmarket near Cambridge, solemn engagements were concluded, a general council of the army (with representatives of the soldiers as well as of the officers) was constituted, and a contingent went to seize the artillery in Oxford and to lay hold of the king. In agreeing to the last move, Cromwell acted under pressure from a revolutionary group within the lower ranks of the army.

Cromwell and his able son-in-law, Henry Ireton, who was also a general officer, now attempted to carry through a triangular negotiation for a settlement among the army, the parliament, and the king, having, so it appeared, most of the cards in their hands. But they were very conscious of the imminent threat of national anarchy. They wished to preserve the institutions of both monarchy and parliament and to protect established property rights against the underswell of discontent from radical-minded agitators. They therefore evolved as an instrument a "written constitution" which, being in draft form, was known as the "Heads of the Proposals." This scheme was aimed not at establishing parliamentary supremacy at the expense of all the former rights of the monarchy, but at making the king's power broadly subservient to that of parliament and the power of parliament broadly amenable to the wishes of the constituencies, as well as restricting the rights of the government over the liberties of the individual. According to the terms of this instrument, parliaments were to be held once every two years and seats were to be redistributed so as to get rid of the smaller (or "rotten") boroughs. Parliament ignored this elaborate plan and stuck to its own "Propositions of Newcastle." To please the army, whose prisoner he was, Charles I expressed his own preference for the "Heads of the Proposals"; but already he was preparing a grand coup. He hoped to escape from his captivity and by promising a period of temporary Presbyterian supremacy in England to revive his cause with the help of Scottish arms. The growing antagonism between the English parliament and the army gave him confidence. If his enemies were divided and crushed, he could be a real king again.

The position of the army leaders was made difficult by the fact that even more radical constitutions were being advocated by John Lilburne's democratic followers, known as "the Levellers," and by his allies in the ranks of the army, known as the soldiers' agents or "Agitators." An incipient republican movement was already appearing. The Levellers' proposals were first put forward in what was known as their "large petition"; many social reforms were advocated in a leaflet entitled *The Case of the Army Truly Stated* and a democratic republican scheme set out in the first *Agreement of the People*, published in October 1647. An important meeting of the Council of the Army was held at Putney near London at the end of this same month in which a serious attempt was made to reconcile the "Heads of the Proposals" with the "Agreement of the People." Although Cromwell, who acted as chairman of the meeting, exerted his influence in favor of conciliation, the majority of the high-ranking officers were afraid that Lilburnian democracy would mean both anarchy and the destruction of private property. These meetings broke up with no decision taken. Soon after they did so, the news was received that the king had escaped to the Isle of Wight and there on December 26 signed an "engagement" with a number of leading Scotsmen who promised to send an army into England to restore him to his throne as a Presbyterian king. In that same confused autumn the army, before it withdrew to Putney, had marched on London and coerced the majority in the Commons, forcing the Presbyterian leaders to flee from Westminster. Thus when the second civil war broke out the king confronted a confused enemy with his newly forged Royalist-Presbyterian alliance.

At first therefore the outlook seemed rosy for the king. In the north the Royalists rose against the Parliamentary government and occupied such towns as Pontefract and Scarborough. In Wales a Presbyterian colonel gave the signal for revolt by proclaiming his new allegiance at Pembroke Castle, where he was the governor; in London part of the navy mutinied and went over to the king's side; in Kent at Maidstone and in Essex at Colchester dangerous risings broke out. Thus the limited forces of the New Model Army were fully stretched in southern England and Wales as the Scottish Engagers were making ready to cross the border. But the discipline, experience, and mobility of the Parliamentarian veterans told. The English Royalist revolts were not concerted to coincide with the Scottish invasion, which did not take place until July. The king had no Rupert or Montrose to direct his operations. The first Duke of Hamilton, who led the Scottish army, was an incompetent with a seamy past whose very mission was repudiated by Argyll, the principal Covenanters, and the Kirk. While Fairfax crushed the southern risings, Cromwell, after obtaining the surrender of Pembroke, made a forced march to join his subordinate, Major-General John Lambert, in Yorkshire. Together they crossed the Pennine hills from Yorkshire into Lancashire and defeated the larger Scottish-Royalist army piecemeal in a series of battles beginning at Preston. By September such Scots as were not already prisoners were heading back for the border. Cromwell turned and followed them, and in October came to terms with Argyll and the Covenanters in Edinburgh. The defeat of Hamilton and his Engagers and the internal divisions in Scotland meant that the smaller kingdom was in effect at the mercy of the victorious party in England.

While the second civil war was being fought, the House of Commons, freed from the presence of Cromwell and other Independent leaders, was still hoping to come to an agreement with the king. A motion that no further negotiations should be carried on with him, which had been passed in the previous year, was revoked; Denzil Holles himself went to the Isle of Wight to beg the king to capitulate to their demands before the New Model Army again bore down on Westminster. Again the king procrastinated and thereby sealed his fate.

Now the wrath in the army was general. Stirred up by Leveller pamphlets, which sought the trial of the king by the existing law of the land, and by the fact that the king and the Royalists had broken the word they had given at the end of the first civil war not to take up arms again, the soldiers considered Charles I to be a Man of Blood, and guilty of a great crime. Both the army under Fairfax in the south and that under Cromwell in the north petitioned for the king's trial and asked that no further negotiations with him be pursued. Insofar as any one man promoted and directed this policy, it was not John Lilburne, the Leveller leader, but Henry Ireton, an austere Puritan whose regiment had been among the first to publish a "remonstrance" and who had himself sent his resignation to Fairfax as a protest against the continued parliamentary negotiations with the king. Ireton had hoped that parliament and the king might make a constitutional compromise on the basis of the "Heads of the Proposals," which he himself had largely drawn up. The Levellers, for their part, still hoped that their own democratic scheme, now modified and known as the third "Agreement of the People," would be accepted by the army and by parliament as a constitutional settlement and put into effect before the king was put on trial—but Lilburne was opposed to a trial by any extraordinary means.

Events were moving too fast for these paper schemes to be seriously discussed. Men were lit by anger and by a desire for immediate retribution. To the Puritan mind the astonishing victories which had so rapidly put an end to the second civil war pointed to providential guidance. The New Model Army had been shown to contain God's chosen people. "Let us look into providences," wrote Cromwell at this time, "surely they mean somewhat, they hang so together; have been so constant, so clear and unclouded." So the army was sanctified in what it did. By early December 1648 the House of Commons was again "purged" of its Presbyterians and the decision was taken that impartial justice must be done upon all offenders.

The House of Commons passed an ordinance for bringing the king to trial on January 1,1649. One hundred and thirty-five commissioners were appointed to serve in Westminster Hall under the presidency of one John Bradshaw. Far fewer served than were nominated and fewer still ultimately signed the king's death warrant. Yet the result of the trial was certain, since the king refused to recognize the validity of the court. So long as the commissioners were satisfied that the king had taken part in an act of war against his people, they were bound to find him guilty. The king stood by the ancient rights of the monarchy as he conceived of them. When he was told that he had violated his oath to the people who had elected him king, he retorted that England had never been an elective kingdom. A king, he said, could be tried by no superior jurisdiction, for he himself was supreme; and his cause, he claimed, was that of the freedom and liberty of all the people of England. His most revealing remark was made in his speech from the scaffold, when he said that he did not believe that the happiness of the people lay in sharing government, "subject and sovereign are clean different things."

All this was indeed capable of producing prolonged historical argument. England had in fact over a long period been an elective monarchy. Kings had been bound by their coronation oaths from the time of King Henry I and had been deposed for their violation of them. The Tudors, even King James I, for all his bluster about the "divine right of kings," had acquiesced in parliament's sharing in "sovereignty." On the other hand, if King Charles I had cared to look back far enough into history he would certainly have found monarchs—Alfred the Great, for example—who stood for the liberty of the people as a whole. Historical arguments like these led nowhere for either side, although they were used alike by the Royalists, by Sir Edward Coke and his disciples, and by the democratic Levellers. Much of it was little more than historicism at its worst. In fact here was the culmination of a revolutionary situation that had been boiling up in Britain for over one hundred years, ever since King Henry VIII had broken with the pope of Rome and declared himself the head of the English Church as well as of the state, and ever since Mary, Queen of Scots, was affianced to a French prince. In earlier times ineffective or unpopular rulers had been deposed or killed by the great magnates of the realm, who chose successors from among themselves. Now new classes had arisen—new judges, new executioners, men of wider and sometimes nobler ambitions, wielding a different kind of Christian vengeance. To give these new classes an exact name is not possible, but they were not the old aristocracy. Many of them were "puritans"; some of them were not out of the top drawer. To say that "the people" killed "their king" is obviously untrue. Yet within the rank and file of the New Model Army and also in the scattered but substantial Leveller following throughout the land there were certainly men of more than one class or calling who believed that it was just to put the king on trial and punish him for his crimes.

Other men and women wept and prayed for him the day he died and afterward. To them he was a saint, and the angels crowned his son. King Charles I himself, knowing, in the last analysis, that he had failed as a ruler, hoped to preserve the monarchy as an institution by his very act of martyrdom when his head fell upon the block on January 30, 1649. In this he proved successful; for the English monarchy has continued—though threatened in every century—until present times. But the Parliamentarians won their victory too. The fate of King Charles I on the scaffold in Whitehall was a warning to all his successors. When the same army that had defeated his father brought King Charles II back to England eleven years later, it was not to the old heritage or the old prerogatives. In a limited but definite sense King Charles II was to be a constitutional monarch, indeed a parliamentary king. And after a brief but decisive struggle in the reign of Charles I's younger son, King James II, Britain showed that she had managed through her civil wars and revolution to avoid the real despotisms that prevailed on the European mainland in the seventeenth century, and she had acquired a new method of government that opened the road to later parliamentary democracy.

XLVII

The Interregnum and the Protectorate

The execution of King Charles I left England, as it were, without a constitution. After the second civil war a political transformation had taken place so rapidly that a republic was established almost as if by accident; for apart from a few Levellers and extremists, scarcely anyone had envisaged the complete destruction of the monarchy. It is true that in the debates in the general council of the army both Cromwell and Ireton had agreed that there was no overwhelming theoretical case in favor of one form of government as against any other; during the civil war government by committee had not always been a striking success; and somehow it had always been expected that in the last resort King Charles I or his sons would accept parliament's terms for a limited monarchy. But the decision to put the king to death had meant that no Stuart would now accept the throne under conditions; so an act of parliament was passed abolishing the monarchy altogether, while another act disposed of the House of Lords, which had long been moribund. John Milton, the poet, hastily compiled a treatise to justify the existence of a "free," but oligarchic, "republic."

A Council of State of forty-one members was set up to work in collaboration with the attenuated House of Commons upon the government of the nation. This Council of State, of which John Bradshaw became president, consisted of an able group of men. Extremists were left on one side. Some who were nominated to the council, such as General Thomas Fairfax, at first refused to serve on the ground that they did not wish to be associated with the king's execution or the introduction of a republic instead of a monarchy. But face-saving formulae were worked out, and gradually a slow-moving but by no means incompetent administrative machine was constructed.

The task of the new Commonwealth was no light one. Not only had it to contend with discontented Royalists, but also with John Lilburne and his Levellers, who thought that the cause of the revolution had been betrayed. Leveller views carried much weight in the army, which of course gave strength and security to the new regime. But, as in most revolutions, a few determined men—some of them, like Sir Henry Vane and Sir Arthur Haselrig, fanatical in their outlook—had laid hold of the reins of power, and until they were well in the saddle nothing approaching a free or democratic commonwealth could come into being.

Apart from the question of internal loyalties, the English Commonwealth had enemies abroad. The kings and queens of Europe expressed their abhorrence at Charles I's execution, at least while they were making up their minds about the likelihood of the new government becoming permanent. In Ireland the rebels were still in command, and Royalist agents hoped to fashion an army there to support the Stuart cause. In Scotland the Covenanters also repudiated the king's execution; they felt that no English tribunal had the right to put to death a king of the Scots. They made it clear that if Charles II, a boy of nineteen, would accept the same stringent Presbyterian conditions that had been offered to his father, they would fight for him.

The first thing that the Council of State had to do was to pacify the army. When John Lilburne uttered blood-curdling threats about starting a fresh revolution he was put under arrest, and Fairfax and Cromwell acted resolutely to suppress mutinies or incipient mutinies in the army. The embers of political unrest were stamped out at the expense of a few lives. Next Fairfax and his colleagues persuaded Oliver Cromwell himself to lead an expedition to Ireland. Cromwell was reluctant to go, and first insisted that his soldiers should be guaranteed good pay, supplies, and conditions of service. The situation was extremely dangerous, for the Marquis of Ormonde had at last succeeded in concluding an agreement between the Irish Royalists and the Catholic rebels. He thought he might be able to drive the Puritan forces out of Ireland and organize an expeditionary force to invade England on behalf of the new king. In May 1649 while Ormonde himself was advancing on Dublin, an Irish nationalist leader, Owen Roe O'Neill, who was the nephew of the Earl of Tyrone, occupied Londonderry in Ulster. But in August Ormonde was defeated by the Puritan governor of Dublin, while O'Neill concluded a truce in the north and not long afterward died.

As soon as Cromwell's powerful army landed, Dublin was relieved and the remaining Royalists withdrew north to Drogheda. Cromwell summoned the governor of Drogheda to surrender "to the end that effusion of blood may be prevented." The governor fought it out, defended the breaches blown by Cromwell's canon, and inflicted heavy losses on Cromwell's assault columns. As a punishment and a warning to other Irish garrisons, Cromwell gave orders that all those found in arms in the conquered city should be put to the sword. Fewer than two thousand men perished and for the time being at least this awful example saved lives: two other towns were voluntarily evacuated. Cromwell then turned south and besieged the port of Wexford. Here also many of the garrison soldiers were slaughtered along with a number of innocent citizens.

During the winter Cromwell's men suffered severely from medical casualties, but by the summer of 1650 much of southern Ireland was in English hands. Cromwell then handed over the military government of Ireland to his son-in-law, Henry Ireton, and after a series of sieges most of the country was subdued. The policy of the English republican government toward the Irish did not differ much from that of its predecessors. Altogether about two-thirds of the land was confiscated and the native Irish told in effect to go to hell or Connaught. In fact wholesale transplantation could not be carried out and the Irish often stayed where they were as servants of the new English settlers. The English government aimed at introducing an enlightened system of justice and equality of trade. A large number of English soldiers settled in Ireland, and like the English before them were usually converted within two generations to the Irish way of life. Prohibitions of mixed marriages were ignored and conversions to Roman Catholicism recorded. But the Puritans were not prepared to consent to the open celebration of the Mass. The large-scale confiscations of Irish property, the proscription of the native religion, and the heavy punishment inflicted on Irish soldiers by Cromwell were all sources of much future resentment among the Irish people against every English government.

As soon as Cromwell returned to England from Ireland he was required to lead another army north against the Scottish Covenanters. King Charles II had at first been reluctant to agree to the Covenanters' demands and hoped either the Irish or the Royalist hero, the Marquis of Montrose, would help him to regain his father's throne. But Montrose was eventually defeated and hanged in Edinburgh, while Cromwell's victories in Ireland had dashed Royalist hopes there. Finally, the young king gave way and signed the Covenant (with tongue in cheek, as the Scots recognized) and a Scottish army was raised to do battle on his behalf.

Meanwhile the reluctant republican, General Fairfax, had resigned his post as commander-in-chief. The majority of the Council of State had wanted him to wage a preventive war against the Scots; for it was felt unwise to allow a Scottish force to harry the north of England for a fifth time. Fairfax, however, said that he would not engage in an unprovoked war against fellow Puritans. He retired to his home in Yorkshire to grow roses; and Cromwell was promptly appointed commander-in-chief in his place.

Cromwell's army crossed the Scottish border in July. It was evidently hoped that a show of force and a well-phrased appeal to the Scottish Covenanters not to take a malignant king to their bosoms might lead to a more or less peaceful Anglo-Scottish settlement. However, the Scots, who had beaten the English so often in recent years, were as certain as the English Puritans that God would fight upon their side. They emptied the south of supplies, withdrew to Edinburgh, and defied Cromwell to come at them. After six weeks of campaigning in which Cromwell was largely outmaneuvered and during which he lost many of his men through illness, the two armies confronted each other at Dunbar, thirty miles east of Edinburgh. Here Cromwell's inferior army surprised and defeated the Covenanters and took ten thousand prisoners. The Scots abandoned the Edinburgh line and withdrew to Stirling and the line of the river Forth. The humiliation of the leaders of the Kirk who had interfered with the operations redounded to the benefit of Charles II, who on January 1, 1651 was crowned king at Scone and appointed nominal commander-in-chief of the Scottish army.

The winter brought campaigning to a standstill and Cromwell himself was taken ill. When at length he recovered, he devoted himself to the problem of how to force the Scots out of Stirling. This he succeeded in doing by an outflanking movement, but when he threw the bulk of his army across the Forth, Charles II and the Scots made the obvious riposte and moved over the border into England. The Council of State in England was profoundly alarmed. Would there be a race for London with the Scottish army picking up Royalist sympathizers on the way south? But Cromwell and his fellow generals knew what they were doing. A son-in-law of Cromwell, Charles Fleetwood, had already raised a reserve army in the south. Cromwell overtook and surrounded the royal army in the city of Worcester, where it was overwhelmed by superior numbers. King Charles II, who had behaved courageously in the battle, managed to escape his enemies and finally reach safety in France. The battle of Worcester marked the end of the third civil war and strengthened the English republic, enabling it to face with confidence all its remaining enemies both at home and overseas.

Although Scotland, like Ireland, was still a thorn in the side of the Commonwealth, the English army of occupation, which for much of the rest of the Interregnum was under the command of a former Royalist, General George Monck, managed to maintain law and order and suppress insurrections; in due course the government of Scotland was subjected to that of the Commonwealth as a whole, but the Scots received equal trading rights and representation of a sort in Westminster. The Scotsman Gilbert Burnet, who later became an English bishop, was to write: "We always reckon those eight years of usurpation a time of great peace and prosperity."

During the first three years of the Interregnum the government of England itself had not been unsuccessful abroad or at home. Prince Rupert, who had proved himself as fine a sailor as he was a soldier, had first been chased away from the seas around Ireland and then from Portugal, where he carried out a commerce-destroying war against the English Commonwealth. The republican navy commanded the seas and made a deep impression upon the rulers of Europe who now began to recognize the new English government. Undeclared wars nevertheless existed against both France and Portugal, while an open war began in 1652 against the Dutch republic. This war was unpopular with some of the leading English Puritans, including Cromwell himself, who regarded it as a conflict with a sister Protestant state. It arose partly out of maritime squabbles and partly because of political differences.

At home the republican government did its duty according to its lights. It endeavored to provide for internal security and to overcome the trend toward unemployment when the armies were disbanded. But it made little progress in the direction of social or law reform, for which there had been great pressure, especially from the Levellers. An Act of Oblivion, which should have contributed to a general pacification, was clogged with exceptions. A feeling arose among the leaders of the army that the comparatively small group of politicians that exerted real influence over the remnants of the House of Commons elected in 1640 —popularly known as "the Rump"—was self-interested and not fundamentally concerned over reforms of any kind. In every way progress appeared to be slow—even in reaching a settlement about the Church —and this provoked criticism on all sides. In August 1652 the army openly began to show its dissatisfaction with the proceedings in parliament and expressed its wishes not only for reform in Church and state but also for a financial settlement to meet the claims of officers and men. The House of Commons agreed only to appoint a committee to draw up a bill for new elections to be held at some unspecified date in the future.

Oliver Cromwell himself, both as commander-in-chief and a leading member of parliament and the Council of State, worked, as he had done in 1647, for conciliation. But undoubtedly he was influenced by the general feeling that at least some of the principal civilians were self-interested, if not corrupt, and he was offended by the continuation of the Dutch war. Long and complicated negotiations were carried on between the leaders of the army and parliament. But the most that the civilians would accept was that fresh blood should be introduced into the House of Commons, and not that there should be a general election. In the end Cromwell lost patience, and in April 1653 he forcibly dissolved the Rump Parliament, which had been sitting for over twelve years. He followed this by breaking up the Council of State. Its president, John Bradshaw, then said to Cromwell: "Sir, we have heard what you did in the House this morning, but before many hours all England will hear it. But, sir, you are mistaken to think that parliament is dissolved, for no power under heaven can dissolve them but themselves. Therefore take notice of that."

Nevertheless the army's breaking of the House of Commons appears to have been not unpopular in the country. The charges circulated by the army that its members had been corrupt were widely believed. The refusal of the House to dissolve itself appeared to lend point to these accusations. But Cromwell and his friends had no clear idea about what they wanted to put in its place. They certainly did not care at this stage to arrange for a general election, nor did Cromwell himself want to substitute a military dictatorship, although his friend, Major-General John Lambert, favored a small administrative committee to act as an executive for the time being. Lambert was overruled, and instead a nominated assembly was established, consisting chiefly of tried Puritans who were chosen by the independent churches.

This Puritan assembly or "Parliament of Saints," which first met in the summer of 1653, consisted of 129 nominees from England, five from Scotland, and six from Ireland—the first "Commonwealth" parliament. The Nominated Assembly, although it contained a number of intelligent and dedicated men, was amateurish in its approach to government. Its extreme proposals—such as the immediate abolition of the court of chancery and the system of paying for the Church with tithes—were regarded, particularly by Lambert, who led the opposition to the radicals, as too revolutionary and impracticable. Behind the scenes Lambert drew up a new constitution, based to some extent upon the earlier "Heads of the Proposals," providing for the establishment of a Lord Protector as executive (as the Duke of Gloucester and the Duke of Somerset had been in former times), an elective parliament, and a Council of State which should share with the Protector the right to control the armed forces and initiate legislation when parliament was not sitting. A fixed revenue was laid down, while toleration was guaranteed to all Christians except Roman Catholics and Anglicans. This was a conservative political scheme, aimed at imposing a system of checks and balances to prevent, on the one hand, extreme radicalism and, on the other, military dictatorship. When by a small majority the Nominated Parliament was persuaded to surrender its powers to the commander-in-chief from whom it had originally received them, Cromwell agreed to give Lambert's scheme a trial, and in December 1653 Oliver Cromwell was proclaimed Lord Protector of England, Scotland, and Ireland under this new constitution, which was known as the "Instrument of Government."

✿ THE CROMWELLIAN PROTECTORATE

During its early months the first Protectorate government was successful in its work. Peace was concluded with the Dutch on the understanding that Charles I's grandson, the child William, Prince of Orange, should be permanently excluded from high office in Holland. Compensation was paid to English merchants who had suffered from Dutch naval depredations, and the Dutch navy agreed to salute the British flag in British waters. Treaties were also made with Sweden, Denmark, and Portugal, all of considerable benefit to British commerce. Union with Scotland was completed after a rising in the Highlands had been suppressed. Peace negotiations were opened with France, with whom an undeclared war had been in progress at sea. Plans were drawn up to attack the Spanish empire "beyond the line" in accordance with precedents established in the reign of Queen Elizabeth I. Cromwell sent his son-in-law, Charles Fleetwood, to Ireland as Lord Deputy to replace his other and abler son-in-law, Henry Ireton, who had died there in

1651. At home, proposals were worked out for law reform and the establishment of Puritan ecclesiastical system in England and Wales. Thus when the first Protectorate parliament met at Westminster in September 1654 Cromwell could claim that the new government had carried out a successful foreign policy and had promoted peace and liberty of conscience at home.

The new parliament was less interested in good government than in constitutional problems—in who should rule and not how to rule. It had been freely elected (except for thirty members each from Scotland and Ireland who were virtually nominees of the English army) and contained at least a hundred members of the former "Long Parliament." Since the "rump" of that parliament had been forcibly dissolved by Cromwell and the army, these men were unlikely to acquiesce supinely in the "Instrument of Government" promulgated by the army leaders. Sir Arthur Haselrig and the oligarchic republicans, who had been the rulers of the country after King Charles I's execution, soon won control over the House and aimed to tear the new constitution to shreds. Cromwell, however, insisted that the members must accept four constitutional "fundamentals" which, he thought, were essential: these were that the government must be carried on jointly by a single person and by parliament, that parliaments should not become perpetual, that liberty of conscience should be maintained, and that the control of the armed forces should be shared by the executive and parliament. After some bitter disputes, about 300 out of the 400-odd members signed a "recognition" of the Protectorate government and afterward there was a fairly even balance between a court party and a country party in the House. Almost the whole of the session was devoted to constitutional squabbles, and when Cromwell dissolved the House in January 1655 (the earliest date that he could) he accused the members of creating "divisions" and "discontents" and giving encouragement both to avenging Royalists and subversive Levellers.

Soon after the dissolution a Royalist insurrection broke out and the government had to face the problem of how to maintain internal security while engaging upon foreign war. It was decided, again apparently upon John Lambert's advice, to raise a horse militia for policing purposes in eleven groups of counties in England and Wales, each group to be under the command of trusted soldiers with the local rank of major-general, and to pay their cost out of a capital levy of 10 per cent upon the property of all known Royalists. This was intended as a temporary expedient to strengthen local defense and local government, but it savored of military despotism. Meanwhile two naval expeditions had been sent out: one, under the command of the brilliant Robert Blake, was instructed to enforce respect for the British flag in the Mediterranean and to round up French privateers; and the other, under an admiral and a general who quarreled with each other, was ordered to seize one of the Spanish islands in the West Indies as a punishment upon the Spaniards for not permitting free trade in their empire. Blake's expedition was a triumph and impressed the French with British naval might; the West Indian expedition was a disappointment to Cromwell since it only managed to lay hold of what was thought to be the barren island of Jamaica. It also inevitably brought about a full-scale war against Spain, and ultimately forced the Protectorate government into alliance with France.

The heavy cost of the Spanish war compelled the Protectoral government to ask a parliament for money, just as the Stuart kings had done before. Everything was tried to obtain a House of Commons friendly to the Protectorate. The major-generals of the Horse Militia exerted such influence as they could; borough charters were altered so as to provide safe seats for the government's supporters; and finally, by a doubtful interpretation of one of the clauses in the "Instrument of Government," the Council of State examined the electoral returns and excluded ninety-nine of the members who had been elected, while others withdrew from the House as a protest against this highhanded action. Of the 200 members who were left about half were officials, army officers, and Cromwell's own relations. No previous ruler of England, except perhaps Queen Mary I, had so effectively molded a House of Commons to suit his own interests. Yet in spite of all this, the new House showed itself to be resolutely independent—a fact of the highest significance in British history. Even Oliver Cromwell, backed by his army, could not—any more than Queen Elizabeth I—subdue the critical temper of the gentry and middle classes.

The Commons agreed to vote money for the continuation of the war against Spain, but at the same time they rejected a proposal to perpetuate the system of internal government through the major-generals. The civilian leaders in the new House now proposed that in order to restore stability and establish a recognizable form of constitutional government Cromwell himself should accept the title and obligations of a king. At the same time it was proposed that a new upper house should be created and the powers of parliament strengthened at the expense of those of the Council of State. Furthermore a modest fixed revenue was to be written into the new constitution, while parliament was to be given definite control over the election returns so that the executive branch could no longer shut out members whom it did not like.

Cromwell, who was always anxious to clothe his rule in some acceptable garb and not be considered "arbitrary," was at first attracted by the arguments of the lawyers and others in favor of this written form of Puritan monarchism, but the army leaders and the old republicans were violently opposed to it. To accept the scheme in its entirety—it was commonly known as the "Humble Petition and Advice"—would have meant that the Lord Protector would have had to abandon all his own old friends and followers—the generals who had fought by his side in the civil wars, the veteran soldiers of the New Model Army, and the Independent preachers and their congregations, which had trusted him. Ultimately, and with some reluctance, he therefore refused the crown, but agreed to the rest of the new constitution.

So it was that in January 1658 the House of Commons met again with the previously excluded members in their places and many of the Lord Protector's friends and officials wafted away to form the nucleus of the new upper house. This grouping completely transformed the character of the Commons, who were now extremely critical of Cromwell, his government, and the two-chamber constitution; indeed their aim was to overthrow the Lord Protector and reconstitute an oligarchic republic. Vainly Cromwell appealed to the members in the name of patriotism and Christianity to give full backing to the war against the Spanish monarchy, which he saw as the instrument of the pope and the Counter Reformation, and to join in his schemes for a European Protestant union. "If God shall not unite your hearts and bless you," he concluded, "it will be said of this poor nation *Actum est de Anglia*—England is finished." Sir Arthur Haselrig and his friends retorted defiantly: "Princes are mortal, but the Commonwealth lives forever."

Both inside and outside the House of Commons a vehement agitation began against the government, while the Royalists rejoiced. Cromwell believed that he was confronted with a threat of imminent anarchy and invasion, so he peremptorily dissolved his second parliament. Thus the latest Puritan constitutional experiment collapsed. Cromwell and his Council of State continued to govern as best they could until September 1658, when the Lord Protector, prematurely old, died at the age of fifty-nine.

It is usually said that Cromwell achieved nothing constructive by his government of Britain; but at least his army and navy made the name of England respected throughout the world of his time. "I am for old Noll," wrote the poet Andrew Marvell a decade later, "He made England great and its enemies tremble." English soldiers campaigned in the Spanish Netherlands, fighting alongside the French, and as the price for their aid King Louis XIV handed over to the English Commonwealth the valuable port of Dunkirk, thus erasing the memory of the loss of Calais by Queen Mary I. By dint of personal efforts Cromwell laid the basis for a flourishing English colony in Jamaica, the first colony ever to be established by direct government action. Supported by the republican navy under Blake and perhaps by the Navigation Act policy (an act of 1651 had given monopoly rights to English ships carrying imported goods), English commerce and shipping expanded. At home too there was a high degree of economic prosperity during the Protectorate. Above all, Cromwell fulfilled the promises he had made to establish wide liberty of conscience. He had prevented a Presbyterian system from being fastened upon England, just as he had helped to destroy the bishops, and the tradition of independent churches and congregations was to help nurture English liberties in the eighteenth and nineteenth centuries. The Jews were allowed to come back to England officially for the first time since they were expelled by King Edward I. Cromwell interfered personally to protect the lives of religious extremists—men like the Quaker James Naylor and the Unitarian John Biddle—when they were menaced by the intolerance of those Puritan fanatics who regarded themselves as orthodox Christians. Even the holding of the old Anglican services and Roman Catholic Masses in private houses was generally accepted by the authorities in England during the last days of the Protectorate. Cromwell was able to claim, as it were, for his own epitaph that he had not been unsuccessful in preventing any one sect from tyrannizing over another. Therein lay his real contribution to the liberty of the individual.

Whatever may be thought of the Protectorate in constitutional terms, therefore, its foreign policy had been notable, it had brought a period of peace and prosperity at home, and it had offered more religious liberty than the nation had known before. England, Scotland, and Ireland had been united under one Commonwealth government. Moreover, never could any anointed king defy parliament or successfully impose autocracy. Such was the legacy of the Interregnum—no mean achievement. Much but not all was lost when, after Oliver Cromwell's death, anarchy supervened and King Charles II was restored to the throne of his father.

XLVIII

The Restoration of Charles II

Oliver Cromwell had held the Protectorate government together by his own resolution and popularity with the Puritan army. His son Richard, whom he named as his successor under the powers conferred upon him by the "Humble Petition and Advice," was not a soldier, had not served in the civil wars, and had left his political education until it was too late. The result was that he had enemies in the army and among the old republicans and even the extreme sectarians, for he was not a Puritan like his father: indeed he was a simple country gentleman rocketed upward by Oliver's fantastic success. The leaders of the army, headed by Richard's own brother-in-law, Charles Fleetwood, were anxious to regularize its position as a state within a state. Hence they wanted the post of commander-in-chief to be divorced from that of Lord Protector and required that no officer should be cashiered except by court-martial. The civilian republicans, on the other hand, were quite determined, now that Oliver was dead, to throw off the tutelage of the army which had twice prevented the establishment of a "pure Commonwealth." It was the balancing of these groups against each other that alone enabled the Cromwellian Protectorate to continue for eight months under Lord Richard.

When a new parliament met in January 1659 it was clear that a majority of the members supported the continuation of the Protectorate, but all the more active members were republicans, some of them oligarchs like Haselrig, a few with democratic sympathies. In this parliament attacks were launched against the army, especially against the former major-generals of the horse militia, while deliberate attempts were made to work up an agitation against the government outside parliament by playing on the sympathies of the junior officers and the extreme sectarians. But the leaders of the army defied alike the Protector, the parliament, and the mutterings of their own rank and file. When a resolution was passed in parliament insisting that no general meetings of the army should be held without special permission while parliament was sitting, Fleetwood replied by demanding the dissolution of parliament itself. Finding himself deserted by those over whom he was the commander-in-chief, Richard was compelled to give way and in April dissolved the two houses. This entailed the ending of the Protectorate; but the army leaders suddenly found that they had been left without any government to put in its place. Thus in May the Rump of the old Long Parliament was recalled to Westminster; and the Commonwealth, much as it had existed after the execution of King Charles I, was restored. The old Rumpers were no more favorable to the pretensions of the army than the Protectorate parliament had been: in fact, though they appointed Charles Fleetwood to be commander-in-chief, they were careful to retain in their own hands the right to nominate, through commissioners, all the officers both in the army and the navy. Thereby they hoped to put an end for all time to military pressure upon government. Leading Cromwellians were then cashiered and the new Council of State was so constituted that the military party was in a permanent minority.

The army leaders were not yet beaten. John Lambert, the able Yorkshireman who had once been Oliver Cromwell's right-hand man but had been retired when he opposed the "Humble Petition and Advice," had re-emerged from the shadows and played a more important part than the weak and vain Fleetwood. He rallied the rank and file of the army in England against the leaders of the Rump by demanding that all their long outstanding grievances should be met. But what strengthened the hand of the army was the revival of royalism. Encouraged by the differences among their enemies, a Royalist group of conspirators planned a rebellion, in which it enlisted the sympathies of many Presbyterians. The revolt broke out prematurely in Cheshire under a Presbyterian Royalist named Sir George Booth. Lambert crushed Booth and then took advantage of his victory to menace the Rump. In October his soldiers surrounded Westminster and obliged the Rump to disperse.

John Lambert proved to be no Oliver Cromwell. He commanded no loyalties and stood for no principles. The military showed themselves incapable of governing and were confused by the ambitions of their own generals. In Scotland the ex-Royalist, General George Monck, who had been faithful to Oliver Cromwell and to his son Richard, now used his power against Lambert. He refused to let his soldiers sign petitions sent across the border and announced that it was his policy always to be loyal to the civil power. Meanwhile a republican rising took place in London and Sir Arthur Haselrig won Portsmouth over to his side. Once again the Rump reassembled and appointed Monck commander-in-chief. Monck purged his army and concentrated it on the Scottish frontier. Then slowly he marched his men into England. In York he was welcomed by the former commander-in-chief, Lord Fairfax, who had become a convinced Royalist. As Monck's men wended their way south,

Lambert's soldiers vanished like a puff of smoke, while addresses were received by Monck from different parts of the country demanding that he should call a "free parliament." The city of London announced that it would pay no more taxes until the vacancies in the existing Rump Parliament had been filled. Although Monck in a sense obeyed the orders of the Rump to enforce obedience on the city, he was impressed by the wave of feeling in London and elsewhere in favor of the restoration of the Stuarts. He told the Rump to admit its secluded members—in other words the Royalists and Presbyterians—and said that it must not sit beyond May, so that a free parliament might be elected in its place. A "convention," consisting of two houses, duly met at the end of April 1660.

Ever since his escape from the field of Worcester, King Charles II, in exile in various parts of Europe, had plotted to regain his throne, but he had no money and few friends and spent much of his time in frivolity. The Anglo-French alliance had dashed his first hopes and he had then secretly gone to the Spanish border to try to persuade the Madrid government to place troops and supplies at his disposal. The Spaniards had said that they could not invade England unless a port were given to them. Royalist conspirators assisted, curiously enough, by the democratic Levellers, had tried hard to fulfill this condition. In fact the king's older and wiser advisers, headed by his Lord Chancellor, Sir Edward Hyde, later the first Earl of Clarendon, hoped that the king would be restored to his own people without foreign assistance. When they learned of Monck's quarrel with Lambert they brought pressure to bear on Monck through his brother, who was an Anglican clergyman, and his wife, a former laundress of Presbyterian persuasions. The king agreed to publish a declaration from Breda in Holland in which he promised that he would leave to a future parliament many important decisions of policy and that he would grant "a liberty to tender consciences." This declaration was read and approved in the convention. The Presbyterians hoped that they would be comprehended within the restored Church of England, and since they always had monarchist sympathies, they welcomed this declaration. The Parliamentarians saw that the new king was committed to constitutional rule. Ordinary men and women thought that the traditional government and the rule of law were preferable to the anarchy that had prevailed during the past two years. Thus the Stuart restoration was carried through without bloodshed and virtually without resistance. In May 1660 King Charles II landed peaceably at Dover from The Hague and was welcomed by General Monck and presented by the local mayor with a copy of the Bible. Maypoles were set up, toasts of loyalty were drunk, and the Royalists polished their

silver and hastened to press their claims at court. But the shadow of
Cromwell's army and the Puritans stretched far ahead into the new
reign.

Six main problems confronted the Restoration government: the future
of the army, religion, and finance, the settlement of landed property,
the return to the monarchical constitution, and the punishment of offenders against the Stuart kings. The first question was whether King
Charles II should retain a standing army to uphold his position. In
spite of the loyalty of the commander-in-chief, General Monck, now
created Lord Albemarle, it was obviously extremely dangerous to leave
in being a force so long dedicated to Cromwellian or republican ideas;
it seemed, on the whole, safer to disband the existing army as quickly
as possible and not to try to raise another in its place. In fact, one or
two regiments, including Monck's old regiment, to be known as the
Coldstream Guards, were retained. But the rest of the army was paid
off by a special parliamentary vote and thereafter presented little trouble.

Religion was altogether a different question. In his declaration at
Breda the king had promised liberty of conscience, and the Presbyterians, who had played an important part in his restoration, had high
hopes. The king and his leading minister, Clarendon, were not intolerant,
and toyed with the notion of a modified episcopal system which should
enable the Presbyterians to be comprehended within the Church of England. On the other hand, most of the principal Anglicans were Laudians,
fully determined to revive the ideals of their martyred chief. A conference held at the Savoy Palace in London, in which the Presbyterians
took part, broke down, and the first parliament of the new reign showed
itself to be vehemently anti-Puritan, far more so than the court. A Cor-
poration Act was passed excluding from the municipalities all who refused to take the sacrament according to the rites of the Church of
England. In 1662 a new Act of Uniformity required a revised common
prayer book again to be used in all the churches. Those clergy who failed
to comply were excluded from their livings. It has been estimated that
as many as one-fifth were affected. Thus was nonconformity created
in England.

A series of subsequent acts of parliament imposed restrictions upon
the services of the nonconformists: for example, the Five Mile Act of
1665 forbade excluded ministers to live in or visit any corporate town
or other place where they had previously officiated. Nonconformists
were shut out from the universities and deprived of other civil rights.
These acts were known collectively as "the Clarendon Code," although
in fact the Earl of Clarendon was not enthusiastic about them. He was,
however, much concerned to prevent disorder and commotions from

upsetting the new government. In fact, apart from one or two extreme sects, such as the Fifth Monarchy Men (they believed in the imminent return of Christ to earth), who staged a rising in the city of London, the nonconformists accepted their fate with resignation. In time they became considerably dispirited under the impact of persecution. Many clergy hastened to acquiesce in the demands of the Church so as to preserve their own livelihoods. Most of the old fervor was damped, but enough of the devotion of the old sectarians, especially among the Baptists and Quakers, remained among humble people for nonconformity to be permanently absorbed into the British way of life both at home and in America.

Finance was a tricky question. The new parliament voted the king sufficient money to pay off the army and settle his own debts, but the debts of the Commonwealth government, amounting to over £2,000,000, were not paid. The king finally gave up his old prerogative rights, such as the earnings of the Court of Wards and knighthood fines, in return for the yield from the new excise tax, which had first been imposed during the Interregnum and was now kept as a permanent source of revenue. He also enjoyed customs duties, but not the "assessment" or land tax, which had been a regular feature of Cromwellian finances, an efficient, and, on the whole, fair tax, but very unpopular among the gentry who served in the House of Commons. The consequence was that though the king was promised a revenue of £1,200,000 a year (Cromwell had nearly twice as much as this), he never in fact received that amount. This compelled him to adopt a number of expedients to make both ends meet, including the sale of the port of Dunkirk to France, though it had been the trophy of English fighting men. It also, in the long run, drove him to accept subsidies from the king of France.

The property settlement did not contribute to the king's popularity either. The lands belonging to the Crown and the Church were restored. So too were properties directly confiscated by the Commonwealth governments for acts of treason against them. But where lands had been sold so that fines could be paid—and of course such lands had often changed hands several times—no legal enactment was, or perhaps could be, made to secure compensation for Royalists who had suffered by the sales, and it was left to individuals to regain their possessions by litigation as best they could. On the whole, modern research suggests that there was no revolutionary change in the ownership of land as a result of the civil wars. In many cases ingenious arrangements had been made whereby Royalists still managed to retain effective control over their own properties or to buy them back through nominees soon after they had been sold. We know that some Cromwellian soldiers and administrators did improve their position as a result of speculations in land during the Interregnum, but many, such as General John Lambert and Martin Noell, who was a leading Cromwellian merchant, lost practically all that they had acquired.

As to the constitution, it was accepted that all the acts to which king Charles I had given his assent, even under pressure, retained their validity. It was agreed that the position as it existed in 1641 was to be restored; the old prerogative courts, largely built up by the Tudors, remained abolished; some acts passed during the Interregnum—such as the Navigation Act of 1651—were re-enacted in a new form. No serious attempt was made to retain the constituency reforms or the union with Scotland. An Act of Union had to wait for fifty years, while parliament stayed virtually unreformed until 1832.

On the whole, the punishment of offenders against the Stuart monarchy was mild. The king had placed the onus of punishment upon parliament. A number of individuals were excluded from an act of indemnity, chiefly those who had taken part in the trial of King Charles I. Altogether only thirteen men, including Major-General Thomas Harrison, who gloried in his part, and Sir Henry Vane, who had not in fact served in the trial, were put to death. A number of others, such as Major-General John Lambert, were imprisoned or exiled. The blind poet, John Milton, who had constituted himself the outspoken apologist for the republic, escaped all punishment through the intervention of his friends.

The comparative clemency shown toward leading republicans, the disbandment of the Cromwellian army, the nature of the land settlement, and the virtual acquiescence of the new government in the establishment of religious nonconformity (the treatment of nonconformists varied from place to place according to the feelings of the local magistrates) all contributed to the relative placidity of the early years of King Charles II's reign. There were a number of isolated plots or risings, but they were easily suppressed. The king recognized his dependence upon a parliament elected in 1661, originally known as the Cavalier Parliament, which was filled with enthusiastic Royalists and other gentry anxious to climb upon the bandwagon. The ardors and excitements of the civil wars had passed away for the time being, and most people were willing to see if the restoration of the monarchy would give them prosperity and peace.

The king himself was not a fanatic. A dark man with a large nose, over six feet tall, he had been a good-looking boy, but had grown into a rather ugly, if strangely attractive, man. He was a dilettante, inclined to be lazy but capable of bursts of energy. Good-looking women and entertaining rogues gave him pleasure, but scarcely influenced his policies. If he had any principles, they were to maintain his throne and his dynasty intact. He refused to sacrifice either his brother, James, when he became unpopular because of his conversion to the Roman Catholic faith, or his Portuguese queen, whom he married in 1662, when it was suggested that he should divorce her since she bore him no children. Thus he could be obstinate; but, like other Stuart monarchs, he would sacrifice his servants ruthlessly—the Marquis of Montrose and the Earl of Clarendon were cases in point—and he allowed judicial murders to be carried out at the time of the so-called Popish Plot, though he obviously did not believe in it. Puritan historians have tended to blame him for faults which many other kings had: his real weaknesses have often been overlooked. On the other hand, his congenital idleness and determination not "to go on his travels again" contributed to the evolution of British constitutional monarchy.

During the early years of the reign King Charles II depended upon Clarendon, who was his Lord Chancellor, and another of the old guard, Thomas Wriothesley, Earl of Southampton, who was Lord Treasurer. Unlike Oliver Cromwell, who had a brilliant Secretary of State in John Thurloe, Charles II had two secretaries who divided the spheres of foreign affairs between them. Clarendon received most of the blame for an unsuccessful foreign policy. The sale of Dunkirk was placed at his door (his house in Piccadilly was nicknamed Dunkirk House) and so was the war against the Dutch republic which broke out in 1664. This was due to rivalries over seas, commerce, and colonies. It is said to have been "the clearest case in history of a purely commercial war." The English navy had been allowed to decline since Cromwell's days; the French were the allies of the Dutch; the Dutch warships proved more maneuverable, while in 1665 the English government was distracted by a great plague, of which nearly 70,000 people died, and in 1666 by a great fire which destroyed much of London. Moreover the Cavalier Parliament soon showed itself to be suspicious of the administration, which was poorly represented in the House of Commons. It demanded that money voted by it should be specifically appropriated to use in the war, and later the administration was accused of malversation by a committee of accounts. After the Dutch had inflicted humiliating defeats on the English navy both at Chatham and on the Thames, a treaty of peace was signed at Breda in July 1667 which, on the whole, was of small benefit to England.

The lack of success in the Dutch war brought about the fall of the Earl of Clarendon, who had many enemies, notably one of the Secretaries of State, Lord Arlington. The king now found Clarendon tiresome, and he was made a scapegoat. An attempt to impeach him resulted in his leaving the country and spending his last years completing a famous *History of the Rebellion,* a work of art as well as of history. Clarendon's fall was a turning point in the reign. Henceforward Charles II governed through a number of ministers, playing off their rivalries against each other, while he himself presided over the Privy Council. He also came to be the client of the French monarch, partly because of his need of money, but even more because he was attracted by the successful autocracy of Louis XIV of France, the "Roi Soleil." But first he showed his independence by permitting a Triple Alliance to be concluded with the Dutch republic and the king of Sweden, aimed at preventing French aggrandizement in the Spanish Netherlands. Such expansion would have threatened English as well as Dutch security.

The French king put the blame for this alliance against him on the Dutch, and was determined to disrupt it and obtain his revenge. He used his sister-in-law, who was also King Charles II's sister, Henriette, an intriguing and much-loved woman (except by her husband), as an intermediary. In June 1670 a treaty was signed at Dover whereby King Charles II agreed not only to attack Holland in alliance with France but also to declare himself a Roman Catholic when the affairs of his kingdom permitted him to do so. In return he was to receive a French subsidy and, if necessary, French troops to sustain the conversion. There is little doubt that King Charles II had small intention of carrying through this plan, which involved deceiving even some of his own ministers, who signed with France a camouflage treaty from which the Catholicizing clauses were omitted. This episode cast a dark cloud over the reign. Informed men, such as the poet Andrew Marvell, gradually came to suspect the existence of a secret popish plot engineered by the king and some of his pro-Catholic clique against his largely Protestant subjects. No historian, not even one who admires King Charles II, has yet produced a convincing defense of the policy of the secret treaty of Dover. It was a blow to public confidence from which the Stuart dynasty never fully recovered.

XLIX

Charles II and the Rise of Political Parties

The Cavalier Parliament that had been elected in 1661 continued for eighteen years, although during that time it was actually sitting for only sixty months. To begin with, it had contained a large number of Royalists, whose devotion to the service of their sovereign was only mitigated by their rabid Anglicanism, but inevitably under the impact of time and events many changes had taken place in its character and composition. It lasted as long as it did because a Triennial Act passed in 1664 stipulated only that the king must call a new parliament within three years of the dissolution of the previous one, and made no provision either for preventing long prorogations or for machinery to enforce the regular summoning of new parliaments. Nevertheless this parliament maintained its powers and privileges. In effect, it enforced control over its own composition. The franchise remained as it had been before the Interregnum, the forty-shilling freeholder having a vote in the county, and a varying and usually restricted franchise existing in the different boroughs. The king's right to create new parliamentary boroughs, a right frequently exercised during the Tudor period, was successfully challenged and the total number of representatives in England and Wales remained unchanged between 1677 and 1832. Although the condition imposed by the Triennial Act of 1641 that parliaments should meet every three years was abandoned, in fact none of the intervals between the parliaments that met during King Charles II's reign were longer than a few months. Broadly, it may be said that during this reign the position of parliament in relation to the king, and of the House of Commons in particular, was stronger than it had ever been before in British history. For the king in parliament had been substituted (in the words of Miss Betty Kemp) "a trinity of King, Lords, and Commons."

By the time this long parliament was dissolved the character and attitude of the Commons had startlingly changed; out of over 500 members, 200 new ones had been introduced at by-elections. Its early royalist fervor had been cooled by events, and distrust of the administration grew apace. The policies of the king's government after the dismissal of the Earl of Clarendon in relation to finance, foreign policy, and religion had all provoked violent criticism.

At the beginning of 1672 the king had got into financial difficulties, partly because his promised revenue had failed to materialize, partly because of the cost of the first Dutch war, and partly through personal extravagance. It was therefore decided to withhold interest on a debt of £1,000,000 owed to London bankers. This step undermined public confidence, damaged business, and brought about bankruptcies. Such was the prelude to King Charles II's second war against the Dutch, which began in March in fulfillment of the treaty of Dover.

Furthermore, in order to keep the promises he had given to King Louis XIV of France, Charles II now published a Declaration of Indulgence (a similar but abortive declaration had been published in 1662) whereby as Supreme Governor of the Church he suspended all the existing penal laws against both nonconformists and Roman Catholics. This was a genuine relief to nonconformists who had suffered from sporadic persecutions, but the declaration revived latent anti-Catholic feelings and incited the Anglican House of Commons to demonstrate its independence of the Crown. It demanded and obtained the passing of a Test Act which prohibited anyone who failed to take the sacrament according to the accepted usages of the Church of England or who refused to declare himself against the doctrine of transubstantiation from holding either civil or military office. In return for the king's assent to this act the House voted a sum of £1,200,000 to be raised by taxes toward the cost of the new war.

Once again the war against the brave and stubborn Dutch people, led by King Charles II's nephew, Prince William of Orange, was a failure. The naval battle of Texel fought in August 1673 saved the Dutch from an English invasion from the sea and from the blockading of their ports. By the next year England had withdrawn from the war and left the French to carry on alone.

The Test Act of 1673 had resulted in important changes in the king's ministry. His brother James, Duke of York, who had become a Roman Catholic, had been obliged to give up his post as Lord High Admiral, in which he had served with some distinction, and other ministers who had been concerned with the secret treaty of Dover also retired. Sir Thomas Osborne, best known as Lord Danby, a Yorkshire Royalist, became Treasurer and tried to rally the Anglicans behind Church and king, but the Duke of York's marriage to an Italian Roman Catholic princess was not popular (he had formerly been married to a daughter of the Earl of Clarendon) and the heavy expenditure of men and money in the fruitless Dutch war had lowered the prestige of the government.

Danby's task was rendered doubly hard because the king was not loyal to him. He carried on a personal foreign policy. In 1675 he came to an agreement with King Louis XIV that if parliament pressed for a war against France, he would dissolve it in return for a fresh subsidy. This was the first of three secret agreements; for King Louis XIV thought it worth while to pay modest sums of money for English neutrality while he was engaged in his critical struggle against the Dutch. A "country party," opposed to all Catholicizing and Francophile measures, was being created: active moves were demanded against the aggressive French king, who was beginning to threaten the whole of Europe. While Charles II refused to give up his prerogative rights of making peace and war, in 1677 he permitted his niece Mary, daughter of the Duke of York by his first wife, to be married to Prince William of Orange. However much he might depreciate it, this was a diplomatic blow to Louis XIV, who promptly stopped the trickle of subsidies into Charles II's pockets. Parliament, however, voted the king money and ships to make war upon the French, and, when no positive steps were taken to this end, ministers were attacked and accusations brought that a conspiracy was being engineered in Whitehall to set up a Roman Catholic despotism with French assistance.

King Charles II refused to submit to such pressure. The French king, for his part, at first tried to bribe the parliamentary opposition to the Crown so as to neutralize England with a threat of civil war, but then he agreed to renew the subsidies to King Charles II in return for his benevolent neutrality. Eventually in August 1678 a treaty was concluded at Nimweguen between the French and the Dutch, which gave the French some substantial benefits and left England revealed as a cipher in international affairs.

The growing distrust of the king and his Roman Catholic brother and the general fear of French influences exemplified both in parliament and outside paved the way in 1678 for an extraordinary outburst of political agitation, which is known in history as "the Popish Plot." The story, invented by a defrocked naval chaplain named Dr. Titus Oates, was that a Jesuit plot had been completed to assassinate Charles II, massacre Protestants, and set up a Roman Catholic government with the Duke of York as king. The death, apparently by murder, of the London magistrate before whom these wild accusations had been laid seemed to lend substance to the story. So did the seizure of papers belonging to a former secretary of the Duke of York. The king was too indolent or cowardly to intervene to stop the blaze. The story was believed by the Privy Council and by parliament when it resumed its sittings in the autumn of 1678. Anthony Ashley Cooper, the first Earl of Shaftesbury, who had at one time served Oliver Cromwell and at another been a minister of King Charles II, constituted himself the leader of the opposition in parliament, which, shocked and disillusioned, fed eagerly on the plausible lies of Titus Oates. A number of Roman Catholics, including the queen's doctor, were impeached for treason and some of them were put to death. Danby was thrust into the Tower of London; the English ambassador in Paris revealed the king's dealings with Louis XIV, in which Danby had reluctantly acquiesced; the Duke of York was compelled to leave the country; and even the king's Portuguese queen was threatened with prosecution. To save them and to gain a respite, King Charles II was obliged first to prorogue and then to dissolve the very parliament which had once delighted him by its exuberant loyalty.

Thus after nineteen years the spirit of the Parliamentarians of King Charles I's reign rose like a phoenix from the ashes. Old Cromwellians and republicans swaggered in the London taverns. In spite of a strict licensing law, subversive pamphlets were published. Shaftesbury created a "Whig" party dedicated to excluding the Roman Catholic Duke of York from succession to the throne. A new civil war seemed more than likely.

The king kept his head. He allowed the national hysteria to burn itself out. Meanwhile he washed his hands of the Duke of York and the Earl of Danby, but saved them both from extreme punishment for their supposed offenses. At the same time he neutralized and divided the opposition by inviting Shaftesbury and others to sit on an enlarged council to transact all the nation's business. In fact, however, the king had no intention of following the advice of his new councilors and preferred to trust men like Lawrence Hyde, Earl of Rochester, and the Duke of York's brother-in-law, whom he made first Lord of the Treasury, and Robert Spencer, Earl of Sunderland—recommended to him by the most permanent of his mistresses, the French Duchess of Portsmouth—whom he appointed Secretary of State. Sunderland is said to have acted as a mediator between the king and the leaders of the Country Party. The aim was to let the storm of excitement die down and then "dish the Whigs."

Thus gradually during the last seven years of King Charles II's reign the Whig frenzy gave way to the Royalist or "Tory" revenge. "This period," writes Sir Keith Feiling, "created the very names of Whig and Tory, linked the development of party strife to the older principles of Civil War, and in a fierce orgy of debate, pamphleteering, and propaganda, fixed the traditional lines of divisions for another generation." The principal object of the Whigs was to exclude James, Duke of York, from the succession by statute. To prevent this, the king dissolved one after another three parliaments which were elected between 1679 and 1681. In the first of these parliaments an Exclusion Bill was carried in the Commons before the king ordered its prorogation. This first parliament was memorable for the fact that it passed a Habeas Corpus Amendment Act which put an end to certain anomalies that had prevented a prisoner from being brought before the courts upon the issue of a writ. The next House of Commons also passed an Exclusion Bill, but it was thrown out by the House of Lords. The third parliament met in Oxford in order that it might be freed from the pressure of the London mob; but the Whigs came to the university city in armed bands and once again the king was prompt in dissolving it.

The Whig leaders, thwarted of their Exclusion Bill by the stubbornness of the king and the obstruction of the Lords, turned from constitutional procedures to conspiratorial action. They had found a Protestant hero in the king's illegitimate son, James Scott, Duke of Monmouth, who had made a name for himself by suppressing a rebellion in Scotland. It was claimed that the king had actually been married to Monmouth's mother during his early exile (she was long since dead, but proofs of the marriage were said to exist in a black box) and that therefore he was the rightful heir to the throne. Monmouth, a weakling, allowed himself to be pushed forward by Shaftesbury as a possible successor to the throne and even went on royal tours or "progresses" in different parts of the country. John Dryden, the poet laureate, ridiculed both Monmouth and Shaftesbury in his brilliant satirical poem *Absalom and Achitophel;* the court party recovered its nerves; the Duke of York was allowed to return from exile; various borough charters were remodeled in the Tory interest and Tory sheriffs were installed in office in the city of London. All this offset the influence of the Whig leaders who had been organizing Green Ribbon clubs and "brisk boys" to press the Duke of York's exclusion and to advocate Monmouth's claims. After a life of intensive intrigue, the Earl of Shaftesbury, who had for a time been imprisoned, fled abroad and died in Holland. The Duke of Monmouth then hastened to make his peace with his father.

Other Whig leaders were now accused of conspiring to murder the king in the so-called Rye House Plot. It was said that a number of old Cromwellians had planned the assassination from this house, which lay near Charles II's route to and from the Newmarket horse races. There was little substance to the story (any more than there had been in Oates's tales of the Popish Plot) and no real evidence that such austere Whigs as William, Lord Russell, or Algernon Sydney were implicated, but they were tried and put to death. Thus the Tories achieved their revenge and the Whigs gained their earliest martyrs.

The government of Rochester and Sunderland, assisted by the Marquis of Halifax—known to history as "the great Trimmer," he had done much to prevent the Duke of York's exclusion—was able to carry on without parliament, especially since King Louis XIV, now engaged in fresh acts of aggression, still thought it worth his while to neutralize England by furnishing her king with subsidies. More important was an expansion of the customs revenue. The judicial bench was subservient, juries were hand-picked, and a small standing army was raised. Thus the opposition to the court was menaced and crushed; James, Duke of York, came back to the king's side and the Earl of Danby was released from prison. Prince William of Orange, who had for years constituted himself the focus of resistance in Europe to the ambitions of King Louis XIV of France, had congratulated King Charles II and the future King James II on their escapes from Whig assassination and said that he upheld the cause of legitimacy. After all, James was his father-in-law. By the truce of Ratisbon, concluded between King Louis XIV and the Habsburg emperor in 1684, the French king appeared to have reached the summit of his power, and the rays of his "sunshine" seemed to warm and embrace the once troubled but now triumphant Stuarts. King Charles II was happily ruling without a parliament, much as his father had done half a century earlier; he was the comfortable pensionary of France; and all his enemies were dead or in exile. Might not he at last be able to establish a form of personal government in London similar to that which prevailed in Versailles? The "constitutional monarch" of the earlier part of the reign might be transmuted into a benevolent autocrat. The intrigues of that time were so complicated and so mysterious that no one knew the answer. But just at the time that this question was being asked King Charles II died unexpectedly of a stroke and the government passed into the hands of his less-flexible and fanatical brother. Before the story of his overthrow is related, an attempt will be made in the next four chapters to paint a picture of Britain in the seventeenth century.

L

Economic and Social Life in Seventeenth Century England

During the first half of the seventeenth century there were few notable changes in the character of social and economic life in England. The impulses, especially toward commercial expansion, that had first been strongly experienced in the Elizabethan age continued. A high level of prosperity seems to have prevailed until about 1620, when the Thirty Years' War in Europe disrupted trade. Economic well-being returned again during the 1630's, partly because the country remained at peace. A depression coincided with the first civil war and was aggravated by it. Oliver Cromwell's firm rule and prestige abroad contributed to economic revival in the middle fifties, but an extremely severe world depression occurred in 1659. Confidence was regained after King Charles II was restored to the throne.

How far government policies influenced the economic life of the country is hard to gauge. It may be supposed that in what was primarily an agricultural country the weather, bringing good or bad harvests, was still a principal factor in creating booms or slumps, while foreign wars, such as the war in Germany in the twenties and the Dutch wars in 1652, 1664, and 1672, could be extremely damaging to commerce. Two particular actions of the Crown had an adverse effect on commerce and industry. The first was King James I's decision to grant to Sir William Cockayne and his associates a patent to dye and finish woolen cloth before its exportation. This was buttressed by a prohibition in 1614 of the export of undyed and undressed cloth. Cockayne had promised King James I £300,000 a year for the privilege. It was a severe blow to the Merchant Adventurers' Company and to other trading organizations that had been concerned with selling undressed cloth abroad. Cockayne's company proved unsuccessful; the cloth was poorly dyed; and in any case it was not what foreign customers wanted from England. The Dutch, who had been valuable customers, actually prohibited the importation of dyed cloth and set up their own cloth manufacturing industry. The English cloth industry took years to recover. Similarly King Charles I, also because of his pressing financial needs, aimed to break the monopoly of the East India Company, which had built up an excellent business in the Far East, by patronizing a rival company known as the Courteen syndicate in which the king himself held shares, and by interfering with the business of the older company. The Courteen association damaged the reputation of British traders in India and nearly ruined commerce with the Far East.

The question of monopolies and patents was a difficult one which complicated English economic affairs in the first half of the seventeenth century. Protests had been made against monopolies in Queen Elizabeth I's last parliaments. King James I granted to courtiers and others the right to issue licenses, for example, to ale houses; he also legitimately granted patents for new industrial processes; and finally exclusive rights were conferred by him on a number of trading companies. It was not easy to draw the line between a justifiable patent and an unfair monopoly; moreover it was generally recognized by all governments that companies engaged in foreign trade which established and paid ambassadors (who in later times would have been called commercial attachés), set up forts to protect their trading posts, and provided armed merchant ships for protection against privateers or pirates were entitled to exclusive privileges. When a Statute of Monopolies was passed in 1624, such companies were exempted from it. Although monopolies were, on the whole, more often attacked than defended by radical thinkers, the experiment made during the Interregnum of virtually throwing open all overseas trade did not work. Oliver Cromwell himself clearly recognized the importance of distinguishing between a monopoly and a patent.

Unquestionably the growth of commerce was a feature of economic life in the later seventeenth century. It is said that 3,000 merchants used the Royal Exchange in the reign of King Charles II, while under Cromwell Londoners like Martin Noell, Maurice Thompson, Thomas Vyner, and others had a real impact on economic policy. London continued to grow in size and wealth out of all proportion to other towns. It is generally accepted that the population of England and Wales had reached a figure of over five million by 1688 and that one-tenth of it was concentrated in greater London. Even the terrible fire of London in September 1666, which covered nearly 450 acres and in which over 13,000 houses were destroyed, caused only a temporary setback. In fact, the rebuilding of the city improved its amenities, even though Sir Christopher Wren, the chief architect, was not given a free hand and his proposals for a new St. Paul's Cathedral were not fully accepted. It was laid down that in future houses should be built of brick or stone instead of wood, while many of the more unsanitary hovels of the past were cleared away. Thus some of the features of the older London that had contributed to the rapid spread of the plague in 1665 were removed. In addition to the new St. Paul's, which was not completed until the reign of Queen Anne, a new Guildhall and Royal Exchange and many lovely new churches and fine halls were built. London came to be regarded as one of the most beautiful as well as richest and largest cities in the world. During the latter part of the reign of King Charles II its coffee houses and taverns became the meeting places of an active, restless, and energetic society, where embryo political parties met and scientists and artists conversed.

Other towns remained small in comparison with the "great wen" of London, although a number of ports benefited from the growth of commerce. Bristol in the west with a population of about 30,000 was now the second largest town, though York and Newcastle in the northeast were its rivals. Newcastle had the advantage of the growing coal trade; for it was from there that coal was sent by sea to London. Bristol was a center for cloth exports; Plymouth in the southwest remained a port of departure to the New World. But the bulk of the population was concentrated in the south of England around London. All governments, from that of King James I onward, were worried over the sprawling character of London, even though outside the city proper it was still quite rural. Acts were passed aimed at checking the number of new buildings there, but these were ineffective.

The growth of London and the development of commerce must not be allowed to obscure the fact that England still remained essentially agricultural. About half the land was under cultivation and four-fifths of the population were employed in agricultural work. Industrial progress was slow and should not be exaggerated. Wool, tin, and corn were the most valuable exports after cloth, apart from re-exports of goods imported from America and India; manufactured articles were not important. The most significant advance on the land was the draining of much of the fen country in eastern England. The work was begun under King Charles I, who granted a patent to the Earl of Bedford: he employed a Dutch engineer to carry out the scheme. Dikes were built, rivers widened and deepened, canals constructed, and the land drained by sluices. The work took many years to complete. Both Cromwell and Charles II displayed an interest in it, but it was interrupted from time to time by the rioting of the local inhabitants whose primitive livelihoods were threatened. At one time John Lilburne, the Leveller leader, acted as a spokesman for the indignant fenmen. Eventually, however, a great deal of land was reclaimed, although it was not until the nineteenth century that all the engineering problems were solved.

Apart from the draining of the fens, enclosures of land continued to improve tillage or extend pasture. During the reign of King Charles I the last acts against enclosure became law; afterward it was recognized both in official circles and among enlightened publicists that it was necessary to get rid of the old mixed-strip methods in favor of hedged fields. Progress was most rapid in the area around London. These counties profited from their proximity to the huge city market. But it was remarkable that in the reign of King Charles II, which was known as an age of experiment and scientific curiosity, such small advances in agricultural techniques were recorded. Mr. David Ogg writes that "many later innovations were foreshadowed in the books and pamphlets of the time": questions of manures and fertilizers, of rotation of crops and the provision of new cattle foods were discussed; the Royal Society, founded in 1660, concerned itself with the history and practice of agriculture; but nothing much was actually done. Even the potato, discovered in America, was only used as fodder. England lagged behind other countries; although the agitation over enclosures had decreased toward the end of the century, experts still quarreled, chiefly over the relative value of growing corn and rearing sheep. The government tried to promote stability in the corn market by prohibiting export in time of dearth and granting bounties in times of plenty, which was agreeable enough to the yeomen and gentry. But, as Dr. Trevelyan observes, "the big landowners, in the generation immediately following the disturbance of the Civil Wars, had not enough confidence in the future, nor enough capital or credit, not enough personal interest in agriculture to take the lead in land improvement on a large scale, like their descendants" in the eighteenth century. The owners of great estates spent much of their money on lavish display and entertainment, on new flowers, trees, and shrubs. Many amateurs, from Sir Francis Bacon to John Evelyn, discussed and praised gardens and trees. The Dutch introduced the tulip, the Huguenot refugees brought in new floral ideas, and the aristocracy imitated the fountains and statues, the avenues and orangeries of Louis XIV's France. Out of all this emerged the formal English garden.

If capital was not accumulated and employed for the improvement of methods of agriculture, it was certainly forthcoming for commerce and industry, in which it seemed possible to get rich quickly. Money was obtained from the exploitation of patents, by the managing of the public revenue, and above all from fees or perquisites at court. An examination of the careers of men who lent money to the government, such as

Edward Backwell or Sir Robert Vyner, or of statesmen employed in the king's service, like Sunderland or Godolphin, shows how capital sums might be collected in that way. Although money lending goes back to very early times—Italian financiers lent large sums to King Edward I—banking seems to date from about the middle of the seventeenth century. The bankers included goldsmiths, scriveners, and perhaps the Jews then readmitted to England. They paid interest on deposits, discounted bills of exchange, and made short-term loans to their customers; they also lent money to the government. The uncertainties induced by the civil wars persuaded men to leave their money on deposit in banks, although aristocrats like the earls of Bedford were still keeping their money locked up in a big trunk. The establishment of an early fire insurance company was an example of a novel form of investment at that time. The coal and iron industries, which required a good deal of fixed capital, offered other means for investment. Trading companies like the East India Company, which at one time issued stock of such a kind that both the capital and the profits were repaid to the participants after a few years, offered another type of investment. The rate of interest fell from 10 per cent at the beginning of the century to 8 per cent during the Interregnum and 6 per cent during the reign of King Charles II. Even the so-called "stop of the Exchequer" in 1671, when the government suspended the payment of interest on money which had been borrowed from the goldsmiths and other bankers, did not long damage the new credit structure. In fact it may be said that private banking in a modern sense and regular commercial investment both date from the reign of King Charles II.

As we have seen, the Merchant Adventurers suffered a setback in the reign of King James I from which the company never fully recovered; but other companies concerned with the export of cloth and the import of necessities, like timber and tar for ship building, or of luxuries, such as silks and wine, progressed and flourished. The East India Company was allowed to export bullion because with it it was able to buy valuable articles for re-export, such as spices, pepper, and saltpeter for gunpowder. The Royal Africa Company, which grew out of the smaller Guinea Company and received a royal charter in 1662, imported ivory and gold or sold slaves to the West Indies and America. The Levant Company, which had begun, like the East India Company, as a joint-stock organization, traded with the Turkish empire and imported silks, spices, and currants. The Eastland Company did business in the Baltic and competed with the Merchant Adventurers in the export of cloth. Smaller and less successful companies were the Muscovy Company, which was shut out from Russia during the Interregnum, and the Greenland Company, which specialized in whale oil. The Hudson Bay Company, trading in furs, was founded in 1670. Attempts to establish a West India Company failed, while the trade with France and Spain was generally open. Various committees and councils of trade were testimony to the government's concern with commerce and industry. Altogether much business was done that was highly profitable to merchants and investors: it is estimated that after the Restoration the total value of exports and re-exports from England amounted to about £4,000,000 a year in value, compared with seven or eight million in the first half of the eighteenth century.

While the character of these exports—cloth, corn, fish, lead, tin—was fairly limited, the variety of imports was immense. In addition to such necessities as naval stores and pepper and spices for preserving food during the winter, tea, coffee, and tobacco were being imported for the first time; sugar, wine, and silk came in (although Huguenot settlers were building up a native silk industry); tortoise shell came from Jamaica, children's daggers from Bilbao, singing birds from Rotterdam. English governments were anxious that these imports be brought in as far as possible in English ships. The Navigation Act of 1651 had confined imports either to English ships or to ships belonging to the country from which the imports came. The object of this restriction was partly to encourage the ship-building industry and the provision of seamen for the royal navy, but it was also apparently intended to wrest part of the carrying trade from the Dutch. The East India, Levant, and Eastland companies, which mainly used their own shipping facilities, favored the navigation acts, although other companies or interests, such as the Merchant Adventurers and the colonial merchants, were opposed to them. The act of 1651 was partially enforced during the Interregnum; a more stringent act, more clearly defining the nature of an English ship and forbidding all trading with English colonies in foreign bottoms, was passed in 1660. This act also stated that certain "enumerated commodities," such as sugar and tobacco, might be exported from the colonies only direct to England or to English possessions so as to create an entrepôt trade. The navigation acts, although unpopular with many people, especially in the colonies, seem on the whole to have been enforced, but they had unfortunate repercussions; for example, they drove Dutch competition into other channels.

Thus industry, commerce, and shipping, if sometimes rudimentary in character, started to expand in seventeenth-century England. Foreign trade in particular made progress. How far this should be credited to government action—to the kind of paternalism exemplified by the royal charters and the navigation acts—may be questioned. Some historians have attributed the advance to the beginnings of genuine religious toleration in the latter half of the century. The Puritans, it has been said, made good business men. Others have suggested that the Jews and nonconformists, after the Restoration excluded by law from public life, were stimulated to devote their abilities to economic enterprise. At the same time state control over industry was relaxing. This may have had evil consequences for the poorer classes, who seem to have been worse off because of exploitation once the government became more disinterested than they had been under Queen Elizabeth I and the early Stuarts. The Elizabethan poor law system, when unmitigated, tended to restrict mobility of labor (since the parishes were responsible for the poor and did not want to be burdened with wandering beggars) and to limit freedom without materially providing for popular welfare.

A recent investigation by Professor W. K. Jordan suggests that the problem of poverty and unemployment in the seventeenth century was much larger than has generally been realized and that the poor became more and more dependent on private charity. Poverty was particularly marked in London, and the social consciences of the rising merchant class and the gentry were offended by it, inspiring them to give to charity on a large scale. It is estimated that in the middle of the century over 50,000 "unfortunate beings were at all times being relieved in their houses or wholly supported by the great alms-house endowments vested in this most generous age." One-tenth of the whole charitable wealth of the country was contributed to experiments on the social rehabilitation of the poor. Preoccupation with the poor, particularly in the towns, was an outstanding characteristic of the post-Reformation period. The problem was great and real.

Whether it is exact to say that in the years before the revolution of 1688 the rich were growing richer and the poor were growing poorer may be open to argument. Perhaps Englishmen were better off in employment than workers in most countries in the world of their time. The compact family units that owned small farms or shops or modest businesses for the most part enjoyed a fair standard of living with reasonably good food to eat and ale to wash it down; but poverty was widespread and the common people had little say in public affairs; when they tried to express themselves politically, as they did at the time of the Leveller agitations of 1648–50 or of the Duke of Monmouth's invasion which was to come in 1685, they were easily crushed. It was their masters, not the common people, who were to eject King James II and who were still to rule through the eighteenth century.

LI

Education and Culture in the Seventeenth Century

The seventeenth century was a remarkable age in English literature, above all in poetry, the outstanding British contribution to the arts of the world. The century opened in the reflected light of Elizabethan glory, although the reign of King James I—the Jacobean age—had its own distinction. The Protestant Reformation gave the nation and posterity two unique Puritan writers, John Milton and John Bunyan, but it also gave birth to authors in the service of the Anglican Church of such diverse genius as the poet George Herbert and the historian of his own times, Edward Hyde, first Earl of Clarendon. In spite of some interruption during the civil wars, the continuous history of the theater stretches from William Shakespeare to William Congreve. Prose ranged from the majestic appeal of Milton's *Areopagitica* for the freedom of the press to the intimate memories of John Aubrey, Samuel Pepys, and John Evelyn. Political writing in the seventeenth century began with pamphleteering and ended with satire. Although the dust may lie upon some dreary seventeenth-century writings, such as the interminable sermons that are to be found in the huge Thomason collection in the British Museum or described in the complete edition of Evelyn's memoirs, a vast amount of the literature—even some of the politics and theology—can be and still is read today.

It may be supposed that this body of literature owed relatively little to the educational system of the time. Neither in the schools nor in the universities was it a period of much progress. Men as different as Milton and Aubrey, Comenius and Hartlib talked about reforming and improving English education, but very little was done. Shakespeare never went to a university; Milton profited little from his days at Cambridge. There was much self-education; printing had improved, books were plentiful, and men liked to read. The grammar school remained the basic educational establishment: it was here that revolutionaries like Pym, Cromwell, and John Lilburne were first impressed with the Puritan outlook. These schools offered a road to all the professions, and they were handsomely supported by the middle class. A boy might go first to a primary school, where he was supposed to be taught reading, writing, and arithmetic. Although many new grammar schools were founded in the century, their curriculums remained largely unchanged. Their traditional aim was still to instruct clerics. Thus Latin grammar remained the staple diet. Schoolmasters as a whole were a despised class, sometimes stupid and often brutal. Children, one schoolmaster admitted, were not instructed in the "true use of learning" but "only to construe and parse a little." Such schools are said to have been "nurseries of piety . . . preparatory to trade." In general the grammar schools, reckoned to have been the pride of early England and the Tudor age, had entered into a period of decline; many of them were out of date, bound by statutes designed for a world that had passed away.

The universities were not in much better shape. It is true that there were increasing demands for higher education: it was proposed that new universities should be set up in Manchester, Durham, and London, while Oxford had new colleges at the outset of the century in Wadham and Pembroke. The system of colleges (instead of hostels) was now well under way, and they were often attended by gentlemen who received special privileges: even Oliver Cromwell, who was the son of a modest country gentleman, was a Fellow Commoner of Sidney Sussex of Cambridge and allowed to dine at the high table. Like the schools, the universities were handicapped by their curriculums (although a recent book argues that this can be exaggerated). Archbishop Laud, when he was chancellor, tried to tighten up the discipline at Oxford, but his success was limited. Licentiousness, intellectual sterility, and idleness were keynotes at both universities. Not a great deal of trouble was taken over boys of sixteen or so who came to the colleges. New topics were taboo; democratic ideas were frowned upon; the civil wars interrupted progress and contributed afterward to conservatism. In the reigns of the later Stuarts the colleges were often the playthings of politics. But toward the end of the century the universities housed many eminent scholars who derived benefit from their common intercourse and from the splendid libraries: the Bodleian was not formed until 1602. The university's real weakness was as an educational institution, not as a center of scholarship. The Inns of Court, after the civil wars, no longer made up for the deficiency: they ceased to provide instruction for students or to insist on the residence of fledgling lawyers.

Bishop Burnet wrote of this age that the English gentry were "for the most part the worst instructed, and the least knowing of any of their rank I ever went amongst." Burnet was a Scot; his country, with a fifth of the population of England, had four universities, and education there was undoubtedly better. The tendency among the members of the aristocracy was to provide private tutors, who were mere servants, for their sons, and after they had finished at the university, if they went there, to send them upon a "grand tour" of Europe, which broadened their minds and emptied their pockets. Girls sometimes had tutors too —Lucy Apsley said she had eight—but in general they were taught only the arts calculated to make them into good wives, such as needle-work and music. The "bluestockings" of the age—Margaret Lucas, second wife of the Duke of Newcastle, for instance—were exceptional and usually eccentric.

For all classes the Bible was prescribed reading. At the Hampton Court conference of 1604 King James I had agreed to its translation into English: a syndicate of scholars was appointed for the purpose; they produced a work of synthesis in which much use was made of the earlier translation by William Tyndale, one of the first Puritans. Un-doubtedly this so-called "authorized version" was widely read—"the great book of the poor and unlettered, the one book that every house-hold was sure to possess"—and although there have been differences of opinion about its impact on English prose, many of its phrases were certainly absorbed into common speech. The tidal wave of pamphlets written by William Prynne, John Lilburne, and thousands of others that swept the country in the 1640's was indebted to it. It was one of the few books that Cromwell read. Two other books, which owed much to the Reformation, were Sir Walter Ralegh's *History of the World* and John Bunyan's *Pilgrim's Progress*. The *History of the World,* written by Ralegh when he was imprisoned in the Tower of London, had a didactic purpose: it purported to justify God's ways to man. It only covered the period from the creation to 130 B.C.; yet it was nearly suppressed as being "too saucy in censuring princes." A valuable yeoman's diary that has survived (that of Adam Eyre, a Yorkshireman) shows that men of his class spent whole days reading, happily absorbed in such tomes as that of Ralegh.

The most famous prose works to appear at the beginning of the century were the *Essays* of Sir Francis Bacon and the *Anatomy of Melancholy* by Robert Burton, a rector and an Oxford don. Bacon was influenced by Montaigne, whose writings had just been translated into English. The *Essays* were first published in 1600, but were later added to and revised. They were examples of "table talk," a phrase later used as a title by lawyer John Selden for a witty collection of expanded epigrams. Burton's book, though equally entertaining, had a more serious purpose than Bacon's *Essays*. Burton's aim, in the days before psychology, was to inquire into the vagaries of the human mind. In the field of prose, the middle of the century was dominated by theology and politics, ranging through the sermons or "pulpit oratory" of John Donne and Lancelot Andrewes, the books of John Milton defending divorce and the freedom of the press (the latter arising out of criticisms of his divorce pamphlets), the pamphlets of the Levellers and their associates—William Walwyn, Gerrard Winstanley, and the like, and the works of the Cambridge Platonists and their predecessors, William Chillingworth, who wrote *The Religion of Protestants* (1638), and Jeremy Taylor, the author of *The Rule and Exercise of Holy Living* (1650), *Holy Dying* (1651), and a *Discourse on the Liberty of Prophesying* (1647). Several authors, better known as poets, also wrote superlative prose. George Herbert's *A Priest to the Temple or The Country Parson, his Character, and Rule of Holy Life* was published posthumously. Andrew Marvell's *The Rehearsal Transpos'd* and *Account of the Growth of Popery and Arbitrary Government in England* were both highly effective essays in controversy. John Bunyan, a self-educated Bedfordshire tinker, wrote a great many books besides his masterpiece, *Pilgrim's Progress,* of which the best known is *Grace Abounding.* Later in the period came two delightfully written books, free from theology or party politics—Isaac Walton's *The Compleat Angler* (Walton also wrote brief lives of poets, most of whom he had not met) and John Aubrey's *Brief Lives* (1669–96), which was edited and published posthumously.

Above all, this was the age of poetry. The poets are too numerous to list or evaluate. Poetry in the seventeenth century began with Michael Drayton, an Elizabethan veteran in the Spenserian tradition, and ended with the poet laureate John Dryden, who lost his post when he turned Roman Catholic. Some critics would claim that Robert Herrick was the finest of the Caroline poets; others would give the first place to John Donne. Both of them were country parsons. Herrick was a lyrical poet in the classical tradition and a master of the rhymed couplet; John Donne, who early in life lost his post and was sent to prison because of his marriage, later took orders and in 1621 became dean of St. Paul's. Only four of his poems were published in his lifetime but many more after his early death: religious poems, love poems, satires, and elegies. His satires were harsh, witty, and lucid; his love poems, being "metaphysical" in character, were not always understood. John Dryden said of him: "he affects the metaphysics not only in his satires but in his amorous verses where nature only should reign; and perplexes the fair sex with nice speculations of philosophy when he should engage their hearts and entertain them with softnesses of love." Yet Donne's brilliant conceits and novel verses influenced Dryden himself and many later poets, and—like the poetry of John Skelton—have proved to be to the taste of our own generation. Besides Donne and Herrick, there were many other Caroline poets, mostly of Cavalier sympathies— Thomas Carew, Sir John Suckling, George Herbert, Richard Crashaw, Thomas Traherne, Francis Quarles, Edmund Waller, Abraham Cowley. The complete list is long: there was, for example, Sir John Denham, an indifferent Royalist poet, who asked King Charles I to spare the life of the Parliamentarian poet George Wither, on the ground that "while George Wither lived, he should not be the worst poet in England."

John Milton, it has been said, might have been reckoned yet another Cavalier poet had he died before the civil war. In *Comus,* the masque that he wrote in 1634, which was set to music by Henry Lawes, and in *Lycidas,* an elegy for a lost friend, there was not a great deal to distinguish him from his early contemporaries. Nor did his themes differ from those of, say, Crashaw or Cowley. In his middle life he turned to prose and to the service of the Commonwealth as the Latin secretary of the Council of State. He did not lead a happy life; his first marriage was a mistake, and in 1652 he became blind. After escaping punishment as a rabid republican and apologist for regicide, he turned to writing his three epics, *Paradise Lost, Paradise Regained,* and *Samson Agonistes.* Here he demonstrated his original genius, for the poems reveal the interplay of Puritanism and rationalism. Their sweeping grandeur, their lofty themes, and their art and learning all contributed to their success. They were admired by men of letters as different as Dryden and Addison. They may have lacked suppleness, humor, and variety, but the tragic themes, the vast canvas, and the magnificent blank verse preserved them for ages despite their queer theology.

John Dryden, born in 1631, was a poet in a different vein from Milton. He was far more a man of the world. No recluse, he bestrode the literary scene of the later half of the century. He lacked Milton's austerity of approach and consistency of beliefs. He earned a name by writing an elegy about Oliver Cromwell, but soon trimmed his sails with another poem welcoming back King Charles II. A High Tory, he made a profound impression with his satire, *Absalom and Achitophel* (1681), attacking the Whig leaders, even though it was published anonymously. In the reign of King James II he became a Roman Catholic. The Glorious Revolution ended his public life and he died in 1700. He was not only a prolific poet, but an energetic translator and dramatist as well. Though he frequently used the heroic couplet, his technique was varied. It has been said that he was in fact akin to the metaphysical Caroline poets and that his thought more closely resembled that of Milton than that of his successors, such as Alexander Pope, in the "Augustine age" of Queen Anne's reign.

Though Dryden was a leading satirist, he was only one of many. In the reign of King Charles II satire became one of the handiest weapons of the opposition to the government. On the other side, Samuel Butler (1612–80) mocked the Puritans in his successful *Hudibras,* following in the footsteps of John Cleveland and Abraham Cowley. On the Whig side, Andrew Marvell, who had once been Milton's assistant but later became a member of King Charles II's Long Parliament, stood out head and shoulders above the rest. He warned the public against the dangers of autocracy and of the government's pro-French policy. He was fortunate to die in 1678 before the Royalist revenge destroyed his friends.

Contributions to history, if not historical writing in a modern sense, were a feature of the century. Bacon wrote a *History of the Reign of King Henry VII* and Lord Herbert of Cherbury the *Life and Reign of King Henry VIII.* Thomas May wrote a history of the Long Parliament and Thomas Fuller a history of the Church. Bulstrode Whitelocke, a Commonwealth ambassador, left important memorials. More valuable than any of these were two books, partly personal memoirs and partly public history, which were written in the latter half of the century, but not published until the following century: Lord Clarendon's *History of the Rebellion* and Gilbert Burnet's *History of My Own Time.* Antiquarians like Ashmole left important collections of documents, while another antiquarian, Sir Henry Spelman, invented the word "feudalism." Some of this antiquarianism misled contemporaries. On its basis both Sir Edward Coke and John Lilburne indulged in fantastic theories about the British past. Finally, many memoirs were written, some of rather dubious value, such as those of Denzil Holles, while others, if justificatory pieces, have proved stand-bys to all modern historians. Clarendon's two books—he also wrote his own *Life*—are not merely the material of history but also indestructible literature that will be read so long as the English-speaking peoples are capable of reading.

The popularity of the theater persisted during the reign of King James I and it was equally popular under his grandson, King Charles II. In 1604 all the companies came directly under royal patronage and remained so until 1642. In 1603 there were six theaters in London, but five were built during the reign of King James I and two during that of King Charles I. Even during the Interregnum the Puritans failed to suppress plays altogether, and the first English opera was performed in 1656. The Jacobean age saw the first performance of many of Shakespeare's greatest plays, including *Coriolanus* and *Antony and Cleopatra,* all the tragedies, and the later comedies, culminating in his "magical swan song," *The Tempest.* Shakespeare died in 1616 and the

first folio of his plays was published in 1623. But the reign was dominated by Ben Jonson, at one time a professional actor like Shakespeare
but far more academic in his approach to writing plays. We know
infinitely more about Jonson's life than we do about Shakespeare's. He
was a figure in the round, not afraid to lay down the law, conceited,
talented, coarse, and prolific; a brilliant conversationalist, he expounded
his philosophy to his admirers in the Mermaid and Sun taverns. He
thought that comedies should show restraint and balance, but at first
he was not very successful in putting his theories into practice. His
most effective "comedies of manners" were *The Alchemist* and *Bar-
tholomew Fair*. His exuberant characters were models for the writers
of the next generation.

It is said that Ben Jonson's plays were favorites of King Charles I,
but the plays attributed to Beaumont and Fletcher, usually tragicomedies
that sometimes degenerated into melodrama, were more generally
popular. Philip Massinger (1583–1640), who also collaborated with
Fletcher, was another popular dramatist of the time. His plays verged
on the sensational and his tragedies influenced the so-called "Restoration drama," but his best play was a comedy, *A New Way to Pay Old
Debts*.

With the return of the king and the discomfiture of the Puritans in
1660, the theater took on a new lease of life. Before the civil war the
theaters were open and women's parts were generally played by boys.
Now the theaters were roofed in and scenery was used. The Theatre
Royal in Drury Lane became the principal playhouse: here women
actresses, of whom the most notorious was King Charles II's mistress,
Nell Gwyn, actually became "stars." The king was fond of the theater
and so were his cronies at court, such as the second Duke of Buckingham and John Wilmot, Earl of Rochester, who themselves tried their
hands as dramatists. Patrons tended to favor heroic dramas and
lascivious comedy, but the plays of Shakespeare and Jonson were revived; the plays of Dryden contained some distinguished writing; and
while William Wycherley's comedies, such as *The Country Wife,* were
to shock the Victorians they have found admirers in our own less-
inhibited age. On the whole, however, these plays lacked the quality of
the plays of Elizabethan and Jacobean times, and by 1682 the popularity of the stage had diminished. However, it has left the memory of
the poetic genius of Dryden and the musical genius of Henry Purcell.

The building of beautiful country houses continued actively from
the time of Queen Elizabeth I to the civil wars. Gradually the Gothic
yielded before what was called the Renaissance or Palladian style. The
great halls, which had long been the principal feature of big country

houses, gave way to vestibules and dining and drawing rooms. The central courtyard disappeared into the background. A famous example of the Palladian style is Inigo Jones's banquet house in Whitehall, which was decorated with a ceiling by Rubens; another is the piazza at Covent Garden in London: a third is Wilton House in Wiltshire. All three have survived. Wilton House contains elaborate internal decoration with carved figures, cornices, and a beautiful mantelpiece and panels filled with the portraits of the Herberts, who owned it. Plaster work, heraldic designs, emblems of birds and beasts: all these were the typical decorations in the seventeenth-century manor. Tapestries, sculpture, and carpets were imported to enhance the manor house's grandeur. A tapestry factory was started at Mortlake in Surrey by Flemish weavers, and there were a few rather indifferent English sculptor-masons. Trestle tables came in to replace the more solid oak structures of earlier times; chairs were richly upholstered; huge postered beds were often the most valuable pieces of furniture in the house.

In Inigo Jones (1597–1652) and Christopher Wren (1632–1723) England had two notable architects. Inigo Jones has been called "the most important English artist of the seventeenth century." Wren, though a very practical man, believed in the political significance of noble public buildings. The Sheldonian Theatre in Oxford, Chelsea Hospital, and some of the London churches are among his monuments. After the Restoration there was an outburst of new buildings of all kinds, from great houses and university colleges to village inns and almshouses. Brick was much more commonly used than ever before and at this time sash windows were introduced.

Britain did not have much to show in painting to compare with her poetry and native versions of Renaissance architecture. In the first half of the century the painters with most appeal were foreigners, such as Sir Anthony Van Dyck, Sir Peter Lely, Marc Gheerhaerts, Daniel Mytens, and Cornelius Johnson. King Charles I was a patron of painting and his personal collection contained many Italian masterpieces; it was sold during the Interregnum to pay the debts of parliament. King Charles I persuaded Van Dyck to come to England, and he painted all the leading figures at court, as Lely later painted the courtiers and ladies of King Charles II's court. William Dobson is reckoned the best of the native painters; others, like Robert Walker, were little more than poor imitators of Van Dyck: Walker sometimes could not even be bothered to think of his own designs or even costumes and bodies, and lifted them unashamedly from the work of the Van Dyck studio. There was, however, a school of miniaturists, including Nicholas Hilliard, who had painted Queen Elizabeth I; Samuel Cooper, who painted Oliver Cromwell and King Charles II; William Faithorne; the two Olivers; and the two Hoskinses. What the country badly needed was genre and landscape painting. To recapture a picture of Britain in the seventeenth century, posterity is dependent largely on mediocre woodcuts or prints. Even the history of the royal navy was recorded pictorially by a Dutchman.

On the whole, this was a cultured and prosperous age. The reign of King Charles II can be studied more intimately, at least so far as the court and society are concerned, than any previous reign in the diaries of Pepys and Evelyn and in the memoirs of the Verneys, the Hattons, Sir John Reresby, and many others. There was a high standard of taste, good books and plays were appreciated, buildings were dignified without being extravagant, food and furnishings were rich, and the artistic achievements of Holland, France, and Italy were welcomed. It has been said that there was a real aristocracy that "elevated the whole nation." "They built commodious and classical houses for themselves and their posterity, filled them with treasures of art, encompassed them with walled gardens to catch the sunlight, made fountains, parterres and grottoes, and planted walks of beech and sycamore." The laborers and artisans who constituted the bulk of the population worked from dawn to dusk to supply the needs of the gentry, drank a glass of ale when they could afford it, which was not often, and pondered a brighter life in the world to come. It was not a democratic age, but for the few it was a good one. In the discussions of the Royal Society, founded in 1660, scientific and political ideas were being examined and formulated which foreshadowed what Britain was to become in more modern times.

LII

Music Through the Seventeenth Century

Early English music consisted of liturgical song, that is to say the plainsong of western Europe, the songs of minstrels, and the songs of the common people. No secular English music earlier than the twelfth century has been preserved, and there was little that was distinctive about early church music. The Venerable Bede mentioned that in 680 Benedict Biscop, the abbot of Wearmouth in Northumbria, brought a singer from Rome "that he might teach in his monastery the system of singing throughout the year as it was practised at St. Peter's in Rome." However, some of the earliest two-part music in existence is preserved in the eleventh-century "Winchester troper." By the thirteenth century there were songs with English words, which have come down to us, notably the six-part rota or "canon," "Sumer is icumen in," and a considerable amount of church music, mostly from the neighborhood of Worcester; the "Sumer" manuscript also contains some two-part instrumental dances. Treatises on the theory and practice of music written by English monks also date from that same period.

A popular type of song in the fifteenth century was the carol, often a two-part song with a three-part refrain, of which the so-called Agincourt song, *"Deo gratias,"* is an example. Much of the repertory of the Chapel Royal (the choir of the royal household) of King Henry IV and King Henry V has also come down to posterity, along with the work of many named composers, including the king himself ("Roy Henry" was probably Henry IV) and, most outstanding of all, John Dunstable, who died in 1453. Dunstable, who was in the service of King Henry V's brother, the Duke of Bedford, regent of France, spent most of his life abroad; and his influence, together with that of Power and other English musicians in Paris or at the Burgundian court, led to the adoption by other European composers of the relatively simple euphonious style that had always characterized English part-music.

After the expulsion of the English from France, English music followed its own course, developing a highly ornamental style analogous, it is said, to that of the English architecture of the same period. It was only in the reign of King Henry VIII that the influence of the Netherlands masters, such as Josquin des Prés, began to make itself belatedly felt in England, for example in the work of Fayrfax (1464–1521) and Taverner (c. 1495–1545). King Henry VIII himself was a keen musician and composer, though an undistinguished one. According to the chronicler Hall he was accustomed to occupy himself with "singing, dancing . . . playing . . . and setting of songs and in making ballads." He performed on the lute, the harpsichord, and the recorder or flute. A manuscript of organ music survived from the early fourteenth century, and in early Tudor times English keyboard music, either for virginal (a type of harpsichord) or organ, flourished at the hands of a number of composers. By the time of Queen Elizabeth I's reign the repertory of keyboard music was large.

The leading church composers of the generation after Taverner were

Christopher Tye (c. 1500–1573), Robert Whyte (c. 1530–74), and Thomas Tallis (c. 1505–85). Tye is said to have been musical tutor to King Edward VI, and Whyte was Tye's son-in-law. Tallis was the ablest and most versatile of the three. All of them wrote both Masses and Latin motets for the Roman rite and English anthems or service music for the new Anglican one. Even Tallis' pupil, William Byrd (1543–1623), greatest of all the Tudor musicians, a member of Queen Elizabeth I's Chapel Royal but a Roman Catholic all his life, composed Latin Masses and English services and anthems with equal mastery. The effects of the Reformation on music were harmful in some respects: many manuscripts preserved in the monasteries were lost forever. Plainsong was garbled in adaptation to English words, as in Merbecke's *Booke of Common praier noted* (1550). The Calvinistic psalm settings became particularly popular in, and characteristic of, Scotland.

Toward the end of the sixteenth century an Italian form of secular part-song, the madrigal, became immensely popular. Madrigal singing was a popular social pastime, and more-or-less Italianate madrigals were composed by Byrd, Morley (who was also a writer publisher), Weelkes, Wilbye, Orlando Gibbons, and numerous other musicians, after which the madrigal was superseded in popularity by the "ayre" (published in alternative versions, for four singers or for soloist with accompaniment on the lute), of which the greatest master was John Dowland. Of the other composers of this rich period, John Bull, organist of Antwerp cathedral when he died in 1617, and Giles Farnaby were essentially writers for the keyboard. Orlando Gibbons was a remarkable all-around musician of the Jacobean age, as Byrd had been of the late-Elizabethan.

The brothers Henry and William Lawes and the instrumental composer John Jenkins stood out in the reign of King Charles I. During the reign of the early Stuarts the new Italian style of vocal music known as the recitative, which paid more attention to "just note and accent" than to melodic beauty, made its first impact upon England, especially in the hands of Henry Lawes, who wrote the original music for Milton's *Comus*. Masques such as *Comus*—amateur entertainments with songs and dances, often performed at court—had been popular since Elizabethan times and endured until long after the Restoration.

The civil wars were a blow to ecclesiastical music: the organs were largely silenced, in some cases even destroyed, and choirs were dispersed. But Oliver Cromwell himself was a lover of music. Ernest Walker wrote that "we may fitly date the never-ceasing stream of English music publications from the Commonwealth." John Playford published the first edition of *The English Dancing Master* in 1651; the opera *The Siege of Rhodes,* with libretto by Sir William Davenant, who produced it in London, and music by Matthew Locke and others, was first performed in 1656. John Hingston, a pupil of Orlando Gibbons, was organist to Lord Protector Oliver; and when Cromwell's daughter Frances was married the forty-eight violins that played and the "mixed dancing" scandalized the more extreme Puritans.

After the Restoration the organs were played again everywhere, but essentially it was a period of flourishing secular music, reflecting the growing materialism of the age and the taste of the court. The Chapel Royal was reformed: King Charles II sent one of his choristers, Pelham Humfrey, to study under Lully, an Italian by birth naturalized in France, a composer of ballets and operas as well as other music. Stage music became popular, and the first public concerts were given (although Cromwell gave state concerts in Whitehall Palace). The St. Cecilia's Day concert, begun in 1683, became popular and has been revived in modern times.

The greatest of English composers—some say of all time—was Henry Purcell, who lived from 1659 to 1695. His father had been a musician and he himself was appointed organist at Westminster Abbey in 1680. His music ranged over every known form of composition, from such church music as his "Te Deum" and "Jubilate in D" to his opera, *Dido and Aeneas*. He wrote music for works of Shakespeare and Dryden; he composed odes to St. Cecilia, he wrote fantasias for viols, sonatas for violins, and suites for the harpsichord as well as a vast quantity of vocal music. His work as a whole was a unique fusion of contemporary French and Italian styles with the English tradition. He towered above his age, and while he had some notable contemporaries, such as John Blow, whose anthems are still performed today, he had no immediate successor.

LIII

Scientific and Political Ideas Through the Seventeenth Century

Although some plausible claims have been put forward on the basis of recent historical research, it can hardly be maintained that much scientific progress was made during the early years of the history of Britain.

The Venerable Bede, it has been suggested, was one of the first English scientists because he did some practical calculations about the Christian calendar and drew a fantastic picture of the universe. In the twelfth and thirteenth centuries Latin translations not only of Greek scientific works but also of some Arabic mathematical writings became available in England, and men like Robert Grosseteste, the first chancellor of Oxford University, and his pupil Roger Bacon wrote on physics, optics, and meteorology, largely by way of commentaries on Aristotle. At Merton College, Oxford, astronomy, mathematics, and medicine were studied. William of Ockham was among the few who resisted the typical scholastic line of argument and urged that observed data should be related. Even as late as the fifteenth century little new was discovered in the fields of science.

In fact, throughout early history scientific theories remained largely under the influence of Aristotle, while free thinking about the nature of the universe was subject to the authority of the Roman Church. The earth was believed to be the center of the universe: the gravitational theory was to the effect that all heavy bodies tended to fall to the earth's center. In medicine, diagnosis had long been based on the state of the stars or of the invalid's urine; treatment consisted mainly of bloodletting or a varied and ingenious use of herbs. Anatomy was dependent upon ancient texts, classical or Arabic. Alchemy sought for the elixir of life; surgery was experimental and optimistic; at the beginning of the seventeenth century barbers were the principal surgeons and certainly killed more patients than they cured. Even well-known doctors like Sir Theodore Mayerne used earthworms. Sir Thomas Browne believed in witches. Mayerne also thought that one might as well enjoy himself while he could because one was not likely to live very long.

One of the first persons to question traditional scientific views was a remarkable man, Francis Bacon, who was not only a statesman and lawyer and King James I's Lord Chancellor but also a historian, an educationist, a prosodist, and a scientist. In his *New Atlantis* he wrote that that land was happiest where the scientist was ruler; in his *Advancement of Learning* he advocated a complete study of man, of his mind as well as his body, and anticipated later psychology; of his *Novum Organum* (1620), in which he pleaded for an elaborate system of inductive reasoning, King James I said it was like the peace of God—it passed all understanding. Bacon, who died in 1626, attacked both Aristotle and Plato, pointing out that it was because of their influence that scientific knowledge had made, as he thought, so little progress since the days of antiquity. He believed that men should lay aside philosophy until what he called "experimental history" had been prepared. By this he meant that a body of experiment should be applied to all the problems of nature; he suggested that the questions of gravity, of the rotation of the heavenly bodies, and of the character of heat and light deserved re-examination. He was excessively optimistic about the speed at which such scientific progress could be achieved. He thought that the earth was stationary and he underestimated the importance of mathematics. Nevertheless, his teaching was exceptionally stimulating to his age; he realized that experiments required organizing and he spoke of the need for minds to be washed clean of "opinion"—of bias, prejudice, and ancient lore. As John Aubrey wrote, "he rang the bell that called the wits together."

Two physicians also contributed novel ideas at the beginning of the seventeenth century. One was William Gilbert, who wrote a book called *De Magnete* which suggested new ideas about gravitation: he has been described as "the father of electrical science." The other was William Harvey, who went to the University of Padua, one of the advanced posts of science in his day, became physician extraordinary to the king, and practiced anatomy. In his *De Motu Cordis* he put forward a novel theory about the circulation of the blood. Previously it had been thought that the liver was the central motivating force in the body and that the blood moved to and fro in the veins. Harvey argued that the movement of the blood was constantly in a circle and was brought about by the beat of the heart.

Although previous to the middle of the seventeenth century English scientific thought had been somewhat confused by the theories of the French philosopher René Descartes, who believed that the mind and body were entirely separate, that the body was a machine, and that the soul was located in the pineal gland, by the middle of the century, largely under the impulse of Bacon and the freedom of thought resulting from the civil wars, a scientific surge forward took place. Among those associated with it were Dr. John Wilkins, warden of Wadham College, Oxford, who became a brother-in-law of Oliver Cromwell and later a bishop, Dr. John Wallis, a professor of geometry, Dr. Jonathan Goddard, a physician, and Samuel Foster, a professor of astronomy at Gresham College. These men first met together in Oxford to discuss scientific ideas at Wadham and elsewhere. Their meetings became known as the "invisible" or "philosophical" college. About 1659 this Oxford society moved to London and in 1660 became the nucleus of the Royal Society, which has been the heart of British science ever since.

The Royal Society first began holding weekly meetings in November 1660 at three o'clock in the afternoon. The admission fee was ten shillings and the members included statesmen as well as savants. With the encouragement of King Charles II, the society aimed "to consult and debate concerning the promotion of experimental learning." Members included the Roman Catholic Sir Kenelm Digby, who invented a "powder of sympathy"; Elias Ashmole, the antiquarian; Sir William Petty, one of the first statisticians; the poet Edmund Waller; and Robert, Earl of Sunderland, as well as many early scientists. Members were expected to read papers: John Evelyn concerned himself with engraving and etching, Petty with the history of various trades, Goddard with the anatomy of wood. Committees were formed and correspondence entered into with foreign scientists; Latin was still the international language, so that foreign students were able to read the works of Harvey and Newton as they were written. Experimental programs were drawn up; for example, members were asked to "try by an hour glass whether a pendulum clock goes faster or slower on the top of a hill than below." As can be seen from the nature of the membership, there was a good deal of dilettantism in the early days of the Royal Society; astronomy had not yet shaken itself free from astrology or chemistry from alchemy, and many aristocrats, from Digby to the second Duke of Buckingham, thought all that was needed was a good laboratory to solve the secrets of mankind. Nevertheless, progress was attained. The Honorable Robert Boyle, the son of the Earl of Cork, did experiments with an air pump and showed that air was necessary for life and combustion. He rejected Aristotle's theory that chemistry was based on only four elements and he investigated the structure of matter. Robert Hooke, author of *Micrographia* (1665) and the curator of the Royal Society, was one of the first to practice artificial respiration; Richard Lower (1631–91) was among the first to perform a blood transfusion.

The English scientists of the time owed a great deal to the Dutch glass industry, which gave birth to both the microscope and the telescope. The University of Leiden became the medical center of western Europe and was attended by Dutch doctors and by English doctors who came over and were naturalized. In 1681 a Royal College of Surgeons was founded in Edinburgh. Improved knowledge of anatomy, which has been traced back to the Italian artist Leonardo da Vinci, aided surgery, and gradually its practice became less barbarous and dangerous, while both medicine and chemistry were slowly freed from the stranglehold of mysticism.

Although the scientific revolution did not take place as rapidly as the Baconians hoped it would, undoubtedly the progress made in the early years of the Royal Society was extraordinary. It should no doubt be largely attributed to the freedom of thought promoted during the Interregnum and persisting afterward, in spite of the Clarendon Code and the Laudian reaction. English scientists were able to draw upon, digest, and develop discoveries abroad that are associated with the Renaissance and with the work of men like Copernicus, Galileo, Brahé, and Kepler. Once men ceased to believe that the earth was the center of the universe all sorts of new vistas opened; age-old problems were looked at in an entirely different way. Gilbert's magnetism suggested the hypothesis of a gravitational pull, and Isaac Newton, who was born in 1642, finally reached the solution of "universal" gravitation—a pull that decreased in proportion to the square of the distance.

Newton was a mathematician and physicist of genius, perhaps the greatest Englishman of his age. Alexander Pope later wrote:

> Nature and Nature's Law lay hid in Night,
> God said, Let Newton be! and all was Light.

Newton established the binomial theorem, introduced literal indices, invented the calculus, developed the theory of equations, founded tidal theory, wrote on optics, and created hydrodynamics. Following Bacon, he stressed an atomic theory which helped to explain the nature of light and color. In his *Principia,* published in 1687, he formulated a fundamental law of mechanics. The theory of universal gravitation and the mechanistic explanation of the human body slowly destroyed the ancient scholastic interpretation of the world. Newton himself, however, devoted much of his time to theology and was not prepared to admit that God was merely a mechanic who had wound up the clock; he believed there were opportunities for Him to intervene later in scientific processes. Boyle also attacked the mechanistic views of Descartes. Yet because of the impact of science, the Church toward the end of the seventeenth century was driven to the defensive. A group of theologians at Cambridge tried to reconcile the theories of Bacon, Descartes, and others with Christianity, which it thought might be justified in the light of pure reason. The advance of scientific knowledge, culminating in Newton's synthesis of 1687, undermined many traditional beliefs in both science and metaphysics and, like the political revolution of 1688, opened the road into modern Britain.

⠿ GROWTH OF POLITICAL IDEAS

Political ideas, like scientific ones, made revolutionary progress in the seventeenth century. Until the Reformation political philosophers had been chiefly concerned with the relations between the Church and the state. But William of Ockham in the fourteenth century, having by his extreme "nominalism" separated divine questions from worldly ones, worked out a purely secular theory of the state. John Wycliffe, who was influenced by William of Ockham, also regarded government in secular terms. But nothing comparable to later political theories emerged except in some of the discussions that ranged around the relations between the king and his councilors, for example in the reign of King Edward II. Both the churchmen and the lawyers maintained that the king was not "sovereign" in the later Austinian sense. The monarch, they held, was "under the law." Henry de Bracton had maintained this position as early as the thirteenth century and Sir John Fortescue, who, like Bracton, was a judge, observed in the fifteenth century that "the King of England cannot alter or change the laws of the realm at his pleasure." The Romans might contend that what pleased the king had the force of law, but in England—home of the common law—even though the king was accepted as the head of the "body politic," his authority was limited.

That was the usual view. In sixteenth-century England, it has been said, "there was hardly a trace of absolutist beliefs." Although the Tudors had successfully built up a nation-state and a national government, not only was the power of the monarch conceived to be limited by the common law or customs of the realm, but the specific rights of parliament were beginning to receive recognition. In *De Republic Anglorum,* written by the statesman and diplomatist Sir Thomas Smith and published after his death in 1583, Smith wrote that parliament could "legitimize bastards, establish forms of religion ... alter weights and measures." Both Catholics and Puritans rejected any suggestion that the rights of the monarch were supreme or absolute, but sixteenth-century opinion was divided over the question whether subjects possessed a right of rebellion if their ruler violated the laws of God or man. William Tyndale, the early Puritan, had indeed emphasized the necessity to obey the king, as Luther had done before him, but some Protestants and Jesuits urged that if their religion were threatened a monarch could be overthrown and even assassinated.

The writings of two influential political thinkers abroad had a considerable impact on England in the seventeenth century: these were Niccolò Machiavelli and Jean Bodin. Machiavelli looked at the problems of government in a highly practical way and tended to separate politics from ethics. Bodin was practical too; unlike the majority of earlier thinkers, he believed that in a well-ordered state there must exist a recognizable and virtually unlimited authority to make laws which he called the "sovereign power." He believed that power to be needed so that a state could serve its proper end, the pursuit of virtue.

This notion of a purely political state possessing undivided sovereign power took time to percolate into English thinking; sovereignty was little discussed in the first half of the seventeenth century, even though Bodin's *Republic* was published in 1573. Neither Sir Thomas Smith nor any of his contemporaries wrote in terms of undivided political authority in the state. On the contrary, the doctrine of "mixed monarchy," a political system in which both king and parliament were conceived as having their own rights, was still widely accepted on the very eve of the English civil wars. Religious ideas continued to dominate political thought. All power came from God; everyone from the prince to the humblest father of a family was supposed to obey the divine will and exercise divinely approved authority. The literature of protest, from More's *Utopia*, was directed against political or social practices which were regarded as a betrayal of God's laws or the laws of nature. King and parliament both ruled by divine right; and the subject had to obey the powers that were, because that too was the will of God; hence rebellion, even against a wicked monarch, was, as many writers urged, a sin.

It has sometimes been said that King James I claimed for himself a "divine right" to rule, and that this was an entirely novel political doctrine. It is said that his argument was that because his authority derived from the mysterious will of his Maker it must necessarily be unlimited. Whatever King James I intended (and it is disputed what he did intend) when he published his book *The Trew Law of Free Monarchies* in 1598 before he came to England, it is certain that his actual conduct betrayed no such extravagant political notions. He specifically repudiated the doctrine that the king was above the law. What both the two early Stuart monarchs did assert, however, was that they possessed "prerogative" powers which enabled them to override the law in times of national emergency. They were perfectly well aware that they were bound by their coronation oaths, as most kings had been before them, to recognize and obey the immemorial customs of the land. They also accepted that parliaments had the right to make laws and vote taxes. On the other hand, they knew that the kings of England had in distant times been the sole lawmakers and that ways existed to raise money without holding parliaments.

The prerogative rights of the Stuart kings were upheld by the courts of law on the basis of clearly defined precedents in a number of cases examined by the courts, notably Bate's case and Hampden's case; but to the prerogative Sir Edward Coke and others opposed an older and wider concept, common law of the realm, which embodied the wisdom of the ages. This in turn produced the notion of a "fundamental law" built up of a body of rights or privileges upon which no king might infringe. Coke reminded readers of his law books that King William I had promised to uphold the ancient laws of the land, that King Henry I and

King Henry II had undertaken by their coronation oaths to abolish all evil customs contrary to the law, that King John had sworn to the Great Charter, and so on; at the same time Sir Henry Spelman and other antiquaries of the first half of the seventeenth century contributed to building up the notion of an ancient constitution, to which all English kings had submitted, thus providing what has lately been called an early Whig interpretation of history. Thus arose a contest between those royal prerogatives to which the early Stuarts had clung and the "fundamental laws" of the realm, which were the battle cry of the revolutionaries.

While the king's prerogatives came under attack, so too did the authority of the Church. Early pleas for religious toleration were heard less among the avowedly Puritan sects (or the Presbyterians, who wished to capture the Church intact) than among a number of latitudinarian thinkers of the orthodox persuasion, if Hooker may be considered orthodox— men like John Hales, William Chillingworth, and Benjamin Whichcote. Both King James I and King Charles I realized that their own position depended on that of the episcopal hierarchy which was responsible for disciplining the Church; and such religious factors sharpened the political struggle.

When the civil war broke out propagandists on both sides agreed that both the king and parliament had their just rights; the difference was over their nature and their limits. The king, said the parliamentarians, was a king by contract, his powers were limited by the "ancient constitution" or by the "fundamental laws," and if he ruled arbitrarily and exceeded his rights, his subjects were entitled to resist him. Such were the arguments of authors like Philip Hunton in his *Treatise of Monarchy* (1643) and William Prynne in his *Sovereign Power* (1642). Henry Parker, a brilliant and original thinker, went much further: he believed that since parliament was representative of the responsible classes in the country, it was "sovereign" or at any rate should be because it was so in fact. In his view, the king only wielded his power as a trustee for the nation, of which parliament was the embodiment. Queen Elizabeth I, he thought, had recognized that and had governed accordingly; but King Charles I had ruled ineptly, neglected the true interests of his kingdom, and tried to compensate for the weakness of his government by putting forward claims to unlimited prerogatives. Other parliamentarian apologists did not go so far as Parker: Henry Robinson, for example, was content with the pragmatical argument that the monarchy had proved itself a failure, had been extravagant, wasteful, and stupid, and considered that the country would be fortunate if it replaced the king with an aristocratic republic such as the ones that worked so admirably in Holland and Venice. A more idealistic view was presented by John Milton in his *Tenure of Kings and Magistrates* (1649). Unlike Coke, Prynne, and others, Milton did not rely upon the fundamental laws of the past, but boldly justified the king's execution by "that general and primary law" which, according to the will of God, nature, and reason, made the people's good the supreme end of the state.

Even most of King Charles I's apologists shared in the general insistence during the civil wars that the king was not a "sovereign" and that his prerogatives were not absolute or divinely bestowed. In the early days of the Long Parliament men like Edward Hyde and John Culpepper had agreed with John Pym and Denzil Holles that the monarchical powers must be restricted and the rights of parliament clearly defined. Such royalist writers as Henry Ferne and Dudley Digges admitted that the power of the monarch was strictly limited by law. Ferne emphasized that those who were supporting the king were not trying to defend "an absolute power in him" or "to raise him to an arbitrary way of government." They turned the doctrine of the "fundamental law" or constitution against their opponents: it was fundamental, they argued, that the king and parliament were "co-ordinate" and that the king's consent was necessary to all the laws of the land. Thus in the first half of the seventeenth century most writers on political questions agreed that a "mixed monarchy" was the best form of government, provided that it was loyally worked. The only exceptions were the realistic Henry Parker and the Leveller leaders like John Lilburne and John Wildman who advocated a fully democratic republic. The advocates of an aristocratic republic, like Milton, Vane, and Henry Robinson, scarcely came into the open until the king was dead, when such a republic seemed to them to be the obvious substitute for the "mixed monarchy." But about this time two highly original and ingenious apologists for absolute monarchy were writing: these were Sir Robert Filmer and Dr. Thomas Hobbes.

Although Sir Robert Filmer's book *Patriarcha or A Defence of the Natural Power of Kings against the Unnatural Liberty of the People* was not published until 1680, it was written much earlier. It can be seen from its title that its argument would not have appealed to the more legalistic royalists of that generation, for Filmer based his far-reaching defense of monarchy on history, tradition, and status. He stated that from the time of Adam and Eve men had been accustomed to being governed by a patriarchal ruler, whether it was Adam, who rather unsuccessfully ruled over Eve, Noah, who ruled over the animals in the Ark, or Charles I, who exercised paternal authority during the eleven-year holiday from parliaments. Far from being so by contract, Filmer argued, kings were kings by virtue of status, a status divinely approved and historically upheld. In Stuart England the family, whether rich or

poor, was the natural unit in the community, and its members were subject to the father; the king was the father of them all, and his will must
be obeyed and not questioned. Thomas Hobbes, whose *Leviathan or
The Matter, Form and Power of a Commonwealth Ecclesiastical and
Civil* was first published in 1651, was more subtle in his approach. Hobbes
reckoned himself a mathematical philosopher, but he was not a Baconian;
he did not believe in experiments, but in definitions. "In the first place,"
he wrote, "I put for a general inclination of all mankind a perpetual and
restless desire of power after power that ceaseth only in death." If men
were left alone in that struggle for power the results would be anarchy,
bloodshed, and destruction. Therefore, he urged, men are inevitably
obliged to agree together to surrender their power to one man or to one
government that can reduce all their conflicting wills to one. This was
"the great Leviathan, called a Commonwealth or State, which is but an
artificial man." The Leviathan is a sovereign power in a more complete
sense than is the sovereign power of Bodin: it is absolute, indivisible,
and unbreakable. The men who create the monster do not retain any
rights for themselves except that of being able to defend their own lives
against it. A right of rebellion is inadmissible; for if the "sovereign" is
overthrown, so too is the state. What the Leviathan commands is law,
what he decides is justice. Hobbes was impressed by the disorder of the
world into which he was born and felt that in the Leviathan he had found
a logical solution to it. It was a materialist solution; for Hobbes was a
materialist and an atheist. To him religion was the opium of the masses
distributed by the government to maintain the obedience of its subjects.
He argued that the best government was that of a single man rather than
an assembly that was likely to be quarrelsome and corrupt. Thus he
justified the absolute authority of monarchy; and although in fact he was
a supporter of the Stuarts, his arguments were equally applicable to a
Cromwellian dictatorship.

Hobbes's defense of absolute monarchy did not appeal to the tastes of
royalists. Besides dabbling in mathematics and theology, Hobbes was
one of the first English philosophers to put forward a purely mechanistic interpretation of human life; but he rejected the dualism of Descartes
and asserted that the body was everything. Although his *Leviathan* was
burned in Oxford and the Anglican leaders of King Charles II's reign
attempted to refute him, it is his political ideas that have survived. Once
his premises were accepted his theories were less easy to refute and more
logical than most of his critics imagined.

Apart from the democratic and radical theories of the Levellers, the
communist view of Gerrard Winstanley and "the Diggers," and the
oligarchic views of Henry Ireton, Henry Vane, and John Milton (the

first of whom argued in a somewhat Hobbesian way), the outstanding political philosophy of the mid-seventeenth century was that of James Harrington. Unlike Hobbes, Harrington believed in a "mixed constitution" and stressed the importance of a balance of power within the state. He thought that the anarchy of the times was owing not to a struggle for political supremacy but to a divergence between the actual distribution of political and economic power in the kingdom. He saw that the monarchy had declined in strength because the king had ceased to be able to manage on his own revenues, and believed that an aristocratic government rather than a plutocracy was the best substitute for monarchy. He therefore proposed that there should be an agrarian law whereby no one man should own landed property of greater value than £2,000 and that marriage settlements should be limited. He advocated a written constitution providing for an executive to execute, a senate to debate, and a popular assembly to vote upon the proposed laws. Members of the senate should be chosen by rotation and votes taken by ballot. Thus there would be a government that was a cross between monarchy and oligarchy and the kingdom would be made safe from the perils of a leveling democracy, since it would be leveled to start with.

The Commonwealth of Oceana, in which Harrington set out his ideas, was published in 1656, and during 1659 a Rota Club was formed which met at a coffee house in Westminster to discuss Harrington's scheme. To this club many of the leading savants of the time belonged, as they did also to the Royal Society. Indeed most of the republican writers of this confused age, including John Milton, were profoundly influenced by the brilliance and sweep of Harrington's theories and evidently accepted his opinion that the civil war had arisen because of a change in the ownership of landed property. One of Harrington's disciples, Henry Nevile, reproduced many of Harrington's arguments in his *Plato Redivivus,* published after the existing licensing laws were suspended in 1679. Nevile urged a stringent reduction in the powers of the monarch on the ground that recent changes in the distribution of property had made the English constitution obsolete. It was also in the 1680's that Algernon Sidney, a republican who had been opposed both to Cromwell and to King Charles II, wrote his *Discourses concerning Government,* which aimed at both refuting Filmer and stating the case for government by a "natural aristocracy."

The latter part of the reign of King Charles II was indeed prolific in political as well as scientific ideas. In addition to those of Filmer, Nevile, and Sidney, there were the ideas of George Savile, Marquis of Halifax, one of King Charles's ministers, anonymously published in his *Character of a Trimmer* (1684). Halifax himself had played a large part in preventing the passage of the exclusion bills against James, Duke of York, but on the other hand had approved of the Test Acts, which kept the Roman Catholics out of public office. He did not approve of the alliance with France. His philosophy was that the state could best be preserved by a moderate, balanced policy; he was the advocate of the middle way or the golden mean; he was ready to place limitations on the powers of the monarchy (limitations less extensive than those advocated by Nevile) in order to ensure the safety of the people and safeguard private property. By some he has been linked with Edmund Burke as one of the most notable of British conservative political thinkers.

Another outstanding political philosopher of this period was John Locke, who, like most of the others, might be considered a scientist as well as a philosopher. His books were not published until after the revolution of 1688, but he had formulated his main political ideas before then. His two *Treatises on Government,* though they may have been revised after the revolution, were probably written in 1681 or 1682 in reply to Filmer. Like Hobbes and Halifax, Locke was a utilitarian, and, unlike Filmer, he believed in a social-contract theory of the state. God, he said, had given men "natural rights" which they had enjoyed before governments existed, and they had agreed to institute governments for specified common interests, above all for the protection of life and property. Thus a contract was made between society and the government; and men retained the right to overthrow the government if it violated the principles for which it had been established. To him liberty was one of the natural rights with which men had been endowed by their Creator; the security that they procured by setting up a state should increase and not diminish that liberty. Thus Locke rejected alike Filmer's benevolent patriarchy and Hobbes's all-powerful Leviathan. Like Harrington, he considered that a balance was needed within the structure of the government and that the powers of the executive, the legislature, and the judiciary should be separated. In his view, the powers of the state should be limited; it should be no more than a trusteeship to ensure the protection of life, liberty, and property. Locke's system of checks and balances was to make a profound impression upon posterity and to influence Thomas Jefferson when he was thinking about the constitution of the United States of America. Locke was the father of Whig political philosophy, the most persuasive of all the advocates of a mixed constitution and one of the theorists whose views contributed to the climate of opinion which was ultimately responsible for the expulsion of King James II.

King James was unable to realize that times had changed since his grandfather had succeeded Queen Elizabeth I, that after all the turmoil of civil war and restoration the monarch could no longer expect to have his own way without the support of parliament and informed opinion, that new classes of people were arising, and that fresh kinds of scientific and philosophical thinking had penetrated London society, stemming from the Invisible College and the Rota Club of the 1650's; for good or for ill, materialist and utilitarian outlooks were challenging the tenets of Laudian Anglicanism and Jesuitical Roman Catholicism. It was a new world from which the scholastic fogs were slowly lifting. Like a hero of Greek tragedy, the new king of England and Scotland, blinded by stubborn pride and misled by the atmosphere of triumphant Tory loyalty in which his brother had died, moved toward his fate. And Whiggism, whether deriving from the legalistic romanticism of Coke or the utilitarian common sense of Locke, was to pervade British history for many years to come.

LIV

James II and the Revolution of 1688

An air of inexorable tragedy, then, brooded over the reign of King James II. When at the age of fifty-one he came to the throne, the Stuart monarchy had never seemed more secure; yet within three years he had lost his Crown and retired into exile, while a constitutional settlement had reduced the powers of English kings for all time. Some historians have traced the course of events back to the civil wars, emphasizing that the settlement of 1688 was the logical conclusion to the revolution that began in 1640. Others have seen it as a milestone on the road that led to the sovereignty of parliament, a road that had been opened four centuries earlier. To some it was an episode in a class war: a new gentry and a new aristocracy were asserting their authority over a reactionary king. To others again it was a practical demonstration of the truth of the political philosophies of Algernon Sidney and John Locke. Obviously there is substance in all these arguments, but the personal factor cannot be neglected: King James stands out as an almost predestined victim of his fate.

Although a few years earlier both the House of Commons and many leading public men had done their utmost to exclude him from the succession, the new king was at first greeted with enthusiasm. In his younger days he had proved himself a good soldier and sailor and a capable administrator, even if he had not made himself popular when he acted as his brother's representative in Scotland. He was known to be serious-minded, and was "a great enemy to drinking, gaming, and all such pleasures as were obstructive to business." "An honest and sincere man . . . . a great and good Englishman" were other tributes. He had inherited a trace of his father's stutter, but this gave his speech a judicious and impressive air. On the other hand, a contemporary French observer noted that he was lacking in self-control and always behaved with arrogance. He had a weakness for women, even ugly ones, but was guided ultimately by Jesuits. Far less adaptable, if more hard-working, than his elder brother, he dedicated his abnormal exertions to one supreme end: the reconversion of his kingdom to the Church of Rome.

That aim was not at first generally recognized, even if it were suspected. His religion of course was known; he attended the Mass openly; but he promised to defend the Church of England. After his coronation, with a curtailed ceremony, had taken place in April 1685, writs for a parliament were at once issued. When it met on May 19 it was found to contain very few of the old Whigs. The Earl of Sunderland, whom the king retained as his principal Secretary of State (he assured the king of his Roman Catholic sympathies), had proved himself extraordinarily adept in producing a parliament of courtiers, more royalist than any since the sixteenth century. In his opening speech the king told his hearers of his English heart and of his determination to uphold the national liberties; but he added, with truculence, that members of parliament must not think that they could ensure his attention to their wishes by rationing him with supplies of money, for that "would be a very improper method." This was taken calmly and liberal grants agreed upon. In any case parliamentary loyalty was enhanced by the fact that the kingdom was at once threatened with invasion by rebels.

The surviving Whig leaders had been driven into exile toward the end of the previous reign and, being somewhat out of touch, naturally assumed that there would be wide resistance to the accession of a Roman Catholic king. The ninth Earl of Argyll aimed to rally the Covenanters in Scotland, while the Duke of Monmouth with a few men and a tiny fleet managed to land in the west of England, where he raised a scratch army of four thousand to fight on his side for the cause of Protestantism. It was the common people—the smallholders and tradesmen of Somerset and Devonshire—who enlisted under the banner of "the Protestant Duke," not the richer gentry. Although the two invasions had neither been properly concerted nor their objects clearly defined, the government was alarmed. When Lord Churchill, personal servant of the new king (later to become celebrated as the first Duke of Marlborough), reached Somerset with two regiments, he reported that "unless speedy course be taken, we are like to lose this country [i.e., county] to the rebels." In fact Churchill clung doggedly to the duke's footsteps and finally defeated him at the night battle of Sedgemoor in July. Meanwhile Argyll had been captured after a hopeless march on Glasgow and promptly executed. The government had received a nasty jolt. Dutch republicans had connived at the invasions and Prince William of Orange, the king's son-in-law, had played an ambiguous part, though he had agreed to send over British regiments paid by the Dutch to help. A fierce revenge was taken not merely on Monmouth himself, who was put to death, and his friends, but on many humble people. The Lord Chief Justice, George Jeffreys, who had formerly been a Crown prosecutor under Charles II, "made a campaign in the west" and inflicted punishments at his "Bloody Assizes." Many men were brutally whipped and imprisoned or heavily fined (the fines to procure pardons were shared between Jeffreys himself and the king) and many were sold into slavery.

The relatively easy victory strengthened King James II's personal ambitions. He received much advice from his brother monarch, King Louis XIV of France, whom he admired. Louis XIV told him to repeal the Test and Habeas Corpus Acts and to show his gratitude to Providence for his victories by at once establishing the "true faith" in England. The French king himself was already setting a splendid example of the art of wholesale conversion: under the influence of his pious morganatic wife, Madame de Maintenon, he repealed the Edict of Nantes—which had guaranteed toleration to the French Protestants—closed their churches, and forced those who refused to submit into prison or exile. James II dismissed the "trimmer," Halifax, from his council and put Sunderland in his place; Jeffreys was appointed Lord Chancellor. He depended upon the leading Anglicans, who were headed by two sons of the first Earl of Clarendon, to be faithful enough to their announced policy of "nonresistance" to an anointed king to acquiesce in an openly Catholicizing policy. He did not realize that they might experience a conflict of loyalties.

Parliament had adjourned in July, and it reassembled in November 1685. The king now clarified his objectives. He had already safeguarded his position to some extent by securing the promise of subsidies from France, while rather foolishly trying to blackmail the French king by renewing an Anglo-Dutch alliance first concluded in 1678. Sunderland, now a consistent advocate of the French alliance, pocketed bribes and pressed the king on his extreme courses. Parliament was informed that it was the king's wish, because of the failure of the local militia in resisting Monmouth's invasion, to raise a large standing army in which Roman Catholics were to be employed. The loyal Commons showed themselves unexpectedly restless over these demands, reduced the sums of money that were asked for, and attempted to impose conditions. The king was angry. A bold M.P. even said: "We are all Englishmen and not to be frighted out of our duty by a few high words." He was committed to the Tower of London: this was one of the last attempts to restrain the right of free speech among members of parliament. The House of Lords, where Henry Compton, the Bishop of London, constituted himself the leader of opposition, was even more doubtful about the royal proposals. The king refused to tolerate criticism and prorogued his only parliament, which never met again. This episode was revealing of the temper of the nation, for the very House of Commons which James II himself had said did not contain more than 40 (out of 513) members of whom he did not approve had exhibited independence. It would not stomach Roman Catholic domination and it feared a standing army.

The king hardened his heart and went his way. He had an army of over 20,000 men, many of whom he encamped on Hounslow heath to overawe London; the soldiers were Protestants but many of the officers were Roman Catholics, some of them Irish. To establish his right to appoint such officers, contrary to the Test Act of 1673, a collusive action was brought against the Catholic colonel Sir Edward Hales in the Court of King's Bench. The judges, who held their offices at the royal pleasure, found that the king had a right to dispense with the laws since "all the laws of England are the King's law." As Supreme Governor of the Church, King James II appointed an ecclesiastical commission with the notorious Jeffreys as its president to impose discipline. This commission suspended Compton from his functions as Bishop of London: the archbishopric of York was kept vacant; and the Archbishop of Canterbury, William Sancroft, was an old man. Thus the Church was virtually leaderless.

Still the Anglicans could not be shaken from their old beliefs. Although a few courtiers were converted to the king's religion, the mass of English Churchmen spurned temptations. In 1686 a national collection on behalf of the French-Protestant refugees from the wrath of Louis XIV brought in £40,000.

While King James II proceeded to build up an army and a navy officered by Roman Catholics, to appoint a Catholic as Lord Lieutenant of Ireland, to silence Anglican critics, to seek more conversions, to force Catholic chancellors on university colleges, and to suspend the Test Acts, he strove to appeal to nonconformists as well as to his own fellow religionists with a Declaration of Indulgence (April 1687) which permitted them to enjoy freedom of public worship. Abroad the situation was changing, and not in the king's favor. King Charles II, during the last years of his reign, when he appeared to be moving toward an autocracy, had leaned heavily upon the support of King Louis XIV, who was incomparably the most powerful monarch in western Europe, in complete command of his own government, and at the height of his glory. But he had provoked the fears and enmity of other princes and states whose territories he had invaded or threatened in order to enlarge the greatness of France. Also, he had been unable to convert the truce of Ratisbon, which he had concluded with the emperor, into a permanent peace, and the rulers of Germany were again becoming apprehensive and restive. The Habsburg emperor had been previously too distracted by the menace of the Turks in the east to put up much resistance to French aggression from the west. In 1686 the storming of Buda in Hungary turned the tide and the reconquest of Hungary from the Turks had begun. Meanwhile, under the leadership of the emperor a number of states banded together in a defensive group called the League of Augsburg. More important than this, one of the rising German princes, the Hohenzollern Elector of Brandenburg, had changed sides: having once been a French ally, he now came to terms both with the emperor and with the Dutch. When at the beginning of 1688 Louis XIV started to interfere with the affairs of the Electorate of Cologne, as he had already done with those of the Elector Palatine, it looked as if the French intended to advance their frontier to the Rhine, and Germany was up in arms. All this gave encouragement to Prince William of Orange, the old foe of Louis XIV. For some years he had been unable to stir up his Dutch compatriots to a renewal of the war against France. But now, supposing he could bind together a grand alliance against France and even bring England into it, might not a unique opportunity present itself to stem French aggression?

Such a war would not be a religious one, for Catholic nations were ranged on both sides. Nevertheless, the attacks on Protestants both by Louis XIV and by James II inspired religious sympathies in Holland and elsewhere beyond the Rhine. The pope himself—Innocent XI—deprecated the idea of reviving religious warfare and through his agents, who included a cardinal and a legate, he tried to damp down King James II's growing fanaticism, with which some of the older English Roman Catholic families were in any case far from pleased. Louis XIV also quarreled with the Papacy. Thus at the very time when King James II was driving his Catholicizing policy furiously forward, other European governments were concerning themselves over the situation in England. France itself was prevented by German enmity from affording protection to the kingdom which had for so long been her client state.

Prince William of Orange regarded England chiefly as a piece upon the chessboard of Europe. But he had a declared interest, for his wife, Princess Mary, was the heiress presumptive to the English throne. Early in 1687 he sent over one of his most trusted diplomatic agents, Everard van Weede, Lord of Dykveld, as ambassador extraordinary to expostulate with King James II over his pro-French tendencies and to report upon the outlook in England. Dykveld talked to a large number of people, especially to Protestant leaders who were worried about the royal policy. King James II laughed at his fears. When Dykveld returned, he brought back letters in which some of King James's most influential subjects told Prince William of Orange of their hopes from him. Naturally the Dutch Stadtholder began to contemplate intervention in English affairs.

King James II was now planning to summon an anti-Reformation parliament to reverse the decisions taken in the reign of King Henry VIII. The question was whether such a parliament could be fashioned to do the king's will. The boroughs could certainly be subjected to pressures, but what of the counties? Several of the Lords Lieutenant were changed and were ordered to call together the principal local magnates to find out if they would agree to the repeal of the Test Acts or assist in the election of members of parliament pledged to repeal the tests and if they would actively support the king's Declaration of Indulgence. Evasive answers were received from almost every county; the three questions only provoked a universal distrust of the king's intentions. Only a small portion of the population was avowedly Roman Catholic; the gentlemen of England indicated that they had no wish to renew their allegiance to the pope.

Nevertheless, the king pushed remorselessly on his course. In May 1688 he published a second Declaration of Indulgence, to which he added a promise that a new parliament would be called that November. He ordered that his new declaration should be read out in every church in the land. The Archbishop of Canterbury and six other bishops presented a petition to the king asking him to withdraw his order on the ground that his exercise of a power to suspend the Test Acts was itself illegal. When the petition was printed and distributed, the bishops were arrested and charged with seditious libel before the Court of King's Bench. At the dramatic trial that followed, the bishops adopted a bold line in their defense, the judges were divided, and the verdict was left entirely to the jury. The nation was electrified when the bishops were acquitted.

Even before this momentous trial Prince William of Orange had made up his mind to intervene and had let it be known that if he received an invitation from men of influence to come over to England in support of the Protestant cause he would do so. The acquittal of the bishops was followed by another unexpected event. In July 1688 the queen, hitherto childless, gave birth to a son, who was to be known later as the Old Pretender. This was a critical occurrence, for now a Roman Catholic royal dynasty had been founded. Some claimed that the birth could not have been legitimate. Dr. Esmond de Beer writes:

Queen Mary's pregnancy was from the start a matter of dispute: Roman Catholics augured that the child would be a son, while Protestants suspected papistical fraudulence. From various motives the queen never allowed Princess Anne to examine her. The child was born unexpectedly early, and the queen's labour was short; Anne who was next in succession to the princess of Orange, was absent at Bath, and Archbishop Sancroft, one of the principal *ex-officio* witnesses to the birth of the heir to the crown, was a prisoner in the Tower. Almost all the witnesses of the birth were Roman Catholics who had never possessed, or Protestants who had forfeited, public confidence.

Princess Anne voiced her suspicions. The invitation to William and Mary said that the birth was generally believed to have been spurious. Although they had sent their congratulations, they later announced their doubts. In any case, they made ready to come to England.

Neither King James II nor King Louis XIV suspected any immediate danger of a revolutionary assault. Although the French king had given warning of unusual activity in the Dutch dockyards, he did not think an invasion could be undertaken before the spring of 1689. But Prince William got ready to move as soon as he knew that King Louis XIV had been drawn into a war against the emperor upon the Upper Rhine in Germany. On October 10 Prince William published a declaration explaining that his intention was to call a free parliament, to safeguard Protestantism, and to preserve the Protestant succession. King James, at last thoroughly alarmed, did his best to conciliate the Church of England and to soothe his subjects by promising an imminent meeting of parliament. London and other towns were given back their ancient charters; the suspension of the Bishop of London was removed; the ecclesiastical commission was abolished; and a general pardon was proclaimed. But it was all done too late and under the impact of fear: "plums for the children," said the contemptuous Whigs. The king's navy failed him and his army betrayed him. In November 1688, on the anniversary of the Gunpowder Plot, Prince William landed unopposed in Devonshire. Then he occupied Exeter and marched to confront his father-in-law, who took up headquarters at Salisbury.

Here King James II quickly recognized that everything around him was falling to pieces. Among those who signed the invitation to Prince William were Tories—such as Lord Danby—as well as Whigs. Danby raised a force in Yorkshire, and other risings took place in Nottingham, in Cheshire, and elsewhere. The king's officers began deserting him, including the long-trusted Lord Churchill, whose wife induced Princess Anne to abandon her father. King James II, after consulting his advisers in London and resolving that his position was hopeless, remembered his father's fate and attempted to flee the country. To the embarrassment of his son-in-law, he was caught in Kent and sent back to London. Prince William, now at Windsor, refused to confer with him and instead allowed him to leave for France on board a fishing smack. Such was the bloodless and ignominious end to his reign.

All King James II's elaborate schemes had collapsed like a castle of cards. His pro-Catholic administration disintegrated (he had dismissed the once-indispensable and now panic-stricken Sunderland in October); his army had deserted him; his own children had turned against him; his kingdom as a whole no longer wanted him. A convention was called, following the precedent of 1660, to decide upon a fresh constitutional settlement. Should the king be recalled to his throne on strict conditions? Should a regency be set up? Should King James's flight be construed as a "demise" of the Crown, permitting his elder daughter, Princess Mary, to succeed? Or should it be interpreted as an act of abdication allowing the convention to choose whom it wished to take over the government? After much discussion it was determined that the throne was "vacant," and Prince William made it clear that he was expecting to rule as well as reign, though his wife might share the royal title. Thereupon the Crown was offered jointly to William and Mary and the succession declared to be in the hands of their children or, if there were none, it was to pass to King James II's other Protestant daughter, Princess Anne. The Scottish parliament was not concerned with any subterfuges to quiet conservative opinion; William and Mary were elected to the throne of Scotland. At the same time a Declaration of Rights was drawn up. This laid down that henceforward England was never again to be governed by a Roman Catholic prince; that rulers must, by the terms of their coronation oaths, observe the laws agreed upon in parliament—these could no longer be "suspended"; parliament was to meet every year; the discipline of the army was to be ensured by annually renewable "Mutiny Acts." All this meant that a limited monarchy had been created.

The transfer of the Crown to William and Mary required the imposition of a new oath of allegiance on officeholders. The demand was painful to the Archbishop of Canterbury and other leading clerics who had genuinely believed in the Anglican doctrine of nonresistance. They became known as Nonjurors. An attempt was made, but soon abandoned, to bring back the nonconformists (who had, in general, turned against the later Stuarts, despite their blandishments) into the Anglican fold. Instead a Toleration Act was passed, which at last made nonconformity open and legal; it recognized the chapel and the Quaker meeting house. Roman Catholics, however, were still left under grave disabilities. Thus a political and religious settlement was achieved in England; but trouble continued for William and Mary for some time both in Scotland and in Ireland, where King James II had irreconcilable adherents. Moreover, everything had to be done in a great hurry; for King Louis XIV turned against William and Mary. In November he declared war on Holland. Later England was at war with France, a war that lasted, on and off, for twenty-five years.

For some thirty years political philosophers and pamphleteers had, as we have seen, been advocating theories of constitutional or "mixed" monarchy. John Locke, the common-sense, utilitarian, secular philosopher, had been the acknowledged prophet of the revolution who emphasized the responsibility of the executive to fulfill an implied trust between sovereign and people. Too much need not be made of these theoretical ideas. The facts of the growing independence of parliament—and the classes represented in parliament—and the increasing grip of Protestantism and nonconformity upon the minds of the British people are writ large in the history of the seventeenth century. So too are a distaste for autocracy, for militarism, and for the dragooning of the human mind. Finally, in an age which witnessed the beginnings of scientific thinking and of rational humanism, men were becoming more realistic and more tolerant. A spirit of expansion, adventure, and discovery was fed by a vigorous nationalism. Not far ahead lay the emergence of a great power and of two empires that circled the globe.

LV

Toward a British Empire

After King William III and Queen Mary II came to the throne of England and Scotland, a war began against France which has sometimes been called the second Hundred Years' War because it continued intermittently until the final defeat of Emperor Napoleon I in 1815. During that period Britain built and lost one empire and then created another. The beginnings of these empires date from the seventeenth century.

The motives for overseas expansion were not so much political in a narrow sense as economic and religious. The jealousy engendered by the Spanish treasure fleets, bringing their rich cargoes from the New World, which had moved the Elizabethans to piracy and war, was reinforced by envy of the rise of the Dutch, who by their enterprise and hard work throughout the world had created a thriving commerce and a busy carrying trade. Both nations depended upon colonies or military outposts. After the conclusion of the war with Spain in 1604 and after a treaty of peace had been signed between the Dutch and the Spaniards in 1611, the minds of Englishmen of vision, especially of ambitious London merchants, turned to the possibility of following in the footsteps of these rival colonizers. They had few concrete advantages to begin with: the discoveries and claims of the Cabots, the traditions of English sea power, the fisheries in Newfoundland, the trading stations of the East India Company. But England and Ireland lay upon the routes to America and the West Indies, and the explorations and adventures of the later Elizabethans had provided a fund of knowledge. The writings of Richard Hakluyt and others inspired thoughts of yet-unplumbed El Dorados; the progress of trade and agriculture had brought an accumulation of funds available for speculative investments.

The economic aspects were clear and simple, but a religious motive existed as well, although it should not be overstressed. Although ideas of religious toleration were in the air in the first half of the seventeenth century, they were not yet put into practice. The repressive policy of Archbishop Laud made sectarian Puritans seek a new land where they might enjoy their faith in freedom. Some Scottish Presbyterians and English Roman Catholics felt the same urge. Sometimes economic and religious considerations were inextricably mixed. It has been suggested that Puritan beliefs gave men a peculiar vocation for the pursuit of new trades and ventures. Finally, governments were willing to export political prisoners and criminals to populate and cultivate colonial possessions.

At the beginning of the seventeenth century the old colonies deliberately and, to a limited extent, successfully created were in Ireland. In its early years the heads of two clans in Ulster, the earls of Tyrone and Tyrconnel, preferred to abandon their vast properties there rather than give their obedience to the Lord Deputy. Their lands were confiscated and sold in parcels to planters. The Scots seized this opportunity, partly from religious motives, and a Presbyterian colony was then founded in Ulster, whose existence has colored the history of Ireland ever since. At the same time an energetic group of business men in London dispatched settlers and built the town of Londonderry. Plantations were established in other parts of Ireland, such as Wexford, during the first quarter of the century, but despite the cheapness of the land only a limited number of colonists were forthcoming from England. This colonization had the backing of the government, which hoped to strengthen Protestantism in Ireland and to reinforce the political power of the Dublin administration. The Earl of Strafford was a strong believer in the virtues of plantation and aimed to extend it to Connaught, but he met with great opposition from the existing proprietors. When he won his way and appointed "undertakers," settlers were shy. Archbishop Laud commiserated with Strafford that "he should want men in Ireland and that the while there should be here [in London] such an universal running to New England and God knows whither." Only Scots remained anxious to settle and they were no longer wanted. Neither had the Puritans any wish to come under the iron rule of Strafford. In fact the early history of the Irish plantations showed that the desire for religious freedom was an important factor in inducing men to emigrate across the Atlantic, for, on the surface, Ireland was a far more convenient and attractive country for settlement than America.

During the Interregnum a strong impulse was given to the colonization of Ireland. In 1642 the English parliament set aside 2,500,000 acres of Irish land to satisfy adventurers who advanced money for the reconquest of Ireland, and in 1652 an act confiscated the lands of all Catholic owners who had taken part in the rebellion of 1641. A survey was carried out, and two-thirds of the land of Ireland is said to have changed hands. Oliver Cromwell wrote when he was at Wexford that it was to be wished "that an honest people should come to plant here" and he invited the "godly" in New England to leave their American homes for Ireland. Many of his soldiers settled in Ireland, since Irish lands were used as a substitute for paying them their arrears. Thus the Restoration government inherited a complicated problem. The existence of colonies of Ulster Scots or Cromwellian soldiers was not welcome to the king, but it was not easy to extrude them or even desirable to do so, so long as they behaved. Indeed in the reign of King Charles II Ireland must have seemed an ideal colony. It had a large and obedient population; its revenues increased so that the full costs of its administration could be met; and the constitutional system originally introduced by Sir Edward Poynings persisted, so that Irish parliaments were not difficult to handle. In the twelfth Earl and first Duke of Ormonde Charles II had a Lord Lieutenant of the highest capabilities who managed for a time to hold the heterogeneous population of English and Scottish settlers and native Irish together. The history of Scotland under King Charles II was far less happy, for the discontent and restlessness of the Covenanters contributed to the ultimate overthrow of King James II.

While colonies were being founded in Ireland during the reign of King James I, the scheme for colonizing Virginia, which had failed in the reign of Queen Elizabeth I, was revived. In April 1606, two years after he had signed the peace treaty with Spain, the king constituted a royal council for Virginia to supervise its colonization. Two companies of adventurers offered to participate, one in London, the other in Plymouth. The Plymouth settlement was soon abandoned, but the London company persevered in the face of all sorts of obstacles. The first permanent English colony in America was set up at Jamestown on Chesapeake Bay in April 1607. The area, covered with swamp and forest, did not look too inviting, but the colonists had an energetic leader in Captain John Smith and excellent backing from London. Later a strict governor gave the colony a sense of discipline, a boatload of women brought fresh inspiration to the toiling colonists, and though no gold was discovered there, as had been hoped, tobacco proved to be a paying crop. In 1624 the Virginia Company was dissolved by King James I, and a royal charter issued by King Charles I in the following year provided for the appointment of a royal governor and a council vested in the Crown. Population and trade then expanded. During the latter half of the century, in consequence of the Navigation Acts policy, the Virginians were compelled to send their tobacco to England for sale or re-export. Whether this "enumeration" of tobacco, as it was called, was a genuine grievance or not, by 1688 Virginia had become a prosperous British colony with a population, including slaves, of about 100,000 inhabitants.

The first permanent proprietary colony to be founded in America was Maryland, north of Virginia. The founder was one of the original members of the Virginia Company, the first Lord Baltimore, who had been converted to Roman Catholicism. Although its charter provided for the establishment of Anglicanism in Maryland, in fact all Christian religions were tolerated. The second Lord Baltimore made his peace with Cromwell and also retained his position as proprietor after the Restoration. Like Virginia, Maryland depended mainly on tobacco exports and enjoyed a modest prosperity.

Before the foundation of Maryland in 1632, the moribund Plymouth Company of Virginia was reconstituted and organized an expedition of colonists to New England. These settlers were extreme Puritans or separatists, who, because of their desire to separate from the Church, had originally left their homes in Lincolnshire and elsewhere to migrate to Holland. The London syndicate drove a hard bargain with these Puritans, who had to undertake to work the land in common for seven years in order to pay off the cost of their voyage. About one hundred of them landed from a ship called the "Mayflower" in November 1620 and are known to history as the Pilgrim Fathers. Their colony was called New Plymouth after the English port from which they sailed; it was ultimately absorbed into the Massachusetts Bay Company, which founded a larger colony in 1630. Here in a flat wide country bordering the Atlantic they fished, grew corn, and built up a Bible Commonwealth. They survived their early struggles and by 1642 the two colonies of New Plymouth and Massachusetts had some 20,000 inhabitants. Other colonies, offshoots from this "New England," were established in the 1630's— New Hampshire, Maine, Connecticut, and Rhode Island. Rhode Island obtained a charter from parliament and was the most liberal and democratic of all the early American colonies. These New England colonies, it has been pointed out, arose not out of any deliberate desire for imperial expansion or even overseas economic development but because of the deep schism in the Church of England which was among the causes of the civil wars. These colonies were exceptional in another way, for they came to be ruled by the stockholders themselves and not indirectly by a proprietary group in London.

During the civil wars four of these colonies entered into a pact known as the New England Confederation. They did not consult London about this. They wanted the Parliamentarians to win the war, but they had already manifested a spirit of independence and had no wish for close relations with the mother country. Virginia and Maryland were Royalist in sympathies, but had to acquiesce in Parliamentary rule, especially after an act had been passed in 1650 forbidding all commercial intercourse between England and pro-Royalist colonies. In the reign of King Charles II Carolina was founded and became a center for smuggling with New England. In 1664 during the second Dutch war the colony of New Netherlands, with a capital in New Amsterdam, was captured without much difficulty by an expeditionary force from New England and was renamed New York. In 1681 a proprietary colony was founded by William Penn and a Quaker syndicate and was named Pennsylvania, while in 1682 New Jersey, originally forming part of a large grant made to James, Duke of York, after the defeat of the Dutch, was split into two colonies, which were to be reunited again in 1702.

King James II displayed considerable interest in the American colonies. In 1686 he sent Sir Edmund Andros, who had previously represented him in New York, to become governor of all the New England colonies. Andros ruled with a firm hand, enforcing both religious toleration and the full rigor of the Navigation Acts. In 1688 he received orders to extend his rule to New York and New Jersey; but when the revolution drove King

James II from his throne, a rising took place in Boston, the capital of Massachusetts, and thus the Jacobite Dominion of New England came to a sudden end.

Although the American colonies, in the light of later history, rightly loom large in the story of the seventeenth century, to an English administrator of the time they seemed far less important than Ireland or even Bermuda and the West Indies. Bermuda was settled accidentally after Sir George Somers and other leaders of an expedition to Virginia were shipwrecked there in 1609. They discovered a colony of wild hogs, left there originally by a Portuguese navigator, and upon this somewhat unpromising basis a colony was built, receiving its first royal charter in 1615. In 1625 a small expedition arrived at Barbados in the West Indies, which soon began to flourish on sugar cultivated by Negro slaves. Barbados was the most Royalist of the colonies during the civil wars; afterward it became the home of a fabulous aristocracy. A Puritan attempt to found a godly colony on Providence Island (now known as Santa Catalina) failed in 1641, but the seizure of Jamaica from the Spaniards by a Cromwellian force in 1654 proved ultimately to be the means for expanding British rule over the West Indies. The Bahamas were planted in the reign of King Charles II, and by the end of the century the whole group of Caribbean islands was doing a good trade in sugar, molasses, tobacco, cotton, and other commodities. Though the cocoa crop, once the pride of the West Indies, failed when disease killed the trees and though a profitable business in buccaneering at the expense of the Spanish empire was stopped by a treaty in 1670, these colonies, ruled, like the American colonies, by a governor and assemblies under royal charter, became a bright jewel in the English Crown and long remained so.

The only English possession in north Africa in the seventeenth century was Tangier, which had been acquired as part of the dowry of King Charles II's Portuguese queen. It was hoped that it might be developed as an entrepôt for trade with the Barbary states, but it was isolated and expensive to maintain; when the king was unable to effect its sale, it was evacuated in 1683. Bombay was also acquired by the marriage treaty, but in 1668 it was granted by charter to the East India Company; it became the headquarters of the company in 1687. A large factory was also developed at Madras, where the fort was strengthened in 1677. After the Restoration the East India Company received a new charter and henceforward operated as a permanent joint-stock company whose ups and downs were reflected in its dividends. The company had to contend with many difficulties following the decline of the Mogul empire and the rise of the warlike Mahrattas; it was also threatened by Dutch rivalries and Dutch wars. But it had a number of brilliant servants, and it laid the foundations of the British empire in India. The Royal Africa Company, founded in 1672 after a predecessor had gone bankrupt, also enjoyed a period of prosperity in the reign of King Charles II, profiting chiefly from the export of slaves to the West Indies and to America, but in the 1680's its dividends fell. One other lonely outpost of the first British empire which flourished in the seventeenth century was Newfoundland. A governor was appointed and a fortification built at St. John's, the largest of the small settlements there, in 1630, but the fisheries remained a bone of contention with France and the dispute about its ownership was not finally settled until the eighteenth century.

Can it be said that the English governments in the seventeenth century had any consistent colonial policy? The fact was that the colonies were so scattered and the means of communication with them were so poor that it was impossible for any real control to be exercised from London. Moreover, the civil wars and the Interregnum interrupted the evolution of policy. On the whole, therefore, the English colonies of this age enjoyed a high degree of independence. They were virtually freed from taxation except for a five-per-cent tax on the value of their exports, and they could make their own laws. They were subject to the Crown and not to parliament, although of course they were ruled by parliament for a time after the execution of King Charles I. When the Confederation of New England was founded, no permission was sought from the home government. The Navigation Acts, which imposed restrictions on the exports and carrying trade of the colonies, were bitterly resented and frequently evaded. Broadly, the colonies were regarded in fact as organs for the promotion of English commerce. It was originally hoped that the American colonies would provide precious metals and timber and stores needed for royal navy; King James I had not approved of tobacco, which proved to be one of their most profitable crops. It was expected that their goods would be fetched and carried in English ships and the system of "enumerated commodities"—such as tobacco and sugar—was intended to make England into the most important entrepôt in the world without being damaging to colonial trade. King Charles II's administration, however, was aware that the relations between the mother country and its independent-minded colonies might easily become delicate. John Evelyn recorded discussions in the Council for Foreign Plantations when the fear of the New England colonies "breaking away from all dependence on this nation" was seriously considered. Historians have since argued that it was precisely because the Council for Foreign Plantations and later the Board of Trade, which were responsible for colonial government, interfered with the colonies so little that they endured so long.

On the whole, seventeenth-century English governments preferred not to raise awkward constitutional questions, and governors of the colonies, although they might be worried by inquiries from Whitehall, knew that it was more essential to please their subjects than to pacify the home government. But the exclusive commercial policy promoted from England was a source of grievance, and it has been said with justice that "imperial progress . . . did not settle administrative problems, but helped to accumulate them." Such was the colonial legacy of England in the eighteenth century.

LVI

Britain in 1688: Conclusion

Although the word "Britain" was used in the seventeenth century, Britain did not yet exist as a constitutional entity, for statutory union with Scotland did not come until 1707 nor union with Ireland until 1801. Both these countries, though dependent upon England, retained their own parliaments and governors—Royal Commissioners in Scotland and Lords Lieutenant in Ireland. The colonies or plantations were very loosely administered from London and, except for the policy embodied in the Navigation Acts, were left to local governors and assemblies to rule.

The population of England in 1688 has been estimated at about 5,500,-000, that of Ireland at 2,000,000, that of Scotland at under 1,000,000, and that of the colonies at over 250,000. This total population of the British empire of under 9,000,000 may be compared with some 18,000,-000 or 19,000,000 inhabitants in King Louis XIV's France, 6,000,000 in Spain, and 2,500,000 in the Dutch Republic. These arithmetical facts spelled the relative imperial decline of Spain and Holland in the eighteenth century and the coming costly struggle with a resurgent France.

In Ireland—in effect, the largest of the British plantations—in spite of various restrictions there was a fair degree of general prosperity: exports of cattle, fish, cloth, and wool paid for imports and stimulated commerce and shipping. In Scotland it was far otherwise. Under the Cromwellian Protectorate free trade and comparative peace had brought a good deal of economic advantage to the northern part of Britain, but it suffered a setback at the time of the Restoration. First the Rescissory Act had brought about the abolition of all the arrangements flowing from its temporary union with England in one Commonwealth; the abolition of free trade with England and with the English overseas possessions had injured foreign trade; finally, the return to episcopacy had provoked restlessness among the Presbyterian Covenanters, whose leader, the first Marquis of Argyll, had been executed at the Restoration. Turbulence prevailed. In 1666 the Covenanters had attacked Edinburgh, but had been defeated in the Pentland Hills. The Earl of Lauderdale, who for a time was Royal Commissioner, had then imposed a system of coercion and had quartered a "highland host" in the Lowlands. The assassination of James Sharp, Archbishop of St. Andrews, in 1679 led to further repression. In that year the Covenanters again suffered defeat at the battle of Bothwell Bridge. The rule of James, Duke of York, which followed that of Lauderdale in the eighties, was also strict and unpopular; so was the rough behavior of John Graham of Claverhouse and his dragoons.

On the whole, the standard of living in Scotland was pitifully low, though that of education was high. There was a noticeable absence of timber, especially in the Highlands. The ordinary people are said to have lived on beer, broth, and bannocks. The largest town, Edinburgh, had a population of only about 20,000; it was not the beautiful city it is today; Glasgow, with half its population, was then more attractive. On the whole, the Stuart era in England was a disaster for Scotland, and when King James II exerted his influence to try to Catholicize the country (in 1686 the Lord Chancellor and secretaries of State for Scotland all declared themselves to be Roman Catholics), it merely inclined the majority of the people, outside the Highlands, to turn with relief to King William III.

In England, London and its environs, with a population of over one-half million, dominated the country and enjoyed much business. Bristol, Norwich, and Newcastle, the next-largest towns, were very small in comparison with the capital. The wealth of the country was concentrated in the south, in spite of the beginnings of the coal and cotton industries in the north. It has been estimated, on the basis of certain taxation returns, that the north had only one quarter the wealth of the south. In general, towns were overcrowded and disease spread rapidly among the poor. The average life-expectancy is said to have been thirty years; over one-third of the children born died before they were six. Smallpox, typhus, tuberculosis, rickets, and syphilis were common, and medicine was still mainly experimental. The extent of the national poverty is not easy to measure, but it appears to have been substantial; Gregory King thought that over a million people, about one-fifth of the entire population, were in occasional receipt of alms. Out of the poor rate nearly a million pounds a year was spent, and it is known that very large sums were distributed in one form or another by private charity. The poor and unemployed ate meat only once a week; their usual meal consisted of bread and cheese, the bread being made of rye, not of wheat. Wages paid amounted to only a shilling or two a day, sometimes with food, sometimes without. Small farms, small businesses, and shops constituted the social units of the time, and it is possible that this characteristic patriarchy had its good as well as its bad side. But life was short and uncertain: only slowly were the inventions and discoveries of the early age of science making an impact upon the common man.

The country was still predominantly rural. Emphasis is sometimes laid on the expansion of the coal industry, for the annual production of coal in 1688 had been estimated at about 3,000,000 tons. Most of this was not used in industry, however, but for domestic heating, by those who could afford it, to compensate for the difficulty in obtaining timber. Coal was carried not only by sea but along rivers by barges and then delivered by pack horse. Roads were not good, particularly in the north of England, and in the extreme west they were impassable in winter. The poorness of most roads and of transport in general and the concentration of a huge population in London and the south gave rise to a particularism in the provinces, where the rich and great exerted a profound political and social influence. The aristocracy and the leading gentry furnished the ruling classes and the membership of parliament. Their country houses and spas, where they lived a leisured life, may still be seen today—and indeed from them Britain continued to be ruled for many generations, at least until the first German war. South and north spoke almost a different language, as they did at the time of the Norman Conquest and were to do during the so-called Industrial Revolution of the eighteenth century and afterward. The south was in fact so much cut off from the north and from Scotland that it was possibly more affected by its proximity to the French and Dutch civilizations and cultures than by being the capital of "Britain."

✦ AN ADOLESCENT AGE

In the field of religion, after the immediate "Laudian" reaction at the Restoration, toleration extended slowly and painfully, while superstition declined. The rise of the Latitudinarian or Broad Church movement in the Church of England, though it was foreshadowed during the reign of King Charles I, may be definitely traced from the reign of his son. The High Church movement did not die, and it was to be partly absorbed by the Nonjurors after 1688, but it received a severe blow from the blatant Catholicizing policies of King James II. Works on natural theology began to be published and utilitarian ethics advanced. Men like Lord Herbert of Cherbury and Dr. Thomas Hobbes even began to sow doubts about the truths of the Christian religion among educated people, while the political arguments for state religion were more freely used. However, it would be a mistake to imagine that because King Charles II himself was easygoing and some members of his court set a bad example of social behavior, there were not many very sincere practicing Christians at the center of public affairs; for every Buckingham or Sunderland, with his openly cynical conduct, might be found dozens of Evelyns, Reresbys, Hydes, and the like, devoted women, stainless clergy, and even rising scientists, like Robert Boyle and Isaac Newton, who fervently upheld the Christian faith. But superstition was to some extent reduced by the climate of the times. One of the last executions for witchcraft in England took place at Exeter in 1685, though belief in witchcraft persisted strongly in Scotland, Ireland, and the New England colonies.

In general it has been said that "latitudinarianism and the authority of the new science, the growing cult of reason and scepticism which was beginning to chasten every kind of confident fanaticism made men more willing to question their own assumptions and consequently hesitant to punish those of their fellow men." It was because of this growing toleration that nonconformity survived the repression of the first years of King Charles II's reign, though it suffered severely in the process. Oliver Cromwell's famous chaplain, Dr. John Owen, before his death noted that "there were great and woful decays in the churches, in church members, in professors of all sorts" and that many Christians found it "hard to keep up their former pitch." The Reverend Richard Baxter also thought he detected signs of a Puritan twilight. Naturally those who had lived through the exciting, prosperous days of the Puritan supremacy in the middle of the century took a pessimistic view; in fact nonconformity struggled through to achieve legal toleration in 1688, even though its adherents remained excluded from political and university life. The attitude of mind of the dissenters was also to play a full part in the eighteenth and nineteenth centuries—as it still does today. On the whole, the milder outlook in religion, the emphasis laid upon its ethical content, which was to increase as the seventeenth century reached its close, and the importance attached to "the candle of reason"—lighting many of the Holy Scriptures—all sustain the telling phrase used by Mr. David Ogg that this was "an adolescent age."

Thinking men in general had become less concerned with the ritual side of religion than was the fanatical and perhaps half-mad King

James II, but the fires that had burned at Smithfield in the reign of Queen Mary I had not been forgotten. Men who considered such matters did not want a revival of persecution or a close alliance with Catholic France or Spain or the restoration of allegiance to the Papacy. This was why, even though he changed the Lords Lieutenant of the counties and exerted every kind of pressure and cajolement, King James II was unable to exact sufficient promises from the electorate that if he called another parliament it would abolish the Test Acts against the Roman Catholics that had been passed in his brother's reign. The investigations that were carried out on his behalf by the Lords Lieutenant proved conclusively that the fate of his program was settled. The persecution of the Protestants in France when King Louis XIV revoked the Edict of Nantes caused a genuine and widespread fear of the consequences of such a policy. The very soldiers encamped at Hounslow to overawe London had cheered when the bishops were acquitted for refusing to support it. Mutiny and desertion had been forecast even earlier by informed foreign observers when they saw how furiously the king was driving. Even Jesuits had remarked upon his dependence upon blockheads and sycophants. Gradually the confidence of the nation in its government was undermined. In April 1687 John Evelyn had noted in his diary the state of confusion that followed the Declaration of Indulgence, while the nonconformists refused to be seduced into allying themselves with "papists." Sir John Reresby, who was loyal to the king to the end, noted in York that "neither the gentry nor common people seemed much afeard or concerned" at the coming of the Prince of Orange. That the revolution which the Dutchman headed was on behalf of a free parliament, the preservation of the Protestant religion, and the government as established by law was accepted by nearly all classes and in almost every part of the country. It is not possible to sustain the view that the "Glorious Revolution" was carried out by the aristocracy in its own interest, though naturally it furnished the leaders.

The Bill of Rights was not a revolutionary document in the same sense as were the sweeping decisions that were taken by the French Revolutionaries of 1789 or by revolutionaries who have conquered great nations in modern times, but certain powers employed by King James II and all earlier monarchs to suspend statute law were declared both illegal and pernicious. The abolition of the standing army in time of peace, the guarantees for the regular holding of parliaments, in which freedom of speech was assured, and the bans imposed upon prerogative courts that undermined the ordinary judicial system all contributed to the evolution of what we now call constitutional government.

But constitutional government needs to be worked. It might have been thought that after the legislation agreed to in 1640 and 1641 and the warning given by the execution of King Charles I clear and effective limitations in the powers of the monarchy within an understood constitutional and legal framework would have been accepted. In fact the task of the Puritan rebels had to be completed in 1688. Though much that the later Stuarts claimed the right to do had been done by Queen Elizabeth I, times were seen to have changed since her death. Since then the British people had not been fortunate in the wisdom of their rulers. They could scarcely rejoice in the fanatical King James II, even if in the eyes of some he were a saint, like Edward the Confessor or Henry VI. Nor in fact did they take to James's dour son-in-law with much enthusiasm, although he had already proved himself to be a hero. Early British history must, unhappily, be largely the record of kings, the ruling class, and their publicists, for beyond that all too little is known about the ways and the thoughts of the ancestors of Englishmen. Up to 1688 the feelings of ordinary people seldom revealed themselves except in mute protests or isolated and hopeless risings.

Nevertheless, nations no doubt receive mostly what they deserve. In carrying through the revolution of 1688 the British people showed themselves for what they were—neither sheep nor sycophants. Since then there have been no other great political revolutions. Reforms have so far been achieved with little violence; peaceful social and economic changes have taken place. Finally, in the twentieth century has evolved a Welfare State ruled by a democratic parliamentary government that is now required to solve the problems of the Nuclear Age.

SUGGESTED READINGS

GENERAL

The standard bibliographies are C. Gross, *The Sources and Literature of English History from the earliest times to about 1485* (1915), a new edition of which is now being planned; Conyers Read, *Bibliography of British History, Tudor Period, 1485–1603* (1958); and Godfrey Davies, *Bibliography of British History, Stuart Period, 1603–1714* (1928), now being revised by Dr. Mary Frear Keeler. The *Annual Bulletin of Historical Literature,* published by the Historical Association of London, and A. T. Milne, *Writings on British History,* bring these bibliographies up to date. For the purposes of ordinary students of British history, the elaborate bibliographies printed in the *Oxford History of England,* edited by G. N. Clark, are sufficient. Helps recommended for students are *Handbook of British Chronology* (1939), edited by F. M. Powicke and others, which is now being revised, and *Handbook of Dates for Students of English History,* edited by C. R. Cheney (1945).

The *Oxford History of England* is now complete for this period, except for the volume on *The Fifteenth Century* which is promised from Professor E. F. Jacob. Though these volumes vary in quality and the first is slightly out of date, they are indispensable, and my debt to them is obvious. They are listed below under separate headings. For a briefer, livelier, and less expensive presentation of English history, students may be referred to the volumes in the *Pelican History of England,* which are also listed below. Another series, published by Longmans and edited by W. N. Medlicott, also promises to be excellent, but is far from complete. A series published by Methuen includes a first-class book on the Tudor period by G. R. Elton, which is now being revised.

The best single-volume histories of England are perhaps those by Dr. G. M. Trevelyan, O.M. (1927), and Sir Keith Feiling (1953). The former is written from a radical point of view, the latter is more conservative.

EUROPEAN BACKGROUND

If Oxford is the prime source for British history, Cambridge furnishes much of the background. *The Cambridge Medieval History* and *The Cambridge Modern History* should be consulted. The latter is in the process of being entirely rewritten as *The New Cambridge Modern History,* under the general editorship of G. N. Clark. The first two volumes, *The Renaissance 1493–1520,* edited by G. R. Potter (1957), and *The Reformation 1520–1599,* edited by G. R. Elton (1958), have already appeared. There is also a *Cambridge History of the British Empire* (1936). J. A. Williamson, *A Short History of British Expansion* (1953) and *The Foundation and Growth of the British Empire* (1953) are useful introductions. For Britain's neighbor, France, reference may be made to Professor Albert Guérard's admirable volume in the same series as my book.

SOCIAL AND ECONOMIC HISTORY

The standard work is Ephraim Lipson, *The Economic History of England;* Vol. I, *The Middle Ages* (1956); Vols. II and III, *The Age of Mercantilism* (1948); but it is arranged by subjects and is somewhat old-fashioned. J. H. Clapham, *Concise Economic History of Britain to 1750* (Cambridge, 1949), is a good short introduction. *The Cambridge Economic History of Europe* (1952) contains chapters on Britain. L. F. Salzman, *English Industries of the Middle Ages* (1923) and *English Trade in the Middle Ages* (1931), as well as other books on the later periods, may be consulted. G. M. Trevelyan, *English Illustrated Social History* (1952), does not begin until the age of Chaucer. C. S. Orwin and C. S. Orwin, *The Open Fields* (1954), is stimulating, but has been criticized. Books about the manor are numerous, but tend to be too precise.

LEGAL AND CONSTITUTIONAL HISTORY

A standard book is W. S. Holdsworth, *History of English Law* (1956), but it is said to be weak on the early period. T. F. T. Plucknett, *A Concise History of the Common Law* (1943), is a good introduction. Constitutional history is covered by J. E. A. Jolliffe, *The Constitutional History of Medieval England* (1937), and Sir David Keir, *The Constitutional History of Modern Britain* (1960). The former is controversial and difficult.

ECCLESIASTICAL HISTORY

The volumes edited by W. Hunt and W. R. W. Stephens entitled *History of the Church of England* (1901) are sound but somewhat dated. J. R. H. Moorman, *A History of the Church in England* (1953), is a good short introduction. M. D. Knowles in *The Monastic Order in England* (1949) and other later books on the religious orders gives the most recent and impartial survey of the English monastic system until its dissolution.

LITERATURE AND THE ARTS

For literature, reference may be made to *The Cambridge History of English Literature* (1932) and, for an introduction, to the *Cambridge Concise History of English Literature;* for the arts, to *The Oxford*

History of English Art and the relevant volumes of the *Pelican History of Art*. A. Lane Poole, *Medieval England* (Oxford, 1958), and *Shakespeare's England,* ed. C. T. Onions (Oxford, 1916), cover most aspects of art and social life in the period under review. There are also various relevant volumes in the Home University Library, now taken over by the Oxford University Press.

MUSIC

Ernest Walker, *A History of Music in England* (1952), and H. C. Colles, *The Growth of Music* (Oxford, 1950), are both useful works of reference; F. Harrison, *Music in Medieval Britain* (1958), is the latest word on that subject. A *New Oxford History of Music* is being published.

SCIENCE

See H. Butterfield, *Origins of Modern Science 1300–1800* (1949), A. C. Crombie, *The History of Science, A.D. 400–1650* (1961), and W. C. D. Whetham, *A History of Science* (1948).

DOCUMENTS

Professor D. C. Douglas is editing a series of useful *English Historical Documents* which give extracts, in translation where necessary, from laws and literature. Several volumes, including the first two on Anglo-Saxon and Norman times, have already been published. The constitutional documents edited by W. Stubbs, R. W. Prothero, S. R. Gardiner (all Oxford), and C. Grant Robertson (Methuen) are still extremely useful. G. R. Elton, *The Tudor Constitution* (Cambridge, 1960) has now superseded J. R. Tanner, *Tudor Constitutional Documents.*

WALES, SCOTLAND, AND IRELAND

J. E. Lloyd, *History of Wales* (1930) and *A History of Wales from the Earliest Times to the Edwardian Conquest* (1939), may be recommended. P. Hume Brown, *History of Scotland* (1911), is still as good as any. Edmund Curtis has written a *History of Ireland* (1952) and *A History of Mediaeval Ireland, 1086–1513* (1942). There is also a book on *Ireland under the Tudors* (1890) and one on *Ireland under the Stuarts* (1916) by R. Bagwell.

The following list of books by periods is necessarily a very small selection. On the whole, I have limited myself to the more up-to-date books on each period of a fairly general character, which may be of value to students. That is why I have omitted famous books by Stubbs, Froude, Gairdner, Gardiner, and others, not because such books are not worth reading, but simply because they need to be considered in the light of later scholarship. In most cases I have given the dates of the latest editions. Where I do not give the place of publication, it may be assumed to be London.

I have also not attempted to list any articles; but to have the latest information the files of *The English Historical Review* and *The Economic History Review* must be consulted. More popular articles will be found in *History* and *History Today*. The publications of the Historical Association are also of the greatest value. To name two recent examples, Joan Thirsk on *Tudor Enclosures* and Edward Miller on *The Origins of Parliament* are extremely enlightening. The Historical Association also publishes useful select bibliographies as "Helps for Students of History."

✿ BOOK I — EARLY TIMES

GENERAL

R. G. Collingwood and J. N. L. Myres, *Roman Britain and the English Settlements* (Oxford, 1937).

I. A. Richmond, *Roman Britain* (1960).

F. M. Stenton, *Anglo-Saxon England* (Oxford, 1947).

D. Whitelocke, *The Beginnings of English Society* (1952).

THE BEGINNINGS

Undoubtedly the best introductions are Cyril Fox, *The Personality of Britain* (1947), and Stuart Piggott, *British Prehistory* (1949). There are also of popular appeal J. and C. Hawkes, *Prehistoric Britain* (1947), and Jacquetta Hawkes, *Early Britain* (1949). T. D. Kendrick, *The Druids* (1927), and R. J. C. Atkinson, *Stonehenge* (1956), throw fitful gleams on a difficult subject. V. Gordon Childe, *Prehistoric Communities of the British Isles* (1947), is stimulating.

ROMAN BRITAIN

Of books on Roman Britain there is no end. Here are some of them:

E. Birley, *Roman Britain and the Roman Army* (Kendal, 1953).

G. C. Boon, *Roman Silchester* (1957).

A. R. Burn, *Agricola and Roman Britain* (1953).

Julius Caesar, *The Conquest of Gaul*, ed. S. A. Handford (1951).

M. P. Charlesworth, *The Lost Province* (Oxford, 1959).

A. Fox, *Roman Exeter* (1952).

F. Haverfield, *The Romanization of Roman Britain* (Oxford, 1923).

F. Haverfield and G. MacDonald, *The Roman Occupation of Britain* (Oxford, 1924).

T. Rice Holmes, *Ancient Britain and the Invasion of Julius Caesar* (1907).

I. A. Richmond, *Roman Britain* (1947).

Tacitus, *Britain and Germany* (Penguin ed., 1948).

R. E. M. Wheeler, *Prehistoric and Roman Wales* (1925).

ANGLO-SAXON ENGLAND

By far the best book is R. H. Hodgkin, *A History of the Anglo-Saxons* (Oxford, 1952). Sir Arthur Bryant's *The Story of England: Makers of the Realm* (1953) sweeps one forward in an exciting way. Good popular biographies, both by E. S. Duckworth, are *St. Dunstan of Canterbury* (1955) and *Alfred the Great and his England* (1957). L. M. Larson has written on *Canute the Great* (1912), but some of his opinions are arguable. For art, see D. Talbot Rice, *English Art 871–1100* (1952), and G. Baldwin Brown, *The Arts in Early England* (1937). M. and C. H. B. Quennell, *Everyday Life in Anglo-Saxon, Viking and Norman Times* (1926), is a good popular book. The standard texts, Bede, *A History of the English Church and People* (Penguin, 1953), and *The Anglo-Saxon Chronicle*, ed. G. N. Garmonsway (Oxford, 1955), are available in these up-to-date versions.

✿ BOOK II — MIDDLE AGES

GENERAL

F. Barlow, *The Feudal Kingdom of England 1022–1216* (1955).

H. Cam, *England Before Elizabeth* (1950).

G. G. Coulton, *Medieval Panorama* (1940).

H. A. L. Fisher, *Political History of England 1485–1547* (1906).

A. Lane Poole, *From Domesday Book to Magna Carta 1087–1216* (Oxford, 1951).

F. B. Marsh, *English Rule in Gascony* (1912).

M. McKisack, *The Fourteenth Century 1307–1399* (Oxford, 1959).

A. R. Myers, *England in the Late Middle Ages* (1959).

C. Oman, *Political History of England 1377–1485* (1906).

E. Perroy, *The Hundred Years War* (1951).

F. M. Powicke, *Medieval England* (1931).

F. M. Powicke, *King Henry III and the Lord Edward* (Oxford, 1947).

F. M. Powicke, *The Thirteenth Century 1216–1307* (Oxford, 1953).

J. H. Ramsay, *Lancaster and York* (1892).

J. H. Ramsay, *Genesis of Lancaster* (1913).

H. Rashdall, *Universities of Europe in the Middle Ages* (Oxford, 1936).

A. L. Smith, *Church and State in the Middle Ages* (Oxford, 1913).

D. M. Stenton, *English Society in the Early Middle Ages* (1952).

BIOGRAPHIES

S. Armitage Smith, *John of Gaunt* (1904).

E. F. Jacob, *Henry V and the Invasion of France* (1947).

S. Painter, *The Reign of King John* (1949).

F. M. Powicke, *Stephen Langton* (1928).

A. Steel, *Richard II* (Cambridge, 1941).

F. M. Stenton, *William the Conqueror* (1915).

W. L. Warren, *King John* (1961).

H. B. Workman, *John Wyclif* (Oxford, 1926).

CONSTITUTIONAL HISTORY

J. F. Baldwin, *The King's Council in England during the Middle Ages* (1913).

S. H. Chrimes, *An Introduction to the Administration of Medieval England* (Oxford, 1952).

W. S. McKechnic, *Magna Carta* (Glasgow, 1914).

F. Pollock and F. W. Maitland, *The History of English Law* (Cambridge, 1911).

G. O. Sayles, *The Medieval Foundations of England* (1948).

T. F. Tout, *The Place of Edward II in English History* (1936).

R. F. Treharne, *The Baronial Plan of Reform 1258–63* (Manchester, 1932).

B. Wilkinson, *Constitutional History of Medieval England* (1958).

SOCIAL AND ECONOMIC HISTORY

H. S. Bennett, *Life in the English Manor* (Cambridge, 1960).

M. W. Beresford, *The Lost Villages of England* (1954).

G. C. Coulton, *Chaucer and his England* (1937).

Ed. J. Gairdner, *The Paston Letters* (1904).

C. Oman, *The Great Revolt of 1381* (Oxford, 1906).

E. Power, *The Wool Trade in Medieval English History* (1941).

L. F. Salzman, *English Industries in the Middle Ages* (1923).

L. F. Salzman, *English Life in the Middle Ages* (1926).

F. M. Stenton, *The First Century of Feudalism* (1932).

ART AND LITERATURE

H. S. Bennett, *Chaucer and the Fifteenth Century* (1947).

T. S. Boase, *English Art 1100–1216* (Oxford, 1953).

P. Brieger, *English Art 1216–1307* (Oxford, 1957).

J. Evans, *English Art 1307–1461* (Oxford, 1948).

W. P. Ker, *English Literature: Medieval* (1912).

M. Rickert, *Painting of Britain: The Middle Ages* (1954).

O. E. Saunders, *English Art in the Middle Ages* (1932).

R. W. Southern, *The Making of the Middle Ages* (1953).

F. Wormald, *The Survival of Anglo-Saxon Illumination after the Norman Conquest* (1944).

❀ BOOK III — THE TUDOR AGE: THE REFORMATION

GENERAL

G. Baskerville, *English Monks and the Suppression of the Monasteries* (1937).

S. T. Bindoff, *Tudor England* (1961).

J. B. Black, *The Reign of Elizabeth* (Oxford, 1959).

G. R. Elton, *England under the Tudors* (1955).

P. Hughes, *The Reformation in England* (1950).

M. M. Knappen, *Tudor Puritanism* (1935).

J. D. Mackie, *The Earlier Tudors 1485–1558* (Oxford, 1957).

G. Mattingley, *The Armada* (1959).

H. Maynard Smith, *Pre-Reformation England* (1938).

H. Maynard Smith, *Henry VIII and the Reformation* (1948).

C. Morris, *The Tudors* (1955).

A. F. Pollard, *Political History of England 1547–1603* (1913).

F. M. Powicke, *The Reformation in England* (1941).

Conyers Read, *The Tudors* (1936).

A. L. Rowse, *The England of Elizabeth* (1950).

A. L. Rowse, *The Expansion of Elizabethan England* (1955).

E. G. Rupp, *The English Protestant Tradition* (1947).

J. A. Williamson, *Maritime Enterprises 1485–1558* (1913).

J. A. Williamson, *The Tudor Age* (1953).

BIOGRAPHIES

R. W. Chambers, *Thomas More* (1935).

A. G. Dickens, *Thomas Cromwell and the English Reformation* (1959).

T. F. Henderson, *Mary Queen of Scots* (1905).

J. E. Neale, *Queen Elizabeth* (1934).

A. F. Pollard, *Thomas Cranmer and the English Reformation* (1904).

A. F. Pollard, *Henry VIII* (1920).

A. F. Pollard, *Cardinal Wolsey* (1929).

D. B. Quinn, *Raleigh and the British Empire* (1947).

Conyers Read, *Mr Secretary Cecil and Queen Elizabeth* (1956).

Conyers Read, *Lord Burghley and Queen Elizabeth* (1960).

A. L. Rowse, *Sir Richard Grenville* (1937).

W. Schenk, *Reginald Pole, Cardinal of England* (1950).

Beatrice White, *Mary Tudor* (1935).

Stephan Zweig, *The Queen of Scots* (1935).

CONSTITUTIONAL HISTORY

J. W. Allen, *A History of Political Thought in the Sixteenth Century* (1928).

S. T. Bindoff, J. Hurstfield, and C. H. Williams, eds., *Elizabethan Government and Society* (1961).

G. R. Elton, *The Tudor Revolution in Government* (1959).

J. E. Neale, *The Elizabethan House of Commons* (1949).

J. E. Neale, *Elizabeth and her Parliaments 1559–1581* (1953).

J. E. Neale, *Elizabeth and her Parliaments 1584–1601* (1957).

K. M. Pickthorn, *Early Tudor Government* (1934).

SOCIAL AND ECONOMIC HISTORY

Mildred Campbell, *The English Yeoman under Elizabeth and the Early Stuarts* (1961).

G. N. Clark, *The Wealth of England from 1491 to 1760* (Oxford, 1947).

J. U. Nef, *The Rise of the British Coal Industry* (1932).

R. W. Prothero, *English Farming Past and Present* (1936).

L. F. Salzman, *England in Tudor Times* (1926).

R. H. Tawney, *Agrarian Problem in the Sixteenth Century* (1912).

R. H. Tawney, *Religion and the Rise of Capitalism* (1938).

ART AND LITERATURE

C. H. Baker and W. G. Constable, *English Painting in the 16th and 17th Century* (1930).

E. K. Chambers, *A Short Life of William Shakespeare* (1935).

C. S. Lewis, *English Literature in the 16th Century exclusive of Drama* (1954).

E. M. W. Tillyard, *The Elizabethan World Picture* (1943).

✿ BOOK IV — STUART TIMES: THE ENGLISH REVOLUTION

GENERAL

Maurice Ashley, *England in the Seventeenth Century 1603–1714* (rev. ed. 1961).

G. N. Clark, *The Later Stuarts 1660–1714* (Oxford, 1956).

G. Davies, *The Restoration of King Charles II* (1955).

G. Davies, *The Early Stuarts 1603–1660* (Oxford, 1959).

K. Feiling, *British Foreign Policy, 1660–1672* (1930).

William Haller, *Liberty and Reformation in the Puritan Revolution* (Columbia, 1955).

J. P. Kenyon, *The Stuarts* (1958).

David Ogg, *England in the Reign of Charles II* (Oxford, 1955).

David Ogg, *England in the Reigns of James II and William III* (Oxford, 1955).

G. M. Trevelyan, *England under the Stuarts* (Pelican, 1960).

C. V. Wedgwood, *The Great Rebellion* (1955 seq.).

BIOGRAPHIES

Maurice Ashley, *The Greatness of Oliver Cromwell* (1957).

Arthur Bryant, *King Charles II* (1960).

Maurice Cranston, *John Locke* (1957).

J. H. Hexter, *The Reign of King Pym* (1942).

F. M. G. Higham, *Charles I* (1932).

J. P. Kenyon, *Sunderland* (1958).

H. Trevor Roper, *Archbishop Laud* (1940).

F. C. Turner, *James II* (1949).

C. V. Wedgwood, *Strafford* (1935).

D. H. Wilson, *King James VI and I* (1956).

B. H. G. Wormald, *Clarendon* (Cambridge, 1951).

CONSTITUTIONAL HISTORY

W. Aiken and B. Henning, eds., *Conflict in Stuart England* (1960).

J. W. Allen, *English Political Thought 1603–1660* (1938).

G. E. Aylmer, *The King's Servants* (1961).

J. W. Gough, *The Social Contract* (Oxford, 1936).

J. W. Gough, *Fundamental Law in English History* (Oxford, 1955).

Margaret Judson, *The Crisis of the Constitution* (1949).

Betty Kemp, *King and Commons 1660–1832* (1957).

W. M. Mitchell, *The Rise of the Revolutionary Party in the English House of Commons 1603–1629* (Columbia, 1957).

J. R. Tanner, *English Constitutional Conflicts of the Seventeenth Century 1603–1689* (Cambridge, 1928).

A. S. P. Woodhouse, *Puritanism and Liberty* (1938).

SOCIAL AND ECONOMIC HISTORY

Arthur Bryant, *The England of Charles II* (1960).

M. James, *Social Problems and Policy during the Puritan Revolution, 1640–1660* (1930).

David Mathew, *The Age of Charles I* (1951).

W. Notestein, *English People on the Eve of Colonization 1603–1630* (1954).

R. D. Richards, *The Early History of Banking in England* (1929).

R. H. Tawney, *Business and Politics under James I* (Cambridge, 1958).

ART AND LITERATURE

H. Grierson, *Cross Currents in English Literature of the Seventeenth Century* (1929).

E. Waterhouse, *Painting in Britain 1530–1790* (1953).

C. V. Wedgwood, *Seventeenth Century English Literature* (1950).

Margaret Whinney and Oliver Millar, *English Art 1625–1714* (Oxford, 1953).

Basil Willey, *The Seventeenth Century Background* (1950).

LIST OF SOVEREIGNS

Name	Dynasty or House	Reign
Egbert [1]	Saxon	829–839
Ethelwulf	Saxon	839–855
Ethelbald	Saxon	855–860
Ethelbert	Saxon	860–866
Ethelred I	Saxon	866–871
Alfred the Great	Saxon	871–899
Edward the Elder	Saxon	899–925
Athelstan	Saxon	925–939
Edmund	Saxon	939–946
Eadred	Saxon	946–955
Edwig	Saxon	955–959
Edgar	Saxon	959–975
Edward the Martyr	Saxon	975–979
Ethelred II the Unready	Saxon	978–1016
Edmund Ironside	Saxon	1016
Canute (or Cnut)	Danish	1016–1035
Harold I Harefoot	Danish	1035–1040
Hardecanute	Danish	1040–1042
Edward the Confessor	Saxon	1042–1066
Harold II	Saxon	1066
William I	Norman	1066–1087
William II	Norman	1087–1100
Henry I	Norman	1100–1135
Stephen	Norman	1135–1154
Henry II	Plantaganet or Angevin	1154–1189
Richard I	Plantagenet	1189–1199
John	Plantagenet	1199–1216
Henry III	Plantagenet	1216–1272
Edward I	Plantagenet	1272–1307
Edward II	Plantagenet	1307–1327
Edward III	Plantagenet	1327–1377
Richard II	Plantagenet	1377–1399
Henry IV	Lancaster	1399–1413
Henry V	Lancaster	1413–1422
Henry VI [2]	Lancaster	1422–1461
Edward IV	York	1461–1483
Edward V	York	1483
Richard III	York	1483–1485
Henry VII	Tudor	1485–1509
Henry VIII	Tudor	1509–1547
Edward VI	Tudor	1547–1553
Mary	Tudor	1553–1558
Elizabeth I	Tudor	1558–1603

[1] King of Wessex and "ruler of Britain."

[2] During the Wars of the Roses (1455–1485) Henry VI was restored to the throne for a short period, from Oct. 5, 1470 to his death May 21, 1471.

RULERS OF SCOTLAND (FROM 1005)

Name	Reign
Malcolm II	1005–1034
Duncan I	1034–1040
Macbeth	1040–1057
Lulach	1057–1058
Malcolm III	1057–1093
Donald Bane	1093–1094
Duncan II	1094
Donald Bane (restored)	1094–1097
Edgar	1097–1107
Alexander I	1107–1124
David I	1124–1153
Malcolm IV	1153–1165
William the Lion	1165–1214
Alexander II	1214–1249
Alexander III	1249–1286
Margaret of Norway	1286–1290
(Interregnum)	1290–1292
John de Baliol	1292–1296
(Interregnum)	1296–1306
Robert I (Bruce)	1306–1329
David II (Bruce)	1329–1371

House of Stuart

Robert II	1371–1390
Robert III	1390–1406
James I	1406–1437
James II	1437–1460
James III	1460–1488
James IV	1488–1513
James V	1513–1542
Mary	1542–1567
James VI [1]	1567–1625

SOVEREIGNS OF GREAT BRITAIN (FROM 1603)

James I (VI of Scotland)	Stuart	1603–1625
Charles I	Stuart	1625–1649
[Commonwealth, 1649–1660]		
[Oliver Cromwell, Lord Protector, 1653–1658]		
[Richard Cromwell, Lord Protector, 1658–1659]		
Charles II	Stuart	1660–1685
James II	Stuart	1685–1688
[Revolution of 1688]		

[1] Became James I of England in 1603 (see next Table).

Abbot, George, Archbishop of Canterbury, 320
Aberdeen, 333–34
Abergavenny, Lord, 167
Abergavenny, Prior of, 115
Aberystwith, 153
Aclea, battle of, 34
Acton Burnell, statute of, 121
Adrian IV, Pope, 113
Adrian VI, Pope, 206
Advertisements, Book of, 258
Adwalton moor, battle of, 343
Aelfric, 50, 59–60
Aelle, 24–25
Africa, 285, 287, 288; *see also* Royal Africa Company
Agincourt, battle of, 157
Agnellus, Fra, of Pisa, 115
Agreement of the People, 353
Agricola, Julius, 14, 16–17, 20, 43
Agriculture, 57, 85, 117, 143, 189–90, 193, 230–31, 277–78, 303, 385
Albany, 1st Duke of, 152, 177
Aldheim, 60
Alençon, Duke of, 262, 264
Alexander II, Pope, 75
Alexander III, Pope, 92
Alexander VI, Pope, 285
Alexander III, King of Scots, 112
Alfonso III, King of Aragon, 121
Alfred the Great, King of the English, 34–43, 45
Allen, William, 297
Alton, treaty of, 80
Alva, Duke of, 260–61, 264
Ambrosius Aurelanus, 24
America, 34, 285, 289, 384, 386, 422
Amicable Grant, the, 206
Amiens, Mise of, 109
Anabaptists, 221
Ancrum, battle of, 248

Andrewes, Lancelot, Bishop of Ely, 392
Andros, Sir Edmund, 424
Anglesey, isle of, 13, 14, 176
Anglo-Saxon Chronicle, 24, 40, 47, 51
Anglo-Saxons, 20–26, 57–61
Anjou, 62, 88, 97, 106, 156
Anjou, Duke of, 261
Anne, Princess, later Queen of England, 418–19
Anne Boleyn, Queen, wife of Henry VIII, 216–17, 219, 224, 235
Anne of Cleves, Queen, wife of Henry VIII, 225, 227
Anselm, Archbishop of Canterbury, 78–79, 81–82
Antonine wall, the, 16
Antwerp, 191, 286
Appelant, Lords, 149–50
Appian, quoted, 19
Apsley, Lucy, 391
Aquitaine, 88, 94, 97, 105, 129–30, 133, 156, 158
Architecture, 87, 116, 140–41, 192, 299, 395–96
Ardes, treaty of, 228
Argyll, Archibald, 9th Earl of, 413–14
Argyll, Archibald Campbell, 8th Earl of, and Marquis, 334, 338, 354, 428
Aristotle, 401
Arlington, Henry Bennet, 1st Earl of, 374
Armada, the Spanish, 271–72
Arms, Assize of, 92
Army, the, 136, 371, 415; *see also* Fyrd
Arran, James Hamilton, 2d Earl of, 247–49
Arran, James Stewart, Earl of, 310

Art, Oge McMurrough, 179
Arthur, "King," 24, 41
Arthur, Prince, of Brittany, 90, 97
Arthur, Prince, son of Henry VII, 198, 215
Arundel, Richard, 4th Earl of, 148–50
Arundel, Thomas, Archbishop of Canterbury, 150, 152
Ascham, Roger, 295
Ashdown, battle of, 36
Ashingdon, battle of, 53
Ashmole, Elias, 403
Aske, Robert, 223
Asser, 40, 43
Athelney, 40
Athelstan I, King of Wessex, 34
Athelstan II, King of the English, 47–48, 55
Atrebates, 12, 17
Aubrey, John, 297, 389, 392, 402
Augsburg, league of, 416
Avebury, 6
Azores, 274, 285, 289

Babington plot, 269
Bachelors, Knight, 108
Backwell, Edward, 386
Bacon, Francis, Viscount St. Albans, 268, 274, 278, 281, 293, 297, 302, 318, 320, 385, 394–401, 404
Bacon, Roger, 401
Bahamas, 425
Ball, John, 146
Balliol, John, 123–24
Baltic, the, 386
Baltimore, 1st Lord, 423
Baltimore, 2d Lord, 423
Banking, 386
Bannockburn, battle of, 126
Barbados, 425
Barfleur, 130
Barlow, Frank, quoted, 74
Barlow, Roger, 287
Barnet, battle of, 171
Barrow, Henry, 265–66
Barton, Elizabeth, 220

Bastwick, John, 333
Bate's case, 406
Bath, 17, 24–25, 50
Bath, Order of the, 152
Battle abbey, 87
Bayonne, 130, 204
Beaton, David, Cardinal, 228, 247–48
Beaufort, Edmund, 2d Duke of Somerset, 165–66
Beaufort, Henry, Bishop of Lincoln, and Winchester, 153, 155, 161, 164
Beaufort, John, 1st Duke of Somerset, 162, 164
Beaufort, Thomas, Marquis of Dorset, 153
Beauforts, the, 153
Beaumont, Francis, 395
Beaumont, Robert, Earl of Leicester, 84
Bec, "compromise of," 228
Becket, Thomas, Saint, Archbishop of Canterbury, 92–93, 114, 116, 143
Bede, the Venerable, 22, 40, 59–60, 398, 401
Bedford, John, Duke of, 157–58, 169
Bedford, 4th Earl of, 384, 386
Beer, 193
Belgic tribes, 8
"Benevolences," 315
Berengaria, Queen, wife of Richard I, 95
Berkeley castle, 128
Berkhampstead, 72
Bermuda, 425
Berners, Lord, 296
Bertha, Queen, wife of King Ethelbert of Kent, 27–28
Berwick, pacification of, 334
Berwick on Tweed, 123, 248
Berwick, treaty of, 132
Bess of Hardwicke, Countess of Shrewsbury, 280
Biddle, John, 367
Bigbury, 10
Bigod, Hugh, 108

Bigod, Roger, 4th Earl of Norfolk, 108
Bill of Rights, the, 431
Bindoff, Professor S. T., quoted, 231
Bishops, 60, 75, 86, 139, 340, 367
Bishops, case of the seven, 417
"Bishops wars," 335–36, 340–41
Black death, the, 131–32, 139, 143–44, 188, 193
Black Prince, the, 128, 131–34
Blake, General Robert, 364, 367
Blois, treaty of, 262
"Bloody Assizes," the, 414
Bodin, Jean, 305, 405–6, 409
Bodleian library, 390
Bodley, Sir Thomas, 296
Bohemia, 316
Bombay, 425
Boniface VIII, Pope, 124, 138
Bonner, Edmund, Bishop of London, 236–37, 243
Booth, Sir George, 369
Bordeaux, 106, 132, 164, 165
Boston, 425
Bosworth, battle of, 175
Bothwell, James Hepburn, Earl of, 252
Boudicca, Queen of the Iceni, 13–14
Boulogne, 20, 228, 234
Bourchier, Lord, 167
Bouvines, battle of, 99
Boyle, Robert, 403–4, 430
Bracton, Henry de, 107, 117, 405
Bradshaw, John, 355, 358, 362
Brandenburg, Elector of, 416
Brandon, Charles, 3rd Duke of Suffolk, 227
Brazil, 288
Brecknoch, 229
Breda, declaration of, 370
Breda, treaty of, 374
Brest, 204
Bretwaldas, the, 25–26, 31–32, 55
Brian Boru, King of the Irish, 45, 112
Brigantes, 12–14
Bristol, 141

Bristol, 1st Earl of, 324, 428
Bristol channel, 24, 176
Britain, prehistoric, 4–8
Britain, Roman, 8–21, 25–26
Britons, Count of the, 21
Brittany, 47, 62, 80, 88, 97, 105, 132, 198, 274
Browne, Robert, 265
Browne, Sir Thomas, 401
Bruce, Edward, 178
Bruce, Robert, King of Scots, 124, 126–28
Bruce, Robert, Lord of Annandale, 123
Bruges, battle of, 98
Brunanburh, battle of, 48
Bruno, Giordano, 305
Bryant, Sir Arthur, quoted, 91
Bucer, Martin, 238
Buchanan, George, 309
Buckingham, George Villiers, 1st Duke of, 174, 317–18, 322–28, 337
Buckingham, George Villiers, 2nd Duke of, 403
Buckinghamshire, 328
Bull, John, 399
Bunyan, John, 389, 392
Burgh, Hubert de, Justiciar, 103–5
Burgundians, the, 153, 156, 158, 170
Burnet, Gilbert, 361, 390, 394
Burton, Henry, 333
Burton, Robert, 391
Bury St. Edmund's, 147
Butler, James, Earl of Wiltshire, 167
Butler, Samuel, 394
Buxton, 17
Byrd, William, 399

Cabot, John, 286
Cabot, Sebastian, 286–87
Cade, Jack, 165 ff., 181
Cadiz, 271, 323
Caedmon, 60
Caen, 130, 158

Caerleon, 14, 20
Caerwent, 20
Caesar, Julius, 3, 8, 9–12
Caister, castle, 141, 181
Calais, 131, 133, 156–57, 162, 165, 187, 198, 205, 228, 253, 255
Calais, treaty of, 132
California, 288
Calvin, John, 236, 249
Calvinists, 261
Cambrai, League of, 203
Cambridge University, 116, 142, 147, 180, 212
Camden, William, 296
Campeggio, Cardinal, 216
Campion, Edmund, 267
Camulodunum, *see* Colchester
Canada, 286
Canterbury, 10, 27–29, 34, 116, 141, 143, 146, 280
Canute, King, 52–53, 57, 59, 62
Cape of Good Hope, 288
Caracalla, Roman emperor, 19
Caratacus, 13
Carausius, Roman emperor, 20
Carberry hill, battle of, 176
Cardiff, 20
Cardigan, 176
Carew, Chief Justice, 324
Carew, Thomas, 393
Caribbean, 289, 425
Carlisle, 82, 112
Carmarthen, 176
Carnarvon, 122
Carolina, 424
Carr, Robert, Earl of Somerset, 314
Carthusians, 139, 212
Cartwright, Thomas, 258, 265
Case of the Army Truly Stated, 353
Cassivellaunus, 10
Castile, 148, 150, 285
Castles, Norman, 72
Cateau-Cambresis, treaty of, 255
Catherine, Queen, wife of King Henry V and of Owen Tudor, 156, 158, 176

Catherine of Medici, Queen, 262
Catholic League, the, 316
Catuvellauni, 10, 12–14
Cavendish, Thomas, 289
Caxton, William, 180, 192
Ceawlin, 25
Cecil, Robert, 1st Earl of Salisbury, 268, 274, 275, 283, 304, 314
Cecil, William, Lord Burghley, 254, 257, 261, 267, 270, 275, 280, 281, 286, 295, 302, 304
Celts, 7, 19, 26
Cerdic, 24
"Cessation, the," 345
Chancellors, 84, 207, 226
Chancery, 136, 207, 208
Chantries, 236, 294
Charity, 388, 429
Charlemagne, Emperor, 33, 40
Charles, Archduke of Austria, 257
Charles of Anjou, 121
Charles the Bad, King of Navarre, 132
Charles the Bold, Duke of Burgundy, 170–71
Charles V, Emperor, 206, 214, 227, 231
Charles I, King of England, 317, 318
Charles II, King of England, 360, 370–81, 393
Charles IV, King of France, 127, 129
Charles V, King of France, 137
Charles VI, King of France, 150, 153, 156
Charles VII, King of France, 158–59, 161
Charles VIII, King of France, 196, 198
Charles IX, King of France, 261
Chartley, 269
Chartres, 159
Chatham, 288, 292, 374
Chaucer, Geoffrey, 139, 142–43, 180
Chesapeake bay, 286, 289, 423

Cheshire, 4, 369
Chester, Ranulf, Earl of, 83–84
Chichester, 24
Chile, 285
Chillingworth, William, 336, 382, 407
Chippenham, 36–37
Christ Church, Oxford, 229, 295
Christian IV, King of Denmark, 319
Christianity, *see* Church of England, etc.
Churchill, John, later 1st Duke of Marlborough, 414, 419
Church of England, 49, 59–60
Churls or ceorls, 57
Circumspecte agatis, 120
Cirencester, 25
Cissbury, 7
Cistercians, 114, 212
Civil War, first, 341–48; second, 354–55
Clare, Gilbert de, 8th Earl of Gloucester, 109–10
Clare, Gilbert de, 1st Earl of Pembroke, 84
Clarence, Dukes of, 159, 162, 170, 172, 179
Clarendon, Assize of, 91
Clarendon, Constitution of, 92, 93
"Clarendon Code," 371, 403
Claudius, Roman emperor, 12–13, 20
Clement VII, Pope, 216, 218
Clergy, behavior of, 59–60, 210
Cleveland, John, 394
Clifford, Lord, 167
Clito, William, 80
Clontarf, battle of, 45, 112
Cloth industry, 143–44, 191, 206, 264, 279, 382–83
"Clubmen," 348
Cluniacs, 211
Clyde, river, 14, 25, 43
Coal, 280, 386, 429
Cobham, Lord, 167
Cockayne, Sir William, 382
Cognac, treaty of, 206

Coke, Sir Edward, 274, 318, 320, 325, 356, 394, 406, 412
Colchester, 12–14, 17, 354
Colet, John, 213, 293
Colonies, 387
Columbus, Christopher, 285
Comenius, 389
Commerce, 191, 384–85, 387
Commines, 12
Committee of Safety, 340
Committee of the Two Kingdoms, 345
Commodus, Roman emperor, 16
Common Prayer, Book of, first, 236–37; second, 237, 254, 265
Commons, House of, 136, 154, 183–84, 232, 254, 256, 258, 264–68, 283, 304–5, 311, 376–80
Commutation of Labour services, 143
Compton, Henry, Bishop of London, 415, 418
Condé, Prince de, 255
Congregation, Lords of the, 249
Congreve, William, 389
Connaught, 45, 112–13, 422
Connecticut, 424
Constantine, Roman emperor, 18, 20
Constantius, Roman emperor, 20
Constitutio domus regis, 81
Convocation, 219–20, 236, 238
Conway, 151
Conway, treaty of, 122
Cooper, Samuel, 396
Coritani, 12
Cork, 292
Cormac Mac Art, 45
Cornovii, 12
Cornwall, 12, 24–25, 33, 48, 196, 234, 237, 343, 345
Coronation ceremony of King Edgar, 50
Coulton, G. G., quoted, 143
Council for Foreign Plantations, 426–27
Council of the Army, 352–54
Council of Fifteen, 108

Council, King's, 104–5, 107, 119, 182, 201, 208
Council of the North, 337
Council of State, 358
"Country party," 378–79
Courteen Association, 383
Court of Chancery, 138
Court of Common Pleas, 138
Court of Exchequer, 89, 97, 132, 136, 313, 328, 332
Court of King's Bench, 119, 138, 217, 324
Court of Wards, 328
Covenant, Solemn League and, 351
Covent Garden, 396
Coventry, 168
Cowley, Abraham, 393–94
Cranfield, Lionel, Earl of Middlesex, 315, 317–20
Cranmer, Thomas, Archbishop of Canterbury, 224
Crashaw, Richard, 393
Craupius, Mount, battle of, 14
Crécy, battle of, 131, 157
Crime, 192
Cromwell, Oliver, 155, 219, 236, 321, 327, 332, 338–39, 342–65, 382–83, 393, 400, 422
Cromwell, Richard, 368–69
Cromwell, Thomas, Earl of Essex, 218–25, 231, 235
Crown lands, 197, 207
Crozon, 274
Cuba, 285
Culpepper, Sir John, 408
Cumberland, 112
Cunobelin, 12–13, 17
Curia Regis, 81
Cyprus, 95

Dalkeith, 334
Danegeld, 36, 52, 56, 72, 91
Danelaw, the, 52
Danes or Vikings, 34–38, 47–49, 52–54, 58–59, 73
Danzig, 280
Darnley, Lord, 251–52, 257–58
Davenant, Sir William, 399

David I, King of Scots, 83–84, 112
David II, King of Scots, 129, 132
Deal, 196
Debasement of coinage, 230
De Beer, Esmond, quoted, 418
De Burgos, 178
Declaration of Rights, 419
Declarations of Indulgence, 377, 416–17, 431
De donis conditionalibus, 120
Dee, Dr. John, 287
Dee, river, 50
Defender of the Faith, 215
Degeangli, 12
De haeretico comburendo, 154, 213
Deira, 25
Dekker, Thomas, 296, 299, 311
De la Pole, Edmund, Earl of Suffolk, 196
De la Pole, John, 2d Duke of Suffolk, 195
De la Pole, Michael, 1st Earl of Suffolk, 148
De la Pole, William, 1st Duke of Suffolk, 166
De la Vere, Robert, Earl of Oxford, 148–49
Deloney, Thomas, 296
Denbigh, 228
Denham, Sir John, 393
Denmark, 73, 323–24, 363
Deptford, 196
Derby, 47, 58
Dermot, King of Leinster, 113
Descartes, René, 402, 404
Despenser, Hugh, 127
Devereux, Robert, 2d Earl of Essex, 274–76
Devereux, Robert, 3rd Earl of Essex, 342–47
Devon, 12, 24, 33, 38, 234, 343, 413, 418
Dialogus de scaccario, 91
Dieppe, 156
Digby, Sir Kenelm, 403
Digges, Dudley, 408
Diocletian, Roman emperor, 20

Dispensations Act, 219
Dobson, William, 396
Dobuni, 12
Domesday book, 75–76
Dominicans, 115
Don John of Austria, 264, 270
Donne, John, 392
Dorset, 24
Douai, 258
Doughty, Thomas, 288
Douglas, James, 4th Earl of Morton, 319
Douglases, 177
Dover, 56, 64, 72, 103, 272
Dover, treaty of, 375
Drake, Sir Francis, 267, 268, 271, 273–74, 287, 288–89, 292, 304
Drama, 192, 298–99, 394–95
Drayton, Michael, 392
Drogheda, 200, 359
Druids, 7, 13, 18, 27
Dryden, John, 380, 392–93
Dublin, 45, 48, 113, 291, 333, 359
Dudley, Edmund, 203
Dudley, Guildford, 239
Dudley, John, Earl of Warwick and Duke of Northumberland, 233–38, 251
Dudley, Robert, Earl of Leicester, 251, 256, 266, 267, 274, 280, 286, 295
Dumnonii, 12
Dunbar, battles of, 123, 360
Duncan, King of Scots, 111–12
Dundee, 124
Dunkirk, 367, 372, 373
Dunstable, John, 398
Dunstan, St., Archbishop of Canterbury, 49–51, 53
Durham, 4, 334
Durham cathedral, 87, 259
Durotiges, 12
Dutch wars, 367, 374, 377, 382, 426
Dykveld, Lord of, 417

Eadred, King of the English, 48
Eadwig, King of the English, 48
Ealdormen, 56

East Anglia, 21, 24, 29, 33, 35, 37–38, 58, 148, 239, 279, 300, 332, 348
Eastern Association, 344
East India Company, 280, 284, 382, 386, 425
East Indies, 285
Eastland Company, 280, 288
Ecfrith, King of Northumbria, 43
Edgar, King of the English, 45, 48–51
Edgar the Atheling, 72, 112
Edgecote, battle of, 170
Edgehill, battle of, 342–43
Edinburgh, 26, 149, 200, 228, 247, 249, 310, 333–34, 360, 428
Edington, battle of, 37
Edith, Queen, wife of Edward the Confessor, 63–64
Edith, Queen, wife of Henry I, 79
Edmund, Earl of Lancaster, 121, 123
Edmund I, King of the English, 48–49
Edmund Ironside, 53
Education, 115; *see also* schools, Oxford, Cambridge
Edward, Earl of Warwick, 195–96
Edward, King of the English, 51
Edward "the Confessor," King of the English, 54, 62–66
Edward I, King of England, 104, 118–26, 144
Edward II, King of England, 125–28, 150, 152, 167, 176
Edward III, King of England, 129–34, 144, 167, 179
Edward IV, King of England, 167–71, 178, 182, 203
Edward V, King of England, 173–74
Edward VI, King of England, 227, 233–239
Edward the Elder, King of the English, 47
Edwin, Earl of Mercia, 70, 72–73
Edwin, King of Northumbria, 26, 28–29, 32, 73

Egbert, King of Wessex, 33–34, 72

Egremont, Lord, 167

Elbing, 280

Eleanor, Queen, wife of Henry II, 89

Eleanor, Queen, wife of Henry III, 104

Eleanor of Castile, 106, 141

Eliot, Sir John, 319, 323–28, 340

Elizabeth, daughter of James I, 316–17

Elizabeth I, Queen of England, 227, 229, 239, 242, 246, 253–76, 286, 293, 300, 302–5, 310, 321, 327, 330, 363, 365

Elizabeth of York, wife of Henry VII, 174, 195, 198

Eltham, 207

Elton, Dr. G. R., quoted, 187, 197, 211, 232, 283

Ely, 82, 147

Emma, Queen, wife of Ethelred "the Unready," 52–54, 62

Emmanuel College, Cambridge, 295

Empson, Richard, 203

Enclosures, 202, 230, 233, 277–78, 303, 385

"Engagement," the, 354

English language, 88

"Enumerated commodities," 387, 423

Epidemics, 188

Epping Forest, 86

Erasmus, Desiderius, 192–93, 213, 293

Eric Bloodaxe, King of Norway, 48

Essex, 86, 146–47, 191, 274

Essex, Earls of, *see* Devereux

Etaples, treaty of, 199, 201

Ethandun, battle of, *see* Edington

Ethelbald, King of Mercia, 32–33

Ethelbald, King of Wessex, 34

Ethelbert, King of Kent, 26–29, 39

Ethelfleda, "the Lady of the Mercians," 47

Ethelfrith, King of Northumbria, 26

Ethelred, Ealdorman of Mercia, 37, 38

Ethelred, King of Wessex, 36

Ethelred "the Unready," King of the English, 51–53, 56

Ethelwald, 47

Ethelwulf, King of Wessex, 34

Eton, 180, 295

Euphues, 296

Eustace, Count of Boulogne, 64

Eustace the monk, 103

Evelyn, John, 385, 389, 403, 431

Evesham, battle of, 109, 111

Exchequer, the, 89, 91, 136; *see also* Court

Exchequer, stop of the, 348

Excise, 348

Exclusion, 379–81, 411

Exeter, 4, 36, 72, 418, 430

Exeter Cathedral, 140

Eyre, Adam, 391

Fairfax, Sir Thomas, afterwards 3rd Viscount, 342, 345–48, 358–60, 369

Falaise, 158

Falkirk, battle of, 124

Falkland, Viscount, 338

Farnaby, Giles, 399

Fauconberg, Lord, 167

Fayrfax, Robert, 398

Feiling, Sir Keith, quoted, 379

Felton, John, 326

Fens, draining of the, 384

Feorm, 56

Ferdinand I, Emperor, 31

Ferdinand II, Emperor, 316

Ferdinand V, King of Aragon, 197, 204

Ferne, Henry, 408

Field of the Cloth of Gold, 187, 206

Fieschi, Cardinal Ottobuono, 110

Fifth Monarchy Men, 372

Filmer, Sir Robert, 408–9, 411

Finance, Public, 273, 313, 323, 328

Finch, Lord Keeper, 335
Fines, Statute of, 202
Fire of London, 374, 383
"Fish Days," 257
Fisher, H. A. L., quoted, 194, 214, 316
Fisher, John, Bishop of Rochester, 213, 217, 220, 221, 224
Fitz Count, Brian, 83
Fitzgerald, James, Earl of Desmond, 291
Fitzherbert, Sir Anthony, 277
Fitz Peter, Geoffrey, Justiciar, 96, 97
Fitz Walter, Robert, Lord of Dunmow, 99
Fitzwilliam, Sir William, 292
"Five Knights Case," 324
Flambard, Ranulf, Bishop of Durham, 78–79
Flanders, 73, 149
Fleetwood, General Charles, 361, 363, 368–69
Fletcher, John, 299
Flodden, battle of, 205
Florence, 197
Food, 192–93
Forced loans, 325
Forfar, 43
Formosus, Pope, quoted, 39
Fortescue, Sir John, 405
Forth, river, 14, 360
Fotheringay Castle, 269–70
Fox, Richard, Bishop of Winchester, 203
France, 48, 105, 121, 123, 129–34, 154–65, 197–99, 205–6, 228, 241, 250, 420, 430
Francis I, King of France, 205–6, 228, 241, 250
Francis II, King of France, 248, 250
Franciscans, 115, 146
Frederick II, Emperor, 106
Freedmen, 57
Friars, 115, 146, 211, 212
Frisians, 3, 22
Frobisher, Martin, 271, 287, 292

Froissart, Sir John, 128, 131, 296
Fyrd, 70

Gaels, 45
Gama, Vasco da, 285
Gardens, 19, 385
Gardiner, Stephen, Bishop of Winchester, 226, 236–37, 240–42
Garter, Order of the, 132
Gascony, 105–6, 117, 121, 122, 129, 130, 133, 143
Gate Fulford, battle of, 70
Gaveston, Piers, 125–26
General Assembly of the Church of Scotland, 250
Geneva, 249, 265
Gentry, 188–89, 281, 302–3, 390
Geoffrey, Count of Anjou, 81–82, 84
Gerald of Wales, quoted, 111, 117
Gheeraerts, Marc, 300, 396
Gibbon, Edward, quoted, 18, 132
Gibbons, Orlando, 399–400
Gilbert, Sir Humphrey, 287, 289, 295
Gilbert, William, 402, 404
Gilbertine nuns, 114
Gildas, 23–27
Glamorgan, 229
Glasgow, 414, 428
Glastonbury, 49, 53
Glendower, Owen, 152, 153, 156, 176
Gloucester, 13–14, 17, 25, 110, 141, 344
Gloucester Cathedral, 140
Gloucester, Humphrey, Duke of, 159–64, 296
Gloucester, Robert, Earl of, 83–84
Goddard, Dr. John, 402–3
Godolphin, Sidney, 386
Godwine, Earl of Wessex, 63–65, 75
"Golden Hind," 288–89
Gondomar, Count, 317–18
Gorboduc, 296, 299
Goring, Lord, 342, 348

Gower, John, 142
Grafton, Richard, 297
Graham, James, Marquis of Montrose, 334, 347, 360, 373
"Grand Remonstrance," 339
Gravelines, 272
Great Charter, *see* Magna Carta
Great Contract, 313–14
Great Council, *see* Magnum Concilium
Greek, 295
Greene, Robert, 296
Greenland Company, 387
Greenwich, treaty of, 247
Gregory I, Pope, 27–29, 40, 59
Gregory VII, Pope, 75
Gregory IX, Pope, 114
Gregory XIII, Pope, 268
Grenville, Sir Richard, 274, 289, 292
Gresham, Sir Thomas, 299
Gresham College, 296
Grey, Lady Catherine, 256
Grey, Lady Jane, 239, 240, 242
Grey, Lord of Ruthin, 153
Grey, Sir Richard, 173
Grimbald, 40
Grindal, Edmund, Archbishop of Canterbury, 265–66
Grocyn, William, 294
Grosseteste, Robert, Bishop of Lincoln, 115–16, 401
Guala, 103, 114
Guesclin, Sir Bertrand, 133
Guiana, 318
Guienne, 97, 162, 164, 204
Guilds, 191, 284
Guinea, 386
Gunpowder plot, 313
Guthrum, 36–38
Gwyn, Nell, 395
Gwynedd, 43, 176

Habbakkuk, H. J., quoted, 281
Habeas Corpus Amendment Act, 380, 414
Haddington, 233–34, 248
Haddon Hall, 300
Hadrian, Roman emperor, 14, 16; his wall, 16, 20, 43

Hadrian I, Pope, 33
Hainault, Sir John de, 127, 131
Hakluyt, Richard, 286, 289, 296
Hales, John, 407
Hales, Sir Edward, 415
Hales, Sir Robert, 147
Halidon Hill, battle of, 129
Halifax, Marquis of, 381, 410–11, 414
Hall, Edward, 297
Haller, William, quoted, 332
Hamilton, 1st Duke of, 354
Hampden, John, M.P., 328, 406
Hampshire, 24, 37, 80, 86
Hampton Court Palace, 299, 320; conference at, 391
Hanseatic League, 171, 191, 280
Harding, Stephen, 114
Hardwick House, 300
Harfleur, 156–57, 162, 165, 174
Harlech, 153
Harold I, King of the English, 54
Harold II, King of the English, 56, 62, 64–66, 70–72, 110
Harold Bluetooth, 52
Harold Hardrada, King of Norway, 70
Harrison, William, quoted, 192, 297
Harthacanute, King of Denmark, 56
Hartlib, Samuel, 389
Haselrig, Sir Arthur, 358, 364, 366, 368–69
Hastings, battle of, 70–71
Hastings, Lord, 173
Hatfield Chase, battle of, 32
Hatton, Sir Christopher, 286
Hawkins, Sir John, 271, 273–74, 288–89, 292
Hawkins, William, 287
"Heads of the Proposals," 353, 363
Hengist, 23
Henrietta Maria, Queen, wife of Charles I, 319, 321–22
Henriette, sister of Charles II, 375
Henry, Earl of Lancaster, 130, 132

Henry I, King of England, 77, 79–82, 110–11
Henry II, King of England, 81, 84, 87–94, 113, 121, 178
Henry III, King of England, 103–9, 116, 118
Henry IV, King of England, 149–54, 179, 181, 398
Henry V, King of England, 152, 154–58, 180–81
Henry VI, King of England, 159–71, 173, 181
Henry VII, King of England, 174–80, 187, 193, 194–95, 286
Henry VIII, King of England, 199, 203–6, 216–32, 235, 291–92, 295, 301, 398
Henry I, King of France, 62, 78
Henry II, King of France, 241, 245, 248
Henry III, King of France, 268
Henry IV, King of France, 262, 273–74
Henry, Prince, son of King James I, 321
Henry the Navigator, 285
Herbert, George, 389, 392–93
Herbert, William, Earl of Pembroke, 298
Herbert of Cherbury, Lord, quoted, 221, 394, 430
Hereford, 110
Herefordshire, 63
Hereward "the Wake," 73
Herrick, Robert, 392
Hertford, Earl of, 227
Hertfordshire, 14
High Commission, 328, 337
Highlanders, Scottish, 334, 428
Hilda, Abbess of Whitby, 31
Hilliard, Nicholas, 396
Hingston, John, 400
Hinxton Down, battle of, 34
Hobbes, Dr. Thomas, 408–9, 430
Hodgkin, R. H., quoted, 31
Holbein, Hans, 300
Holgate, Robert, Archbishop of York, 237
Holinshed, Raphael, 297
Holland, *see* United Provinces

Holland, Henry, Duke of Exeter, 167
Holles, Denzil, 355, 394, 408
Holstein, 22
Holyroodhouse, 248
Homildon Hill, battle of, 152
Honorius, Pope, 29
Hood, Robin, 86
Hooke, Robert, 403
Hooker, Richard, 293, 296–97, 302, 407
Hooper, John, Bishop of Gloucester, 237, 245
Hopton, Lord, 342–43, 349
Horsa, 23
Hoskins, Doctor W. G., 283
Hotspur, Henry, 153
Housecarles, the, 56
Howard, Frances, 317
Howard, Lord Charles, of Effingham, 271–72
Howard, Thomas, Duke of Norfolk, 225
Howard, Thomas, Earl of Suffolk, 327
Hudson Bay, 286–87
Hudson Bay Company, 387
Huguenots, 255, 261
Hull, 341
Humber, river, 25–26, 37
"Humble Petition and Advice," 366, 368–69
Humfrey, Pelham, 400
Hungary, 316
Huntingdon, Earl of, 280
Hunton, Philip, 407
Hyde, Edward, 1st Earl of Clarendon, 338, 370–375, 389, 394, 408
Hyde, Lawrence, Earl of Rochester, 379, 381
Hygiene, 192

Ice Ages, 5
Iceni, 12–13
Impositions, 313
"Independents," 331, 354
India, 285
Industry, 57, 191, 284
Ine, King of Wessex, 39

Innocent II, Pope, 83
Innocent III, Pope, 98, 114
Innocent IV, Pope, 106, 114
Innocent XII, Pope, 416
Inns of Court, 120, 296, 302, 390
"Instrument of Government," 364
Iona, 27
Ireland, 29, 45–47, 112–13, 150, 178–80, 200, 229, 275, 291, 337, 345, 351, 358–60, 422, 427
Ireton, Major General Henry, 355, 363, 409
Iron, 57
Isabella, Queen, wife of Edward II, 125, 127
Isabella, Queen of Castile, 197, 199
Isle of Wight, 20, 24, 70, 146, 190, 228, 272, 354, 355
Italy, 197, 204, 205

Jacob, E. F., quoted, 155
Jamaica, 367
James I, King of England, 252, 267–69, 275, 305, 307–20, 323, 330, 382, 383, 389, 406, 423
James II, King of England, 377–80, 411–19, 438
James I, King of Scots, 161–62
James II, King of Scots, 162, 177
James III, King of Scots, 178
James IV, King of Scots, 178, 199, 205, 227
James V, King of Scots, 228, 247
Jamestown, 423
Jane Seymour, Queen, 225
Java, 288
Jefferson, Thomas, 411
Jeffreys, George, Lord Chief Justice, 414
Jenkinson, Anthony, 287
Jerusalem, 94
Jesuits, 267, 405, 413
Jews, 94, 121, 367, 387
John, King of England, 94–102, 112–13, 161, 171, 178, 208
John of Gaunt, Duke of Lancaster, 133–34, 145, 148–49, 150, 177

John of Salisbury, 117
Johnson, Cornelius, 396
Jolliffe, J. E. A., quoted, 181
Jones, Inigo, 329, 396
Jonson, Ben, 299, 395
Jordan, W. K., quoted, 388
Judges, 119, 137, 181
Julius II, Pope, 203, 215
Julius III, Pope, 244
Justices of the Peace, 137, 181, 202
Justiciars, 81
Jutes, 28

Katherine (Howard), Queen, wife of Henry VIII, 227
Katherine of Aragon, Queen, wife of Henry VIII, 198–99, 204, 215, 217, 220, 224–25, 240
Katherine (Parr), Queen, wife of Henry VIII, 227, 253
Kenilworth, Dictum of, 109
Kenneth MacAlpin, 43
Kent, 8, 9, 24, 26–29, 33, 37, 64, 70, 146–47, 196, 354
Kett, Robert, 234
Kildare, Earls of, 178, 180, 195, 200, 202, 229
Kilkenny, statute of, 179
Kilpeck church, 87
King, Gregory, 428
King's College, Cambridge, 180
Kingston on Thames, 47; peace of, 103
Kinsale, 275
Knights Hospitallers, 114
Knights' service, 74, 82
Knights Templars, 115
Knowles, David, quoted, 115
Knox, John, 237–38, 247–52, 309

Labourers, statute of, 132
Lacy, Hugh de, 113
Lambarde, William, 139, 142
Lancashire, 279, 342, 354
Lancaster, 82
Lancaster, Dukes and Earls of, *see* Edmund, Henry, John, and Thomas

Langland, William, 139, 142
Langport, battle of, 348
Langton, Stephen, Archbishop of Canterbury, 98–104
Langton, Walter, Bishop of Lichfield, 125
La Roche-aux-Moines, 99
La Rochelle, 99, 325–26
Latimer, Hugh, Bishop of Worcester, 88, 115–16, 142, 295, 403
Latin, 88, 115–116, 142, 295, 403
Laud, William, Archbishop of Canterbury, 320, 326, 328, 331–32, 390, 422
Lauderdale, Earl of, 428
Laurentius, Archbishop of Canterbury, 29
Law, 58, 91, 119
Lawes, Henry, 393, 399
Lawes, William, 399
Lawyers, 303
Lead, 57
Lee, Rowland, Bishop of Lichfield and Coventry, 228
Le Havre, 255–56
Leicester, 58, 349
Leith, 249
Leland, John, 193, 296
Lely, Sir Peter, 396
Lennox, Esmé Stuart, Earl of, 309
Leo IV, Pope, 35
Leo X, Pope, 206
Leofric, Earl of Mercia, 63, 65
Leslie, Alexander, Earl of Leven, 334, 344
Levant Company, 280, 387
"Levellers," the, 3, 53, 361, 364, 370, 388, 392
Lewes, battle of, 109
Lewis, C. S., quoted, 344
Lilburne, John, 355, 384, 391, 394, 408
Lily, William, 294
Linacre, Thomas, 293
Lincoln, 17, 58, 83
Lincoln Cathedral, 116
Lincolnshire, 141, 223
Lindisfarne, 31, 40

Lisbon, 271
Literature, English, 141–42, 296–99
Llewellyn ap Gruffyd, 107, 111, 122
Lloyd, J. E., quoted, 43, 176
Locke, John, 411–12, 420
Locke, Matthew, 400
Loire, river, 88
Lollards, 138, 140, 154, 156, 213, 215, 248, 330
London, 14, 17, 20, 25, 34, 36, 38, 47, 58, 71, 87, 100, 188, 277, 280, 296, 304, 335, 339, 341, 343, 384, 428
London Bridge, 71, 124, 147, 165
Londonderry, 422
Longchamp, William, Justiciar, 94–95
Lords, House of, 119, 139, 232, 244, 254, 302, 337–38, 358, 380, 415
Lothian, 95, 112, 129
Louis VI, King of France, 80
Louis VII, King of France, 88–89
Louis VIII, King of France, 101–2, 105
Louis IX, King of France, 104–7
Louis XI, King of France, 169, 170–71, 198
Louis XII, King of France, 204–5
Louis XIV, King of France, 375–76, 414–20, 430
Lower, Richard, 403
Lucas, Margaret, Duchess of Newcastle, 391
Lucy, Richard, 93
Ludlow, 168
Lully, Jean Baptiste, 400
Luther, Martin, 214–17, 224, 405
Lydgate, John, 180
Lyly, John, 296

Macbeth, King of Scots, 111
Machiavelli, Nicolo, 405
Mackie, J. D., quoted, 199
Madras, 425
Madrid, 319, 322
Magellan Straits, 288–89

Magna Carta, 100–102, 105, 107, 117, 124, 137, 327

Magnum Concilium, 104, 107, 117

Magnus, King of Norway, 63

Magnus Intercursus, 202

Maiden Castle, 7

Maidstone, 354

Maine (U.S.A.), 424

Maine (France), 62, 80, 88, 97, 106, 156, 164

Maitland, William, Lord of Lethington, 250

Malcolm II, King of Scots, 45, 111

Malcolm III, King of Scots, 73, 78, 79, 111–12

Mandeville, Geoffrey, Earl of Essex, 86

Manfred, Count, 106

Map, Walter, 117, 119

Mare, Sir Peter de la, 139, 145

Margaret, Queen of Anjou, 164–66, 169–71

Margaret, Queen of Scotland, 112

Margaret of Burgundy, 195

Margaret (Tudor), Queen, wife of James IV, King of Scots, 200

Marignano, battle of, 205

Marlborough, statute of, 109

Marlowe, Christopher, 293, 299

Marshal, William, Earl of Pembroke, 97, 103, 104

Marsiglio of Padua, 223

"Martin Marprelate" pamphlets, 332

Marvell, Andrew, 375, 392, 394

Mary, Princess, sister of Henry VIII, 204, 227

Mary I, Queen of England, 216, 227, 237, 239–47, 304

Mary II, Queen of England, 378, 417, 419

Mary, Queen of Scots, 228, 233, 247–52, 254, 256, 257–61, 268–70, 295

Mary of Lorraine, Queen, 249

Maryland, 423–24

Massachusetts Bay Company, 424–25

Massinger, Philip, 395

Matilda, "Empress," 80–84, 112

Matilda, Queen, wife of Stephen, 82–83

Matilda, Queen, wife of William I, 62, 73

Maurice, Prince, 342–43

Maximilian I, Emperor, 196–99, 205

Maximilian II, Emperor, 260

Maximilian of Bavaria, 316

Maximinian, Roman emperor, 20

May, Thomas, 394

Mayerne, Sir Theodore, 401

"Mayflower, the," 424

Meath, 45

Medina del Campo, treaty of, 198

Medina Sidonia, Duke of, 271–73

Medway, river, 13

Melanchthon, Philipp, 235

"Mercantilism," 284

Merchant Adventurers Company, 279–80, 284, 382, 386, 387

Merchants, 121, 303, 313

Mercia, 25, 29, 32, 36–37, 47

Merton College, Oxford, 116

Messina, treaty of, 95

Mexico, 285

Middlesex, 8

Middlesex, Earl of, *see* Cranfield

Middle Stone Age, 5

Milan, 197, 206

Mile End, 146, 148

Milford Haven, 124

Milton, John, 373, 389, 392–93, 407–8, 410

Monasteries, 40, 49, 59, 87, 115, 139, 211–12

Monasteries, suppression of, 221–22, 230, 294

Monck, General George, Earl of Albemarle, 361, 369–71

Monmouth, Duke of, *see* Scott

Monopolies, 383

Montacute, 300

Montague, Edward, Earl of Manchester, 342

Montague, Richard, Bishop, 324, 326

Montaigne, Michel de, 391

Montfort, Simon de, Earl of Leicester, 105–6, 109, 111, 119
Montgomery, 228
Montgomery, treaty of, 111
Montrose, Marquis of, *see* Graham
Moray, *see* Stewart
Morcar, Earl of Northumbria, 65, 70
More, Sir Thomas, 190, 213, 217, 219–21, 228, 293, 406
Moreton Old Hall, 300
Mortimer, Edmund, 134
Mortimer, Roger, 128, 179
Mortmain, statute of, 120
Morton, John, Bishop of Ely, 73
Mount Badon, battle of, 24
Mountjoy, Lord, 275, 292
Mount Snowdon, 43
Mowbray, John, 3rd Duke of Norfolk, 167
Mowbray, Thomas, 1st Duke of Norfolk, 150
Mulcaster, Richard, 294, 295
Munster, 45, 275, 292
Music, English, 397–400
"Mutiny Acts," 419
Myers, A. R., quoted, 183

Naples, 197–98
Nashe, Thomas, 296
Navarre, 204
Navigations Acts, 367, 373, 387, 423–24, 426
Navy, 292, 301, 323
Naylor, James, 367
Neale, Sir John, quoted, 257, 302
Neile, Richard, Archbishop of York, 329
Nene, river, 101
Netherlands, 198–99, 202, 207, 220, 231, 255, 260, 270
Netherlands, revolt of the, 262
Netherlands, Spanish, 270, 332, 361, 375
Nevile, Henry, 410–11
Neville, George, Archbishop of Canterbury, 170
Neville, Ralph, Earl of Westmorland, 167

Neville, Richard, Earl of Warwick, 167, 168–71
Neville, Richard, Earl of Westmorland, 152
Neville's Cross, battle of, 132
Newark, 101, 348
Newburn, 336
Newcastle, treaty of, 129
Newcastle, William Cavendish, Marquis of, 342, 345
Newcastle upon Tyne, 16, 112, 248, 280, 334, 343, 350, 386, 428
New College, Oxford, 134
New England, 332, 422, 424, 426
New Forest, 78, 86
Newfoundland, 286
New Hampshire, 424
Newmarket, 352, 380
"New Model Army," 347
Newton, Isaac, 403–4, 430
New York, 424
Nimwegen (Nimeguen), treaty of, 378
"Nineteen Propositions," 340
Noell, Martin, 373, 383
Nombre de Dios, 285, 288
"Nominated Assembly," 363
Nonjurors, the, 420, 430
Norfolk, 234
Norfolk, Duke of, 226, 228
Norfolk, 4th Duke of, 258–60, 266
Norfolk, Earl of, 124
Normandy, 52, 61–62, 72–74, 84, 97, 99, 102, 105, 133, 156–58, 162, 164
Northampton, 100
Northampton, Assize of, 91
Northampton, battle of, 168
Northampton, Earl of, 112
Northampton, treaty of, 128
Northumberland, 117, 152
Northumberland, Duke of, *see* Dudley
Northumberland, Earl of, Henry Percy, 152, 153
Northumbria, 24–25, 31–33, 35, 48
Norton, Thomas, M.P., 264

Norway, 45, 52–53, 70, 73
Norway, Maid of, 123
Norwich, 188, 428
Nottingham, 35, 128, 174, 419

Oates, Titus, 379
Oblivion, Act of, 361
Ockham, William of, 142, 213, 401, 404–5
O'Connor, Turlock More, 112
Odo, Bishop of Bayeux, 72, 77
Offa, King of the English, 33, 39, 43
Offa's dyke, 33, 43, 111
Ogg, David, quoted, 385, 430
Olaf Fryggvason, 52
Olaf the White, King of Norway, 45
Oldcastle, Sir John, 155
Oman, Sir Charles, quoted, 147
Ordainers, Lords, 126
Ordinance of Eltham, 207
Ordovices, 12
Orinoco, 291, 318
Orkneys, 178
Orleanists, 153, 156–57
Orleans, 161
Ormonde, Marquis of, 345, 359, 422
Osborne, Thomas, Lord Danby, 377, 419
Oswald, King of Northumbria, 29, 31
Oswy, King of Northumbria, 31
Otterburn, battle of, 177
Otto IV, Emperor, 98
Otto the Great, 48
Ouse, river, 24
Owain Gruffyd ao Cynan, 111
Owen, John, 430
Owen Roe O'Neill, 359
Oxford, 39, 47, 142, 143, 212, 222, 295
Oxford, Earls of, *see* De la Vere
Oxford, Provisions of, 108–9, 117
Oxfordshire, 234
Oxford University, 116, 390

Pacific, 288
Painting, English, 141, 300

Palatinate, 316–19
Palatine, Elector, 314, 316, 319
Paris, 34, 37, 130, 158
Paris, Matthew, 107, 116
Paris, treaty of, 106, 109
Parishes, 49
Parisi, 12
Parker, Henry, 407–8
Parker, Matthew, Archbishop of Canterbury, 254, 258, 265
Parliament, "Cavalier," 376
Parliament, evolution and origins of, 104, 118–19, 135, 183, 232
Parliament, "Good," 134
Parliament, "Long," 336–62, 369–70
Parliament, "Merciless," 149
Parliament, Protectorate, 364–65
Parliament, "Reformation," 217–20
Parliament, "Short," 335
Parliament "of Saints," 363
Parma, Duke of, 264, 267, 271–72
Pastons, 181
Paul III, Pope, 224
Paul IV, Pope, 245
Paulet, Sir Amyas, 268–69
Paulinus, Archbishop of York, 29
Paulinus, Suetonius, 13
Pavia, battle of, 206
Peacham, Henry, 281
Peada, King of Mercia, 29
Peasants, *see* Agriculture
Peckham, John, Archbishop of Canterbury, 122, 124
Peers, 188, 280, 302
Pembroke, 110, 229, 354
Pembroke College, Oxford, 390
Pembrokeshire, 6, 176
Penda, King of Mercia, 29, 32, 33
Penn, William, 424
Pennsylvania, 424
Pepys, Samuel, 389
Persia, 287
Perth, 310
Peru, 285, 291
Peter, King of Aragon, 121

Peterborough cathedral, 116
Peterhouse College, Cambridge, 116
"Petition of Right," 326–27
Petty, Sir William, 403
Pevensey Bay, 24, 70
Philip I, King of France, 73
Philip IV, King of France, 121–22
Philip VI, King of France, 129, 130–31
Philip II, King of Spain, 241–43, 255, 266, 270–71
Philip III, King of Spain, 275
Philip IV, King of Spain, 275
Philip Augustus, King of France, 93, 95–98, 121
Philip of Burgundy, 199
Philippa of Hainault, Queen, wife of Edward III, 128
Picts, 20, 21, 23, 43
Pilgrimage of Grace, 304
Pinkie, battle of, 233, 248
Pius V, Pope, 259
Plague, the great, 374
Plautus, Avlus, 13
Playford, John, 399
Pluralism, 139
Plymouth, 272, 288, 323
Plymouth, New, 423
Poitou, 97, 99, 105, 122
Pole, Reginald, Cardinal, 220, 223–24, 244–47, 254
Pollard, A. F., quoted, 208, 223, 302
Poll taxes, 146
Ponet, John, Bishop of Winchester, 237
Pontefract, 151, 354
Ponthieu, 131, 133
Poor laws, 278–79, 388
Population, 427
Portsmouth, 130, 326, 341
Portsmouth, Duchess of, 379
Portugal, 148, 264, 285, 286, 361, 363
Poverty, 278, 283, 428
Power, Eileen, quoted, 191
Powicke, Sir Maurice, quoted, 108

Poynings, Sir Edward, 200–201, 422
Praemunire, statutes of, 139
Prague, 316
Prayer Book, *see* Common
Presbyterians, 266, 310, 320, 333, 350, 351, 367, 407
Preston, battle of, 354
Prices, 229–30, 279
Privy Council, 375
"Prophesyings," 330
"Propositions of Newcastle," 353
Protestant Union, 316
Provisors, statutes of, 138
Prynne, William, 332, 391, 407
Purcell, Henry, 400
Puritans, 256, 265, 268, 295, 305, 311, 315, 320, 330–33, 371, 387, 407, 423, 440
Purveyance, 312
Putney, 354
Pym, John, 318, 320, 325–26, 336–41, 344, 408
Pyrenees, 88
Pytheas of Marseilles, 3

"Quakers," 372
Quarles, Francis, 393
Queen's College, Cambridge, 180
Quia emptores, 120
Quinn, D. B., quoted, 291
Quo warranto, 120

Radcot Bridge, battle of, 149
Radnor, 229
Raegnald, 47
Ragman's Roll, 123
Ralegh, Sir Walter, 268, 289, 291, 292, 297, 301, 391
Raleigh, Sir Walter, quoted, 301
Ratisbon, truce of, 416
Ravenspur, 151
Read, Conyers, quoted, 194
Reading, Berkshire, 36, 343
Recusancy, laws, 266
Reeves, 56
Regnans in excelsis, Bull, 259
Regni, 12
Regularis concordia, 50

Religion, introduction of Christianity into Roman Britain, 18, 19; introduction into Anglo-Saxon England, 27–32, 39
Renard, Simon, 241
Reresby, Sir John, 430–31
Rescissory Act, 428
Rheims, 260
Rhode Island, 424
Rhodri the Great, of Wales, 43
Rhys ap Gruffyd, 111
Rich, Edmund, Archbishop of Canterbury, 105
Richard, Duke of Cornwall, 104, 106, 114
Richard, Duke of York, 162–68, 179, 183
Richard, Earl of Pembroke, 113
Richard I, King of England, 85, 94–96, 100, 112
Richard II, King of England, 145–56, 167, 177, 179
Richard III, King of England, 171–75
Richborough, 13, 20
Richelieu, Cardinal, 319, 322
Ridley, Nicholas, Bishop of London, 237–38, 245
Ridolfi plot, 261
Ripon, treaty of, 336
Rivaux, Peter des, 105
Rizzio, David, 252
Roanoke Island, 289
Robert II, King of Scots, 177
Robert III, King of Scots, 152, 177
Robert of Jumièges, Archbishop of Canterbury, 63
Robinson, Henry, 407–8
Roches, Peter des, Bishop of Winchester, 92, 105
Rochester, 37
Roger, Bishop of Salisbury, 83
Roger of Wendover, 117
Rogers, John, 244
Rollo, founder of Normandy, 52, 61
Roman Catholics, 258, 266, 268, 273, 310, 322, 363, 367, 411, 415–16

Roman Empire, 12–21, 23
Romanization of Britain, 17–26
Roman republic, 8
Roses, Wars of the, 166–81, 187
Rota Club, 410
Rouen, 158, 174
Roundway Down, battle of, 344
Rowse, Dr. A. L., quoted, 281, 294, 301
Roxburgh Castle, 177
Royal Africa Company, 386, 426
Royal Society, 397, 402–3
Rubens, Sir Peter Paul, 329, 396
"Rump," *see* Parliament, "Long"
Runnymede, 100–101
Rupert, Prince, 322, 342, 369
Rupp, E. G., quoted, 213, 235
Russell, William, Lord, 380
Russia, 287, 386
Rutland, Edmund, Earl of, 107
"Rye House plot," 380–81

St. Aidan, 31, 43
St. Albans, 147
St. Albans, battles of, 168
St. Alphege, 53, 59
St. Andrew's, Archbishop of, 178
St. Augustine, 27–28, 40
St. Columba, 27, 43, 45
St. David, 27
St. James's Palace, 299
St. Joan, 161, 164
St. John's College, Cambridge, 195
Saint-Lo, 130
St. Mungo, 43
St. Oswald, 50
St. Patrick, 27, 45
St. Paul's Church, London, 29, 173, 198, 383–84
St. Paul's School, London, 29, 295
St. Thomas, *see* Becket
St. Valéry, 70
Salisbury, 24, 418
Salisbury, Bishop of, *see* Roger
Salisbury, oath of, 73–75
Salisbury Cathedral, 116
Salt, 57

Sancroft, William, Archbishop of Canterbury, 415, 417, 419

Sandwich, 168

San Juan de Ulloa, 285, 288

Santa Cruz, Marquis of, 271

Savoy conference, 371

Sawtré, William, 154

Saxon Shore, Count of the, 20, 21

Say, Lord, 165

Scapula, Ostorius, 13

Scarborough, 126, 345, 354

Schleswig, 22

Schools, 180, 294, 390

Scone, 124

Scotland, 14, 16, 25, 43–44, 47, 98, 104, 108, 111–12, 123, 129, 152, 177–78, 196, 199, 200, 204, 233, 247–50, 270, 311, 333, 338, 340, 344–46, 360–61, 363, 373, 419, 422–24, 427

Scotland, Church in, 74, 248

Scots, 20–21, 23, 25, 48

Scott, James, Duke of Monmouth, 380–82, 388, 413–14

Scriptorium, 55

Sculpture, English, 116, 141

Scutage, 82, 136

Sedgemoor, battle of, 414

Selden, John, 391

"Self-Denying" ordinance, 352

Severn, river, 47

Severus, Roman emperor, 16–17, 19

Seymour, Edward, Earl of Hertford and Duke of Somerset, 247, 248, 253

Seymour, Thomas, 253

Shaftesbury, Anthony Ashley Cooper, Earl of, 378–80

Shakespeare, William, 293, 295, 297–99, 302, 315, 394

Sharp, James, Archbishop of St. Andrews, 428

Sheriffs, 56, 58, 89, 137

Sherwood forest, 86

Shetlands, 178

Ship money, 328–29

Shire courts, 58

Shrewsbury, 110

Sicily, 95, 114, 121

Sidney, Sir Philip, 293, 296, 297–98, 302

Sidney Sussex College, Cambridge, 295, 390

Sierra Leone, 288

Sigismund, Emperor, 157

Silchester, 17–18, 20

Silures, 12

Simnel, Lambert, 195

Siward, Earl of Northumbria, 63, 72

Six Articles, the, 226–27, 243

Sixtus VI, Pope, 270

Skelton, John, 203, 297, 392

Skye, 27

Slaves, 57, 76

Smith, Captain John, 423

Smith, Sir Thomas, 302, 405–6

Smithfield, 154–55

Smithson, Robert, 300

Snowdon, Mount, 122

Solemn League and Covenant, 344

Solway, river, 78

Solway Moss, battle of, 228, 247

Somers, Sir George, 425

Somerset, 37, 413, 414

Somerset, Dukes of, *see* Seymour

Somerset, Earls of, *see* Carr

Somme, river, 131

Spain, 197, 200, 204, 207, 260, 270, 285, 286, 318–19, 334, 363–64

Speed, John, 297

Spelman, Sir Henry, 394, 407

Spenser, Edmund, 281, 293–94, 297

Stainmore, battle of, 48

Stamford, 58, 100

Stamford Bridge, battle of, 70

Standard, battle of the, 83, 112

Stanley, Lord, 173, 175

Staple towns, 144, 191

Star Chamber, 182, 202, 208, 221, 266, 324, 328, 332, 337

Stenton, Sir Frank, quoted, 53, 57, 65

Stenton, Lady, quoted, 85
Stephen, King of England, 82–112
Stewart, Lord James, Earl of Moray, 249, 250–52, 258, 261
Stigand, Archbishop of Canterbury, 64, 75
Stilicho, 21
Stirling, 360
Stirling Bridge, battle of, 124
Stoke, battle of, 202
Stone Ages, 4–6
Stonehenge, 6
Stonors, 181
Stow, John, 297
Stratford, John, Archbishop of Canterbury, 128, 142
Strathclyde, 25, 43, 45, 47–48
Straw, Jack, 146
Strickland, William, 264–65
Strongbow, *see* Richard, Earl of Pembroke
Stuart, Arabella, 314
Stuart, Esmé, Earl of Lennox, 267
Stuarts, 177
Studland church, 87
Submission of the Clergy, Act for, 219
Subsidy, 207
Suckling, Sir John, 393
Sudbury, Simon, Archbishop of Canterbury, 146–47
Suffolk, 147
Suffolk, 1st Duke of, *see* Brandon
Suffolk, Earls of, *see* De la Pole, Howard
Sugar, 426
Sunderland, Robert Spencer, Earl of, 379, 381, 386, 403, 413–14, 419
Supplication against Ordinaries, 219
Supremacy, Acts of, 220, 254
Surrey, Earl of, 124, 187, 203, 205
Sussex, 12, 24, 33, 63
Sussex, Earl of, 259
Sweden, 363

Swein, son of Earl Godwine, 63, 64
Swein the Forkbeard, King, 52
Swindon, 24
Switzerland, 254
Sydney, Algernon, 380, 410, 412

Tacitus, quoted, 9, 12, 14
Talbot, John, Earl of Shrewsbury, 167
Tallis, Thomas, 399
Tara, 45
Taverner, John, 398
Taylor, Jeremy, 392
Ten Articles, the, 224
Terra Australis, 287–88, 291
Test Acts, 377, 411, 414–15, 417
Tettenhall, battle of, 47
Tewkesbury abbey, 87, 141
Tewkesbury, battle of, 171
Texel, battle of, 377
Thanes (thegns), 56
Thanet, isle of, 28, 35, 101
Theatres, *see* drama
Theobald, Count of Blois, 82
Theodore of Tarsus, Archbishop of Canterbury, 31–32, 49, 59
Theodosius, Roman emperor, 21
Thérouanne, 204
Thirty-nine Articles, the, 235, 238, 255
Thirty Years' War, 315–16, 341, 349, 382
Thomas, Earl of Lancaster, 125–27
Thompson, Maurice, 383
Thorne, Robert, 287
Thorpe, John, 300
Throckmorton plot, 267–68
Thurloe, John, 373
Tilbury, 271
Tillyard, Dr., quoted, 294, 301
Tithe, 56
Tobacco, 426
Togodurus, 13
Toledo, treaty of, 380
Toleration Act, 420
Tonnage and poundage, 197, 323

"Tories," the, 380
Tostig, Earl of Northumbria, 65, 70
Toulouse, 88
Touraine, 88, 97, 156
Tournai, 205
Tower of London, 72, 79, 132, 146, 152, 155, 196, 225, 257, 260
Towns, 58
Towton, battle of, 170
Traherne, Thomas, 393
Trajan, Roman emperor, 16
Treasurers, 81
Trevelyan, G. M., quoted, 385
Triennial Act, 376
Trinity College, Cambridge, 295
Trinovantes, 12, 14
Triple Alliance, 375
Troyes, treaty of, 158–59
Tudor, Jasper, Earl of Pembroke, 167, 170, 177
Tudor, Owen, 176–77
Turks, 97, 197, 386, 416
Turloch More, see O'Connor, 112
Turnham Green, 343
Tusser, Thomas, 277
Tweed, river, 45, 122, 205
Tyburn, 221
Tye, Christopher, 399
Tyler, Wat, 146
Tyndale, William, 215, 226, 244, 391, 405
Tyrone, Earls of, 275, 292, 421

Udall, Nicholas, 295, 299
Ulster, 45, 113, 200, 275, 292, 421
"Undertakers," 314
Uniformity, Act of, first, 237, second, 238, third, 371
United Netherlands, 267, 275, 418–19
Universities, 390; see also Cambridge and Oxford

Van Dyck, Sir Anthony, 322, 329, 396
Vane, Sir Henry, the Elder, 337

Vane, Sir Henry the Younger, 344, 351, 373, 408–9
Venice, 197, 204
Verulamium, 14, 20
Vervins, treaty of, 275
Vesci, Eustace de, Lord of Alnwick, 99
Vespasian, Roman emperor, 14
Vienne, Jean de, 133
Vikings, see Danes
Villeins, 85, 143, 144, 147
Virginia, 289, 291, 423–25
Vortigern, 23
Vyner, Sir Robert, 386
Vyner, Sir Thomas, 383

Wadham College, Oxford, 390
Wakefield, battle of, 168
Wales, 13–14, 16, 21–25, 27, 41–42, 48, 78, 98, 104, 108, 110–11, 122–23, 152, 156, 171, 175–76, 228–29, 344, 354, 364
Wales, Principality of, 122
Wales, Statute of, 122, 175–76
Walker, Edward, quoted, 399
Walker, Robert, 396
Wallace, Sir William, 124
Waller, Edmund, 393
Waller, Sir William, 342–43, 345, 349
Walsingham, Sir Francis, 261–62, 266, 269, 286, 304
Walter, Hubert, Archbishop of Canterbury, 95–97
Waltheof, Earl of Huntingdon, 72–73
Walton, Izaak, 392
Walworth, William, 146
Walwyn, William, 392
Warbeck, Perkin, 195–96, 199
Wareham, Dorset, 36
Warham, William, Archbishop of Canterbury, 203, 218
Warwick, Earls of, see Neville
Wash, river, 20, 24
Waterford, 196, 292
Webster, John, 299
Wedgwood, C. V., quoted, 334, 338

Wedmore, "treaty of," 37

Wells Cathedral, 116, 140

Wentworth, Paul, 257

Wentworth, Peter, 264

Wentworth, Thomas, Earl of Strafford, 321, 325, 328

Wergild, 39, 56, 91

Wessex, 24, 29, 33–34, 56

West Indies, 285, 292, 365, 386, 425, 426

Westminster, Provisions of, 108

Westminster Abbey, 66, 72, 78, 82, 89, 104, 116, 140–41, 295

Westminster Assembly, 351

Westminster Hall, 119, 355

Wexford, 422

Whichcote, Benjamin, 407

"Whig" party, 379–80

Whitby, conference of, 31

White Horse tavern, Cambridge, 215

Whitelocke, Bulstrode, 394

White Mountain, battle of, 316

Whitgift, John, Archbishop of Canterbury, 273, 330

Whyte, Robert, 399

Wildman, Sir John, 408

Wilfrid, St., 31–32

Wilkins, John, 402

William I, "the Conqueror," King of England, 62–77, 110–11

William II, "Rufus," King of England, 74, 76–80, 111

William III, of Orange, King of England, 363, 377, 381, 414, 416–17

William, Prince, son of Henry I, 80–81

William of Malmesbury, 117

William of Poitiers, 71

William of Sens, 116

William the Lion, King of Scots, 112

William the Silent, Prince of Orange, 262, 264, 268

Willikin of the Weald, 103

Wilmot, John, Earl of Rochester, 395

Wilson, Thomas, 281

Wilton house, 396

Winchester, 48, 54–55, 78, 83, 134, 142

Winchelsea, Robert, Archbishop of Canterbury, 124, 126

Windsor, 132, 152, 343, 419

Wine, 117, 191–93

Winstanley, Gerrard, 392, 409

Witan, the, 55

Wither, George, 393

Wogan, Sir John, 178

Wollaton Hall, 299–300

Wolsey, Thomas, Cardinal, 205–8, 213, 215–18, 223, 231, 295

Women, 57, 390

Woodstock, Thomas, Duke of Gloucester, 148–49

Wool, 143, 144, 191, 382, 384

Wool taxes, 139, 197

Worcester, 39, 54, 75, 101

Worcester, battle of, 361

Wren, Sir Christopher, 383, 396

Wriothesley, Thomas, Lord Chancellor, 1st Earl of Southampton, 233–34

Wriothesley, Thomas, 4th Earl of Southampton, 294, 373

Wroxeter, 20

Wulfhere, King of Mercia, 32

Wyatt, Sir Thomas, 242–43, 253, 297

Wycherley, William, 395

Wycliffe, John, 134, 138, 140, 142, 148, 153, 210, 213, 404

Wyndeville, Elizabeth, Queen, wife of Edward IV, 169, 173

Wyndeville, Richard, Earl of Rivers, 167, 173

Yeomen, 184, 189, 281

York, 14, 16, 17, 20, 29, 45, 47, 48, 58, 65, 70, 188, 258, 333, 334, 339, 345, 369, 384

York, Duke of, *see* Richard

York Minster, 140

Yorkshire, 73, 151, 153, 170, 173, 223, 332, 341, 345, 354

Zwingli, Ulrich, 214, 224, 236